Combatting Misinformation and Global Nation's False Narratives Through Education

Goran Ilik
University "St. Kliment Ohridski", Bitola, North Macedonia

Mladen Karadjoski
University "St. Kliment Ohridski", Bitola, North Macedonia

Ice Ilijevski
University "St. Kliment Ohridski", Bitola, North Macedonia

Blagoj Nenovski
University "St. Kliment Ohridski", Bitola, North Macedonia

IGI Global
Scientific Publishing
Publishing Tomorrow's Research Today

Published in the United States of America by
IGI Global Scientific Publishing
701 East Chocolate Avenue
Hershey, PA, 17033, USA
Tel: 717-533-8845
Fax: 717-533-7115
Website: https://www.igi-global.com E-mail: cust@igi-global.com

Library of Congress Cataloging-in-Publication Data
Names: Ilik, Goran, editor. | Karadjoski, Mladen, 1983- editor. | Ilijevski, Ice, 1986- editor. | Nenovski, Blagoj, 1987- editor.
Title: Combatting misinformation and global nation's false narratives through education / edited by: Goran Ilik, Mladen Karadjoski, Ice Ilijevski, Blagoj Nenovski.
Description: Hershey, PA : IGI Global Scientific Publishing, [2026] | Includes bibliographical references. | Summary: "The book contributes to existing research by compiling and analyzing empirical evidence on the effectiveness of various educational interventions in combating misinformation. By presenting best practices and lessons learned from different educational contexts, it offers a valuable resource for researchers, educators, and policymakers seeking to understand what works and what does not in the fight against misinformation"-- Provided by publisher.
Identifiers: LCCN 2024056676 (print) | LCCN 2024056677 (ebook) | ISBN 9798369396018 (hardcover) | ISBN 9798369396025 (paperback) | ISBN 9798369396032 (ebook)
Subjects: LCSH: Media literacy--Study and teaching--Case studies. | Misinformation--Study and teaching--Case studies. | Disinformation--Study and teaching--Case studies. | LCGFT: Case studies.
Classification: LCC P96.M4 C566 2025 (print) | LCC P96.M4 (ebook) | DDC 302.23--dc23/eng/20250203
LC record available at https://lccn.loc.gov/2024056676
LC ebook record available at https://lccn.loc.gov/2024056677

British Cataloguing in Publication Data
A Cataloguing in Publication record for this book is available from the British Library.

This book is dedicated to the spirit of collaboration, the strength of friendship, and the enduring pursuit of knowledge that binds us together.

In our joint endeavors—whether in the quiet rigor of scientific inquiry or the vibrant challenges of life—we have shared not only ideas and ambitions, but also trust, laughter, and purpose.

May this work stand as a modest tribute to the bonds we have forged and the discoveries yet to come.

With gratitude and respect,

Prof. dr sc Goran Ilik

Editorial Advisory Board

Table of Contents

Detailed Table of Contents

Education has long played a pivotal role in shaping political narratives, and in recent years, the Western Balkans have become a critical arena for geopolitical influence between the European Union and China. Both actors strategically leverage educational initiatives as instruments of soft power to expand their reach and assert their visions within the region. This chapter explores how the EU and China utilize education not only as a means of engagement but also as a conduit within the complex ecosystem of disinformation that characterizes the Western Balkans. By analyzing these educational efforts, the chapter sheds light on how they intersect with, reinforce, or challenge competing disinformation narratives, ultimately influencing the political and social fabric of the region.

The chapter discusses the implications that social media age has on modern political and social processes, examines dangers of disinformation and fake news, and analyses different approaches to countering them. Social media literacy is considered as one of the key tools to respond to the perils of false information on social media platforms, by giving users competences and skills to discern between facts and falsehood. Different concepts in literature and overview of relevant research on the topic are reviewed. The chapter concludes the discussion with the considerations on the so called "post-truth" era and offers recommendations for steps forward, both in countering negative effects of disinformation, and in possible future research on social media literacy.

In the new era of today, Generative AI (GenAI) and media literacy, are inseparably linked. GenAI has both the potential to transform the world of media, but also the opportunity to challenge the status quo and help users with malicious intents create misinformation and disinformation easier than ever. This chapter addresses this intersection. It begins with an overview of GenAI's origins and its growing influence on media production, journalism, and creative industries. The discussion then shifts to the new challenges posed by AI-generated misinformation, deepfakes, bias, and intellectual property concerns, all of which contribute to the erosion of trust in media. The chapter also examines opportunities for enhancing media literacy in the age of AI, including educational initiatives, policy interventions, and collaborations between tech companies and educators, all to show that the issue of GenAI and media literacy is of importance and requires careful consideration.

This chapter explores how disinformation is propagated by scholars who act as Foreign Information Manipulation and Interference (FIMI) agents. Focusing on the Venezuelan presidential elections of July 2024, it analyzes the behavior of a network of Ibero-American academics and intellectuals who actively disseminated regime-aligned narratives online. This chapter shifts attention to digital advocacy, where academic credibility is leveraged to legitimize authoritarian propaganda. Using the framework of Public Diplomacy in authoritarian contexts, the study applies a mixed-methods design combining quantitative and qualitative content analysis with Social Network Analysis (SNA). The dataset comprises all posts on X (formerly Twitter) from 17 selected individuals between July 15 and August 1, 2024. The findings reveal how academic figures contribute to disinformation campaigns, calling for greater scholarly engagement with the risks of authoritarian influence in knowledge production and democratic discourse.

This study aims to examine media content in the Republic of North Macedonia to identify the presence and use of disinformation and misinformation, and to explore the relationship between media literacy education and public perceptions of these phenomena. Employing a mixed-methods approach, the research integrates both qualitative and quantitative methods across two distinct studies with complementary objectives. The findings indicate a significant presence of disinformation and misinformation within North Macedonian media, alongside a notable deficiency in the audience's ability—particularly among youth—to critically assess and verify online content. The study offers valuable insights into the current media environment and provides actionable recommendations for enhancing media transparency and combating false narratives through targeted media literacy education initiatives.

Deepfake technology, initially developed for interactive entertainment, has increasingly become a tool for influencing voter behavior, making its impact particularly significant in the context of the 2024 elections. This relevance is heightened by the occurrence of multiple national elections held concurrently with the European Parliament (EP) elections. In response, various countries have introduced legal frameworks to address the challenges posed by deepfakes. This chapter examines these national legal approaches and analyzes their interaction with the broader European Union (EU) legal system in combating disinformation and promoting voter participation. It provides a concise overview of the evolution of deepfake technology, demonstrates its role in voter manipulation through disinformation campaigns, and evaluates the EU's strategic measures aimed at mitigating the adverse effects of deepfakes. Ultimately, the chapter underscores the importance of coordinated legal and policy efforts to safeguard democratic processes across the EU and its member states.

Chapter 7

This chapter investigates students' perceptions, knowledge, and attitudes toward deepfake technology, including its potential misuse and related protection and reporting mechanisms. The research employs a focus group discussion involving 10 students from five faculties at the University "St. Kliment Ohridski" – Bitola: Faculty of Law, Faculty of Education, Faculty of Technical Sciences, Faculty of Information and Communication Technologies, and Faculty of Biotechnical Sciences. Preliminary findings indicate that while students are generally familiar with the concept of deepfakes, they lack sufficient skills to accurately identify deepfake content. To the best of our knowledge, this is the first study in North Macedonia to examine students' awareness and understanding of deepfake technology. Based on these results, the chapter offers recommendations aimed at enhancing public awareness and improving students' ability to recognize and respond to deepfake materials effectively.

Chapter 8

The role of digital media in disseminating information has attained a prominent position in society. Though social media and other platforms promise a democratic space, in reality, it has been an easy ground for powerful entities with resources to sow the seeds of propaganda with the help of manipulated information. The dominance of incorrect information in the form of misinformation, disinformation, and fake news is evident. This chapter analyses the scenario of the UK and the USA in brief, with a primary focus on India, which has been the nucleus of the informational crisis, palpable during elections, COVID-19, and in general. Further, the paper attempts to identify the factors that flare up the menace of misinformation,

The widespread dissemination of misinformation, amplified by social media, presents a significant threat to democracies and societies globally. False narratives distort reality, manipulate public opinion, and undermine trust in institutions. Addressing this challenge requires a dual approach that combines legal regulation and educational empowerment. This chapter examines existing and emerging legal frameworks aimed at curbing the spread of harmful misinformation, alongside educational strategies designed to enhance individuals' critical thinking skills and their ability to discern fake news. It also reviews the roles of international organizations and governments in implementing solutions such as stricter regulations on social media platforms, accountability measures for content, public awareness campaigns, media literacy programs, and fact-checking initiatives. By integrating legal and educational efforts, societies can become better equipped to navigate the complex information environment of the digital age and foster a more informed and resilient citizenry.

This study examined how group discussions affected prospective teachers' metacognitive confidence and decision accuracy when classifying AI-based educational technology news as real or fake. A quasi-experimental design was used with 20 prospective teachers. Before evaluating the news, participants completed measures of news media and AI literacy. They then classified eight news articles individually, in groups, and again individually. Findings showed that group discussions significantly affected confidence and accuracy, with group confidence exceeding individual confidence after discussion. However, accuracy was more consistent for real news than fake news. News media and AI literacy had a small effect on initial judgments and a limited effect after discussion. The results highlight the need to integrate media and AI literacy into teacher education to improve decision making in collaborative learning, while highlighting the complexity of group dynamics in addressing misinformation about AI.

Preface

INTRODUCTION

In an age where information flows with extraordinary speed and reach, the challenge is no longer merely accessing knowledge—but discerning truth from falsehood. The proliferation of misinformation and false narratives has emerged as a pervasive threat to the integrity of public discourse, the resilience of democratic societies, and the foundations of global cooperation. These threats transcend national borders, political systems, and cultural contexts, influencing how individuals perceive the world, make decisions, and engage in civic life.

This book, *Combatting Misinformation and Global Nations' False Narratives Through Education* responds to this urgent and complex challenge. It examines the pivotal role education plays in navigating the evolving global information landscape, empowering individuals to become critical thinkers, responsible media consumers, and informed citizens.

From the rise of artificial intelligence and algorithmically generated content to the manipulation of social media and the orchestrated spread of disinformation, the book examines the multifaceted ways misinformation is created, disseminated, and believed. Importantly, it also offers a roadmap for resistance—grounded in education. Through the lens of pedagogy, curriculum design, digital literacy, civic education, and ethical frameworks, the chapters within offer diverse and interdisciplinary strategies for equipping learners of all ages with the tools they need to engage meaningfully and discerningly in today's complex media ecosystem.

The contributors to this volume—educators, researchers, practitioners, policymakers, and thought leaders—bring together international perspectives and innovative approaches that highlight both the challenges and the opportunities in countering false narratives through education. Collectively, they argue that education is not merely an antidote to misinformation but a proactive force for cultivating resilient democracies and fostering global understanding.

This book is intended for a wide readership, including academic scholars, education professionals, decision-makers, and students. It serves as a resource and a call to action—for those who recognize that the battle for truth is not only being fought in newsrooms and courtrooms but also in classrooms, lecture halls, and informal learning spaces worldwide.

In today's world, the topic of combatting misinformation and false narratives through education sits at the crossroads of some of the most pressing global challenges—information integrity, democratic resilience, technological disruption, and global security.

We are living in an era often described as a "post-truth" age, where emotions and personal beliefs frequently overshadow facts in shaping public opinion. The unprecedented speed and scale of information dissemination, particularly through digital platforms and social media, have created fertile ground for misinformation, disinformation, and propaganda to thrive. From election interference and public health crises to geopolitical conflicts and climate denialism, false narratives have had real-world consequences—undermining trust in institutions, fueling polarization, and distorting democratic processes.

This issue is global, affecting every region regardless of political, economic, or cultural context. False narratives can be domestically generated or internationally orchestrated, often using sophisticated technologies such as deepfakes, bots, and AI-generated content. The result is a highly volatile and manipulated information environment in which truth competes against an ever-expanding web of distortions.

Amid this complexity, education emerges as a powerful, long-term solution. While fact-checking and platform regulation are necessary short-term measures, only education can equip individuals with the critical thinking skills, digital literacy, and civic awareness needed to resist manipulation sustainably. This makes the topic deeply relevant to governments, civil society, international organizations, and educators in particular.

As nations grapple with how to safeguard democracy, uphold public trust, and protect social cohesion, this topic provides a framework for proactive and preventive action. It emphasizes that building a society capable of resisting falsehood begins not with censorship but with cultivating knowledge, judgment, and ethical reasoning.

This topic is not only timely but essential. It speaks to the core of how societies will function in the digital age—and whether truth, democracy, and informed citizenship can prevail in an increasingly chaotic information landscape.

CHAPTER OVERVIEW

Each chapter adds unique value to this discourse:

The chapter **"Education as a Geopolitical Tool: EU and China's Competing Strategies in the Western Balkans Disinformation Narrative"** by *Goran Ilik, Vesna Shapkoski, and Mladen Karadjoski* explores the role of education in the geopolitical contest between the European Union and China. Through strategic educational initiatives, both powers aim to shape public perception and influence political orientation in the Western Balkans. This chapter examines how these efforts frequently intersect with disinformation dynamics, revealing the intricate relationship between soft power, education, and narrative control in a region characterized by historical volatility.

Complementing this geopolitical lens, the chapter **"Evaluating the Impact of Education on Misinformation Suppression: A Stock-and-Flow Simulation Approach"** by *Ilija S. Hristoski* applies a systems-thinking model to simulate the effects of education on reducing misinformation in digitally connected societies. Utilizing a Stock-and-Flow simulation, the study models three key variables—Misinformed Individuals, Well-Informed Individuals, and Educational Resources—and explores how changes in educational interventions impact the broader information landscape. The results underscore the importance of sustained resource investment and educational effectiveness in shaping public understanding and combating the dissemination of misinformation. This chapter offers valuable quantitative insights for decision-makers seeking to design evidence-based policies for mitigating misinformation.

The chapter **"Student Perceptions and Knowledge of Deepfake Technology in North Macedonia"** by *Blagoj Nenovski, Ice Ilijevski, and Angelina Stanojoska* offers an empirical perspective on how university students understand digital manipulation technologies—specifically deepfakes. Based on focus group discussions with students from five faculties at the University "St. Kliment Ohridski" – Bitola, the study reveals that although most students are aware of the existence of deepfakes, they lack the technical skills and critical literacy to recognize such content with confidence. As one of the first studies of its kind in North Macedonia, this chapter underscores the urgency of integrating digital literacy and misinformation awareness into university curricula. The authors offer practical recommendations for raising awareness and improving protective mechanisms against technologically sophisticated forms of disinformation.

In **"Teaching Media Law in the Era of Disinformation and Hybrid Threats: Navigating the Infodemic,"** *Vesna Poposka and Goran Ilik* examine how the pedagogy of media law must evolve to meet the challenges of our time. They argue that beyond legal theory, media law education must address the ethical, strategic, and societal implications of the information disorder caused by hybrid threats and infodemics.

Emphasizing freedom of expression, resilience, and responsible communication, the chapter proposes curriculum reforms and interdisciplinary teaching approaches that foster these values. These changes aim to equip future media professionals, legal experts, and citizens with the tools to understand and counteract disinformation within complex and rapidly shifting environments.

The chapter **"Exploring the Legal Framework and Education for Protection and Promotion of Truthful Information"** by *Pranjal Khare, Vishambhar Raghuwanshi, and Paridhi Sharma* examines how legal regulation and education must work in tandem to counter misinformation. The authors analyze international and national legal frameworks, explore strategies such as accountability mechanisms, fact-checking initiatives, and media literacy programs, and advocate for a harmonized approach that enhances critical awareness while safeguarding fundamental freedoms.

In **"The Role of Media Literacy Education in Countering Disinformation and Misinformation: Exploring the Capability of Youth and Media in North Macedonia to Recognize False Narratives,"** *Agron Vrangalla, Agron Kurtishi, Arta Xhelili, and Avni Remzi Avdiu* investigate the landscape of disinformation within North Macedonia's media environment and assess the effectiveness of media literacy education, particularly among young audiences. Using a mixed-methods approach, the study reveals a significant gap in young people's ability to evaluate online content despite their high exposure to misinformation. This chapter offers actionable insights and policy recommendations to enhance media literacy curricula and strengthen youth's capacity to navigate today's complex digital information ecosystem.

"The Role of Education in Combating Cybercrime in the Asia-Pacific: Tackling Misinformation and Disinformation in Australia" by *Leo S.F. Lin, Geberew Tulu Mekonnen, Mladen Zecevic, Duane Aslett, and Douglas M.C. Allan* explores the critical function of education in addressing cybercrime, with a focus on misinformation and disinformation challenges faced in Australia. This chapter highlights the importance of digital literacy and critical thinking education in equipping individuals to navigate complex online environments, identify trustworthy information, and resist malicious content. By emphasizing ethical standards and adaptive educational strategies, it provides valuable insights for shaping policy and educational frameworks across the Asia-Pacific, aiming to strengthen societal defenses against the evolving threats of cybercrime and information manipulation.

"Influenced by the Group: AI Misinformation Detection by Prospective Teachers" by *Gamze Türkmen* examines the effect of group discussions on the confidence and accuracy of prospective teachers in distinguishing between real and fake AI-related educational news. Using a quasi-experimental design, the study reveals that collaborative discussions significantly boost participants' confidence, although improvements in accuracy are more pronounced for real news than for misinformation. The findings underscore the importance of embedding both media literacy and AI literacy into teacher education programs to enhance critical evaluation skills. Additionally, the chapter highlights the nuanced role of group dynamics in shaping decision-making processes, emphasizing the complexity of combating AI misinformation in educational contexts.

"Media Literacy in Times of Advanced GenAI: New Challenges and Perspectives" by *Elena Shalevska* explores the intricate relationship between generative artificial intelligence (GenAI) and media literacy in today's rapidly evolving information landscape. The chapter traces the development of GenAI and its transformative impact on media creation, journalism, and the creative industries while critically addressing the new risks posed by AI-generated misinformation, deepfakes, bias, and intellectual property challenges. It emphasizes how these emerging threats contribute to declining trust in media and highlights innovative educational strategies, policy measures, and collaborative efforts between technology and education sectors. Ultimately, the chapter emphasizes the need to reassess and enhance media literacy frameworks to address the challenges presented by advanced AI technologies effectively.

"Combating Misinformation, Disinformation, and Fake News: A Comparative Study of the USA, UK, and India" by *Pallav, S. M. Aamir Ali, and Anuttama Ghose presents a comparative analysis of how misinformation, disinformation, and fake news spread* through digital media platforms across three influential democracies. While briefly examining the UK and US contexts, the chapter focuses extensively on India, where the informational crisis has intensified during critical events, such as elections and the COVID-19 pandemic. It identifies key factors that exacerbate the spread of false information on social media and critically evaluates regulatory responses and their effectiveness. The chapter concludes by proposing practical countermeasures to manage better and mitigate the pervasive impact of manipulated information in these diverse socio-political environments.

"Scholars as Disinformation Agents: Unmasking Academic Propaganda for Authoritarian Venezuela" by *Michel Navarro and Juan Cristóbal Demian* investigates the troubling role of certain academics as active agents in foreign information manipulation and interference (FIMI). Focusing on the Venezuelan presidential elections of July 2024, the chapter uncovers how a network of Ibero-American scholars strategically disseminated regime-supportive narratives via social media platforms, particularly on X (formerly Twitter). By leveraging their academic authority, these individuals helped legitimize authoritarian propaganda, blurring the lines between scholarship and political advocacy. Employing a rigorous mixed-methods approach that includes content and social network analysis, the study highlights the complexities of digital advocacy in authoritarian contexts and calls for increased vigilance and responsibility within the academic community to safeguard democratic discourse from such covert influence operations.

"Politics and Democracy in the Age of Misinformation" by *Svetlana Veljanovska* addresses the profound challenges misinformation poses to democratic societies today. The chapter explores the increasingly blurred lines between truth, propaganda, and manipulation in public discourse, highlighting how populism often exploits these ambiguities to capture widespread attention. It critically examines the complex relationship democracy holds with truth, questioning the very value of truth when it is marginalized or dismissed in political debate. The work highlights the dangers of disinformation as a deliberate form of deception that threatens not only informed dialogue but also the foundational principles of democracy itself, raising urgent questions about the resilience and future of democratic governance in an age dominated by misinformation.

"Digital Global Village: Literacy in the Age of Social Media and 'Post-Truth'" by *Goran Bandov* and *Nikolina Herceg Kolman* explores the profound effects social media has on political and social dynamics in today's world. The chapter examines the dangers posed by disinformation and fake news, highlighting the crucial role of social media literacy in enabling users to distinguish fact from fiction. By reviewing key concepts and relevant research, the authors shed light on effective strategies to combat misinformation within the broader context of the "post-truth" era. The chapter concludes with practical recommendations for advancing social media literacy initiatives and directions for future research to address the ongoing challenges of digital misinformation.

"Deepfakes Risks and Challenges in the Context of National and European Parliament Elections" by *Viktorija Soņeca* addresses the growing threat posed by deepfake technology in the electoral processes of 2024. Recognizing the potential of deepfakes not only for entertainment but also for influencing voter decisions, the chapter highlights the increased urgency of this issue during simultaneous national and European Parliament elections. It reviews national legal frameworks established to tackle deepfake-related disinformation and analyzes their interaction with EU-level legislation. Through a concise history of deepfake technology, the chapter illustrates its use in disinformation campaigns targeting voters. It evaluates the EU's strategies designed to counteract these threats and safeguard democratic participation across member states.

CONCLUSION

This book makes a significant contribution to the evolving field of misinformation, disinformation, and media literacy by providing a multidisciplinary and international perspective on the challenges posed by the digital information environment. Through diverse case studies, theoretical analyses, and empirical research, the volume offers innovative approaches to understanding how education, legal frameworks, technology, and social dynamics interact to shape the spread and suppression of false information. Ultimately, this book not only advances academic debate but also contributes practical solutions to one of the defining challenges of our digital age.

Taken together, the chapters in this volume reflect the multifaceted nature of today's information crisis and underscore the pivotal role of education in defending truth, trust, and transparency. This book is a valuable resource for educators, policymakers, legal professionals, communication experts, civil society organizations, and researchers dedicated to restoring integrity in the global information landscape. By highlighting both the vulnerabilities and the opportunities that define our digital age, it calls on all sectors of society to invest in education as a cornerstone of democratic resilience and informed global citizenship.

Goran Ilik
University "St. Kliment Ohridski", Bitola, North Macedonia

Mladen Karadjoski
University "St. Kliment Ohridski", Bitola, North Macedonia

Ice Ilijevski
University "St. Kliment Ohridski", Bitola, North Macedonia

Blagoj Nenovski
University "St. Kliment Ohridski", Bitola, North Macedonia

Chapter 1

Education as a Geopolitical Tool:

EU and China's Competing Strategies in the Western Balkans Disinformation Narrative

Goran Ilik
https://orcid.org/0000-0003-3501-1386
University "St. Kliment Ohridski", Bitola, North Macedonia

Vesna Shapkoski
https://orcid.org/0000-0002-7705-2808
University "St. Kliment Ohridski", Bitola, North Macedonia

Mladen Karadjoski
https://orcid.org/0000-0002-1942-1804
University "St. Kliment Ohridski", Bitola, North Macedonia

ABSTRACT

Education has long played a pivotal role in shaping political narratives, and in recent years, the Western Balkans have become a critical arena for geopolitical influence between the European Union and China. Both actors strategically leverage educational initiatives as instruments of soft power to expand their reach and assert their visions within the region. This chapter explores how the EU and China utilize education not only as a means of engagement but also as a conduit within the complex ecosystem of disinformation that characterizes the Western Balkans. By analyzing these educational efforts, the chapter sheds light on how they intersect with, reinforce, or challenge competing disinformation narratives, ultimately influencing the political and social fabric of the region.

DOI: 10.4018/979-8-3693-9601-8.ch001

INTRODUCTION

The Western Balkans, a region historically marred by political instability, economic volatility, and contested identities, has emerged as a key geopolitical arena for external powers seeking to expand their influence. Among the most prominent actors in this evolving landscape are the European Union (EU) and the People's Republic of China, which have adopted multifaceted strategies to assert their presence. Often overlooked in traditional geopolitical analyses, education has become a strategic instrument through which these actors pursue their respective visions for the region.

The EU, positioned as a normative power and long-standing partner in the Western Balkans, has embedded education at the core of its broader integration agenda. Initiatives such as Erasmus+, the Bologna Process, and regionally targeted programs are designed to elevate the quality and compatibility of higher education and foster democratic values, the rule of law, and institutional transparency. These educational efforts aim to create pro-European constituencies, cultivate reform-minded elites, and enhance the region's alignment with EU norms and standards.

China's approach, by contrast, is embedded in its Belt and Road Initiative (BRI) and emphasizes principles of mutual benefit, non-interference, and respect for sovereignty. Through scholarships, academic partnerships, and the establishment of Confucius Institutes, China is extending its soft power and offering an alternative development model. These educational channels are carefully crafted to nurture pro-Chinese sentiment, legitimize China's global leadership ambitions, and counter-narratives that portray China as a threat to liberal democratic order.

Crucially, both actors recognize the role of education in shaping public perceptions and combating—or, conversely, disseminating—disinformation. The EU has increasingly invested in media literacy, critical thinking, and civic education to build resilience against authoritarian narratives, particularly those from China.

China is governed by an authoritarian regime, with the Chinese Communist Party (CCP) tightly controlling government, media, religion, education, and civil society. Under Xi Jinping, power has been highly centralized, and years of crackdowns have severely weakened independent NGOs and human rights advocacy.

China has been accused of using educational and cultural platforms to propagate state-sanctioned narratives that downplay human rights concerns and depict the West as fragmented and in decline. In this context, education is a development tool and a geopolitical influence conduit.

This chapter critically examines the competing educational strategies of the EU and China in the Western Balkans, analyzing how these initiatives intersect with broader narratives of disinformation, political alignment, and regional transformation.

LITERATURE REVIEW

The Western Balkans have emerged as a strategic region in the geopolitical contest between the European Union (EU) and China. China's growing presence in the area is reflected through various economic, cultural, and educational initiatives, which regional actors and international observers closely monitor. For instance, Balkan Investigative Reporting Network (2021) launched an online platform dedicated to tracking China's activities in the region, highlighting the breadth and complexity of its involvement. Recent scholarly work has increasingly scrutinized the implications of China's development assistance in the Western Balkans, particularly regarding its influence on democratic governance and national decision-making processes.

Ana Krstinovska (2022a; 2022b) underscores critical concerns regarding transparency and political conditionality in the context of Chinese development assistance to the Western Balkans, drawing attention to the governance challenges that such aid may pose. While Chinese-funded projects have become increasingly visible across the region, scholarly engagement with this phenomenon remains limited. Many aid-funded initiatives are frequently misrepresented as foreign direct investments, obscuring their actual nature and implications. Recent findings suggest that although Chinese assistance may contribute to short-term economic development, it concurrently undermines democratic institutions and facilitates China's political leverage by aligning recipient states' decision-making with its broader foreign policy objectives.

Culturally, China is fostering soft power through institutions such as the Confucius Institutes in North Macedonia, Serbia and Bosnia and Herzegovina (The Geopost, 2024; University of Sarajevo, 2025; University "Ss. Cyril and Methodius" in Skopje, 2025), and via art performances like those reported in Albania (China Daily, 2015). Educational ties are further deepened through Chinese government scholarships (Education Department of the PRC in Serbia, 2015) and partnerships with regional universities (Western Balkans University, 2024). This approach is supplemented by public diplomacy and propaganda, as identified by the United States-China Economic and Security Review Commission (2023), which warns of China's global strategy to shape public narratives.

The Belt and Road Initiative (BRI), as described by McBride, Berman, and Chatzky (2023), has had both infrastructural and environmental consequences in the Western Balkans, with the highway project in Montenegro serving as a prominent example (Kajosevic, 2020). Environmental watchdogs, such as Petkova (2021), have detailed the ecological impacts of such projects, raising questions about the sustainability of Chinese-led investments.

In contrast, the EU's strategy focuses on democratic standards, human rights, and capacity building. The European Commission (2021; 2024) and its instruments like Erasmus+ aim to strengthen youth mobility, academic cooperation, and values-based education across the Western Balkans, aligning the region more closely with European norms. The European Universities Initiative and related policy frameworks (European Commission: DG EAC, 2024) emphasize regional integration through joint university alliances. Reports by the European Parliament (2022) and European Union (2023) underline the EU's strategic concern over Chinese influence, potentially undermining the EU's normative leverage.

The rising importance of media and information literacy is also underscored in the regional context. Reports by EAVI (2017) and Goodman (2021) advocate for stronger media literacy networks in Macedonia and Europe more broadly, especially as disinformation and foreign influence pose growing threats. Institutions like Human Rights Watch (2019) and Freedom House (2020) have cautioned against China's suppression of academic freedom, which has international ramifications.

Furthermore, cultural fascination with the Chinese language and culture is rising, particularly among the youth, as noted in Liuliu, Wenwen, and Wei (2023). These soft power efforts contribute to the broader narrative of China as a benign partner, counterbalancing more critical Western portrayals. Still, researchers like Zeneli (2023) argue that China's presence in the Western Balkans complicates the region's EU accession process by promoting alternative governance models and economic dependencies.

Finally, efforts like the Youth Guarantee schemes discussed by the European Training Foundation (2024) and civic platforms such as We Balkans (2023; 2024) show how the EU invests in long-term human development, which contrasts sharply with China's project-driven engagements.

The literature reflects a growing academic and policy interest in understanding the EU's and China's dual influence in the Western Balkans. While the EU emphasizes governance, democratic standards, and regional integration, China's influence is exerted through economic infrastructure, cultural diplomacy, and educational exchange, with potentially ambivalent effects on the region's political alignment and development trajectory.

METHODS

This chapter employs a qualitative comparative case study methodology to examine the educational strategies pursued by the European Union and China in the Western Balkans. It operates on the premise that education serves not only as a means of fostering human capital but also as a strategic instrument of soft power.

Within this framework, the chapter explores how educational initiatives are utilized to advance broader geopolitical objectives and shape or counteract regional disinformation narratives.

The research is grounded in document analysis and a review of secondary sources, including policy papers, official declarations, programmatic frameworks, and academic literature. This methodological approach enables a multi-dimensional investigation of how education contributes to the ongoing contest for normative and political influence between the EU and China.

The Western Balkans—comprising Albania, Bosnia and Herzegovina, Kosovo, Montenegro, North Macedonia, and Serbia—serve as the geographical focus due to their geopolitical relevance, ongoing EU accession processes, and increasing engagement with China's Belt and Road Initiative (BRI). The region presents a strategically significant context where Western and non-Western interests intersect amid relatively weak institutional frameworks and heightened susceptibility to disinformation.

While preparing this chapter, the authors used ChatGPT to refine the text's English language. Following this tool, the authors carefully reviewed and edited the content as necessary and assumed full responsibility for the final version of the chapter.

EU EDUCATIONAL INITIATIVES

The European Union (EU) has long recognized education as a pivotal tool for fostering unity, promoting shared values, and combating disinformation. In the context of the Western Balkans, a region marked by historical divisions and external influences, the EU's educational initiatives aim to strengthen pro-European sentiment, counter malign narratives, and support broader foreign policy objectives. Therefore, the EU employs a multifaceted approach to leveraging education as a geopolitical instrument in the Western Balkans, aiming to promote its "axiological (value) framework" (Ilik and Adamczyk, 2017, p. 11) and bolster resilience against disinformation. This strategy encompasses programs like Erasmus+, collaborations with European universities, and initiatives that intertwine education with the EU's broader foreign policy objectives in the region.

Erasmus+ and Mobility Programs

Erasmus+, the European Union's flagship education, training, youth, and sports program, is a cornerstone of the EU's efforts to foster closer educational collaboration among countries worldwide. By offering scholarships, exchange opportunities, and capacity-building initiatives, Erasmus+ creates vital people-to-people connections and serves as a platform for promoting European values such as pluralism, democracy, human rights and freedoms, and the rule of law.

Regarding benefits for the Western Balkan countries, Erasmus+ facilitates mobility opportunities for students, academics, and young professionals from the Western Balkans to engage with European universities and institutions (European Commission, 2020).

These exchanges enhance participants' academic and professional experiences and immerse them in the EU's cultural and social values. Between 2015 and 2020, for example, over 23,000 individuals from the Western Balkans took part in Erasmus+ mobility programs. Participants gained exposure to European teaching methods, academic standards, and collaborative learning environments, which many described as transformative experiences (European Commission, 2021). Such mobility opportunities often create ripple effects. Upon their return, participants frequently act as ambassadors for European ideals, sharing their knowledge and experiences with their home communities. This role is particularly important in fostering critical thinking, media literacy, and resilience against disinformation—key challenges in a region often targeted for external disinformation campaigns.

One of the Erasmus+ program's distinguishing features is its emphasis on inclusivity. The program actively encourages participation from individuals of diverse socio-economic backgrounds, ensuring that disadvantaged groups, such as rural or underprivileged students, can access these opportunities. By prioritizing inclusivity, Erasmus+ fosters equitable access to high-quality education and builds bridges between diverse communities across the EU and the Western Balkans.

Beyond individual mobility, Erasmus+ fosters long-term institutional collaborations through funding for joint degrees and academic partnerships. Programs like "Capacity Building in Higher Education" (CBHE) under Erasmus+ have been instrumental in modernizing curricula, improving teaching methodologies, and strengthening research capacities in the Western Balkans. In line with the Sustainable Development Goals (SDGs) and the Paris Agreement, this action supports the relevance, quality, modernization and responsiveness of higher education in third countries not associated with the Program in addressing socio-economic recovery, growth and prosperity and reacting to recent trends, in particular, economic globalization but also the recent decline in human development, fragility, and rising social, economic and environmental inequalities (European Commission, 2024, p. 326). For example, through CBHE, universities in the region have adopted innovative teaching methods, such as blended learning and digital classrooms, which align with European standards. These projects often involve collaborative partnerships between multiple universities, NGOs, and industry stakeholders, ensuring that educational reforms are comprehensive and responsive to local and global challenges. Erasmus+ has also been a key driver in establishing joint degree programs, which allow students to earn qualifications recognized across multiple countries. These programs not only enhance the employability of graduates but also promote academic excellence and cross-cultural understanding.

By equipping participants with critical thinking skills, Erasmus+ helps address the growing challenge of disinformation in the Western Balkans. Students and young professionals returning from Erasmus+ programs often bring back a heightened awareness of media literacy and democratic principles. These experiences empower them to counteract false narratives and contribute to more informed public discourse in their home countries. Furthermore, the broader impact of Erasmus+ extends beyond the immediate benefits to individuals and institutions. The program strategically strengthens the EU's relationship with the Western Balkans, fostering trust and mutual understanding. Erasmus+ contributes to the region's socio-economic development and alignment with EU integration goals by enabling knowledge transfer and promoting European educational standards.

The Role of European Universities

European universities play a pivotal role as hubs for intellectual exchange, research innovation, and cross-border collaboration, often serving as extensions of the European Union's strategic objectives. These institutions actively foster narratives that align with EU values, such as democracy, human rights, and the rule of law, while addressing challenges like disinformation and social polarization, particularly in neighboring regions like the Western Balkans. European universities partner with their Western Balkans counterparts to develop research programs and curricula emphasizing critical skills for navigating the modern information ecosystem. For instance, initiatives often focus on critical media literacy, digital skills, and civic education—key areas for empowering students and communities to resist and counteract disinformation campaigns. Furthermore, European universities frequently organize conferences, workshops, and academic forums that bring together scholars, practitioners, policymakers, and students from the EU and the Western Balkans. These events foster dialogue on shared challenges and opportunities, such as combating disinformation, strengthening democratic institutions, and promoting regional stability.

One significant example of an initiative directly involving European universities is the European Universities Alliances Initiative - an ambitious EU initiative to establish alliances between higher institutions across Europe to benefit their students, staff and society.

At the national level, Germany (67) and France (64) have the highest number of higher education institutions participating in European Universities alliances, followed by Spain (56) and Italy (46). This corresponds with these countries being among the largest EU Member States and having many HEIs with an Erasmus Charter for Higher Education (ECHE) (European Commission, 2025, p. 82) (Figure 1).

Figure 1. Relative share of higher education institutions (HEIs) in alliances per country, expressed as a percentage of national institutions holding an Erasmus+ charter for higher education (ECHE), as of January 2025 (European Commission, 2025, p. 82).

Figure 2 presents the distribution of alliances based on the types of member institutions. It reveals that over half of the alliances comprise comprehensive universities, while nearly a quarter comprise mixed memberships. The remaining alliances—about one in five—are composed of universities of applied sciences or are specialized groupings, such as technical universities, art schools, or distance-learning institutions (European Commission, 2025, p. 85).

Figure 2. Number of alliances by type of member institutions (European Commission, 2025, p. 85).

By developing long-term structural, strategic and sustainable cooperation between the higher education institutions in the European universities alliances, the initiative aims to improve the international competitiveness of higher education institutions in Europe and promote European values and identity (European Commission, 2024).

Students can get a degree through these alliances by combining their studies in several European countries. The initiative can benefit higher education institutions more than any previous cooperation projects. As of the summer of 2024, 65 European universities involving more than 570 higher education institutions from all parts of Europe were part of the initiative, creating opportunities and transforming higher education (European Commission, 2024).

By leveraging their intellectual resources, reputations, and extensive networks, European universities contribute significantly to promoting the EU's normative agenda. They act as intermediaries, facilitating knowledge transfer and capacity-building efforts that align with EU priorities. For example, universities often include components in their programs that emphasize democratic governance, media freedom, and cross-cultural understanding—values that resonate with the EU's vision for a stable and prosperous neighborhood.

These collaborations also serve to strengthen local expertise and institutions. For instance, partnerships have resulted in the publication of research papers, policy briefs, and educational resources that directly address disinformation and its societal impacts. The focus on evidence-based approaches helps establish credibility and fosters trust between EU institutions and communities in the Western Balkans.

The role of European universities extends beyond education and research; they contribute to creating a resilient information ecosystem. By investing in partnerships with the Western Balkans, they help build the region's capacity to address the challenges of disinformation, ensuring that citizens are equipped to engage with information in an increasingly digital world critically. These efforts support the EU's broader geopolitical interests and strengthen the ties between the EU and its neighboring regions, fostering mutual understanding and cooperation.

Intersecting Education and Foreign Policy

The EU's educational initiatives in the Western Balkans are deeply interwoven with its foreign policy objectives, particularly its commitment to the region's European integration and stabilization. By investing in education, the EU aims to build local capacity, promote alignment with European standards, and strengthen resilience against external influences. These efforts shape a pro-European identity, foster regional stability, and counter disinformation and authoritarian narratives propagated by geopolitical rivals such as Russia and China.

Education serves as one of the EU's most effective soft power tools in the Western Balkans, helping to promote its values of democracy, good governance, human rights, and the rule of law. By integrating these principles into educational initiatives, the EU addresses regional challenges and counters the influence of other global actors pursuing alternative engagement models. For example, while China's

Confucius Institutes promote Chinese culture, language, and state-centric narratives, EU programs emphasize transparency, inclusivity, and democratic governance. Similarly, Russian-funded cultural initiatives often promote narratives that challenge the EU's legitimacy in the region. In response, EU education programs aim to provide an alternative vision rooted in pluralism, critical thinking, and civic responsibility.

The European Union has implemented several initiatives to foster a pro-European identity among young people in the Western Balkans, promoting democratic values, active citizenship, and media literacy. One such initiative is the "Young European Ambassadors" (YEA) platform, a creative network of young activists from the Western Balkans. YEAs engage in various activities, including organizing events and workshops that promote activism, learning, and personal development (We Balkans, 2024). These efforts aim to build bridges of trust and understanding, fostering a sense of European identity among the youth in the region.

The European Training Foundation (ETF) has also promoted the EU's Youth Guarantee in the Western Balkans. This initiative aims to offer young people employment, work-based learning, or further education or training within four months of leaving education or becoming unemployed. By bringing together various stakeholders, the Youth Guarantee seeks to facilitate the school-to-work transition and encourage active participation in governance processes (ETF, 2024).

The EU's educational engagement in the Western Balkans also mitigates the region's susceptibility to geopolitical rivals. Educational initiatives focused on critical media literacy equip citizens to discern such disinformation and reinforce trust in European institutions. Moreover, the EU's capacity-building programs, such as those under Erasmus+, help local institutions modernize and align with European standards, reducing dependency on external actors. For instance, the EU has funded collaborative projects with universities in Serbia and North Macedonia to strengthen their research capacities and foster regional cooperation in digital education and sustainable development.

While other actors like China and Russia use educational and cultural diplomacy to project influence, the EU differentiates itself by promoting inclusivity, pluralism, and evidence-based education. Its emphasis on fostering democratic resilience and critical thinking provides a compelling alternative to authoritarian models. The EU bolsters its vision of a unified and stable Europe by equipping individuals and institutions in the Western Balkans with the skills and knowledge to thrive in an interconnected world.

China's Educational Outreach

China has increasingly leveraged education as a strategic tool to expand its influence in the Western Balkans, a region pivotal to its Belt and Road Initiative (BRI) and global geopolitical ambitions. Moreover, Chinese investment in the region has expanded significantly. A Balkan Investigative Reporting Network report released in December 2021 identified 122 Chinese projects valued at approximately $31 billion (27.6 billion euros) (Zeneli and Mejdini, n.d.).

By establishing Confucius Institutes (as an exponent of Chinese soft power), facilitating academic exchanges, and providing scholarships, China seeks to enhance its soft power, foster cultural affinity, and promote narratives that challenge Western dominance. Joseph Nye (2012) defines soft power as "an ability to affect others to get the outcomes one wants, and that can be done by coercion, payment or attraction". For the first time, soft power as part of Chinese policy was mentioned in October 2007 by former president Hu Jintao in his keynote speech at the 17th National Congress of the Communist Party of China (Babulik, 2024).

A key component of China's soft power strategy in the Western Balkans is educational and cultural diplomacy, most notably represented by the Confucius Institutes. These institutes function as international cultural hubs established by the Chinese government through its National Office for Teaching Chinese as a Foreign Language, aiming to promote Chinese language culture and foster mutual understanding abroad (Babulik, 2024).

The Role of Confucius Institutes

Confucius Institutes (CIs) are a key component of China's educational and cultural diplomacy (soft power), strategically designed to promote Chinese language, culture, and bilateral cooperation. CIs operate under the umbrella of Hanban (the Office of the Chinese Language Council International, a branch of the Chinese Ministry of Education), which in 2020 renamed itself the Center for Language Education and Cooperation (CLEC).

CIs are often embedded within local universities, allowing China to project soft power globally. Beijing has established Confucius Institutes throughout the Western Balkans, with the first institute in the region opened in Belgrade in 2006 and the rest after the establishment of the BRI: Two in Serbia at state universities of Belgrade (2006) and Novi Sad (2014), at the University of Tirana in Albania (2013), at Ss. Cyril and Methodius University in Skopje in North Macedonia (2013), at the University of Sarajevo (2015) and the University of Banja Luka (2018) in BiH and the University of Montenegro in Podgorica (2017) (Zeneli, 2023).

Confucius Institutes focus primarily on teaching Mandarin and organizing cultural events that showcase Chinese traditions. These activities, such as Chinese New Year celebrations, calligraphy workshops, traditional music performances, and tea ceremonies, are designed to foster a favorable perception of Chinese cultural heritage.

- The Confucius Institute at the University of Novi Sad in Serbia has been instrumental in promoting Mandarin language education and cultural exchange programs. According to a 2023 article by the Global Times, the institute aims to serve as a bridge for Serbian students to learn about Chinese culture and language. The institute organizes various cultural activities, including Chinese language classes and events where students can engage in traditional Chinese practices such as making dumplings and preparing hotpots. These initiatives have deepened students' appreciation for Chinese culture and strengthened the friendship between China and Serbia (Global Times, 2023).
- The Confucius Institute of Tirana was established in 2013. Apart from setting up Chinese courses at different levels, the Confucius Institute regularly launches a series of activities to promote Chinese culture and help students gain better insight into Chinese society (China Daily, 2015).
- In Bosnia and Herzegovina, Confucius Institutes actively collaborate with local governments and academic institutions to organize exhibitions and exchange programs that promote mutual understanding and goodwill. For instance, the Confucius Institute at the University of Sarajevo successfully held the 2025 Spring Festival Gala on 4 January 2025. The event featured cultural performances, exhibitions of teaching achievements, and activities such as Chinese calligraphy and painting, providing a window for local people to understand Chinese Spring Festival culture (UNSA, 2025).
- The Confucius Institute at Ss. Cyril and Methodius University in Skopje is a significant platform for cultural and academic exchange between North Macedonia and China. For instance, in October 2017, the Confucius Institute co-organized the 3rd China-CEE Conference in Ohrid, focusing on "The Role of Human Capital in the One Belt One Road Initiative." This event was a collaborative effort involving Ss. Cyril and Methodius University in Skopje, the Faculty of Economics – Skopje, the Institute of Economics – Skopje, and the University of Ljubljana's Faculty of Economics. The Chinese Academy of Social Sciences and the Institute for European Studies in Beijing supported the conference, highlighting the institute's commitment to promoting mutual understanding and cooperation.

In addition, Beijing promotes the creation of Confucius Classrooms at primary and secondary schools: The Government of Serbia has started a pilot project for the introduction of the Chinese language into 31 primary and secondary schools in the country, a project that started in 2012 involving more than 2500 students; More than 700 students are involved in similar courses in Montenegro, with similar numbers in Republika Srpska; In Albania, Confucius classrooms were set up in several high schools in Tirana since 2013 (Zeneli, 2023).

While Confucius Institutes present themselves as centers for cultural exchange, critics argue that their activities often extend beyond neutral cultural promotion. Instead, they serve as platforms to advance Beijing's strategic interests, particularly in regions like the Western Balkans, where China seeks to expand its economic and geopolitical influence. One of the most common criticisms of Confucius Institutes is their avoidance of sensitive topics, such as China's human rights record, the treatment of Uyghurs, the situation in Tibet, or issues surrounding Taiwan and Hong Kong. This selective approach to engagement has raised concerns about academic freedom and intellectual transparency; Universities hosting these institutes are sometimes pressured to avoid hosting events or discussions critical of China (Human Rights Watch, 2019). Furthermore, critics argue that the presence of Confucius Institutes can compromise the independence of host institutions. Allegations of censorship and self-censorship have surfaced in universities where CIs operate, leading to debates about the balance between academic autonomy and international collaboration (Human Rights Watch, 2019).

The activities of Confucius Institutes in the Western Balkans align with China's broader strategy of expanding its influence in politically significant regions but less integrated into Western alliances. With its strategic location and aspirations for development, the Western Balkans provides an ideal setting for China to position itself as a partner in economic growth and cultural exchange. Through cultural initiatives and language programs, CIs often create a favorable impression of China among local populations. This "soft" approach to diplomacy contrasts with other global actors' hard power tactics and gives China a competitive edge in the battle for influence. Furthermore, by engaging with students and young professionals, Confucius Institutes aim to cultivate a generation of future leaders who are familiar with and sympathetic to Chinese culture and policies. This long-term strategy shapes perceptions and fosters pro-China sentiments within key demographics.

China's approach through Confucius Institutes contrasts with the EU's educational initiatives in the Western Balkans. While the EU emphasizes inclusivity, pluralism, and critical thinking, Confucius Institutes focus on cultural promotion within a controlled narrative framework. For example, whereas EU-funded programs encourage open governance and human rights dialogue, CIs often sideline such discussions, focusing instead on presenting an idealized image of China.

Academic Exchanges and Scholarships

China's academic exchange programs and scholarships represent a significant mechanism for fostering influence in the Western Balkans, strategically aligning with Beijing's broader geopolitical and economic objectives. Through initiatives such as the Chinese Government Scholarship, students from the region are invited to pursue higher education in China, often on fully funded programs. The Chinese government has set up a series of scholarship programs to sponsor international students, teachers, and scholars studying and conducting research in Chinese universities. China Scholarship Council, entrusted by the Ministry of Education of the People's Republic of China, is responsible for the enrollment and administration of Chinese Government Scholarship programs (Education Department of the Embassy of PRC in Serbia, 2015). Two hundred seventy-nine designated Chinese universities offer various academic programs in Science, Engineering, Agriculture, Medicine, Law, Economics, Management, Education, Liberal Arts, Philosophy, History, and Fine Arts for scholarship winners at all levels (Education Department of the Embassy of PRC in Serbia, 2015). These opportunities expose Chinese academic environments while fostering long-term goodwill and networks supporting bilateral cooperation.

The Chinese Government Scholarship program has been a significant instrument in engaging the Western Balkans, offering students opportunities to study at prestigious Chinese institutions such as Tsinghua University, Peking University, and Fudan University. For instance, Fudan University offers various scholarships to international students, including the Chinese Government Scholarship, the Confucius Institute Scholarship, and the Shanghai Government Scholarship (Fudan University, 2025).

Approximately $1.5 billion has been allocated to development aid across a variety of projects, including grants for public administration support, agricultural modernization donations, school initiatives, funding for Confucius Institutes through Hanban, debt relief, training programs, as well as cooperation in police and military sectors—particularly in Bosnia and Herzegovina and Serbia (Zeneli, 2023) (see Figure 3).

Figure 3. China's development money (loans and grants) in the Western Balkans, 2000-2017 (Zeneli, 2023)

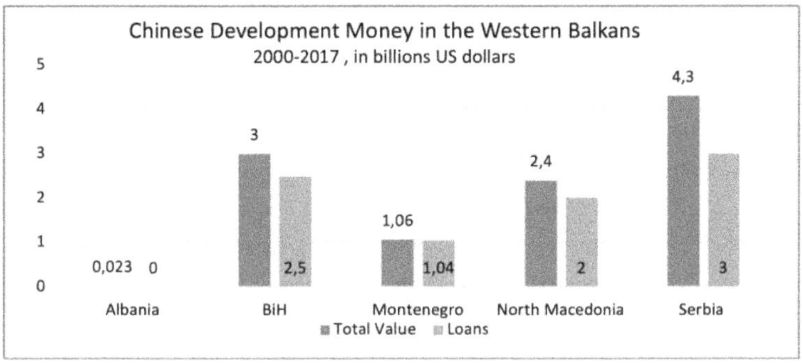

Academic scholarships are critically important for spreading the pro-Chinese sentiment among the academic community. Many students who study in China return with favorable impressions of the country. Immersed in an academic and cultural setting that emphasizes China's achievements, they often develop a sense of admiration for its rapid economic growth and technological advancements. Upon returning to their home countries, these alumni frequently become informal ambassadors for China, influencing public opinion, media narratives, and even policymaking. An important part of the role of this scholarship is the alumni networking. These networks serve as conduits for soft power, reinforcing positive perceptions of China among political, academic, and business leaders.

In addition to scholarships, China collaborates with universities in the Western Balkans through joint research programs, faculty exchanges, and institutional partnerships. These collaborations often focus on areas that align with China's strategic priorities, such as technology, infrastructure, and environmental sustainability.

Academic links between China and Western Balkan countries are growing and are characterized by an increasing range and intensity of interactions between national academies of sciences. This includes cooperation agreements with local institutions, new academic programs, regular exchanges of personnel, joint research projects, and new teaching positions (Zeneli, 2023). For instance, the University of Donja Gorica (UDG) in Montenegro has signed agreements with ten universities in China. It has implemented student and staff exchanges with three of them: Xihua University, Beijing Union University, and Southwestern University of Finance and Economics. Companies from China that cooperate prominently with the University of DonjaGorica include Sichuan Road and Bridge Group Corp and Sichuan Tianfu Bank. (European Parliament, 2022, 6). Another example is Western Balkans University from Albania, which, in February 2024, announced the signing of a cooperation agreement with Zhejiang Normal University in China. This agreement includes collaboration in research and scholarly activities, such as cooperative research and joint workshops on topics of common interest (WBU, 2024).

Academic exchanges are integral to China's broader soft power strategy in the Western Balkans, complementing its economic and cultural diplomacy. By investing in education, China gains goodwill among students and academics and cultivates a generation of future leaders who are familiar with and sympathetic to its policies and culture. This long-term investment in human capital creates a base of individuals who may later support or facilitate stronger bilateral ties with China. Many academic collaborations are aligned with China's Belt and Road Initiative. Joint research projects and educational exchanges often focus on infrastructure development, digital transformation, and green energy—key areas where China seeks to position itself as a global leader. China's educational programs offer an alternative engagement model in a region traditionally influenced by the European Union and the United States. By promoting its narrative of development and modernization, China provides a counterweight to Western norms and values, appealing to countries seeking diversified partnerships.

China's academic exchanges, including scholarships and joint research programs, are often viewed as opportunities for mutual learning. However, concerns have been raised regarding the nature and impact of these initiatives. Expanding joint research projects and faculty exchanges with Chinese institutions has prompted discussions about academic dependency. A U.S.-China Economic and Security Review Commission report highlights that the China Scholarship Council (CSC), affiliated with China's Ministry of Education, significantly facilitates these exchanges. The report suggests that such arrangements could influence participating institutions' academic freedom and independence (USCC, 2023, 37).

China's academic exchanges and scholarships in the Western Balkans demonstrate the country's strategic use of education as a soft power tool. By fostering academic and cultural ties, China strengthens its regional influence and advances its geopolitical and economic goals. However, the long-term implications of these programs, particularly regarding academic freedom and the balance of influence in the Western Balkans, remain topics of ongoing debate.

Counter-Narratives and Disinformation

China's educational outreach in the Western Balkans is not solely about fostering cultural understanding or academic collaboration. It also serves as a platform for disseminating counter-narratives that challenge Western dominance and promote China's global vision. Through carefully curated messaging, Beijing seeks to position itself as a reliable and equitable partner, contrasting with perceptions of Western paternalism or inconsistency.

China's approach in the Western Balkans emphasizes themes of mutual respect, non-interference, and "win-win" cooperation. Since the 1990s, "all the WB countries have received China's development assistance through grants and, except for Albania, also loans" (Krstinovska, 2022, p. 231).

Chinese-funded media outlets and academic forums often emphasize the positive impacts of China's investments in infrastructure projects, such as roads, bridges, and energy initiatives, as well as technological advancements like 5G implementation by companies like Huawei. These narratives typically portray China as a development partner focused on delivering tangible results without imposing political or ideological conditions. For instance, China's Belt and Road Initiative (BRI) is presented as a means to enhance connectivity and economic development in participating countries (McBride et al., 2023). In contrast, China's messaging sometimes subtly critiques Western powers by framing them as paternalistic or overly focused on imposing values rather than addressing practical needs. China's influence has expanded over the last decade in the Western Balkans, aligning with Beijing's geoeconomic and diplomatic vision. A key tool in promoting engagement with Western Balkans countries has been the "16+1" initiative with Central and Eastern European countries, established in 2012 and later tied to support the BRI (Zeneli, 2023). China's regional strategic communications often highlight the efficiency and mutual benefits of Chinese-led projects, contrasting them with Western institutions' more conditional and value-laden approaches. This framing aims to position China as a pragmatic partner committed to infrastructure development and economic growth, appealing to countries seeking rapid development without the political stipulations commonly associated with Western aid and investment.

China has strategically employed educational initiatives, including seminars, workshops, and university partnerships, to promote its perspectives in the Western Balkans. Confucius Institutes often organize events highlighting China's Belt and Road Initiative (BRI). These seminars present the BRI as a significant opportunity for economic development in the Western Balkans, emphasizing benefits such as infrastructure modernization and job creation. For instance, the Confucius Institute in Niš, Serbia, has actively promoted Chinese culture and fostered discussions on economic cooperation (The Geopost, 2024). While these initiatives aim to foster mutual understanding, concerns have been raised about the potential for promoting selective narratives that emphasize China's positive role in global affairs while downplaying critical perspectives.

China has actively shaped public discourse in the Western Balkans to promote favorable perceptions of its regional role. In Serbia, "ironclad friendship" is frequently used to describe the strong bilateral relations between China and Serbia.

This phrase underscores the mutual support and cooperation between the two nations (Yuwei, 2023). During the COVID-19 pandemic, China's assistance to Serbia was prominently highlighted. Serbian President Aleksandar Vučić personally received Chinese vaccines (as part of the Chinese "vaccine diplomacy" during the COVID-19 pandemic) at the airport, emphasizing the quality of the vaccines and the deep friendship between the two countries (Shumei and Yuwei, 2021). These efforts are part of China's broader strategy to enhance its image and influence in the Western Balkans, portraying itself as a reliable partner committed to mutual development and support. China has dedicated its resources entirely "to improving its international position and image. During the initial stage of the global COVID-19 pandemic, China's aid, mainly consisting of medical supplies and staff, was urgently aimed mainly at the countries and regions that were hit the hardest, but also the ones that had a history of stronger relations with China in recent years, such as Italy and Serbia" (Ilik and Shapkoski, 2022, p 112).

Furthermore, graduates of Chinese universities often play a key role in disseminating these narratives. Having been exposed to curated educational and cultural experiences in China, they frequently return home with favorable views of the country's governance model and global initiatives. Alumni networks organize events and discussions reinforcing positive narratives about China, further embedding these perspectives within local communities.

In some instances, China's counter-narrative efforts overlap with disinformation campaigns aimed at discrediting Western actors. Chinese-funded media outlets in the Western Balkans have occasionally portrayed the European Union (EU) and the United States (U.S.) as entities facing internal challenges and declining influence. This narrative aims to position China as a stable and reliable partner in contrast to Western powers. For instance, China's strategic interests in the Western Balkans are often highlighted in the Belt and Road Initiative (BRI) context, emphasizing economic cooperation without the political conditions typically associated with Western aid.

Discussions about the environmental impact of Chinese-funded projects in the Western Balkans are often downplayed or reframed to emphasize economic benefits. Reports indicate that Chinese investments in energy and infrastructure have led to significant environmental concerns.

However, local media coverage, influenced by Chinese partnerships, tends to focus on job creation and economic growth, minimizing environmental and social costs (Petkova, 2021).

China's engagement in the Western Balkans has been scrutinized, particularly concerning transparency, academic integrity, and local resistance. Critics argue that China's selective dissemination of information through sponsored publications and academic programs distorts public discourse by presenting an overly positive and one-sided view of its role in global and regional affairs. The Balkan Investigative

Reporting Network (BIRN) has highlighted the need for greater transparency regarding China's regional activities, noting that many projects lack sufficient public oversight (BIRN, 2021). Integrating Chinese-funded materials and perspectives into academic curricula raises concerns about academic freedom and the potential suppression of critical viewpoints on human rights, democracy, and governance. While specific instances in the Western Balkans are less documented, similar global patterns suggest the need for vigilance to maintain academic integrity. While many in the Western Balkans appreciate China's economic contributions, skepticism remains about the long-term implications of its involvement. Concerns about debt sustainability, environmental degradation, and labor practices have sparked protests and debates in countries like Montenegro and Serbia. For example, in Montenegro, the construction of the Bar-Boljare highway, funded by a Chinese loan, has raised issues regarding debt dependency and environmental impact (Kajosevic, 2020). These concerns underscore the importance of transparency, academic freedom, and sustainable practices in international collaborations to ensure that partnerships with China benefit the Western Balkans without compromising local interests and values.

The educational strategies deployed by the European Union and China in the Western Balkans significantly influence disinformation narratives, shaping public perceptions of global powers and their roles in the region. While the EU primarily uses education to promote democratic values and resilience against disinformation, China's approach often involves advancing narratives that challenge Western dominance. The following section critically examines how these educational interventions mitigate or exacerbate disinformation, with case studies from countries in the region illustrating their impacts in greater detail.

The EU's Role in Mitigating Disinformation

The European Union has taken a proactive role in combating disinformation, particularly in the Western Balkans, where a combination of historical vulnerabilities and modern technological trends heightens the risk of misinformation spreading. These efforts are centered on educational initiatives, partnerships, and regulatory approaches to foster media literacy, enhance critical thinking, and promote European values such as the rule of law, human rights and freedoms, democracy, multilateralism, etc.

Media literacy is foundational to the European Union's strategy to counter disinformation. Programs such as Erasmus+ and Horizon Europe have expanded beyond academic exchanges to include targeted initiatives designed to empower individuals and institutions with tools to identify and combat misinformation.

In North Macedonia, the EU supported the establishment of a Media Literacy Network by the Agency for Audio and Audiovisual Media Services (AVMS) in 2017. This network includes 35 stakeholders, including ministries, state institutions, higher education institutions, and civic associations. The network aims to promote media literacy across various segments of society (EAVI, 2017).

Media literacy programs play a significant role in the fight against disinformation. A 2021 report by the European Digital Media Observatory (EDMO) emphasized that a critically and digitally literate public is much more likely to assess information effectively, thereby reducing the spread of false or misleading content (Goodman, 2021, p. 2).

However, despite its proactive stance, the EU faces significant obstacles in its fight against disinformation. Although impactful, many EU initiatives remain underfunded, which limits their scalability and reach. Expanding media literacy programs to rural or underserved areas is particularly challenging. Political instability and polarization in the Western Balkans can undermine the implementation of EU initiatives. Sometimes, disinformation campaigns are politically motivated or tied to local elites, complicating efforts to foster trust and collaboration. Furthermore, in regions where Euroscepticism is growing, there is often resistance to EU-led initiatives. For example, some disinformation narratives in the Western Balkans countries depict the EU as imposing external values incompatible with local traditions, undermining media literacy programs' credibility.

China's Role in Exacerbating or Shaping Disinformation

China has increasingly utilized educational and cultural initiatives in the Western Balkans to advance its geopolitical interests. While these programs ostensibly promote academic and cultural exchange, they often shape narratives that align with China's strategic objectives, subtly promoting its development model while challenging Western institutions and norms. Confucius Institutes have become a cornerstone of China's educational outreach globally, including in the Western Balkans. These institutes offer a range of activities, including Chinese language classes, cultural workshops, and academic seminars to foster an understanding of Chinese culture and history.

However, they conduct their activities using a selective narrative that promotes a favorable image of China while subtly critiquing Western policies and media. For instance, public lectures may question the objectivity of Western media, framing it as biased or overly critical of China's global initiatives. A 2020 report by Freedom House highlighted how such approaches contribute to soft power strategies, influencing local perceptions and creating an environment receptive to China's geopolitical goals.

China's educational and cultural outreach often aligns with broader disinformation efforts. This is particularly evident in how Chinese-funded programs frame the BRI as a solution to regional economic underdevelopment. However, these narratives downplay concerns about debt dependency, lack of transparency, and environmental impacts.

CONCLUSION

This study has explored the nuanced role of education as a strategic instrument of geopolitical influence in the Western Balkans, comparing the European Union's and China's approaches. The EU's educational initiatives—anchored in democratic values, critical thinking, and institutional transparency—represent a deliberate effort to foster societal resilience and embed European norms. In contrast, while facilitating cultural and academic exchange, China's educational engagement also serves as a vehicle for projecting alternative governance models and contesting the liberal democratic values of the EU.

It can be concluded that China's intent in the Western Balkans region, and possibly more broadly in Europe, is to portray a distorted and selective image of the European Union to relativize and diminish its significance in the eyes of the local population and political actors. In this context, China uses education and disinformation as key tools of influence to achieve its geopolitical interests and strengthen its position in these regions. This strategy is part of China's broader policy to enhance its international image while undermining European unity and influence. Education, in this geopolitical contest, becomes a critical arena where the European Union and China engage in competing strategies. While the EU promotes education as a means to support democratic values, transparency, and integration, China often leverages educational initiatives and cultural exchanges to propagate narratives that challenge the credibility and appeal of the EU. This dual use of education reflects a broader disinformation narrative in the Western Balkans, where competing influences seek to shape public opinion and political alignment through targeted messaging. Understanding these conflicting approaches is essential for recognizing the broader geopolitical dynamics and developing effective responses to safeguard the region's democratic resilience and alignment with European integration.

To preserve the integrity of the region's educational sphere, it is imperative to strengthen local capacities in critical media literacy and ensure that all international academic cooperation upholds transparency, mutual respect, and pluralistic values. Regional policymakers, educational institutions, and civil society actors must collaborate to build an educational environment resistant to disinformation and authoritarian drift.

While this study adopts a qualitative and interpretive methodology to capture the depth and context of educational geopolitics in the region, it acknowledges limitations, including the lack of survey-based data and potential interpretive constraints due to language barriers in accessing Chinese policy sources. Future research could benefit from empirical studies involving student and public perceptions and deeper engagement with primary sources in the original languages.

In an era of intensifying global competition, the Western Balkans must navigate competing educational agendas with strategic discernment. By prioritizing inclusive, democratic, and critically engaged educational frameworks, the region can transform education from a field of external contestation into a pillar of internal cohesion, democratic resilience, and sustainable development.

REFERENCES

Babulík, M. (2024). China's influence in the Western Balkans. *Strategic Analysis*. Retrieved May 24, 2025, from https://www.strategicanalysis.sk/chinas-influence-in-the-western-balkans/

Balkan Investigative Reporting Lab. (2021). BIRN presents online platform on China's activities in Western Balkans. https://balkaninsight.com/2021/12/15/birn-presents-online-platform-on-chinas-activities-in-western-balkans/

Balkans, We. (2023). Serbia's leap into the Erasmus Plus programme: Fostering mutual understanding and opportunities. https://webalkans.eu/en/stories/serbias-leap-into-the-erasmus-plus-programme-fostering-mutual-understanding-and-opportunities/

Balkans, We. (2024). Discover the YEA Network. https://webalkans.eu/en/yea/

China Daily. (2015). Chinese art troupe presents gala performance in Albania. https://www.chinadaily.com.cn/culture/2015-10/26/content_22287211.htm

Education Department of the Embassy of the People's Republic of China in the Republic of Serbia. (2015). Introduction to Chinese Government Scholarships. https://serbia.lxgz.org.cn/serbia/lxzg/2021090910330183206/index.html

European Association for Viewers Interests (EAVI). (2017). Media literacy network in the Republic of Macedonia. https://eavi.eu/media-literacy-network-in-the-republic-of-macedonia/

European Commission. (2020). *EU–Western Balkan cooperation through Erasmus+*. https://ec.europa.eu/assets/eac/erasmus-plus/factsheets/regional/westernbalkans-regional-erasmusplus-2020.pdf

European Commission. (2021). Erasmus+ program impact report: Western Balkans. https://ec.europa.eu/assets/eac/erasmus-plus/factsheets/regional/westernbalkans-regional-erasmusplus-2020.pdf

European Commission. (2024a). Erasmus + programme guide, Version 1 (2024): 28-11-2023 (p. 326). https://erasmus-plus.ec.europa.eu/sites/default/files/2023-11/2024-Erasmus%2BProgramme-Guide_EN.pdf

European Commission. (2024b). The European Universities alliances in action. https://education.ec.europa.eu/education-levels/higher-education/european-universities-initiative/about

European Commission, Directorate-General for Education, Youth, Sport and Culture, & PPMI. (2025). Report on the outcomes and transformational potential of the European Universities initiative (Authors: Manja Klemencic, Sabine Hoidn, Hanne Shapiro, Dragana Avramov, Hans de Wit, Simone Ravaioli NC-02-24-860-EN-N). Publications Office of the European Union. https://doi.org/DOI: 10.2766/32313

European Commission, Directorate-General for Education, Youth, Sport and Culture. (2024). *European universities: A key pillar of the European education area*. Publications Office of the European Union. https://data.europa.eu/doi/10.2766/521265

European Parliament. (2022). China's strategic interests in the Western Balkans – Briefing (p. 6). https://www.europarl.europa.eu/RegData/etudes/BRIE/2022/733558/EPRS_BRI%282022%29733558_EN.pdf

European Training Foundation. (2024). Taking forward Youth Guarantee schemes in the Western Balkans. https://www.etf.europa.eu/en/news-and-events/news/taking-forward-youth-guarantee-schemes-western-balkans

European Union. (2023). EU annual report on human rights and democracy in the world 2022 country updates (pp. 12-13). https://www.eeas.europa.eu/sites/default/files/documents/2023/2022%20EU%20Annual%20Human%20Rights%20and%20Democracy%20Country%20Reports_0.pdf

Freedom House. (2020). Freedom in the World reports – China, 2020. https://freedomhouse.org/country/china/freedom-world/2020

Fudan University. (2025). International students office – Scholarships. https://iso.fudan.edu.cn/isoenglish/16210/list.htm

Goodman, E. (2021). Media literacy in Europe and the role of EDMO. *European Digital Media Observatory*. https://edmo.eu/wp-content/uploads/2022/02/Media-literacy-in-Europe-and-the-role-of-EDMO-Report-2021.pdf

Human Rights Watch. (2019a). China: Government threats to academic freedom abroad. https://www.hrw.org/news/2019/03/21/china-government-threats-academic-freedom-abroad

Human Rights Watch. (2019b). The Chinese government cannot be allowed to undermine academic freedom. https://www.hrw.org/news/2019/11/08/chinese-government-cannot-be-allowed-undermine-academic-freedom

Ilik, G., & Adamczyk, A. (2017). Finalité politique or just a step forward: The Lisbon Treaty and the identity of the European Union as a global actor. *Journal of Liberty and International Affairs*, *3*(Supp. 1), 9–25. https://e-jlia.com/index.php/jlia/article/view/89

Ilik, G., & Shapkoski, V. (2022). The EU's response vs. Chinese vaccine diplomacy in Central and Eastern Europe. *Eastern Journal of European Studies*, 13(2), 99–115. https://doi.org/https://ejes.uaic.ro/articles/EJES2022_1302_ILI.pdfDOI: 10.47743/ejes-2022-0205

Kajosevic, S. (2020). Montenegro forced to extend deadline for Chinese to finish highway. *BIRN*. https://balkaninsight.com/2020/09/30/montenegro-forced-to-extend-deadline-for-chinese-to-finish-highway/

Krstinovska, A. (2022a). Chinese influence in North Macedonia. *Center for European Policy Analysis (CEPA)*. https://cepa.org/comprehensive-reports/chinese-influence-in-north-macedonia/

Krstinovska, A. (2022b). China's development assistance to the Western Balkans and its impact on democratic governance and decision-making. *Journal of Liberty and International Affairs*, *8*(1), 229–242. DOI: 10.47305/JLIA2281229k

Liuliu, X., Wenwen, W., & Wei, F. (2023). Falling in love with Chinese language. *Global Times*. https://www.globaltimes.cn/page/202309/1298681.shtml

McBride, J., Berman, N., & Chatzky, A. (2023). China's massive Belt and Road Initiative. *Council of Foreign Relations*. https://www.cfr.org/backgrounder/chinas-massive-belt-and-road-initiative

Nye, J. S. (2012). China and soft power. *The South African Journal of International Affairs*, *19*(2), 151–155. DOI: 10.1080/10220461.2012.706889

Petkova, M. (2021). The environmental impact of Chinese projects in the Western Balkans. *Association for International Affairs (AMO)*. https://chinaobservers.eu/wp-content/uploads/2021/11/CHOICE_policy-paper_Environmental-Impact_A4_07_web.pdf

Shumei, L., & Yuwei, H. (2021). Chinese COVID-19 vaccines gain more international recognition. https://www.globaltimes.cn/page/202101/1213083.shtml

Ss. Cyril and Methodius University Skopje, Institute of Economics. (2017). International cooperation. https://www.ek-inst.ukim.edu.mk/en/international-collaboration

The Geopost. (2024). Expansion of the Confucius Institute in Serbia despite controversies in Europe and the USA. https://thegeopost.com/en/news/expansion-of-the-confucius-institute-in-serbia-despite-controversies-in-europe-and-the-usa/

United States China Economic and Security Review Commission. (2023). Section 2: Battling for overseas hearts and minds: China's united front and propaganda work (p. 37). https://www.uscc.gov/sites/default/files/2023-11/Chapter_2_Section_2--Chinas_United_Front_and_Propaganda_Work.pdf

University of Sarajevo. (2025). The Confucius Institute of the Sarajevo University successfully held the 2025 Spring Festival Gala event. https://www.unsa.ba/en/novosti/confucius-institute-sarajevo-university-successfully-held-2025-spring-festival-gala-event

University "Ss. Cyril and Methodius" in Skopje. (2025). Confucius Institute. https://ukim.edu.mk/en/sostav/nauchni-instituti/institut-konfucij/

Western Balkans University. (2024). WBU has signed a cooperation agreement with Zhejiang Normal University in China. https://wbu.edu.al/en/news/wbu-has-signed-a-cooperation-agreement-with-zhejiang-normal-university-in-china

Yuwei, H. (2023). China-Serbia ironclad friendship sets a model of shared fulfillment: Serbian deputy PM. *Global Times*. https://www.globaltimes.cn/page/202305/1291032.shtml

Zeneli, V. (2023, June 23). Chinese influence in the Western Balkans and its impact on the region's European Union integration process. *Europe's Futures*. https://www.iwm.at/blog/chinese-influence-in-the-western-balkans-and-its-impact-on-the-regions-european-union

Zeneli, V., & Mejdini, F. (n.d.). Countering Beijing's regional influence. *Per Concordiam*. Retrieved May 24, 2025, from https://perconcordiam.com/china-in-the-balkans/

ADDITIONAL READING

Ilik, G., & Adamczyk, A. (2017). Finalité politique or just a step forward: The Lisbon Treaty and the identity of the European Union as a global actor. *Journal of Liberty and International Affairs*, *3*(Supp. 1), 9–25. https://e-jlia.com/index.php/jlia/article/view/89

Ilik, G., & Shapkoski, V. (2022). The EU's response vs. Chinese vaccine diplomacy in Central and Eastern Europe. *Eastern Journal of European Studies*, 13(2), 99–115. https://doi.org/https://ejes.uaic.ro/articles/EJES2022_1302_ILI.pdfDOI: 10.47743/ejes-2022-0205

Krstinovska, A. (2022). China's development assistance to the Western Balkans and its impact on democratic governance and decision-making. *Journal of Liberty and International Affairs*, *8*(1), 229–242. DOI: 10.47305/JLIA2281229k

KEY TERMS AND DEFINITIONS

Belt and Road Initiative: This concept refers to China's ambitious global development strategy to enhance regional connectivity and economic integration through large-scale infrastructure projects, trade networks, and investment across Asia, Africa, Europe, and beyond. Launched in 2013, the Belt and Road Initiative combines economic diplomacy, soft power projection, and strategic partnerships.

Confucius Institutes: This concept refers to educational and cultural organizations established worldwide, primarily funded and supported by the Chinese government, intending to promote Chinese language learning and culture abroad. Confucius Institutes serve as platforms for cultural diplomacy by offering language courses, cultural events, and academic exchanges. While they enhance China's soft power and global influence, these institutes have also been subjects of debate and scrutiny regarding academic freedom, political influence, and the promotion of China's strategic interests in host countries.

Cultural Diplomacy: This concept refers to the practice of using a country's cultural assets—such as art, music, literature, language, traditions, and heritage—as a means to promote mutual understanding and build positive relationships with other nations. Cultural diplomacy seeks to create dialogue and exchange that transcend political and economic differences, enhancing a country's soft power by showcasing its identity and values.

Disinformation Campaigns: Disinformation campaigns are often conducted through various media channels, including social media, news outlets, and online platforms, and can be used as tools of political influence, propaganda, or hybrid warfare. Their goal is to create confusion, polarization, and distrust within societies or between countries, thereby destabilizing democratic processes and weakening social cohesion.

Educational Diplomacy: This concept involves using educational exchanges, collaborations, and initiatives as tools to build and strengthen diplomatic relationships between countries. Educational diplomacy leverages academic partnerships, student and faculty mobility, joint research projects, and cultural programs to promote mutual understanding, trust, and cooperation.

Erasmus+: This concept denotes the European Union's flagship program for education, training, youth, and sport, designed to promote mobility, cooperation, and innovation across member states and partner countries. Erasmus+ enables students, educators, and institutions to participate in exchanges, joint projects, and capacity-building activities, fostering intercultural dialogue and enhancing skills and employability. The program supports the development of a European Education Area and contributes to social inclusion, lifelong learning, and active citizenship by connecting diverse communities through education and collaboration.

European Universities Alliances: This concept refers to collaborative networks of universities across Europe that work together to strengthen higher education, research, and innovation on a continental scale. These alliances aim to foster academic mobility, joint degree programs, shared resources, and cross-border research projects, enhancing the quality and competitiveness of European higher education.

European Values: This concept encompasses the fundamental principles and norms that guide the political, social, and legal systems of the European Union and its member states. These values include respect for human dignity, freedom, democracy, equality, the rule of law, and human rights. They reflect a commitment to peaceful coexistence, pluralism, tolerance, and the protection of minority rights, forming the basis for building inclusive and just societies.

Euroscepticism: This concept describes the critical attitude or opposition toward the European Union and its policies, institutions, or integration processes. Euroscepticism ranges from calls for reform within the EU to outright rejection of EU membership or cooperation. Euroscepticism influences political discourse and electoral dynamics within member states and shapes the broader debate on the future direction and legitimacy of the European project.

Global Powers: Global powers shape international relations and the global order through their capacity to project power, form alliances, and set agendas that affect multiple regions and countries. Their influence extends beyond their borders, impacting global security, trade, diplomacy, and governance. The term highlights the importance of hard power (military and economic strength) and soft power (cultural and ideological appeal) in maintaining and expanding their global reach.

Soft Power: This concept refers to the ability of a country or actor to influence others not through coercion or payment but through attraction and persuasion. Unlike hard power, which relies on military or economic force, soft power operates by winning hearts and minds, creating legitimacy, and fostering cooperation.

Chapter 2
Digital Global Village:
Literacy in the Age of Social Media and "Post-Truth"

Goran Bandov
https://orcid.org/0000-0003-4644-4582
University of Zagreb, Croatia

Nikolina Herceg Kolman
https://orcid.org/0000-0002-3171-8985
University of Zagreb, Croatia

ABSTRACT

The chapter discusses the implications that social media age has on modern political and social processes, examines dangers of disinformation and fake news, and analyses different approaches to countering them. Social media literacy is considered as one of the key tools to respond to the perils of false information on social media platforms, by giving users competences and skills to discern between facts and falsehood. Different concepts in literature and overview of relevant research on the topic are reviewed. The chapter concludes the discussion with the considerations on the so called "post-truth" era and offers recommendations for steps forward, both in countering negative effects of disinformation, and in possible future research on social media literacy.

INTRODUCTION

Social media literacy is a relatively new concept, which is gaining more focus and relevance in literature with growing threats and consequences of online misinformation and "alternative" facts. Within the last decade, social media have become

DOI: 10.4018/979-8-3693-9601-8.ch002

a formidable political and social tool, with power to decide elections, manipulate masses on a worldwide scale, and even endanger global health and global security. This brought us into the disinformation age, as Coper (2022) calls this social media mayhem, which is dangerously fracturing modern democratic societies and is threatening to disintegrate liberal democracy even in the most resilient environments.

Coper (2022) differentiates this false information on social media into three groups: misinformation (unintentional), disinformation (deliberate) and malinformation (presenting facts in malicious way by manipulating the context). This disinformation age is not just sowing mayhem here and there, bringing politicians to power, or bringing them down. These new technologies can be weaponized in any political or social context and often go undetected.

When we look at the information chaos on social networks it seems that "facts" mostly fit into one of Coper's three categories. However, the most vicious are those that have intent to mislead and deceive, especially in the widespread atmosphere of distrust and disdain for formal institutions.

The term "fake news" became a worldwide known phenomenon with the 2016 presidential elections in the USA as "viral posts based on fictitious accounts made to look like news reports" (Tandoc et al., 2017a, p. 138). Alcot and Gentzkow (2017, p. 213) defined fake news as "news articles that are intentionally and verifiably false and could mislead readers". Another definition is by Rochlin (2017, p. 388): "a knowingly false headline and story [that] is written and published on a website that is designed to look like a real news site and is spread via social media".

All definitions point out to one common feature – something that is fabricated and is spread as a fact. Another element should be added – this fake news is always spread with certain agenda. And precisely for this reason social media literacy is so vital. Social network platforms have, mostly to boost their profit, aided the spread of fake news, with rewarding such content and through design of elaborate algorithms. This became evident after the 2016 USA election and Brexit.

The research conducted by American Library Association (ALA) showed that 80 percent of the middle school students cannot tell the difference between sponsored content and real news, and that 75 percent cannot discern between real and false news on Facebook. Furthermore, only 30 percent could detect a bias in news reporting (ALA, 2021). This means that only a small percentage of young people are capable to differentiate facts from fake news. That fact has serious implications for the future of the democratic system, considering that critical thinking and understanding of media content is crucial for democratic culture.

It is, therefore, essential to develop skills that will make social media users less susceptible to misinformation and more capable of recognizing fake information. This phenomenon is, of course, much more complicated, and it has to do with the downfall of democratic political culture and the crisis of liberal democracy in general.

The tools for "enlightened" use of social media are just one small part of a much bigger picture; nonetheless, they might prove crucial for survival of democracy in the 21st century. One such tool is the concept of social media literacy.

METHODS

The chapter is conceptualised as an academic article, aiming to synthesize the literature on media and social media literacy, giving also the overview of relevant concepts and definitions on the subject (see, e.g., Green, Johnson, & Adams, 2006). There are four main types of literature reviews: traditional (narrative) literature review, rapid review, scoping review and systematic review (Grant, Booth, 2009). This chapter is combination of traditional (narrative) review and scooping review, as it synthetizes literature on the topic, but also offers conclusions on possible further research.

A traditional (narrative) literature review is a thorough and critical evaluation of the research on a topic. It is commonly utilized to summarize and integrate current studies, pinpoint knowledge gaps, and set the stage for new investigations. This method also offer flexibility, a wide scope, holistic examination, comprehensive insight, and an in-depth analysis of the topic. On the other hand, scoping reviews chart the available research on a subject, identifying key ideas, theories, evidence sources, and research voids (Arksey & O'Malley, 2005). This method is mainly employed to ascertain the existing breadth of literature. Once the scoping review analysis is complete, a more detailed synthesis uses the analytical framework of a traditional (narrative) literature review, as this paper does.

MEDIA LITERACY IN GLOBAL VILLAGE: DEFINITIONS AND RELEVANCE FOR SOCIAL MEDIA

The idea that mass media would forever change the world we live in and intertwine us on an unimaginable scale goes back to the seminal work of Marshal McLuhan and his concept of "global village" (1964). Central to his concept was the idea that mass media have the ability to overcome all boundaries and to connect people from every corner of the world into what McLuhan termed a "global village" (McLuhan, 1964). McLuhan's concept is very relevant and applicable to today's world of social media. "Global village" has, in fact, never been as connected as it is today when we experience everything in real-time, while never more people had the chance to have their say and be a part of every news and every event via their comments and posts on social media feeds. At the same time, it has never been easier to manipulate people, as it is sometimes very hard to distinguish between facts and “alternative facts” on social media. Even videos can today be completely fake, with AI and deep-fake technologies that achieve uncanny resemblance to real people.

The term “village” was by no means accidental, and McLuhan chose it for a good reason. This new and unprecedented connectedness would not automatically turn people into a cosmopolitan, open-minded global citizens; the opposite can also happen – thus the term “villagers”. Nowadays social media realm very much resembles a village, albeit a medieval one - tribalistic tendencies, closed groups of “kindred spirits”, distrust in anyone from outside the group, modern “shamans” followed blindly without any evidence to their wisdoms, a ubiquitous virtual violence and lack of common sense – all of which are features of this new entangled information web.

One of McLuhan famous claims is “medium is the message”, which basically means that it is not about content, at least not in terms what content meant in print media, but rather about the entire experience of watching or listening to the news (see McLuhan 1964, p. 9). In other words, “effect involves the total situation, and not a single level of information movement” (McLuhan 1964, p. 26). Probably most compelling and applicable to today’s world of social media is McLuhan’s warning that people were not prepared to encounter mass media. “We are as numb in our new electric world as the native involved in our literate and mechanical culture”, he wrote (McLuhan 1964, p. 16). McLuhan saw the reason for that in the fact that, despite living in this electrical global village, people still think in terms of pre-electric age (McLuhan 1964, p. 25).

Another important term of McLuhan’s theory is new “central nervous system” that mass media have created. As he puts it: “Today, after more than a century of electric technology, we have extended our central nervous system itself in a global embrace, abolishing both space and time as far as our planet is concerned” (McLuhan, 1964). This “central nervous system” has become tremendously powerful after the invention of social media. The potential for manipulation and disinformation is almost unlimited, and, as we have witnessed, it was already used with raving success in several prominent cases – Brexit, January 6 Capitol Hill insurrection, conspiracy theories on vaccines and on climate change, just to name a few most infamous.

Georgiadou (1998) found that Internet in its beginnings did not fit into the picture of McLuhan’s global village. Mostly because it declared individualism as the supreme principle (Georgiadou, 1998). There is nothing individual about social media, on the other hand, which is exactly why we are dealing with fake news and misinformation on such scale.

The Aspen Institute (2022) defines media literacy as the ability to use media content sensibly. This simple, yet, very up to the point definition, covers only partially the scope and influence of social media. Furthermore, most definitions and frameworks of media literacy focus on the user's ability to consume and interpret media content and messages (Buckingham et al., 2005).

The UNESCO Media and Information Literacy Curriculum for Teachers (UNESCO, 2011), commonly known as MIL framework, encompasses six main competences:1. Understanding the role of media and information in democracy; 2. Understanding media content and uses; 3. Accessing information effectively; 4. Critically evaluating information and its sources; 5. Applying new and traditional media formats; 6. Situating the socio–cultural context of media content. (UNESCO, 2011).

In the EU, media literacy is defined within the digital competences framework. The European Commission's Joint Research Centre (JRC) first introduced this framework in 2013, and in 2022, the framework was updated to its current form, DigComp 2.2.

The Digital Competence Framework (DigComp 2.2) links social media competencies with security and wellbeing (Vuorikari et al., 2022). Digital competence, as one of the key competences for lifelong learning, was first defined in 2006, and after an update of the Council Recommendation in 2018, the definition is the following: "Digital competence involves the confident, critical and responsible use of, and engagement with, digital technologies for learning, at work, and for participation in society. It includes information and data literacy, communication and collaboration, media literacy, digital content creation (including programming), safety (including digital well-being and competences related to cybersecurity), intellectual property related questions, problem solving and critical thinking." (Vuorikari et al., 2022, p. 3).

DigComp 2.2 delineates 21 competencies grouped within five thematic areas:

- Information and data literacy: To articulate information needs, to locate and retrieve digital data, information and content. To judge the relevance of the source and its content. To store, manage, and organize digital data, information and content (skills such as browsing, searching and filtering data, information and digital content, evaluating data, information and digital content, managing data, information and digital content).
- Communication and collaboration: To interact, communicate and collaborate through digital technologies while being aware of cultural and generational diversity. To participate in society through public and private digital services and participatory citizenship. To manage one's digital presence, identity and reputation (skills such as interacting through digital technologies, engaging in citizenship through digital technologies, collaborating through digital technologies, netiquette, managing digital identity).
- Digital content creation: To create and edit digital content. To improve and integrate information and content into an existing body of knowledge while understanding how copyright and licenses are to be applied. To know how

to give understandable instructions for a computer system (skills such as developing digital content, integrating and re-elaborating digital content, copyright and licenses, programming).
- Problem solving: To identify needs and problems, and to resolve conceptual problems and problem situations in digital environments. To use digital tools to innovate processes and products. To keep up-to-date with the digital evolution (skills such as solving technical problems, identifying needs and technological responses, creatively using digital technologies, identifying digital competence gaps). (Vuorikari et al., 2022)

Most of the researchers agree on several core principles of media literacy (Yousman, 2008): all media messages are constructed, media messages are constructed with creative language that has its own codes and rules, different people interpret the same message differently, media have their own values and positions, most media messages are created to gain power and/or profit. Furthermore, media literacy encompasses the ability to access, analyse, evaluate, and create communication in a mediated context (Aufderheide, Firestone, 1993; Livingstone, 2004).

All these categories are still relevant in the age of social media, but nowadays it takes different sets of skills and cognitive abilities to master each of them. Social media are nothing like what we have seen before, in terms of their reach and multifaceted nature. With traditional media, there was not much difference between different issues of print media or various TV networks, but each social media has their own specific rules which require that users master certain sets of skills for information management, both in creating content and consuming it. Furthermore, there is much more need for fact checking and for skills to discern between reliable and unreliable sources.

Most of the core principles on traditional mass media apply to social media, however, not to all content and not at all times. New media, especially social media, have opened unimaginable possibilities for users to create their own content, both independently and within other people's content, including media content and content produced by other organizations and individuals. Thus, the lines between "users" and "creators" of content are blurred and, even more relevant; these roles completely and constantly overlap.

According to American Library Association media literacy is:

- the ability to access, analyse, create and act using all forms of communication,
- the ability to access, share and create media across multiple formats and platforms while utilizing critical thinking skills to evaluate the purpose and potential impact of the material,

- understanding how various groups are represented in the media, including whose stories are highlighted and whose are marginalized,
- understanding media ownership structures and its impact on what we see. (ALA, 2020)

Concepts designed for "old" mass media, and even early new media, are, therefore, inadequate for this new world of social media. At the same time, dangers that this new "disinformation age" (Coper, 2022) brings, require prompt and comprehensive approach and integration of social media into educational system. It is, therefore, necessary to develop a new theoretical framework for social media literacy.

Cho et al. (2024) detected several important limitations of media literacy concept, which renders it inadequate for social media research. The first limitation refers to the commonality of content, or difference in possibility for content curation. The content on mass media is given in entirety to consumers, and they have no influence on that content (Cho et al., 2024). They can select between different channels or print media issues and thus change the content they consume, but there is no space for individuality or feedback.

The different nature of content curation on social media requests different competencies and skills. Social media literacy, as Cho et al. stress (2024), requires an emphasis on the self and a willingness and ability to examine our own role in the analyses and evaluation of media content. Second limitation refers to the boundary between user and media (Cho et al., 2024). In traditional concepts of media literacy, developed for mass media, the media and users are strictly and completely separated. Social media and their users cannot be so strictly separated, and there are no clear boundaries between them.

The third limitation deals with different units of reality and mutability of identity. In mass media, the real world and the media world are two different realms. This means that the media world is inhabited by experts that create the content and message, while the real world is inhabited by receivers who interpret the content and messages. On the other hand, on social media there are no two distinct realms. Likewise, the world of social media is multifaceted, with mass media, individual users, institutions, organizations, all producing content and receiving it at the same time, both on local and global level (Cho et al., 2024).

The fourth limitation has to do with the direction of influence. With the mass media and their concept of literacy influence goes in one direction, from the media to the user. On social media the influence is multi-directional (Cho et al., 2024). Social media go beyond boundaries of previous power domains, knowledge, skills and available technology (Cho et al., 2024). The fifth limitation refers to the shifting locus of responsibility. In the mass media setting, responsibilities are almost entirely on the media, which have all the knowledge, technological infrastructure, and means of creation and production of the content. In social media, users are also responsible for the content, through two roles, engagement with the content that others create, and second, the creation of content which represents ideas, beliefs or sentiments of individuals or groups (Cho et al., 2024). That is one of the reasons why it is so hard to guarantee that the content on social media is factual and true.

Heyneman (2021) recommends following steps to address the challenges of inadequate literacy for social media:

- Schools should create a certificate of media competence at each level of education, asa criterion of completion before advancing to the next level.
- The certificate of media competence should be divided into three levels: beginning, emerging and mastery.
- The certificate should be based on whether the source of information is identified as more or less trustworthy.
- The certificate of media competence should be utilized outside of schools, similar to a driver's license, and it might be used as a criterion for an application for employment in the civil service or to enter the military.

Heyneman's recommendations have very broad implications, especially the part on the "certificate of media competence" as a condition to enter civil service or military, However, considering consequences that illiteracy in this context might have for our common future, it doesn't seem completely unreasonable.

On a lighter note, John Spencer proposed checklists and recommendations for educators dealing with fake news, which he named "The 5 Cs of Critical Consuming" (Spencer, 2016):

1. Context – Look at the context of the article. When was it written? Where does it come from? Have the events changed since then? Is there any new information that could change your perspective?
2. Credibility – Check the credibility of the source. Does the site have a reputation for journalistic integrity? Does the author cite credible sources? Or is it satirical? Is it on a list of fake news sites? Is it actually an advertisement posing as a real news story?
3. Construction. Analyse the construction of the article. What is the bias? Are there any loaded words? Any propaganda techniques? Any omissions that you should look out for? Can you distinguish between the facts and opinions? Or is it simply all speculation?
4. Corroboration: Corroborate the information with other credible news sources. Make sure it's not the only source making the claim. If it is, there's a good chance it's actually not true.

5. Compare: Compare it to other news sources to get different perspectives. Find other credible sources from other areas of the ideological or political spectrum to provide nuance and get a bigger picture of what's happening.

LITERATURE REVIEW: RESEARCH ON SOCIAL MEDIA LITERACY IN LITERATURE

In the aftermath of fake news crisis after the USA2016 presidential election and Brexit, most critics focused on Cambridge Analytica and their illegal data collection about Facebook users, while requests towards social networks regulations were mostly technical and asked for modifications of their algorithms (Tagg, Seargeant, 2021). There was still little focus on the aspect of social media literacy. As Buckingham (2019) noted, the approach to digital literacy was functional, focusing on skills for critical evaluation of information, which would equip social media users to discern between facts and fake news.

Tagg and Seargeant (2021) argue that approach to social media literacy and learning skills to become critical reader should also take into account that literacy is shaped by socio-cultural factors and political motivations (Cope and Kalantzis, 2009). Furthermore, they argue that higher education institutions should educate students on how people process, share and consume information on social media and that these institutions should prepare them for their roles as critically engaged citizens (Tagg, Seargeant, 2021).

In their research, Tagg and Seargeant explored the connection between their interviewees' online practices and their critical language and media awareness through the sociolinguistic concept of context design (Tagg, Seargeant, 2021). In doing so they conceptualized media awareness as fluid, constantly developing process, dependent on their interactions on social media. Thus, critical awareness of social media users develops over time with their experience and interactions on social media, which, in turn, shape their actions on social media. Therefore, they emphasize that, in preparing social media literacy programs, higher education institutions should take into account social nature of the social media use. This would equip users better to recognize social dynamics and resist those that are manipulative and dangerous.

This social approach recognizes that users' interactions on social media affect, albeit inadvertently, information flow and news consumption and shape their engagement with political issues and their decision to share or not to share certain information. Therefore, they argue for wider approach to social media literacy, which goes beyond classroom, and recognizes both the role of social interactions on users' behaviour on social networks and the role that social media literacy has in society (Tagg, Seargeant 2021).

Cho et al. (2024) conceptualized social media literacy by proposing content dimensions and competency dimensions. The elements of content dimensions are "Self" – the knowledge and awareness of our own role on social media, of our engagement, consumption and creation of content; "Medium"- the understanding of the nature of social media platforms, and the prevailing rules guiding interactions on social media, including political economy; and the "Reality" - the awareness that there are multiple realities on social media as well as the multiple criteria to judge whether content is real or true. The content dimensions are complemented with competency dimensions: analysis, valuation, and contribution. Cho et al. state two ways in which their concept is different from media literacy concepts in literature. First, their concept reconceptualises the relationship between the user and the media. Second, it recognizes that media literacy goes beyond skills or competencies, by including awareness and understanding of "self", i.e. the individual role in the world of social media (Cho et al., 2024).

Tandoc et al.(2021) developed a social media literacy scale which encompasses different skills, ranging from technical (skills needed to meet technical requirements of social media – creating and deleting account, posting content, deleting unwanted content), relational (social relations on social media – copyright laws governing social media platforms, handling conflicts on social media), to informational and algorithmic awareness and privacy (fact checking and sources checking, awareness that what we see on social media is controlled and that advertisements are targeted to our preferences) (Tandoc et al., 2021).

The research found that social media users vary in social media literacy competencies based on age, gender, education, income, and frequency of social media use. Frequency of social media was positively associated with all four competencies. The research suggests continuing research and broadening understanding of aspects of the informal learning contexts that can best promote social media literacy. Their research found that women, for some reason, report lower competencies, which could, as authors note, be due to self-perception and the fact that women tend to underestimate their abilities and competences. The research also showed that older users have confidence in the aspect of social relations aspect, but not so much in their technical and privacy competences, and algorithmic awareness. Formal education was, on the other hand, positively associated with privacy and algorithmic awareness. The authors, therefore, call for interventions and training targeting specific groups and focus on social media literacy competences they feel they lack the most (Tandoc et al., 2021).

Heiss, Nanz and Matthes (2023) further developed this scale into multidimensional scale – social media information literacy (SMIL) that measures six literacy dimensions: navigation, curation, appraisal, comprehension, creation, and social interaction, and one meta-factor – social media. Their research showed that high levels of education were strongly connected to high levels of all literacy skills (except curation), with the strongest relationship to comprehension. On the other hand, frequent use of social media was associated with increase in all skills, except for the appraisal and comprehension (Heiss, Nanz and Matthes, 2023). Thus, low levels of education and high level of social media use equals the lowest level of comprehension and the highest level of susceptibility to fake news, disinformation and misinformation on social media.

This indicates, as Heiss, Nanz and Matthes (2023) concluded, that comprehension on social media requires more formal education, or at least, more training. Growing up with social media and knowing all technical skills from an early age is not sufficient for development of social media information literacy. Moreover, educational gaps may widen over time, and, therefore Heiss, Nanz and Matthes (2023) conclude that the level of formal education is positively correlated with the level of social media literacy. This also suggests that social media literacy education is vital, especially for those with low levels of formal education. As authors rightly noted, critically appraisal of sources and content features, and understanding of causal links is vital for detecting disinformation and misinformation (Heiss, Nanz and Matthes, 2023).

Yanqing Sun and Juan Xie's (2024) study revealed that psychological factors—such as motivations like passing time, socialization, entertainment, and altruism—and two forms of trust, namely trust in information and trust in social media, influence social media users' inclination to share misinformation and disinformation (Sun, Xie, 2024). This research is intriguing because it demonstrates that some motives for spreading false information can be altruistic, aiming to warn or assist others. Past experiences have shown that these kinds of misinformation can be extremely hazardous.

Consequently, the authors suggest that relevant authorities clarify facts, rectify misinformation, and timely provide accurate information, particularly during emergencies or public crises (Sun, Xie, 2024). They also recommend that social media platforms continue collaborating with independent fact-checking organizations. However, after Mark Zuckerberg disclosed that Facebook, Instagram, and Threads will cease this practice (Isaac and Schleifer, 2025), this recommendation seems impractical. The authors emphasize the importance of warning flags and labels as valuable tools to reduce individuals' trust in misinformation and thus their likelihood of sharing it (Sun, Xie, 2024). They conclude that education on social media literacy should aim to enhance users' ability to navigate social networks and locate reliable, verified information (Sun, Xie, 2024).

Their research also found that older people and women are more likely to spread misinformation about health, while younger people and men are more likely to share misinformation about politics. The authors propose an online media literacy program which would incorporate a fact-checking game, as an experiential learning program

(Sun,Xie, 2024). Their findings indicated that these games have a positive effect on students' ability to discern unreliable and misleading information. In their research, the "game-only group" scored significantly higher in cognitive skills related to information lecture groups and control groups (Sun, Xie, 2024). Another measure they propose is to include reflective learning processes in games. That means that game educational materials should include a post-game reflection (Sun, Xie, 2024).

They also point to a very important feature of social media and, accordingly, the need to adapt education for social media literacy. We should, as they advise, view literacy practices on every social network as different and unique. Social media literacy should also be perceived as cognitive process that develops critical thinking skills, supports the development of writing and literacy skills, and can lead to improved cognitive and metacognitive processes (Sun, Xie, 2024).

As opposed to these views, which emphasize individual use and skills, social media literacy should also focus on social and political aspects of social media (Sun, Xie, 2024). As the authors highlight, social media literacyis an "inherently political act". In this concept, social media can be a platform for social change (i.e., #MeToo), and critical resistance, and give voice to marginalized groups in fight for their rights (Sun, Xie, 2024).

Manca et al. (2021) provide several recommendations for researchers and educators to integrate into curriculum to enhance social media literacy. Their first suggestion is to incorporate learning theory into social media literacy courses. The authors caution that omitting learning theory may lead to only a shallow comprehension of how meaning is constructed and evolves (Manca et al., 2021). By utilizing learning theory, researchers and educators can critically evaluate their own perceptions and beliefs about the impacts of social media literacy, and cultivate new insights through social media engagement (Manca et al., 2021).

Their second recommendation advises that understanding literacy and literate practices should not be viewed solely as individual activities. Instead, these should be recognized as skills and practices that rely on the context, which include the influence of corporations. This notion of "surveillance capitalism" described by Zuboff and Schwandt (Zuboff, Schwandt, 2019), where large corporations gather user data, should encourage researchers to explore the connection between individual abilities and the socio-economic and cultural context influenced by social media companies (Manca et al., 2021). This perspective suggests that social media literacy goes beyond just technical skills or critical thinking to assess online sources and content. It also requires an understanding of how global companies, through their platform designs and algorithms, exploit human behaviour to generate profit (Krutka et al., 2019).

The third recommendation is for teachers and researchers to begin to consider how socioeconomic context produces meaning and behaviour on social networks. This recommendation requires scholars to stop thinking locally when linking socio-economic context to social media literacy, as well as to question current notions of global and local, as social media link people across time and space, thus challenging traditional understanding of local and global (Manca et al., 2021).

Wei et al. (2023) conducted research to explore the relationship between social media literacy levels and the tendency of social network users to share false information. They discovered that an individual's desire for status and trust in social media significantly influenced the sharing of fake news. Additionally, this relationship was more pronounced among users with lower social media literacy levels. These findings highlight the importance of social media literacy skills as crucial tools in combating the spread of false news on social media.

On the other hand, Sakya et al. (2021) found that social media literacy alone may not be sufficient for users to differentiate between true and false information. Their study showed that individuals who primarily relied on Facebook for Covid-19 information were less informed about the issue compared to those who sourced their information from various other channels and platforms. In a similar vein, Granderath et al. (2021) observed that social media users often overestimated their knowledge regarding Covid-19. Sakya et al. (2021) concluded that relying on social media as the primary source resulted in misinformation and a lack of proper understanding about Covid-19. This effect was further exacerbated by conspiracy theories and misleading narratives spread on these platforms by certain groups (Viswanath et al., 2020). These studies underscore a critical aspect of social media literacy: the ability to discern truth from misinformation is strongly linked to "offline" literacy, which encompasses a person's overall knowledge and education on topics discussed and shared in social networks.

Tandoc et al. (2023) study tested interventions to curb fake news in adolescents age group. The study showed that the intervention was effective in the short-term, however, for long-term effects and long-term ability to recognize fake news, students had to be motivated to participate. They concluded, therefore, that future research should explore which factors could contribute to motivation and the willingness of adolescents to critically engage in social media content evaluation (Tandoc et al., 2023).

Orosz et al.(2024) also found that learners who went beyond passively consuming information and engaged in reflective observation and abstract conceptualization had better learning outcomes in social media literacy education. This prompted them to propose learning environments that 1) maximize the opportunities for learners to practice recommended actions in specific cyber risk contexts and minimize the affordances that may elicit irrelevant actions; 2) provide proper scaffoldings to help learners translate knowledge into actions; 3) allow more sophisticated data capturing and triangulation mechanisms to accurately detect learners' behaviours towards learning goals (Orosz et al., 2024).

Perez et al. (2023) conducted research of scientific literature on the use of social media in higher education teaching and learning from 2009 to 2021. They found that Computers & Education and Education and Information Technologies published the most articles on social media as a teaching and learning tool. The word student was the most commonly used word in the abstracts (n = 2,156), followed by social media (n = 1,077), use (n = 1,043), Facebook (n = 858), and learning (n = 667). These results show that most studies focused on Facebook as social network (n = 858), followed by Twitter the (n = 274). The term "social media" appears in literature from 2016, at first linked with terms such as "data", "educational use", and "educational tool". Since 2018 focus of research shifts to "attitudes", "influence", "intention", "performance", or "satisfaction" (Perez et al., 2023).

Perez et al. identified four research trends: 1. From 2010–2014 – focus on Facebook as a community of practice, blog, and for informal learning; 2. From 2014–2016more emphasis on Facebook as a tool for the educational learning process;3. 2016–2018, the term "social media" dominates, studies were still focused on social media as educational tool; From 2018 onwards, studies focused on research of "attitudes", "influence", "intention", "performance", or "satisfaction" (Perez et al., 2024). Perez et al. (2024) conclude that future studies should focus on "best practice" for integrating social media into pedagogy and formal education.

BEYOND SOCIAL MEDIA LITERACY: "POST-TRUTH" ERA

In 2018the European Commission published the Code of Practice on disinformation, which was signed by all major social networks and platforms - Facebook, Google, Twitter, and later joined by Microsoft and TikTok, as well as by advertisers. This was the first time ever that major online global players agreed upon a self-regulatory standard to fight disinformation (European Commission, 2018). The 2018 Code of Practice comprised objectives set out by the Commission earlier that year, by setting 21 commitments in different domains, from transparency in political advertising, demonetization of spreaders of disinformation to investing in technologies to support social media literacy and cooperation with governments, scientific community and civil society (European Commission, 2018).

The Code defines disinformation as "verifiably false or misleading information which, cumulatively: Is created, presented and disseminated for economic gain or to intentionally deceive the public; and may cause public harm, intended as threats to democratic political and policymaking processes as well as public goods such as the protection of EU citizens' health, the environment or security." (European Commission, 2018). After series of reports in following years, a new, improved and strengthened Code was signed in 2022. The strengthened Code of Practice has 44 commitments and 128 specific measures, in the following areas: Demonetization - cutting financial incentives for purveyors of disinformation, Transparency of political advertising, Ensuring the integrity of services, empowering users, Empowering researchers, Empowering the fact-checking community, Transparency centre and Task-force, Strengthened Monitoring framework, Structural Indicators, Cooperation during elections (European Commission, 2022).

It remains to be seen whether signatories will continue to follow through on commitments of the Code. The CEO of Meta Mark Zuckerberg already announced that Meta is done with independent fact-checking practice. But, even before, there were obvious signs that he is about to quit "the nice guy" act. Trump's profile was quietly reinstated in 2023 with additional monitoring and fully restored in 2024 before the election (Clarke, 2025). He also sent a letter o Republicans in Congress in August 2024 in which he expressed regret that Meta complied to Biden's requests to censor Covid-19 content (Clarke, 2025). Elon Musk's stance on this issue has been notorious for a while now, and his platform X, former Twitter, has played an important role in Trump's presidential campaign. In 2023, YouTube, X and Meta stopped labelling or removing posts that repeated Trump's claims. YouTube announced it would stop removing videos falsely saying that 2020 presidential election was stolen from Trump (Clarke, 2025).

It has been theorized for a long time that negative content provoking strong emotions is alluring to people, especially online. Social networks depend on users' engagement, so they naturally promote such content for their own gain and profit (Ryan, 2012, Munn, 2020, Lee et al., 2024). That is the reason why false information aimed at certain groups spreads like wildfire on social media. Social networks have, thus, become, not just a handy tool for spreading an agenda, but also a weapon against vulnerable groups, if not deliberately, then by their very design and wish of their owners to earn more. In other words, the effects of social media on democratic societies are beyond the reach of social media literacy.

Buckingham (2019) warned about the limitations of social media literacy and the dangers of assigning too much power to that concept. Fake news, as Buckingham noted, often function as political propaganda or even "cyberwarfare". However, oftentimes motivation is primarily economic. These political and economic motivations may also be blurred (Buckingham, 2019). The recent developments suggest that motivation behind fake news is often both political and economic - sometimes fake political agenda is promoted simply because it provokes engagement on social networks, and, consequently more profit for their CEOs. But, as Trump's presidential campaign demonstrated, this coupling of interests can be more sinister. The tech CEOs can promote political agenda or politicians in order for them to gain political power and adopt policies in their favour, as was the case with Elon Musk and his platform X. Furthermore, he is now attempting to affect election results in EU member states using his platform, again with the same agenda. Fake news phenomenon should, therefore, be placed in the wider context of the online political economy (Buckingham, 2019).

Another interesting concept is the so-called "post-truth" era (Keyes, 2004, Buckingham, 2019). Post-truth, defined by Oxford English Dictionary as "relating to circumstances in which people respond more to feelings and beliefs than to facts" (Oxford English Dictionary, 2016). The post-truth was Oxford English Dictionary word of the year in 2016, while American comedian Stephen Colbert in the role of his conservative talk show host persona in "The Colbert Report" popularized another word with similar meaning - "truthiness". "Truthiness", as used by Colbert, "is the truth as we wish it to be, what we know in our gut as opposed to what we know in our brain". In post-truth era facts are a matter of opinion or as Colbert sarcastically puts it, a matter of our "gut feeling". Therefore, there are no facts any longer.

This has profound implications not only for politics, but also for science and social interactions in general. Timothy Snyder warned us to believe in truth to safeguard democracy: "To abandon facts is to abandon freedom. If nothing is true, then no one can criticize power because there is no basis upon which to do so. If nothing is true, then all is spectacle" (Snyder, 2017, p. 65). In post-truth era politicians in particular have not only made false promises or tried to manipulate public debate, but actually told outright lies, and managed to do so with impunity (Buckingham, 2019). A claim of Donald Trump that he was the one who won the election in 2020 led to something that seemed unimaginable in the USA up to that point – a violent insurrection in Washington DC, USA (Levitsky, Ziblat, 2023). These types of politicians, use untrue as legitimate tactic to destroy democratic institutions for short-term personal gain (Finchelstein, 2024). Analysing Putin's Russia's effect on democracy in Europe and America, Timothy Snyder writes about "assault on factuality", which he calls "implausible deniability" - denying what everyone knows to be true and thus creating alternative reality in Russia and dilemmas in European and American media (Snyder, 2018, p.163).

In such political and social environment and "clear and present" danger to democratic systems worldwide, it is not unusual for the scientific community to try and detect a problem and offer simple and effective solution to that problem, Thus, social networks have come into the focus, as media that spreads these dangerous lies and agendas, and social media literacy is seen as a tool for debunking those lies, and sometimes even as magical panacea to the issues that our democracies face (Buckingham, 2019). As Buckingham further warns, this tendency oversimplifies problems, overestimates the influence of media and underestimates complexity of educational system (Buckingham, 2019).

Fake news is phenomenon much broader than the social media users' ability of critical thinking and discerning between facts and lies, and people will not stop believing in fake news just because they were taught to fact-check or think rationally. Buckingham (2019) suggest it is not just the matter of spotting fake news, but also of identifying form of bias in all media and all sources of information, recognizing, before anything else, that bias is inevitable. We all have our own biases based on our prejudices or preconceptions, and what social networks do, more than anything else, they create "bias bubbles" by exposing us almost exclusively to the content that confirms our biases (Buckingham, 2019).

Bias can also be expressed in what is reported on and what is ignored, in the agenda setting and framing of topics. This is an even more powerful form of bias because they are harder to detect and, therefore, harder to resist. Bias can also be motivated by profit – journalist and media report on the issues that users find interesting, which in the era of the internet news portals and social networks is easy to find out. Moreover, people will pay to consume things that confirm their biases or will not pay to consume what conflicts them (Buckingham, 2019).

Buckingham (2019) also sees some pedagogical problems with education on social media literacy and dealing with fake news – the matter of discerning between credible sources online. As he warns, it is much more difficult to assess the reliability of online sources than it was with traditional media. In any case, deciding on this issue requires knowledge on topic, not just on the manner it was presented. And even if educators are knowledgeable on the issues, it is hard to expect that students will have the same experience, knowledge, or even interest in the topic, especially in those that are of most concern – political, scientific and social (Buckingham, 2019). Even if social media skills can be learned in classroom, very few people regularly fact-check online sources. (Buckingham, 2019).

Buckingham (2019) also points to epistemological problems, in determining and interpreting what the truth is, in the grey area between some absolute truths and absolute falsehoods. All of us are inclined to believe what we want to believe, and in the era of digital media, this is exacerbated by the "filter bubble", or the "echo chamber effect" (Buckingham, 2019). What this means is that social network design and algorithms make it easy for us to filter out the things that we don't believe or don't agree with. Therefore, we might develop false beliefs from exposure to fake news, but fake news might also only reaffirm what we already believe (Buckingham, 2019).

Social media literacy can address a part of the problem but cannot cover the whole picture. Buckingham stresses the role of journalists in this "post-truth" era. He finds that it is their job to be sceptical more than ever, more vigilant and persistent in their pursuit of evidence, but also more transparent themselves (Buckingham,

2019). However, the biggest challenge is the fact that spreading fake news is profitable. Therefore, Buckingham concludes that in order to challenge fake news, we have to challenge digital advertising and global companies that gain profit on this advertising. The first step is to define those companies as media companies and to regulate them as such, with all responsibilities and rules that other media comply with (Buckingham, 2019).

Some other authors turn to solutions that are more practical. Coper (2022) identified seven steps to counter false information on social media. First step is to identify information as false, Coper gives several clues – have you heard of the website with the link before, is the post recent, and who is posting. The second step is to decide what you want to do with the disinformation, whether to just leave it be, as doing anything would do more harm than good. The third step is to report the disinformation to the platform on which it was posted. The fourth step is to decide how to respond – it depends on whether you know the person who posted the disinformation, in that case the next step is to engage privately with them. Coper stresses this point as one of the most important - never engage with disinformation publicly. Sixth step is to tell the truth – telling our own true stories to counter the false ones. Seventh and final step is to talk about disinformation – warning on its dangers (Coper, 2022, p.324-30).

CONCLUSION: A WAY BACK TO THE "TRUTH ERA"?

Second presidential term of Donald Trump poses an unprecedented challenge to democracy, not only in America, but also throughout Europe. Democratic institutions managed to survive his first term, mostly because his power was still curbed by checks and balances, and he was lacking organized support. This time around, he has control of both the Congress and the Supreme Court and is heavily supported by far-right organizations and the right wing of the Republican party. On his first day he issued 45 executive orders, some of which are unconstitutional, such as the one revoking the birth right citizenship. Some others are extremely hostile towards LGBTQ+ minorities (rolling back federal recognition of gender identity), dangerous for world health and fight against climate change (withdrawing from the WHO and the Paris Agreement), or just outright dangerous, such as pardoning over 1500 rioters from January 6 insurrection, even those that attacked the police.

The EU is in particular danger. Populists, or "wannabe fascists", as Finchelstein (2024) named them for their motives to destroy democratic institutions for their own gain and not because they are especially interested in installing long-term fascist regimes, are gaining support throughout Europe. The 2025 is election year for Germany, which is traditionally the frontrunner and champion of the European integration. The 2027 is presidential election year in France, another European power and traditional proponent of the EU as well. Should it happen that the AFD gains enough support in Germany so that the government is impossible without their MPs, and that Marine Le Pen movement wins presidential elections in France, the EU based on the values of liberal-democracy would be in serious danger.

The future seems bleak for democracy and human rights after the presidential election in USA, and now all eyes are on Europe. So, the question is how can the EU and its liberal democracies survive this "post-truth" era, with war on its borders and with hostile administration in a crucial ally country, and what can be done in that regard to strengthen some of the key safeguards of democracy and EU institutions?

The crisis that democracies face today is crisis on a much larger scale than that of fake news and disinformation; it is more than anything else the crisis of democratic political culture and crisis of trust both in democratic institutions and in fellow citizens. Likewise, the crisis of the idea of EU integration is a much broader issue, with roots in inefficiency of the EU structure, decision-making, miscommunication, but also political culture that upheld the idea of European unity and its positive values for more than 50 years.

Nevertheless, social media have played a role in these processes and, therefore, there are possible steps that the EU can take in that regard, while having in mind all limitation mentioned before (Buckingham 2019). First, having in mind political and socioeconomic context, the EU should consider adopting and implementing new regulations on social networks which would define them as media and regulate them as such (Buckingham, 2019). The era of unregulated global dominance of tech multibillionaires, who reap benefits of the system of every democratic, free country, but manage to evade almost all regulations, has probably come to an end. And the EU, with partners such EEA and EFTA countries, Canada, Australia, New Zealand, and some others, could be the one to end this global dominance of online platform companies and what some authors label as digital feudalism (Meinrath et al., 2011).

The EU could enact such a new regulative framework under the shared competencies, within internal market policy. A regulation on that scale and with enormous potential consequences for social platforms would not pass without meeting serious resistance, both from the outside (tech moguls and new Trump administration) and from the inside (populist regimes in EU member states). Therefore, it is highly questionable whether such an endeavour would be successful. Nonetheless, it might be the only long-term step, when it comes to social platforms, that would bring us back to the "truth era".

Second, despite its limitations, social media literacy education should become a part of curricula on all levels of education. As shown by research, social media literacy interventions and education on social media literacy skills had positive effects on development of critical thinking and users' ability to detect fake news

(Heiss, Nanz, Matthes, 2023; Tandoc et al., 2023). However, as Sakya et al. (2021), demonstrated, these online skills should be accompanied by knowledge on topics at hand, both by educators and by students. It would, therefore, be useful that those who teach certain topics incorporate social media literacy skills into their curriculum.

Third, social media literacy education should go beyond teaching a set of technical and communication skills. Curriculum for social media literacy should take into account both the sociocultural (social interaction and relations) and the socio-economic context (political economy of social media) in which social media and its users operate (Tag, Seargeant, 2021; Krutka et al., 2019; Manca et al., 2021).The future research could, thus, focus on developing curricula for social media literacy within formal education and within the process of lifelong learning; further studying causal relations between socioeconomic and sociocultural context and behaviour on social platforms; deepening the understanding on the impact of the political economy of social media on societies in general.

The way back to the "truth era" is not possible without enlightened citizens, equipped with all relevant tools to navigate the complicated world of social media. A social media literate citizens should be able to position themselves between the media and reality in that complicated and interconnected social media context, should be aware of the interactions between themselves and the media and to recognize values that underline these interactions (Cho et al., 2024).In other words, citizens with social media literacy skills should be aware of their role, the role of social media and the context in which their interaction is happening.

REFERENCES

Allcott, H., & Gentzkow, M. (2017). Social media and fake news in the 2016 election. *The Journal of Economic Perspectives*, *31*(2), 211–236. https://www.jstor.org/stable/44235006. DOI: 10.1257/jep.31.2.211

American Library Association. (2020). Media literacy for adults. Architecture of the internet: Programming guide. https://www.ala.org/sites/default/files/tools/content/!%20Media-Lit_Prac-Guide_FINALWEB_112020_0.pdf

American Library Association. (2021). Promising practices: Educational research applied to the shared foundations. https://www.ala.org/sites/default/files/2024-04/AASL_ClassIIResearch_Book_0.pdf

Arksey, H., & O'Malley, L. (2005). Scoping studies: Towards a methodological framework. *International Journal of Social Research Methodology*, *8*(1), 19–31. DOI: 10.1080/1364557032000119616

Aspen Institute. (2022). Medienkompetenz meistern: Tipps von Schüler*innen für Schüler*innen. https://www.aspeninstitute.de/wp-content/uploads/Aspen-Institute-Germany-Handbuch-Medienkompetenz-meistern-Tipps-von-SchuelerInnen-fuer-SchuelerInnen.pdf

Aufderheide, P., & Firestone, C. (1993). Media literacy: A report of the national leadership conference on media literacy. The Aspen Institute. https://www.medialit.org/reading_room/pdf/358_AspenFrwd_Firestone.pdf

Buckingham, D. (2019). Teaching media in a 'post-truth' age: Fake news, media bias and the challenge for media literacy education. Cultura y Educación, 31(2), 1–19. https://davidbuckingham.net/wp-content/uploads/2019/10/post-truth-buckingham.pdf

Buckingham, D., Banaji, S., Carr, D., Cranmer, S., & Willett, R. (2005). *The media literacy of children and young people: A review of the research literature*. Ofcom.

Cho, H., Cannon, J., Lopez, R., & Li, W. (2024). Social media literacy: A conceptual framework. *New Media & Society*, *26*(2), 941–960. DOI: 10.1177/14614448211068530 PMID: 38328341

Clarke, L. (2025). Nobody was tricked into voting for Trump: Why the disinformation panic is over. https://www.politico.eu/article/nobody-tricked-vote-donald-trump-disinformation-panic-over/

Cope, B., & Kalantzis, M. (2009). Multiliteracies: New literacies, new learning. *Pedagogies*, *4*(3), 164–195. DOI: 10.1080/15544800903076044

Coper, E. (2022). *Facts and other lies. Welcome to the disinformation age*. Allen & Unwin Book Publishers.

European Commission. (2018). Code of practice on disinformation. https://digital-strategy.ec.europa.eu/en/library/2018-code-practice-disinformation

European Commission. (2022). Strengthened code of practice on disinformation. https://digital-strategy.ec.europa.eu/en/library/2022-strengthened-code-practice-disinformation

Federal Register. (2025). 2025 Donald J. Trump executive orders. https://www.federalregister.gov/presidential-documents/executive-orders/donald-trump/2025

Finchelstein, F. (2024). *The wannabe fascists: A guide to understanding the greatest threat to democracy*. University of California Press.

Georgiadou, E. (1995). Marshall McLuhan's 'global village' and the Internet [Unpublished manuscript]. https://www.researchgate.net/publication/274383916_Marshall_McLuhan's_'global_village'_and_the_Internet

Granderath, J. S., Sondermann, C., Martin, A., & Merkt, M. (2021). Actual and perceived knowledge about COVID-19: The role of information behaviour in media. *Frontiers in Psychology*, *12*, 778886. Advance online publication. DOI: 10.3389/fpsyg.2021.778886 PMID: 34975667

Grant, M. J., & Booth, A. (2009). A typology of reviews: An analysis of 14 review types and associated methodologies. *Health Information and Libraries Journal*, *26*(2), 91–108. DOI: 10.1111/j.1471-1842.2009.00848.x PMID: 19490148

Green, B. N., Johnson, C. D., & Adams, A. (2006). Writing narrative literature reviews for peer-reviewed journals: Secrets of the trade. *Journal of Chiropractic Medicine*, *5*(3), 101–117. DOI: 10.1016/S0899-3467(07)60142-6 PMID: 19674681

Heiss, R., Nanz, A., & Matthes, J. (2023). Social media information literacy: Conceptualization and associations with information overload, news avoidance and conspiracy mentality. *Computers in Human Behavior*, *148*, 107908. Advance online publication. DOI: 10.1016/j.chb.2023.107908

Heyneman, S. P. (2021). Fake news, fake truth: A new purpose for public schooling. *International Journal of Educational Development*, *87*, 102496. Advance online publication. DOI: 10.1016/j.ijedudev.2021.102496

Isaac, M., & Schleifer, T. (2025). Meta says it will end its fact-checking program on social media posts. New York Times. https://www.nytimes.com/live/2025/01/07/business/meta-fact-checking

Keyes, R. (2004). *The post-truth era: Dishonesty and deception in contemporary life*. St. Martin's Press.

Krutka, D. G., Manca, S., Galvin, S. M., Greenhow, C., Koehler, M. J., & Askari, E. (2019). Teaching "against" social media: Confronting problems of profit in the curriculum. *Teachers College Record, 121*(14), 1–42. DOI: 10.1177/016146811912101410

Leary, T. (1994). *Chaos and cyberculture*. Ronin Publishing.

Lee, J., Kalny, C., Demetriades, S., & Walter, N. (2024). Angry content for angry people: How anger appeals facilitate health misinformation recall on social media. *Media Psychology, 27*(4), 639–665. DOI: 10.1080/15213269.2023.2269084

Livingstone, S. (2004). Media literacy and the challenge of new information and communication technologies. *Communication Review, 7*(1), 3–14. DOI: 10.1080/10714420490280152

Manca, S., Bocconi, S., & Gleason, B. (2021). "Think globally, act locally": A glocal approach to the development of social media literacy. *Computers & Education, 160*, 104025. https://www.researchgate.net/publication/344340527_Think_globally_act_locally_A_glocal_approach_to_the_development_of_social_media_literacy. DOI: 10.1016/j.compedu.2020.104025

McLuhan, M. (1964). *Understanding media: The extensions of man*. McGraw-Hill.

McLuhan, M. (1967). *The medium is the massage: An inventory of effects*. Penguin Press.

Meinrath, S. D., Losey, J., & Pickard, V. (2024). Digital feudalism. *Advances in Computers, 81*, 237–287. DOI: 10.1016/B978-0-12-385514-5.00005-7

Munn, L. (2020). Angry by design: Toxic communication and technical architectures. *Humanities & Social Sciences Communications, 7*(1), 53. Advance online publication. DOI: 10.1057/s41599-020-00550-7

Orosz, G., Faragó, L., Paskuj, B., & Krekó, P. (2024). Strategies to combat misinformation: Enduring effects of a 15-minute online intervention on critical-thinking adolescents. *Computers in Human Behavior, 159*, 108338. Advance online publication. DOI: 10.1016/j.chb.2024.108338

Oxford English Dictionary. (2016). Post-truth. https://www.oxfordlearnersdictionaries.com/us/definition/english/post-truth

Oxford English Dictionary. (2016). Word of the year. https://languages.oup.com/word-of-the-year/2016/

Rochlin, N. (2017). Fake news: Belief in post-truth. *Library Hi Tech*, *35*(3), 386–392. https://www.researchgate.net/publication/318709609_Fake_News_Belief_in_Post-Truth. DOI: 10.1108/LHT-03-2017-0062

Ryan, T. J. (2012). What makes us click? Demonstrating incentives for angry discourse with digital-age field experiments. *The Journal of Politics*, *74*(4), 1138–1152. DOI: 10.1017/S0022381612000540

Sakya, S. M., Scoy, L. J. V., Garman, J. C., Miller, E. L., Snyder, B., Wasserman, E., Chinchilli, V. M., & Lennon, R. P. (2021). The impact of COVID-19-related changes in media consumption on public knowledge: Results of a cross-sectional survey of Pennsylvania adults. *Current Medical Research and Opinion*, *37*(6), 911–915. DOI: 10.1080/03007995.2021.1901679 PMID: 33840315

Snyder, T. (2017). *On tyranny: Twenty lessons from the twentieth century*. Crown.

Snyder, T. (2018). *The road to unfreedom*. Europe, America. Tim Duggan Books.

Spencer, J. (2016). Fake news is a real problem. Here's how students can solve it. https://spencerauthor.com/fake-news-is-a-real-problem-heres-how-students-can-solve-it/

Sun, Y., & Xie, J. (2024). Who shares misinformation on social media? A meta-analysis of individual traits related to misinformation sharing. *Computers in Human Behavior*, *158*, 108271. https://www.researchgate.net/publication/380409062_Who_Shares_Misinformation_on_Social_Media_A_Meta-analysis_of_Individual_Traits_Related_to_Misinformation_Sharing. DOI: 10.1016/j.chb.2024.108271

Tagg, C., & Seargeant, P. (2021). Context design and critical language/media awareness: Implications for a social digital literacies education. *Linguistics and Education*, *62*, 100776. Advance online publication. DOI: 10.1016/j.linged.2019.100776

Tandoc, E. C.Jr, Goh, Z. H., Wong, D. K. J., & Zhang, L. (2023). The good, the bad, and the Internet: Investigating the impact of online prosocial and anti-social behaviours on well-being. *Cogent Social Sciences*, *9*(1), 2225834. Advance online publication. DOI: 10.1080/23311886.2023.2225834

Tandoc, E. C.Jr, Lim, Z. W., & Ling, R. (2017). Defining "fake news": A typology of scholarly definitions. *Digital Journalism (Abingdon, England)*, *6*(2), 137–153. DOI: 10.1080/21670811.2017.1360143

Tandoc, E. C., Jr., Yee, A., Ong, J., Lee, J., Duan, X., Zheng, H., Matthew, C., Ng, J., Lim, C., Cheng, L., & Cayabyab, M. (2021). Developing a perceived social media literacy scale: Evidence from Singapore. International Journal of Communication, 15, 2484–2505. https://www.researchgate.net/publication/352118340_Developing_a_Perceived_Social_Media_Literacy_Scale_Evidence_from_Singapore United Nations Educational, Scientific and Cultural Organization. (2012). Media and information literacy: Curriculum for teachers. https://iite.unesco.org/publications/3214706/

Vishwanath, A., Neo, L. S., Lee, J., Goh, P., & Khader, M. (2020). Cyber hygiene: The concept, its measure, and its initial tests. *Decision Support Systems*, *128*, 113160. Advance online publication. DOI: 10.1016/j.dss.2019.113160

Vuorikari, R., Kluzer, S., & Punie, Y. (2022). *DigComp 2.2: The digital competence framework for citizens—With new examples of knowledge, skills and attitudes (EUR 31006 EN)*. Publications Office of the European Union., DOI: 10.2760/115376

Wei, L., Gong, J., Xu, J., Abidin, N. H., & Apuke, O. D. (2022). Do social media literacy skills help in combating fake news spread? Modelling the moderating role of social media literacy skills in the relationship between rational choice factors and fake news sharing behaviour. *Telematics and Informatics*, *76*, comprobating101910. https://www.researchgate.net/publication/365290679_Do_social_media_literacy_skills_help_in_combating_fake_news_spread_Modelling_the_moderating_role_of_social_media_literacy_skills_in_the_relationship_between_rational_choice_factors_and_fake_news_shari. DOI: 10.1016/j.tele.2022.101910

Wordorigins.org. (n.d.). Truthiness. https://www.wordorigins.org/big-list-entries/truthiness

Yousman, B. (2008). Media literacy: Creating better citizens or better consumers? In Andersen, R., & Gray, J. (Eds.), *Battleground: The media* (pp. 238–247). Greenwood Press., https://newmediagr.wordpress.com/wp-content/uploads/2009/10/17171370-battleground-themedia.pdf

Zuboff, S. (2019). *The age of surveillance capitalism: The fight for a human future at the new frontier of power*. Profile Books.

KEY TERMS AND DEFINITIONS

Disinformation: All false information spread on social media, with the intent to deceive (unlike misinformation, which is not deliberate).

Education: A process of acquiring and/or teaching skills and knowledge.

Fake News: False information and made-up stories that are spread as factual. They usually originate from a fake news portal and form there enter the mainstream media.

Global Village: The world interconnected by mass media.

Media: Means of mass communication, including traditional (TV, print, radio) and New media (Internet – news portals, social networks, video portals, podcasts).

Media Literacy: Technical, communication and social skills and knowledge required to receive and interpret media content and messages.

Post-Truth Era: A phenomenon that gained popularity after US presidential election in 2016 and Brexit, referring to a widespread notion that facts are a matter of opinion and emotions. The term "post-truth" is not new, but post-truth era, or post-truth politics, refers to a recent period in the development of liberal democracies, coinciding with the growing power of social media.

Social Media: Social networks that have characteristics of media, but unlike with traditional media, there is no clear distinction between creators and users and social interaction is their most prominent feature.

Social Media Literacy: Technical, communication and social skills and knowledge required to create, receive and interpret social media content and messages.

Chapter 3
Media Literacy in Times of Advanced GenAI:
New Challenges and Perspectives

Elena Shalevska
https://orcid.org/0000-0002-3270-7137
Faculty of Education, University "St. Kliment Ohridski", Bitola, North Macedonia

ABSTRACT

In the new era of today, Generative AI (GenAI) and media literacy, are inseparably linked. GenAI has both the potential to transform the world of media, but also the opportunity to challenge the status quo and help users with malicious intents create misinformation and disinformation easier than ever. This chapter addresses this intersection. It begins with an overview of GenAI's origins and its growing influence on media production, journalism, and creative industries. The discussion then shifts to the new challenges posed by AI-generated misinformation, deepfakes, bias, and intellectual property concerns, all of which contribute to the erosion of trust in media. The chapter also examines opportunities for enhancing media literacy in the age of AI, including educational initiatives, policy interventions, and collaborations between tech companies and educators, all to show that the issue of GenAI and media literacy is of importance and requires careful consideration.

INTRODUCTION

The landscape of media consumption and production is undergoing a profound transformation due to the rapid advancements in artificial intelligence, particularly in the realm of **Generative AI (GenAI)**. This emergent technology enables machines

DOI: 10.4018/979-8-3693-9601-8.ch003

to create content—ranging from text, images, and videos to music and code—with a level of sophistication that often mimics human creativity. Tools such as OpenAI's GPT series for text generation and DALL·E for image synthesis are at the forefront of this revolution. These technologies are not only enhancing creativity and productivity but are also fundamentally changing how we interact with and interpret media.

However, the rise of GenAI brings with it unprecedented challenges, particularly in the context of media literacy. As AI-generated content becomes more prevalent, it is becoming increasingly difficult for media consumers to distinguish between content created by humans and that generated by machines. This presents new challenges for truth, authenticity, and trust in the information people encounter daily. In a world where fake news, deepfakes, and synthetic media can be produced at scale, the importance of media literacy has never been greater.

Media literacy has traditionally focused on equipping individuals with the critical thinking skills needed to evaluate media sources, understand biases, and engage responsibly with information. However, the rise of GenAI requires a reevaluation and expansion of these competencies. Consumers now need to be literate not only in identifying misinformation and bias but also in understanding the inner workings of AI technologies, the ethical implications of their use, and the ways in which AI-generated media can manipulate perceptions.

This chapter explores how media literacy must adapt in the age of GenAI, addressing both the opportunities and risks that this new technology presents. It will examine how GenAI is reshaping media industries, what new skills are required for media consumers to navigate an AI-driven media ecosystem, and how educational frameworks must evolve to address these challenges.

Objectives of the Chapter

1. **To provide an overview of Generative AI and its impact on media production and consumption**
2. **To explore the new challenges GenAI poses for media literacy**
3. **To identify the expanded competencies required for media literacy in the GenAI era**:
4. **To discuss the ethical implications of GenAI in media**
5. **To propose educational and policy responses to GenAI challenges**

In a world increasingly dominated by AI-driven media, understanding the dynamics of GenAI is essential for becoming a discerning and informed media consumer. This chapter aims to contribute to that understanding by offering insights into how media literacy can evolve in response to the opportunities and challenges posed by Generative AI.

Generative AI (GenAI): The Origin Story

In recent years, Generative AI (also dubbed as GenAI) has become a buzzword – the very thing that has captured the imagination of technologists, creatives, and businesses alike. Suddenly, everything became AI-focused and everyone wanted to try it out. Its rapid development and widespread adoption have sparked both excitement and concern, as GenAI promised to revolutionize the world and how we create and interact with content.

But where did this transformative technology come from? To truly understand its impact, we need to take a step back and discuss how this type of AI came to be. The roots of Generative AI can be traced back to the early days of artificial intelligence research in the mid-20th century, when pioneers like Alan Turing began exploring the idea of machines that could mimic human thought. However, it wasn't until the advent of machine learning and neural networks in the 1980s and 1990s that the foundations for GenAI were really and trully laid. Early experiments with generative models, such as Markov chains and simple autoencoders, hinted at the potential for machines to create content, but these systems were rudimentary and limited in scope, and absolutely nothing like the models available today. (Kaplan, 2024)

The real breakthrough came with the rise of deep learning in the 2010s, fueled by the availability of massive datasets, powerful computing resources, and innovative algorithms like Generative Adversarial Networks (GANs) and transformers. GANs, introduced by Ian Goodfellow in 2014, revolutionized the field by pitting two neural networks against each other – one generating content and the other evaluating its authenticity. This adversarial process enabled the creation of increasingly realistic outputs, from images to text. And the world was changed! (Kaplan, 2024)

The release of OpenAI's GPT-2 in 2019 marked another turning point. GPT-2 was the very portrayal of all of the potential of large-scale language models and their ability to generate coherent and contextually relevant text (Brown, 2020). This was followed by GPT-3 in 2020, which stunned the world with its ability to write essays, code, and even poetry. Around the same time, tools like DALL·E and MidJourney were introduced – tools that showed how GenAI can create visual art, by generating stunning images from simple text prompts. These advancements were not just technical feats; they signaled a cultural shift, as GenAI began to permeate industries and redefine creativity (Wingström et al., 2023).

So, generally speaking, GenAI refers to a class of artificial intelligence systems designed to create new content, such as text, images, video, music, or code, by learning patterns from large datasets. These models can produce content that mimics human creativity, often indistinguishable from what a person might create. Key examples include language models like OpenAI's GPT series, which generate human-like text, and DALL·E, which creates images from textual descriptions. Other tools, such as deepfake generators, allow the manipulation of video and audio, often leading to hyper-realistic outputs (Koperniak, 2022).

Over the past few years, GenAI has evolved rapidly, transforming various fields like journalism, design, entertainment, and marketing. It can now write essays, compose music, design logos, and even generate entire movie scenes, all with minimal human input. These advancements are reshaping content creation, reducing production costs, and speeding up processes across industries. However, they also raise critical questions about authenticity, ownership, and the potential for abuse.

As these AI systems become increasingly sophisticated, their influence on media and society grows. They not only augment human creativity but also introduce significant challenges, such as the creation of highly realistic misinformation and the erosion of trust in media. From its humble beginnings in academic research to its current status as a global phenomenon, Generative AI has come a long way – and its journey is far from over. As we stand on the brink of a new era defined by AI-driven creativity, one thing is clear: the future of content creation and media creation will never be the same.

Why Media Literacy in the Context of GenAI?

In an era where AI-generated content is literally everywhere, media literacy has taken on a new level of urgency and complexity. Traditionally, media literacy focused on teaching students how to critically assess and engage with information in its various forms—whether news articles, advertisements, or social media posts (Potter, 2016). However, with the rise of GenAI, the landscape of media consumption has shifted dramatically. And so has the need of the media literacy curriculum. The line between what is human-made and AI-generated is blurring, and with it comes a host of new challenges and responsibilities for media consumers.

Today, people face challenges like never before. Navigating the media landscape is becoming more and more complex as AI systems can now generate fake news stories, create manipulated videos (deepfakes), and produce fabricated images that are often indistinguishable from reality. This makes the ability to discern truth from falsehood more complex than ever before. Traditional skills like critical thinking and source evaluation, while still essential, are no longer sufficient on their own. People must now develop the ability to recognize AI-generated content, understand the mechanisms behind its creation, and critically assess the biases or limitations inherent in the systems that produce it. Take a look at this "article":

Trump's Wildest Plan Yet: Draining the ENTIRE Gulf of Mexico to Build 'Trump Ocean City' – Critics Say It's a Disaster Waiting to Happen!

In a shocking announcement today, former U.S. President Donald Trump revealed an ambitious plan to "drain the Gulf of Mexico" and convert the seabed into new land for commercial and residential development. Speaking at a rally in Florida, Trump claimed the project would create "millions of jobs" and "unlock trillions of dollars in economic potential."

"The Gulf of Mexico is just sitting there, wasted space," Trump said. "We're going to drain it, build the most beautiful cities you've ever seen, and make America richer than ever before. It's going to be huge."

According to the proposal, the U.S. government would partner with private companies to construct a massive network of dams and pumps to remove water from the Gulf. The exposed seabed would then be developed into luxury resorts, shopping centers, and residential neighborhoods. Trump also hinted at plans to build a "Trump Ocean Resort" as the centerpiece of the project.

Environmental experts have slammed the idea, calling it "scientifically impossible" and "environmentally catastrophic." Dr. Emily Carter, a marine biologist, warned that draining the Gulf would devastate marine ecosystems, disrupt global weather patterns, and lead to irreversible damage to coastal communities.

Despite the backlash, Trump's supporters have rallied behind the idea, with many calling it a "bold vision for America's future." Social media platforms are already buzzing with hashtags like #DrainTheGulf and #TrumpOceanResort, as supporters and critics debate the feasibility and ethics of the plan.

The White House has yet to comment on the proposal, but sources close to the administration suggest that the idea is being "seriously considered."

ChatGPT, 5 seconds, one prompt and a handful of clicks. That's all it took to create this completely fake, fabricated piece of news – a piece of news that looks rather authentic upon first glance! This example serves as a great reminder why, in the age of GenAI, where tools like GPT models and deepfake generators can produce highly convincing text, images, and videos, media literacy is more critical than ever.

Moreover, GenAI introduces a host of ethical dilemmas that media literacy must address. Questions about the ethical use of AI in journalism, concerns over intellectual property rights, and the societal impact of AI-created misinformation are just the tip of the iceberg. For instance, who is accountable when an AI-generated article spreads false information? If people find and spread the Trump fake news above, who should be the one blamed, the prompter, the model, the developers, or the government? How do we ensure that AI tools are used responsibly in creative industries without stifling innovation? These questions show why we all need to better understand AI and GenAI models' role in media production and consumption.

What to do? The answer is simple (yet the implementation is much more nuanced!): Expand the media literacy curriculum. To navigate this new reality, there is a growing need to expand media literacy to include AI literacy. This means educating the public not only on how AI works but also on how it can be manipulated and how it influences the media they consume. Understanding the technical underpinnings of AI, such as how large language models are trained or how deepfake algorithms operate, can help students, as well as the general public engage with content more critically and responsibly (Koperniak, 2022).

Because, in this rapidly changing landscape, media literacy is no longer just about consuming information—it's about understanding the tools and systems that create it. By integrating AI literacy into media education, we can empower individuals to navigate the complexities of the digital age with confidence and critical awareness. The stakes are high, but so are the opportunities: a media-literate society is one that can harness the benefits of GenAI while mitigating its risks, ensuring that the future of media remains informed, ethical, and trustworthy.

The Role of GenAI in Media Production

Generative AI is revolutionizing the world of media production, transforming industries by automating tasks that were once the sole domain of human creativity. The rise of advanced AI models like OpenAI's GPT-4 and DALL·E has not only broadened the scope of what machines can produce but also introduced new dynamics in how media is consumed, created, and understood. So, what exactly can GenAI do and why has it completely transformed journalism and news media, as well as creativity and artistic expression?

What Generative AI Can Actually Do: An Overview

Generative AI systems have unlocked a vast array of possibilities for content creation by mimicking human creativity (Russel et al. 2020). At the core of these systems are deep learning models that analyze vast amounts of data to generate new, highly realistic content—whether text, images, music, or even videos (Kaplan, 2024). OpenAI's GPT-4, for instance, has the ability to generate well-structured essays, dialogue, and even code with minimal prompts, while DALL·E produces detailed images from text descriptions, pushing the boundaries of what machines can create. Other AI tools like MidJourney and Stable Diffusion also enable users to generate creative content with unprecedented ease.

These systems have revolutionized industries ranging from marketing and journalism to entertainment and gaming (Dhamani et al., 2024). In advertising, AI-generated content allows companies to rapidly produce targeted campaigns, creating ads that are personalized to individual preferences. For example, a clothing brand might use AI to generate thousands of unique ad variations tailored to different demographics, ensuring maximum engagement. In the visual arts, tools like DALL·E have democratized creativity, enabling users without technical artistic skills to create professional-level artwork with a simple text prompt. Imagine typing "a futuristic cityscape at sunset with flying cars" and receiving a stunning, high-resolution image in seconds.

In video production, AI can generate realistic landscapes, characters, and even entire scenes, drastically cutting down on production costs and time. For instance, AI-powered tools like Runway ML allow filmmakers to create special effects or edit footage with minimal effort, making high-quality production accessible to independent creators.

However, while the benefits of GenAI are clear, there are growing concerns about its broader implications for authorship, authenticity, and creativity. As AI systems become more adept at generating content, distinguishing between human-made and machine-generated creations becomes increasingly challenging (Musiol, 2024). This raises questions about what constitutes originality in an era where AI can mass-produce creative works, as well as how humans fit into the creative process when machines can replicate, and in some cases surpass, human efforts in generating new content.

The Impact on Journalism and News Media: Can Robots Run the Newsroom?

Generative AI is having a profound impact on journalism and the news media. "Robots" are now included in both news production and news consumption. But the good news is, though there are definitely downsides, it's not all bad. AI-driven tools have enabled newsrooms to streamline many aspects of the content production process. Automated journalism, also known as "robot journalism," has gained traction, with AI systems capable of generating news reports on topics like sports, weather, and financial updates with minimal human input. This automation allows journalists to focus on more nuanced and investigative work while routine stories are handled by AI.

For instance, tools like Wordsmith from Automated Insights can generate entire news articles from structured data, producing reports that are difficult to distinguish from those written by humans. Similarly, news agencies such as Reuters and The Associated Press have experimented with AI-driven reports to cover high-volume but low-complexity stories. AI-generated summaries, live updates, and data-driven reports are helping newsrooms manage the increasing demand for real-time information.

But it's not all rainbows and butterflies. The rise of GenAI in journalism also introduces several challenges to do with bias and objectivity – as AI systems are only as neutral as the data they are trained on; loss of human judgment – as AI-generated content often lacks context, and the ethical consideration that human journalists bring to complex issues; and of course, misinformation and deepfakes – the most alarming development is the potential for AI to be misused in the creation of disinformation. Deepfakes—AI-generated videos or audio recordings that convincingly mimic real people—have already been used in attempts to spread false information and manipulate public opinion. The technology's ability to create hyper-realistic fake content poses a significant risk to the integrity of news media, eroding public trust and making it harder to separate fact from fiction. The rapid evolution of GenAI only means one thing: all parties involved, including journalists, media organizations, and the public have to develop new skills in detecting AI-generated misinformation and ensuring that automated journalism maintains ethical standards. And to answer the previous question: No, as of now, robots *cannot* run the newsroom.

Creativity and Artistic Expression Through GenAI: The Art of AI-Generated Masterpieces

Generative AI has become a powerful tool for creative expression, blurring the lines between machine-assisted production and human creativity (Musiol, 2024; Wingström et al., 2023). From visual art and music composition to literature and game design, AI is unlocking new avenues for artistic innovation. For instance, DALL·E can produce all kinds of visual designs from simple text prompts, while AIVA and Amper Music allow users to compose original music scores tailored to specific styles and emotions.

The democratization of creative tools through AI is one of the most profound shifts in the creative industries. Individuals without formal artistic training can now use AI to generate high-quality artwork, music, and even films. This is particularly significant in fields like advertising and video game design, where rapid content creation is key to maintaining a competitive edge. In the realm of literature, AI models like GPT-4 can generate poetry, short stories, and even long-form narrative pieces, pushing the boundaries of what machines are capable of producing in the realm of creative writing.

And yet again, this rise in AI-driven creativity raises important questions:

- Can AI Truly Be Considered Creative? While AI systems can generate content that mimics human creativity, they do so by learning patterns from preexisting data rather than by experiencing or interpreting the world in the way humans do. This leads to a philosophical debate about whether AI-generated content is truly "original" or merely an imitation of human creativity.
- What Is the Role of the Artist? As AI increasingly automates the creative process, the role of human artists, writers, and designers may shift from that of creators to curators or directors of AI-generated content. This change may require a rethinking of what it means to be a creative professional in an AI-driven world.

Moreover, the growing prevalence of AI-generated art and media has sparked debates about intellectual property (Kaplan, 2024; Musiol, 2024). If an AI system generates a piece of artwork or music, who owns the rights to that work? And if the AI was trained on copyrighted material, does the output constitute an infringement of those rights? What do you think?

Shifts in the Creative Industries: How AI is Redefining What It Means to Be Original

As AI-generated content becomes ever-present, creative industries are facing a fundamental shift in how they operate. We may also need to redefine what constitutes "original" work, too. AI can work and can work fast. The sheer volume of AI-generated content risks overwhelming human creators. So, if humans aren't as fast, what of them? There may a new role for human creators: that of the editor or curator, refining and personalizing AI-generated content rather than crafting it from scratch.

This redefinition of creativity challenges the traditional models of authorship and ownership in artistic production. Moving forward, creative professionals will likely need to balance AI's efficiency with human originality, focusing on how they can guide and enhance AI-generated content while maintaining their own unique voice and style.

New Challenges in Media Literacy Due to GenAI

Regardless of who the creative director of AI content is, what cannot be overstated is that AI-driven tools of now have become increasingly sophisticated. Thus, media consumers must adapt to new realities where distinguishing between real and AI-generated content is more difficult than ever. So, what are the key challenges introduced by GenAI, including the proliferation of misinformation and deepfakes, the ethical issues surrounding bias and fairness, intellectual property concerns, and the overall erosion of trust in media?

AI-Generated Misinformation and Deepfakes

One of the most urgent and troubling challenges introduced by GenAI is the introduction of AI-generated misinformation and deepfakes. Misinformation has always been a concern in media (Lewandowsky, 2017), but AI has dramatically increased its scale, sophistication, and impact. AI tools can now generate highly convincing, but entirely fabricated, news articles, social media posts, audio clips, and even videos that seem indistinguishable from authentic sources. Deepfakes, defined by OED (2023),"any of various media,esp. a video, that has been digitally manipulated to replace one person"s likeness convincinglywith that of another, often used maliciously to show someone doing something that he or shedid not do", pose a particular threat due to their ability to distort reality in ways that human eyes and ears struggle to detect.

The danger of AI-generated misinformation is magnified by its ability to spread rapidly across digital platforms (Dobber 2021). Fake news stories, for instance, can be automatically tailored to specific audiences by AI algorithms. Social media networks also amplify this problem by providing fertile ground for the rapid spread of fake news, which is often designed to elicit emotional reactions. Here's one piece of news that was generated for the purpose of this chapter. It looks truly believable, yet is completely fake:

New Study Links COVID-19 Vaccine to Severe Heart Conditions in Young Adults, Experts Warn

By Emily Carter, Health Correspondent

A groundbreaking study has uncovered alarming links between the COVID-19 vaccine and an increased risk of severe heart conditions in young adults, sparking widespread concern among medical professionals.

The research, reportedly conducted by a team of scientists from the Global Health Research Institute (GHRI), claims that individuals under the age of 35 who received the mRNA vaccine are at a "significantly higher risk" of developing myocarditis, a rare but potentially life-threatening inflammation of the heart muscle.

Dr. Steven Michaels, a cardiologist and outspoken critic of vaccine mandates, stated in an interview, "This study raises serious questions about the safety of these vaccines. While the benefits may outweigh the risks for older populations, we cannot ignore the data showing harm among younger age groups."

The report, which has yet to be peer-reviewed, cites a sharp rise in hospital admissions for cardiac-related issues within three months of vaccine distribution. It also alleges that health authorities failed to adequately investigate early warning signs.

Adding to the controversy, Dr. Lisa Hoffman, a researcher at the Center for Vaccine Transparency, called for immediate action: "It's crucial that we pause and reassess the risks associated with these vaccines. Transparency and public trust are at stake."

Despite these claims, major health organizations such as the World Health Organization (WHO) and the Centers for Disease Control and Prevention (CDC) continue to endorse the COVID-19 vaccines as safe and effective. In response to the report, a CDC spokesperson dismissed the findings as "misleading and based on flawed data."

However, skepticism is growing among the public, with many taking to social media to share personal anecdotes and concerns. One user wrote, "My brother started having heart issues just weeks after his second dose. Why aren't we talking about this more?"

The study has reignited debates over vaccine mandates, with critics accusing pharmaceutical companies and governments of prioritizing profit over safety.

As the controversy unfolds, experts urge the public to consult reliable sources and wait for additional research before jumping to conclusions.

(generated by DeepSeek, prompted by the author)

Upon first glance, this piece of news looks truly authentic. It features the name of an expert, it includes statements from both professionals and members of the general public, and it even has a name of the author/journalist who wrote it. In many regards, this text is not that different from the hundreds of texts we encounter online daily. And yet, it is completely and utterly false – filled with AI hallucinations and the user's malintent. The only way to check it is for one to do one's due diligence: Google all of the names mentioned, compare sources, research data, critically approach the information shared etc.

Though this is absolutely a valid reason to worry, we must revert back to deepfakes that take this challenge to a more dangerous level (Helmus, 2022). AI-tools aimed at generating such videos make it possible for users to create realistic-looking videos or even audio clips of different public figures doing things they never actually did or making statements they never actually made. This technology has already been used to deceive the public in various contexts, from political elections to financial scams. Deepfakes can distort public perceptions of reality, undermine political leaders, and tarnish individual reputations, all while being almost impossible for the average viewer to detect without specialized tools.

Alongside deepfakes, voice cloning also poses a threat (Helmus, 2022). As a kind of a subset of deepfake technology, such cloningenables users to replicate the voices of well-known personalities through various apps like Celebrity Voice Cloning and Voicer Famous AI Voice Changer. Unfortunately, this technology has been exploited for fraudulent activities. For instance, Helmus (2022) notes an instance when a UK energy firm's CEO received a call from someone mimicking his superior's voice, instructing him to transfer €220,000 to a Hungarian supplier's account. Believing the call to be genuine, he complied.

What does all of this mean for media literacy? It is clear that the implications are profound. It is also worth noting that traditional strategies for identifying misinformation, such as checking sources or verifying facts, though still valid, are becoming less effective against AI-generated content that mimics legitimate media. Consumers must now develop advanced skills, including recognizing the subtle indicators of AI manipulation, using AI-detection tools, and becoming familiar with the risks and biases inherent in the AI models that create such content.

In much the same way, AI-generated misinformation contributes to confirmation bias by allowing bad actors to create content that conforms to specific political or social narratives, making it even harder for individuals to critically assess the truthfulness of what they encounter. The sheer volume and plausibility of this false information are eroding public trust in media, undermining democratic debate, and fueling divisive narratives across society.

To counter this, a number of AI-based disinformation detection tools have been developed – tools such as Microsoft's Deepfake Detection Tool, GPT Zero, and Google's AI-powered fact-checking initiatives. Though these tools are useful in their own ways, they unfortunately have many limitations, particularly as AI-generated content continues to evolve. AI detection systems are often playing catch-up with increasingly sophisticated synthetic media, leading to an arms race between those seeking to create disinformation and those trying to stop it.

This means that manual fact-checking is needed more than ever before. Researchers have developed various methods to identify AI-generated content, including analyzing inconsistencies in image or audio features, such as artifacts or anomalies not typically found in human-created media (Agarwal et al., 2019; Wang et al., 2020). For instance, deep learning-based forensic tools can detect AI-generated faces by identifying subtle differences in facial features and lighting. Individuals, in much the same way, should look for inconsistencies in narratives, textual flow, and stylistic choices in texts, as well as unnatural movements, speech patterns, or background distortions in videos and audio. But that, unfortunately, may not be enough. This is why cross-referencing information with reputable sources and verifying the context of media remains crucial. A healthy skepticism, coupled with a critical eye for detail may just be the answer to the AI content conundrum.

The Evolution of Misinformation

In the Internet-of-things age, misinformation has evolved from simple text-based falsehoods to sophisticated, multimodal synthetic content. For example, deepfake videos have been used to manipulate political discourse, such as the fabricated video of Ukrainian President Volodymyr Zelensky appearing to surrender during the Russia-Ukraine conflict (NPR, 2022). Similarly, AI-generated text can produce convincing news articles or social media posts, making it increasingly difficult for individuals to discern fact from fiction (Chu-Ke, 2024). The scale and speed at which such content spreads are amplified by social media algorithms, which prioritize engagement over accuracy (Vosoughi et al., 2018).

The scariest thing is that misinformation continues to evolve in the GenAI era. And one of the most concerning trends is the rise of hyper-personalized misinformation, where GenAI tailors content to exploit individual vulnerabilities based on data from social media profiles and browsing histories (Chu-Ke, 2024). This not only increases the effectiveness of misinformation campaigns but also erodes trust in authentic media. For example, the proliferation of synthetic content has led to a phenomenon known as the "liar's dividend," where even genuine information is dismissed as fake (Chesney & Citron, 2019). Globally, these trends have significant implications, from election interference to social unrest.

Bias, Ethics, and Fairness in AI-Generated Media

A more subtle but equally significant challenge posed by GenAI is the issue of bias in AI-generated media. While AI systems can produce vast amounts of content, they are only as neutral as the data on which they are trained (Noble, 2018). Because AI models learn from human-created datasets, they often inherit the biases and prejudices present in the original data. This can result in the perpetuation of harmful stereotypes, inequities, and imbalances in representation across AI-generated media.

For example, AI models trained on datasets that disproportionately feature certain racial, gender, or socioeconomic groups may generate content that reflects and reinforces existing societal biases. Stereotypical depictions of marginalized communities, for instance, may be reproduced in AI-generated images, texts, or videos, leading to unfair or harmful representations. In journalism, AI-generated news articles may skew toward certain narratives or fail to capture the complexity of issues affecting underrepresented groups due to biased training data.

Moreover, algorithmic bias is not always visible to consumers, making it a particularly insidious challenge for media literacy (Noble, 2018). For instance, AI-generated content might seem neutral at first glance but could subtly prioritize certain perspectives over others, reinforcing dominant social, political, or cultural views. This creates the risk of echo chambers, where AI tools reinforce existing biases by continually presenting users with content that aligns with their pre-existing beliefs. Here's an example. A recent study, by Dr. Kelly Choong, an advertising researcher and senior lecturer for Edith Cowan University, focusing on Midjourney's portrayal of Olympic Athletes found that men were five times more likely to be featured in images than women, with 82.86% of the images depicting men and that the model relied on cultural stereotypes, such as depicting the Australian team with kangaroo bodies and koala heads, and the Nigerian team in traditional attire (Edith Cowan University, 2024). This best shows how AI can contribute to inaccurate representation that reinforces existing stereotypes.

Ethically, these issues raise similar critical questions as above: Who is responsible for biased AI-generated content? Should blame rest with the creators of the AI models, the organizations that use them, or the consumers who rely on them? There is also the question of ownership and accountability: if an AI system produces harmful or biased media, can its creators be held accountable, or does responsibility fall on the human users of the technology?

Whatever the answer may be, one thing is for sure: people must improve their understanding of the ethical issues associated with AI-generated media. This includes recognizing the obvious limitations and biases of AI systems and engaging critically with AI-generated content by asking questions about its source, fairness, and inclusivity.

Discussion

Have you noticed any biases in AI output?

Who should be responsible for addressing the biases outlined above, and what steps can be taken to make AI systems more equitable?

Intellectual Property and Copyright Concerns

When you generate an image using an AI tool, do you, or should you own the copyright? If one creates a poem (such as the one below) by using a long prompt, many details about the form, rhyme scheme, metaphors and other literary devices etc. should they be able to claim it as their own? Take a look at this poem:

time leans in
the clock is a drunkard
slurring seconds,
tripping over the edge
of my shadow—
this body,
a house with doors
that no longer shut,
letting the weather in.
(generated by ChatGPT-4o, prompted by the author)

Should the author of the prompt be considered the author of the poem? It is evident that the emergence of GenAI has introduced new legal and ethical challenges related to intellectual property and copyright. AI models, especially those that generate creative content, are trained on large datasets, which often include copyrighted works such as books, images, music, and films. This raises difficult questions about ownership and rights over the content that AI systems produce: if an AI-generated artwork is inspired by millions of copyrighted images, who owns the rights to the final product? Is it the AI developer, the user who gave the prompt, or the creators whose works were used in training the AI?

This ambiguity over ownership is particularly concerning for artists, musicians, writers, and other creators who rely on intellectual property protections to safeguard their work. AI systems like Stable Diffusion or MidJourney, for example, can generate art that mimics the styles of well-known artists, sometimes blurring the line between derivation and originality. Does this constitute plagiarism, or is it a transformative process that creates new, original work?

Of course, some regulatory bodies have recognized these challenges. Some existing laws such as the EU's Digital Services Act and proposed legislation like the U.S. Copyright Office's recommendation on digital replicas, show how difficult it is to navigate this evolving legal landscape (Perkins Coie, 2022; U.S. Copyright Office, as cited in Perkins Coie, 2022). The U.S. Copyright Office has emphasized that AI-generated content is not automatically copyrightable, human authorship is still needed for protection to be valid, and *"Text prompts alone do not establish authorship"* (U.S. Copyright Office, as cited in Commlaw Group, 2025).

DISCUSSION

In what ways do you think AI complements or threatens traditional forms of human creativity in industries such as journalism, art, and entertainment? Can AI ever truly "create," or is it simply imitating human creativity?

The Erosion of Trust in Media

It is safe to say that media trust has been declining in recent times (Funk et al.. 2024) but with the widespread use of GenAI in media production this erosion of trust in media, particularly in journalism is getting more prominent. We have established that AI-generated content has become more sophisticated and harder to distinguish from human-made work, and with this, public skepticism about the authenticity and reliability of information has grown. This is particularly problematic in democratic societies, where trust in the media is essential for informed public debate, decision-making, and, of course, accountability.

All of the things detailed above – deepfakes, AI-generated misinformation, and the use of AI in automating journalism – contribute to this erosion of trust. As AI takes on more roles in automated journalism, there are concerns that the human elements of empathy, judgment, and context are being lost in the process. While AI can efficiently generate factual reports on routine subjects like sports or financial updates, its limitations in understanding complex social or political issues mean that AI-generated journalism might fail to provide the depth and context that human reporters offer.

It goes without saying that addressing this trust deficit is crucial. Consumers need to be equipped with the tools to critically engage with media, including the ability to identify and analyze AI-generated content. This may involve learning to use AI-detection technologies, understanding the inherent limitations of AI, and recognizing the subtle ways AI can manipulate media.

Discussion

As AI-generated content becomes more prevalent, what role do you think media literacy will play in maintaining or restoring trust in traditional and digital media? What can be done to rebuild trust when it has been compromised by AI-generated misinformation?

Opportunities and Potential Solutions

As we have already established, Generative AI GenAI has introduced a new era of media production, filled with both challenges and opportunities. As we confront the risks posed by AI-generated misinformation, deepfakes, and biases, we must also explore how these technologies can be used to actually improve media literacy. The easiest way would be to update educational frameworks, improve the collaboration between tech companies and educators, and adopt realistic long-term strategies. Only then can we can create a more informed and resilient media-consuming public.

Teaching Media Literacy in the Age of GenAI

As GenAI integrates into media, media literacy must evolve to include AI literacy. Traditional media literacy emphasizes critical thinking—evaluating sources, recognizing bias, and understanding media influence (Paul & Elder, 2017). In the AI era, these skills must also cover how AI-generated content is created, manipulated, and spread.

Recognizing AI-generated content is crucial but difficult. Deepfake detection and AI-authorship identification require spotting inconsistencies or unnatural artifacts. Research shows people struggle with this: Jakesch et al. (2023) found participants correctly identified AI-generated text only 52% of the time, while Groh et al. (2022) reported a 40% misclassification rate for AI-generated faces, worsening with higher-quality images.

Beyond detection, media literacy must address AI's ethical challenges—bias, journalism ethics, and copyright. Educators should foster discussions on AI's role in reinforcing social inequalities and ethical media use.

It is important to acknowledge, in this regard, that while media literacy education is essential, not all communities have equal access to the resources needed to navigate (and teach about) AI-generated content. Digital divides, economic disparities, and educational gaps create many barriers to AI literacy – barriers that need to be not only recognized, but also actively targeted. Inclusive strategies must be implemented – strategies like mobile-based learning platforms, AI literacy workshops in public places, and multilingual AI education resources – to make digital literacy programs accessible to all.

Discussion

Do you think you're able to successfully detect AI-geenrated content? How do you know what's real?

What is more difficult to detect, in your opinion, textual content, pictures or videos?

AI as a Tool for Media Literacy

Though it may sound counterintuitive, GenAI itself can be a powerful tool that can help improve media literacy education. AI itself can be used to teach media literacy by providing tools that help individuals better assess and interpret media. For example, AI-powered detectors can be used to check whether something is AI-generated. Though these detectors are not fully reliable as of now, AI systems continue to develop and we can hope for better detection algorithms in the years to come.

Another way AI can improve media literacy education is through **personalized learning**. In fact, this is one of the chief benefits of using AI in education in any context. (Beck, 1996; Tahiru, 2021; Anders, 2023; Skrabut, 2023 etc.) AI-driven educational platforms can tailor learning experiences based on the user's skill level and knowledge gaps. These tools can offer interactive exercises that help users practice spotting AI-generated misinformation, with immediate feedback to improve learning outcomes. This kind of personalized, adaptive learning is particularly useful for engaging younger generations, who are growing up in an AI-saturated media environment and require practical, hands-on approaches to media literacy. Take a look at this. We asked ChatGPT to generate explanations of what fake news are at different age levels:

Explaining “fake news” to different age groups –

For a 5-year-old:

Fake news is like when someone tells you a made-up story and pretends it’s real. Imagine if your friend told you that dinosaurs are coming back tomorrow—sounds exciting, right? But it’s not true! Fake news is like that, but on the internet or TV, where people sometimes say things that aren’t real to trick others.

For an 18-year-old:

Fake news is false or misleading information spread online, on TV, or in newspapers, often to make people believe something that isn’t true. Sometimes, it’s done for fun (like pranks), but other times, it’s meant to confuse people or make them angry. For example, if someone spreads a post saying a famous singer has died when they haven’t, it can cause panic. That’s why it’s important to check reliable sources before believing or sharing news.

For a 40-year-old:

Fake news refers to deliberately misleading or false information spread through various media channels, often to manipulate public opinion, generate clicks, or serve political and financial interests. It can take many forms, such as fabricated stories, distorted facts, or misleading headlines. For example, during elections, fake news articles may falsely claim a candidate has done something scandalous to sway voters. Being media-literate and verifying sources is crucial to avoiding misinformation.

(generated by ChatGPT-4o, prompted by the author)

This adaptability helps learners at any stage—whether they're young children or adults—grasp any concept (in this case, the concept of fake news) in a way that resonates with their level of understanding. As they progress through personalized lessons, the AI can continuously adjust the complexity of explanations, to keep them challenged and motivated. In this way, AI is not just a challenge to media literacy but can also be a powerful ally in equipping students and people, in general, to navigate the complexities of modern media.

Discussion

What are the advantages and potential drawbacks of using AI-powered tools to teach media literacy? Do you think AI tools themselves could introduce bias or misinformation in the educational process?

Collaborations Between Tech Companies and Educators

The media literacy issue can also be tackled through improved collaboration between technology companies and educators. Tech companies can help provide resources, and insights but also help by being truly and really transparent about how their AI models function and the potential risks they pose to media consumption. These partnerships can extend to professional development for educators, too. As AI technology continues to evolve, teachers need and will continue to need ongoing training to help them stay up to date with the latest developments. Tech companies can contribute by offering workshops, seminars, and resources that help educators integrate AI literacy into their curricula.

Discussion

If you're a teacher, have you gotten any formal AI training? If you're a student, do you find that your teachers are knowledgeable about AI models and AI, in general?

Long-Term Strategies for Strengthening Media Literacy in an AI-Driven World

AI will continue to be part of our lives in the years to come, too. So, preparing for the future of media in the age of GenAI should also mean adopting long-term strategies that promote lifelong learning in media literacy. AI-driven media is not static—it will continue to evolve, introducing new challenges and complexities that require ongoing education and adaptation. As a result, media literacy must be seen as an ongoing process that extends beyond formal education into community and workplace settings.

One effective strategy is to promote media literacy as a lifelong skill, making educational resources available in public libraries, community centers, and online platforms. Media literacy should also be framed as a social responsibility. Encouraging public discourse on the ethical use of AI, the integrity of media, and the challenges posed by AI-generated content can help build a more resilient society now and in the future.

Finally, governments and educational institutions must commit to ongoing research and development in media literacy education by exploring new pedagogical approaches, testing the effectiveness of AI-driven educational tools, and continually updating curricula as AI technologies evolve.

Looking Ahead—The Future of AI in Media and Media Literacy

As Generative AI continues to transform media production, journalism, and creative industries, it is crucial to consider how these changes will unfold in the future. While it is difficult to even attempt to predict the future in times changing as fast as these, anticipating certain AI developments, can help us be better prepared for a future where AI plays a central role in shaping the media we consume and create.

The Future of AI in Media and Journalism: Some predictions

AI is already reshaping journalism by automating routine tasks like transcription and data analysis, allowing journalists to focus on complex work (CNTI, 2025). As AI advances, it may generate entire narratives, videos, and immersive experiences with minimal human input. Future AI developments may extend beyond text, video, and image generation to include advanced AR and VR. As AI-driven immersive experiences become common, media consumers must develop new forms of literacy to recognize and interpret AI-generated content.

AI may also be used to combat misinformation. Disinformation is intentionally deceptive, while misinformation is shared without malicious intent (Wardle et al., 2017). AI could enhance detection of deepfakes and manipulated content using machine learning, blockchain, and pattern recognition.

Global Governance and Policy Initiatives: The Role of International Bodies

As AI continues to disrupt media, robust policy frameworks and media literacy programs are essential. Policymakers at national and international levels should integrate AI literacy into formal education—either as a standalone course or within existing curricula—to equip media consumers with the skills to navigate AI-generated content. Governments increasingly recognize that AI literacy is vital for protecting democratic systems and mitigating misinformation.

Global organizations like UNESCO have been proactive in advocating for media and information literacy (MIL), emphasizing AI literacy as a key component. UNESCO's AI Futures Lab (2024) and similar initiatives promote a multi-stakeholder approach, involving governments, educators, and tech companies in shaping inclusive and accessible media literacy programs. These efforts are crucial for marginalized communities, who are more vulnerable to misinformation and algorithmic biases.

AI's role in political manipulation is a growing concern. For instance, in a campaign collage, Republican presidential candidate Ron DeSantis included AI-generated images of Donald Trump with Anthony Fauci, deliberately blurring fact and fiction. Similarly, in April 2023, the Republican National Committee released an AI-generated ad depicting hypothetical crises under a second Biden term (Bond, 2023). These cases highlight how generative AI can be weaponized in political campaigns.

Regulatory efforts are beginning to take shape. The EU AI Act (2024) addresses safety, transparency, and non-discrimination, banning high-risk AI applications like social scoring and real-time biometric identification, except in limited law enforcement cases (Europarl, 2025). However, more comprehensive frameworks are needed. A multi-stakeholder approach—engaging governments, media organizations, tech companies, and civil society—is essential to balancing innovation with accountability and preventing regulatory capture by powerful AI firms.

CONCLUSION

As Generative AI continues to reshape media production, journalism, and the creative industries, the importance of media literacy has never been greater. AI's ability to generate realistic content—from text and images to immersive experiences—introduces new opportunities for innovation, but also raises significant challenges.

These include the rise of AI-generated misinformation, deepfakes, biases in AI-driven media, intellectual property concerns, and the erosion of public trust in the media.

To meet these challenges, media literacy must evolve to include AI literacy, equipping individuals with the tools to recognize, critically engage with, and ethically navigate AI-generated content. This requires a rethinking of education systems, where traditional media literacy is supplemented by AI detection skills, ethical frameworks, and a deep understanding of the societal implications of AI in media.

At the same time, AI itself offers potential solutions. AI-driven tools can help in detecting misinformation, personalizing education, and designing responsive curricula, creating new opportunities for collaboration between educators, tech companies, and policymakers. Long-term strategies for strengthening media literacy must include ongoing education efforts, partnerships between public institutions and industry, and the development of global governance frameworks to regulate AI's influence in media.

Looking ahead, the future of AI in media will require a careful approach: one that combines ethical oversight, public engagement, and continuous learning to ensure that society can harness AI's potential while mitigating its risks. As we navigate this complex landscape, media literacy will be a crucial tool in safeguarding democracy, public trust, and social cohesion in the digital age.

REFERENCES

Agarwal, S., Farid, H., & Guo, H. (2019). Protecting world leaders against deep fakes. *Proceedings of the IEEE Conference on Computer Vision and Pattern Recognition Workshops,* 38-45.

Anders, B. (2023). *ChatGPT AI in Education: What it is and How to Use it in the Classroom*. Sovorel Publishing.

Beck, J., Stern, M., & Haugsjaa, E. (1996). Applications of AI in Education. *XRDS: Crossroads. The ACM Magazine for Students*, *3*(1), 11–15.

Brown, T. B.. (2020). Language models are few-shot learners. *Advances in Neural Information Processing Systems*, *33*, 1877–1901.

Chesney, R., & Citron, D. (2019). Deepfakes and the new disinformation war: The coming age of post-truth geopolitics. *Foreign Affairs*, *98*(1), 147–155.

Chu-Ke, M.F, C. & Dong, Y.. (2024). Misinformation and Literacies in the Era of Generative Artificial Intelligence: A Brief Overview and a Call for Future Research. *Emerging Media* 2(1).

CNTI – Center for News. Technology and Innovation. (2025). *Artificial Intelligence in Journalism.* Retrieved from: https://innovating.news/article/ai-in-journalism/ on 19.3.25.

Coie, P. (2022). *The EU's Digital Services Act: A Paradigm Shift for Online Intermediaries.* Retrieved from: https://perkinscoie.com/insights/update/eus-digital-services-act-paradigm-shift-online-intermediaries

Dobber, T., Metoui, N., Trilling, D., Helberger, N., & de Vreese, C. (2021). Do (Microtargeted) Deepfakes Have Real Effects on Political Attitudes? *The International Journal of Press/Politics*, *26*(1), 69–91. DOI: 10.1177/1940161220944364

Edith Cowan University. (2024). *Hidden Biases: Midjourney's Portrayal of Olympic Athletes by Country.* ECU Online. Retrieved from: https://studyonline.ecu.edu.au/blog/hidden-biases-ai-portrayal-olympic-athletes on 4.1.25.

Europarl (2025). *EU AI Act: first regulation on artificial intelligence.* Retrieved from: EU AI Act: first regulation on artificial intelligence | Topics | European Parliament on 20.3.25.

Funk, A., Vesteinsson, K., & Baker, G. (2024). T*he Struggle for Trust Online.* Retrieved from: https://freedomhouse.org/report/freedom-net/2024/struggle-trust-online on 28.1.25.

Helmus, C. T. (2022). Artificial intelligence, deepfakes, and disinformation: A primer. *RAND Corporation.* Retrieved from: https://www.rand.org/content/dam/rand/pubs/perspectives/PEA1000/PEA1043-1/RAND_PEA1043-1.pdf on 15.1.25.

Kaplan, J. (2024). *Generative Artificial Intelligence: What Everyone Needs to Know.* Oxford University Press.

Koperniak, S. (2022). *Fostering media literacy in the age of deepfakes.* MIT Open Learning.

Lewandowsky, S., Ecker, U. K. H., & Cook, J. (2017). Beyond misinformation: Understanding and coping with the "post-truth" era. *Journal of Applied Research in Memory and Cognition, 6*(4), 353–369. DOI: 10.1016/j.jarmac.2017.07.008

Musiol, M. (2024). *Generative AI - Navigating the Course to the Artificial General.* New Jersey.

Noble, S. U. (2018). *Algorithms of Oppression: How Search Engines Reinforce Racism.* NYU Press. DOI: 10.18574/nyu/9781479833641.001.0001

NPR. (2022). *Deepfake video of Zelensky could be 'tip of the iceberg' in info war, experts warn.* Retrieved from: https://www.npr.org/2022/03/16/1087062648/deepfake-video-zelenskyy-experts-war-manipulation-ukraine-russia on 17.12.24.

Paul, R., & Elder, L. (2014). *Critical Thinking: Tools for Taking Charge of Your Professional and Personal Life.* Pearson.

Potter, W. J. (2016). *Media Literacy.* SAGE Publications.

Rini, R. (2020). Deepfakes and the Epistemic Backstop. *Philosophers' Imprint, 20*(24), 1–16.

Russell, S. J., & Norvig, P. (2020). *Artificial Intelligence: A Modern Approach* (4th ed.). Pearson.

Shalevska, E. (2024). The Future of Political Discourse: AI and Media Literacy Education. *Journal of Legal and Political Education, 1*(1), 50–61. Advance online publication. DOI: 10.47305/JLPE2411050sh

Skrabut, S. (2023). *80 Ways to Use ChatGPT in the Classroom: Using AI to Enhance Teaching and Learning.* Stan Skrabut: Self Published.

Tahiru, F. (2021). AI in Education: A Systematic Literature Review. *Journal of Cases on Information Technology, 23*(1), 1–20. DOI: 10.4018/JCIT.2021010101

The CommLaw Group. (2025). *U.S. Copyright Office Releases Reports Addressing Digital Replicas and Copyrightability of AI-Generated Content.* Retrieved from: U.S. Copyright Office Releases Reports Addressing Digital Replicas and Copyrightability of AI-Generated Content—Part 3 Covering AI Model Training Remains to Be Published | The CommLaw Group on 20.3.25.

UNESCO. (2025). *UNESCO-MICA hold summit on media and information literacy in AI age.* Retrieved from: https://www.unesco.org/en/articles/unesco-mica-hold-summit-media-and-information-literacy-ai-age on 20.3.25.

UNESCO. (n.d.) *Media and Information Literacy.* Retrieved from: https://www.unesco.org/en/media-information-literacy on 5.1.25.

Vosoughi, S., Roy, D., & Aral, S. (2018). The spread of true and false news online. *Science, 359*(6380), 1146–1151. DOI: 10.1126/science.aap9559 PMID: 29590045

Wang, S., Wang, O., Zhang, R., & Tao, X. (2020). CNN-generated images are surprisingly easy to spot... for now. *Proceedings of the IEEE/CVF Conference on Computer Vision and Pattern Recognition*, 8692-8701. DOI: 10.1109/CVPR42600.2020.00872

Wardle, C., & Derakhshan, H. (2017). *Information Disorder: Toward an Interdisciplinary Framework for Research and Policy Making*. Council of Europe.

Wingström, R., Hautala, J., & Lundman, R. (2023). Redefining Creativity in the Era of AI? Perspectives of Computer Scientists and New Media Artists. *Creativity Research Journal*. Advance online publication. DOI: 10.1080/10400419.2022.2107850

ADDITIONAL READING

Chapman University. (n.d.). Bias in AI||. Available at: https://www.chapman.edu/ai/bias-inai.aspx

Dhamani, N., & Engler, M. (2024). *Introduction to Generative AI.* Manning Publications.

Franklin Pierce Center for Intellectual Property, 57(3). Available on:

Friedman, Batya and Nissenbaum,Helen. 1996. —Bias in computer systems||. ACM Trans.

Helmus, C. T. (2022). Artificial intelligence, deepfakes, and disinformation: A primer. RAND Corporation. Available at: https://www.rand.org/content/dam/rand/pubs/perspectives/PEA1000/PEA1043-1/RAND_PEA1043-1.pdf

Kaplan, J. 2024. Generative Artificial Intelligence: What Everyone Needs to Know. Oxford

Koperniak, S. (2022). *Fostering media literacy in the age of deepfakes.* MIT Open Learning.

Musiol, M. (2024). Generative AI - Navigating the Course to the Artificial General

Sainsbury, M. (2024). Generative AI is outpacing media literacy and it's leaving people vulnerable, new research finds. Decrypt. Available at: https://decrypt.co/245283/generative-ai-outpacing-media-literacy-leaving-people-vulnerable

Vinchon, F., Lubart, T., Bartolotta, S., Gironnay, V., Botella, M., Bourgeois-Bougrine, S., Burkhardt, J.-M., Bonnardel, N., Corazza, G. E., Glăveanu, V., Hanchett Hanson, M., Ivcevic, Z., Karwowski, M., Kaufman, J. C., Okada, T., Reiter-Palmon, R., & Gaggioli, A. (2023). Artificial Intelligence & Creativity: A Manifesto for Collaboration. *The Journal of Creative Behavior, 57*(4), 472–484. Advance online publication. DOI: 10.1002/jocb.597

Wingström, R., Hautala, J., & Lundman, R. (2023). Redefining Creativity in the Era of AI? Perspectives of Computer Scientists and New Media Artists. *Creativity Research Journal.* Advance online publication. DOI: 10.1080/10400419.2022.2107850

KEY TERMS AND DEFINITIONS

Algorithmic Bias: Algorithmic bias refers to systematic and unfair discrimination that can occur in AI systems due to biased training data or flawed algorithms. These biases can lead to skewed outputs, reinforcing stereotypes or unequal treatment based on race, gender, or other characteristics. In generative AI, biases in the data used to train models can affect the fairness of the content generated (Nobel, 2018)

Artificial Intelligence (AI): Artificial Intelligence is a branch of computer science focused on creating systems capable of performing tasks that would normally require human intelligence. These tasks include problem-solving, decision-making, visual perception, language understanding, and learning from experience. AI systems use algorithms to process data and improve their performance over time without explicit human programming (Russel, 2020)

Critical Thinking: Critical thinking is the process of analyzing, synthesizing, and evaluating information to guide decision-making and belief formation. In media literacy, critical thinking skills are essential for assessing the credibility of sources, identifying bias, and determining the validity of AI-generated content (Paul & Elder, 2014).

Deepfakes: Deepfakes refer to AI-generated or manipulated audio and video content that is designed to look or sound like real people, often with the intent of misleading or deceiving viewers. These technologies use deep learning techniques, particularly generative adversarial networks (GANs), to create realistic fake media that can manipulate public opinion, spread misinformation, or harm individuals' reputations (Chesney et al. 2019).

Disinformation: Disinformation refers to deliberately false or misleading information spread with the intent to deceive or manipulate an audience. Unlike misinformation, which may be spread unintentionally, disinformation is crafted with the goal of misleading viewers. AI-generated disinformation, such as deepfakes or fabricated news articles, can have widespread and damaging effects, particularly in political or social contexts.

Generative Artificial Intelligence (GenAI): Generative AI refers to a subset of AI that focuses on creating new, original content by learning from existing data. This can include text, images, audio, or video. Examples of GenAI include models like GPT-4 for generating human-like text and DALL·E for creating images from text descriptions. These systems use deep learning algorithms, particularly neural networks, to generate outputs that mimic human creativity (Brown, 2020)

Media Literacy: Media literacy refers to the ability to access, analyze, evaluate, and create media in a variety of forms. It encompasses understanding how media messages are constructed, the intent behind them, the techniques used to convey information, and the potential impact on audiences. In the context of Generative AI (GenAI), media literacy extends to recognizing AI-generated content and understanding its implications in terms of authenticity, misinformation, and ethics (Potter, 2016).

Misinformation: Misinformation is false or inaccurate information that is spread, regardless of intent to deceive. With the rise of generative AI, the ability to quickly and convincingly generate false information has increased, contributing to the spread of fake news, manipulated images, or deepfakes that mislead the public (Lewandownsky, Ecker, Cook, 2017).

Chapter 4
Scholars as Disinformation Agents:
Unmasking Academic Propaganda for Authoritarian Venezuela

Michel Navarro
https://orcid.org/0009-0005-8242-3668
Corvinus University of Budapest, Hungary

Juan Cristóbal Demian
https://orcid.org/0009-0009-5090-7405
Corvinus University of Budapest, Hungary

ABSTRACT

This chapter explores how disinformation is propagated by scholars who act as Foreign Information Manipulation and Interference (FIMI) agents. Focusing on the Venezuelan presidential elections of July 2024, it analyzes the behavior of a network of Ibero-American academics and intellectuals who actively disseminated regime-aligned narratives online. This chapter shifts attention to digital advocacy, where academic credibility is leveraged to legitimize authoritarian propaganda. Using the framework of Public Diplomacy in authoritarian contexts, the study applies a mixed-methods design combining quantitative and qualitative content analysis with Social Network Analysis (SNA). The dataset comprises all posts on X (formerly Twitter) from 17 selected individuals between July 15 and August 1, 2024. The findings reveal how academic figures contribute to disinformation campaigns, calling for greater scholarly engagement with the risks of authoritarian influence in knowledge production and democratic discourse.

DOI: 10.4018/979-8-3693-9601-8.ch004

INTRODUCTION

Authoritarian regimes have refined their strategies to shape audience perceptions. Propaganda and disinformation campaigns aimed at national and international audiences are meticulously crafted to legitimize and secure their rule. At the same time, these regimes work tirelessly to discredit critics, portraying dissenting voices as unreliable or hostile (Walker & Ludwig, 2017).

While the internet and traditional media remain the primary tools for spreading propaganda and disinformation, other seemingly less far-reaching mechanisms, such as cultural exchanges and international conferences, can be equally effective. These spaces foster personalized connections between authoritarian regimes and foreign civil society actors, establishing bonds that are often more resilient and enduring (Kalathil & Boas, 2003).

Authoritarian propaganda has also penetrated the academic world, influencing research and scientific discourse (Cilano Peláez et al., 2021). Nowadays, studies carried out by academics, think tanks, and intelligence agencies highlight strategies employed by regimes such as China, Cuba, and Russia to recruit academics and intellectuals into their spheres of influence (Camero Guevara et al., 2023). Once aligned, these individuals act as both producers and disseminators of propaganda, targeting foreign audiences to legitimize authoritarian narratives (Brady, 2015).

This chapter examines the role of Ibero-American academic and intellectual circles in disseminating pro-regime propaganda online during the Venezuelan national elections in July 2024. The case is particularly relevant, as linguistic and cultural barriers frequently obstruct external researchers from comprehending the intricate dynamics of these communities. The study further investigates the actions and narratives employed by a group of such individuals throughout the electoral process, offering a detailed temporal analysis. Finally, it calls attention to a concerning trend: the infiltration of disinformation into academic discourse, a phenomenon that erodes institutional credibility and public trust.

Our guiding research question was: *What narratives did foreign academics and intellectuals affiliated with Venezuela's regime promote during the country's elections?*

This study is framed by Public Diplomacy, a core concept in International Relations that examines state strategies to influence foreign audiences through non-state actors. To analyze the data effectively, the research applies mixed-methods content analysis alongside social network analysis, providing a comprehensive understanding of the collected dataset.

Given the insufficient scholarly examination of academics supporting authoritarian regimes in Latin America, the Venezuelan case holds particular significance. Consequently, several vital subjects remain unaddressed here, highlighting a limitation and potential pathway for subsequent studies.

This chapter is organized as follows: It first examines the growing tendency of authoritarian regimes to engage foreign audiences and the central role of propaganda and disinformation in their strategies. The methodological framework is then outlined to ensure clarity and transparency in the research process. The analysis then shifts to the Venezuelan case, exploring the regime's connections with foreign actors, its strategic objectives, and its mechanisms of influence. A contextualization of the events surrounding the July 28, 2024, elections follows, providing necessary background for the study. The final sections present the research findings, followed by a discussion that critically assesses their implications, concluding with key takeaways and areas for further research.

Propaganda: A Weapon in the Hands of Autocrats

Authoritarian regimes, characterized as governments not chosen through free and fair electoral processes (Frantz, 2018), share distinct commonalities despite their differences. One notable feature is their intense focus on maintaining power, often concentrated in a small elite. This focus leads to a heightened sensitivity to threats, both internal and external (Dukalskis, 2021). Internally, dissent, political opposition, and ideological divergence are perceived as existential threats to their legitimacy. Any deviation from the official narrative is swiftly suppressed to maintain control. Externally, they view sanctions imposed by international organizations and foreign governments as assaults on their sovereignty and stability. However, one of the most persistent and insidious threats comes from their own citizens abroad. Diaspora communities—often composed of exiled activists, journalists, and dissidents—serve as voices that challenge state-controlled narratives, expose human rights violations, and rally international pressure (Marton & Navarro, 2024).

To address external threats and consolidate their position internationally, authoritarian regimes have adopted strategies beyond traditional state-to-state diplomacy (Cull, 2008). In a manner similar to democracies, they have expanded their approach to include what is commonly referred to in International Relations as Public Diplomacy. This concept encompasses tools and strategies that allow governments to engage with foreign citizens. The theory has since been refined to include a two-stage framework: the first focuses on communication strategies aimed at influencing foreign publics, while the second involves leveraging non-state actors to create domestic pressure on foreign governments to align with the regime's interests (Gilboa, 2008). As a result, Public Diplomacy strengthens the ability of authoritarians to deceive and disrupt other nations.

A wide range of methods can be employed to establish connections with foreign audiences, with cultural promotion being among the most effective. Governments often prioritize activities such as organizing music festivals, art exhibitions, and film screenings abroad, as well as establishing cultural centers and institutes to teach their language. Public Diplomacy also encompasses civil initiatives, including humanitarian aid, development programs, the management of social media campaigns, and the broadcasting of national media content in foreign languages. Moreover, these strategies frequently target educational institutions, academics, and intellectual circles.

Although democracies and authoritarian regimes conduct Public Diplomacy, the aims are not the same. Democratic countries use Public Diplomacy as a communication bridge between their domestic and foreign societies (Gilboa, 2008). It is a means of demonstrating, promoting, and educating others about its cultural identity, ways of life and values, and of creating strong ties of partnership, having a two-way nature. When a democratic state reaches out to civil society in a foreign country, it is equally receptive to reciprocal engagement from the counterpart.

In contrast, authoritarian regimes employ fundamentally unidirectional Public Diplomacy strategies (Gilboa, 2008). Their primary objective is to influence foreign audiences while simultaneously restricting the flow of external information within their own borders. This often involves implementing strict censorship measures and imposing barriers to restrict engagement with foreign actors. Moreover, the information disseminated by authoritarian regimes is frequently biased and lacks credibility (Taylor, 2011), so their goal is to manipulate global perceptions by controlling narratives that align with their interests (Walker & Ludwig, 2017).

Experts believe that the communication strategies of authoritarian regimes rely on propaganda, which rejects logic and credibility in favor of emotional appeals and the exploitation of human biases to create bonds (Baines & O'Shaughnessy, 2020). Leveraging their structural advantages, authoritarian regimes use propaganda to misinform, destabilize, and polarize societies, making it a cornerstone of their modern hybrid warfare (Camero Guevara et al., 2023).

Disinformation—understood as the deliberate dissemination of false or misleading information to manipulate public opinion on specific issues—constitutes a tool within broader propaganda strategies (Baines & O'Shaughnessy, 2020). Although its use is not exclusive to authoritarian regimes, these actors tend to deploy it in a more coordinated, state-sponsored manner. The advent of digital technologies and the rise of social media platforms have significantly altered disinformation's landscape.

Traditional propagandistic outlets, such as Russia Today or Venezuela's TeleSur, have given way to a more diffuse and networked information environment (Polegkyi, 2023). Algorithms on social media now serve to amplify disinformation by targeting users within ideologically aligned echo chambers, reinforcing narratives and polarizing public discourse (Mejías & Vokuev, 2017).

The shift toward a decentralized propaganda environment has elevated the strategic importance of high-profile individuals in shaping public discourse. Under the concept of *Foreign Information Manipulation and Interference* (FIMI), authoritarian regimes engage influential figures—such as academics, artists, and influencers—to disseminate regime-aligned narratives (European External Action Service [EEAS], 2023). These individuals act as informal agents of influence, guiding online conversations toward outcomes favorable to authoritarian interests.

These operations may occur continuously—promoting positive imagery of the regime—or be strategically activated during critical junctures, such as during electoral periods, as examined in this chapter. It is important to clarify that a FIMI actor is not merely expressing personal views under democratic norms. Rather, FIMI involves coordinated actions aimed at legitimizing authoritarian leadership, disseminating disinformation, discrediting opponents, exacerbating societal divisions, and eroding trust in democratic institutions (EEAS, 2023).

As disinformation tactics evolve, they have become central to "hybrid threat" strategies designed to undermine democratic societies (EEAS, 2023). These strategies have proven effective for manipulating public opinion in geopolitical conflicts, including Russia's aggression in Ukraine and Azerbaijan's campaigns in Nagorno-Karabakh (Polegkyi, 2023). In other regions, particularly in Latin America and Africa, such campaigns have also served to erode public trust in liberal democracies and promote the notion that Western democratic systems are in decline or inherently unstable (Rouvinski, 2022).

Therefore, the following section explores an essential dimension of disinformation operations: the engagement of academics and intellectuals in support of authoritarian regimes outside their classrooms. Operating as FIMI actors, these individuals contribute to coordinated online campaigns that disseminate regime-endorsed narratives to influence public discourse.

Autocrats and Academic Circles

Authoritarian regimes do not limit themselves to using state capacities to spread propaganda and disinformation; they also attract individuals and institutions to further disseminate their narratives. When academics and intellectuals are drawn into these networks of influence, the benefits for authoritarian regimes are substantial. First, their professional expertise and rhetorical skills enhance their credibility, making the public less likely to question their assertions (Downs, 1957). Second, foreign academics and intellectuals can effectively communicate with audiences in their home countries, leveraging the emotional and psychological dimensions of propaganda (Taylor, 2011). Third, their participation in debates—whether on television, at conferences, or on social media—often dilutes and undermines genuine academic discourse.

The influence of academics in shaping the perspectives of future generations cannot be overstated. University classrooms, where decision-makers and officials are formed, can serve as spaces for indoctrination, embedding cognitive biases that favor authoritarian regimes. Academics and intellectuals further amplify these narratives through their personal networks, multiplying the reach of propaganda.

Through their work, disinformation and false narratives infiltrate academic literature, sometimes gaining enough traction and becoming the dominant narrative within scholarly communities. Furthermore, authoritarian regimes exploit the prestige and foreign status of their collaborators to showcase international legitimacy and support to their domestic audiences. The motivations for supporting authoritarian narratives vary from personal gain to ideological alignment, as some individuals believe they are championing a noble cause.

Specific characteristics help to establish a framework for identifying propagandistic behavior (Robin, 2024). Firstly, the propagandist often engages in such activities due to material incentives or the public recognition it offers. Secondly, propagandists tend to disregard or distort the realities on the ground, opting instead to portray a parallel reality aligned with the interests of the sponsoring state. Their narratives consistently echo the official discourse, avoiding counterarguments or criticism, and present authoritarian institutions and leaders as credible sources. Additionally, their rhetoric often relies on emotional appeals and prejudices, designed to manipulate the audience's reasoning. Like authoritarian regimes, they attach derogatory labels to critics and opponents of the regime. Having established these criteria, the following section outlines the methodology employed and details the subjects of this investigation.

METHODOLOGY

Participants were selected through a rigorous and systematic process to ensure alignment with the study's objectives. The initial pool of candidates was drawn from Spanish-speaking academics and intellectuals who met the following criteria: (1) they self-identified as experts or knowledgeable commentators on Venezuelan political and social issues; (2) they were not Venezuelan citizens; (3) they were professionally affiliated with educational institutions, think tanks, or other intellectual enterprises;

and (4) they had participated in Venezuelan state-controlled or sympathetic media, offering commentary on Venezuelan topics.

The initial selection process identified 57 individuals. To ensure the availability of sufficient publicly available data for analysis, only those with identifiable and active X (formerly Twitter) accounts were included. This further refinement resulted in a final sample of 17 participants. The reduced sample ensured the availability of publicly accessible content while maintaining a focus on individuals actively engaged in public discourse on Venezuelan issues. Primary data were collected and anonymized for ethical reasons from the identified accounts (see Table 1) over the period from 15 July to 10 August 2024.

A closer examination of the sample revealed that many individuals have close ties with high-ranking members of the Venezuelan regime, including the President Nicolás Maduro. Three serve as regular or occasional contributors to state-run media outlets such as *TeleSur*. All are linked to organizations known for their ideological alignment with Chavismo, and most operate their own communication platforms or collaborate with far-left publications. Additionally, investigative reports have identified several of these individuals as active participants in the transnational dissemination of disinformation campaigns orchestrated by the Venezuelan regime (Ubertalli, 2025).

Table 1. List of academics and intellectuals analyzed (Source: Author's own collection)

Name	Country	Profession
BRA01	Brazil	Journalist and Intellectual
ARG01	Argentina	Intellectual and Academic
MEX01	Mexico	University Professor
ARG02	Argentina	International Analyst/Journalist
ESP01	Spain	University Professor
ESP02	Spain	University Professor and Former Politician
ARG03	Argentina	University Professor
ARG04	Argentina	University Professor
ESP03	Spain	University Professor
CUB01	Cuba	Intellectual
CUB02	Cuba	Intellectual
ESP04	Spain	Intellectual
ARG05	Argentina	University Professor
ARG06	Argentina	International Analyst/Journalist
ESP05	Spain	Essayist, Journalist

continued on following page

Table 1. Continued

Name	Country	Profession
CHI01	Chile	Intellectual
ESP06	Spain	University Professor

A predefined set of keywords was applied to the dataset[1] to isolate content directly addressing Venezuela's election. This filtering process reduced the total dataset from 2,810 tweets to 1,425 tweets segmented into three temporal phases: pre-election (15–27 July), election day (28 July), and post-election (29 July–10 August). Additional data sources, such as academic publications, media, and government reports were incorporated to contextualize findings.

This chapter applied a mixed-methods content analysis, chosen for its ability to systematically code and interpret digital text. Recognized for its methodological rigor and replicability (Trimble & Sampert, 2010), this approach is especially relevant to studies involving social media. Given the relevance of Twitter (now X) in shaping political discourse, this approach aligned with previous studies analyzing social media in political contexts (Small, 2011).

To examine tweet frequency and volume across temporal phases, the quantitative content analysis employed text pre-processing techniques, including cleaning, tokenization, and lemmatization via Python and Word2Vec, with manual verification. Semantic analysis further explored the dominant narratives, hashtag patterns, and the most frequently mentioned actors.

To understand the context and intentions behind the tweets, qualitative content analysis was conducted using the 5D methodology, which measures foreign manipulation and interference strategies (EEAS, 2023). Tweets were evaluated against trustworthy sources reporting on events at the time of publication and classified into one of five categories: *Dismiss*, *Distort*, *Distract*, *Dismay*, or *Divide*. A brief Social Network Analysis (SNA) was employed to reinforce the findings and evaluate the hypothesis of coordination or cooperation among the studied actors. The analysis focused on identifying clusters, pinpointing central figures, and exploring the dynamics of their online interactions (Grandjean, 2016).

The Venezuelan Case

In February 1992, an unknown military officer named Hugo Chávez led a coup d'état against the democratically elected president Carlos Andrés Pérez. In prison, Chávez later admitted that he had also participated in the preparation of a second coup attempt in November of the same year (Gonzalez, 2025). Both incidents resulted in an unspecified number of casualties, leaving a legacy of violence and instability.

Chávez remained in prison for barely two years before receiving an amnesty. These events are critical to understanding the broader themes explored in this chapter.

In the 1998 national elections, Hugo Chávez was elected president of Venezuela, presenting himself as a moderate reformist committed to addressing the nation's entrenched corruption. However, his moderate rhetoric quickly gave way to an ideologized agenda (Ponniah & Eastwood, 2011). Chávez unveiled his vision of building socialism in Venezuela and spearheading a regional movement to counterbalance U.S. influence and dismantle the neoliberal order that had dominated Latin America (Ellner, 2014).

A segment of the academic community responded positively to Chávez's project. Venezuela was envisioned as a leading force for Latin America's leftward turn (Kingsbury, 2016), and as a central actor in a globally relevant geopolitical project: post-hegemonic regionalism. This framework for regional integration sought not only to counter U.S. "imperialism" and the perceived injustices of neoliberalism but also to foster proactive cooperation through the creation of institutions like ALBA, UNASUR, and CELAC (Clemente, 2017).

Marta Harnecker, a Chilean Marxist theorist who played a significant role in Salvador Allende's administration, became one of Hugo Chávez's key advisors. In her writings, Harnecker underscored the importance of deploying media propaganda to counteract the "counter-revolutionary" and "fascist" narratives propagated by the opposition (Harnecker, 2004). She explicitly endorsed the censorship of opposition media as a necessary measure to "ideologically educate the population" (Harnecker, 2004).

Chávez's era was classified by other academics as an example of "competitive authoritarianism" (Alarcón & Hidalgo, 2024). For them, Venezuela had the characteristics of a system in which elections and limited freedoms for the opposition existed primarily to enhance the regime's legitimacy. Propaganda was central to this approach, with the regime focusing on controlling media platforms, educational systems, and academic institutions to consolidate its legitimacy and sustain its popularity. In the absence of legitimacy and popularity, the regime could still survive sustained by its clientelist networks of influence and control. Alternatively, should this strategy fail, the regime resorts to political repression and autocratization as a last resort (Alarcón & Hidalgo, 2024).

The post-2013 period marks a critical juncture in Venezuela's political development. Following Chávez's death, Nicolás Maduro assumed leadership as his designated successor. The opposition achieved a landmark victory in the 2015 National Assembly elections, obtaining 65.27% of the ballots (Semana, 2015). The erosion of popular support was compounded by a deep economic and migration crisis (Nagy, 2020). In response, Maduro intensified repression and shifted decisively towards outright authoritarian rule (Alarcón & Hidalgo, 2024). Between 2016 and 2020,

Maduro governed by decree, and in the 2020 parliamentary elections—conducted with minimal opposition participation and a voter turnout of only 30.18%—the regime secured 67.6% of the ballots(BBC Mundo, 2020). This outcome symbolized the regime's consolidation of authoritarian power (Nagy, 2020).

While Venezuela experienced severe political, social, and economic upheaval, Nicolás Maduro strengthened the regime's propaganda and disinformation ecosystem (Suárez Pérez & Ponce de Leon Rosas, 2021). Central to this effort is *TeleSur*, an international television network based in Venezuela that plays a key role in promoting pro-regime messages while simultaneously supporting the geopolitical objectives of allied nations such as Cuba, China, Iran, and Russia (Puyosa, 2023). It has also been leveraged to target governments with tense relations with the Venezuelan regime (Puyosa et al., 2023). By exaggerating their social and economic crises, *TeleSur* aims to fuel discontent, magnify internal divisions, and delegitimize opposing governments. Furthermore, it offers a stage for foreign academics and intellectuals to participate as salaried hosts or as invited "experts."

The Venezuelan propaganda ecosystem also incorporates extensive bot farms, operating thousands of fake accounts on social media to artificially generate trends aligned with the regime's objectives (Puyosa, 2017). This has been identified as a key tool to influence political processes beyond Venezuela's borders (Puyosa, 2017). The regime's foreign influence spans a range of activities, including the dissemination of false content targeting unfavored candidates, orchestrating inorganic support for preferred political actors, and, in some cases, directly financing political parties abroad.

This ecosystem enabled Nicolás Maduro to address both domestic and international audiences. Between 2021 and 2023, the regime's communication strategy for Venezuelans centered on portraying economic adjustments as evidence of effective governance and leadership (Mawad, 2024). This narrative aimed to project an image of stability and economic renewal, encouraging members of the Venezuelan diaspora to return by promoting the perception of emerging opportunities. Simultaneously, regime propaganda sought to discredit opposition leaders by labelling them as "vendepatrias" (sellouts), fascists, pro-Yankee agents, or even more extreme defamatory labels (Medianálisis, 2023). Opposition figures were systematically blamed for the nation's challenges, including economic sanctions, social unrest, and political divisions.

The strategy for foreign audiences was primarily designed to generate empathy and deflect accountability. Venezuelan propaganda blamed "American imperialism" for attempting to subvert the sovereign will of the Venezuelan people. The economic collapse, deterioration of healthcare services, hunger, and the broader humanitarian crisis were portrayed as direct consequences of U.S. actions and those of other neo-colonial powers. International media outlets not subject to regime control were dismissed as purveyors of "fake news." These narratives were framed as part of a broader capitalist conspiracy aimed at destabilizing and overthrowing the government. In this context, foreign academics and intellectuals play an important role due to their direct links with the Venezuelan regime, as will be explained in the following subsection.

Foreign Academics and Intellectuals Within the Chavismo Influence Network

Hugo Chávez, who frequently identified himself as Fidel Castro's ideological heir, enjoyed acceptance within academic and intellectual circles (Vicent, 2006). Among other factors, this can be attributed to Cuba's enduring influence over these communities (Cilano Peláez et al., 2021). Chávez not only adopted Castro's ideological framework but also inherited and sustained a well-established and active network of influence that spanned Spanish-speaking university, academic, and intellectual circles. These Cuban networks active in Ibero-America since the 1960s (Amorín, 2022), were strategically integrated into Chávez's propaganda efforts. Their mobilization was facilitated through the alliance between the Cuban and Venezuelan regimes, reflecting their aligned political and ideological goals.

Since its inception, the Venezuelan regime integrated the educational system into its broader ideological project, aiming to consolidate political control and safeguard its agenda (Rojas & Ángel, 2017). While pledging to expand educational access for marginalized sectors, the regime embedded an ideological framework within state-owned universities, research centers, and academic institutions. Educational institutions that resisted alignment with the regime faced financial cuts, while those that supported its agenda received preferential funding (Rojas & Ángel, 2017). Additionally, universities were encouraged to affiliate with CLACSO (Consejo Latinoamericano de Ciencias Sociales), a regional network of academics and intellectuals, often criticized for its ideological bias and its silence regarding the authoritarian practices of leftist regimes in Latin America (Chaguaceda & Rouvinski, 2024).

The Venezuelan academic and educational ecosystem provides activities and incentives, including conferences, scholarships, and opportunities for publication in state-affiliated journals and publishing houses. Foreign academics and intellectuals invited to Venezuela often receive VIP treatment, with all expenses covered. These visits feature curated programs where participants meet high-ranking public officials, gain exposure through state-controlled media, and are taken on guided tours of selected communities to reinforce the carefully crafted narrative of the regime's social and political achievements. Through these initiatives, the Venezuelan regime cultivates loyalty and goodwill among the beneficiaries. As a result, they end up promoting the regime's narratives, contributing to its broader propaganda and disinformation campaigns.

The Venezuelan strategies also involve the creation of intellectual organizations and think tanks. One prominent example is the *Red de Intelectuales y Artistas en Defensa de la Humanidad* (Network of Intellectuals and Artists in Defense of Humanity), established in 2003 with the support of Hugo Chávez. From its inception, the organization brought together members from over 50 countries with the stated aim of fostering solidarity for social and political struggles. However, it has also served as a platform for advocacy in favor of the Venezuelan regime, framing its actions as part of an "offensive resistance" (REDH, 2023).

Other institutions, such as the *Centro Internacional Miranda* (International Miranda Centre, 2006) and *the Instituto Samuel Robinson* (Samuel Robinson Institute, 2020), illustrate a more sophisticated approach. Operating under the guise of scientific think tanks, these centers finance and engage domestic and foreign experts to discredit countries and institutions supporting a democratic transition in Venezuela. Simultaneously, they actively promote narratives favoring allies, notably China, Cuba, Iran, Nicaragua, and Russia.

International congresses held in Venezuela play a strategic role in constructing and disseminating the regime's social and political myths. Framed within a progressive discourse of empowering the Global South, these events serve as platforms to propagate narratives against foreign governments and political adversaries. There, the Venezuelan opposition is branded as an accomplice of imperialist forces or as fascist. Simultaneously, ideologists associated with the regime openly advocate for international mobilization and solidarity to exert pressure on foreign governments in support of the regime's political objectives.

These events are organized on a regular basis to ensure consistent engagement between Venezuelan authorities and foreign circles under its influence. For example, just a few months before the elections, the regime hosted a highly publicized event designed to mobilize its foreign affiliates and equip them with narratives to reproduce in the lead-up to the elections. The *Encounter for a Social World Alternative* conference took place in Caracas from April 18 to 20, attracting over 300 delegates from 60 countries (Clarín, 2024). Coordinated by high-ranking Chavista officials, the event featured President Nicolás Maduro, who personally moderated a two-hour panel alongside other prominent figures from Latin American political and intellectual circles.

The consolidation of an international intellectual support network has been central to the Chavista regime's propagandistic strategy. Over the past two decades, foreign academics and intellectuals have been engaged through direct relationships, institutional cooperation, and recruitment into state-controlled media, organizations and think tanks. During critical junctures—such as elections or domestic unrest—

these individuals have been instrumental in promoting favorable narratives and discrediting opposition voices.

Even as many former sympathizers have distanced themselves, a loyal core continues to act as unofficial spokespersons for the Venezuelan regime. They serve as commentators in international media, produce scholarly work that reinforces official narratives, and appear at public events advocating regime perspectives. Through collective activity on social media, they amplify propaganda while drawing on the perceived authority of their academic positions. They also use their social media platforms to engage in coordinated campaigns that leverage their academic credentials to amplify Venezuelan government propaganda. Their roles, as outlined in the theoretical section, strongly align with the methods typically employed by FIMI actors.

The individuals studied in this chapter belong to this particularly committed group within Ibero-American academic circles that support the Venezuelan regime. Their participation in online campaigns during the July 2024 elections, especially through X, warrants detailed examination. To meaningfully assess the disinformation they disseminated, it is first necessary to understand what was actually taking place in Venezuela at the time. The next subsection offers a reality check by presenting independent accounts from reputable academic and international institutions. This will pave the way for the following section's analysis of the narratives these individuals helped propagate.

Elections and Fraud

For the presidential elections held on July 28, 2024, Nicolás Maduro had all the advantages necessary for victory—except popular support. Following an agreement signed in Barbados, where Maduro committed to holding transparent and free elections, the U.S. relaxed sanctions on Venezuela. However, the regime showed no genuine intent to honor these commitments (Infobae, 2024a). María Corina Machado, the indisputable winner of the opposition primaries in October 2023 with over 92.5% of the vote, was banned by a so-called "independent" Venezuelan court from holding any elected political office (Freedom House, 2024). Moreover, her designated successor was disqualified from registering as a candidate due to an alleged "technical error."

In an unexpected turn of events, the Venezuelan opposition united behind Edmundo González as the candidate. Maria Corina Machado tirelessly took to the streets in support of González, bypassing the regime's imposition of pseudo-news, censorship, repression, and other measures specifically designed to undermine him.

The Venezuelan presidential election campaign, which officially ended on July 25, was marked by the severe restrictions imposed by the regime (Infobae, 2024b). The members of María Corina Machado's team were arbitrarily detained. Airlines operating in the country did not allow them to board their flights, forcing them to drive everywhere. The campaign routes were also blocked by trucks, police checkpoints and, in some places, tons of earth, which meant that they had to walk for hours or take boats to reach the areas they had been blocked off. The regime also systematically closed restaurants and hotels where the opposition stayed for rest.

Unsatisfied with simply undermining the electoral campaign of its primary rival, the regime imposed additional barriers. It violated the constitutional rights of the Venezuelan diaspora—numbering up to 8 million—by restricting their ability to vote abroad, allowing only 1% of them to participate (Centenera et al., 2024). Days before the election, the regime closed the land borders with Colombia and Brazil, hindering emigrants from physically returning to vote in their hometowns (Reuters, 2024). Moreover, the regime denied authorization and also arrested some foreign independent observers who sought to monitor the elections (Carter Center, 2024).

Edmundo González emerged victorious in the presidential elections, winning between 65% and 67% of the vote according to independent estimates (Edison Research, 2024). This outcome was corroborated by the opposition, which secured over 80% of the tally sheets as evidence (Corrales & Kronick, 2025). Nonetheless, Nicolás Maduro's government refused to concede defeat, declaring himself the winner. Maduro maintained his grip on power by exploiting his control over the military, the judiciary, and the National Electoral Council (CNE) (Corrales & Kronick, 2025).

The electoral fraud drew significant international condemnation. The Organization of American States (OAS) recognized the fraudulent nature of the election (El País, 2024a), while the Carter Center, an observer of the process, stated the elections "cannot be considered democratic" (Carter Center, 2024). The United Nations also initiated an investigation into human rights abuses tied to the elections (El País, 2024b). Despite widespread criticism, allied regimes and pro-Chavist organizations like *Casa de las Américas* (TeleSur, 2024) and the *Network of Intellectuals and Artists in Defense of Humanity* (2024) openly supported Maduro's contested victory.

FINDINGS

Dissecting Tweet Activity: Frequency, Dominant Narratives, Key Actors and Patterns

The dataset offered insights into the engagement patterns of academics and intellectuals on social media. The studied timeframe overlapped with major global events, such as the Paris Olympics, French elections, an attack on Donald Trump during the U.S. presidential campaign, the Russian invasion of Ukraine, and the Israeli-Palestinian conflict. Despite the breadth of international developments,

Venezuela remained central to the discourse, with 1,426 tweets—50.75% of the total—focused on the country.

Participants were categorized into three tiers based on their activity levels. The most prolific contributors included CHI01 (215 tweets), ESP04 (172), ESP06 (156), MEX01 (142), ESP03 (120), ESP01 (110), and ESP05 (107). Moderately active contributors featured ARG02 (84), CUB02 (80), BRA01 (78), ARG05 (55), ESP02 (37), and ARG01 (31). The least active group comprised ARG04 (15), ARG03 (11), CUB01 (6), and ARG02 (6).

Tweet activity from 15 to 27 July increased steadily, peaking at 85 posts on 27 July, just before Election Day (see Figure 1). On 28 July, a significant surge occurred, with 147 tweets recorded. CHI01 led with 27 tweets, followed by ESP04 (19) and BRA01 (13). Contributors such as ESP02, ESP05, and ESP06 exceeded ten tweets each, while CUB02 (10), ARG05 (9), and ESP02 (3) demonstrated moderate levels of engagement. In total, 14 authors participated on election day, reflecting heightened interest.

From 29 July to 10 August, tweet activity intensified, surpassing pre-election levels. The most active day was 29 July, with 164 tweets, driven by debates over the election results. ESP04 posted 24 tweets, followed by CHI01 (22) and BRA01 (18). ESP06 maintained engagement with 19 tweets on 2 August and 12 on 10 August, highlighting the persistent focus on post-election narratives.

Figure 1. Tweet activity of the scholars studied from July 15 to August 10, 2024 (Source: Authors' depiction)

Figure 1

Tweet Activity of the Scholars studied from July 15 to August 10, 2024.

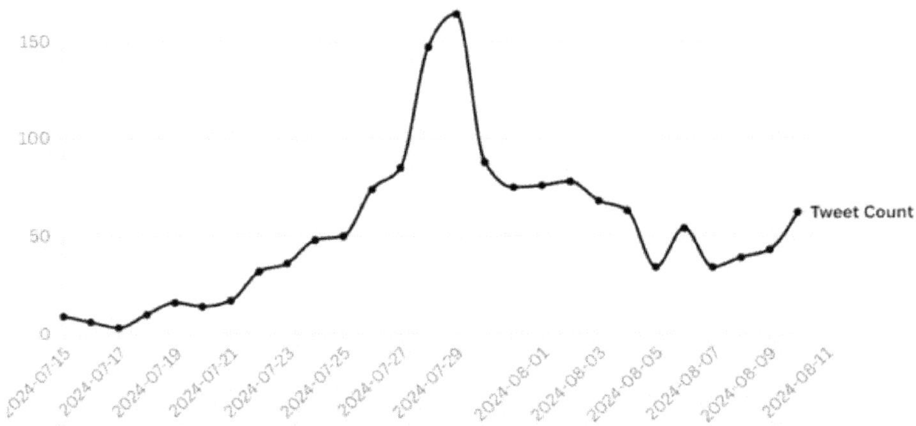

Note. Disinformation activity increased exponentially in the days leading up to the elections and remained moderately high afterward, indicating a strategy aimed at counteracting the negative international attention the Venezuelan regime was receiving in the media.

Source: Data compiled by the authors from X.

Semantic analysis of the dataset revealed clear patterns in narratives tied to Venezuela's electoral process, resulting in four key clusters. The dominant cluster, "**Maduro**," featured terms such as people, president, power, country, government, and democracy. Opposing this was the "**Opposition**" cluster, characterized by frequent use of descriptors like ultra-right, extreme-right, fascist right or the coup-mongers right. This cluster included references to electoral fraud allegations and opposition leaders Edmundo González and María Corina Machado.

The "**Election**" cluster surfaced as the third significant grouping, emphasizing terms that reinforced the credibility of Venezuela's electoral process. Key terms included *electoral process*, **acts**, *the Electoral National Council* (CNE*), results*, *people's decision*, and *people's choice of candidate*. The fourth cluster, titled "**External Actors**," captured references to global engagement, featuring terms like international audiences, the world, the United States, international media, recognition of the elections, and Elon Musk.

The dataset's 393 hashtags also shed light on key narratives. Over half (53.69%) focused on Venezuela's electoral process, with frequent use of *#Venezuela* and *#VenezuelaElige.*[2]A notable 19.34%, representing 76 hashtags, endorsed Nicolás

Maduro, with terms like *#MaduroPresidente*, *#GalloNico*, and *#VamosNico*,[3] reflecting the contributors' ideological bias. Hashtag usage evolved during the study period. Early on, sovereignty and the electoral process were central themes. On 28 July, electoral-specific hashtags saw a significant rise. Post-election, hashtags shifted to promoting legitimacy and non-intervention, exemplified by *#HandsOffVenezuela*, *#RespectVenezuela*, and *#VenezuelaPeaceAndJustice*.[4] The hashtag *#VenezuelaHasAlreadyDecided*[5] encapsulated claims of conclusive electoral results.

Interactions on the X platform played a role in amplifying the narratives of the 17 accounts. Nicolás Maduro's account was retweeted or cited 143 times, dwarfing the 14 retweets of opposition candidate Edmundo González. Opposition leader María Corina Machado was cited more often, with 28 mentions. This imbalance reveals a clear preference for Maduro's narrative over those of his opposition, highlighting a significant asymmetry in coverage.

In the dataset, the most frequently mentioned and retweeted profiles were directly linked to the Venezuelan regime. Nicolás Maduro's account was a central hub, often amplified alongside other high-ranking officials, such as Diosdado Cabello, Minister of Interior, Justice, and Peace; the National Electoral Council (CNE), heavily influenced by the regime; Yvan Gil, Minister of Foreign Affairs; and Delcy Rodríguez, Vice President of the Republic.

The reinforcement of these narratives came from a cluster of pro-regime media and propagandist accounts. Leading this cluster were influential platforms like *VNV Radio*, *TeleSur*, and the program *Con el Mazo Dando*. Additionally, propagandist accounts linked to Cuban and Venezuelan regimes—dedicated to spreading disinformation in favor of authoritarian states—were among the most shared and cited.

Foreign politicians and academicians form a third cluster of interactions. Gabriel Boric, President of Chile, and his Foreign Minister, Alberto van Klaveren, were the most cited figures, underscoring Chile's critical stance and leadership in rallying regional opposition to Venezuela's electoral irregularities. Following closely was Brazilian President Lula da Silva, another influential figure. Rubén Martínez Dalmau, a Spanish legal scholar, also stood out for his active participation in debates with several individuals analyzed in this study.

Through the analysis, dominant narratives were revealed and grouped by temporal phases:

Pre-Election Narratives Observed (July 15–27, 2024)

1. Electoral Integrity and Transparency
    - Reassurances of international observers safeguarding the electoral process.
    - Framing Venezuela's electoral system as a model of transparency.

- Highlighting concerns about opposition strategies, such as pre-emptive fraud claims.

2. Maduro's Leadership and Chavismo
   - Leveraging Hugo Chávez's legacy to bolster political messaging.
   - Declaring Maduro's imminent and decisive victory.
   - Depicting widespread mass support for Maduro.
   - Framing Chavismo as a pillar of stability and legitimacy.
   - Reinforcing the ideological importance of the Bolivarian Revolution.

Narratives Advanced on Election Day (July 28, 2024)

1. Electoral Transparency
   - Highlighted orderly voting and international observer endorsements, anticipating detailed results from the CNE.
2. International Validation
   - Calls for the international community to recognize the legitimacy of Venezuela's elections.
3. Geopolitical Contestation
   - Framing the elections as emblematic of a broader ideological conflict between multipolarity and unipolarity.
4. Opposition Allegations
   - Accusing the opposition of fraudulent actions and promoting conspiracy theories.
5. Media Scrutiny
   - Critiquing media outlets for perceived biases and delegitimizing narratives.

Post-Election Narratives Observed (July 29–August 10, 2024)

1. Allied Support and International Criticism
   - Noted robust support for Maduro from allies such as China, Russia, and Cuba, as well as recognition from OPEC.
   - Presented initiatives like those by Lula, Obrador, and Petro as a conflict resolution approach.
   - Contrasted this with the rejection from Western countries, driven by political and economic concerns.
2. Opposition Narratives
   - Rejected fraud allegations by opposition forces as lacking evidence and designed to destabilize.

- Highlighted warnings about the use of violence by opposition groups.
- Critiqued misinformation campaigns and fake news promoted on social media platforms.
- Compared opposition reactions to global right-wing trends of rejecting electoral outcomes.

3. Defending Sovereignty
    - Positioned Venezuela as resisting imperialist pressures to safeguard its sovereignty.
    - Pointed to accusations against the OAS and the U.S.for interference.
    - Framed the elections as a reflection of global ideological clashes between imperialist and multipolar visions.

A Qualitative Approach to Rhetorical Strategies

A detailed review of the tweets uncovered deliberate efforts to bolster Nicolás Maduro's regime. No tweets openly criticized or scrutinized the actions taking place at the time. Instead, all authors showed consistent alignment with official narratives, using their platforms to support these positions, justify actions, or redirect focus to unrelated issues (see Figure 2). Using the "5D methodology" (Dismiss, Distort, Distract, Dismay, and Divide), this section examines examples of how these voices strategically frame their messages.

Figure 2. Percentage allocation of the '5D' methodology (Source: Authors' depiction)

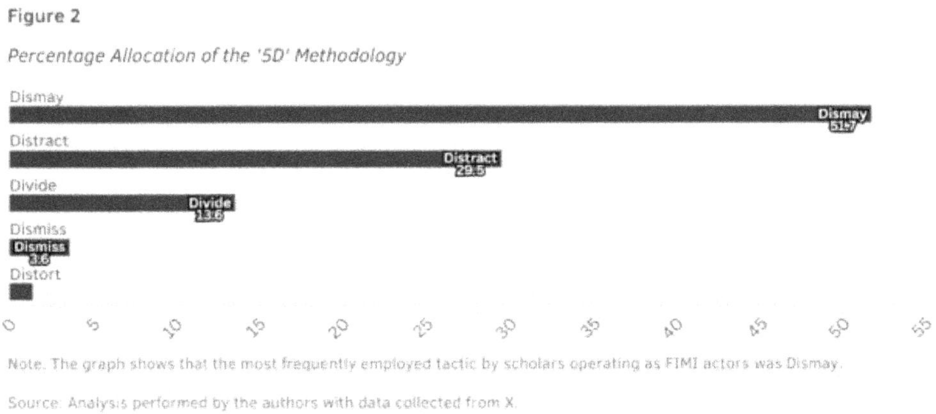

“**Dismay**” refers to the sowing of fear or discouragement to delegitimize the opposition and strengthen one's own position. This mechanism is observed when narratives warn of catastrophic scenarios (violence, civil wars, invasions) if the political adversary triumphs or if the public discredits the official version. In the dataset, the academics studied resort to a vocabulary that predicts chaos, “bloodbaths” or coups d'état, projecting the idea that the defeat of Chavismo would lead to a national collapse.

These narratives relied on warning the audiences of catastrophic outcomes if Maduro were defeated.MEX01 published that the right wing “sings frauds of what has not happened” and urged to be “alert” before a presumed media operation to use fraud as a “pretext” for the opposition to generate chaos. (19 July 2024). Similarly, ARG01 invoked alarming historical parallels, predicting a “bloodbath” under opposition rule, drawing comparisons to infamous Latin American dictatorships (26 July 2024). BRA01 further contributed to this rhetoric, alleging that the opposition was plotting a “fascist cybernetic coup” in coordination with external powers (5 August 2024).

Beyond domestic concerns, the pro-regime rhetoric extended to framing Venezuela as a target of global imperialist aggression.ESP03 frequently referenced “soft coups” and potential invasions by international forces, painting a picture of an international conspiracy against Venezuela (28–30 July 2024). ESP01 echoed these sentiments, linking opposition victories to the threat of civil wars or foreign military interventions backed by imperialist powers (24 July 2024). This messaging cultivated a pervasive sense of external threat, positioning the regime as the sole defender of Venezuelan sovereignty and stability.

They also portrayed the opposition as inherently violent and incapable of accepting electoral defeat.ESP04 reinforced this notion by echoing claims that the “extreme right” fundamentally rejected democracy (23 July 2024). BRA01 suggested that a loss by the opposition would inevitably lead to unrest and coup attempts (26 July 2024). To support these claims, they often recycled old imagery of protests and destruction, portraying opposition activities as precursors to chaos.

This study also identified the use of the “**Distract**” tactic, which diverts attention through frequent references to global conflicts, including Israel-Palestine, the Ukraine war, or political developments in other countries. Rather than engaging with domestic electoral concerns, the authors compared Venezuela's alleged problems to global injustices. For example, ESP01 calls a potential opposition victory a “victory of Israel’s genocidal regime,” while ESP03 equates supporting María Corina Machado with endorsing Israeli policies. By highlighting these international disputes, the conversation shifts away from calls for electoral transparency and toward denouncing perceived foreign meddling or hypocrisy.

On August 4, ESP03 questioned via his X account: *"How can the same people who fabricated lies about Iraq, Libya, the Atocha bombings, oppose sanctions on Israel, and manipulate the media convince you that Venezuela should be destroyed? Another round of lies?"* *Likewise, on August 10, ESP06 stated: "While Israel murders innocent civilians with the West's approval. We're supposed to trust their advocacy for democracy in Venezuela? Ridiculous."*

This rhetorical strategy reframed any critique of the Venezuelan regime as part of a broader imperialist scheme, making accusations of electoral fraud appear secondary or unimportant. As a result, local demands (e.g., requesting electoral rolls) are overshadowed by moral or ideological debates about conflicts abroad. Thus, "**Distract**" redirected the attention from specific electoral issues to more global controversies, complicating efforts at objective scrutiny of Venezuela's political process.

The "**Divide**" tactic seeks to intensify societal antagonisms by framing the population into two opposing and irreconcilable groups: "them" (the opposition) versus "us" (the regime and its supporters). This strategy thrives on derogatory terms, sweeping generalizations, and pejorative descriptions of opponents. Its primary goal is to deepen divisions, obstructing reconciliation efforts while reinforcing unity within the pro-regime faction.

The analysis of the dataset revealed a recurring use of divisive language. A significant pattern (shared by ARG04, ARG05,CUB01, CUB02, ESP02 and others) involved harsh, pejorative terms directed at the opposition, such as "fascist" and "Nazi-fascist." For instance, ARG02 responded to critical users with phrases like "disgusting fascist" and "degenerate fascist" (10 August 2024). Furthermore, divisive rhetoric extends beyond individual insults, portraying the opposition as a monolithic, hostile and radical entity; and therefore, the single idea of dialogue was futile. The repeated mention of the "ultra-right Venezuelan opposition" collapses distinctions between moderate and extremist factions, creating a narrative of a single, uncompromising adversary. BRA01 reinforced this framing by asserting that "*Venezuelan fascists behave like Bolsonaro's supporters*" (29 July 2024), equating the opposition with violent and chaotic groups. ARG04 contributed to the misleading portrayal of the election as a class conflict, stating, "*Campaign closing in Venezuela: For socialism we will triumph!!! Tremble oligarchs!!!! You will not return!!!!*" (July 26, 2024).

The "**Dismiss**" tactic, characterized by personal attacks or ad hominem remarks, was widely employed across the dataset. This approach is particularly potent within polarized contexts where credibility is a prime currency. It also stifles the space for nuanced conversations about electoral integrity or social conditions in Venezuela. In this case, authors mocked critics of the Venezuelan regime, branding them with terms like "nauseating flunky" or "Pop-Up Venezuela Analysts." Instead of engaging in debate, they chose to delegitimize the messengers through insults, inhibiting critical discourse. Many authors criticized media outlets and journalists by name, particularly those from their home countries. Two examples come from MEX01, who posted on August 3: "*Enough of the sold-out press. No more hucksters of mediocrity... Enough of mercenary fugitives from journalism schools.*" On August 9, he retackled on the same topic arguing: "We need to make an organized -and thorough- effort to put the bourgeois media packs in their place. Their shamelessness and mediocrity are unacceptable. Their hypocrisy and their "war journalism." *Their role as assassins of the truth is a crime against humanity.*"

Another observed tactic, "**Distort**," involves manipulating facts or sources to support a biased narrative. Some actors disseminated false information or quoted reputable sources out of context to bolster claims of Maduro's imminent victory. For instance, ESP04 retweeted a post by Franco Vielma, a known pro-regime propagandist, alleging that the Atlantic Council had acknowledged a clear victory for Maduro:

"*The opposition will not say it, but recently the Atlantic Council, (...) in a public report addressed to Biden, estimated as a 1st Scenario that Maduro would win the elections cleanly.*"

This claim was factually incorrect. The report was neither addressed to President Biden nor did it assign higher probability to this scenario. Forecasting reports inherently consider multiple possibilities without prioritizing any specific outcome. Nonetheless, the claim was weaponized to distort public understanding and falsely imply international validation of Maduro's victory.

On election day, 28 July, another distortion was circulated. This involved the supposed findings of a U.S.-based polling firm, *Lewis and Thompson*, which claimed Maduro's victory was imminent. This narrative was promoted by ARG02, CHI01 and ESP05. For instance, ARG02 tweeted at 7 pm: "*In an election that runs from 6 am to 6 pm, U.S. pollster Lewis & Thompson, based in Miami, gives 55% of the votes to Nicolás Maduro, 34% to Edmundo González, with Antonio Ecarri in third place with 8%. (...).*"

However, as reported by Infobae (2024c), this polling firm was entirely fictitious. It had been established only 19 days before the election, and its X account had been active for just nine days. This suggested that the entity was orchestrated by the Venezuelan regime to lend legitimacy to the electoral process. The distortion was carefully crafted. Posing as a foreign firm based in the U.S. with an English name lent an aura of credibility and neutrality, making the narrative more persuasive. The fabricated data served to portray Maduro's victory as not only legitimate but also internationally recognized, thereby shielding the regime from deeper scrutiny. By sharing this disinformation on their online platforms, the studied accounts not only expanded its reach but also enhanced its perceived credibility among their followers and media.

In sum, all these tactics worked together to suppress critical voices, amplify polarization, and present government support as the only safeguard against chaos and external threats. Critics were invalidated through personal attacks, facts were twisted or fabricated to fit the agenda, and references to foreign conflicts diverted the attention from electoral controversies. Alarmist rhetoric predicting coups or violence aimed to create dismay among audiences, while labeling opponents as "fascists" or "conspirators" fostered societal polarization.

A Collaborative Effort

The findings indicate that, regardless of geographic distance—from Spain to Brazil or Mexico to Chile—all studied individuals are interconnected within a shared network comprising various clusters. Figures like ARG01, BRA01, ESP03, and ESP04 are personally connected to Nicolás Maduro, while individuals such as CUB02, CHI01, and MEX01 maintain ties to senior Venezuelan officials. Others are involved with organizations founded by Chavismo, contribute to regime-controlled media outlets, or use their personal platforms to disseminate messages aligned with the regime's narrative.

By cross-referencing with secondary sources, it was confirmed that many of the individuals participated in congresses and events financed by the Venezuelan regime. Furthermore, during the election, individuals such as ARG02, BRA01, CHI01, ESP01, and ESP03 were present in Venezuela. They were either invited as international observers to "guarantee" the impartiality of the electoral process or engaged in covering the events for their respective audiences. While serving as international observers, they attended pro-Maduro events, and appeared in interviews with regime-friendly media, openly displaying their biases.

Figure 3. Network graph of coordinated online disinformation among identified academics (Source: Authors' depiction)

Figure 3

Network Graph of Coordinated Online Disinformation Among Identified Academics

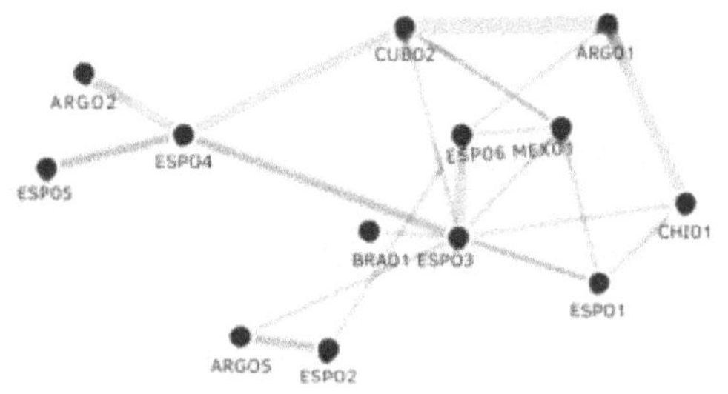

Note. Among the network of 17 scholars studied, 14 are actively involved in coordinated dissemination of mutually reinforcing disinformation. ESP03 emerges as the central hub, exhibiting the highest number of simultaneous interactions with the others.

Source: Network Analysis performed by the authors with data collected from X.

Online interactions among the studied individuals revealed a coordinated effort to reinforce narratives and propagate pro-regime messaging to their audiences (see Figure 3). The dataset highlighted ESP03 as the key figure in the network, with the highest number of interactions. His discourse and ideas, prominently shared on social media and offline, were subsequently adopted and spread by others within the network.

CONCLUSION

The Venezuelan regime under Nicolás Maduro exemplifies how autocracies strategically co-opt academics and intellectuals to manufacture legitimacy and deflect scrutiny. By cultivating personal relationships with these individuals, the regime integrates them into its broader propaganda apparatus, transforming their academic authority into a tool for political validation. During the election, these figures used their academic credentials to legitimize the regime narrative of normalcy.

This chapter has illustrated that instead of acting as independent analysts, these intellectuals have become active participants in a state-orchestrated disinformation campaign. Despite varying levels of engagement among the 17 academics and intellectuals analyzed, all systematically reproduced and amplified narratives aligned with the Venezuelan regime's propaganda. Functioning as key nodes in Maduro's unidirectional Public Diplomacy efforts, they sought to shape discourse in their home countries, influence public opinion, and pressure foreign governments into passively accepting Venezuela's fraudulent elections.

Moreover, the remarkable flexibility of the narratives employed by pro-regime academics and intellectuals stands out. They adapted their discourse according to the regime's shifting needs at different phases of the electoral process. In the pre-election period, their messaging was triumphalist, portraying Chavismo as the pillar of Venezuelan stability and progress. They championed the integrity of the electoral system and positioned Maduro's victory as inevitable, seeking to establish a preemptive defense against accusations of fraud.

On election day, pro-regime intellectuals worked to both validate the process and discredit any criticism. Reports of irregularities were dismissed as opposition propaganda or Western media distortions. The rhetoric shifted from celebrating democracy to aggressively delegitimizing dissent. Post-election, the discourse became overtly geopolitical, portraying the opposition as imperialist agents rather than a legitimate political force. Maduro's contested victory was framed as a stand against neocolonial subjugation.

Another observation in this study is that pro-regime academics and intellectuals did not engage in straightforward political debate. Instead, they strategically redirected discussions about electoral fraud and democratic rights into ideological arguments that favored the Venezuelan regime. This maneuver was not incidental but a deliberate effort to remove factual events from scrutiny and reframe them within a broader ideological confrontation.

Andrés Villavicencio, a pro-democracy advocate who witnessed the election firsthand, argues that the regime's tactic of reframing facts into ideological struggles is a defensive move—an attempt to sidestep damning evidence. While such rhetoric is crafted to secure automatic backing from international left-wing networks, in Venezuela's case, this strategy has lost traction, as disillusionment with the regime grows even among former sympathizers.

The declining effectiveness of Venezuelan regime propaganda can be credited to the sustained resistance of activists, journalists, and independent academics who have exposed its disinformation strategies. These actors have countered official narratives not through rhetoric, but with empirical data and critical analysis. Yanina Welp, for instance, directly confronted ESP03—the central actor of the studied disinformation network—on X, methodically debunking his contradictions and misleading claims.

Two other important points arise from this research. First, there is clear evidence of coordination and cooperation among the individuals analyzed, both online and in physical spaces. These intellectuals not only converge at conferences, podcasts, and interviews to promote the Venezuelan regime's interests, but also actively reinforce each other's narratives on social media to maximize reach. Second, this coordination transcends geographic boundaries, with particularly strong hubs of academic and intellectual support for Chavismo observed in Argentina and Spain.

Their advocacy for an authoritarian regime carries a profound moral contradiction. Except for those residing in Cuba, all of them live and work in democratic societies—albeit some in fragile ones—where they enjoy rights and freedoms unavailable to Venezuelans. This disconnect is striking given their attempts to frame themselves as credible interpreters of Venezuelan public sentiment. Despite never having to endure the consequences of dictatorship firsthand, they assume the role of authoritative voices on Venezuela's reality, shaping narratives that ultimately serve the regime's interests rather than those of the people they claim to represent.

As a final reflection, it is imperative to increase awareness of how disinformation circulates within academic and intellectual spaces to defend authoritarian regimes. This study calls for further research into how similar dynamics unfold across other authoritarian contexts, shedding light on the mechanisms that enable propaganda to infiltrate scholarly discourse. Moreover, academics, students, and the broader public should approach favorable narratives about autocratic states with scrutiny—questioning not only the message but also the affiliations and interests of those promoting it.

REFERENCES

Alarcón, B., & Hidalgo, M. (2024). Venezuela: La lógica de la supervivenciaautocrática. *Revista de Ciencia Política, 44*(2), 463–489. DOI: 10.4067/s0718-090x2024005000121

Amorín, S. (2022). Uruguay y la "cuestióncubana":Diplomacia, movilizaciónpolítica y radicalizaciónanticastrista en los sesenta. *EncuentrosUruguayos, 15*(1), 90–124. DOI: 10.55509/ayer/896

Baines, P., & O'Shaughnessy, N. (2020). Towards the measurement of Islamist propaganda effectiveness: A marketing perspective. In Baines, P., O'Shaughnessy, N., & Snow, N. (Eds.), *The SAGE handbook of propaganda* (pp. 223–242). SAGE Publications. DOI: 10.4135/9781526477170.n15

Brady, A. M. (2008). *Marketing dictatorship: Propaganda and thought work in contemporary China*. Rowman&Littlefield.

Camero Guevara, Y., Chaguaceda Noriega, A., Diaz Torres, I., González Arenas, B., González Marrero, C., Hernández, H. E., Puerta Riera, M. I., & Thiemann, L. (2023). *Sharp power y redes intelectuales: La presencia de Cuba en América Latina* [Sharp power and intellectual networks: Cuba's presence in Latin America]. Editorial Dunken.

Carter Center. (2024, July 30). Statement on Venezuela's 2024 presidential election [Press release]. *The Carter Center*. https://www.cartercenter.org/news/pr/2024/venezuela-073024.html

Centenera, M., Mella, C., & Gómez Vega, R. (2024, July 28). Sólo el 1% de los venezolanos en el exteriorpuedevotar en las eleccionespresidenciales. *El País*.https://elpais.com/america/2024-07-27/solo-el-1-de-los-venezolanos-en-el-exterior-puede-votar-en-las-elecciones-presidenciales.html

Chaguaceda, A., & Rouvinski, V. (2024, September 10). Russia's capture of intellectual elites in Latin America. *Wilson Center*.https://www.wilsoncenter.org/blog-post/russias-capture-intellectual-elites-latin-america

CilanoPeláez. J., Chaguaceda, A., Puerta, M., VieraCañive, E., & González, C. (2021). *Cuba en Latinoamérica: Presencia e influencia cubanas en espacios académicos y plataformas generadoras de pensamiento*. Gobierno y AnálisisPolítico AC.

Clarín. (2024, April 25). Encuentro para una Alternativa Social Mundial del ALBA CTP reunió en Caracas a los pueblos del sur global. *Clarín*.https://www.elclarin.cl/2024/04/25/encuentro-para-una-alternativa-social-mundial-del-alba-ctp-reunio-en-caracas-a-los-pueblos-del-sur-global/

Clemente, D. (2017). El regionalismo post-hegemónico en perspectiva crítica: Una mirada neogramsciana. Brasil, Venezuela y la opción contra-hegemónica. *Observatorio Latinoamericano y Caribeño, 1*(1), 110–130.

Cull, N. J. (2008). *The Cold War and the United States Information Agency: American propaganda and public diplomacy, 1945–1989*. Cambridge University Press. DOI: 10.1017/CBO9780511817151

Downs, A. (1957). *An economic theory of democracy*. Harper &Row.

Dukalskis, A. (2021). *Making the world safe for dictatorship*. Oxford University-Press. DOI: 10.1093/oso/9780197520130.001.0001

Edison Research. (2024). *Edison Researchconductsexitpoll in Venezuela* [Report]. Edison Research.https://www.edisonresearch.com/edison-research-conducts-exit-poll-in-venezuela/

El País. (2024a, July 30). La OEA denuncia la aberrante manipulación de las elecciones de Venezuela en un proceso sin garantías. *El País*.https://elpais.com/america/2024-07-30/la-oea-denuncia-la-aberrante-manipulacion-de-las-elecciones-de-venezuela-en-un-proceso-sin-garantias.html

El País. (2024b, October 15). La ONU acusa al gobierno de Maduro de cometer crímenes de lesa humanidad en las elecciones. *El País*.https://elpais.com/america/2024-10-15/la-onu-acusa-al-gobierno-de-maduro-de-cometer-crimenes-de-lesa-humanidad-en-las-elecciones.html

Ellner, S. (2014). *LatinAmerica's radical left: Challenges and complexitiesofpoliticalpower in thetwenty-firstcentury*. Rowman&Littlefield.

European External Action Service (EEAS). (2023). *1st EEAS report on foreign information manipulation and interference threats: Towards a frameworkfornetworkdefence*.EEAS. https://www.eeas.europa.eu/sites/default/files/documents/2023/EEAS-DataTeam-ThreatReport-2023.pdf

Freedom House. (2024). *Venezuela: Freedom in theWorld 2024* [Report]. Freedom House.https://freedomhouse.org/country/venezuela/freedom-world/2024

Gilboa, E. (2008). Searchingfor a theoryofpublicdiplomacy. *The ANNALS ofthe American AcademyofPolitical and Social Science, 616*(1), 55–77. https://doi.org/ DOI: 10.1177/0002716207312142

Gonzalez, A. (2025, January 9).¿Cómo llegó Nicolás Maduro al poder en Venezuela y cuánto tiempo lleva?*CNN*.https://cnnespanol.cnn.com/2025/01/09/venezuela/como -llego-maduro-poder-venezuela-orix

Grandjean, M. (2016). A social networkanalysisof Twitter: Mappingthe digital humanitiescommunity. *Cogent Arts & Humanities*, *3*(1), 1171458. DOI: 10.1080/23311983.2016.1171458

Harnecker, M. (2004). *Venezuela: Una revolución sui géneris*. El Viejo Topo.

Infobae. (2024a, September 11). El derroche de Maduro en la campaña electoral ahora es la nueva amenaza para su régimen. *Infobae*.https://www.infobae.com/ venezuela/2024/09/11/el-derroche-de-maduro-en-la-campana-electoral-ahora-es -la-nueva-amenaza-para-su-regimen/

Infobae. (2024b, May 16). El régimen de Maduro clausuró un hotel para evitar que Edmundo González y María Corina Machado se hospeden en su visita al estado Aragua. *Infobae*.https://www.infobae.com/venezuela/2024/05/16/el-regimen -de-maduro-clausuro-un-hotel-para-evitar-que-edmundo-gonzalez-y-maria-corina -machado-se-hospeden-en-su-visita-al-estado-aragua/

Infobae. (2024c, July 28).El chavismo difundió en las redes sociales resultados de falsos boca de urna de una encuestadora que no existe. *Infobae*.https://www.infobae .com/venezuela/2024/07/28/el-chavismo-difundio-en-las-redes-resultados-falsos-de -boca-de-urna-de-una-encuestadora-que-no-existe/

Kalathil, S., & Boas, T. C. (2003). *Open networks, closed regimes: The impact of the internet on authoritarian rule*. Carnegie Endowment for International Peace.

Kingsbury, D. V. (2016). Frompopulismtoprotagonism (and back?) in Bolivarian Venezuela: Rethinking Ernesto Laclau'sOnPopulist Reason. *Journal of Latin American Cultural Studies*, *25*(4), 495–514. DOI: 10.1080/13569325.2016.1230939

Marton, P., & Navarro, M. (2024). At thecrossroads: The Cuban American NationalFoundation and theendoftheColdWar. In Thomasen, G., Békés, C., & Rácz, A. (Eds.), *ThePalgravehandbookofnon-stateactors in East-West relations* (pp. 277–292). Palgrave Macmillan., DOI: 10.1007/978-3-031-40546-4_14

Mawad, T. F. (2024). Maduro, las elites y la «perestroika» venezolana. *Nueva Sociedad*.https://nuso.org/articulo/venezuela-elites-Maduro-fedecamaras/

Medianálisis. (2023, December 13).#CiberAlianzaAlDescubierto: Desinformación y ataques en línea con tinte de género.*Medianálisis.*https://www.medianalisis.org/ciberalianzaaldescubierto-desinformacion-y-ataques-en-linea-con-tinte-de-genero/

Mejías, U., & Vokuev, N. E. (2017). Disinformation and the media: The case ofRussia and Ukraine. *Media Culture & Society*, *39*(7), 1027–1042. DOI: 10.1177/0163443716686672

Mundo, B. B. C. (2020, December 7). Venezuela:Laoposiciónlograuna victoria histórica al ganar las eleccionesparlamentarias.*BBC Mundo.*https://www.bbc.com/mundo/noticias-america-latina-55212032

Nagy, S. G. (2020). Maduro Venezulája [Maduro's Venezuela]. In Zs. Csikós& E. Horváth (Eds.), *Diktátorokésdiktatúrák a Karibtérségben* [Dictators and dictatorships in theCaribbeanregion] (pp.131-145). L'HarmattanKiadó.

Polegkyi, O. (2023). Russiandisinformation and propaganda before and after the-invasionofUkraine. *RocznikInstytutuEuropyŚrodkowo-Wschodniej*, *21*(1), 91–107. DOI: 10.36874/RIESW.2023.1.6

Ponniah, T., & Eastwood, J. (2011). *Therevolution in Venezuela: Social and politicalchangeunder Chávez*. Harvard UniversityPress.

Puyosa, I. (2017). Political bots on Twitter in #Ecuador2017 presidential campaigns. *Contratexto*, *27*(027), 39–60. DOI: 10.26439/contratexto.2017.027.002

Puyosa, I. (2023, September 6). Pro-Russian BRICS narratives in LatinAmerica-prosperedduringsummit lead-up. *DFRLab.*https://dfrlab.org/2023/09/06/pro-russian-brics-narratives-in-latin-america-prospered-during-summit-lead-up/

Puyosa, I., Marín Vázquez, M., & Fivenson, A. (2023), *Contrarrestar las operaciones de información de actoresautoritarios en Latinoamérica*(pp. 18–30). NationalEndowmentforDemocracy (NED Studies). https://www.ned.org/wp-content/uploads/2023/12/NED_FORO-Countrarestar-Operaciones-AMLAT.pdf

REDH. (2023, August 9). A 20 años de la fundación de la Red de Intelectuales y Artistas en Defensa de la Humanidad y a 40 años de la democracia en Argentina. *Humanidad en Red.*https://humanidadenred.org/a-20-anos-de-la-fundacion-de-la-red-de-intelectuales-y-artistas-en-defensa-de-la-humanidad-y-a-40-anos-de-la-democracia-en-argentina/

Reuters. (2024, July 26). Venezuelans abroad say they are struggling to register to vote. *Reuters.*https://www.reuters.com/world/americas/venezuelans-abroad-say-they-are-struggling-register-vote-2024-07-26/

Robin, M. (2024). Are propagandistscombatants?Analysingtheethical status of propagandists in warfare. *Reviewof International Studies,* 1–20. https://doi.org/DOI: 10.1017/S0260210524000044

Rojas, N., & Ángel, S. (2017). "Estancamiento paradójico": La ciencia política en los tiempos de la Revolución Bolivariana. *Anuario Latinoamericano: Ciencias Políticas y Relaciones Internacionales, 5*, 157–172. DOI: 10.17951/al.2017.5.157

Rouvinski, V. (2022). Russia in LatinAmerica: A frameworkofanalysis. In *Rethinking post-ColdWarRussian–Latin American relations* (1.ª ed., p. 17). Routledge. https://doi.org/DOI: 10.4324/9781003183372

Semana. (2015, December 6).Elecciones en Venezuela: Oposición gana Asamblea Nacional 17 años después.*Semana.*https://www.semana.com/mundo/articulo/elecciones-en-venezuela-oposicion-gana-asamblea-nacional-17-anos-despues/452639-3/

Small, T. A. (2011). What the hashtag? *Information Communication and Society, 14*(6), 872–895. DOI: 10.1080/1369118X.2011.554572

Suárez Pérez, D., & Ponce de León Rosas, E. (2021, March). *Digital autocracy: Maduro's control of the Venezuelan information environment.* Atlantic Council, DFRLab. https://dfrlab.org/wp-content/uploads/2021/04/DigitalAutocracyVEN-FINAL.pdf

Taylor, P. M. (2011). Ethics and international propaganda. In Fortner, R. S., & Fackler, P. M. (Eds.), *The handbook of global communication and media ethics* (Vol. II, pp. 912–932). Wiley-Blackwell. DOI: 10.1002/9781444390629.ch46

Trimble, L., & Sampert, S. (2010). *Mediating Canadian politics.* Pearson Prentice Hall.

Ubertalli, O. (2025, January 17). Quand le dictateur Maduro fait la « leçon » au « Point ».*Le Point.* https://www.lepoint.fr/monde/quand-le-dictateur-maduro-fait-la-lecon-au-point-17-01-2025-2580184_24.php

Vicent, M. (2006, August 7). Chávezcalifica a Fidel Castro de "Papa de los revolucionarios": Cuba se mantieneatenta a los mensajes sobre la saluddelcomandante.*El País.*https://elpais.com/diario/2006/08/07/internacional/1154901612_850215.html

Walker, C., & Ludwig, J. (2017). *Sharp power: Rising authoritarian influence.* National Endowment for Democracy. https://www.ned.org/wp-content/uploads/2017/12/Sharp-Power-Rising-Authoritarian-Influence-Full-Report.pdf

KEY TERMS AND DEFINITIONS

Academics: Scholars and educators conducting research and teaching at universities.

Authoritarianism: A governance system in which power is centralized, and political and civil rights are suppressed.

Chavism: The political movement and ideology rooted in Hugo Chávez's Bolivarian Revolution in Venezuela.

Disinformation: Intentionally false or misleading information spread to deceive or manipulate audiences.

FIMI Actors: Entities coordinating Foreign Information Manipulation and Interference to influence public opinion.

Intellectuals: Thinkers who critically engage with and shape cultural, social, or political discourse.

Propaganda: Systematically crafted messages designed to persuade or mobilize support for a cause.

Venezuela: A South American country defined by its Bolivarian political model and oil-dependent economy.

ENDNOTES

1 The dataset includes tweets, replies and retweets made between July 15 and August 10, 2024.

2 #VenezuelaVotes

3 #MaduroPresident, #NicoTheRooster, and #GoNico

4 *#ManosFueraDeVenezuela*, *#VenezuelaSeRespeta*, and *#VenezuelaPazYJusticia*

5 *#VENEZUELAYADECIDIO*

Chapter 5
The Role of Media Literacy Education in Countering Disinformation and Misinformation:
Exploring the Capability of Youth and Media in North Macedonia to Recognize False Narratives

Agron Vrangalla
https://orcid.org/0000-0001-9621-0229
Mother Teresa University, North Macedonia

Agron Kurtishi
https://orcid.org/0000-0002-0430-0380
Mother Teresa University, North Macedonia

Arta Xhelili
https://orcid.org/0000-0001-5345-9948
Mother Teresa University, North Macedonia

Avni Remzi Avdiu
https://orcid.org/0009-0000-3646-0963
Mother Teresa University, North Macedonia

DOI: 10.4018/979-8-3693-9601-8.ch005

ABSTRACT

This study aims to examine media content in the Republic of North Macedonia to identify the presence and use of disinformation and misinformation, and to explore the relationship between media literacy education and public perceptions of these phenomena. Employing a mixed-methods approach, the research integrates both qualitative and quantitative methods across two distinct studies with complementary objectives. The findings indicate a significant presence of disinformation and misinformation within North Macedonian media, alongside a notable deficiency in the audience's ability—particularly among youth—to critically assess and verify online content. The study offers valuable insights into the current media environment and provides actionable recommendations for enhancing media transparency and combating false narratives through targeted media literacy education initiatives.

INTRODUCTION

Spreading false narratives in the media is one of today's biggest global challenges. "Disinformation", "misinformation," and "fake news" are three similar notions with few differences, but they can be confused by users. Unlike fake news, which is fabricated to appear true, disinformation results from inaccurate and incomplete news reporting. Misinformation also refers to news that is not accurate but comes as a result of unintentional errors that are not done to cause harm, such as fake news and disinformation. Disinformation does not mean something false has been invented, but it is not exactly what the media presents. This way, unverified things are added, facts are manipulated, and certain things may be removed due to the media's bias or the circles that have ordered it. Thus, in most cases, disinformation is intended, and someone who wants to achieve a certain goal stays behind it. In some cases, disinformation appears as a manipulation of the source of information, as a deliberate distortion of it. Some of the disinformation comes through written texts, some through audio and video, and others through their combination.

Disinformation is created for various reasons. The nature of disinformation reflects the intentions of its creators. Most commonly, disinformation involves extracting fragments or inserts from their original context to alter the meaning in a way that suits the author. At times, disinformation is used to divert attention from important issues. In such cases, corrupt politicians or business groups may be behind these efforts. Sometimes, the goal of disinformation is not to convince but to create confusion. This confusion is intended to disorient people and generate sensationalism.

Besides its serious implications, disinformation increasingly takes on an entertaining character, often incorporating humor. Although earlier technologies were simpler, such manipulations for ideological purposes were also carried out during monist regimes. Many political figures were discredited or eliminated by retouching photos, manipulating facts and texts, or secretly editing recordings. With the advancement of digital technology, these manipulations have become more sophisticated and convincing.

The Internet has become a cheap but powerful weapon of disinformation. Likewise, the possibility of disseminating and spreading disinformation through social networks is now even greater. Moreover, disinformation spread on the Internet is dangerous because of the speed of its distribution. For a short time, they can change public opinion and very easily create strong negative emotions. Likewise, their inevitable evil is the harm that follows until the untruth is confirmed. Through disinformation, hateful language, and xenophobic, racist, chauvinist and misanthropic actions can be increased. In this way, it has become one of the most used tools in hybrid warfare. It can easily cause serious problems; it can destroy someone's dignity and reputation, cause damage to innocent individuals and groups, change people's perceptions, encourage dangerous and harmful behavior and adversely affect people's health.

Disinformation was all too common during the coronavirus pandemic. During this period, all kinds of information were distributed, which influenced the increase of stress and depression. Disinformation is more frequent when the general political, economic, social and security situation is difficult, especially during unrest or conflict. Public damage from disinformation can cause significant societal problems; it can damage democratic processes, political decision-making, economic and social well-being and security. A large part of the population worldwide is concerned about disinformation. The victims of misinformation are mainly children, young people and uneducated adults.

There are several ways to investigate whether a piece of information is disinformation: when the content is altered - the news source or visual content is altered in a way that is designed to mislead, the content is fabricated and contains outright lies, the context is false, when the source content is fragmented, deleted or distorted and when we have false links and when the title is not consistent with the visual part and the textual content. The ease of mind concerning the belief in disinformation is also related to "mental shortcuts" and the lack of media education. "Mental shortcuts" are rooted in our brain just like a path that we know by heart; they also operate when it is desired to extract the content of the text through the title without reading it. Through proper media literacy, the individual can avoid being a victim of disinformation, having a critical attitude towards any information, thinking about the news and not reacting immediately, checking other news sources, verifying the date of publication, making sure the author is a well-known and respectable name, whether the title matches the content and whether the text is consistent with the logical flow of what has been published. At the global level, there are several ongoing large-scale projects to create efficient fact-checking programs through which computer algorithms would enable the verification of the authenticity of information and the detection of disinformation.

In this context, as a well-known search engine, Google has created a fact-checking tool that enables the search of a global database of textual and visual content published on various Internet platforms. Due to the many damages that have resulted from disinformation, any approach that deals with their problem is complex and requires detailed analysis, which we intend to achieve through this study.

However, before thinking about ways to achieve media literacy for audiences, it is necessary to understand the audience's current state regarding media and information literacy. It is more than important to analyze the needs of the audience. From this point of view, it is necessary to examine the level of audience knowledge and needs.

Several studies have examined the issue of false reporting in North Macedonian media. A study conducted by Transparency International (2024) has looked at Macedonian legislation and how disinformation is regulated through media self-regulation. A survey report on youth news consumption, disinformation recognition, and civic engagement in North Macedonia conducted by the Institute of Communication Studies (2023) found that youth consider themselves able to recognize disinformation in the media. However, over half may have shared disinformation without knowing it (Serafimovska & Cherepnalkova-Trajkoska, 2023). Serafimovska and Cherepnalkova-Trajkoska (2023) studied whether media literacy can lead to more successful recognition of disinformation in media (primarily online news). The main objective was to establish the individual factors, motives and barriers for identifying and countering disinformation. Halili, Disha, Bajrami and Ibrahimi (2023) have explored the role of media and information literacy in countering disinformation in North Macedonia. However, none of the recent studies have used a triangulation of content analysis and quantitative research to examine the relationship between the capacity to recognize disinformation and media literacy education.

Therefore, this study aims to examine media content in the Republic of North Macedonia to recognize the use of disinformation and misinformation, as well as determine the relationship between media literacy education and public perceptions regarding misinformation and disinformation.

LITERATURE REVIEW

The Rise and Impact of Misinformation and Disinformation in the Digital Age

In the digital age, the spread of misinformation and disinformation has emerged as one of the serious social issues that has altered the core of how information is created, disseminated, and consumed. Social media platforms, instant messaging services, and online news outlets have increasingly become primary vectors for spreading misinformation and disinformation. It is reflected that false news spreads far quicker and reaches larger populations compared to actual news; this fact is reflected in studies that revealed the likelihood of false news stories to be retweeted was 70% more than that of actual news and reached the initial 1,500 people six times as fast (Vosoughi, Roy, & Aral, 2018).

The very basic difference between misinformation and disinformation starts with their definitions. Misinformation refers to false information shared without malicious intent, while disinformation is deliberately created and disseminated to cause harm or achieve specific objectives (Wardle & Derakhshan, 2017). This distinction helps explain the varying motivations and impacts behind different types of false information campaigns. Recent research has extended this taxonomy to include malformation-genuine information shared with intent to harm and missing information, which involves deliberately omitting key facts (Freelon & Wells, 2020).

The architecture of digital platforms plays a fundamental role in the amplification of false information. Engagement-based algorithms, designed to maximize user interaction, often prioritize sensational and emotionally charged content over factual information. These systems create what Pariser 2011originally described as "filter bubbles", where users are primarily exposed to information that confirms their beliefs. Further research by Zimmer et al. (2019) demonstrates how such digital architectures contribute to the construction of "epistemic bubbles" and "echo chambers," rendering correction efforts increasingly difficult.

The psychological mechanisms that drive the dissemination of misinformation are highly complex and multilevel. Confirmation bias is one of the basic human cognitive tendencies identified by Nickerson (1998), where people accept information that supports their belief system and reject contradictory evidence. Emotional triggers, especially fear, anger, and outrage, garner more engagement and increase the likelihood of sharing. Additionally, motivated reasoning explains how people process information in ways that support their desired conclusions rather than seeking objective truth (Pennycook & Rand, 2021).

Recent global events have demonstrated the real-world impact of false information. During the COVID-19 pandemic, false claims about treatments, vaccines, and the virus's origins undermined public health efforts and fuelled vaccine hesitancy. For example, an analysis by Islam et al. (2020) documented more than 2,300 reports of pandemic-related misinformation in 87 countries during the first three months of 2020 alone. This so-called "infodemic" has had measurable effects on health outcomes, with studies by Loomba et al. (2021) showing direct correlations between exposure to false information and vaccine hesitancy. In politics, disinformation campaigns have influenced elections, sow discord, and polarize societies. It also shows how conspiracy theories, "Pizzagate," can result in actual physical harm and violence to the living and cause social unrest, as elaborated by Lewandowsky et al. (2020).

Approaches towards stemming the flow of misinformation and disinformation have followed technical and social paths, including deploying automated fact-checking systems, machine learning-based detection models, and content moderation tools to stem the flow of fake content. Thus, media literacy education and critical thinking training are long-term strategies that could enhance one's ability to verify sources of information and differentiate fake from real. However, these measures face challenges in reaching audiences immersed in alternative information ecosystems (Wardle & Derakhshan, 2017).

Platform policies and regulatory frameworks continue to evolve in response to these challenges. Social media companies have implemented content warnings and account suspensions, though questions remain about their effectiveness and implications for free speech. International cooperation in addressing cross-border disinformation campaigns has become increasingly important, particularly in combating state-sponsored operations (Benkler, Faris, & Roberts, 2018).

This is why the role of professional journalism and fact-checking organizations has become more important than ever. Such institutions are the necessary counterweights to false information, even though they struggle to reach audiences increasingly immersed in alternative information ecosystems. Trust networks and credibility indicators foster the ability of users to identify reliable sources of information, though the effectiveness varies across demographic groups and cultural contexts (Pennycook & Rand, 2021).

Emerging technologies present both challenges and opportunities in the fight against false information. Artificial intelligence and deepfake technology make it increasingly difficult to distinguish authentic content from sophisticated fabrications (Chesney & Citron, 2019). However, these same technologies offer potential solutions for detecting and countering false information at scale (Westerlund, 2019). Therefore, the continuous evolution of social media platforms and communication technologies would suggest a constantly changing landscape of false information, to which adaptive and innovative response strategies must be designed.

The economic impact of false information has become a growingly evident factor. According to an estimate by the Global Disinformation Index (2020), through advertisers, $235 million is poured into websites spreading disinformation every year, unaware that it does so. Research by Tambini (2017) indicated that the attention economy incentivizes perverse rewards in creating and spreading false information.

The aftermath of fake news is as evident in the immediate- socially and politically- as it is in a broader perspective through public health, economic stability, and social cohesion. Understanding broader implications frames urgency while balancing approaches that preserve open dialogue and free expression. Since these issues continue to fester, developing effective countermeasures lies squarely in the hands of researchers, technology companies, policymakers, and civil society organizations.

The Rise and Impact of Misinformation and Disinformation in North Macedonia

Misinformation and disinformation have become pervasive in North Macedonia, a country described by a complex socio-political landscape and a rapidly changing media environment. The digital age amplifies the spread of false information, while social media platforms are at the forefront of shaping public discourses. This literature review looks at the key themes, examples, and relevant studies setting the dynamics of misinformation and disinformation in perspective within the North Macedonian context.

The COVID-19 pandemic underlined the vulnerability of North Macedonia to health-related misinformation. Blazhevski and Rizankoska (2020) documented that false claims concerning treatments, vaccines, and the virus's origin circulate on platforms like Facebook. Such narratives lower the ambition of public health efforts, promoting vaccine hesitancy and erosion of public trust in health authorities. This report also identifies the role of social media algorithms in amplifying sensational content, which often exceeds the reach of official health communications.

Foreign influence operations have been among the major sources of disinformation in North Macedonia. Cvetkovska et al. (2021) reported the existence of a structured network spreading pro-Russian narratives during moments of political instability. Social media platforms were used to polarize public opinion, thus undermining democratic institutions. The findings agree with Bradshaw and Howard's global inventory (2019), which reported similar tactics in other Balkan countries.

Political polarization has maintained the flow of disinformation in North Macedonia. As pointed out by Majhosev and Bakev in 2019, "partisan media often distribute such false narratives to advance the interests of their political groups." This has resulted in the loss of public confidence in traditional media, where unverified information spreads so fast. According to the European Commission's Progress Report for 2021, more independence of the media would counter such trends.

Low levels of media literacy have been considered one of the pivotal factors in disseminating misinformation. Apostolov and Jankulovski (2018) indicated the need to include media literacy education in the national curriculum to develop critical abilities for information assessment among citizens. By the time when Trpevska and Micevski (2022) reported partial improvements in these activities, media literacy was still underfinanced and barely widespread.

Social media has turned out to be a vector of false information in North Macedonia. Trpevska and Micevski (2022) highlight how platform algorithms promote sensational content while META.mk Network (2023) documents the development of fact-checking initiatives to counter misinformation. The effects have been promising in the fight against disseminating false information, though the reach is limited.

The 2021 Progress Report of the European Commission on North Macedonia underlined that media regulation and independence remained challenging. The report underlined that a stronger legal framework was needed to address disinformation without compromising press freedom. Similarly, the IREX Media Sustainability Index 2020 underlined that support for independent journalism was necessary to counter false information.

The spread of misinformation and disinformation in North Macedonia illustrates more general global trends, but specific features of the socio-political process in the country further contextualize it. An appropriate response to such challenges requires complex solutions that involve media literacy education, robust regulatory frameworks, and the enhancement of independent journalism. Additionally, there is a need for further research on how developing technologies, such as AI or deepfakes, shape the information landscape.

The Role of Media Literacy Education in Countering Disinformation and Misinformation

In an age of unparalleled excess of information, media literacy education has taken center stage in fighting against the onslaught of untruths. This literature review examines media literacy education's effectiveness, methods, and challenges in building resilience to misinformation and disinformation.

The concept of media literacy has undergone a radical transformation in the digital age. Ashley, Maksl, and Craft (2017) say that traditional media literacy frameworks must be updated to respond to the contemporary challenges of social media and digital platforms. Their study has shown that critical thinking skills, which are particularly designed for digital environments, are a must in identifying false information. Building on this, Khan and Idris (2019) develop a more holistic framework that combines old and new media literacies, with an important thrust being given to knowledge of platforms' algorithms and how they curate content.

Recent scholarship has provided some compelling evidence of the effectiveness of media literacy education. For instance, in a large-scale experiment, Guess, Nyhan, and Reifler (2020) found that brief media literacy interventions can reduce the likelihood of sharing false information by as much as 25%. Likewise, Brodsky et al. (2021) found improved means of assessing source credibility and recognizing possible misinformation among pupils receiving systematic media literacy education.

The pedagogical dimensions of media literacy education have been explored in great depth. McGrew et al. (2018) underline some important competencies that curricula of media literacy should comprise, such as lateral reading, source verification, and understanding the business models of digital platforms. Huguet et al. (2022) emphasize the role of hands-on learning experiences since students learn fact-checking and source evaluation more successfully through practical exercises than through theoretical instruction alone.

Understanding platform dynamics has become critical in media literacy education. Boyd and Zou (2021) examined the influence of social media algorithms on information exposure and called for the inclusion of platform mechanics instruction in media literacy programs. Their study found that students who understood algorithm-driven content were more prepared to recognize probable biases and manipulation.

Cross-Cultural and Global Perspectives

Media literacy education has unique challenges in different cultural contexts. Lee and Xenos (2023) analyzed media literacy initiatives across multiple countries, finding that successful programs must be culturally adapted while keeping core critical thinking principles. Their study highlighted the importance of considering local media ecosystems and cultural norms when designing literacy interventions.

Integrating media literacy into formal education systems has brought about opportunities and challenges. Martinez-Costa and Rodriguez (2021) analyze different integration models, ranging from stand-alone courses to cross-curricular approaches. Their results suggest that embedding media literacy across many subjects yields better results than isolated interventions.

Emerging technologies continue to pose new challenges for media literacy education. For instance, Zhang and Thompson (2022) examine how artificial intelligence and deepfake technology now call for new approaches in media literacy education, arguing that incorporating technical literacy alongside traditional critical thinking skills is necessary. In addition, Carlsson (2023) addresses the challenge of keeping media literacy curricula current in an evolving information landscape.

The literature demonstrates that media literacy education is crucial in building societal resilience against misinformation and disinformation; it does work under certain conditions pertaining to pedagogical approach, cultural context, and relation to emerging technologies. Thus, the way forward in this field of research is to develop scalable, culturally appropriate methodologies able to keep up with the pace of technological change.

Case Studies of Successful Media Literacy Programs

One of the most successful examples in the world is Finland's national media literacy program, which has been implemented since 2016 across all levels of education. Marin and Koivula (2022) described how the Finnish approach integrates critical thinking with digital skills from elementary through secondary education. The program resulted in a 47% improvement in students' ability to identify false information over three years.

McGrew and Wineburg (2023) evaluated the Stanford History Education Group's COR curriculum, which instructs students in the methods of professional fact-checkers to evaluate online information. The curriculum was implemented in 76 high schools; students who participated were found to be twice as likely to identify misleading online content compared to control groups correctly.

Vanderhoven et al. (2021) researched this transnational project in seven European countries. The program trained over 500 media coaches, reaching 15,000 students, thus showing a multiplier effect for media literacy education.

RESEARCH Methodology

The study uses multiple methods and data sources to develop a comprehensive understanding of fake narratives in North Macedonia's media and the capacity of the youth to detect them. The study applies qualitative and quantitative research in two separate studies with different objectives.

The themes and categories that emerged in the qualitative study were used to develop the research instrument for the second study within this research. A survey was administered to 237 randomly selected students. In line with the study's hypothesis, the sample was divided into two groups: one that has attended at least one media related course and the second group with no media literacy education. The quantitative study examined the relationship between media literacy education and public perceptions of disinformation and misinformation. This second study aimed to prove if media literacy education impacted students' acquisition of the necessary skills to recognize misinformation in news.

Study 1

Method

The qualitative study examines the lack of transparency and the spread of disinformation and misinformation in the North Macedonian media during the first 100 days of the Mickoski government. The main objective of the qualitative research is to contextualize disinformation, misinformation and transparency issues within the media landscape of RMV by content analysis of the media coverage from this period. Some key themes explored include the state budget, inflation, state destabilization, ethnic divisions and others. For content analysis, are taken 12 media outlets, namely 6 national televisions (Sitel, Kanal 5, 24 Vesti, Alsat M, Tv21 and Klan Macedonia) as well as 6 informational web portals (nistori.com, actual.mk, telegrafi.com, slobodenpecat. mk, sdk.mk and plusinfo.mk). Other media outlets are not excluded in episodic cases as well.

Since qualitative content analysis involves a systematic review of textual descriptions and can trace trends, themes and biases in media descriptions (Schreier 2012), it was chosen as the most appropriate MCD method.

The analysis is conducted in three stages:

Phase 1: Gathering and Extraction of the Data

- Qualitative study of the broadcasting volumes of twelve prominent media, inclusive of six national television broadcasters (Sitel, Kanal 5, 24 Vesti, Alsat M, Tv21 and Klan Macedonia) together with six information websites (nistori.com, actual.mk, telegrafi.com, slobodenpecat. mk, sdk.mk and plusinfo.mk)
- Term: The first one hundred days of the Mickoski Government
- Languages Spoken: Macedonian and Albanian
- Media Used: Television and Internet

Phase 2: Development of Coding Process

- Some hierarchy of coding scheme was developed which alone concentrated on:
- Political language variables
- Ethnic groups in the media
- Fact-checking with existing data
- Narrative biases and framing

Phase 3: Application of the Coding Scheme to the Collected Materials

- Implementation of the coding scheme to the gathered data
- Comparison of the narratives

The methodology systematically examines how media outlets frame political issues, particularly those involving ethnic relations and governmental policies (Mayring, 2014). This approach is particularly valuable for analyzing complex political discourse in multicultural contexts, as it identifies subtle biases and varying interpretations across different media sources (Krippendorff, 2013).

The coding process involves multiple iterations and cross-verification of findings to ensure reliability. This systematic approach helps maintain objectivity while examining sensitive topics such as ethnic representation and political tensions in media coverage.

This part of the research addresses three primary questions:

1. How do media outlets in North Macedonia cover major political and economic developments across ethnic and linguistic lines?
2. What patterns of misinformation emerge in the coverage of government policies and initiatives?
3. How do existing media structures influence transparency and accountability in reporting?

ANALYSIS

Media Attention after Elections: The Albanian Flag Divides the Approach in Government

The 2024 elections, just like the previous ones, were notable due to how national events influenced political dialogue and media coverage of the nation. The issue surrounding the usage of the Albanian flag in public institutions was a very controversial topic that different political representatives hotly contested.

Maksim Dimitrievski, the chair of the ruling ZNAM political party, threatened in a speech that ZNAM would leave the Government if the ministers of the VLEN coalition continued to fly the flag of Albania. The media reported it promptly (Time.mk, 2024).

The portal of the daily "SlobodenPeçat" published the article titled "Discord in the government because of the flag, after only 8 days." (SlobodenPečat, 2024). This title creates divisiveness among not only the coalition partners but also on ethnic grounds.

"Nistori" portal reported this article with the "purpose of safeguarding the flag" presented a title that also puts the parties into the therapeutic rule of twos. "Opposition and Position – Albanian parties react to Makis Dimitrievski about the Albanian flag" (Nistori, 2024). In this case, the portal in question rather effectively tried to restate with a little variation the sentiments expressed by the Alban Government and the opposition about the Alban flag, which agreed against the root of the Albanian flag.

Most of the other Macedonian media houses picked up Dimitrievski's comments in a fair manner. They also brought out the voice of Bilall Kasami, the leader of the BESA Movement, who responded to Dimitrievski's allegations by saying he had no power to tell him how to use the national flag. TV 21 and other Albanian media put enormous emphasis on the coverage of this issue. They called on the ministers from the VLEN coalition, ordering the latter to go to the next coordination meeting, which was meant to clarify that other presentations were only targeted at the convention of government programs.

The way media handled the flag issue 'spoke' of an ethnocentric perspective, notably concerning the selected ethnicity or religion and culture', which always tends to be sensitive. Such a matter pointed to the persistent problem of media enclosure of professionalism and ethics in their reporting practice (IMA.mk, 2024).

Media Controversy: The "Balancer" Mechanism and Administrative Representation of The State

The focus of the government administration's attention on the "balancer" mechanism has opened up a serious discussion over the relations between the partners of the government coalition, namely VMRO-DPMNE and ZNAM on one side and the VLEN coalition on the other. The dispersal focuses on altering the mechanisms to provide equality of representation across the public service (IMA.mk, 2024).

Minister for Digital Transformation Stefan Andonovski announced that the balancer numbers now reflect the 2021 Census projection of the resident population within the country. This is important because the alienated Albanian ethnic group makes up only 24% of the population against 29% of the total population if non-residents are included.

- Media coverage of this development varied significantly along ethnic lines:

Macedonian media reported the change largely in positive terms. Thus, for example, TV 24 (24.mk, 2024) and Alsat's Macedonian portal (Alsat.mk, 2024) titled "Balancer went to history," while "Sloboden Pecat" underlined a movement toward professionalism being more significant than ethnic quotas (Sloboden Pecat, 2024).

- Albanian-language media took a more critical stance. TV Shenja highlighted the reduction in Albanian representation (Shenja.tv, 2024), while TV 21 focused on the resulting coalition tensions (TV21, 2024). TV Klan Macedonia noted how the changes would decrease Albanian representation from 29.54%, which was established under former Minister Admirim Aliti (TV Klan Macedonia, 2024).

The reaction of the VLEN coalition to these changes, especially after the strong statement by Ziadin Sela, was followed with particular attention. "Revista" portal characterized the position of VLEN as subordinate, particularly in light of ZNAM's defense of Minister Mincev's decision to adjust the representation percentages. The case underlines the persistent challenge of balancing ethnic representation in the public administration of North Macedonia, with deep divisions within the governing coalition over approaches to administrative reform and ethnic representation.

"Destabilization" Allegations: A Closer Look

On August 1, 2024, Prime Minister Mickoski accused DUI of being "a threat to peace and stability in Macedonia" and announced plans for government action to safeguard the nation's "sovereignty and territorial integrity," which he claimed were at risk.

With all the unfounded claims and speculations on "destabilization" in the media, not a single word has been said about the real activities of the Government regarding the threats. The Prime Minister has repeatedly insinuated that serious crimes are being plotted against the state. Meanwhile, neither MVR nor the prosecution has reported any confirmed information or news about their subsequent actions.

That continuous flow of "state destabilization" statements Mickoski dominated the media in August. Most of them were published as an argument, not as speculation. This is how a story gets told without professional filtering.

Fact Check: Analysis of State Debt Claims and Media Coverage

The statements by Prime Minister Mickoski regarding North Macedonia's state debt have raised questions about the accuracy and consistency of government communications. In a news conference alongside the Minister of European Affairs Murtezani, Mickoski cited that the previous Government had raised the state debt by 4 billion euros from 2018 to 2023. Records from the official Ministry of Finance, however, show different data of an increase from 4.344 million to 7.256 million euros, amounting to 2.912 billion euros-a more than 1 billion euro difference from what the Prime Minister mentioned (Government of the Republic of North Macedonia, 2024).

A notable contradiction emerged between Mickoski's public stance and subsequent policy decisions. While expressing opposition to "putting the country and unborn generations in debt," he announced plans for 1.5 billion euros in new borrowing shortly after taking office – 1 billion following the election and an additional 500 million after assuming the role of Prime Minister.

However, it was matched pound for pound in the media's response-investigative reporting deficiencies. Broadly, news media did very little cross-referencing of claims made by the prime minister with official financial data. They neither examined apparent discrepancies between what he said and his actions nor serious corruption issues concerning misuse of public money that have surfaced. Even fewer journalists have been asking whether any criminal investigations have taken place over misappropriation of budget or whether anyone has been formally charged in courts.

This story presents an urgent need for severe fact-checking and extensive journalistic research, especially regarding claims about the state budget and suspected cases of fiscal delinquency. A lack of more serious media scrutiny points to bigger challenges in ensuring transparency and accountability in managing and reporting public finances (IMA.mk 2024).

Economic Recovery Claims: A Statistical Analysis

Prime Minister Mickoski's recent statements about inflation control have prompted a detailed examination of economic data and government communications. Following a media headline on August 28, 2024, which proclaimed that his administration had "stopped inflation," closer analysis reveals a more nuanced economic reality (Sitel.mk, 2024).

During public appearances, including a TV interview and a speech in Makedonska Kamenica, Mickoski discussed his economic vision, expressing a preference for deflation while acknowledging historical inflation challenges. He referenced past double-digit rates of 15-18% and claimed credit for stabilizing the economy, suggesting current inflation rates had decreased to approximately 3%. However, official statistical data tells a different story.

The economic timeline shows inflation peaked at 19.8% in October 2022, gradually declining to 3.2% by June 2024 and reaching 3.0% in July 2024, though with a notable 0.7% monthly increase. This data reveals that the substantial inflation reduction occurred before Mickoski assumed office on June 28, 2024. In fact, during his administration's first full month, July 2024, inflation showed a slight uptick, contradicting claims about stopping economic "free fall."

The disparity between government statements and economic data underscores the crucial role of media in providing accurate economic reporting. Journalists are responsible for verifying government claims against official statistics, contextualizing economic trends, and carefully distinguishing between correlation and causation in policy outcomes. The current situation demonstrates how attributing the inflation decrease to recent government actions misrepresents the economic timeline and overlooks pre-existing trends contributing to the country's economic stabilization (IMA.mk, 2024).

DISCUSSION

These findings indicate complex points of intersection between media narratives, political discourse, and ethnic relations that have been in evidence within North Macedonia since the elections in 2024. This analysis may present critical insight into how media framing, political controversies, and ethnocentric reporting shape public perceptions and influence political stability.

Media Framing and Ethnocentric Reporting

The dispute over the Albanian national flag symbolizes the role of the media in raising the level of ethnic and political tensions. Most media with an ethnocentric approach, especially in the framing of the flag issue, pointed to problematic objectivity and professionalism within the multiethnic environment. For example:

- Macedonian-language media frequently framed the dispute as one which jeopardized governmental stability and focused on the attitude of the ZNAM party.

Meanwhile, in Albanian-language media, the counter-framing was a defense of cultural identity that united opposition and government voices against Dimitrievski's comments. This polarized coverage only heightened ethnic divisions and indicated the impact the media might have on political discourse. A lack of balanced coverage and critical analysis indicates the need to upgrade the standard and practice of journalism.

Political Controversies and Coalition Dynamics

It further highlights the coalition's fragility, such as in debates on the so-called "balancer" mechanism and the flag controversy that revealed the sharp division within the coalition itself. In fact, given the deep-seated ethnic and political divisions in such coverage, the media could not develop a neutral space to bring people closer and build the necessary consent toward effective governance.

Lack of Investigative Reporting

Prime Minister Mickoski's statements on state debt and economic recovery show a big difference between his words and the official data. The fact that the media did not critically analyze and verify these claims indicates deeper investigative reporting inadequacy. This gap undermines the media's watchdog role and contributes to disseminating unverified information.

Broader Implications

The observed dynamics have far-reaching implications, including political stability, interethnic relations, and the ongoing democratic process in North Macedonia. Such ethnocentric media reporting, coupled with a lack of critical analysis, may further polarize society and undermine public confidence in the media and political institutions. Handling these challenges is crucial for consolidating an inclusive and cohesive society.

Study 2

The main objective of this study is to identify the role of media education in countering and raising awareness about misinformation and disinformation. In this regard, the study poses two research questions:

> Research question 1: What is the level of vulnerability to misinformation and disinformation of youngsters in North Macedonia?
> Research question 2: Does media education have a role in countering misinformation and disinformation?

To answer this question, we pose the hypothesis:

> *H1:* There is a correlation between media education and vulnerability to misinformation and disinformation.
> *H2:* Students who have pursued a media course will be less vulnerable to misinformation and disinformation than those who have not.

Method

Study 2 used a survey method to examine the relationship between media literacy education and public perceptions of disinformation and misinformation. This second study aimed to prove if media literacy education impacted students' acquisition of the necessary skills to recognize misinformation in news. The quantitative method produced data that can be statistically examined and allows conclusions to be drawn based on a representative sample of North Macedonian youth. The data were collected online by utilizing Google Forms. The survey was conducted between November 2024 and January 2025. The sample size included 237 participants (66 males, 171 females, Mean age 20.65 years) (Table 1).

Table 1. Sociodemographic composition of the sample (N=237) (Authors' depiction)

	Adolescents	
	N	%
Gender		
Male	66	27.8
Female	171	72.2
Place of residence		
Urban	117	49.4
Rural	120	50.6
Ethnicity		
Macedonian	3	1.3
Albanian	233	98.3
Roma	1	0.4
Age		
18	9	3.8
19	80	33.8
20	60	25.3
21	32	13.5
22	24	10.1
23	29	13.5

The themes and categories that emerged in the qualitative study were used to develop the research instrument for the quantitative study. The questionnaire contained 20 open-ended questions divided into two sections: a demographic section and a section regarding news media literacy. The second section measured respondents' experience with disinformation and misinformation and their capability to identify truthful information.

The questionnaire was coded and then entered into the SPSS 20.00 data system. After inserting the data into the system, tests were run for reliability, descriptive, and inferential statistics.

RESULTS

Descriptive Statistics

Research question 1: What is the level of vulnerability to misinformation and disinformation of youngsters in North Macedonia?

Descriptive statistics on the items measuring North Macedonian youngsters' experience with misinformation and disinformation answer this research question.

When asked if they had experienced believing information from media that later turned out to be false, 40% of the respondents answered positively, saying that they had experienced this situation very often, followed by 35% sometimes. Only 4.6% of the respondents answered that they have never had an experience being misled about information on media. Those numbers indicate great chances of vulnerability to misinformation and disinformation (Table 2).

Table 2. Vulnerability to misinformation and disinformation (Authors' depiction)

It happens that people believe some information from the media, but later it turns out that it was false. How often doe this happen to you?					
		Frequency	**Percent**	**Valid Percent**	**Cumulative Percent**
Valid	Sometimes	83	35.0	35.0	35.0
	Very often	95	40.1	40.1	75.1
	Rarely	48	20.3	20.3	95.4
	Never	11	4.6	4.6	100.0
	Total	237	100.0	100.0	

Regarding the source they have encountered, as seen in Table 3, as more prone to false information on media, 61.2% of the respondents declared that social networks were spreading intentionally misleading and false information, followed by 29.5% online media/portals, 1.7% newspapers and only 1.3% TV (Table 3).

Table 3. Perceptions regarding new media pronto misleading and false information (Authors' depiction)

Where do you usually encounter news that you think is intentionally misleading or false? In:					
		Frequency	**Percent**	**Valid Percent**	**Cumulative Percent**
Valid	Social networks	145	61.2	61.2	61.2
	Online media portals	70	29.5	29.5	90.7
	TV	3	1.3	1.3	92.0
	Newspapers	4	1.7	1.7	93.7
	Don't know/ Refuse to answer	15	6.3	6.3	100.0
	Total	237	100.0	100.0	

The table above provides descriptive statistics for each item of the level of media education concerning identifying and checking for disinformation and disinformation.

Table 4. Descriptive statistics of education regarding identifying and checking false information (Authors' depiction)

Knowledge in regard to detecting and checking misinformation and disinformation	**I never do it**	**Rarely**	**Occasionally**	**Often**	**Regularly**	**Mean**	**SD**
I always check all news from several different sources to make sure it is accurate	7.6	26.2	29.1	25.7	11.4	2.45	1.21
I am not only interested in the information, but I always check the bigger picture and the context behind it.	8.4	24.1	28.7	25.3	13.5	2.54	1.23
I always check the source of the media content I have access to.	4.2	26.2	33.8	16.0	19.8	2.43	1.19

continued on following page

Table 4. Continued

Knowledge in regard to detecting and checking misinformation and disinformation	I never do it	Rarely	Occasionally	Often	Regularly	Mean	SD
Read how other media outlets have reported the story	5.5	28.3	25.3	21.1	19.8	2.49	1.24
Check the publication date	7.6	21.5	21.1	24.9	24.9	2.76	1.25
Research the media outlet that reported the news/story	7.2	22.4	31.6	24.5	14.3	2.52	1.19
Evaluate the quality of the language used	8.0	16.0	32.1	22.4	21.5	2.73	1.19
Search for the original source of the information	8.4	17.7	25.3	27.8	20.7	2.77	1.20
Use fact checkers for the information I read	13.1	18.6	35.0	20.7	12.7	2.67	1.28

The percentage examination for each item shows that the greatest agreement has been reached in these items: 50% of the respondents check for the publication date in order to see if it is up-to-date information, 49% search for the source of the information, 44% evaluate the quality of the language the news is written in order to evaluate professionalism, 41% read how other media outlets have reported the story, and 39% check for the bigger picture and the context behind the News (Table 4). On the other hand, they rarely or never check all news from several sources to ensure it is accurate or read how other media outlets have reported the story (34%). Those percentages reveal a moderate knowledge of identifying and checking for disinformation and misinformation.

This knowledge level corresponds with their formal education regarding media subjects. Only 38% of the respondents had a media-related course during their studies, and only 20.3% participated in an educational program related to false and true information in media. With an agreement of 74%, they considered it highly important to introduce the subject of "Media Education" into primary school curricula.

Inferential Statistics

Research question 2: What is the relationship between media education and the capability of countering misinformation and disinformation?

The above hypothesis will provide an answer to this research question:

H1: There is a correlation between media education and vulnerability to misinformation and disinformation.

H2: Students who have pursued a media course will be less vulnerable to misinformation and disinformation than those who have not.

The Leven test will be used to test these hypotheses and see if there are differences in the vulnerability toward disinformation and misinformation, according to formal education regarding media. Thus, an Independent T-test will be conducted to compare the two groups' average on the independent variable (Follow media course/study program). In comparing the arithmetic means in the first part of Table 5. it can be seen that 90 students have an average knowledge of detecting misinformation and disinformation, meaning neither positive nor negative, with 2.54 from 1 minimum to 5 maximum. In comparison, 147 students who have not followed any media course have similar knowledge, with an arithmetic mean of 2.62. From these data, we can see that the averages are approximately the same, which indicates that youngsters who have followed a media course and those who have not have a similar score on capabilities to detect and check misinformation and disinformation.

The second part of the table shows the data for the Leven test. The P value of the t-test is .485. This is greater than 0.05, a common indicator of significance, indicating no significant differences between the two groups. So, there are no differences in the capabilities of respondents who have pursued a media course and those who have not been trained in detecting misinformation and disinformation. The comparison of the averages shows that both groups have similar capabilities towards detecting misinformation and disinformation (average 2.6), so we can conclude that the differences between respondents who have pursued a media course and those who have not in terms of capabilities to detect false information are not statistically significant (Table 5).

Table 5. Inferential statistics regarding Media education and countering misinformation and disinformation (Authors' depiction)

	During your studies, did you take any media-related courses?	N	Mean	Std. Deviation	Std. Error Mean
Media Education	Yes	90	2.6251	.89790	.09465
	No	147	2.5444	.83940	.06923

Independent Samples Test

		Levene's Test for Equality of Variances		t-test for Equality of Means						
		F	Sig.	t	df	Sig. (2-tailed)	Mean Difference	Std. Error Difference	95% Confidence Interval	
									Lower	Upper
Media_edu	Equal variances assumed	1.996	.159	-.699	235	.485	-0.08065	.11538	-.30795	.14665
	Equal variances not assumed			-.688	178.558	.492	-.08065	.11727	-.31205	.15075

According to the results obtained from descriptive statistics and Leven tests, it can be concluded that there is no difference between students who have pursued a media course and those who have not pursued capabilities to detect false information, so both groups are neither proficient nor incapable of detecting false information. In conclusion, the data does not support the hypotheses in answering research question no. 2.

DISCUSSION

This study aimed to examine North Macedonian youth's knowledge of misinformation and disinformation and its relationship with attending a formal course regarding media studies. The research results showed that previous formal education in regard to media did not play any role in their capabilities to detect false information. It is worth emphasizing that youth's capability to detect misinformation and disinformation is scored as average and there is a need to enhance their skills. At the same time, the number of students who have attended media courses or training regarding detecting false information was very low.

Limitations

The first limitation of this research is related to external validity. The sample was very small, and the results could not be generalized to the entire population. A larger sample would have provided more reliable results and statistically significant findings. Being a non-random sample may also be a limitation. A random sample would have provided more objective and unbiased answers. Mo Moreover, the sample did not represent the ethnic diversity of North Macedonia. The survey was shared among multicultural respondents; however, the number of respondents from Macedonian nationality was unsatisfactory, which does not allow us to generalize the results. A larger and more diverse population should include all nationalities in North Macedonia.

Despite the limitations, the present study extends the current literature investigating the relationship between media education and encountering misinformation and disinformation in North Macedonia. It also contributes to the evidence that media education and capabilities to detect misinformation and disinformation must be considered. Educative programs and training courses should be implemented to teach the youth to detect and check for false information in media.

This study underlines the media's vital role in shaping current political and social processes in North Macedonia. Overcoming the challenges highlighted by this analysis will help all the stakeholders work toward creating more balanced, ethical, and transparent media, which is a necessary condition to further democratic development and interethnic harmony within the country. Results revealed that North Macedonian media is not an exception when false news is in question.

Moreover, respondents showed average knowledge in detecting and checking for false information. Thus, investing in media literacy and education is crucial for fighting misinformation, disinformation and fake news. If media literacy becomes mandatory in schools and universities, it will empower young people to become more aware of false news in the media. Integrating media literacy into strategic plans of the Ministry of Education needs to become a priority in providing the digital generation with the necessary skills to deal with all types of media. And methods of false news checking.

CONCLUSION

Living surrounded by the virtual world with all its deceptive capacities means not distinguishing the real world from the fake one. The possibilities for fabricating the unreal as real have been so powerfully sophisticated by digital technology that man has no choice but to constantly ask: "Is this true?" and "Is this possible?" In addition to the numerous digital possibilities for distorting the contents of photographs and videos through Artificial Intelligence, the possibilities of voice manipulation, setting in motion at the will of the persons with whom the staging of a scene is intended, and other forms have been perfectly added. These manipulative forms are increasingly moving towards perfection, to the point where the unreal will seem more real than the real. So, the world is moving towards creating a virtual reality that is more real than the natural, non-virtual reality. In such circumstances, the likelihood of disinformation, misinformation, and fake news will increase their credibility. The ethical dilemmas surrounding this possibility remain whether people will be more entertained, confused or finally annoyed. Now that these manipulative forms are at the stage of perfection, it can be said that people are oscillating between being confused and entertained by them.

The roots of the causes of arriving at this level of society must be sought in the very nature of the capitalist system, the flaws of which have been thoroughly analyzed in the works of Marx, the neo-Marxists of the Frankfurt School, the social psychologist Erich Fromm, Herbert Marcuse and others, which, due to the nature of the work, we cannot exaggerate in them. However, the current socio-psychological dilemmas that have already arisen after all these dizzying changes in the "information society" are that if this trend continues to spread with the dimensions and speed that it is already opening up, then where will we be as human beings after a few decades or a century. In fact, what will be our status in relation to technology, others, and even ourselves...?! All these dilemmas and questions, while it is not too late, should be addressed now with a balanced media education strategy so that the younger generations know how to face the challenges of this development so that this development can be put to the service of their usefulness and good, and not on the contrary - to their detriment. Otherwise, the manipulative elements will not stop and will act linearly in accordance with the progress of digital technology.

Manipulative methods through disinformation, misinformation, and fake news, as well as traps through tempting offers with the aim of hacking bank accounts through various transactions and other psychological and material blows, are and will remain a constant concern for their challenge in the future. Recently, fake profiles on social networks have been trending in North Macedonia, which allegedly offers extremely effective medicines for some problematic diseases. The peculiarity of these pages is that they have been opened recently and are widely spread through the payment method they make on social networks to sponsor the widest possible distribution of their propaganda. They improvise that eminent names in the world and local medicine speak about the one hundred percent success of the drugs. Due to people's health problems, their clickability is very high, but the number of customers who fall into the traps is also considerable. Hence, media education would stop the manipulators and close the paths to their success.

Faced with the multitude of online manipulative platforms, media education is the only preventive and promising way to protect children from manipulative evils. Policymakers worldwide will need to set a framework with some of the key points of our time to create legal certainty regarding the use of AI and clarify the responsibilities of the media, especially on social media platforms. The EU has already adopted key regulations to this end, such as the General Data Protection Regulation and the Digital Services Act, and the planned AI Act will also make an important contribution to minimizing the risks posed by AI and strengthening the protection of fundamental rights.

Recommendations

Based on the issues identified, the following recommendations are made:

1. Enhanced Quality of Journalism: Media should establish strict ethical standards and ensure a balanced and objective approach to reporting, especially on sensitive ethnic and cultural matters.
2. Capacity Building Among Journalists: Training programs on investigative reporting and fact-checking should be arranged for journalists.
3. Media Literacy: The need for public awareness regarding biased reporting and the use of multiple sources for verification of information should be promoted, including media education as an obligatory subject in the academic curricula of both primary and secondary education.
4. Policy Interventions: Policymakers have to consider the introduction of a regulatory framework that could assure media accountability and transparency.

REFERENCES

Alsat.mk. (2024, December 30). *Balanserotzaminuvavoistorijata [The balancer goes into history]*. Retrieved from https://alsat.mk/mk/balanserot-zaminuva-vo-istorijata/

Apostolov, G., & Jankulovski, M. (2018). Media literacy and fake News in North Macedonia. *The Journal of Medical Research, 11*(3), 56–72.

Ashley, S., Maksl, A., & Craft, S. (2017). News media literacy and political engagement: What's the connection? *The Journal of Media Literacy Education, 9*(1), 79–98. DOI: 10.23860/JMLE-2017-9-1-6

Benkler, Y., Faris, R., & Roberts, H. (2018). *Network propaganda: Manipulation, disinformation, and radicalization in American politics*. Oxford University Press. DOI: 10.1093/oso/9780190923624.001.0001

Blazhevski, T., & Rizankoska, J. (2020). Social media disinformation during COVID-19: A case study of North Macedonia. *Southeast European and Black Sea Studies, 20*(4), 595–617.

Bradshaw, S., & Howard, P. N. (2019). *The global disinformation order: 2019 global inventory of organised social media manipulation*. Project on Computational Propaganda.

Brodsky, J. E., Brooks, P. J., Scimeca, D., & Galati, P. (2021). Improving college students' fact-checking strategies through lateral reading instruction in a general education civics course. *Cognitive Research: Principles and Implications, 6*(1), 1–18. DOI: 10.1186/s41235-021-00291-4 PMID: 33788064

Chesney, R., & Citron, D. (2019). Deepfakes and the new disinformation war: The coming age of post-truth geopolitics. *Foreign Affairs, 98*, 147.

Cvetkovska, S., Belford, A., Silverman, C., & Methodieva, A. (2021). *Russian disinformation networks in the Balkans: A study of media manipulation in North Macedonia, Serbia, and Kosovo*. Digital Forensic Research Lab.

European Commission. (2021). *North Macedonia 2021 Report: Progress on media freedom and pluralism* (SWD(2021) 294 final). Brussels: European Commission.

Fokus.mk. (2024, December 30). *(ИНТЕРВЈУ) Мицкоски: ДУИ јазагрозуваинтеретничкатаслика и претставувазаканапомирот и стабилноста! [Interview - Mitskoski: DUI endangers the interethnic image and poses a threat to peace and stability]*. Retrieved from https://fokus.mk/intervju-mitskoski-dui-ja-zagrozuva-interetnichkata-slika-i-pretstavuva-zakana-po-mirot-i-stabilnosta/

Freelon, D., & Wells, C. (2020). Disinformation as political communication. *Political Communication, 37*(2), 145–156. DOI: 10.1080/10584609.2020.1723755

Guess, A. M., Nagler, M. H., Tucker, J., Reifler, J., & Sircar, N. (2020). A digital media literacy intervention increases discernment between mainstream and false news in the United States and India. *Proceedings of the National Academy of Sciences of the United States of America, 117*(27), 15536–15545. DOI: 10.1073/pnas.1920498117 PMID: 32571950

Halili, A., Palloshi-Disha, E., Bajrami, D., & Ibrahimi, Sh. (2023). Media and information literacy education in the age of disinformation: SEEU professor and student perceptions. *Media and Communication Review, 2*, 56–65.

Huguet, A., Kavanagh, P. B., Sultana, A., Leung, T., Tran, L. M., Rosen, M. L., & Downey, G. (2022). Evaluating the effectiveness of digital media literacy programs: A systematic review and meta-analysis. *Psychological Bulletin, 148*(3), 193–226.

IMA.mk. (2024, August 21). *(ANALIZË) Media njësojsipolitika: Përplasjeetnikem-biçështjetëndjeshme [(ANALYSIS) Media as politics: Ethnic clashes over sensitive issues].* Retrieved from https://ima.mk/sq/2024/08/21/analize-media-njesoj-si-politika-perplasje-etnike-mbi-ceshtje-te-ndjeshme/

IMA.mk. (2024, August 31). *ПремиеротМицкоскикакоизворнанепотврдениинформацииздржавендолг, инфлација, дестабилизација [Prime Minister Mickoski as a source of unconfirmed information about state debt, inflation, destabilization].* Retrieved from https://ima.mk/2024/08/31/premierot-miczkoski-kako-izvor-na-nepotvrdeni-informaczii-za-drzhaven-dolg-inflaczija-destabilizaczija/

IREX. (2020). *Media Sustainability Index 2020: North Macedonia*. IREX.

Islam, M. S., Sarkar, T., Khan, S. H., Mostofa Kamal, A.-H., Hasan, S. M. M., Kabir, A., Yeasmin, D., Islam, M. A., Amin Chowdhury, K. I., Anwar, K. S., Chughtai, A. A., & Seale, H. (2020). COVID-19-related infodemic and its impact on public health: A global social media analysis. *The American Journal of Tropical Medicine and Hygiene, 103*(4), 1621–1629. DOI: 10.4269/ajtmh.20-0812 PMID: 32783794

Khan, M. L., & Idris, I. K. (2019). Recognise misinformation and verify before sharing: A reasoned action and information literacy perspective. *Behaviour & Information Technology, 38*(12), 1194–1212. DOI: 10.1080/0144929X.2019.1578828

Klan Macedonia, T. V. (2024, December 30). *Minçevndryshoillogaritjetpërbalancuesin, uletpërqindja e shqiptarëve, rritet e maqedonasve [Mincev changed the calculations for the balancer, Albanian percentage decreases, Macedonian increases].* Retrieved from https://tvklan.mk/mincev-ndryshoi-llogaritjet-per-balancuesin-ulet-perqindja-e-shqiptareve-rritet-e-maqedonasve/

Krippendorff, K. (2013). *Content Analysis: An Introduction to Its Methodology* (3rd ed.). SAGE Publications.

Lee, N. M., & Xenos, M. (2023). Toward a global understanding of media literacy education: Insights from cross-cultural research. *Communication Education*, *72*(1), 1–21.

Loomba, S., de Figueiredo, A., Piatek, S. J., de Graaf, K., & Larson, H. J. (2021). Measuring the impact of COVID-19 vaccine misinformation on vaccination intent in the UK and USA. *Nature Human Behaviour*, *5*(3), 337–348. DOI: 10.1038/s41562-021-01056-1 PMID: 33547453

Majhosev, A., & Bakev, M. (2019). Media freedom and disinformation in North Macedonia: Challenges and perspectives. *Balkan Social Science Review*, *13*(1), 63–80.

Marin, V. V., & Koivula, A. (2022). Media literacy education in Finland: Integrating critical thinking and digital skills. *The Journal of Media Literacy Education*, *14*(1), 1–15.

Martinez-Costa, C., & Rodriguez, R. (2021). Media literacy in formal education: Challenges and opportunities. *Comunicar*, *29*(66), 9–19.

Mayring, P. (2014). *Qualitative Content Analysis: Theoretical Foundation, Basic Procedures and Software Solution*. Beltz.

McGrew, S., Breakstone, J., Ortega, T., Smith, M., & Wineburg, S. (2018). Can students evaluate online sources? Learning from assessments of civic online reasoning. *Theory and Research in Social Education*, *46*(2), 165–193. DOI: 10.1080/00933104.2017.1416320

McGrew, S., & Wineburg, S. (2023). Improving students' ability to identify misinformation online: Lessons from the COR curriculum. *The Journal of Media Literacy Education*, *15*(1), 1–15.

META. mk Network. (2023). *Fact-checking initiatives in North Macedonia: Annual report 2023*. Skopje: META.

24. mk. (2024, December 30). *Balanserot zaminuva vo istorijata [The balancer goes into history]*. Retrieved from https://24.mk/details/balanserot-zaminuva-vo-istorijata

Nickerson, R. S. (1998). Confirmation bias: A ubiquitous phenomenon in many guises. *Review of General Psychology*, *2*(2), 175–220. DOI: 10.1037/1089-2680.2.2.175

Nistori. (2024, December 30). *Opozitë e pozitë, partitëshqiptareireagojnë Maksim Dimitrievskitpërflamurinshqiptar [Opposition and position, Albanian parties react to Maksim Dimitrievski about the Albanian flag].* Retrieved from https://nistori.com/opozite-e-pozite-partite-shqiptare-i-reagojne-maksim-dimitrievskit-per-flamurin-shqiptar/

Pariser, E. (2011). *The filter bubble: What the Internet is hiding from you*. Penguin Press.

Pennycook, G., & Rand, D. G. (2021). The psychology of fake news. *Trends in Cognitive Sciences*, *25*(5), 388–402. DOI: 10.1016/j.tics.2021.02.007 PMID: 33736957

Schreier, M. (2012). *Qualitative Content Analysis in Practice*. SAGE Publications. DOI: 10.4135/9781529682571

Serafimovska, E., & Cherepnalkova-Trajkoska, J. (2023). (2023). Vulnerability to Disinformation of Diverse Groups of Citizens in North Macedonia. *Institute of Communication Studies*https://cdn.iks.edu.mk/wp-content/uploads/2023/04/ranlivost-na-dezinformacii-en.pdf?_gl=1*b38uyy*_ga*MTU1NTQ0OTU4MC4xNzE2NjMzMzI2*_ga_0E19CX2514*MTczNTI0MDMwMi4xMC4xLjE3MzUyNDA0NDIuNTguMC4w

Sitel.mk. (2024, December 30). *Мицкоски: Запрена е инфлацијата, сеработи настабилизацијанаинституциите [Mickoski: Inflation has been stopped, work is being done on stabilization of institutions].* Retrieved from https://sitel.com.mk/mickoski-zaprena-e-inflacijata-se-raboti-na-stabilizacija-na-instituciite

SlobodenPečat. (2024, December 30). *РаздорвоВладатаноради ЗНАМ(е) посамо 8 дена [Discord in the Government over the flag after only 8 days].* Retrieved from https://www.slobodenpecat.mk/razdor-vo-vladata-poradi-zname-po-samo-8-dena/

TV21. (2024, December 30). *Përplasjemes VLEN dhe ZNAM: Ulja e përfaqësimit-tëshqiptarëvenëadministratëshkaktonrevoltëtepartnerët e koalicionitqeverisës [Clash between VLEN and ZNAM: Reduction of Albanian representation in administration causes revolt among government coalition partners].* Retrieved from https://tv21.tv/perplasje-mes-vlen-dhe-znam-ulja-e-perfaqesimit-te-shqiptareve-ne-administrate-shkakton-revolte-te-partneret-e-koalicionit-qeverises/

Tambini, D. (2017). *The attention economy and the law*. Media Policy Brief 22. London School of Economics and Political Science.

Time.mk. (2024, December 30). *Димитриевски: ЗНАМ ќеизлезеодВладатаако повторноминистритеодВредиистакнаталбанскознаме [Dimitrievski: ZNAM will leave the government if VREDI ministers display the Albanian flag again]*. Retrieved from https://time.mk/c/e7085289af/dimitrievski-znam-ke-izleze-od-vladata-ako-povtorno-ministrite-od-vredi-istaknat-albansko-zname.html

Transparency International Macedonia. (2024). *(Dis)information spread online in the pre-election period.* https://transparency.mk/wp-content/uploads/2024/05/disinformation-spread-online-in-the-pre-election-period.pdf

Trpevska, S., & Micevski, I. (2022). *Digital media manipulation in the Balkans: Mapping disinformation ecosystems in North Macedonia*. Southeast European Media Observatory.

Vanderhoven, E., Raes, A., Montrieux, H., Rotsaert, T., & Schellens, T. (2021). Developing a media literacy program for secondary education: Challenges and opportunities. *The Journal of Media Literacy Education*, *13*(1), 1–13.

Vecer.mk. (2024, December 30). *Димитриевски: Акоповторносеистакнеалбанскотознаме, ЗНАМ ќејанапуштиВладата [Dimitrievski: If the Albanian flag is displayed again, ZNAM will leave the Government]*. Retrieved from https://www.vecer.mk/makedonija/dimitrievski-ako-povtorno-se-istakne-albanskoto-zname-znam-kje-ja-napushti-vladata/

Vest.mk. (2024, December 30). *Димитриевски: Акоповторносеистакнеалбанскотознаме, ЗНАМ ќејанапуштиВладата [Dimitrievski: If the Albanian flag is displayed again, ZNAM will leave the Government]*. Retrieved from https://vest.mk/dimitrievski-ako-povtorno-se-istakne-albanskoto-zname-znam-kje-ja-napushti-vladata/

Vlada na Republika Severna Makedonija [Government of the Republic of North Macedonia]. (2024, December 30). *ВладанаРепубликаСевернаМакедонија: Балансеротзаминувавоисторијата [Government of the Republic of North Macedonia: The balancer goes into history].* Video]. YouTube. https://www.youtube.com/watch?v=P5Pq739NbSA

Vosoughi, S., Roy, D., & Aral, S. (2018). The spread of true and false news online. *Science*, *359*(6380), 1146–1151. DOI: 10.1126/science.aap9559 PMID: 29590045

Wardle, C., & Derakhshan, H. (2017). *Information disorder: Toward an interdisciplinary framework for research and policy making*. Council of Europe Report DGI(2017)09.

Westerlund, M. (2019). The emergence of deepfake technology: A review. *Technology Innovation Management Review*, *9*(11), 39–52. DOI: 10.22215/timreview/1282

Zhang, B., & Thompson, A. (2022). Deepfakes and media literacy: Toward a framework for navigating synthetic media. *New Media & Society*, *24*(5), 1165–1182.

KEY TERMS AND DEFINITIONS

Deepfake: Refers to synthetic media generated using artificial intelligence to create realistic but fake audio, video, or images used in disinformation.

Disinformation: Refers to false or misleading information deliberately created and disseminated to deceive, manipulate public opinion, or influence social and political outcomes. Disinformation is often used for propaganda, political manipulation, or economic gain and can be spread through various media, especially digital platforms and social networks.

Echo Chambers: Refers to digital or social media environments where users are exposed primarily to opinions and information that align with their existing beliefs.

Fact-Checking: Refers to verifying the factual accuracy of information, often conducted by journalists or specialized organizations.

Fake News: Refers to fabricated or intentionally distorted news stories presented as legitimate journalism. Fake news is designed to mislead, attract attention, or provoke emotional responses, often influencing public opinion or generating financial profit through clicks and shares.

Filter Bubbles: Refer to situations where algorithms tailor online content to individual users based on past behavior, limiting exposure to diverse perspectives.

Infodemic: Refers to a rapid and far-reaching spread of accurate and inaccurate information, particularly during crises like the COVID-19 pandemic.

Media Literacy: This refers to the ability of individuals to critically access, analyze, evaluate, and create media messages in various forms. Media literacy empowers people to recognize bias, distinguish credible information from falsehoods, and make informed decisions in a complex media environment.

Media Self-Regulation: Refers to the practice by which media institutions develop and enforce internal standards and ethical guidelines to maintain credibility and accountability.

Misinformation: Refers to inaccurate or incorrect information that is shared without malicious intent. Unlike disinformation, misinformation is not purposely deceptive but can still cause confusion, misunderstanding, or harm, particularly when it spreads widely through social media or other communication channels.

Motivated Reasoning: Refers to a psychological phenomenon where individuals form or evaluate information in a biased way that aligns with their desires or preconceptions.

Public Perception: Refers to how the general population interprets and reacts to media messages shaped by media literacy, personal beliefs, and societal context.

Source Credibility: Refers to the perceived trustworthiness and expertise of the individual, organization, or outlet that disseminates information. A credible source is generally recognized as reliable, impartial, and knowledgeable, influencing how audiences interpret and believe the information presented.

Source Manipulation: Refers to altering or misrepresenting the origin or credibility of information to deceive audiences.

Trust in Media: Refers to public confidence in media sources, which affects susceptibility to misinformation and disinformation.

Chapter 6
Risks and Challenges of Deepfakes in National and European Parliament Elections

Viktorija Soņeca
https://orcid.org/0009-0001-6973-9570
Supreme Court of Latvia, Latvia

ABSTRACT

Deepfake technology, initially developed for interactive entertainment, has increasingly become a tool for influencing voter behavior, making its impact particularly significant in the context of the 2024 elections. This relevance is heightened by the occurrence of multiple national elections held concurrently with the European Parliament (EP) elections. In response, various countries have introduced legal frameworks to address the challenges posed by deepfakes. This chapter examines these national legal approaches and analyzes their interaction with the broader European Union (EU) legal system in combating disinformation and promoting voter participation. It provides a concise overview of the evolution of deepfake technology, demonstrates its role in voter manipulation through disinformation campaigns, and evaluates the EU's strategic measures aimed at mitigating the adverse effects of deepfakes. Ultimately, the chapter underscores the importance of coordinated legal and policy efforts to safeguard democratic processes across the EU and its member states.

DOI: 10.4018/979-8-3693-9601-8.ch006

INTRODUCTION

The Member States of the European Union (EU) should be understood as part of a multi-level democracy, operating under three legal systems: a national legal system, an EU legal system, and international law. This creates a need for synergies between these systems (Levits, 2024). However, this chapter will focus solely on the synergy between the national and EU legal systems. Citizens, through their participation in European Parliament (EP) elections, influence who is elected to the EP and, consequently, who represents their interests at the EU level. Article 10(1) and (2) of the Treaty on European Union (TEU) indicates that the operation of the EU is based on representative democracy, allowing citizens to have direct representation at the EU level through the EP.

Democracy must rest on the free will of citizens to shape their own political, economic, social, and cultural systems, along with their active engagement in all aspects of life.Therefore, it is essential to prioritize the role of information - not only ensuring the right to access information but also the information that guides decision-making by both citizens and parliamentarians. Access to information is vital, as it directly influences an individual's understanding of events, shapes their worldview, and informs the decisions they make based on that understanding (UN General Assembly Resolution, 2015). However, it is equally crucial to be aware of the risks of disinformation, and especially deepfakes. This includes the information encountered during interactions on social media platforms or search engines.Therefore, the quality of information, its dissemination methods, and the communication techniques employed through digital technologies are crucial for both national and EU elections, as well as for comprehending the synergy between the two(Topsümer, Durmuş, Yılmaz, 2023).

LITERATURE REVIEW

This chapter is aimed at readers interested in the interplay between national and EU legal systems concerning disinformation related to elections. In today's context, it would be ill-advised to view national and EP elections in isolation from the advantages and possibilities afforded by digital technologies, especially during pre-election campaigns (Borz, Francesco, 2024; Hoferer, Böttcher, Hans J. Herrmann, Gersbach, 2020; DGI(2017)11).Consequently, this chapter highlights that the adoption of innovative solutions has been a persistent practice, although the definition of what constitutes innovation tends to evolve over time. A notable historical example is Dwight Eisenhower's victory in the U.S. presidential election against Adlai Stevenson, which was significantly aided by interactive television advertisements. At that time, Eisenhower employed a strategic advertising approach that involved frequent broadcasts to reach a broader electorate, whereas Stevenson favored 30-minute television briefings that aired late at night, limiting his audience.In the present day, and particularly in recent years, deepfake technology - also referred to as "synthetic media" - have become widely utilized in pre-election campaigns (Vaccari, Chadwick, 2020).

This chapter illustrates that the application of deepfake technology can differ depending on its intended use. Given that deepfake technology can influence not only interactive entertainment but also voter behavior, its significance increased in light of the 2024 elections, making it one of the most debated topics as numerous countries had elections planned alongside the EP elections. In this chapter the Republic of Latvia (Latvia) is highlighted for a more detailed analysis because it enacted amendments to two laws: the Pre-election Campaign Law and the Criminal Law, and these amendments address the use of artificial intelligence (AI) systems and deepfakes in pre-election campaigns and their potential effects on the electoral process.

Moreover, within the context of the EP elections, Latvia represents a significant case study. Despite being an EU member since 2004, there has been a disconnect between national election regulations and those governing EP elections. This misalignment enabled the election of former MEP Tatjana Ždanoka, who has been linked to Russian intelligence services for over a decade, as referenced in the EP resolution B9-0128/2024. Furthermore, this chapter will offer a brief overview of the history of deepfakes, exploring their use in influencing voters and shaping decisions within the realm of disinformation, with an emphasis on the impact of deepfake technology.

DEEPFAKE EVOLUTION FROM LOW-QUALITY IMAGE TO REALISTIC VIDEO

In this subchapter is proposed a brief examination of the evolution of deepfake technology, highlighting key turning points. This historical overview is essential to illustrate that, prior to the use of deepfake technology to influence democratic processes in national and EU level, the associated risks could have been anticipated and proactively addressed by monitoring the technology's advancements and responding accordingly in advance (*ex ante*), rather than reacting *post factum*.Nevertheless, the aftermath has prompted a number of legislative measures at the EU level (for example, AI Act,Digital Services Act), as well as national laws enacted by individual countries. For example, in the French Republic (France), Article 27 of the French Freedom of the Press Act prohibits the publication, dissemination, or reproduction of false news, as well as falsified, fabricated, or falsely attributed material if it is done for malicious purposes and disturbs or is likely to disturb public peace. The infringement of this provision is punishable by a fine of €45,000. An additional example is the Hellenic Republic, where the dissemination of fake news is criminalized if it creates public fear, particularly when such news is spread via the internet.To be precise,anyone who publicly disseminates false news, whether through the internet or other means, resulting in fear among an indefinite number of people or within a specific group or category, and consequently forces individuals to take unplanned actions or cancel plans-which poses a risk of damaging the economy, the country's defense capacity, or public health-shall be punished with imprisonment of up to three years or a fine. The actual owner or publisher of the medium through which these actions were committed shall face the same penalties.

From a historicalperspective, one of the first widely recognized videos that creates the illusion of a person performing an action they never actually did is the "Hitler jig". In this video, Hitler appears to dance absurdly, even though he merely tapped his foot and raised it too high in the original footage. At that time, such video manipulation was achieved using traditional methods like scissors and glue, unlike today's automated processes that leverage AI for editing and content generation. Specifically, in 1940, the Armistice of Compiègne was signed in the carriage of the French Marshal to emphasize Germany's victory over France, recalling the previous 1918 armistice that had seen Germany as the losing party. Hitler, in a moment of joy, tapped his foot during the signing, and this brief action inspired two filmmakers to repeatedly edit the footage to make it look as if he was performing a comical dance, which later became known as the "Hitler jig".

A significant development in the realm of deepfakes occurred in 1997, when Video Rewrite introduced the capability to alter video content, enabling the lip movements of one person to sync with an audio track spoken by someone else. This innovation created the impression that the person in the video was conveying an entirely different message than in the original footage (Kertysova, 2018; Thies, Zollhöfer, Stamminger, Theobalt, Nießner, 2016).Currently, lip synchronization technology is being adopted in the film industry, allowing actors to perform in multiple languages while maintaining consistent facial expressions. Conventional translation methods frequently fail to accomplish this, as they either depend on a separate voice actor to translate the dialogue or utilize subtitles, which can divert viewers' attention from fully immersing themselves in the movie (Theobalt, 2018).A notable example of this technology in action is a campaign against malaria featuring David Beckham, who speaks in nine different languages in the video.

From a computer science perspective, it was in 2014 when several researchers published a paper introducing "generative adversarial networks" (GANs), which are the foundational technology behind deepfakes (Goodfellow, Pouget-Abadie, Mirza, Xu, Warde-Farley, Ozair, Bengio, 2014; Nan-Run, Tian-Feng, Xin-Wen, Jun-Yun,

2023). In simple terms, a GAN consists of two AI algorithms that compete against one another to produce entirely new images. The first algorithm, known as the generator, receives random data to create a new image, while the second algorithm, the discriminator, evaluates the image against known data (such as established images or faces). This competitive interaction compels the generator to produce highly realistic images intended to deceive the discriminator (Pupillo, Fantin, Ferreira, Polito, 2021).

The next key advancement came in 2015, when GANs were integrated with multilayer convolutional neural networks to enhance image recognition capabilities and facilitate the generation of fake images (Cornelisse, 2018).However, it is vital to emphasize that the quality of these generated images at that time was not sufficiently high (Radford, Metz, Chintala, 2015). In 2016, GANs were combined to enhance the reliability of generated images, aiming to make them appear more realistic. However, challenges with image quality persisted. For instance, this method made it feasible to alter facial features in images, such as creating depictions of individuals with or without glasses. Nonetheless, these generated images could readily be recognized as fakes due to their inferior quality (Liu, Tuzel, 2016).The year 2017 marked a significant turning point, primarily by introducing a solution to enhance the quality of generated images (Mallya, Wang, Liu, 2022).The first deepfake videos emerged for both interactive and adult content (Ajder, Patrini, Cavalli, Cullen, 2019),utilizing the likenesses of well-known actors. A notable case involved a pornographic video that featured the face of actress Scarlett Johansson. By 2018, advancements allowed deepfake technology to be applied not just to facial features, but to the entire body as well (Westerlund, 2019).

Moreover, it's important to mention ChatGPT as well, which represents a form of generative AI, a tool that allows users to input prompts and receive human-like textgenerated by AI. Both deepfaketechnology and ChatGPT represent generative models (Mitra, Mohanty, Kougianos, 2024) While deepfake technology synthesizes realistic visual media, ChatGPT is designed to generate coherent and contextually relevant textual content. They exhibit the capacity to create content that can sometimes be indistinguishable from real human output, thereby posing similar challenges in terms of authenticity and trustworthiness (Mubarak, Alsboui, Alshaikh, Inuwa-Dute, Khan, Parkinson, 2023).In 2018, OpenAI released the first model in the GPT series (Radford, Narasimhan, Salimans, Sutskever, 2018). "GPT-1 was a major move forward in AI development because it enabled computers to comprehend textual material in a more natural manner than before. This generative language model was able to learn a wide variety of connections and gain immense knowledge on a varied corpus of contiguous text" (Yenduri, Srivastava, Maddikunta, Jhaveri, Wang, Vasilakos, Gadekallu, 2023.). In 2019, OpenAI followed up with GPT-2, which was both larger and more capable than its predecessor. Initially, the full release of this model was withheld due to concerns about potential misuse, such as the generation of misleading information (Partha Pratim Ray, 2023).

Then a significant milestone occurred in November 2022 with the launch of ChatGPT, a fine-tuned version of GPT-3 specifically designed for interactions with users. In March 2023, OpenAI introduced GPT-4, which featured advanced capabilities compared to earlier models, including improved contextual understanding, creativity, and better alignment with user intent in conversations. For instance, one of the most notable capabilities of GPT-4 is its proficiency in understanding and generating responses that are nuanced and relevant to the context.Additionally, it should be noted that Microsoft announced in 2023 that ChatGPT-powered features would be integrated into Bing.Furthermore,OpenAI also launched the ChatGPT API, enabling developers to incorporate ChatGPT functionality into their applications.

As a result,in 2024, the electoral process, for example, in the U.S. saw a significant shift with the emergence of new information-sourcing methods, particularly through conversational generative AI chatbots.Traditionally, users relied on search engines like Google to access a variety of information sources, but platforms such as OpenAI's ChatGPT are starting to shift and take on a role in this area as well. However, there is a difference in using ChatGPT depending on factors such as age and education level. Statistics on ChatGPT usage show a monthly average of around 1.7 billion visitors, which is still 98% lower than Google's traffic. This disparity can be attributed to the fact that ChatGPT is a relatively new tool, while Google has been a well-established resource for a longer period.

However, any incorrect answer to a simple question can hinder a user's ability to exercise their voting rights, depending on the person's reliance on the generated response.Furthermore, misleading or biased information regarding voting rights or electoral procedures can undermine voter confidence in the democratic process (Harper, Aboulafia, Linzer, 2024). It is crucial to emphasize that the main issue lies in the use of deepfake technology to threaten elections, as manipulated content containing misleading or false information spreads online, can sway public opinion and affect voters' choices (Battista, 2024).Therefore, as society faces an ever-growing array of information sources, it is essential for individuals to acquire the tools and skills necessary to navigate this intricate landscape. There is no straightforward solution to fighting disinformation.However, through sustained, systemic efforts, it is possible to foster societal resilience by enhancing media, digital, and civic literacy. This, in turn, will empower individuals to develop critical thinking abilities and effectively recognize and counter disinformation, as relying solely on legal acts will not address the problem.

For instance, the Organisation for Economic Co-operation and Development (OECD) highlights in its Recommendation of the Council on Information Integrity the necessity of creating and implementing initiatives aimed at both children and adults. These initiatives should concentrate on raising awareness about the threats posed by disinformation and information manipulation, promoting media and information literacy skills and improving civic and scientific literacy. It is also essential to establish training programs for educators and advance media and information literacy within adult education and lifelong learning initiatives. Consequently, these efforts will contribute to increasing awareness and cultivating skills that enable individuals to leverage opportunities while acknowledging and understanding the potential risks related to AI-generated content (OECD/LEGAL/0505).

In addition, in 2024, the EC initiated a series of actions aimed at raising awareness about the dangers of disinformation and the manipulation and interference of foreign information. In collaboration with the European Regulators Group for Audiovisual Media Services, which consists of all 27 national independent regulatory bodies overseeing audiovisual services, a joint communication campaign was created to educate individuals about these risks. Additionally, the EC has published a new toolkit that provides actionable guidance for teachers and educators, including effective strategies to help them explain disinformation and information manipulation to students and youth, empowering them to recognize and combat these issues.

However, while initiatives and recommendations serve as useful guidelines, it is crucial to integrate these tools and awareness programs into schools and higher education institutions to benefit students, children, teachers, and lecturers. This can be achieved through an interdisciplinary approach that, on one hand, explains disinformation and deepfakes and how to identify them, and, on the other hand, fosters an understanding of digital tools and their available options.This integration will ensure that the available resources are effectively utilized in practice, as education serves as a vital countermeasure against disinformation. Therefore, while deepfake technology is not a new concept, its growing accessibility and the improved quality have heightened the urgency for appropriate responses (OECD, 2024).In light of the threats these pose to democratic processes, both national governments and the EU are compelled to tackle the risks linked to deepfakes. This response should encompass not only legal measures but also the education of children and adults. Such an approach will enhance individuals' capacity to assess the authenticity and origins of AIgenerated information and other content disseminated across social media platforms or search engines.

DISINFORMATION IN CONTEXT OF DEEPFAKES: LATVIA'S EXAMPLE

Disinformation

Information that is not only published but also accessible to individuals is of paramount importance in shaping public opinion, as it creates opportunities for both citizens and society as a whole to participate in political and legislative debates and to actively express their views.In doing so, they are executing their fundamental rights. However, to effectively exercise these rights, it is essential to provide the public with understandable, accessible, relevant, timely, trustworthy, transparent, accurate, and comprehensive information. This is important because not only do national public administrations have social networking accounts, but EU-level institutions do as well, and almost anyone can post and share a wide range of content on social media. Therefore, given the vast variety of information available, individuals should be able to rely on and easily understand the information published by national and EU-level institutions or other reliable sources. Otherwise, individuals may choose to believe unverified information simply because it is presented in an understandable format. In such cases, the risk of disinformation, especially in the context of deepfakes, will be particularly prevalent (Vaccari, Chadwick, 2020).

Looking into the definition of disinformation, the EC has stated that it is important to distinguish between illegal content as defined by law and content that is harmful but not illegal. Furthermore, it is crucial to determine whether there is an intention to deceive, cause harm to the public, or gain an economic advantage. In the absence of such an intention - such as when individuals share false information with friends and family in good faith - the content may be regarded as misleading information. In contrast, the existence of such an intention would qualify the content as disinformation (Join(2020) 8 final). Additionally,given that disinformation can be part of a hybrid threat, and disinformation is only one element of a broader set of activities that may include various tactics un techniquesin terms of a hybrid threat,organizations such as NATO understands the mentioned term as false or inaccurate information disseminated deliberately to manipulate the opinions and actions of others.Therefore, as OECD has defined,"disinformation refers to verifiably false, manipulated, or misleading content that is knowingly and intentionally created and/ or shared, including through co-ordinatedinauthentic behaviour, to deliberately deceive, manipulate or inflict harm on a person, social group, organisation or country" (OECD/LEGAL/0505).

As disinformation is particularly effective on social networks, largely due to users' lack of knowledge in detecting false content (Katkovska, 2024), there have been attempts to establish a legal framework addressing the issue of disinformation

(Jonins, Dvorovijs, 2024).For example, the EC defines disinformation in guidelines which is soft law as verifiably false or misleading information that is created, presented and disseminated for economic gain or to intentionally deceive the public, and may cause public harm. Public harm comprises threats to democratic political and policy-making processes as well as public goods such as the protection of EU citizens' health, the environment or security(COM(2018)236). The aim of disinformation is to distract and divide, to plant seeds of doubt by distorting and falsifying facts, thus confusing people and weakening their faith in institutions and established political processes (JOIN/2019/12 final).Howeverregarding the EC definition,it is important to note that particular definition lacks specific criteria, which may lead to various issues for those applying it in practice. This observation highlights the necessity for not only authorities but also individuals to be aware of the extent of the discretion they are granted and the manner in which it should be exercised. Without proper guidance and criteria for the correct and consistent application of the legal provisions in relation of disinformation, officials tasked with enforcing the law may struggle to determine which actions are punishable (Jonins, 2021).Moreover, the absence of specific criteria against which their actions can be assessed would hinder individuals' understanding and ability to predict which statements or information would qualify as disinformation (CCPR/C/GC/34).

Given this complexity, defining the limits of this specific definition raises concerns, particularly since an opinion, as a subjective assessment, can be formed from both true facts and erroneous news or false information. Thus, including the specific concept (Case No SKC-98/2017; CCPR/C/GC/34)in legal provisions may inadvertently undermine one of the objectives of a democratic state governed by the rule of law - to ensure pluralism of democracy. Furthermore, such an approach could severely restrict freedom of expression. However, as suggested by the EC, this stance would contradict the ideals of a healthy democracy, which relies on an active civil society and public participation in decision-making (Report on the Public Consultation for the European Democracy Action Plan (EDAP), 2020).A healthy democracy depends on the ability of citizens to access diverse forms of verifiable information that enable them to formulate their views on various political issues. Inthisway, citizenscanparticipateinpublicdebateandexpresstheirviewsin a freeandfairpolitical process.

Additionally, the selection of tools to address disinformation must respect the fundamental rights grounded in the EU's core values, as outlined in the Charter of Fundamental Rights. Simultaneously, the principle of self-defensive democracy should be taken into account, which emphasizes the need to prevent the misuse of democratic instruments-such as freedom of expression-to erode democracy itself. In a state that upholds the rule of law and democracy, claiming human rights and freedoms cannot be leveraged to undermine or dismantle democracy or the principles and values that define a democratic society. The stability and effectiveness of the democratic system are ensured by the notion of "self-defending democracy," which exists in harmony with and is balanced by fundamental rights(Pleps, Engīzers, Soņeca, 2024, pp.233. - 234).

On one hand, freedom of expression is one of the essential foundations of a democratic society. It applies not only to information or ideas that are favorably received or considered harmless but also to those that offend, shock, or disturb particular individuals or sections of the population. The exercise of this freedom is subject to restrictions that must be interpreted narrowly, and their necessity must be convincingly demonstrated.On the other hand,the right to freedom of expression is not absolute and does not imply permissiveness, although it is crucial for exercising institutional power and public participation (CDL-AD(2013)011).

In this context, it is important to bear in mind that Article 10(2) of the European Convention on Human Rights provides little scope for restricting political speech or debate on matters of public importance, even on the grounds of national security. This means that the justification of "protection of national security" put forward by the state should be interpreted narrowly and must always be proportionate. The assessment of whether certain statements constitute disinformation must be contextual and individual; it cannot be abstract or general. It must be possible to distinguish between news and opinion and take into account the purpose of the author of the statement. Measures aimed at limiting the dissemination of information will be more proportionate than those in which the state seeks to block information outright (Rāviņa, Šantare, 2024).

It is important to note that disinformation is merely one of the tactics employed by third countries to disrupt national and EU democratic processes. The OECD has highlighted that foreign influence can significantly transform a nation's political landscape, affecting not only its domestic and foreign policies but also its electoral systems, economic interests, and its capability to safeguard national security (OECD, 2021). When the interests of foreign governments are presented transparently, these third country ideas can positively contribute to public discourse and enhance international engagement (2023/0463(COD)). However, when foreign interests are covertly represented, they can disrupt EU democracies by manipulating public opinion to sway political decisions, ultimately harming the political integrity of both Member States and the EU as a whole.

It should be noted that, as the EP mentioned in one of its resolutions, there have been instances where the MEPs have utilized EP resources to advocate for activities directly or indirectly associated with foreign interference. A significant incident occurred in December 2022 when the Belarusian state propaganda channel STV accessed EP premises, including the VoxBox video-recording facility. Consequently, several MEPs produced pro-Kremlin and anti-EU disinformation content using

EP facilities. Moreover, some MEPs have employed Russian nationals loyal to the Putin regime as interns, registered parliamentary assistants, and group advisors, continuing this practice even after Russia's aggression against Ukraine began. A notable case is Elizaveta Peskova, the daughter of Dmitry Peskov, who interned for an MEP (2024/2548(RSP)). However, such developments erode voter confidence in democratic processes and therefore influence their decision-making.

Amendments in Latvia's National Laws

As there is an undeniable synergy between national legal systems and the EU legal system, disinformation must be considered in the context of both national and EU legal frameworks, as evidenced, for example, by the recent amendments to the Latvia's Criminal Law at national level, which criminalise the use of deepfake technologies in electioneering. As the annotation of the draft law states, "[t]he draft law is designed to criminalise attempts to influence the outcome of elections through the use of deepfake technology and to ensure the right of voters to participate in fair and free elections. [...] Over the last few years, photo, video and audio materials produced by deepfake technologies have become an integral part of electoral campaigns" (DraftLaw "Amendments to theCriminalLaw" (No: 535/Lp14)). Therefore, Article 90.[2] of Criminal law currently states that for the production or dissemination of deliberately false discrediting information, using deepfake technology, in relation to a candidate for a public office who is elected, appointed or confirmed by the Parliament (Saeima), if committed during the process of election, appointment or confirmation of a public office holder as provided by law, shall be punishable by deprivation of liberty for a term not exceeding five years or by temporary deprivation of liberty or by probation supervision or by community service.

Moreover, taking into account the risks of disinformation, the President of Latvia E. Rinkēvičs sent to theParliament (Saeima) the draft law "Amendments to the Pre-election Campaign Law". According to the annotation of the draft law, amendment was drafted because as "fair elections are possible only if the public receives comprehensive information on candidates, lists of candidates, political parties [..]. Last but not least, this electioneering must contain only truthful information. [...] The increasing use of modern technologies, including AI systems, offers political organisations (parties) unprecedented opportunities to reach voters, including through online chat rooms and targeted calls. However, whatever the form of electioneering, its content must comply with the requirements of a democratic state governed by the rule of law in order not to cast doubt on the integrity of elections" (Annotation to the draft law "Amendments to the Pre-election Campaign Law"). Thus, this draft law proposed, inter alia, to supplement the Pre-election Campaign Law with Article 3[1], which would provide that "[i]f pre-election campaign material is created in an

AI system or an AI system is used in any other way in pre-election campaigns, this shall be clearly and unambiguously stated" (Draft Law "Amendments to the Pre-election Campaign Law").

Considering the intensity surrounding this particular amendment, it is important to explore the discussions related to it, as these discussions contain valuable insights. In particular, the Center for Public Policy "PROVIDUS" (PROVIDUS), first of all, stressed the need to assess the existing framework and its scope. Secondly, PROVIDUS pointed out that the regulation of pre-election campaigning traditionally does not include a requirement that such campaigning must be truthful. Such a requirement applies to commercial advertisements (Letter from the Public Policy Centre Providus "On the Need to Clarify the Legal Framework on the Use of Artificial Intelligence and Deep Learning Technologies in Election Campaigning", 2024). The Latvian Advertising Association also disagreed with the proposed wording of Article 3^1 of the draft law, pointing out that this would require all electioneering material to be labelled, as virtually all communication material is prepared or distributed using AI. Moreover, referring to PROVIDUS, the Latvian Advertising Association stressed that "freedom of political expression is particularly important for the functioning of democracy and should not be subject to a duty of truthfulness" (Letter from the Latvian Advertising Association "Proposals to the Draft Law "Amendments to the Pre-election Campaign Law" (No 523/Lp14)", 2024).

The State Chancellery, while saying that it supported the draft law, specified that "the wording should be such that it achieves the objective pursued and that this requirement should not apply to all campaign material if AI systems are used in its creation or dissemination" (letter from the State Chancellery "On the Draft Law "Amendments to the Pre-election Campaign Law" (No 523/Lp14)", 2024). Moreover, the State Chancellery also suggested that consideration should be given to adding a provision to the draft law which would impose a general ban on the use of automatically managed or automatically controlled accounts on online platforms for electioneering, as the will of the electorate must be free. Additionallythe State Chancellery explained that it is mostly social media platforms that influence the will of the electorate. This is achieved by artificially increasing, for example, the number of views and comments on the post (content) in order to give the user of the online social media platform a false impression of widespread support for the post and, consequently, for the views expressed therein. Last but not least, there are algorithms that prioritise such posts with artificially increased number of comments or views and make them accessible to an even wider number of users of the online social media platform, which in turn means that a post that may contain both electioneering and manipulated information reaches a significant number of users.The above can be used as a tool to influence the opinions of voters and decision makers.

In light of the objections raised, the proposed Article 3[1] has been clarified. Currently, it states that if, during the pre-election campaigning period, a representation of a person or an event (image, audio or video content) that does not correspond to reality, created by an AI system, is used in paid pre-election campaigning or campaign material, this shall be clearly and unambiguously stated.Furthermore, taking into account the discussion surrounding the mentioned amendment, it has also been proposed to add a sixth paragraph to Article 18 of the law. This addition establish a legal norm stating that atemporaneous use of automated systems for electioneering using fake or anonymous account profiles on social media (a technological platform that allows the creation, publication and dissemination of information through public communication, as well as the creation of communities and interaction based on this content) shall be prohibited.

At the same time, it should be noted that there are several EU legal acts that impact disinformation and deepfakes. Firstly, the AI Act states that content created by an AI system must be labelled in order, firstly, not to give a false impression and, secondly, to reveal the artificial origin of such content.Secondly, the Digital Services Actobliges social media platforms to take action against illegal content. However, while both pieces of legislation - AI Act, Digital Services Act - propose solutions to address the problem of disinformation, there are still many uncertainties regarding how these proposed solutions (e.g., content labeling) will function in practice and their potential effectiveness. For example, Meta has announced that major digital platforms such as Facebook and Instagram will label AIgenerated content created using the most popular generative AI tools (Clegg, 2024). At the same several factors need to be considered in this context. First, this approach will only partially address the issue of deepfakes, as not all AI-generated content will be labeled. In other words, if the generative AI tool used is not included in the list of most popular tools, the content generated by it will remain unlabeled. Secondly, the presence of a watermark is also crucial; if the content generated by the AI does not contain such a watermark, Meta's proposed solution will not be effective in practice. Additionally, it should be noted that generated AI content may not include a watermark, or if it does, it may be relatively easy to remove. One of the simplest methods for removing a watermark is by taking a screenshot. For instance, if an image is generated and a screenshot of that image is taken, the watermark will not be detectable by examining the screenshot (Harris, Norden, 2024). Currently it is too early to assess the effectiveness of the two regulations until it is possible to observe how they will be implemented in practice and how adept the circumvention of the new rules will be. Moreover, it's important to address how content will be detected or labeled, especially when hyper-realistic images are generated that resemble photos of real people. Such images can be used to create fake profiles and actively promote various ideas, including non-democratic ones. Not to mention that Meta announced that Meta is ending its fact-checking program (Horvath, Abbruzzese, Goggin, 2025),although interventions such as Facebook's fact-checking measures were successful in decreasing the belief in false claims and in reducing the frequency with which such content was shared (Hsu., Stuart A. Thompson, 2023).

As a result, the aforementioned national amendments should be viewed in relation to the AI Act and the Digital Services Act to avoid any conflicts between national and EU law. However, at present, national regulations are more detailed compared to the EU framework mentionedand complement each other.

National and EU Legal System Synergy in Context of Elections

As free elections are a hallmark of a democratic polity in this subchapter, democracy and elections in this subchapter will be examined from two perspectives: first, from a national perspective, and second, from EU perspective. This dual approach is proposed because the choices made by voters at the national level not only influence future decisions within the respective country but also affect that country's standing within the EU and beyond. Namely, citizens have the opportunity to influence not only who will represent their interest in national level in every EU Member State (the national parliaments), but also those who will represent their interests at the EU level, as the Council of the EU includes ministers and the European Council consists of heads of state or government.

Moreover, national parliaments play a crucial role regarding the proposals put forth by the EC, ensuring that the EU operates within its competencies as outlined in Article 5 of the TEU. To protect these competencies from being violated, the national parliaments are granted the authority to exercise a monitoring role, as specified in Article 5(3) TEU, along with Protocol No. 1 concerning the role of national parliaments in the EU and Protocol No. 2 regarding the principles of subsidiarity and proportionality. Namely, in the context of national and EU legal systems, the principle of conferral of competences plays a significant role. Articles 3, 4, 5, 6 TFEU define the division of competences between the EU and the Member States, taking into account that, upon becoming an EU member state, a country will have to transfer part of its competences,and the EU can only act within the framework of its assigned competences. This distinguishes, for example, the powers of a national parliament from the powers granted to EU legislators, as "a state has the right to decide for itself in which areas it wishes to issue binding regulations [..]. Comparing the national legislator with the EU legislator[s], one could say that the national legislator has the right to do everything that is not prohibited, but the EU may only act if it is [..] expressly permitted" (Buka, Schewe., Strazdiņš, 2020, p. 89.).

The EU legislator is the EP, where, in accordance with Article 10(2) of TEU, EU citizens are directly represented at EU level, this is achieved through EP elections, and through the EU Council, where, in accordance with Article 16(2) of TEU, each Member State shall have one representative at ministerial level empowered to commit the government of that Member State and to exercise the right to vote. Therefore, through the use of elections:

a) at the national level, members of parliament are elected. This means that voters choose who will carry out the oversight function in relation to EC proposals or initiatives, as such a function is entrusted directly to the national parliaments of the EU member states. At the same time, a government is formed through elections, which decides on issues related to state governance and also represents the country in the Council of the EU, bearing in mind that in the Council of the EU, an EU Member State is represented at ministerial level and the minister of each ministry represents the relevant area in accordance with the competence of the specific ministry;
b) at the EU level, direct representation of EU citizens is ensured by electing members of the EP.

Thus, through elections, citizens decide who will represent their interests in the national and EP, as well as influence what kind of government will be formed and what opinion will be expressed in the EU Council within the framework of the relevant ministry. Consequently, citizens of EU Member States have a direct influence on what decisions will be taken at national level and what their impact will be at EU level, and *vice versa*.

However, the choices made by the electorate and the decisions of their representatives' hinge, in part, on the information available to them. This aspect has gained particular relevance in the digital environment, where platforms such as Facebook, Instagram, and TikTok, as well as search engines like Google and Bing, play a central role. Notably, approximately more than 50% of internet users obtain their information directly through social media (Unesco, 2023; Digital News Report, 2023),which means these users are more susceptible to being manipulated in their choices. This reliance on social media also opens the door for disinformation content creators, such as those utilizing deepfake technology, to deliberately mislead the public and affect decision-making by both citizens and parliament.

Additionally, a study published at the end of 2023 examined the impact of search engines featuring generative AI on the information accessible during election campaigns in Switzerland, Germany, and Bavaria. The study found that one-third of the information provided by the Bing Chat chatbot contained factual inaccuracies (Algorithm Watch, 2023, p. 11). Given that search engines like Google and Bing serve as a primary information source for many individuals, the prevalence of factual errors is a critical concern (Lopatovska, Fenton, M. R., Campot, 2012, pp. 1-11). This is important because the decisions made by citizens, residents, and elected officials on various issues rely not only on their understanding of a democratic state governed by the rule of law, but also on the information they have access to in the digital landscape.

Moreover, there is another significant risk to consider. Specifically, a lack of awareness or understanding regarding how citizens of EU Member States can be directly represented in the EPas well as the interplay between national and EU legal systemsmay lead to scenarios where an individual is barred from participating in national elections yet can still be elected as a MEP. It is important to highlight that the former MEP from Latvia, Ždanoka, was prohibited from national parliamentary elections; however, national lawmakers did not impose the same limitations for EP elections, allowing her to serve as an MEP until 2024. Restrictions are outlined in the Law on the Election of the Parliament, which prohibits individuals who actively participated in organizations associated with the Soviet occupation after January 13, 1991, and whose actions aimed at undermining Latvia's independence, from running in parliamentary elections. However, amendments in Election to the European Parliament Lawwere introduced only in 2022, despite several rulings from the European Court of Human Rights affirming that such national restrictions align with the Convention on Human Rights. Additionally, multiple rulings from the Constitutional Court have stated that this type of prohibition does not conflict with the Latvian Constitution (for example, cases No. 2000-03-01, No. 2005-13-0106, and No. 2017-25-01)(Pleps, Engīzers, Soņeca, 2024, pp.233. - 234).

Therefore, if national legislator would act sooner it would prevent that as the EP has repeatedly stated, while in this position, the mentioned person has expressed a pro-Russian stance, consistently disseminated anti-Latvian and anti-EU messages (2024/2548(RSP)).Thus, this situation exemplifies R. Schuman's assertion that "Europe will not be made all at once or according to a single plan" (Schuman, 1950), highlighting the continual process of European integration and the fact that not all developments contribute positively to the unified Europe initiative. Additionally, it underscores the necessity of comprehending both legal systems and promoting synergy between them, as well as understanding how they interact. This can be achieved by educating individuals about the interconnectedness of national and EP elections and their democratic processes from an early age. The urgency for this education is further emphasized by the reality that even national legislators have struggled to identify the gaps in the national legal framework that have implications for the EU system.

CONCLUSION

Perceptions of political and legislative matters are influenced by engagement with specific informational sources, where the quality and truthfulness of these sources are essential, especially in light of the potential for disinformation. Such information may include not only accurate and verified data but also falsehoods designed to sway the opinions of the public and decision-makers in favor of particular interests and political agendas. The clarity and context of this information are critical, as they affect both the choices made by decision-makers and the broader societal outcomes. Information serves as the foundation upon which decisions regarding specific issues are based. Moreover, dependence on unverified sources, or those lacking in impartiality, in conjunction with a limited understanding of the situation and the information at hand, may lead to decisions that benefit a select group rather than society as a whole, jeopardizing the principles of a democratic state based on the rule of law.

Insufficient information and a weak grasp of processes at both the national and EU levels, as well as the interconnections between them, create significant opportunities for the misuse of institutional power and public engagement to achieve the goals of specific individuals or groups, as exemplified by the situation in Latvia.

The effectiveness of freedom of expression represents a positive obligation of the state. However, since this freedom can be exploited to sway political or legislative outcomes at both national and EU levels, limitations on this fundamental rightare acceptable. Such restrictions must be proportional to a legitimate aim and necessary within a democratic framework, ensuring alignment with the principles of a state governed by the rule of law. Furthermore, they must be in accordance with EU law.

The technology behind deepfakes is inherently neutral; its use is dictated solely by the goals and intentions of those who develop them. This technology has become a tool for spreading disinformation, particularly in cases where external countries interfere with national and EU democratic processes. The information available significantly shapes voters' decisions and the selection of their representatives, which in turn influences future policy choices both domestically and within the EU framework.

To maintain a democratic state under the rule of law, it is crucial to foster meaningful and inclusive participation among citizens, thereby ensuring a well-informed society. People must be cognizant not only of their options but also of the potential factors that could sway those decisions. In this era of transformation, it is vital to acknowledge the risk of manipulation, recognize its occurrence, and take proactive measures to mitigate it -or at least avoid disseminating it.

For society to navigate these challenges effectively, information literacy is essential, which can be cultivated through education for both children and adults.

ACKNOWLEDGMENT

The research is financed by the Project No 5.2.1.1.i.0/2/24/I/CFLA/007 "Internal and External Consolidation of the University of Latvia" of the second round of the Consolidation and Governance Change Implementation Grants within Investment 5.2.1.1.i "Research, Development and Consolidation Grants" under Reform 5.2.1.r "Higher Education and Science Excellence and Governance Reform" of Reform and Investment Strand 5.2 of the Latvian Recovery and Resilience Mechanism Plan "Ensuring Change in the Governance Model of Higher Education Institutions".

REFERENCES

Ajder, H., Patrini, G., Cavalli, F., & Cullen, L. (2019). The State of Deepfakes: Landscape, Threats, and Impact. Available: https://regmedia.co.uk/2019/10/08/deepfake_report.pdf

Algorithm watch (2023). Generative AI and elections: Are chatbots a reliable source of information for voters? Available from: https://algorithmwatch.org/en/wp-content/uploads/2023/12/AlgorithmWatch_AIForensics_Bing_Chat_Report.pdf

Annotation to thedraftlaw "Amendments to thePre-electionCampaignLaw". Available: https://titania.saeima.lv/LIVS14/saeimalivs14.nsf/webSasaiste?OpenView&restricttocategory=523/Lp14

Battista, D. (2024). Political communication in the age of artificial Intelligence: an overview of deepfakes and their Implications. *Society Register*, Vol. 8 No. 2 (2024). Available: https://www.ceeol.com/search/article-detail?id=1251211

Borz, G., & De Francesco, F. (2024). Digital political campaigning: Contemporary challenges and regulation. *Policy Studies*, *45*(5), 677–691. DOI: 10.1080/01442872.2024.2384145

Buka, A., Schewe, C., & Strazdiņš, Ģ. (2020). European Union law. Section I. Institutional Law. Second revised edition. In scientific editorial of K. Gailitis, A. Buka, C. Schewe. *Riga: Publishing house "Tiesunamuagentura"*.

Clegg, N. (2024). Labeling AI-GeneratedImagesonFacebook, InstagramandThreads. Meta. Available: https://about.fb.com/news/2024/02/labeling-ai-generated-images-on-facebook-instagram-and-threads/

COM (2023) 637: Proposal for a DIRECTIVE OF THE EUROPEAN PARLIAMENT AND OF THE COUNCIL establishing harmonised requirements in the internal market on transparency of interest representation carried out on behalf of third countries and amending Directive (EU) 2019/1937/ (2023/0463(COD)).

Cornelisse, D. (2018) An intuitive guide to Convolutional Neural Networks, Available: https://www.freecodecamp.org/news/an-intuitive-guide-to-convolutional-neural-networks-260c2de0a050/

Council of Europe. (2017). Study on the use of internet in electoral campaigns, DGI(2017)11. Available: https://rm.coe.int/study-on-the-use-of-internet/1680796298

Digital News Report (2023). Available: https://reutersinstitute.politics.ox.ac.uk/digital-news-report/2023

European Commision. (2019). Joint communication to the European Parliament, the European Council, the Council, the European Economic and Social Committee and the Committee of the Regions. Report on the implementation of the Action Plan Against Disinformation, JOIN/2019/12 final. Available: https://eur-lex.europa.eu/legal-content/EN/ALL/?uri=comnat:JOIN_2019_0012_FIN

European Commision. (2020). Joint communication to the European Parliament, the European Council, the Council, the European Economic and Social Committee and the Committee of the Regions, Tackling COVID-19 disinformation - Getting the facts right. Join(2020) 8 final. Available: https://eur-lex.europa.eu/legal-content/LV/TXT/?uri=CELEX:52020JC0008

European Commission (2018). Communication from the Commission to the European Parliament, the Council, the European Economic and Social Committee and the Committee of the Regions.

European Parliament. (2024). Joint motion for a resolution on Russiagate: possible Russian interference in the democratic processes of the European Union. (2024/2548(RSP)) Available: https://www.europarl.europa.eu/doceo/document/RC-9-2024-0124_LV.html

Goodfellow, I., Pouget-Abadie, J., Mirza, M., Xu, B., Warde-Farley, D., Ozair, S., & Bengio, Y. (2014). Advances in Neural Information Processing Systems: Vol. 27. *Generative adversarial nets.*, Available https://arxiv.org/abs/1406.2661

Harper, T., Aboulafia, A., & Linzer, I. (2024). Generating Confusion, Stress-testing AI Chatbot Responses on Voting with a Disability, Center for Democracy & Technology. Available: https://cdt.org/wp-content/uploads/2024/09/updated-508-Prep-CDT-Issue-Brief-Chatbot-Responses-on-Disability-Rights-and-Voting-FINAL.pdf

Hoferer, M., Böttcher, L., & Hans, J. (2020). The impact of technologies in political campaigns. *Physica A*, *538*, 122795. Advance online publication. DOI: 10.1016/j.physa.2019.122795

Jonins E. (2021). Cīņa Ar Dezinformāciju Latvijā (I). Journal JuristaVārds, 03.08.2021., No 31 (1193), pp. 11.-18.

Jonins E., Dvorovijs M. (2024). Dezinformācija Latvijā un Ukrainā. Journal JuristaVārds, No 13/14 (1331/1332), pp.11.-16.

Judgment of the Senate of the Republic of Latvia of 6 March 2017 in Case No SKC-98/2017 (C17150712).

Katkovska M. (2024). Kā Atpazīt Dezinformāciju. Journal JuristaVārds No 13/14 (1331/1332), pp. 35.-38.

Kertysova, K. (2018). Artificial Intelligence and Disinformation: How AI Changes-theWay Disinformationis Produced, Disseminated, and Can Be Countered. *Security and HumanRights*, *29*(1-4), 55–81. DOI: 10.1163/18750230-02901005

Law, D. "Amendments to the Criminal Law" (No: 535/Lp14). Available: https://titania.saeima.lv/LIVS14/SaeimaLIVS14.nsf/0/F49CCF01C82F5C2AC2258AD20025B611?OpenDocument

Law, D. "Amendments to the Pre-election Campaign Law". Available: https://titania.saeima.lv/LIVS14/saeimalivs14.nsf/webSasaiste?OpenView&restricttocategory=523/Lp14

Letter from the Latvian Advertising Association. "Proposals to the Draft Law "Amendments to the Pre-election Campaign Law" (No 523/Lp14)". (2024). Available: https://titania.saeima.lv/LIVS14/saeimalivs14.nsf/0/A67A48F4C9B7DDE4C2258B230029D3BD?OpenDocument

Letter from the Public Policy Centre Providus. "On the Need to Clarify the Legal Framework on the Use of Artificial Intelligence and Deep Learning Technologies in Election Campaigning", (2024). Available: https://titania.saeima.lv/LIVS14/saeimalivs14.nsf/0/41EF917932E7BBBDC2258B0100451C4D?OpenDocument

Letter from the State Chancellery. "On the Draft Law "Amendments to the Pre-election Campaign Law" (No 523/Lp14)". (2024). Available: https://titania.saeima.lv/LIVS14/saeimalivs14.nsf/0/EE83C25EC0BE43D5C2258B1F004792D0?OpenDocument

Levits, E. (2024). The European Union, democracy and the risks of populism. *Journal. JuristaVards*, *18/19*(1336/1337), 13–18.

Liu, M. Y., & Tuzel, O. (2016). Coupled generative adversarial networks. *Advances in Neural Information Processing Systems*, •••, 29.

Lopatovska, I., Fenton, M. R., & Campot, S. (2012). Examining preferences for search engines and their effects on information behavior. *Proceedings of the American Society for Information Science and Technology*, *49*(1), 1–11. DOI: 10.1002/meet.14504901110

Mitra, A., Mohanty, S. P., & Kougianos, E. (2024). The world of generative ai: Deepfakes and large language models. *arXiv preprint arXiv:2402.04373.*

Nan-Run, Z., Tian-Feng, Z., Xin-Wen, X., & Jun-Yun, W. (2023). Hybrid quantum-classical generative adversarial networks for image generation via learning discrete distribution. *Signal Processing: Image Communication,* Volume 110, 2023, 116891, ISSN 0923-5965. Available: https://doi.org/DOI: 10.1016/j.image.2022.116891

OECD. (2021). *Lobbyinginthe 21st century: Transparency, Integrityand Access.* OECD Publishing., DOI: 10.1787/c6d8eff8-

OECD. (2024). Recommendation of the Council on Information Integrity, OECD/LEGAL/0505, Adopted on: 17/12/2024. Available: https://legalinstruments.oecd.org/en/instruments/OECD-LEGAL-0505

OECD. (2024). *Facts not Fakes: Tackling Disinformation, Strengthening Information Integrity*. OECD Publishing., DOI: 10.1787/d909ff7a-

Pleps, J., Engīzers, K., & Soņeca, V. (2024). *Latvija. The 2023 Global Review of Constitutional Law*. Published by the Constitutional Studies Program at the University of Texas at Austin. U of Texas Law, Legal Studies Research Paper., Available https://papers.ssrn.com/sol3/papers.cfm?abstract_id=5046787

Pupillo, L., Fantin, S., Ferreira, A., & Polito, C. (2021). *Artificial Intelligence and Cybersecurity. Technology, Governance and Policy Challenges*. Centre for European Policy Studies., Available https://www.ceps.eu/ceps-publications/artificial-intelligence-and-cybersecurity-2/

Radford, A., Metz, L., & Chintala, S. (2015). Unsupervised representation learning with deep convolutional generative adversarial networks. Available: https://arxiv.org/abs/1511.06434

Radford, A., Narasimhan, K., Salimans, T., & Sutskever, I. (2018). Improving Language Understanding by Generative Pre-Training. *Technical Report, OpenAI.* Available: https://cdn.openai.com/research-covers/language-unsupervised/language_understanding_paper.pdf

Rāviņa, K., Šantare, G. (2024) Sabiedrības tiesības saņemt patiesu informāciju demokrātiskā, tiesiskā valstī. Journal JuristaVārds, No13/14 (1331/1332), pp. 31.-34.

Ray, P. P. (2023). ChatGPT: A comprehensivereviewonbackground, applications, keychallenges, bias, ethics, limitationsandfuturescope. *Internet ofThings and Cyber-Physical Systems*, *3*, 121–154. https://www.sciencedirect.com/science/article/pii/S266734522300024X. DOI: 10.1016/j.iotcps.2023.04.003

Report on the Public Consultation for the European Democracy Action Plan (EDAP), (2020). Available: https://commission.europa.eu/document/fe30817d-9ea1-4ec7-ae2b-f80b301df8f7_en

Report "On the role of extra-institutional actors in the democratic system (lobbying)", adopted by the Venice Commission at its 94th Plenary Session (Venice, 8-9 March 2013). CDL-AD(2013)011.

Sharf, Z. (2019). Deepfake Porn Videos Are Using Scarlett Johansson's Face, but She Says It's Useless to Fight Back. IndieWire. Available: https://www.indiewire.com/features/general/scarlett-johansson-deepfakes-face-porn-videos-1202031678/

Tackling online disinformation: a European Approach, COM(2018)236. Available: https://eur-lex.europa.eu/legal-content/EN/TXT/?uri=celex:52018DC0236

Theobalt, C. (2018). Lip-syncingthanks to artificial intelligence. Max - Planck - Gesellschaft. Available: https://www.mpg.de/12226519/synchronisation-facial-expressions-video

Thies, J., Zollhöfer, M., Stamminger, M., Theobalt, Ch., & Nießner, M. (2016). *"Face2Face: Real-Time Face Capture and Reenactment of RGB Videos". 2016 IEEE Conferenceon Computer Vision and Pattern Recognition (CVPR).* IEEE.

Topsümer, F., Durmuş, Y., & Yılmaz, B. A. (Eds.). (2023). *Media and Communication in the Digital Age: Changes and Dynamics.* Özgür Publications., DOI: 10.58830/ozgur.pub234

UN GeneralAssemblyResolutionof 09.04.2015 on "HumanRights, DemocracyandtheRuleofLaw", A/HRC/RES/28/14.

Unesco, (2023). SSurvey on the impact of online disinformation and hate speech. Available at: https://www.unesco.org/sites/default/files/medias/fichiers/2023/11/unesco_ipsos_survey.pdf

United Nations Human Rights Committee. General Comment No. 34: Article 19: Freedoms of opinion and expression, (CCPR/C/GC/34). Available: https://www2.ohchr.org/english/bodies/hrc/docs/gc34.pdf

Vaccari, C., Chadwick, A. (2020). Deepfakes and Disinformation: Exploring the Impact of Synthetic Political Video on Deception, Uncertainty, and Trust in News. *Social Media + Society, 6*(1). https://doi.org/ (Original work published 2020)DOI: 10.1177/2056305120903408

Westerlund, M. (2019). The Emergence of Deepfake Technology: A Review. Technology Innovation Management Review. Available: https://timreview.ca/article/1282

Yenduri, G., Srivastava, G., Maddikunta, P. K. R., Jhaveri, R. H., Wang, W., Vasilakos, A. V., & Gadekallu, T. R. (2023). Generative pre-trained transformer: A comprehensive review on enabling technologies, potential applications, emerging challenges, and future directions. *arXiv preprint arXiv:2305.10435*.

KEY TERMS AND DEFINITIONS

Deepfake Technology: Any AI-generated or modified images, audio, or video content that portrays real individuals, objects, places, entities, or events, while misleadingly appearing genuine or truthful to viewers

Disinformation: Content that is intentionally produced or distributed, which is evidently false, altered, or misleading. This encompasses organized deceptive behavior designed to intentionally mislead, manipulate, or harm individuals, social groups, organizations, or states.

Generative Adversarial Networks (GANs): Are two competing AI algorithms that generate entirely new images. The first algorithm, called the generator, uses random data to create an image, while the second algorithm, the discriminator, assesses the generated image against known data (such as established visuals or faces). This competitive dynamic drives the generator to produce highly realistic images aimed at deceiving the discriminator.

Illegal Content: Any information that, whether on its own or in conjunction with an activity fails to comply with national and EU law.

Online Platform: A hosting service that stores and distributes information to the public at the request of its users.

Self-Defensive Democracy: The legitimate proactive protection of democratic principles against threats of self-destruction. Its goal is to safeguard the democratic framework from individuals who seek to undermine it through means that contradict democratic values. In essence, the concept of self-defensive democracy functions as a legal deterrent; it is not meant for everyday use but to prevent potential dangers to the democratic order.

Chapter 7
Student Perceptions and Knowledge of Deepfake Technology in North Macedonia

Blagoj Nenovski
http://orcid.org/0000-0001-7093-5133
Faculty of Law, University "St. Kliment Ohridski", Bitola, North Macedonia

Ice Ilijevski
Faculty of Law, University "St. Kliment Ohridski", Bitola, North Macedonia

Angelina Stanojoska
http://orcid.org/0000-0002-0587-1222
Faculty of Law, University "St. Kliment Ohridski", Bitola, North Macedonia

ABSTRACT

This chapter investigates students' perceptions, knowledge, and attitudes toward deepfake technology, including its potential misuse and related protection and reporting mechanisms. The research employs a focus group discussion involving 10 students from five faculties at the University "St. Kliment Ohridski" – Bitola: Faculty of Law, Faculty of Education, Faculty of Technical Sciences, Faculty of Information and Communication Technologies, and Faculty of Biotechnical Sciences. Preliminary findings indicate that while students are generally familiar with the concept of deepfakes, they lack sufficient skills to accurately identify deepfake content. To the best of our knowledge, this is the first study in North Macedonia to examine students' awareness and understanding of deepfake technology. Based on these results, the chapter offers recommendations aimed at enhancing public awareness and improving

DOI: 10.4018/979-8-3693-9601-8.ch007

students' ability to recognize and respond to deepfake materials effectively.

INTRODUCTION

Deepfake technology, powered by artificial intelligence (AI), has rapidly evolved, creating a new landscape of digital deception that poses significant challenges to individuals, society, and institutions. This chapter explores university students' perspectives on deepfakes and their ability to recognize deepfakes by working with a focus group study with students from various faculties. The increasing accessibility of deepfake technology has raised concerns about misinformation, privacy, and ethical implications, making it imperative to assess students' awareness, perception, and ability to detect such content.

As deepfake technology becomes more sophisticated, its societal implications grow more significant. Researchers have identified various threats deepfakes pose, including non-consensual imagery, political misinformation, and cybersecurity concerns. Efforts to counteract these threats include legislation, corporate policies, and educational initiatives. A pilot study examining undergraduate students' ability to detect synthetic media revealed that even educated individuals struggle to identify deepfakes with the naked eye, highlighting the need for improved awareness and training to enhance detection skills (Preu et al., 2022).

As a digitally engaged demographic, students are particularly susceptible to deepfake misinformation. A study investigating their trust in deepfake videos on social media found that user knowledge, the platform, and the uploader significantly influenced their perception of credibility. Conversely, comments and accuracy indicators had little effect. This suggests that while students know deepfakes, they still rely on contextual cues rather than content authenticity in evaluating media credibility (Hilmansyah et al., 2024).

The challenge of deepfake detection extends even to students with a background in computer science. A survey of UK university students tested their ability to recognize deepfake videos on mobile devices. Despite being informed that one of the videos was altered, students struggled to identify the manipulated content, with accuracy levels lower than random guessing (Delchev et al., 2024).

The vulnerabilities of various educational stakeholders to deepfake misinformation have also been explored in the context of scientific communication. A nationwide survey found that 27–50% of individuals, including students and educators, struggled to distinguish real videos from deepfakes. Interestingly, educators demonstrated greater susceptibility to deepfakes than students, underscoring the need for targeted interventions to enhance media literacy among those responsible for disseminating knowledge (Doss et al., 2023).

The role of social media platforms in addressing deepfake misinformation has been another point of investigation. A study analyzing public concerns and perceptions of platform responsibility found that while there is a strong demand for deepfake detection tools, individuals' views on platform accountability vary. Notably, concerns about deepfakes were widespread, but some individuals viewed deepfakes as humorous rather than threatening, leading to differing opinions on regulatory measures (Cochran & Napshin, 2021).

Despite the risks, deepfake technology also presents opportunities for controlled experimentation in social science research. A pilot study explored the use of deepfakes to manipulate variables in an experiment on student perceptions of instructors. The findings suggest that deepfakes can be a valuable tool for scientific studies, allowing researchers to vary experimental conditions while maintaining high levels of control systematically. However, ethical considerations must be carefully managed when using deepfakes in research settings (Eberl et al., 2022).

Recognizing the limitations of human perception, some researchers have explored the potential of targeted training programs to improve deepfake detection. A study on audio deepfakes evaluated whether training undergraduate students in linguistic feature recognition could enhance their ability to discern synthetic voices. Results showed that exposure to structured training significantly reduced uncertainty and improved accuracy in identifying manipulated audio content. This suggests that tailored educational approaches can enhance students' ability to detect deepfakes (Bhalli et al., 2024).

Beyond technical detection, deepfakes raise philosophical and ethical questions regarding authenticity, mimesis, and deception. A study on visual arts students examined their critical thinking and awareness of deepfake imagery. The findings indicated that artistic education plays a role in shaping students' understanding of deepfake implications. However, the ethical debates surrounding deepfake usage remain complex, particularly in creative fields where synthetic media can be both an artistic tool and a source of misinformation (Murillo-Ligorred et al., 2023).

Ethical concerns also extend to the engineers and developers responsible for creating deepfake technology. An experimental study investigated how deepfake exposure influences engineering students' moral reasoning and sensitivity. Analyzing students' attentional and emotional engagement with deepfake content highlighted the need for integrated ethics education within engineering curricula to foster critical discussions on the consequences of AI-generated media (Ramachandran et al., 2023).

One major concern regarding deepfakes is their impact on personal anxiety, particularly among social media users. A study on Egyptian university students revealed that despite their high engagement with social networking sites, their awareness of deepfake threats remained low. The findings also indicated that increased exposure to social media did not necessarily correlate with greater awareness of deepfake risks. However, there was a direct relationship between deepfake awareness and personal anxiety levels (Al-Nimr, 2024).

In our previous work, we addressed the definitions, context and usage of deepfakes, the benefits and positive usage and deepfake threats and criminal activities, the software used to create deepfakes and created a deepfake video example intending to strengthen resilience against deepfakes (Nenovski et al., 2023).

In this chapter, we explore students' perceptions, knowledge, and attitudes regarding deepfake technology, its potential misuse, and the protection and reporting mechanisms it provides.

DEFINITION, CONTEXT, AND MISUSE

Deepfakes, a portmanteau of "deep learning" and "fake," have rapidly evolved from a niche technological curiosity to a powerful and potentially disruptive force in our digital landscape. These artificial intelligence-generated media can create stunningly realistic manipulated videos, images, or audio recordings, often depicting people saying or doing things they never actually did.

The technology behind deepfakes has made significant strides since its emergence in 2017. It relies on sophisticated machine learning algorithms and profound neural networks to analyze and synthesize facial movements, expressions, and voice patterns. The most common techniques include face swapping, facial reenactment, and voice synthesis. As of 2025, the technology has become increasingly accessible, with popular generative AI platforms like Midjourney 5.1 and OpenAI's DALL-E 2 providing widely available tools for creating synthetic media.

Merriam-Webster defines a deepfake as an altered image or recording that misrepresents someone. The term 'deepfake' is loosely defined, prompting research into a multidisciplinary definition (Whittaker et al., 2023), a comprehensive overview of various definitions (Altuncu, Virginia, and Li, 2022), and the need for a clearer definition (Cochran and Napshin, 2021).

Deepfakes are manipulated or synthetic audio or visual media that appear authentic (Van Huijstee et al., 2021). These media feature individuals who say or do things they have never said or done. They are produced using artificial intelligence techniques like machine learning and deep learning. Deepfakes are a subset of AI-generated "synthetic media," including video, audio, photos, and text.

While "deepfake" often carries a negative connotation, the technology also has positive applications. Public tools allow for humorous face swaps among friends or swapping movie actors' faces. In news anchoring, digital twin avatars can present news 24/7. In film production, deepfakes reduce retakes, age or de-age actors, and enhance local content realism. Gaming studios can combine deepfake tech with text-to-speech to achieve varied game outcomes. Advertising can cut marketing costs using this technology. Historical figures can be brought to life in education to illustrate their actions and speeches better.

Modern smartphone users often benefit from basic deepfake technologies, such as "beauty filters" that enhance photos. Advanced deepfakes, like face swaps or speech alterations, can be used legally for critique, satire, entertainment, and more. Constructive uses for deepfakes include audio-visual production, human-machine interaction, video conferencing, satire, artistic expression, and medical research or treatment.

Opposite to positive use, several threats can emerge from using deepfake technology, such as disinformation, defamation (creating videos depicting a victim saying things they have never said), identity theft, AI-generated and manipulated content, etc.

Deepfake videos can pose a significant threat when combined with other criminal acts. One well-known real-life example of deepfake pornography involving a public figure is the case of Taylor Swift. In January 2024, deepfake images of the singer began circulating on the X platform. These images originated from a Telegram group dedicated to generating artificial pornographic content of women. These images of Swift were viewed more than 45 million times during the approximately 17 hours they were live on the platform before being taken down. The incident was so severe that X temporarily blocked searches of Swift's name to prevent further sharing of the images (Gilbourne, 2025).

This case highlights the ongoing challenges posed by deepfake technology, particularly its use in creating non-consensual pornographic content of public figures. It also demonstrates the rapid spread of such content on social media platforms and the difficulties in containing it once released.

RESILIENCE AGAINST DEEPFAKES

Strengthening resilience against the pervasive threat of deepfakes demands a comprehensive strategy that spans technological, legislative, and societal dimensions. The authors believe there are four pillars for strengthening resilience against deepfakes. These are raising public awareness, building, implementing, and using better recognition tools, the media and social media company policies, and the government's regulation and decriminalization. These pillars are all interconnected because higher levels of awareness can lead to better recognition tools and vice versa. Different entities can create recognition tools, but the tools created by media and social media companies can have the best vertical integration with their products. Those companies can be stimulated or pressed with better government acts, bills, and laws, leading to better tools and raising public awareness. Better public awareness can be achieved through educational campaigns, media coverage, workshops, and public service announcements. Considering the difference in demographic, social, and cultural factors, this process has to be implemented with various media channels, social platforms, and technicians to reach a wide spectrum of target audiences.

Robust legal frameworks are imperative, ones that outline clear responsibilities and consequences for those involved in the malicious creation or dissemination of deepfakes. Collaboration at the international and industry levels is essential, fostering information sharing, research, and the development of innovative countermeasures. Continuous research and innovation, along with user empowerment through controls and transparency, round out the multi-faceted approach required to fortify society against the insidious influence of deepfakes.

REGULATION AND LEGISLATION IN THE EUROPEAN UNION AND NORTH MACEDONIA

The creation of a deepfake typically involves personal data, and a deepfake that depicts a natural person can be considered personal data since it relates to an identified or identifiable natural person. Personal data may only be processed under certain conditions since everyone has the right to privacy and data protection. The general rules for processing personal data are laid down in the General Data Protection Regulation (GDPR) (Intersoft Consulting, 2013).

One of the documents concerning the discussion of the deepfakes issue is the resolution of May 19, 2021, on "Artificial Intelligence in Education, Culture and the Audio-visual Sector" (www.europarl.europa.eu, n.d.). This resolution puts forth several proactive suggestions. These encompass the significance of heightening awareness about the risks associated with deepfakes and enhancing digital literacy. It also addresses the growing challenge of identifying and labeling false or manipulated content through technological methods. The resolution urges the Commission to establish suitable legal frameworks governing the malicious creation, production, or distribution of deepfakes. Additionally, it advocates for advancing detection capabilities and enhancing transparency on the content displayed to platform users, providing them with increased autonomy to decide upon the information they wish to receive.

The AI Act is the first-ever legal framework on AI that addresses the risks of AI.

The AI Act (Regulation (EU) 2024/1689 harmonized rules on artificial intelligence) is the first-ever comprehensive legal framework on AI worldwide.

This Act sets a clear set of rules for developers and deployers of AI and has a clear package of policy measures and support for developing trustworthy AI. Furthermore, this legal document will ensure that citizens of the EU can trust what AI offers and address specific challenges.

Recently, the adopted Directive (EU) 2024/1385 on combating violence against women and domestic violence, which criminalizes at the EU level several types of cyberviolence based on Article 83 of the Treaty on the Functioning of the European Union (TFEU).

This directive on combating violence against women should be implemented at the latest by June 2027, sets minimum EU standards for criminalizing several serious forms of cyberviolence, and enhances the protection of and access to justice for victims.

Also, EU legislation on the protection of privacy has an impact on cyber violence. For example, the new Digital Services Act obligates big digital platforms in the EU to remove harmful content from their websites. This is instrumental in removing intimate or manipulated images disseminated on the internet without the person's consent.

In North Macedonia, in 2023, the Criminal Code has been amended (Official Gazette of RNM, 36/23) with important changes to the criminal incriminations covered by the Istanbul Convention, such as including a definition of rape and sexual assault based on consent, including gender-based violence as a special type of homicide; criminalization of stalking, sexual harassment, and female genital mutilation (GREVIO Report, 2023).

The working group during 2022 was developing a completely new Criminal Code with amendments to current crimes and new incriminations. The proposed Criminal Code was available for public discussion through the ENER system, but unfortunately, that was the last step in that process. Until today, the Parliament has not adopted this completely new Criminal code.

One of the new proposed crimes is the incrimination of Unauthorized Distribution of Photographic, Film, and Video Recordings of a Sexual Nature.

This provision explicitly criminalizes the publication of intimate photos or videos without consent, with penalties of up to three years in prison. For acts committed against children, the sentence increases to five years. Given that the provision states that it applies to "an identified or identifiable person," the conclusion is that it could also apply in cases of deepfake content.

METHODOLOGY

To achieve the objectives of the given research, our methodology included a focus group data collection technique. The focus group was chosen as a technique due to its ability to stimulate interactive exchange of opinions and ideas, enabling clarification of individual and group perceptions.

The focus group included 10 students from five faculties at the University "St. Kliment Ohridski" - Bitola (Faculty of Law, Faculty of Education, Faculty of Technical Sciences, Faculty of Information and Communication Technologies, and Faculty of Biotechnical Sciences). Participation was voluntary and anonymous.

Furthermore, the structure of the faculty they are studying at, the year of study, the gender structure, and minimal knowledge of the topic were considered as criteria for selecting the participants.

The focus group discussion was organized on February 11, 2025, in the Amphitheater of the Faculty of Law, lasted 90 minutes, and was recorded and moderated by one of the paper's authors. Students have signed a prior consent for audio recording. The data has been anonymized.

The questions during the focus group were developed about these three segments:

- Introduction and topic overview – Explanation of deepfake technology and examples;
- Discussion and scenarios – Exchange of opinions based on hypothetical cases;
- Reflection and recommendations – Summarizing experiences and suggestions for protection.

For this chapter, a qualitative analysis was performed by grouping the responses into thematic categories to understand the student's attitudes better.

DISCUSSION AND RESULTS

From the focus group discussions, it appears that students generally understand the term "deepfake" and associate it with the application of artificial intelligence. Most believe it involves fake videos and photographs of public figures aimed at creating a false impression or spreading disinformation.

One student said: *"Deepfake technology is always associated with using artificial intelligence to edit voices or photographs to create videos that aim to spread falsehoods."*

The students' general opinion is that deepfake videos and photographs are most often shared on social networks such as Facebook, X, Instagram, and TikTok, as well as on digital platforms like YouTube. However, such content is also frequently shared through communication apps like Telegram, Viber, and WhatsApp.

Students' experiences recognizing deepfakes from authentic content and the characteristics that distinguish them indicate that they could recognize deepfakes, most often through certain characteristics such as voice, details related to body movement, facial expressions, background, etc. However, some of them emphasize that recognition depends on the quality of the deepfake content, the expertise of the creator, and the software used.

One student pointed out: *"I can recognize a deepfake video if I carefully follow visual details, such as eye blinking and mouth movement, which sometimes look unnatural."* While another said: *"When I watch deepfake content, I often pay attention to the background, which can often be blurred or the result of using filters."*

To determine the students' ability to recognize deepfake content, six videos of public figures were shown to them within the focus group (in random order), of which three were authentic, and three were deepfakes.

The first video we played was "You Will Not Believe What Obama Says In This Video!" a famous deepfake video by BuzzFeedVideo (2018) in which actor and comedian Jordan Peele impersonates former President Barack Obama in order to highlight the threat of manipulated videos.

For this video, we received a unanimous response from the students, who believed it was a deepfake video. As specific reasons why they believe it is a deepfake video, the students highlighted: 1: "*he did not know what he was talking about*" 2: "*The movement of his mouth*"; 3: "*The way he held his neck*"; 4: "*what he was saying did not make sense*"

The second video we played was "This is not Morgan Freeman" by the channel Diep Nep. This video has been taken down but reuploaded by various channels, including teknoius (2023), another example of an extremely realistic deepfake, in which students saw a digital replica of Morgan Freeman, who speaks and acts like a real person. The original intent of the video was to demonstrate how far technology has advanced in creating hyper-realistic digital personalities.

Starting from this video, we got different responses from three students who thought it was a deepfake and the others who thought it was an authentic video. Focusing on those who thought it was a deepfake, the students noted the following reasons: 1: "*the facial expressions*", 2: "*the head movement*"; 3: "*the body movement, his chest was filled with air the entire time*" and 4: "*the mouth and head do not seem to match, but it is a more realistic video than the previous one*"

This video had a black background, and we asked the students if their answer was influenced by the black background, to which we received the answer that it was not.

The third video we played was "Boris Johnson's speech on Brexit, AI robots and chicken at the UN," which is an authentic video of Boris Johnson's speech at the UN, which was uploaded by The Sun (2019).

All students considered this video to be authentic without a single suspicious element.

The fourth video we played is an example of a high-quality deepfake created by Metaphysic.ai, which demonstrates advanced technology for generating realistic digital faces through its TikTok channel deeptomcruise (2021). In the video, a fake version of Tom Cruise performs natural movements and speaks with convincing facial expressions, with the face, expressions, and voice being almost indistinguishable from the real person.

The level of realism in this video was confirmed by the fact that only 1 of the students thought it was a deepfake video. In contrast, all the other students thought it was a real video, without a single element that would give the video away as being manipulated by AI.

JOE.ie uploaded the fifth video. (2025) on Facebook containing a sequence of an authentic statement by Donald Trump at the World Economic Forum regarding the level of regulation within the European Union for a specific investment project in Ireland that he had planned in the past.

We had equally divided opinions about this video, with five students thinking it was a deepfake and the other five thinking it was an authentic video.

In this case, a text overlay was displayed over Donald Trump's statement, which makes it different from other videos. We asked the students whether placing the spoken text has an effect on the credibility of the video, that is, whether an authentic video makes it more authentic or whether an AI-manipulated video makes it more credible, to which the students reaction was affirmative. One said, "*Yes, just like we watch movies with subtitles*".

The last video played to the students to determine their ability to distinguish deepfake from authentic videos was an authentic video uploaded by The Telegraph (2020), where The Queen addressed her nation regarding the challenges faced by the coronavirus.

For this video, seven students thought it was a deepfake, and three thought it was an authentic video. One of the students who thought it was a deepfake video received a clarification: "*Only the mouth moved, and everything else was stiff, and there were unnatural intervals of blinking with the eyes,*" from one of the students who thought it was authentic because "*there were normal hand movements.*"

Although students were previously confident that they could distinguish authentic from deepfake videos, the results after showing the videos indicate that it is not that simple. Many of them made mistakes in their answers, identifying authentic videos as deepfakes and vice versa, which may result from the previous discussion.

Surprisingly, none of the students knew about tools for detecting deepfake content and had not used such tools before. Using websites and software that analyze videos to detect altered content is very important.

Students' responses to the question about the potential danger and risks of deepfake technology are primarily directed towards a general opinion that this content is concerning, on the rise, and poses the greatest danger to public figures, especially politicians, artists, athletes, and others. Also, some students said they were concerned about the spread of disinformation and compromising content, which could affect someone's reputation and privacy. On the other hand, potential risks include scams for material gain.

One of the students emphasized: *"What worries me most is that deepfake technology can be used to spread fake news and create false compromising videos that can cause great harm to individuals."*

Although focus group participants stated that they had not been directly affected or victims of deepfake technology abuse, they still believe that the danger exists for every individual; many students believe it is very easy for someone to become a victim with the help of advanced technology. This indicates the existence of a perception of the danger of deepfake technology without specific personal examples that negatively affect students.

Most students were unsure whether there is a specific criminal offense in the Criminal Code of the Republic of North Macedonia that sanctions the abuse of deepfake technology. Some believe that existing criminal offenses, such as blackmail, fraud, or misuse of personal data, can be applied in certain cases.

One female student said: *"I do not know if there is a specific provision for deepfake abuses, but I think a special criminal offense should be added to the Criminal Code, as this technology is becoming an increasingly big problem."*

In the discussion with students in the focus group, it was pointed out that they are not sufficiently informed about their rights and how and where they can report abuse of deepfake technology. Most of them said that the police and public prosecutor's office are the institutions where they would turn in case of deepfake technology abuse, but only if it is a serious case and from where they expect concrete measures to be taken for detection and clarification.

One of the students indicated: *"If I become a victim of deepfake abuse, I will hire a lawyer who would help me with the legal procedure."*

None of the students mentioned the Personal Data Protection Agency, possibly due to a lack of information about its role and competencies in such cases. Non-governmental organizations working on digital rights or initiatives to combat online violence were also not recognized as sources of support and advice on how to proceed.

Students generally agree that platforms like Facebook, X, YouTube, Instagram, and TikTok should take proactive measures to prevent disinformation and abuse with deepfake technologies. The need for cooperation with law enforcement agencies to handle such cases more efficiently was also emphasized.

One female student pointed out: *"Deepfake videos containing disinformation, fraud, or harassment should be removed immediately."* Another student believes: *"Social networks should organize campaigns to inform users about deepfake technology, especially on how to recognize it and report abuse."*

Most of the students from the focus group know the procedures and ways of reporting on social networks. However, they believe that these procedures should be simplified and that there should be greater efficiency in the reaction of administrators.

One student pointed out: *"Reporting from a larger number of people is needed for some content or profile to be removed from social networks."*

Most students believe cybersecurity, media literacy, and deepfake technology should be part of formal education as a separate subject or as part of existing subject programs. They recognize the risks of digital threats and the importance of education in this context. However, there are different opinions on the implementation method.

Although they agree on the need for education, none of the students have attended training or other types of education on detecting deepfake abuses. This may result from the lack of such training aimed at students. Only one student had attended media literacy training where content related to deepfakes was not covered.

Students generally agree that universities should take an active role in education about deepfakes through curricular and extracurricular programs. They believe it is very important for students to be educated on ways to recognize deepfake content. Practical workshops and training on deepfake technology's legal, ethical, and technical aspects would help students acquire specific skills for analyzing and recognizing deepfake videos. They also agree that there is a need to organize student debates and discussions about deepfakes that will help raise awareness about potential risks and ways of protection.

RECOGNIZING A DEEPFAKE

To get a feel for the different levels of realism, we reviewed hundreds of deepfake videos available on platforms like YouTube and videos embedded in websites. It is rare to find videos created with an academic approach from the start, with no regard for the software used, the processing tools, the resources used, the amount of data, or the time spent training the models. Analyzing such videos allowed us to get a picture of the state of deepfake and also list the elements by which a deepfake can be recognized.

Context plays a key role in identifying deepfake content, as the inadequacy of the topic or statements concerning the speaker's expected topics or statements may indicate manipulation. If the video has a discussion, attitude, idea or a topic that significantly deviates from the previously known positions of that speaker, there is reason to doubt its authenticity. This is especially relevant for public figures often present on digital platforms, where their opinions and statements are widely documented, allowing for easier comparison and detection of potential inconsistencies. Through the focus group, we realized that one of the main criteria for students when judging whether a video is a deepfake or an authentic one is context, which is one of the main elements for making the decision.

One of the indicators for recognizing a deepfake is the **inconsistency between sound and image quality**. If a video has high-resolution visuals but the audio sounds unclear, robotic or of lower quality, this may indicate manipulation. This difference often comes from using additional AI-based voice synthesis applications, which can lead to unnatural interruptions, imprecise intonation, or inadequate matching of lip movements with spoken words. In the focus group context, the sound was reproduced by the projector on which the videos were played. In our case, all students were exposed to the same sound quality, but we should note that the sound output can be reproduced on different devices that output different quality.

The inadequacy of **background sounds** concerning the visual content can also indicate a deepfake. If certain activities are observed in the video, but the corresponding sounds are absent or replaced with inappropriate audio effects, this may indicate manipulation. For example, if people are clapping in the scene but that specific sound is missing, or the presence of ambient noise in a quiet room that does not match the surroundings, it is likely that the audio was synthesized or manipulated independently. In our case, we chose videos without background sounds so that students could focus primarily on the speaker's sound. Therefore, we cannot comment on how this focus group would perceive this element in their judgment process.

One of the most obvious indicators of a deepfake is the mismatch between the **mouth movement** and the reproduced audio. If the lips of the speaker do not move naturally following the spoken words, it may indicate that the audio was added or separately synthesized. This mismatch can manifest through delays in opening and closing the mouth, incorrect articulation of certain sounds, or stiff movements that do not correspond to natural human expression. Along with context as an element, mouth movement concerning the sound was also a major decision factor for students in our focus group when deciding on the authenticity of videos.

The intensity and naturalness of **eye blinking** are significant indicators for detecting a deepfake. Sometimes, the speaker may blink less frequently than normal or with a noticeable delay, as the generation algorithms may not reproduce the blinking with natural fluctuation. In other cases, unnaturally frequent or irregular blinking may be observed, creating an artificial appearance. These discrepancies arise from the limitations of deepfake technologies, which, in synthesizing the face, do not always accurately capture subtle and spontaneous eye movements, which can lead to anomalies in the expressions. This feature was a deciding factor for some of the students in the focus group, as one of the main elements in the decision-making process in the case of the Queen video.

The coordination between eye movements, facial expressions, body position, and the message conveyed by the speaker is an important indicator for recognizing a deepfake video. In authentic videos, the eyes naturally follow the movements of the head and body, and facial expressions are aligned with the content of the speech. In contrast, inconsistencies are often observed in deepfake videos, such as when the head turns at an angle, but the eyes unnaturally remain directed towards the viewer. This can create an anomaly where certain movements and expressions are not properly integrated, creating artificial and unconvincing visual effects. In the videos played to the students in the focus group, the speakers mostly had a position in which they were addressing the viewer without significant head movement.

Inconsistencies in the **light sources** and the position of shadows on the face and other elements in the scene can be a significant indicators of a deepfake. If the lighting on a person's face does not match the ambient lighting, or if the shadows are placed at different angles than what would be expected based on the position of the light sources, there is a possibility that the video has been manipulated. This inconsistency can be especially noticeable with uneven face shadows, inappropriate skin reflections, or objects in the background that do not respond properly to the scene's light.

The presence of **blurred** or **pixelated** areas and differences in detail between different elements of the face can indicate deepfake manipulation. Certain areas, such as the cheeks, forehead, or jaw, can appear blurred or have less texture than the other facial features. These anomalies are often absent in the entire video but usually appear in certain frames or during specific head movements and facial expressions. The selected three deepfake videos played to the students are some of the most realistic videos available on the internet, which was confirmed by the ability of students to distinguish deepfake from authentic videos. It should be emphasized that professionals created all three deepfake videos.

The difference in the level of detail between the face and the background can indicate deepfake manipulation. In some cases, the face may appear unusually smooth and without fine textures, while the background remains with a normal level of detail, failing to preserve the natural face characteristics. In contrast, in other cases, deepfake technology can produce a face with excessively sharp details that do not match the background, creating an unnatural contrast. Additionally, suppose there are multiple faces in the video, and the face-swapping technique is applied to only one of the faces. In that case, it is possible to notice a discrepancy in the level of detail between different faces. As with the previous point, the selected deepfake videos were created by professionals with the highest level of realism, which further complicated the task of students to distinguish deepfake from authentic videos.

CONCLUSION

The authors have identified numerous malicious and beneficial uses of deepfake technologies in this chapter. Deepfake technologies become problematic when a creator intends to deceive an audience with malicious intent or influence. The authors conclude that the risks posed by deepfake technologies to society are significant yet contingent on specific contexts. Given their dual-use nature, these technologies should be subject to regulation.

In a world with deepfakes, legal action is one of the hardest things for victims. Furthermore, identifying the creator of one's attack is a serious challenge, as attackers often operate under the veil of anonymity. Additionally, victims may find themselves without the necessary resources to initiate legal proceedings, leaving them vulnerable and exposed.

Deepfake technology is rapidly evolving, making it challenging to anticipate its future trajectory accurately. Nevertheless, visual manipulation is certainly a persistent presence. Quick solutions are currently unavailable, and effectively addressing the risks associated with deepfakes necessitates ongoing contemplation and perpetual learning.

Students demonstrate a general understanding of deepfake technology and its association with artificial intelligence. However, their ability to consistently identify deepfakes is limited, highlighting a gap between perceived and actual skills. There is widespread concern about the potential misuse of deepfakes, particularly in spreading disinformation and compromising individuals' reputations. Despite this awareness, students lack knowledge about specific tools and legal frameworks to combat deepfake abuse. They strongly desire more education on this topic, emphasizing the need for universities to play a more active role in preparing students to navigate this emerging technological challenge.

Based on the results from the focus group discussions, it is clear that a comprehensive approach is needed to address the challenges posed by deepfake technology.

Universities should integrate deepfake awareness and broader digital literacy into their curricula. This could involve developing courses or incorporating these topics into existing subjects.

Furthermore, there is a need to develop and promote user-friendly tools for deepfake detection. Tech companies and research institutions should be encouraged to create and make accessible software to help the average user identify manipulated content. These tools should be accompanied by clear instructions and integrated into popular social media platforms.

On the legal front, policymakers should work on legal solutions to specifically address deepfake abuse. This may involve creating new laws or amending existing ones to cover the unique challenges posed by this technology. Clear guidelines on reporting procedures for deepfake abuse should be established and widely shared.

As the primary channels through which deepfakes are created, shared, and amplified, social media platforms hold a pivotal responsibility in addressing the proliferation of manipulated content. Given their scale and reach, these platforms should be actively encouraged—and where appropriate, regulated—to adopt and continuously improve AI-powered detection systems that can automatically flag potentially deceptive deepfake videos and images. Beyond automated detection, social media companies must also enhance and simplify user reporting mechanisms, empowering individuals to quickly report suspicious content. These combined measures would not only reduce the spread of harmful deepfakes but also foster a safer online environment where trust in digital media can be gradually restored.

In parallel, comprehensive public awareness campaigns are urgently needed to raise the general population's understanding of the nature and dangers of deepfakes. These campaigns should go beyond simply warning about risks—they must equip people with practical skills for identifying suspicious content, encourage critical thinking, and promote a healthy skepticism towards sensational or unverified online media. By integrating media literacy into educational curricula and public discourse, societies can build resilience against manipulation, enabling citizens to navigate the digital landscape with greater caution and informed judgment.

Moreover, combating the deepfake challenge requires a coordinated, multi-stakeholder approach that brings together the expertise and resources of universities, technology companies, law enforcement agencies, and policymakers. Universities can lead cutting-edge research to improve detection technologies and better understand the social impact of deepfakes. Tech companies can implement those innovations at scale while shaping ethical standards for AI use. Law enforcement agencies must be equipped with specialized training and tools to investigate and prosecute malicious deepfake creators effectively. Policymakers play a critical role in crafting clear legal frameworks that balance innovation with protection against abuse. Strong collaboration and continuous dialogue among these actors will ensure that responses to deepfake threats remain agile, comprehensive, and aligned with evolving technological realities.

By actively implementing these recommendations, society can move towards building a more informed, resilient, and prepared public. This approach not only mitigates the risks associated with deepfake misuse but also paves the way for harnessing the positive potential of synthetic media technology in fields such as education, entertainment, and communication. Ultimately, a collective commitment to vigilance, education, innovation, and cooperation is essential to safeguarding trust in the digital age while unlocking new possibilities afforded by AI-driven media.

REFERENCES

Al-Nimr, A. M. I. (2024). The relationship between college students' personal anxiety resulting from deepfake threats and the privacy of social media data management. *The Egyptian Journal of Media Research, 2024*(88), 127–189.

Altuncu, E., Franqueira, V., & Li, S. (2022). Deepfake: Definitions, performance metrics and standards, datasets and benchmarks, and a meta-review. arXiv. org.

Bhalli, N. N., Naqvi, N., Evered, C., Mallinson, C., & Janeja, V. P. (2024). Listening for Expert Identified Linguistic Features: Assessment of Audio Deepfake Discernment among Undergraduate Students. arXiv preprint arXiv:2411.14586.

BuzzFeedVideo. (2018, April 17). You Won't Believe What Obama Says In This Video! YouTube. https://www.youtube.com/watch?v=cQ54GDm1eL0

Cochran, J. D., & Napshin, S. A. (2021). Deepfakes: Awareness, concerns, and platform accountability. *Cyberpsychology, Behavior, and Social Networking, 24*(3), 164–172. DOI: 10.1089/cyber.2020.0100 PMID: 33760667

deeptomcruise. (2021, February 25). I love magic! Video]. TikTok. https://www .tiktok.com/@deeptomcruise/video/6933305746130046214

Delchev, K., Safieddine, F., & Hammad, R. (2024). Identification of AI generated deep fake video by Higher Education Students. Lecture Notes in Networks and Systems, 473–489. https://doi.org/DOI: 10.1007/978-3-031-62281-6_33

Doss, C., Mondschein, J., Shu, D., Wolfson, T., Kopecky, D., Fitton-Kane, V. A., Bush, L., & Tucker, C. (2023). Deepfakes and scientific knowledge dissemination. *Scientific Reports, 13*(1), 13429. Advance online publication. DOI: 10.1038/s41598-023-39944-3 PMID: 37596384

Eberl, A., Kühn, J., & Wolbring, T. (2022). Using deepfakes for experiments in the Social Sciences - a pilot study. *Frontiers in Sociology, 7*, 907199. Advance online publication. DOI: 10.3389/fsoc.2022.907199 PMID: 36524213

Hilmansyah, I., Wiryawan, D., & Hartono, H. (2024). Analysis of student trust in the credibility of Deepfake video information on Social Media. 2024 9th International Conference on Information Technology and Digital Applications (ICITDA), 1–6. https://doi.org/DOI: 10.1109/ICITDA64560.2024.10810015

Intersoft Consulting. (2013) General Data Protection Regulation (GDPR). Available at: https://gdpr-info.eu (Access 9.01.2025).

Jade Gilbourne PhD Candidate in Sociology. (2025, January 29). *Taylor Swift Deepfakes: A legal case from the singer could help other victims of AI pornography*. The Conversation. https://theconversation.com/taylor-swift-deepfakes-a-legal-case-from-the-singer-could-help-other-victims-of-ai-pornography-222113

JOE.ie. (2025, January 24). Video]. Facebook. https://www.facebook.com/reel/28397734073174759

Murillo-Ligorred, V., Ramos-Vallecillo, N., Covaleda, I., & Fayos, L. (2023). Knowledge, Integration and Scope of Deepfakes in Arts Education: The Development of Critical Thinking in Postgraduate Students in Primary Education and Master's Degree in Secondary Education. *Education Sciences*, *13*(11), 1073. DOI: 10.3390/educsci13111073

Nenovski, B., Ilijevski, I., & Stanojoska, A. (2023). *Strengthening Resilience Against Deepfakes as Disinformation Threats*. Poland's Experience in Combating Disinformation.

Preu, E., Jackson, M., & Choudhury, N. (2022, October). Perception vs. Reality: understanding and evaluating the impact of synthetic image deepfakes over college students. In 2022 IEEE 13th Annual Ubiquitous Computing, Electronics & Mobile Communication Conference (UEMCON) (pp. 0547-0553). IEEE.

Ramachandran, V., Hardebolle, C., Kotluk, N., Ebrahimi, T., Riedl, R., Jermann, P., & Tormey, R. (2023). A multimodal measurement of the impact of deepfakes on the ethical reasoning and affective reactions of students

teknoius. (2023, July 23). *This is not Morgan Freeman - A Deepfake Singularity* [Video]. YouTube. https://www.youtube.com/watch?v=cJ80z_CzFRA

The Sun. (2019, September 25). *Boris Johnson's speech on Brexit, AI robots and chicken at the UN* [Video]. YouTube. https://www.youtube.com/watch?v=XaN-MbGV4dY

The Telegraph. (2020, April 5). *"We will succeed": Watch the Queen's speech on coronavirus in full* video]. YouTube. https://www.youtube.com/watch?v=_d1YEkcbFwk

Van Huijstee, M., Van Boheemen, P., & Das, D. (2021). *Tackling deepfakes in European policy*. European Parliament.

Whittaker, L., Mulcahy, R., Letheren, K., Kietzmann, J., & Russell-Bennett, R. (2023). Mapping the deepfake landscape for innovation: A multidisciplinary systematic review and future research agenda. *Technovation*, *125*, 102784. DOI: 10.1016/j.technovation.2023.102784

www.europarl.europa.eu. (n.d.) Texts adopted – Artificial intelligence in education, culture and the audio-visual sector. 19.05.2021. Available at: https://www.europarl.europa.eu/doceo/document/TA-9-2021-0238_EN.html (Access 9.01.2025).

KEY TERMS AND DEFINITIONS

Artificial Intelligence (AI): Refers to the branch of computer science focused on developing systems capable of performing tasks that typically require human intelligence. In the context of deepfakes, AI is used to analyze, learn from, and generate human-like visuals, thus enabling the creation of synthetic media that closely mimics the attributes of real people.

Deepfake: Refers to synthetic media created using artificial intelligence, specifically deep learning and neural networks, to manipulate or generate visual content. It enables the creation of hyper-realistic videos in which individuals appear to say or do things they never actually did.

Disinformation: This refers to the intentional creation of false content to deceive or manipulate an audience. Deepfakes have become a powerful tool for disinformation, particularly in political contexts and on social media platforms, where they can rapidly influence beliefs and behaviors.

Media Literacy: This refers to the ability to critically evaluate media content, identify sources, detect manipulation, and understand the intentions behind media production. In the age of deepfakes, media literacy is increasingly essential for recognizing synthetic content and preventing the spread of manipulated information.

Misinformation: This refers to spreading false or misleading information, regardless of intent. In the case of deepfakes, misinformation can be fabricated videos or audio that distort reality and influence public opinion, political discourse, or individual reputations.

Recognition Tools: This refers to technological solutions, often AI-powered, designed to identify and flag manipulated content. These tools assess audio-visual inconsistencies such as unnatural facial expressions or mismatched voice modulation to detect deepfakes and alert users of potential media falsification.

Regulation and Legislation: These refer to the legal frameworks that address the challenges posed by deepfake technologies. These include provisions in EU law, such as the AI Act and the GDPR, and national amendments like those proposed in North Macedonia's Criminal Code, which seek to criminalize synthetic media's malicious use and distribution.

Social Media Platforms: This refers to platforms such as Facebook, Instagram, X, and TikTok. These platforms are the major distribution channels for both authentic and manipulated content. These platforms are central in spreading deepfakes and are increasingly expected to take responsibility by developing detection technologies and content moderation policies.

Synthetic Media Refers to Content: Synthetic media can include videos, audio recordings, images, and even text. Deepfakes are a subset of synthetic media, often used in contexts ranging from satire and entertainment to deception and disinformation campaigns.

Chapter 8
Combating Misinformation, Disinformation, and Fake News:
A Comparative Study of the USA, UK, and India

Pallav Pallav
http://orcid.org/0009-0005-1753-9891
The West Bengal National University of Juridical Sciences, India

S. M. Aamir Ali
http://orcid.org/0000-0002-8686-0217
Symbiosis Law School Pune, Symbiosis International University, Maharashtra, India

Anuttama Ghose
http://orcid.org/0000-0002-7210-4074
School of Law, Dr. Vishwanath Karad MIT World Peace University, Pune, India

ABSTRACT

The role of digital media in disseminating information has attained a prominent position in society. Though social media and other platforms promise a democratic space, in reality, it has been an easy ground for powerful entities with resources to sow the seeds of propaganda with the help of manipulated information. The dominance of incorrect information in the form of misinformation, disinformation, and fake news is evident. This chapter analyses the scenario of the UK and the USA in

DOI: 10.4018/979-8-3693-9601-8.ch008

brief, with a primary focus on India, which has been the nucleus of the informational crisis, palpable during elections, COVID-19, and in general. Further, the paper attempts to identify the factors that flare up the menace of misinformation, disinformation and fake news on social media. Finally, it delves into the scope of its regulation and attempts to produce possible effective countermeasures to tackle incorrect information on social media.

INTRODUCTION

"Trust what you see" has become obsolete in the current era of information manipulation. One of the elements of free speech is the attainment of truth, which is a fulcrum of societal growth. Neutral and genuine information has unparalleled value in a representative democracy. Democratic values and rights are incomplete without access to genuine information. Technological advances fill the communication void between the masses and the government.Tim Berners-Lee, the creator of the World Wide Web, would not have thought of the possibilities and the unprecedented transformation in which humans communicate. The public's dependency on the internet today is incredible. The internet influences every aspect of human life, whether shopping, travelling, education, etc. Social networking sites are one of the most famous outcomes of internet connectivity, and they are popularly known as social media. Itmay be defined as a means of communication (such as social networking websites and microblogging) via which people create online communities to share information, ideas, personal messages, and other content(WordPress, 2020).It can also be defined as a set of internet-based apps built on the conceptual and technological foundations of Web 2.0, enabling the creation and exchange of user-generated content. Further, we may understand "Web 2.0" asan internet platform that enables interactive user participation (Kaplan & Haenlein, 2010).A wide range of social media exists, like Facebook, Instagram, Twitter, and X, that facilitate communication and interactive user participation. On the other hand, Instant messengers like WhatsApp and Telegram enable mass messaging.

As more and more individuals use these platforms to voice their thoughts and acquire news, the social media arena has emerged as a new forum for public discussion of political and social concerns, with many people engaging in vehement debates.Though social media was initially structured to connect people with increased user participation and a vast audience, it has become an information-dissemination tool.It has become a significant medium for gathering information for the public. Evengovernment bodies and political leaders have turned to social media sites like X to broadcast information. Social media fosters free speech and allows individuals unrestricted power to speak their thoughts, which traditional media lacked. It furtherfills the communication gap between the government and the citizens. But even in nations where views on social media's benefits are generally favourable, the majority nevertheless think it has had some negative consequences, most notably dividing and manipulating society. Anonymity and large circulation have allowed it to be an easy platformto spread propaganda. With the popularity of social media among the public, the concern about widespread incorrect information has arisen. Incorrect information in the form of misinformation, disinformation and fake news has become prevalent on social media.So, we may dividethe chapter into four parts to decode the menace ofmisinformation, disinformation and fake news.

This paper follows this structure: The chapter begins with a history of social media and how it transformed the world. Part II of the chapter reviews the literature on 'misinformation', 'disinformation', and 'fake news'. Social media's role in free speech and information change are covered in Part III of the chapter. It also explains 'misinformation', 'disinformation', and 'fake news'. Part IV of this chapter examines the Indian information crisis and government measures to determine cause and effect. Part V examines the US and UK legal responses to "misinformation," "disinformation," and "fake news," showing how they differ. A conclusion and recommendations in Parts VI and VII conclude the chapter.

METHODOLOGY

This article uses automated framing analysis and textual aspect evaluation to assess how manipulated information affected public behaviour after a national event. The study uses critical discourse analysis to explore how misinformation, disinformation, and false news are used to spread propaganda. To understand the practical ramifications, case studies from various political systems were analysed. The research process stressed ethics and included insights from computer science, political science, sociology, law, and ethics. The chapter also compares legal and non-legal measures taken by different nations to combat misinformation, disinformation, and fake news. The investigation covers US, UK, and Indian legal and non-legal tactics. A regulatory solution for misinformation, disinformation, and false news is proposed after a thorough review of policies and laws.

LITERATURE REVIEW

The word "misinformation" is used frequently in the report to describe inaccurate or misleading material produced or disseminated without necessarily having the intention of misleading. On the other hand, when incorrect or misleading material is known to have been produced and circulated with the intent to deceive, it is referred to as "disinformation." The difference in intent is crucial in drawing the line between misinformation and disinformation. Misinformation can be defined as a larger category encompassing incorrect information on social media.

Media disinformation is nothing new; it has existed since the invention of the first writing systems.Although the meaning of the phrase "fake news" is subject to change, it usually refers to obviously misleading material that is released online with the intention of influencing public opinion(Kurtzleben, 2017). Dr. Claire Wardle and Hossein Derakhshan's (2017) definition of "information disorder" includes misinformation and disinformation as two of its main elements. For information to mislead its audience, it need not be expressly incorrect. Even when the material disseminated is not incorrect in and of itself, the promotion and/or censoring of information on specific subjects may skew audience perception.If used literally, the phrase "fake news" would only refer to content that has been created in a news format with false information intended to mislead regarding its source or veracity(Cunliffe-Jones, et al., 2018)

A significant hindrance in combating fake news information is the inability of academics to reach a consensus on a coherent description of it.Fake news is not a new term, and as early as the fourth century, slander was considered a sin by the early Catholic Church. Slanderers may have had their tongues severed as a form of punishment in ninth-century England. With the development of the printing press in the fifteenth century and the increased dissemination of knowledge that followed, defamation laws began to take on their current form. The appeal of sensationalism was always constant (Burkhardt, 2017).

Before defining fake news, it is imperative to distinguish between fake news, misinformation and disinformation; using the term "news" draws the difference. Prior scholarly works can provide insight into the meaning of the term "news." News can be characterised in various ways, including describing a recent, intriguing, and significant event. News is a product of journalism, a profession that provides "independent, reliable, accurate, and comprehensive information" (Tandoc et al., 2018). The presence of news characteristics makes it different from misinformation and disinformation.

The meaning of fake news could be clearer, which leads to a significant misunderstanding of its true nature. In the effort to overcome this, the term "fake news" may be described as inaccurate narratives, factually skewed reports, or other non-existent occurrences that, in a pseudo-journalistic way, portray "statements of fact" as accurate—that is, as opposed to parodies or opinions. The stories' assertions that aren't supported by objectively verifiable facts are essential to fake news. Since 2016, politicians, headline writers, and the general public have widely used the term "fake news," which, if taken literally, would only refer to fabricated information produced in a news format to deceive about its origins or accuracy, to dismiss a wide range of information as false or biased, without having to state the specifics of the information's errors or its accuracy (Aimeur et al., 2023). Although the broader meaning of "fake news" varies, it usually refers to clearly incorrect information released online to influence public opinion. If the available literature on the subject is considered fake news, it may have multiple definitions based on content, mode, ambit and authenticity (Egelhofer & Lecheler, 2019).The subjects of fake news in India are mainlyrelated to politics, crime, health, religion, entertainment, and miscellaneous things. Text, video, and audio are used in different combinations to generate fake news; with the popularity of short videos, it has been widely used for circulating fake news (Al-Zaman, 2021).

TRANSFORMATIVE EVOLUTION: CHANGING DIMENSIONS OF SOCIAL MEDIA PLATFORMS

To comprehend the information issue, we must first understand the platforms that propagate it so quickly. For years, newspapers were people's main source of news and information and a forum for politicians and other non-politicians to express their views and justify their actions. Thanks to electronic media like radio and television, news and information can reach more people faster and more appealingly. Traditional media outlets have spread false information, but source verifiability and traceability have controlled it. Digital technology changed communication. Social media facilitates information manipulation due to anonymity and a lack of verifiability. It has become a major news distribution and consumption channel.

Social media and digital technologies filled the emptiness and inability of people to actively participate in mass communication. People can freely express their opinions on social media due to its fast-paced environment. It influences crowd psychology and group dynamics well. It disrupted global connectedness and revealed internet behaviour. Since it offers public access to information and active conversation, social media is considered 'inherently democratic'. Another theory is that it encourages democratic public engagement. Even marginalised groups can obtain information and participate in public debates about social, economic, and political changes that affect them.

Further, we may lay down that social media, with easy internet access, created a paradigm shift in the role of the public in the distribution of information. People can now actively participate in developing and disseminating information, whereas in the past, they were mainly passive consumers of content rather than active creators or distributors (Chang et al., 2021). The ability of the user to determine what content in their newsfeed is worthy of being shared and reported acts as a personal gatekeeper.As information sharing, social media allows going beyond the confines of institutional publication and broadcast structures and encourages behaviour that deviates from accepted traditional norms.Social media also increased the direct connection between information providers and their audience, elevating them to prominent figures who were observed to deliberately and carefully craft news stories to pique the interest of their target audience.

Political actors worldwide are using social media for everyday political communication between elections to connect leaders and citizens and re-energise the political landscape. It has made politics more inclusive by allowing those formerly excluded due to geography and demographics to participate directly. It has increased public engagement and perspective diversity to unprecedented levels. Since 2006, Twitter has generated and consumed more news than other platforms. Even the government uses it to spread information. Politicians and government officials utilise it to spread information.

So, we find that the new opportunities brought by digital technology have attracted more public engagement than traditional forms of media.It has been witnessed that the user perceives a blurring of the boundaries between news and social media content.It has been apparent that a growing number of people, particularly those between the ages of 18 and 24, get their news via social media. Facebook and Twitter are currently the most significant social media platforms for news regarding engagement and referrals (Roese, 2018).Social media sites, which may not have been intended to be news outlets when they launched, but became one as the Arab Spring progressed. Twitter feeds from the impacted Middle Eastern nations during the Arab Spring created a narrative that refuted the official government accounts of events and gave accurate pictures of what was officially inaccessible. Social media sites were now viewed as reliable news sources rather than just places for social conversations (Tully, 2014).

Social media was meant to support free speech and, in turn, help the growth of democracy. However, it is generally observed that digital democracy is fiction due to its uneven construction, which allows for the potential to transcend established privileged systems while maintaining and duplicating repressive ones. A louder voice can be bought by anonymous private entities with large sums of money to pay for more space for their thoughts. Not every online voice appeals to the same type of readership (Editorial, 2019). There is a dangerous link between money, anonymity, and technology to sway public opinion, advance their goals, and spread false and misleading information. This relationship is not encouraging for democracy, where dependency on social media for information and news has increased significantly. In addition to allowing the spread of a wealth of actual, genuine content, this indiscriminate liberty in the digital space has also made room for fake news, misinformation, and disinformation. A negative consequence of the Internet's ongoing growth and development is that social media platforms have allowed the spread of false information created by third parties (Flick, 2017).

Menaces of Misinformation, Disinformation, and Fake News in India

India is similarly affected by the information crisis. Instead, ignorance, disinformation, and fake news have spread rapidly. The Indian information crisis challenges free speech and the media. Genuine communication and information flow must be strong. Even a marketplace of ideas that supports free speech as truth would fail in the current environment. Free speech was based on the idea that truth will eventually emerge or real knowledge will outweigh false information. Incorrect information spreads quickly and widely with digital technologies. Before being noticed, it will do the desired damage.Chief Justice of India DY Chandrachud highlighted worries about the "unprecedented proliferation of disinformation and hate speech on the internet," posing a severe challenge to traditional ways of comprehending free speech in a democracy.If basic facts cannot be agreed upon, discourse ends, partisanship deepens, and social cohesion fails. Misinformation, Disinformation, and false news can permanently degrade democratic debate, driving a marketplace of free ideas to the edge of collapse beneath the enormous weight of fake stories (Livelaw News Network, 2023).

Incorrect information is generally targeted to push propaganda. It has been observed that perpetrators are using fake news to target protests in India, whether it was CAA concerns or thewell-knownJNU issue (Sudarsanan & Yamuna, 2020; Sidharth, 2019).A debunked Image of two wrestlers smiling while in a police van being detained during a national protest by female Olympic wrestlers demanding that reports of sexual harassment be looked into was used to weaken the support for the protest among the public (Sukumaran, 2023). Numerous Farmer's Protest 2024-related videos became extremely popular on social media. A video showed that certain individuals received payment for the demonstration, which, after Fact Check, was clarified to be untrue (Mitra, 2024). Even the Supreme Court of India (SCI) is not untouched by the menace. It released a statement warning the public about a social media post allegedly referencing the Chief Justice of India. The bogus post featured a picture of CJI DY Chandrachud alongside a false remark encouraging the populace to resist the government (Livelaw News Network, 2023). Another video of CJI went viral on Facebook, claiming that he left the court while the Solicitor General was making arguments. India Today Fact Check discovered that the accusations going viral are untrue. In the middle of the Solicitor General's arguments, neither the CJI nor the other judges left the room. The court was in session for an additional twenty minutes while the CJI adjusted his chair (Tiwari, 2024).

Combatting Fake News During COVID-19

COVID-19 was unprecedented and unprepared for. Everything was challenged-social, financial, economic, and health. People struggled for subsistence. The pandemic was harder to manage in India due to its large population. The deadly virus broke lockdowns and curfews, terrifying people. India saw an unexpected number of infections and deaths. The situation was exacerbated due to social media misinformation. Before India reported the first COVID-19 case in January 2020, social media networks spread fake information regarding its origins, transmission, and treatment. Misleading web messages and WhatsApp forwards led many to believe that India's heat and humidity would keep the virus at bay.

Fake news coloured with communal aspects to ignite communal hate was persistent from the beginning and continued throughout. A dealer with a particular religious background was allegedly spreading COVID-19, according to an audio tape. The offender played a 6-minute, 42-second audio tape in which he implied that a vegetable merchant was offering low-cost produce with the secret goal of spreading COVID-19. The fact-checking group Boom looked into the audio tape and discovered it was fraudulent (Chang et al., 2021).Next, industry participants used misconceptions about immunity boosters to fight COVID-19 to promote their products. Marketing claims for herbal medicines, handwashing solutions, and masks include immunisation-boosting properties. Due to the lack of correct treatment and knowledge about the virus, internet scammers took advantage of people's worry by advertising coronavirus treatments on social media and e-commerce sites. Most recently, Patanjali Ayurved Limited apologised to the SCI for a false advertisement to cure COVID-19 with their ayurvedic medications.

On March 20, 2020, May 7, 2021, and May 21, 2021, the Indian Ministry of Electronics and Information Technology issued timely advisories ordering all social media platforms to stop spreading false COVID-19 information to prevent public panic. On April 4 and 25, 2022, the Ministry of Information and Broadcasting stopped various YouTube channels, news websites, Twitter accounts, and Facebook pages using its emergency authority under Rule 16 of the Information Technology Rules, 2021. These social media networks promote security misinformation on the ground. One explanation was COVID-19 fake news (Faizan & Hussain, 2022). Rajasthan detained a healthcare practitioner for spreading fraudulent COVID-19 case data. Section 54 of the Disaster Management Act of 2005 criminalises the transmission of false information regarding a disaster's breadth, severity, or other aspects that could scare the public. Multiple FIRs and misinformation, deception, and fake news notices were served to offenders.

Combatting Fake News During the Election

COVID isn't simply when India spreads lies and fake news. Indian politics encourages political material on social media. This lets politicians skip traditional media and address the public directly (Allcott & Gentzkow, 2017). India is the world's largest democracy, and elections celebrate democracy. Political participation and information sharing increase on social media during elections. Social media threatens traditional media election coverage due to its flexibility. Traditional media inadvertently absorbs candidate narratives from social media. Politicians still use Twitter mostly to spread information. This rise exceeds political information. Both pro- and anti-government parties are spreading hate speech, propaganda, and misinformation on social media (Aimeur, 2023). Facebook and Twitter political mobilisation messages and self-expressions may encourage self-directed information-seeking and self-serving behaviour. These communications affect voting. Political disagreements frequently match voter opinions of candidates (Mitchell, 2014). Election preppers spread bogus news in many ways. Fake accounts convey political messages and harm religiously sensitive people. Bots employing algorithms to mimic human social media activity and spread fake news about politicians have also grown. Bots can make internet forums seem more popular by introducing a specific idea. When journalists and media outlets need content, bots are extremely detrimental (Nagumotu, 2022).

To convince the public, the same information is presented from several aspects. Even if social media trending, tweeting, and retweeting can be bought, manipulated, or otherwise faked to make a topic seem popular, they determine the worth and dependability of a piece of information (Olaniran & Williams, 2020). The 2024 Lok Sabha elections saw widespread disinformation. In India, bogus news concerning candidates, corruption, and criminal charges circulated. Social media was full of inaccurate political party makeup, alliance, and horse-trading information. Information about election spending and tax evasion was also frequent. ECI 2024 established a grievance redressal process for unsuitable postings notified to the ECI under the election rules, including Section 126 of the Representation of People Act, 1951. The ECI reported that tech platforms removed many incorrect posts during the election season via grievance redressal. War-like awareness and fact-checking were done. It was crucial to identify and stop misinformation, deception, and fake news before it had an impact (Bhadoria, 2024).

The technology behind fake news, misinformation, and misinforming has improved rapidly. Advanced AI can impersonate anyone, including candidates and voters. It's now easy to create an AI avatar or digital twin of a famous politician and make false claims or promises, so people assume this is the party's manifesto platform (Bhadoria, 2024). Political opponents in Telangana and Madhya Pradesh were defamed via deepfake films. (ET Online, 2024). If we reveal the response, the Election Commission will take several steps to combat misinformation, deception, and fake news. Among its efforts was “Myth vs. Reality”. Each state's authorised officers could request that social media posts be removed under IT Act Sections 69(A) and 79(3)(b). Nearly every state appointed officials to investigate locally fabricated information. Every district received intensive instruction on how to manage this threat from the commission. Despite public knowledge and sensitisation, the Chief Election Commissioner warned that social media is a “marketplace of lies.” He recommended users to “Verify before you amplify.” A Voluntary Code of Ethics ensures free, egalitarian, and moral use of social media to protect election integrity. Facebook, WhatsApp, Twitter, Google, and others voluntarily signed the deal through the Internet and Mobile Association of India (IAMAI) industry organisation (HT Correspondent, 2024).

The Menace of Deepfakes

With the advent of new technology, the mode and ambit of misinformation, disinformation, and fake news have changed. Recently, we have witnessed transformative technology appear in the form of deepfake videos. The scope of its utilisationis dangerous in circulating misinformation, disinformation, and fake news. We must highlight the scope of deepfakes in the information crisis, with possible ways to combat it. The ability to produce deepfakes has become easier to obtain over time. The public can access numerous deepfake projects on GitHub, like TensorFlow, which offers the tools needed for simple deepfake creation. Now, it has become very easy for any individual with basic knowledge of the internet to create and circulate deepfake videos.It's now as easy as following a YouTube lesson to learn how to edit a video and create a deepfake.With technology, the maker of a deepfake film can meticulously alter the subject's actions and words to make him seem like he never did them. While early deepfakes featured explicit content, most current popular deepfakes focus on well-known politicians and online personalities (Ajder, 2020).

Pornographic deepfakes have the potential to seriously affect a person's emotions and mental health and even result in harassment of the video's subject. Such videos of Bollywood actresses appear on the internet and social media platforms. In India, Rashmika Mandanna's phoney video recently became viral; she was seen entering an elevator wearing a black dress. In reality, she is swapping faces with British-Indian influencer Zara Patel in a video (Sukumaran, 2023). This was followed by videos of celebs like Alia Bhatt, Ananya Pandey, etc.According to a survey by LocalCircles, a social media platform and pollster that focuses on problems related to public, corporate, and citizen interest, 25% of all videos that people watch turn out to be fraudulent, as reported by 30% of respondents (Jain, 2023). The effects of the deep fake can be frightening, and the use of this technology during times of crisis can be even more harmful.

The Indian government takes deepfakes seriously, especially during elections, when Instagram reels and YouTube clips are popular. It can easily deceive people and skew election results. Due to legal difficulties, deepfake creators cannot be held accountable for spreading misleading information. Due to the rapid spread of digital content across many web channels, deepfake producers can be hard to find. If platforms don't cooperate, the government will rescind Section 79 of the Information Technology Act of 2000 protections. With the "safe harbour clause," they are protected from legal liability for providing third-party data, information, or communication links. Rule 7 of the Information Technology Rules (Intermediary Guidelines and Digital Media Ethics) Code, 2021 and other IT Act, 2000 legislation partially control deepfakes. Privacy invasion is punishable by posting or sharing images of someone else's private property without permission under Section 66E of the Act. The penalty is an INR 2 lakh fine and three years in prison. Sections 67, 67A, and 67B of the IT Act ban and penalise the electronic publication or transmission of pornographic, sexually explicit, and child-oriented information (Mondal, 2024). The BNS has enticing general measures, but none address deep, bogus video circulation. There are legal remedies for deepfake movies, but law enforcement must act quickly. The Digital India Act, which will replace the IT Act of 2000, is expected to include strong government controls on deepfakes.

Factors Escalating India's Information Crisis and Response

After defining misinformation, disinformation, and fake news in relation to specific events, the response has unfolded. We must now determine what has exacerbated the Indian information crisis and how to respond.

Digital literacy

Despite global misinformation, disinformation, and fake news, India has been impacted hard. Internet access has reached distant areas in India, yet social media misuse awareness is poor. This hinders public efforts to combat misinformation, deception, and fake news. Knowledge of misinformation, disinformation, and fake news would greatly improve information crisis response. The state alone cannot raise awareness of the information issue. State and non-state actors must work together. Social media sites must warn users about information emergencies. Their efforts must go beyond information sharing. They should be used with interactive methods. These should be available in local languages on social media to raise awareness. The state must act, and traditional media should be used to spread awareness quickly.

Technology and criminals' transmission methods are changing, therefore vigilance should be ongoing.

Lack of Critical Thinking

Lack of critical thinking in India exacerbates misinformation, deception, and fake news. Creating the ability to examine information before trusting it helps contradict the claim that it is impossible to make everyone aware and keep up with technological innovation. Rapid information diffusion on digital platforms makes it hard to spot inaccurate material before it reaches the public. Basic public behaviour requires critical thinking and information processing. Most Indians trust social media information due to culture and social behaviour. The age barrier to safeguard minors is insufficient; young children use social media, and improper information might harm their growth. Therefore, the development of critical thinking can be focused on the school level itself; this will not only make it easy to inculcate the skill of critical thinking but also counter the problem of underage individuals getting exposed to incorrect information. Critical thinking should be valued over scientific knowledge since individuals can find any fact with a Google search. Online videos and animations can help understand. It will reduce expert information gathering (Sule, 2020).

Lack of Adequate Information

We will also have to consider that the inability to obtain trustworthy data impedes attempts to combat disinformation, and steps to guarantee increased public access to correct information on significant subjects are a must. Countermeasures to tackle the information crisis can be further made effective by removing the barriers to accessible public access to reliable information that aggravates the impact of misinformation in public. People all throughout the world have inadequate comprehension of a wide range of subjects. This is due to "how they think," their ingrained biases and heuristics, and the information they are exposed to. Access to genuine information for the public disrupts the flow of incorrect information. Ensuring access to trustworthy information is crucial to combating false information. Numerous organisations are making a heroic effort to combat this deluge of false information. An endeavour known as Indian Scientists' ISRC produced several infographics about hoaxes that were supported by in-depth research in response to COVID-19, but these types of actions are required on a permanent basis by different agencies giving genuine information (Sule, 2020).

Role of Industry

Disinformation and fake videos will occur; the key is to stop them before they spread. For monitoring, analysis, tracking, and timely response to such situations, a fast response team is needed (Alt News, n.d.). Multiple parties must work together to tackle the information crisis by identifying and reducing inaccurate information. Other than legal action, Fact-checkers are practical and necessary. In reaction to the social media information crisis, these people fight fake news. Famous companies operating include 'Check4Spam', 'Fact Crescendo', 'Logically Facts', 'Newschecker', 'Newsmeter Factcheck', 'Boom', and 'Alt News'. Many Indian fact-checkers have recently formed associations like the Ekta consortium to share best practices and fight disinformation. The Misinformation Combat Alliance announced the Fact-Checking Network (FCN) in November 2023 to create self-governing standards and best practices for Indian fact-checking NGOs. The coalition has also contacted the Indian government to self-regulate fake news online under the IT Rules, 2021. Google's new About This Result feature provides context for search results and helps people choose websites and content. Google Top News and YouTube prioritise reputable material, and the organisation trains Indian media students and journalists to refute online misinformation. With 11 third-party fact-checking partners in India, Facebook's parent company, Meta, has the most worldwide. In November 2023, WhatsApp announced Check the Facts, a safety program with ten Indian fact-checking NGOs, to prevent misinformation on its network. Media stakeholders have consistently recommended self-regulation to combat misinformation, disinformation, and false news. The effectiveness of self-regulation is questionable. Self-regulation includes creating the Digital News Publishers Association (DNPA). Ten of India's leading media businesses created DNPA in response to the I&B Ministry's efforts to promote the digital space. It even advocated government and association cooperation in addition to self-regulation (Bali & Desai, 2019). Some major drawbacks of self-regulation make its efficacy unclear. The entities' sincerity, not the absence of large participants, makes it pointless. Actions against users must also be enforceable. Some argue that social media's bigger user base indirectly serves the public. Traditional government actions against users that hinder free speech have been taken. This empowers social media companies without responsibility (Balkin, 2018).

State Action

Countering fake news, misinformation, and disinformation requires state action. Legal deterrence is essential for offenders. India has many laws to combat misinformation, disinformation, and fake news, but their efficacy is debatable. Section 505 and its subsections of the Indian Penal Code (IPC) are most relevant to fake news. They prohibit and punish any rumours, statements, or reports that incite fear or alarm, induce an offence against the state, or disrupt public peace. Additionally, materials that incite any group to commit state crimes are included. The section also includes publications, remarks, and stories that create fear or hate. Finally, publishing or distributing rumours or alarming news to incite hostility between groups is likewise punishable under this clause. Indian Penal Code 1860 Sections 153, 499, and 500 can be used to punish fake news that incites riots, defames, or falsely scares the public. To prevent misinformation, use IPC Sections 153 and 295. Sections 153 and 295 allow legal action against bogus news that counts as hate speech. The FIR can be filed for wantonly instigating to cause a disturbance under Section 153 and for inflicting harm or defiling a place of worship to insult any class's religion under Section 295. The IT Act's Section 66D tackles electronic communication offences and can govern fake news (Mahitha, 2021). To bridge legal and Internet advancements, the Information Technology (Intermediary Guidelines and Digital Media Ethics Code) Rules 2021 supersede the 2011 Rules and are framed under section 87(2) of the Information Technology Act, 2000. Code 2021 requires social media platforms to allow users to complain and be heard. The rules have been criticised for being excessive and violating free expression from their beginning, and the judiciary is reviewing the case (Jain, 2024). Recently, the SCI remitted all national challenges to the Delhi High Court for resolution in *Agij Promotion of Nineteenonea Media Pvt. Ltd. v. Union of India* (2021). Other special laws, such as the 1951 Representation of the People Act and the 2005 Disaster Management Act, control fake news, misinformation, and disinformation.

Section 197(1)(d) of the Bharatiya Nyaya Sanhita, 2023, which makes it illegal to create or disseminate false or misleading material that endangers India's sovereignty, unity, integrity, or security, has replaced Section 153B of the IPC. Three years in prison, a fine, or both are the possible penalties for this offence. The following conditions must be satisfied for an action to be prohibited by Section 197(1)(d): i) information must be made or published; ii) it must be "false or misleading"; and iii) it must have the effect of "jeopardising" the "unity, sovereignty and integrity or security of India." Though concerns about the definitional crisis and limited scope of the provision have been raised, the limitation of the provision makes it incapable of tackling a variety of incorrect information circulating online. In the midst of a wide range of false information, it was critical to determine how much of it constituted a crime. It is evident that until the false information poses a threat to India's sovereignty, unity, or integrity or amounts to character assassination, no one can be tried or held accountable for disseminating false information. Other than this, it is apparent that the amended provision is the same product in a new package.

The widespread misinformation, disinformation, and fake news have called for new legislation and rules to regulate them in India. Still, any regulation will come with caution in overstepping the fundamental right of freedom of speech and the press (Mishra, 2008). Therefore, any action must be based on solid research. Maintaining the balance between freedom and curbing the menace of information crises is fundamental.

INTERNATIONAL PERSPECTIVES TOWARDS 'MISINFORMATION', 'DISINFORMATION', AND 'FAKE NEWS'

Now that we have a detailed understanding of the information crisis in India and the factors that have elevated its impact, we must consider different approaches adopted by nations to counter the menace of misinformation, disinformation and fake news.

Self-Regulatory Framework for Misinformation and Fake News in the USA

Thanks to technology, the US has become a hub for misinformation and fake news. Social media and the information crisis are major contributors to democracy's decline worldwide, according to several observers (Gubbala et al., 2022). In the studied countries, 57% said social media has helped their democracy, while 35% said it has hurt it. The US is an anomaly, and there are significant cross-national disparities on this question: Social media has hurt democracy, say 64% of Americans. Only 34% think it's helped. More Americans view social media as divisive, making the US an anomaly (Gubbala et al., 2022). With 64% believing social media has hurt democracy, Americans are the most gloomy. Republicans and independents who lean Republican (74%) are more likely than Democrats and Democratic leaners (57%) to see social media's negative influence on politics (Gubbala et al., 2022).

Due to its media self-regulation model, the US handles the information problem differently from India. The US, like the rest of the globe, struggled to reduce misinformation and fake news. Social media has been lauded for promoting free expression, but it also spreads disinformation. Disinformation begins on fringe platforms in the US and spreads to mainstream social media platforms and traditional media outlets like newspapers and TV. New social media networks often claim to be alternatives to Facebook, Twitter, and YouTube. They oppose free expression limits, they say are everywhere on those platforms (Gubbala et al., 2022). Fake news started on small sites and spread on popular platforms. Following the revelation of favourable Phase III vaccine trial findings in November 2019, fringe sites like 4chan and 8kun saw more talk around the Pfizer COVID-19 vaccine. Many of these talks centred on known conspiracies and disinformation. Russia's state media and pro-Kremlin sites are accused of hiding their sources and authenticity. Some connections spread bogus news and misinformation on Twitter and Facebook, resulting in thousands of interactions (Institute for Strategic Dialogue, 2020). Due to the persistent media attention caused by disinformation, prominent news outlets have tried to reassure Americans about COVID-19 vaccination safety and efficacy (Bond, 2020; Brumfiel, 2021). Even if much of this coverage debunked conspiracy theories and falsehoods, the perpetrators achieved their goal of increasing their visibility.

User reaction studies are needed to understand disinformation and fake news. In answer to questions on the 2020 pandemic and other problems, 915 inventors, developers, corporate and policy leaders, scholars, and activists discussed life in 2025. Their broad and nearly universal view is that people and technology will get closer (Vogels et al., 2021). Misinformation spreads as authoritarians and polarised masses fight each other over information. Many respondents worried most about online disinformation, which uses lies and hate speech to create detrimental attitudes and concerns. They fear significant damage to social stability and cohesion and reduced rational deliberation and evidence-based policymaking (Vogels et al., 2021).

Elections also show the danger of misinformation. Like India, the US faces massive misinformation and fake news during elections. Most Americans (69%) follow 2024 presidential election news closely or somewhat. Additionally, 73% of respondents cited semi-regularly erroneous election news coverage (Misinformation, 2024). The 2024 campaign was full of organised efforts to sway voters, distort perceptions, and persuade people to believe negative things about various candidates in a time when public confidence in news reporters is at an all-time low and new generative AI tools make it easy to create and spread fake narratives, images, and videos (West, 2024). A Haitian man in a video was not Haitian. He claimed to have recently arrived in the US and voted in Gwinnett and Fulton counties, but the video was a Russian fraud (West, 2024). Candidates were personally attacked and misinformed. Democratic candidate Kamala Harris was accused of prostitution work and hitting a young child with a car. The Republican candidate, Donald Trump, was likewise accused of sitting on an incontinence pad on a talk program (Steffen, 2024). Misinformation was even spread through videos. The FBI revealed that two films claiming ballot fraud and Doug Emhoff, the husband of Democratic nominee Vice President Kamala Harris, were false. The fake FBI films with the bureau's emblem received many views from real X users. Similar to ongoing Indian misinformation and fake news campaigns to sway elections. The Department of Homeland Security worried that electoral conspiracy theories would incite domestic radicals. The unanticipated flood of misinformation before the election generated fears about weakening public faith in the results and encouraging violence and threats during the campaign and beyond (Wendling, 2024). Fake news and misinformation from AI were also common during the elections. Microsoft warned in late October that Russian actors are continuing to make AI-enhanced deepfake films targeting Vice President Harris. Harris apparently insulted former President Donald Trump in a video. Another case accuses Harris of poaching in Zambia. Finally, a film misrepresenting Democratic vice presidential contender Tim Walz has over 5 million views on X in 24 hours (Riedel et al., 2024).

International disinformation and fake news are evident in the US. As Americans protested police brutality and racism in June 2020, Russian and Chinese media "piggybacked onto hashtags linked to George Floyd... to push divisive messages and criticise Washington's handling of the unfolding crisis" (Scott, 2020). The Department of Homeland Security issued an Intelligence notice to law enforcement agencies, assessing that foreign enemies had used domestic political tensions for geopolitical aims (Margolin & Bruggeman, 2020). The US administration has repeatedly called disinformation a Kremlin weapon. Russia promotes deception and propaganda to maintain information rivalry. This environment promotes the Kremlin's agenda with bogus news. This lies firehose covers everything. Russian aggression includes human rights crimes, environmental policy violations, assassinations, and civilian-killing bombings (US Department of State, 2024).

The US prefers industry- and user-based information crisis responses. Despite various government efforts to curb misinformation, these have little impact. In preparation for the 2020 election, CISA created Rumorcontrol.gov. By providing accurate election protection information, it pre-emptively exposed and warned of election integrity disinformation (CISA, n.d.). In 2020, Russia's cyber efforts and online actors were able to denounce mail-in voting, highlight alleged irregularities, and accuse the Democratic Party of voter fraud to stoke public mistrust in the electoral process. The "big lie" President Trump told about the 2020 election results increased Russian attempts and damaged voter trust in election outcomes (Sanchez &Middlemass, 2022). Through DARPA, the Pentagon is working with many of the nation's major scientific universities to predict deepfakes. No such advances exist to combat deepfakes and reduce their impact (Knight, 2018). In addition to official intervention, Facebook and Twitter have implemented disinformation interventions after government advisories. Disabling accounts and pages that share misinformation, down-ranking pages, groups, and content associated with misinformation, including warning labels and contextual information on misleading posts, and encouraging users to read articles before posting links are among these interventions. The more mysterious down-ranking action, which reduces misinformation's prominence, may be similar (Gillespie, 2022). Shadow banning damages platform confidence (Malhotra et al., 2023). Unlike platform-led interventions, social media users evaluate misinformation based on interpersonal ties with other users, and the

US relies on this to combat fake news. These answers are promising, a study shows. Experimental research suggests that social media corrective messages can minimise misperceptions, and people are more willing to accept corrections from friends than strangers (Malhotra et al., 2023). However, discussing sensitive topics with other users is challenging. This requires the capacity to spot falsehoods, research factual information, and respond to aggressive confrontations. Political discussions online are often avoided to avoid conflict and relationship harm.

Public reactions to disinformation and fake news activities must also be considered. A survey of 11,178 adults from July 26 to August 8, 2021, found that 48% of U.S. adults now believe the government should limit the spread of false information, even by limiting their ability to access and publish content. It rose from 39% in 2018 (Walker & Mitchell, 2021). Even if it limits Americans' ability to access and post content, 59% of adults feel technology companies should limit disinformation online. Three-quarters of the people (39%) would value freedom of information even if it spreads misleading information (Walker & Mitchell, 2021). Thus, state engagement is needed to combat misinformation and fake news. Using non-state actors alone is insufficient.

The National Defence Authorisation Act (NDAA) established the US Cyberspace Solarium Commission (CSC) in Fiscal Year 2019. It provided a recommendation relevant to our study:

Congress should create a Civic Education Task Force, provide more civic education resources, and raise awareness of foreign disinformation. For easier civic education, Congress should create a Civic Education Task Force. The Department of Justice should finance nonprofits that reveal and explain damaging foreign influence campaigns to Americans. Public awareness of foreign deception is also crucial. A government agency should set and implement transparency requirements with congressional approval. Congress should instruct the federal government to amend the Foreign Agents Registration Act. The US Communications Commission should pass new guidelines to clarify who owns what on social media.

Legislative Regulation of Misinformation and Fake News in the United Kingdom

Ofcom discovered that 71% of individuals who have seen fraudulent or misleading content had done so online. Twenty-one percent had seen deception in newspapers or websites/apps, and 43% on TV. The majority of UK citizens (77%) believe it's vital to check multiple news sources, and 71% understand that online content will always contain both fact and fiction (Ofcom, 2024). Four in ten (44%) think modified stories are less accurate. Additionally, 42% believe traditional news agencies intentionally conceal vital stories. Only 32% think journalists behave ethically (Ofcom, 2024).

This statistic illustrates UK disinformation and fake news. Ofcom's 2023 UK news consumption study shows online platforms' information distribution role. Ofcom's 2023 UK news consumption report found that adults prefer broadcast television. This platform is used by 70% of UK adults. On-demand programming increases this to 75%. Online news is the second most popular in the UK, used by 68%. 47% of UK adults get news on social media. Compared to 83% of 16-24-year-olds who consume news online (Todd & Woodhouse, 2024). Internet disinformation in the UK can be assessed using Ofcom's 2021 discussion paper. From September 2018 to August 2020, UK mobile and desktop traffic to 2,093 trustworthy and 177 fraudulent information websites was examined. False information websites get 14 million monthly visits, while trustworthy ones get 2 billion (Ofcom, 2021). We can assess the response now that disinformation and fake news are rampant in the UK, and social media is a contributor.

Like India, UK media laws are complex. The UK's Office of Communications regulates broadcast media, not online journalism. In addition, UK press regulators IPSO and IMMPRESS supervise only newspapers—both traditional and online—that comply with their terms and conditions, which cover a limited number of publications. Despite their massive regulatory mechanisms, none have taken any significant steps to regulate fake news and misinformation. Additionally, generic laws can be used. Defamation, privacy breaches, and incitement to violence, prejudice, or terrorism against disinformation and fake news may be legal. However, hurdles must be overcome, including meeting claim requirements and addressing jurisdiction and enforcement issues when the publisher is unknown or in a foreign jurisdiction (Mukaddam, 2017).

The UK government has taken significant steps to combat misinformation and fake news. The government created the Counter-Disinformation Unit in 2019. Using publicly available data to assess disinformation narratives and patterns, it focuses on UK-targeted content that may threaten public health, safety, or national security. The government developed an Online Media Literacy Strategy and action plan in 2021. The plan used media literacy to strengthen audience resilience to misinformation and disinformation (Todd & Woodhouse, 2024). The Online Safety Act 2023 is the main response to fake news and misinformation (Cipers et al., 2023). It covers Scotland, Wales, NI, and England. The 2023 Act aims to improve user well-being and internet safety. All regulated services must protect customers from criminal content (Todd & Woodhouse, 2024). Under section 71 of the 2023 Act, category one services—the largest platforms to be identified by secondary legislation—must follow their own misleading policies. Moreover, Section 179 of the 2023 Act creates a new fraudulent communications crime. Section 179(1)(c) makes it illegal to send a message with misleading information that is intended to "cause non-trivial psychological or physical harm to a likely audience." The sender must also have no valid reason for sending the communication.

CONCLUSION

Itcan be concludedthat social media's function has altered as the public relies on it for information. Once confined to linking people, social media is now a crucial medium for information dissemination and collection. Additionally, social media has overcome traditional media's public-viewing limits. Public participation in information production. News is now published and broadcast by social media as well as newspapers and news channels. Social media allows direct government-citizen connection. Government and public leaders now publish information on social media. Flexible and fast information sharing on social media has broadened its reach. Undoubtedly, social media facilitates free expression and journalism.

Misinformation, disinformation, and fake news have flourished on social media. The effect and influence have also increased as individuals rely more on social media for information. Misinformation, disinformation, and fake news are not new, but their reach and impact have grown. Perpetrators use social media because of its anonymity and speedy distribution. Offenders can transmit misleading information to the public before it is discovered because to the ability to forward and share information in a self-maintaining cycle. With cheap and accessible internet, social media has grown in popularity. The study found that diversity, politics, ignorance, and technology have generated social media information crises. COVID-19 and elections show how misinformation, deception, and fake news can influence people. With artificial intelligence and deepfake videos, this power has grown.

The paper shows how several approaches have been used to manage information crises, yet none are sufficient. The US uses self-regulation and industry-based approaches with little official interference. However, the UK and India mix self-regulation with legislation. To counteract misinformation, disinformation, and fake news, the public, non-state actors, and state actors need diverse effectors. Despite its deterrent value, regulation and law alone are insufficient. New rules and restrictions are demanded, but excessive regulation curtailing free expression is still opposed. Any new law or regulation must be founded on research, stakeholder input, and the balance between free expression and countering misinformation, disinformation, and fake news. In the document, various laws are in place, but enforcement bodies must act quickly to be effective. Public and law enforcement awareness is key to neutralising misinformation, disinformation, and fake news. Social media platforms must act impartially and honestly to resolve information crises, and the government must distinguish between regulation and control.

Recommendation

After going through different aspects of misinformation, disinformation and fake news, it is apparent that significant steps are required to counter the information crisis on social media. Both state and non-state actors need a holistic approach to combat misinformation, disinformation and fake news.

1. **Independent fact-checking body**- The issue requires the state to establish an independent and autonomous fact-checking entity. For impartiality, the unit must be independent. Politics in appointments or functioning can hinder the flow of accurate information and promote misinformation.
2. **Legislative Action**- To address the information problem, rules and legislation should contain measures against fake news and misinformation. For all types of fake news and misinformation, the government must create policies. The design must also respect free speech and expression. Sharing bogus news and misinformation in good faith requires a tactful response that is not harsh but reduces its spread. The regulatory system has some mechanisms to combat inaccurate information, but law enforcement's slowness needs to be addressed.
3. **Role of Industry-**Social media platforms must respond quickly on government-established fact-checking recommendations and address non-compliance with strict measures. Self-regulation by social media platforms can combat misinformation, but the government must persuade them to operate honestly. Technology has accelerated the spread of false information. Social media platforms must actively develop technologies to trace the source and identify such activities before they have their intended effects. To combat misinformation, disinformation, and false news, the government must invest in technology for the fact-checking unit and law enforcement.
4. **Awareness and critical thinking-**Combating misinformation requires public participation. Government and social media companies must work together to raise awareness of misinformation, disinformation, and fake news in local languages. Critical thinking should be taught in school to help students decipher inaccurate information. Any government or social media action will only work if people are aware and mindful.

REFERENCES

Aïmeur, E., Amri, S., & Brassard, G. (2023). Fake news, disinformation and misinformation in social media: A review. *Social Network Analysis and Mining, 13*(1), 30. DOI: 10.1007/s13278-023-01028-5 PMID: 36789378

Ajder, H. (2020, July 9). Tracer newsletter #58 (09/07/20)-deepfake threat intelligence: A statistics snapshot from June 2020. *Sensity*. https://medium.com/sensity/tracer-newsletter-58-09-07-20-deepfake-threat-intelligence-a-statistics-snapshot-from-june-2020-1af7052e724a

Al-Zaman, M. S. (2021). Social media fake news in India. *Asian Journal for Public Opinion Research, 9*(1), 25–47. DOI: 10.15206/ajpor.2021.9.1.25

Allcott, H., & Gentzkow, M. (2017). Social media and fake news in the 2016 election. *The Journal of Economic Perspectives, 31*(2), 211–236. DOI: 10.1257/jep.31.2.211

Alt News. (n.d.). *Methodology for fact checking*. https://www.altnews.in/methodology-for-fact-checking/

Anderson, J., Rainie, L., & Vogels, E. A. (2021). *Experts say the'new normal'in 2025 will be far more tech-driven, presenting more big challenges* (Vol. 18). Pew Research Center.

Bali, A., & Desai, P. (2019). Fake news and social media: Indian perspective. *Media Watch, 10*(3). Advance online publication. DOI: 10.15655/mw/2019/v10i3/49687

Balkin, J. (2018). Free speech is a triangle. *Columbia Law Review, 118*(7), 2032–2033.

Bhadoria, S. (2024, February 25). *How AI will be a double edged sword in the upcoming Lok Sabha polls*. Mint. https://www.livemint.com/news/india/lok-sabha-elections-2024-how-ai-will-be-a-double-edged-sword-to-boost-fake-news-curb-voting-manipulations-11708705430974.html

Bond, S. (2020, December 10). 'The perfect storm': How vaccine misinformation spread to the mainstream. *NPR*. https://www.npr.org/2020/12/10/944408988/the-perfect-storm-how-coronavirus-spread-vaccine-misinformation-to-the-mainstrea

Brumfiel, G. (2021, June 14). Anti-vaccine activists use a federal database to spread fear about covid vaccines. *NPR*. https://www.npr.org/sections/health-shots/2021/06/14/1004757554/anti-vaccine-activists-use-a-federal-database-to-spread-fear-about-covid-vaccine

Burkhardt, J. M. (2017). Chapter 1. History of fake news. *Library Technology Reports, 53*(8), 5–9. https://journals.ala.org/index.php/ltr/article/view/6497

Chang, L. Y. C., Mukherjee, S., & Coppel, N. (2021). We are all victims: Questionable content and collective victimisation in the digital age. *Asian Journal of Criminology*, *16*(1), 37–50. DOI: 10.1007/s11417-020-09331-2 PMID: 33042290

Cipers, S., Meyer, T., & Lefevere, J. (2023). Government responses to online disinformation unpacked. *Internet Policy Review*, *12*(4). Advance online publication. DOI: 10.14763/2023.4.1736

CISA. (n.d.). *Election security rumor vs. Reality*. https://www.cisa.gov/topics/election-security/rumor-vs-reality

Correspondent, H. T. (2024, March 17). 'Myth vs Reality': EC lays down steps to curb fake news. *Hindustan Times*. https://www.hindustantimes.com/india-news/myth-vs-reality-ec-lays-down-steps-to-curb-fake-news-101710615785656.html

Cunliffe-Jones, P., Diagne, A., Finlay, A., Gaye, S., Gichunge, W., Onumah, C., Pretorius, C., & Schiffrin, A. (2018). Misinformation: One part of a wider information disorder. In *Misinformation policy in Sub-Saharan Africa: From laws and regulations to media literacy* (pp. 114–117). University of Westminster Press. https://www.jstor.org/stable/j.ctv1v3gqw5.20

Editorial. (2019, February 15). Can social media be democratised? *Economic and Political Weekly*. https://www.epw.in/journal/2019/7/editorials/can-social-media-be-democratised.html

Egelhofer, J. L., & Lecheler, S. (2019). Fake news as a two-dimensional phenomenon: A framework and research agenda. *Annals of the International Communication Association*, *43*(2), 97–116. DOI: 10.1080/23808985.2019.1602782

Faizan, N., & Hussain, E. (2022). Fake news in India during COVID-19: Legal study on the spread of fake news via social media. *Jus Corpus*, *3*(1), 254–273.

Flick, D. (2017). Combatting fake news: Alternatives to limiting social media misinformation and rehabilitating quality journalism. *SMU Science and Technology Law Review, 20*(2), 375. https://scholar.smu.edu/scitech/vol20/iss2/17

Gillespie, T. (2022). Do not recommend? Reduction as a form of content moderation. *Social Media + Society*, *8*(3), 20563051221117552. DOI: 10.1177/20563051221117552

Gov. UK. (n.d.). *Fact sheet on the CDU and RRU*. https://www.gov.uk/government/news/fact-sheet-on-the-cdu-and-rru

Gubbala, R. W. Laura Silver, Janell Fetterolf, Christine Huang, Sarah Austin, Laura Clancy and Sneha. (2022, December 6). Social media seen as mostly good for democracy across many nations, but u. S. Is a major outlier. *Pew Research Center.* https://www.pewresearch.org/global/2022/12/06/social-media-seen-as-mostly-good-for-democracy-across-many-nations-but-u-s-is-a-major-outlier/

Institute for Strategic Dialogue (ISD). (2020, June 25). *Anatomy of a disinformation empire: Investigating NaturalNews.* https://www.isdglobal.org/wp-content/uploads/2021/10/20211013-ISDG-NaturalNews-Briefing.pdf

Jain, D. (2024, March 22). Supreme Court transfers petitions pending before various HCs against its rules 2021 to Delhi High Court. *Livelaw.* https://www.livelaw.in/top-stories/supreme-court-petitions-against-it-rules-2021-transferred-delhi-hc-253147

Jain, S. (2023, November 30). The rise of deepfakes: 25 percent of videos that people watch are later found to be fake. *Forbes India.* https://www.forbesindia.com/article/news/the-rise-of-deepfakes-25-percent-of-videos-that-people-watch-are-later-found-to-be-fake/90077/1

Kaplan, A. M., & Haenlein, M. (2010). Users of the world, unite! The challenges and opportunities of Social Media. *Business Horizons, 53*(1), 59–68. DOI: 10.1016/j.bushor.2009.09.003

Knight, W. (2018, May 23). The US military is funding an effort to catch deepfakes and other AI trickery. *MIT Technology Review.* https://www.technologyreview.com/2018/05/23/142770/the-us-military-is-funding-an-effort-to-catch-deepfakes-and-other-ai-trickery/

Kurtzleben, D. (2017, February 17). With 'fake news,' Trump moves from alternative facts to alternative language. *NPR.* https://www.npr.org/2017/02/17/515630467/with-fake-news-trump-moves-from-alternative-facts-to-alternative-language

Livelaw News Network. (2023, August 14). *Supreme court issues alerts about fake news falsely quoting CJI; it says legal action is being taken.* https://www.livelaw.in/top-stories/supreme-court-issues-alert-about-fake-news-being-spread-falsely-quoting-cji-says-legal-action-being-taken-235161

Livelaw News Network. (2023, December 2). *'There's no market place of facts': CJI DY Chandrachud expresses concerns about online disinformation & hate speech.* https://www.livelaw.in/top-stories/cji-dy-chandrachud-expresses-concerns-about-online-disinformation-hate-speech-243497

Mahitha, D. S. (2021). Social media and its regulations in India. *International Journal of Law Management & Humanities*, *4*(6), 1560–1572. https://doij.org/10.10000/IJLMH.112426

Malhotra, P., Zhong, R., Kuan, V., Panatula, G., Weng, M., Bras, A., Sehat, C. M., Roesner, F., & Zhang, A. (2023). User experiences and needs when responding to misinformation on social media. *Harvard Kennedy School Misinformation Review*. Advance online publication. DOI: 10.37016/mr-2020-129

Margolin, J., & Bruggeman, L. (2020, June 11). Intel bulletin warns of 'malign actors' targeting US over George Floyd fallout. *ABC News*. https://abcnews.go.com/US/intel-bulletin-warns-malign-actors-targeting-us-george/story?id=71184163

Mishra, N. K. (2008). Governmental Threats for Media Freedom : Comparative Study of Asian Countries. *Indian Journal of Poultry Science*, *69*(1), 149–156. http://www.jstor.org/stable/41856399

Misinformation - Research and data from pew research center. (2024, October 10). *Pew Research Center*. https://www.pewresearch.org/topic/news-habits-media/media-society/misinformation/

Mitchell, D.-G. (2014). Here Today, Gone Tomorrow? Assessing How Timing and Repetition of Scandal Information Affects Candidate Evaluations. *Political Psychology*, *35*(5), 679–701. http://www.jstor.org/stable/43783812. DOI: 10.1111/pops.12095

Mitra, H. (2024, February 24). Fact Check: Video claiming farmers joining protest in exchange for money turns out to be fake | Know truth. India Today. https://www.indiatvnews.com/fact-check/fact-check-video-claiming-farmers-joining-protest-in-exchange-for-money-turns-out-to-be-fake-know-truth-2024-02-24-918426

Mondal, A. (2024, March 19). India: Deciphering Deepfakes: Navigating The Legal Implications Of Digital Deception. *Mondaq*. https://www.mondaq.com/india/new-technology/1441788/deciphering-deepfakes-navigating-the-legal-implications-of-digital-deception

Mukaddam, F. (2017). *UK Government seeks to tackle the "fake news" problem*. Global law firm. https://www.nortonrosefulbright.com/en/knowledge/publications/4a0c020f/uk-government-seeks-to-tackle-the-fake-news-problem

Ofcom. (2021, January 27). *Understanding online false information in the UK*. Economist discussion paper series, Issue number 2. Ofcom UK. https://www.ofcom.org.uk/siteassets/resources/documents/research-and-data/economic-discussion-papers-/understanding-online-false-information-uk.pdf?v=325850

Olaniran, B., & Williams, I. (2020). Social media effects: Hijacking democracy and civility in civic engagement. In Jones, J., & Trice, M. (Eds.), *Platforms, Protests, and the Challenge of Networked Democracy* (pp. 77–94). Springer International Publishing., DOI: 10.1007/978-3-030-36525-7_5

Online, E. T. (2024, February 24). Fake Lok Sabha Election schedule alert! ECI warns against misinformation. *The Economic Times*. https://economictimes.indiatimes.com/news/elections/lok-sabha/india/fake-lok-sabha-election-schedule-alert-eci-warns-against-misinformation/articleshow/107965334.cms?from=mdr

Reuters (2021, August 18). *Facebook removes dozens of vaccine misinformation 'superspreaders'*. https://www.reuters.com/technology/facebook-removes-dozens-vaccine-misinformation-superspreaders-2021-08-18/

Riedel, A., Whittaker, L., Barnes, R., & Mulcahy, R. (2024, November 20). *Disinformation and deepfakes played a part in the US election. Australia should expect the same*. The Conversation. http://theconversation.com/disinformation-and-deepfakes-played-a-part-in-the-us-election-australia-should-expect-the-same-243373

Roese, V. (2018). You won't believe how co-dependent they are: Or: Media hype and the interaction of news media, social media, and the user. In Vasterman, P. (Ed.), *From Media Hype to Twitter Storm* (pp. 313–332). Amsterdam University Press., DOI: 10.2307/j.ctt21215m0.19

Roth, Y., & Pickels, N. (2020, May 11). *Updating our approach to misleading information*. X Blog. https://blog.twitter.com/en_us/topics/product/2020/updating-our-approach-to-misleading-information

Sanchez, G. R., & Middlemass, K. (2022, July 26). *Misinformation is eroding the public's confidence in democracy*. Brookings. https://www.brookings.edu/articles/misinformation-is-eroding-the-publics-confidence-in-democracy/ (Sanchez & Middlemass, 2022)

Scott, M. (2020, January 1). *Russia and China target U.S. protests on social media*. Politico. https://www.politico.com/news/2020/06/01/russia-and-china-target-us-protests-on-social-media-294315

Sidharth, A. (2019, November 21). How misinformation is being used to undermine JNU students' protest: Alt News compilation, *Alt News*. https://www.altnews.in/how-misinformation-is-being-used-to-undermine-jnu-students-protest-alt-news-compilation/

Silverman, H. (2019). *Helping fact-checkers identify false claims faster*. Meta. https://about.fb.com/news/2019/12/helping-fact-checkers/

Steffen, S. (2024, July 11). *Fact check: Disinformation's impact on the US election.* Dw.Com. https://www.dw.com/en/fact-check-what-role-did-disinformation-play-in-the-us-election/a-70729575

Sudarsanan, T., & Yamuna, S. (2020). 'Fake news' in India – a legal approach. *International Journal of Law Management & Humanities*, *3*(3), 86–94.

Sukumaran, A. (2023. December 07). Deepfakes: Clear and present danger. *India Today*. https://www.indiatoday.in/india-today-insight/story/deepfakes-clear-and-present-danger-2473187-2023-12-07

Sule, A. (2020). COVID-19 and Infectious Misinformation. *Economic and Political Weekly*, *24*(13), 54.

Tandoc, E. C.Jr, Lim, Z. W., & Ling, R. (2018). Defining "Fake News": A typology of scholarly definitions. *Digital Journalism (Abingdon, England)*, *6*(2), 137–153. DOI: 10.1080/21670811.2017.1360143

Tiwari, S. (2024, March 20) Fact Check: Did CJI walk away while Tushar Mehta was speaking? NO, viral claim is false. *India Today*. https://www.indiatoday.in/fact-check/story/fact-check-did-cji-walk-away-while-tushar-mehta-was-speaking-no-viral-claim-is-false-2516874-2024-03-19

Todd, J. T., & Woodhouse, J. (2024, January 15). *Preventing misinformation and disinformation in online filter bubbles*. UK Parliament House of Commons Library. https://commonslibrary.parliament.uk/research-briefings/cdp-2024-0003/

Tully, S. (2014). People you might know: Social media in the conflict between law and democracy. In Patmore, G., & Rubenstein, K. (Eds.), *Law and Democracy: Contemporary Questions*. ANU Press., DOI: 10.22459/LD.12.2014.09

United States Department of State. (2024, February 8). Disarming Disinformation: Our Shared Responsibility. *Global Engagement Center.*https://www.state.gov/disarming-disinformation/

United States Department of State. (2024, June 7). Russia spreads disinformation to cover up its use of chemical weapons in Ukraine. *Global Engagement Center.*https://www.state.gov/russia-spreads-disinformation-to-cover-up-its-use-of-chemical-weapons-in-ukraine/

Walker, M., & Mitchell, A. (2021, August 18). More Americans now say government should take steps to restrict false information online than in 2018. *Pew Research Center*. https://www.pewresearch.org/short-reads/2021/08/18/more-americans-now-say-government-should-take-steps-to-restrict-false-information-online-than-in-2018/

Wardle, C. (2020, February 23). Essential guide to understanding information disorder. First Draft News. https://firstdraftnews.org/wp-content/uploads/2019/10/Information_Disorder_Digital_AW.pdf:contentReference[oaicite:2]{index=2}

Wendling, M. (2024, November 3). Whirlwind of misinformation sows distrust ahead of US election day. *BBC*. https://www.bbc.com/news/articles/czj7eex29r3o

West, D. M. (2024, November 7). *How disinformation defined the 2024 election narrative*. Brookings. https://www.brookings.edu/articles/how-disinformation-defined-the-2024-election-narrative/

WordPress. 2U. (2020, May 28). The evolution of social media: How did it begin, and where could it go next? *Maryville University Online*. https://online.maryville.edu/blog/evolution-social-media/

KEY TERMS AND DEFINITIONS

Disinformation: Incorrect information in any form, like a picture, video, text, or used in combination with intention or malice to mislead. The very motive of spreading disinformation lies in deception.

Fake News: Fake news is intended to mislead. News—relevant public information—is required. Non-public information about an individual will not be shared as news. Additionally, journalism generates news.

Freedom of Speech and Expression: Article 19 (1) (a) of the Indian Constitution guarantees citizens the right to free speech and expression. This indicates that everyone has the right to express their opinions and thoughts openly.

Misinformation: Incorrect information without intention or malice to mislead. To further simplify, it is just incorrect information, which might be possible because of distorted focus or so on.

Chapter 9
Teaching Media Law in the Era of Disinformation and Hybrid Threats:
Navigating the Infodemic

Vesna Poposka
https://orcid.org/0000-0002-4787-3197
Military Academy "General M.Apostolski", Skopje, North Macedonia

Goran Ilik
https://orcid.org/0000-0003-3501-1386
University "St. Kliment Ohridski", Bitola, North Macedonia

ABSTRACT

This chapter explores the evolving role of media law pedagogy in equipping future media professionals and citizens with the necessary tools to navigate this complex information ecosystem. It argues that traditional approaches to teaching media law, often focused on established legal frameworks, must be adapted to address the novel legal and ethical dilemmas presented by disinformation and hybrid tactics, through application of the fundamental principles on freedom of expression in different contexts and understanding of the strategic environment. By adopting comprehensive approach, media law education can empower future professionals and citizens to become informed and responsible, resilient actors in the fight against disinformation and the protection of democratic values. This chapter concludes by suggesting concrete strategies for curriculum development, pedagogical innovation, and interdisciplinary collaboration to effectively address these pressing challenges.

DOI: 10.4018/979-8-3693-9601-8.ch009

INTRODUCTION

Teaching media law in today's world involves addressing the complexities of disinformation and other forms of hybrid threats. As an evolving and rapidly growing legal discipline where several different legal branches already met, adding the challenges of self-regulation and balance of specific human rights in sensitive constellations, media law enforcement is an outstanding challenge, as crucial part of increased awareness for the need of media literacy trainings on every level of education. That requires understanding hybrid threats as a wider phenomenon that combines conventional and unconventional methods, including disinformation campaigns, cyber-attacks, and political subversion.

The globalization of threats is a growing trend. Attempting to suppress one threat creates others through a domino effect. The different emerging forms and specific morphological characteristics of new security threats contribute to the continuous need to change the approach and response. The crisis of values negatively affects the balance between the imperative of freedom and the need for security, narrowing the liberal space of contemporary conceived societies. The crisis of legitimacy in leadership is a transnational problem and generates the creation of new elites. Contemporary security threats, such as hybrid threats and the fight against disinformation, contribute to reducing the democratic capacity of liberal societies and narrowing the scope of civil rights and liberties. Security crises generate new legal norms and narrow the liberal perimeter. This establishes potential threats to media freedom and human rights and liberties. The global changing environment is harshly changing the media landscape. In times of global deception, the liberal perimeter is narrowing. War in Ukraine, disinformation and hybrid threats, pandemic, and energy crises escalated with the crisis of the values upon which our society has been built. In such times, it is of extreme importance to protect media freedom and freedom of expression in general. Legal frameworks are being developed to address disinformation, but these must be balanced with ethical considerations to ensure they do not become tools for political repression. Navigating these issues requires a nuanced approach that protects both the public from the harms of disinformation and the fundamental right to free expression. Social media platforms have a responsibility to prevent the spread of harmful disinformation, but this must be balanced with the protection of free speech. Over-regulation could lead to censorship and stifle legitimate discourse. Platforms like Facebook, Twitter, and YouTube have implemented various content moderation policies to tackle disinformation. However, these measures are often criticized for being either too lenient or too strict, and for lacking transparency. Different countries have different approaches to regulating social media. For example, the European Union's Digital Services Act aims to create a safer digital space by holding platforms accountable for illegal and harmful content (EP,2021). Advances in AI and machine learning offer potential solutions for identifying and mitigating disinformation. However, these technologies are not foolproof and can sometimes lead to false positives, where legitimate content is mistakenly flagged as disinformation.

Recognized in NATO's Bi-strategic Command Concept 2010 (NATO, 2010) hybrid threats are defined as "those posed by adversaries with the ability to simultaneously use adaptive conventional and unconventional means in pursuit of their objectives".

On the other hand, the media landscape is the bloodstream our society relays on. Media are the blood vessels that enable circulation and keep the system alive. During the Prague Spring of 1968, the call for freedom of the press and speech spread through Czech radio broadcasts. The Iranian revolution of 1979 was promoted through the dissemination of speeches on smuggled tapes. News of the 1989 Tiananmen Square protests in China spread by fax. The Ukrainian Orange Revolution of 2004-2005 was promoted through the use of the Internet and cell phones. At the end of the decade, the tools of social protest shifted to Facebook and Twitter, such as the Iranian post-election protests of 2009, the revolutions in Tunisia and Egypt in 2010 and 2011, and other protests in North Africa and the Arab world. After the Russian invasion of Ukraine, it was Elon Musk who launched Starlink to support the people of Ukraine.

That's why it is of immense importance to create an enabling environment for media development and existence, ensuring that neither extreme would happen to humanity as a whole: censorship, erosion of privacy, misbalance of liberty and security, extreme empowerment of specific elites, and so on. An enabling legal and regulatory environment is essential for guaranteeing freedom of expression and, in particular, media freedom. Laws on defamation, hate speech and other areas, that restrict free speech rights, must be drafted as narrow exceptions to the cardinal principle of the free flow of information and ideas. The concept of press credentialing, which was designed to regulate access and grant privileges to journalists working for traditional media outlets, is facing challenges in the digital age (Lai et al., 2023). As media and journalism studies increasingly focus on multimedia and online journalism, it becomes clear that the traditional press credentialing policy needs to adapt to the evolving landscape of journalism.

LITERATURE REVIEW

Media law is a unique blend of international law, national regulations and self-regulation practices and is one of the youngest legal branches. It remains relatively sparse, particularly when it comes to the post-Primakov era and the influence of geopolitical narratives on legal education. While there is a growing body of work on disinformation and its legal implications, most studies focus on regulatory frameworks, platform accountability, and freedom of expression, rather than on how these issues. Existing publications on media law tends to emphasize traditional press freedom and defamation doctrines, with limited engagement with newer challenges such as influencer culture, algorithmic amplification, and cross-border legal strategies like forum shopping.

The regulation of disinformation presents a complex legal challenge, particularly in balancing the imperative to protect democratic discourse with the fundamental right to freedom of expression. Under Article 10 of the European Convention on Human Rights (ECHR), freedom of expression is a cornerstone of democratic society, yet it is not absolute. The European Court of Human Rights (ECtHR) has consistently emphasized the need for any restriction on speech to be lawful, necessary, and proportionate. Disinformation is not just a media or technology issue, it's a human rights issue because it affects how people live, communicate, and participate in society. The regulation of disinformation presents a complex legal challenge, particularly in balancing the imperative to protect democratic discourse with the fundamental right to freedom of expression All of the above has to be taken into consideration when teaching and learning media law. The limitations of the research are the national legal frameworks and their interceptions with international law, as well as the crosscutting of different legal branches that do have effect directly or indirectly such as civil law, criminal law and telecommunications law.

This chapter seeks to fill that gap by integrating doctrinal legal analysis with pedagogical insights, offering a framework for teaching media law that is responsive to contemporary disinformation dynamics and the evolving digital media landscape.

METHODOLOGY

This chapter adopts legal and doctrinal methodology to explore the evolving landscape of media law education in the context of disinformation, particularly in the post-Primakov era. The analysis is grounded in a close reading of key judgments from the European Court of Human Rights (ECtHR), which serve as a foundational legal framework for understanding the balance between freedom of expression and the regulation of harmful content.

In addition to case law, the chapter draws on normative documents and policy guidelines issued by international organizations, including the Council of Europe, EU, NATO, and the OSCE. These texts provide essential context and guidance on media pluralism, legal harmonization, and best practices for safeguarding democratic discourse in an age of digital manipulation. The inclusion of these materials supports a comparative approach, allowing for the identification of common principles and divergences in regulatory strategies. The chapter also incorporates elements of socio-legal analysis by examining how emerging phenomena—such as the rise of influencers, the practice of forum shopping by media actors, and the algorithmic amplification of disinformation—challenge traditional legal categories and shall be considered when syllabuses are prepared. In absence of strict normative regulation, the same principles that apply to freedom of speech shall be applied in the context drawn by the new security architecture, since democracy is exploited and free speech has been used as a weapon through disinformation and hybrid warfare. Anyhow, the intensity of the threat cannot be justification for narrowing the liberal perimeter and the same principle- no matter how wage they are and how complicated the legal and digital landscape are-still apply. So, anyone who teaches or explores media law or contemporary security threats shall be aware of both sides of the medal. The chapter provides an overview on the key questions that should be discussed in any contemporary curriculum from a pedagogical point of view.

NEW SECURITY ARCHITECTURE

A number of state and non-state actors are using an expanding array of hybrid tactics against democracies, targeting their core values and aiming to fracture society and undermine political decision-making. In Europe, this trend was exacerbated in 2022 and 2023 by Russia's ongoing war of aggression against Ukraine. This has been accompanied by hybrid campaigns against the EU and its partners with the primary goal to erode their unity and solidarity with Ukraine (European Commission, 2023). Beyond the devastation in Ukraine, the war has cast a long shadow over global affairs. The rapidly changing security environment has brought a plethora of non-military measures to the fore. These measures have completely changed the nature of hostilities by giving them a hybrid character. With regard to the South Caucasus region, the chasm among the political courses pursued by particular states makes the overall region more susceptible to diverse external threats of a political, economic, military and cultural nature (Iskandarov and Gawliczek, 2022 p.7-9). One of the critical aspects of hybrid threats is the weaponization of information and narratives. Armenia has witnessed how false information, when strategically disseminated, can have a destabilizing impact on society (Melikyan, 2023). Since there is not a foreseeable ending of the war in Ukraine, Russia will continuously empower the foresights of foreign policy rooted in Primakov's legacy. Power is redefined, and the balance of power is out of balance.

Disinformation as a Module of Hybrid Warfare and NATO's Response

As an official doctrine, hybrid warfare was promoted in 2013 by Russian General Valery Gerasimov pointing out that relations between Russia and NATO are the coldest since the Cold War (McKew, 2017). Disinformation, as the origin of the word, despite having Latin roots, has been taken practically from the Russian version, as a term that has been used since 1923 in the Bureau of Stalin. These instruments of power were later basically taken over by the doctrine of Gerasimov, what we know from 2014 onwards, as part of the hybrid warfare that includes cyber warfare. The doctrine of Gerasimov has been practically inherited from Primankov, his predecessor in the area of foreign policy. It develops as a special kind of warfare or as an instrument of soft power. However, much of what is being treated as a "hybrid threat" is not new at all - but strategy and tactics applied in a new way.

Since 2016, NATO has publicly stated that hybrid actions against one or more Allies could lead to a decision to invoke Article 5 of the North Atlantic Treaty. In 2017 Statement, Janis Sarts, Director of NATO Strategic Communications Centre of Excellence on Russian Interference in European Elections in United States Senate Select Committee on Intelligence referred on electoral interference, stating that election meddling is primarily conducted through:

- Financing pro-Russian candidates and political parties and offering the Kremlin media as platform (Estonian EP elections 2009, French Presidential elections 2017)
- Cyber-attacks against candidates Russia perceives as unfriendly
- Malicious disinformation using social media bots and Kremlin-aligned fringe media outlets (USG,2017)

In 2018, as a response toward ongoing developments in strategic environment, NATO has established counter-hybrid support teams to assist member countries in preparing for and responding to hybrid threats. These teams provide tailored assistance, including strategic communications support, to help countries counter disinformation and other hybrid activities . During the COVID-19 pandemic, NATO detected several coordinated disinformation attacks targeting its presence in Latvia, Lithuania, and Poland. These attacks aimed to undermine the legitimacy of NATO's operations and create fear among the local populations (Poposka, 2024 p.10-12).

Balancing Liberty and Security Needs

The various emergent forms and specific morphological characteristics of new security threats contribute to the continuous need to change the approach and response. The crisis of values negatively affects the balance between the imperative of freedom and the need for security, narrowing the liberal space of the contemporary conceived societies. Democratic values are under attack as a result of the changed security constellation. Legislators are increasingly narrowing the circle around the liberal democratic principles and established values at the heart of European democracies. Just as an example, France as a reaction to a series of terrorist attacks on its territory, adopted drastic legal changes in 2016. Thus, for example, Canada which in 2015 adopted new anti-terrorism legislation, led by a Conservative government, in 2017, led by a Liberal government established new powers for the national electronic surveillance agency. In 2017, a controversial amendment to the German Criminal Code came into effect in Germany, expanding the powers of law enforcement to conduct online searches and sources through telecommunications surveillance ("State Trojan"). Measures adopted by states to counter terrorism often pose serious challenges to human rights and the rule of law. In the name of fighting terrorism, repressive measures are used to stifle the voices of human rights defenders, journalists, minorities, indigenous groups and civil society. Resources normally allocated to social programs and development aid are being diverted to the security sector, affecting the economic, social and cultural rights of many – especially the vulnerable. These practices, especially when taken together, have corrosive effects on the rule of law, good governance and human rights, but also on national security, because they provoke social revolt (Poposka, 2021 p.55-70).

Freedom Of Expression and The Practice Of The European Court of Human Rights, As Well As The Margin Of Appreciation And The Three-Part Test;

Freedom of expression is a cornerstone upon which the very existence of a democratic society rests. It is indispensable for the formation of public opinion. It is also a *conditio sine qua non* for the development of political parties, trade unions, scientific and cultural societies and, in general, those who wish to influence the public. It represents, in short, the means that enable the community, when exercising its opinions, to be sufficiently informed. Consequently, it can be said that a society that is not well informed is not a truly free society" (OAS, 1969).

Freedom of expression is guaranteed under Article 19 of the Universal Declaration on Human Rights (UDHR), and more or less in similar terms under Article 19 of the International Covenant on Civil and Political Rights:

"Everyone has the right to freedom of opinion and expression; this right includes the right to hold opinions without interference and to seek, receive and impart information and ideas through any media regardless of frontiers." (UNGA, 1966)

Freedom of expression is also protected in all three regional human rights treaties, Article 10 of the European Convention on Human Rights (ECHR), Article 13 of the American Convention on Human Rights and Article 9 of the African Charter on Human and Peoples' Rights.

Acknowledgement of the need to balance rights, and to prevent people from using their rights as armaments to attack the rights of others, is echoed in Article 5 of the ICCPR, which states:

"Nothing in the present Covenant may be interpreted as implying for any State, group or person any right to engage in any activity or perform any act aimed at the destruction of any of the rights and freedoms recognized herein or at their limitation to a greater extent than is provided for in the present Covenant". (UNGA, 1966)

That is why, freedom of expression affects the notion of balance as no other right. In this manner, it directly affects the media freedom and media law.

The American Convention on Human Rights in Article 13 settles a wider understanding of freedom of expression, stating that:

"1. Everyone has the right to freedom of thought and expression. This right includes freedom to seek, receive, and impart information and ideas of all kinds, regardless of frontiers, either orally, in writing, in print, in the form of art, or through any other medium of one's choice.

2. The exercise of the right provided for in the foregoing paragraph shall not be subject to prior censorship but shall be subject to subsequent imposition of liability, which shall be expressly established by law to the extent necessary to ensure:
   (a) respect for the rights or reputations of others; or
   (b) the protection of national security, public order, public health or morals."(OAS, 1969).

The European Convention of Human Rights and Fundamental Freedoms by the Council of Europe is considered a "golden standard" when it comes to both the preciseness of definition and positive court practice of the European Court of Human Rights.

Article 10 of the Convention is structured in two paragraphs. The first paragraph defines the freedoms protected while the second stipulates the circumstances in which a state may legitimately interfere with the exercise of freedom of expression.

Paragraph 1 thus provides for three components of the right to freedom of expression:

- freedom to hold opinions.
- freedom to receive information and ideas; and
- freedom to impart information and ideas.

These freedoms must be exercised freely, without interference by public authorities and regardless of frontier.

Freedom to hold opinions is a prior condition of the other freedoms guaranteed by Article 10, and it enjoys almost complete protection in the sense that the possible limitations outlined in paragraph 2 are inapplicable. Moreover, the promotion of one-sided information by the state may constitute a serious and intolerable obstacle to the freedom to hold opinions. Under the freedom to hold opinions, individuals are also protected against possible harmful consequences in circumstances where opinions are credited to them following previous public expressions. The freedom to hold opinions includes the "negative freedom" of not being compelled to communicate one's own opinions (ECHR, 1995).

Scope Of The Freedom Of Expression

The scope of the right to freedom of expression under Article 10 of the European Convention on Human Rights has been a subject of interpretation and debate. While Article 10 of the European Convention on Human Rights guarantees the right to freedom of expression, it is important to understand the scope and limitations of this right (Erickson, 2016). One important aspect of the scope of freedom of expression is its application to artistic and symbolic speech. Artistic expression, encompassing various forms such as visual arts, music, literature, and performance art, is deemed to be an integral part of the concept of freedom of expression (CoE, 2023).

Moreover, Article 10 protects not only the substance of the information and ideas but also the form in which they are expressed. Therefore, printed documents, radio broadcasts, paintings, films, poetry, novels or electronic information systems are also protected under this article. Satirical expression has also been granted special protection by the Court. By the same analogy, it shall apply to the online world and disinformation campaigns.

The "expression" protected under Article 10 is not limited to words, written or spoken, but extends to pictures, images, actions and even cultural heritage intended to express an idea or to present information (ECHR, 2022).

The protection given by Article 10 extends to any expression, notwithstanding its content, disseminated by any individual, group or type of media. Anyone who exercises freedom of expression assumes "duties and responsibilities" and their scope "will depend on the situation and the means used" (ZNM, 2017).

In the last few decades, especially in the post-soviet bloc, a trend of so-called "memory laws" emerged. The term "loi mémorielle" (memory law) originally appeared in December 2005, in Françoise Chandernagor's article in Le Monde magazine. Chandernagor protested about the increasing number of laws enacted with the intention of "force(ing) on historians the lens through which to consider the past" (Le Monde, 2005).

'Memory laws' enshrine state-approved interpretations of crucial historical events and promote certain narratives about the past, by banning, for example, the propagation of totalitarian ideologies or criminalizing expressions that deny, grossly minimize, approve or justify acts constituting genocide or crimes against humanity, as defined by international law (CoE, 2018).

In a polarized word torn by different ideologies and interest, it is extremely hard to keep up the balance among freedom of expression and right of others, since the new security perimeter narrowed the space of liberal values. News from different sides of the globe spread faster than ever, as waves, facing the threat of amplifying the violence shared through the news of public interest.

Denmark's government started toward the criminalization of the public mistreatment of religious objects, setting aside free-speech concerns with what one minister called a "targeted intervention" after a spate of public Quran desecrations caused furors in many Muslim-majority countries (The New York Times, 2023), since after a small group of Danish right-wing nationalists filmed themselves burning copies of the holy book, hundreds of Iraqi protesters tried to storm Denmark's embassy in Iran before security forces detached them. With the draft law proposed, burning a Quran under the new law would be an act punishable by fines or up to two years in prison (Al Jazeera, 2023).

In the United States of America, the legal system is quite different and relies on precedent as a source of law. The extensive court practice refers to developing its freedom of expression doctrine, the Supreme Court has differentiated between the different types of speech in establishing what standards and how much protection each category of speech is afforded. Categories of protected speech include pure speech, symbolic speech, political speech, and commercial speech. Unprotected speech itself can be split into multiple subcategories. Other major pure speech areas in which the Supreme Court has created doctrine, standards, and rules include video games, false statements, social protests, civil liability, and parody (Killion, 2019).

The Three-Part Test

The protection of freedom of expression under any circumstances falls under the same criteria-the three part tests. The Court, in assessing the interference with the freedom of expression, uses the three-part test, which is also used in cases concerning Articles 8, 9 and 11 of the Convention. According to Article 10, paragraph 2, domestic authorities in any of the contracting states may interfere with the exercise of freedom of expression where three cumulative conditions are fulfilled:

- the interference (meaning "formality", "condition", "restriction" or "penalty") is prescribed by law;
- The interference must have a legitimate aim meaning that it is aimed at protecting one or more of the following interests or values: national security; territorial integrity; public safety; prevention of disorder or crime; protection of health; morals; reputation or rights of others; preventing the disclosure of information received in confidence; and maintaining the authority and impartiality of the judiciary.
- Interference is necessary in a democratic society, meaning that the restriction must be necessary to secure one of those aims. The word "necessary" means that there must be a "pressing social need" for the restriction. The reasons given by the State to justify the restriction must be "relevant and sufficient" and the restriction must be proportionate to the aim pursued.

The primary role of Article 10 is to protect everyone's freedom of expression.

The term "margin of appreciation" refers to the space for maneuver that the Strasbourg organs are willing to grant national authorities, in fulfilling their obligations under the European Convention on Human Rights (CoE. Int, 2023). Given the diverse cultural and legal traditions embraced by each Member State, it was difficult to identify uniform European standards of human rights. The margin of appreciation gives the flexibility needed to avoid damaging confrontations between the Court and the Member States and enables the Court to balance the sovereignty of Member States with their obligations under the Convention.

The margin of appreciation is a legal doctrine with a wide scope in international human rights law. It allocates to States a certain degree of discretion in determining whether or not a pressing social need exists and, if so, the measures they take to address it. The doctrine articulates the diversities and enables adaptation of the standard in different contexts. The doctrine also takes into account the very different legal systems in European countries, as well as the different approaches to addressing issues that may be taken even in States with the same legal system (Mc. Bride, 2021). The purpose of the margin of appreciation is to balance individual rights with national interests, as well as resolve any potential conflicts. The margin of appreciation is wider for politicians and public personalities. Different margin of appreciation for politicians and public personalities Statements about politicians can be restricted only when this is necessary.

The first requirement of the three-part test – "provided by law "– will be fulfilled only where the law is available and adequately precisely worded. Prescribed by law means that according to this requirement, any interference with the exercise of the freedom of expression must have a basis in national law. As a rule, this would mean a written and public law adopted by parliament. This requirement also refers to the quality of the law. Ambiguous laws or provisions that leave excessive discretion cannot justify limiting a right. Vagueness about what is and what is not covered by specific regulation, especially in the field of media law will have a chilling effect on media professionals, artists and others who see it as their task to provide information on or comment on matters of public interest. As stated in *The Sunday Times v. the United Kingdom:*

- First, the law has to be adequately accessible: the citizen must be able to have an indication that is adequate in the circumstances of the legal rules applicable to a given case.
- Second, a norm cannot be regarded as a "law" unless it is formulated with sufficient precision to enable the citizen to regulate his conduct: he must be able – if need be with appropriate advice – to foresee, to a degree that is reasonable in the circumstances, the consequences which a given action may entail. Those consequences need not be foreseeable with absolute certainty: experience shows this to be unattainable (ECHR, 1979).

The second requirement – "pursues a legitimate aim " – relates to the legitimate aims cited in the second paragraph of Article 10 of the European Convention of Human Rights and Fundamental Freedoms. Necessary in a democratic society means that the "aim" is that specific interest invoked by the state, such as "national security", "order", "morals", "rights of others", etc. The "means" is the particular measure adopted or enforced against an individual exercising his/her right of expression. To prove that interference was "necessary in a democratic society", the domestic courts, as well as the Strasbourg Court, must be satisfied that a "pressing social need" existed, requiring that particular limitation on the exercise of freedom of expression. The first to assess the existence of a pressing social need are the national authorities.

The third requirement – "necessary in a democratic society" – is often key to the assessment of alleged violations. The word "necessary" means that there must be a "pressing social need" for the restriction. The reasons given by the State to justify the restriction must be "relevant and sufficient" and the restriction must be proportionate to the aim pursued. In the case of hate speech legislation, this means that there must be a clear causal relationship between the expression and that no other procedures which may reasonably be expected to prevent such anger, discrimination or violence that are less restrictive then limitation of freedom of expression are available (ECHR, 1999). Legitimate aim can mean many things, such as national security and territorial integrity, public safety and the prevention of disorder or crime, protection of public health and morals, the protection of the reputation or rights of others, preventing the disclosure of information received in confidence, maintaining the authority and impartiality of the judiciary, etc.

One of the key cases where the ground of "national security" was used to restrict freedom of expression is *Observer and Guardian v. the United Kingdom* (ECHR, 1986). In 1986, the two newspapers announced their intent to publish extracts from Spycatcher, a book by Peter Wright, a retired intelligence agent. A former British spy, Peter Wright, wrote a controversial book of memoirs about his time in MI5. The book was called "Spycatcher" and was due to be serialized in newspapers. The British government tried to stop the book being published in the UK and Australia, on the basis that Wright had violated the duty under his employment contract to keep state secrets confidential. However, the book was published in the USA in July 1987.

At the time of the announcement, the book was not yet published. Mr. Wright's book included an account of alleged unlawful activities by the British Intelligence Service and its agents. He asserted that MI5 had bugged all diplomatic conferences in London throughout the 1950s and 1960s, as well as the Zimbabwe independence negotiations in 1979; that MI5 had bugged diplomats from France, Germany, Greece and Indonesia, as well as Mr. Khrushchev's hotel suite during his visit to Britain in the 1950s; that MI5 had burgled and bugged the Soviet consulates abroad; that MI5 had plotted unsuccessfully to assassinate President Nasser of Egypt at the time of the Suez crisis; that MI5 had plotted against Harold Wilson during his premiership from 1974 to 1976; and that MI5 had diverted its resources to investigate left-wing political groups in Britain (CoE, 2017). The attorney general asked the courts to issue a permanent injunction against the newspapers preventing them from publishing extracts from the book. The Observer and The Guardian complained to the Strasbourg organs against the temporary injunctions. The British Government argued that at the time the temporary injunctions were ordered, the information to which Peter Wright had had access was confidential. Had this information been published, the British intelligence service, its agents and third parties would have suffered huge damage following the identification of agents; the relationships with allied countries, organizations and others would also have been damaged; and they would all have ceased to trust the British intelligence service. The Court further found that the temporary injunctions were justified before the publication of the book but not after this point. Wright had breached his duty to keep state secrets confidential. However, the court also ruled that once the book was published in the USA, it had become public knowledge and so any potential damage to national security was already done. Therefore, the government's attempts to keep banning the book were excessive and violated the papers' right to freedom of expression. Once in the public arena, information on national security may not be prohibited, withdrawn, or the authors of the dissemination punished. States are banned from unconditionally defining as classified all information in the area of national security and, consequently, establishing a prior limitation on access to such information. Some information on national security may indeed be classified where there are serious reasons to believe that national security is endangered by allowing it into the public sphere. Moreover, the classified status of information must be limited in time, and the need to maintain this status must be verified periodically.The interest of the public in knowing certain information should also be considered in the process of classifying or declassifying information related to national security.

Another interesting case where the Court limits media freedom based on national security involves two British newspapers *Guardian News and Media Ltd v AB CD* (ECHR, 2014). A trial for suspected of terrorism was supposed to be kept closed for the media and the general public, so the media outlets reacted toward law enforcement agents and judiciary that it does interfere with media freedom. The court decided that the whole trial could not be made public in the interests of national security. However, the court ruled that – in the interest of open justice – some parts of the trial had to be revealed. The cornerstone case for the practice related to Article 10 was settled in 1979 in the judgment of Sunday Times v United Kingdom discussed above. Thalidomide was a drug taken by many pregnant women to alleviate the effects of morning sickness but it also caused serious birth defects in newborn babies. Between 1958 and 1961, thalidomide was prescribed as a sedative for pregnant women. Several women who took the drug during their pregnancy, however, gave birth to children who suffered from deformities. By November 1961, the manufacturers of thalidomide, Distillers Company (Biochemicals) Limited (Distillers), withdrew all drugs containing this ingredient from the British market. Due to this parent filled actions against Distillers. The parents held that the company was "negligent in the production, manufacture and marketing of the drugs" that seriously harmed the health of the newborn babies. The Sunday Times launched a newspaper campaign for the victims of Thalidomide while the court procedures on a national level were not yet disclosed, so the case was settled on the notion that this campaign may affect the court case and potential settlement with the victims. In particular, The Sunday Times published an article on September 24, 1972, titled "Our Thalidomide Children: A Cause for National Shame" (The Guardian, 2021). The article discussed the settlements and characterized such offers as "grotesquely out of proportion to the injuries suffered." Furthermore, the article criticized English law regarding the recovery and assessment of damages among other things. In a footnote to this article, there was an announcement that another article would be published to uncover in more depth the cause of these birth defects. The European Court of Human Rights ruled that there was a breach of the freedom of expression. There was a major public interest in the case and the public had a right to be informed.

In cases concerning the press, the national margin of appreciation is wider and circumscribed by the interest of democratic society in ensuring and maintaining a free press.

The Concept Of Self-Regulation

Given the role of the media as a government watchdog, the regulation of media activities by the state, the very entity being observed, can be challenging. That is why many states have established self-regulatory mechanisms, which set up specific rules for the media and oversee the compliance of those rules through fellow media organizations and journalists. Self-regulatory instruments can take the form of ethics codes, press and media councils and professional guidelines. The general opposition to regulation, outside the media world, rests on two basic assumptions. The first is that the market is a self-correcting set of mechanisms and that interfering with it will produce distortions, inefficiencies and sub-optimal outcomes. The second is that regulation is an intrusion on individual liberty; that individuals know best what is good for them, and that no external state body should impose such choices on them (Finkelstein and Tiffen, 2015 p.946-948). In the case of media, such theses become even more visible and sensitive. As regards the press, Cohen-Almagor states: "As it is unthinkable to allow other agents of power in society to act without proper professional standards, so it is unthinkable to allow journalists to act with complete freedom and oblivious attitude to risks and harmful consequences (Cohen-Almagor, 2014 p.202-207). Media self-regulation is a joint endeavor by media professionals to set up voluntary editorial guidelines and abide by them in a learning process open to the public. By doing so, the independent media accept their share of responsibility for the quality of public discourse in the nation, while fully preserving their editorial autonomy in shaping it (OSCE, 2008).

The "Chilling Effect" Explained

The chilling effect in the media refers to the self-censorship and fear that journalists and media organizations face because of government censorship and pressure. Media professionals may choose to withhold or alter information due to the fear of repercussions from government authorities (Gürkan, 2017 p.56). This chilling effect can severely compromise the freedom of the press and the ability to provide accurate and unbiased information to the public (Hong et al., 2019). Moreover, the chilling effect extends beyond government interference and includes other factors such as the influence of advertisers and the fear of backlash from powerful individuals or groups. Implicit or explicit censorship by the government can lead journalists and media organizations to self-censor their content, avoiding topics or criticisms that may lead to backlash or punishment. This can have a detrimental effect on the media's ability to fulfill its role as a watchdog and hold those in power accountable for their actions. Furthermore, the chilling effect can create a culture of silence and conformity within the media industry, stifling creativity, critical thinking, and diversity of opinions. The chilling effect can still have a long-lasting impact on public trust and the quality of journalism. When the media is perceived as practicing self-censorship, public trust in the media can be eroded (Stępińska, 2021 p.49-63).

From a legal point of view, the chilling effect may be defined as the negative effect any state action has on natural and/or legal persons, and which results in pre-emptively dissuading them from exercising their rights or fulfilling their professional duties, for fear of being subject to formal legal proceedings which could lead to sanctions or informal consequences such as intimidations, attacks or insult campaigns. State action is understood in this context as any measure, practice or omission by public authorities which may deter natural and/or legal persons from exercising any of the rights provided to them under national, European and/or international law, or may discourage the potential fulfillment of one's professional obligations.

The apparent purpose of licensing schemes is usually to ensure that the task of informing the public is reserved for competent persons of high moral integrity. In practice, however, the power to distribute licenses can become a political tool, used to prevent critical or independent journalists from publishing, contributing to the so-called "chilling effect". For this reason, and simply because the right to express oneself through the mass media belongs to everyone, irrespective of qualifications or moral standing, licensing schemes for media workers are considered to be in breach of the right to freedom of expression (Article 19, 2012).

An important source of legal authority on the subject of licensing schemes is an opinion of the Inter-American Court of Human Rights rendered in 1985. It was accepted in the case that licensing was a restriction on freedom of expression. Costa Rica in that specific case argued that a requirement for journalists to become members of a colegio (association) to perform the journalistic profession was legitimate for three different reasons: necessary for public order; promoting higher professional and ethical standards; and third, because the licensing scheme would guarantee the independence of journalists in relation to their employers (IACHR, 1985).

There is an international consensus that criminal defamation is unnecessary for the protection of reputation and must be abolished given its chilling effect on free expression. In General Comment No. 34 concerning Article 19 of the International Covenant on Civil and Political Rights (ICCPR), the UN Human Rights Committee stated: state parties should consider the decriminalization of defamation, and, in any case, the application of the criminal law should only be countenanced in the most serious of cases and imprisonment is never an appropriate penalty (UN, 2011).

Forum Shopping

Forum shopping refers to the practice of the court or jurisdiction that has the most favorable rules or laws for the position being advocated. A party can forum shop when more than one court has jurisdiction over the dispute, choosing the court that gives it an advantage over the opposing party. The forum most favorable to the applicant's case is not always the forum that is most relevant to the dispute. The term forum shopping refers to the practice of bringing defamation lawsuits before courts where it is easiest to sue and where the likelihood of a favorable outcome is the highest, by playing on any possible connection with the court's jurisdiction. This generates an atmosphere where virtually any court in any country may be chosen to launch a libel suit. Defendants (whether individuals or legal entities, such as media) therefore face heightened levels of unpredictability, which creates a chilling effect on freedom of expression. As forum shopping has become more frequent, and its forms more creative in recent years, the phenomenon presents an important concern (CoE, 2019).

The Influencers

Influencers play a significant role in modern marketing by leveraging their social media presence to promote products and services. Their influence can shape consumer behavior and brand perception, and even sharpen political polarities. Influencers are someone (or something) with the power to affect the buying habits or quantifiable actions of others by uploading some form of original—often sponsored—content to social media platforms like Instagram, YouTube, Snapchat, TikTok or other online channels (The Wired, 2019). It is related to branded content on social media and digital marketing. Facebook and Instagram have a set of brand content policies for influencer marketing and endorsements. Branded content may only be posted through Instagram and Facebook and requires the business relationships between influencers and endorsers to be tagged when promoting branded content. The branded tool provided in the business layout of Facebook and Instagram is to be used whenever promoting products and endorsers. In the United States, the Federal

Trade Commission (FTC) treats influencer marketing as a form of paid endorsement. It is governed by the rules for native advertising, which include compliance with established truth-in-advertising standards and disclosure by endorsers (influencers) and is known as the Endorsement Guides (FTD, 2015).

Besides companies, governments also use influencers. A wide range of the global population, particularly Generation Z (often shortened to Gen Z, colloquially known as Zoomers, referring to the generation born in the mid-to-late 1990s), has been relying on social media influencers for all sorts of information. With millions of followers on their accounts, including Instagram, Snapchat, Facebook and others, influencers have not just been working with brands, but also governments. Countries like Egypt and the United Arab Emirates have been using these influencers to spread a positive image of them (The Guardian, 2021).

Although the industry is moving towards standardizing professional expectations and protections for influencers, there is a need for more consistent global regulations to address the cross-border nature of social media. Regulations vary by country but generally focus on transparency and ethical marketing practices.

User-Generated Content

User-generated content (UGC) means that today, everybody can produce their own media or media-like content and distribute it on the Internet without significant financial investment or technical skills. This does not make user-generated content professional journalism, let alone valuable content, but the basic human right to freedom of expression is not reserved for editorial offices or traditional media outlets. It is important to remember that the right to freedom of expression also applies to individual users and citizens, online as well as offline. There is a huge debate over who should control the user-generated environment. The declining level of state control and government regulation in the media sector should be welcomed, as it removes entry barriers and allows more people to express themselves freely. On the other hand, this trend requires more from the individual user when it comes to self-regulation as well as professional and personal considerations of media ethics. To ensure pluralism in the digital age, these concepts, together with a robust enforcement of the human right to freedom of expression, are crucial to addressing unwanted or offensive content more effectively. There has not yet been a common agreement reached on people's rights and responsibilities on the Internet (PEW, 2020).

User-generated content become an integral part of online platforms, providing diverse perspectives and valuable insights. The increasing complexity of society, the acceleration of social change, and the emergence of advanced digital tools have made user-generated content a key source of rich and timely knowledge in business, science, government, the arts, and many other fields. User-generated content, defined as various forms of digital information produced by the general public has proliferated due to the active participation of individual users across multiple platforms (Song & Tian, 2020).

CONCLUSION

Due to the contemporary environment and asymmetric nature of globalized world, media law is constantly developing and broadening, but it does not get recognition and significance in academic sphere. The core principles that underpin freedom of speech are consistent, but their application can vary significantly depending on the context. Contextual differences may include territorial, temporal, and cultural content. Different countries have varying legal frameworks that define and protect freedom of speech. For example, the First Amendment in the United States provides robust protections, while other countries may have more restrictive laws to balance free speech with other societal values. Cultural attitudes towards free speech can influence how it is practiced and perceived. In some cultures, there may be greater tolerance for controversial or offensive speech, while others may prioritize harmony and respect. The rise of digital platforms has transformed the landscape of free speech. Social media allows for rapid dissemination of information but also poses challenges in regulating harmful content and disinformation. In contexts where national security is a priority, there may be more stringent limitations on speech to prevent incitement, hate speech, or other forms of harmful expression. Some jurisdictions impose restrictions on speech to maintain public order and uphold moral standards. This can include laws against hate speech, obscenity, and defamation. The challenge lies in balancing the right to free speech with other important values such as security, public order, and respect for others. This balance is often achieved through legal and regulatory frameworks that vary by context. Understanding these contextual differences is crucial for effectively navigating and advocating for freedom of speech in different environments. Potential stricter regulation may lead to chilling effects. The chilling effect refers to the phenomenon where individuals or organizations refrain from exercising their legal rights, particularly freedom of speech, due to fear of legal repercussions or sanctions, such as self-censorship and reduced investigative journalism (Bedi, 2021).

As for the aspect of teaching media law and media literacy in the new context, it is of utmost importance to incorporate practical exercise and inspire critical thinking among students. Practical exercises, such as moot courts and similar competitions or simulations, can help students apply legal principles to contemporary issues. Incorporate insights from various disciplines, including political science, cybersecurity, and communication studies. This holistic approach can provide a deeper understanding of how hybrid threats operate and how they can be countered. Invite professionals with experience in media law, cybersecurity, and strategic communication to share their insights. This can provide students with practical knowledge and expose them to different perspectives. Emphasize the importance of ethical journalism and responsible reporting. Discuss the role of journalists in combating disinformation and maintaining public trust. Teach students about strategic communications as a tool to counter hybrid threats. This includes understanding target audiences, crafting effective messages, and using digital technologies to disseminate information responsibly. Media law encompasses the legal frameworks that regulate the dissemination of information. It includes laws related to freedom of speech, defamation, privacy, and intellectual property. Understanding media law is vital for strategic communicators to ensure their practices comply with legal standards and for media literacy educators to teach the legal implications of media production and consumption. Media literacy education often includes an understanding of media law to help individuals navigate the legal aspects of media use. This knowledge is crucial for protecting one's rights and understanding the legal boundaries of media production and consumption. Strategic communicators must be aware of media laws to avoid legal pitfalls and ensure their communication strategies are lawful. This includes understanding regulations around advertising, public relations, and digital communications. Categories such as influencers, UGC and forum shopping must be included in the media law syllabus although case by case analysis has to be done and different rules may apply even within the same category.

By integrating those fields into research and practice, professionals can develop more effective strategies to counter hybrid threats and promote a well-informed, resilient public. The ability to adapt to changing conditions is a key characteristic of resilience. This means being flexible and able to adjust strategies and behaviors in response to new information or evolving threats, and as such, the general concept of building resilience rather than simply intercepting or simply countering the malign narratives is of utmost importance. Resilience involves the capacity to endure and resist the impacts of adverse events, whether they are natural disasters, cyber-attacks, or disinformation campaigns.

A resilient public refers to a community or population that can effectively prepare for, adapt to, withstand, and recover from adverse conditions and disruptions. This concept is crucial in the context of hybrid threats, disinformation, and other challenges. A resilient public contributes to national security by reducing the effectiveness of hybrid threats and disinformation campaigns. When people are informed and prepared, they are less likely to be manipulated by false information. By fostering a resilient public, societies can better navigate the complexities of modern threats and ensure a more secure and stable environment.

Investing in training and capacity building for communication professionals and policymakers is crucial. This includes understanding the principles of strategic communications and how to apply them in different scenarios. Well-trained personnel can better identify and respond to hybrid threats.

Utilizing digital technologies and social media platforms allows for rapid dissemination of information and counter-messaging. This also includes monitoring online spaces to detect and respond to emerging threats. Digital tools can amplify the reach of strategic communications and ensure timely responses to disinformation. Adjusting algorithms on social media platforms to reduce the spread of disinformation and promote credible source. Anyhow, human factor needs to engage as additional filter toward ensuring freedom of speech.

Proactively engaging with the public and stakeholders helps build trust and credibility. This involves regular communication and transparency to preempt and mitigate the impact of disinformation. Developing clear, consistent, and credible messages is essential. These messages should be tailored to different audiences to ensure they resonate and counteract the influence of hostile narratives.

Teaching media law can play a significant role in addressing issues related to disinformation and other forms of hybrid threats in contemporary society through educating students about the legal frameworks governing media and freedom of expression helps them understand their rights and responsibilities. This knowledge is crucial for journalists, media professionals, and the public to navigate the legal landscape effectively. Media law education can provide insights into how laws are designed to balance the protection of free speech with the need to prevent harm, such as hate speech and disinformation. Contemporary curriculums shall include training on how to identify and analyze disinformation as well as providing a general understanding of the legal implications of spreading false information and the tools available to counter it. Media law education can extend to public awareness campaigns and community programs that enhance media literacy. This helps the public critically evaluate information and recognize disinformation. Media law education can also be integrated, beyond legal curriculums, with courses in political science, communication studies, international relations and security studies to provide a comprehensive understanding of how legal principles apply in various contexts.

REFERENCES

Article 19 (2011) General Comment No.34: Article 19: Freedoms of opinion and expression, available at https://www.refworld.org/docid/4e38efb52.html

Article 19 (2012) International standards: Regulation of media workers, available at https://www.article19.org/resources/international-standards-regulation-media-workers/

Bedi, S. (2021). The myth of the chilling effect. *Harvard Journal of Law & Technology, 35*(1). https://jolt.law.harvard.edu/assets/articlePDFs/v35/Bedi-The-Myth-of-the-Chilling-Effect.pdf

Cohen-Almagor, R. (2014). After Leveson: Recommendations for Instituting the Public and Press Council' 19. *The International Journal of Press/Politics, 202*(2), 207. DOI: 10.1177/1940161213516680

Council of Europe. (2023) Council of Europe report on the freedom of artistic expression- Free to create: Artistic freedom in Europe, https://rm.coe.int/free-to-create-council-of-europe-report-on-the-freedom-of-artistic-exp/1680aa2dc0#:~:text=Protection%20of%20freedom%20of%20artistic,rights%20as%20provided%20under%20human

Council of Europe. (CoE. Int) (2023) Margin of appreciation, available at https://www.coe.int/t/dghl/cooperation/lisbonnetwork/themis/echr/paper2_en.asp

Council of Europe (CoE). (2017) Dominika Bychawska-Siniarska, Protecting the right to freedom of expression under the European convention on human rights: A handbook for legal practitioners, https://rm.coe.int/handbook-freedom-of-expression-eng/1680732814

Council of Europe (CoE). (2017) Dominika Bychawska-Siniarska, Protecting the right to freedom of expression under the European convention on human rights: A handbook for legal practitioners, available at https://rm.coe.int/handbook-freedom-of-expression-eng/1680732814

Council of Europe (CoE). (2018) Factsheet on memory laws available at https://rm.coe.int/factsheet-on-memory-laws-july2018-docx/16808c1690

Council of Europe (CoE). (2019) Focus on defamation: a new Council of Europe study draws attention to dangers of 'forum shopping' in defamation cases, https://www.coe.int/en/web/freedom-expression/-/focus-on-defamation-a-new-council-of-europe-study-draws-attention-to-dangers-of-forum-shopping-in-defamation-cases

Đurić, L. (2023) Do Companies Have Human Rights? https://geciclaw.com/companies-human-rights/

ECHR. (1979) case of Sunday Times v. The United Kingdom, 6538/74, Council of Europe: European Court of Human Rights, 29 March 1979, https://www.refworld.org/jurisprudence/caselaw/echr/1979/en/14995

ECHR. (1991) The Observer and Guardian v. The United Kingdom, 51/1990/242/313, Council of Europe: European Court of Human Rights, 24 October 1991, https://www.refworld.org/jurisprudence/caselaw/echr/1991/en/18238

Erickson, K. (2016) Defining the public domain in economic terms: Approaches and consequences for policy, available at https://papers.ssrn.com/sol3/papers.cfm?abstract_id=2777407

European Commission. (2023). Annual progress reports on countering hybrid threats. Retrieved from https://defence-industry-space.ec.europa.eu/eu-defence-industry/hybrid-threats_en

European Court of Human Rights (ECHR). (1976) Handyside v. the United Kingdom, 5493/72, Council of Europe: European Court of Human Rights, 4 November 1976, available at https://www.refworld.org/jurisprudence/caselaw/echr/1976/en/40705

European Court of Human Rights (ECHR). (1995) Vogt v. Germany Application no. 17851/91, https://globalfreedomofexpression.columbia.edu/wp-content/uploads/2021/09/CASE-OF-VOGT-v.-GERMANY.pdf

European Court of Human Rights (ECHR). (2022) Factsheet – Derogation in time of emergency https://www.echr.coe.int/documents/d/echr/FS_Derogation_ENG

European Court of Human Rights (ECHR). (2022) Guide on Article 10 of the European Convention on Human Rights - Freedom of expression https://www.echr.coe.int/documents/d/echr/guide_art_10_eng

European Parliament. Directorate-General for Internal Policies of the Union, Wieworra, L., & Godlovitch, I. (2021). The Digital Services Act and the Digital Markets Act: a forward-looking and consumer-centred perspective, European Parliament. https://data.europa.eu/doi/10.2861/447141

Federal Trade Commission (FTD). (2015) Native Advertising: A Guide for Businesses https://www.ftc.gov/business-guidance/resources/native-advertising-guide-businesses

Finkelstein, R., & Tiffen, R. (2015). When does press self-regulation work? *Melbourne University Law Review*, *38*, 944–967.

Gürkan, H. (2017) The Portrayal of Journalists in Turkish Cinema: A Study about Journalism Ethics through Cinema, available at https://hrcak.srce.hr/file/284649

Inter-American Court of Human Rights (IACHR). (1985) Compulsory Membership in an Association Prescribed by Law for the Practice of Journalism, Advisory Opinion OC-5/85 of 13 November 1985, Series A. No. 5, available at https://www.corteidh.or.cr/docs/opiniones/seriea_05_ing.pdf

Iskandarov, K., & Gawliczek, P. (2022). Economic coercion as a means of hybrid warfare: The South Caucasus as a focal point. Security and Defence Quarterly. Retrieved from https://securityanddefence.pl/Economic-coercion-as-a-means-of-hybrid-warfare-The-South-Caucasus-as-a-focal-point,151038,0,2.html

Jazeera, A. (2023) Denmark proposes bill that could see ban on Quran burnings, available at https://www.aljazeera.com/news/2023/8/25/danish-government-proposes-bill-that-would-ban-

Killion, V. (2019) Cong. Research Serv., The First Amendment: Categories of Speech, available at https://crsreports.congress.gov/product/pdf/IF/IF11072

Lai, K., Queiroz, L., Shmerko, V., Sundberg, K., & Yanushkevich, S. (2023) Post-Pandemic Follow-Up Audit of Security Checkpoints.

McBride, J. (2021) The doctrines and methodology on the interpretation of European Convention on Human Rights by the European Court of Human Rights, Council of Europe, https://rm.coe.int/echr-eng-the-doctrines-and-methodology-of-interpretation-of-the-europe/1680a20aee

McKew, M. (2017) "The Gerasimov Doctrine" https://www.politico.eu/article/new-battles-cyberwarfare-russia/

Melikyan, G. (2023) Commentary: Navigating Hybrid Threats in the South Caucasus,available at https://www.commonspace.eu/commentary/commentary-navigating-hybrid-threats-south-caucasus

Miklaucic, M. (2011) NATO countering the hybrid threat https://www.act.nato.int/nato-countering-the-hybrid-threat

Monde, L. (2005) L'enfer des bonnes intentions, par Françoise Chandernagor https://www.lemonde.fr/idees/article/2005/12/16/l-enfer-des-bonnes-intentions-par-francoise-chandernagor_722124_3232.html

NATO. (2010) NATO's Bi-Strategic Command Capstone Concept of 2010 https://www.act.nato.int/images/stories/events/2010/20100826_bi-sc_cht.pdf

Organization of American States (OAS). (1969) "American Convention on Human Rights." Treaty Series, No. 36

OSCE. (2008) The Media Self-Regulation Guidebook, available at https://www.osce.org/files/f/documents/1/d/31497.pdf

PEW Research Centre. (2020) Concerns about democracy in the digital age, available at https://www.pewresearch.org/internet/2020/02/21/concerns-about-democracy-in-the-digital-age/

Poposka, V. (2021). *Меѓународно-правни аспекти за заштита на критичната инфраструктура од современи безбедносни закани, " International Legal Aspects of the Critical Infrastructure Protection Against Contemporary Security Threats"- published by International Vision University*. North Macedonia.

Poposka, V. (2024) A Primer on Hybrid Threats to Critical Infrastructurepublished by PRESPA Institute, available at http://www.prespa-institute.mk/wp-content/uploads/2024/02/EN_Informirana-odbrana_01.pdf

Song, Y., & Tian, X. (2020). Managerial Responses and Customer Engagement in Crowdfunding. *Sustainability (Basel)*, *12*(8), 3389. DOI: 10.3390/su12083389

Stępińska, A. (2021). Factors Affecting Self-Censorship Among Polish Journalists. *Zeszyty Prasoznawcze*, *64*(2 (246)), 49–63. DOI: 10.4467/22996362PZ.21.010.13475

The Guardian. (2016) How Facebook powers money machines for obscure political 'news' sites, available at https://www.theguardian.com/technology/2016/aug/24/facebook-clickbait-political-news-sites-us-election-trump

The Guardian. (2021) Sugar-coated propaganda? Middle East taps into power of influencers, https://www.theguardian.com/world/2021/jan/29/sugar-coated-propaganda-egypt-taps-into-power-instagram-influencers

The New York Times. (2023) Denmark Moves to ban Quran Burning after Muslim Outrage, available at https://www.nytimes.com/2023/08/25/world/europe/denmark-quran-burning.html

The Wired. (2019) The WIRED Guide to Influencers - Everything you need to know about engagement, power likes, sponcon, and trust available at https://www.wired.com/story/what-is-an-influencer/

United Nations. (General Assembly) (1966) "International Covenant on Civil and Political Rights." https://www.equalityhumanrights.com/en/our-human-rights-work/monitoring-and-promoting-un-treaties/international-covenant-civil-and#:~:text=ICCPR%20is%20an%20international%20human,fair%20trial%20rights

USG (United States Government Office) Russian intervention in European elections hearing before the select committee on intelligence of the United States Senat, one hundred fifteenth congress, first session Wednesday, june 28, 2017 available at https://www.intelligence.senate.gov/wp-content/uploads/2024/08/sites-default-files-hearings-s-hrg-115-105.pdf

ZNM. (2017) Freedom of expression through the practice of the European Court of Human Rights https://znm.org.mk/wp-content/uploads/2020/04/Freedom-of-expression-through-the-practice-of-the-European-Court-for-Human-Rights-December-2017.pdf

KEY TERMS AND DEFINITIONS

Disinformation: A form of hybrid threat refers to the deliberate spread of false or misleading information by state or non-state actors to destabilize societies, manipulate public opinion, and undermine democratic institutions—all without engaging in open warfare.

Freedom of Expression: A fundamental human right that protects every individual's ability to seek, receive, and share information and ideas of all kinds, regardless of frontiers, through any media—whether spoken, written, artistic, or digital.

Hybrid Threat: Any strategy that blends conventional and unconventional tactics, including cyberattacks, economic pressure, and information warfare, to achieve political or strategic goals.

Media Law: A law that regulates media production and use. Media law can encompass many different types of media including broadcast television, internet and print media. The practice of media law may involve all of the types of legal issues that might arise during the production or consumption of various types of media.

Media Self-Regulation: Refers to the process by which media organizations and professionals establish and enforce their own standards and codes of conduct, rather than being governed solely by external laws or government regulations.

Syllabus: A document that outlines the structure, content, and expectations of a course. It serves as a contract between the instructor and students, providing essential information about what will be taught and how the course will be conducted.

Chapter 10
Politics and Democracy in the Age of Misinformation

Svetlana Veljanovska
https://orcid.org/0009-0006-5112-4339
University "St. Kliment Ohridski", Bitola, North Macedonia

ABSTRACT

Today, it is increasingly difficult to draw clear boundaries between information and disinformation, between information and propaganda, between public relations and manipulation, and between truth and lies. Public speaking has never required greater courage. One of the dangers lurking in what the media imposes is populism, which becomes a measure of taste for the mass audience. Even in democracy, which is often considered the better side of politics, the relationship with truth is complex and remains unresolved. What value does truth have if it is not part of the public discourse? Disinformation is a form of deliberate deception. If facts and arguments are invalid, if truth no longer matters, if debate is rejected and dialogue is silenced, can we still claim to live in an age of disinformation (lies), or are we witnessing an attack on democracy itself?

INTRODUCTION

In the modern world, information is no longer just a communication or data exchange tool – it is becoming an essential prerequisite for accumulating and maintaining political and economic power. Decisions, policies and strategies created by institutions cannot be considered legitimate without access to accurate, timely and

DOI: 10.4018/979-8-3693-9601-8.ch010

verified information. Therefore, informed citizenship and transparent governance are becoming central elements of a modern, democratic society.

Institutional transparency is increasingly important with the development of digital technologies and global connectivity. It is not just an administrative necessity but an essential value contributing to increased trust between institutions and citizens. In conditions of transparency, relations between the government and the public are characterized by mutual accountability, honesty and openness. This sense of openness creates an environment in which citizens feel that their voice is heard and that their involvement in social processes has real weight.

Transparency also has a practical function: it provides mechanisms for public oversight through which citizens can hold institutions accountable for their actions. This dynamic of accountability reinforces trust and ensures that policies are formulated and implemented in the public interest. As a result, public institutions are encouraged to make decisions ethically and fairly, transparently explaining their motives and actions.

On the other hand, the challenge facing today's democracies is the increasingly aggressive emergence of disinformation – a phenomenon that directly threatens the transparency and integrity of institutions. Disinformation is the deliberate dissemination of false or manipulative information to deceive the public, undermine institutional stability, or gain political or economic advantage. Although such phenomena are not new, their intensity and prevalence have increased significantly in the last decade, primarily due to the exponential growth of the Internet, social media, and digital communication.

In the 21st century, disinformation is becoming a weapon of the new age – destabilizing societies, undermining electoral processes, and spreading fear and distrust. A parallel reality is created through fake news, conspiracy theories, propaganda narratives, and manipulated photos or videos that often seem more believable than the truth. This creates serious consequences – not only distorting public discourse but also directly affecting the capacity of citizens to make informed decisions. Like many other countries, North Macedonia is not immune to this global challenge. Politics, the economy, health, the environment and culture are some areas where disinformation can cause long-term damage.

In this context, the need for transparency becomes even more emphasized. The principle of transparency, which received particular attention in the 1990s with the enlargement of the European Union and the establishment of international democratic standards, is today a key element of any public policy that strives for openness and accountability. Over time, transparency has evolved from an abstract concept into a concrete strategy: it is implemented through freedom of information legislation, public records, digital availability of institutional data, and opportunities for direct citizen participation in decision-making processes.

In addition, transparency is also a powerful tool for combating corruption. Research shows that institutions' openness significantly reduces the likelihood of abuse of power. When information is available, and processes are visible, public officials are encouraged to work with integrity, aware that the public watches their decisions. In contrast, non-transparent governance creates an environment conducive to corruption, clientelism, and institutional abuse.

Although "transparency" can be defined differently, all definitions boil down to one common essence – revealing what was previously hidden from the public. As Davis (1998) puts it, transparency is "lifting the veil of secrecy," and Den Burr describes it as the ability to "see clearly through the windows of an institution." These metaphors point to the need for continuous communication between institutions and citizens and the importance of public officials being aware of their responsibilities.

Birkinshaw (2006) further emphasizes that transparency is a matter of access to information and active public participation in evaluating institutional behavior. For some theorists, transparency is a metaphor for exposing behind-the-scenes political games—a way of bringing light where there is shadow.

For Ball (2009), transparency symbolizes moral accountability and integrity, while Etzioni (2016) emphasizes that the right to information is a key foundation of democratic governance.

Ultimately, transparency is not just a formality but an essential element of any sustainable democracy. It encourages citizens to participate, encourages institutions to behave ethically, and lays the foundation for trust, stability, and long-term development. At a time when misinformation spreads faster than truth and distrust in institutions is growing, transparency remains our strongest ally in defending democratic values.

RESEARCH METHODOLOGY

This study applies a mixed-method approach, combining theoretical framework analysis with secondary data analysis, in order to examine the relationship between institutional transparency, disinformation, and public trust in the media across six Balkan countries: North Macedonia, Serbia, Bosnia and Herzegovina, Albania, Kosovo, and Montenegro.

- Theoretical Framework: The first part of the study is based on a qualitative review of academic literature and policy reports that define and explore key concepts such as institutional transparency, public accountability, media trust, and disinformation. This review draws from political science, media studies, and public administration disciplines to create a conceptual foundation for the empirical analysis.

- Empirical Analysis: The empirical part of the research involves secondary data analysis, using previously collected data from sources such as the European Media Institute, the IREX Media Sustainability Index, and other reputable regional research organizations. The data are analyzed following three central thematic areas, each corresponding to a distinct research question category:

  a. Media Use of News: This dimension investigates how often citizens access news and information, particularly regarding political and social events. It identifies their main sources of news (e.g., television, online media, radio, or print) and patterns in media consumption. This aspect helps contextualize levels of exposure to information and possible disinformation.
  b. Trust in the Media: This section explores citizens' trust and distrust in various media types, emphasizing their perceptions of accuracy, fairness, and completeness in news reporting. It also examines the underlying reasons behind trust/distrust, including attitudes toward public service broadcasters and perceptions of bias, political influence, or professional standards in journalism.
  c. Attitudes and Experiences with the Media: The third focus area analyzes citizens' broader views on whether the media serves the public interest, promotes transparency, protects freedom of speech, and operates independently. It also examines public opinion on the media's role in spreading hate speech, propaganda, and disinformation, providing insights into each country's perceived integrity and social responsibility of media systems.

  d.Comparative and Regional Approach: By comparing results across the six countries, the study identifies regional patterns, national differences, and shared challenges concerning media trust and transparency. This comparative analysis allows a deeper understanding of the interplay between media practices, institutional openness, and citizens' democratic engagement in the Western Balkans.

  e.Limitations: As this is a secondary data analysis, the study is dependent on the scope, methodology, and time frame of the original data sources. Variations in survey methodologies across countries may introduce some limitations in cross-national comparability. Nevertheless, the selected data sources are credible and widely recognized, ensuring a reliable foundation for drawing analytical conclusions.

THE RELATIONSHIP BETWEEN DISINFORMATION AND TRANSPARENCY

Disinformation and transparency are considered inversely proportional, i.e., opposing terms and social phenomena. Disinformation refers to the intentional creation and dissemination of false or misleading information, while transparency is a state of openness and honesty. Transparency helps to build trust and prevent the spread of disinformation.

Disinformation can undermine trust by spreading false, partially false or misleading information. Transparency can be seen as its opponent because it can help prevent false information (Lazer et al., 2018).

This is especially important in the digital age, when disinformation spreads quickly and causes significant harm, undermining trust in institutions with potentially serious consequences.

Hence, the absence of transparency means a deficit in democratic processes while at the same time opening up space for the spread of disinformation and speculation. The lack of transparency of institutions increases the risk of disinformation, which can lead to human rights violations in various ways because it does not allow citizens to monitor government decision-making in an informed manner.

The lack of institutional transparency can lead to the spread of disinformation in several different ways.

1. If institutions are not transparent about their actions and decisions, an environment is created where disinformation can thrive, as people become susceptible to believing false or misleading information when they do not have access to the facts.
2. The lack of transparency can also make it easier for those who tend to spread disinformation. Holding institutions and individuals accountable for the information they share is not easy without transparency.
3. The lack of transparency can make it difficult for people to distinguish between reliable and unreliable sources of information. When institutions are not transparent, people can find it difficult to know whom to trust, making them more likely to believe misinformation that aligns with their beliefs or prejudices.

Institutional transparency is an important component of good governance. It can help promote trust and accountability, balancing efforts to counter disinformation while offering an approach that ensures access to accurate and reliable information while allowing the media and the public to retain their freedom of speech.

The development and spread of information and communication technologies have unfortunately led to an increase in the impact of disinformation with far-reaching political consequences for democratic societies around the world.

The emergence of new media sources associated with digitization has significantly transformed the landscape over the past two decades.

The public is exposed to various sources of information, and instead of better-informed citizens, we have confused consumers of media information. Furthermore, precisely because of the amount of information and media available, citizens create their own media politics; that is, they follow their own media repertoire.

Media and Politics

One of the questions we want to open is: what is happening to politics and democracy in the era of disinformation? Is the media present in implementing politics, and to what extent? Do the media impose or take over the political agenda? What is the consequence of the media's role in the disinformation era?

Today, the media are present in all phases and levels of the political process. Every policy presupposes a confrontation in the public space between different actors, policies, programs and concepts, citizens and authorities, and society and the state.

When reality cannot be changed, then the perception of that reality changes. The media is needed for the widest possible participation in creating political content and to convince people to accept certain decisions.

If citizens are inadequately and untimely informed, especially if they are misinformed, this means that decisions on their part are not made appropriately. Decision-making should result from reflection, which will be created in an appropriate social context, during which the public will reflect on the nature and content of the arguments to consider accurate information and content. (Fishkin 2008, p. 23).

In the Machiavellian sense, according to which "the end justifies the means," media magnates behave as if any mechanism that brings money and votes is permissible." That is why it is not easy today to determine the boundaries between information and disinformation, information and propaganda, public relations and manipulation, and truth and lies.

News is fake "when done intentionally, written to spread disinformation and untruths" (Chayko 2019, p. 98). Then, we speak of intentional untruth or fraud.

Mass media turn the audience into a crowd. In the crowd, individuals lose their individuality and critical awareness and uncritically accept information and suggestions from outside. In "democracy without citizens," the media addresses the audience as a crowd. (Moskovisi 1997, p. 104),

In this context, we must mention the power of the Internet. It has become indispensable in shaping politics and election campaigns. The reality from the media perspective creates a false and incomplete picture of the mood of voters according to the narrow circle of those we like.

Truth in politics has always been suspect because those in power usually try to keep citizens in delusion and ignorance, and they even go a step further by introducing organized lying as a weapon against the truth.

As Badiou (2020) writes: "Once politics finds its legitimate place exclusively in public opinion, it is obvious that the topic of truth is excluded from there" (p. 19).

Societies today are pluralistic, and, as a rule, different opinions should be tolerated. The one who communicates the truth has a problem because he has to overcome disinformation, and it is not easy for the truth to prevail over the crowd's opinion. The dilemma is truth versus false information that undermines trust in state institutions.

Democracy needs active and informed citizens. Politics in a democracy is legitimized by citizens who perceive it as being in line with their interests. In a democracy, truth and power are paramount, and when trust and truth fail, only power remains (Vaidyanathan 2018, p. 26).

In his speech when receiving the Nobel Prize in 2005, Harold Pinter, among other things, emphasized: "As a citizen, I must ask the question: What is truth? What is a lie?" and added: "According to the evidence we have, the majority of politicians are not interested in truth, but in power and staying in power. In order to maintain power, people must remain ignorant of the truth, even of their truth" (Pinter, 2005).

Politicians strive to win the favor of the public. Democratic regimes today, more than ever before in history, offer their citizens assistance, education, social support, social housing, security, stability, etc. The public believes in democratic principles but doubts their application. The public expects too much from politics and does not fully understand it.

Disinformation and Public Discourse

What can be the impact of disinformation on public discourse, electoral processes and citizen awareness?

1. Impact on the public: Disinformation can undermine trust in the media and institutions. If people cannot distinguish true from false information, this can lead to misinforming the public.
2. Elections and politics: In pre-election periods, disinformation is often used to manipulate election results. This can include fake news about candidates or political parties, influencing voters' decisions.

3. Decision-making and strategy: The fight against disinformation should be practiced through collective efforts. It is necessary to educate citizens in media literacy, regulate social media platforms and encourage critical thinking, all to reduce the possibility of spreading disinformation.
4. The role of technology: Technology can be both a blessing and a curse! It can be used for the rapid exchange of information and as a platform for disinformation.

These are just some of the challenges available to citizens, and they should be aware of all the challenges that are part of preserving democracy.

The same information and facts in different interpretations acquire a different meaning and significance. Without interpretation, the facts cannot be learned, and the interpretation depends on the starting point of the interpreter - on his moral, ideological and political understandings.

One explanation is that in politics, it is not the best who win but those who convince the best. There is also a belief that the media do not reflect reality but construct it. (Sartori 2003, p. 171).

The goal that societies strive for is detecting whether and to what extent institutions' (non)transparency can contribute to (the fight against) the spread of disinformation.

The research findings point to numerous challenges in terms of normative-legal, organizational and technological-technical aspects. In overcoming these challenges, the EU's comprehensive approach to tackling disinformation and the EU's general norms acts on institutional transparency and the fight against corruption offer useful guidance.

Their recommendations are aimed at:

- Strengthening the resilience of democratic societies against disinformation,
- Supporting free and independent media and quality journalism,
- Promoting transparency and accountability in online platforms and advertising,
- Strengthening cooperation and coordination between EU Member States and international partners,
- Empowering citizens by improving media literacy and critical thinking skills.

Transparency is considered one of the important prerequisites in the fight against corruption. The relationship between transparency and disinformation is inversely proportional. Transparency has emerged as a counterweight to disinformation due to its role in openness, building trust, preventing false information, and promoting accurate and open information.

In institutional transparency and openness conditions, institutional distrust and the space for the spread of disinformation are reduced. Of course, this does not mean that this space can be eliminated since several other intertwined social actors and processes play a role in spreading disinformation, often not limited to state borders.

Therefore, increasing institutional transparency is the logical step that can be taken to reduce the impact of disinformation.

The absence of institutional transparency means curtailing citizens' right to access information, i.e., marginalization from decision-making and policy-making processes. These tendencies not only do not enable citizens to follow government decision-making in an informed manner but also increase the risk of disinformation.

When institutions are not transparent about their actions and decisions, a lack of institutional transparency can spread misinformation. When people do not have access to the facts, they become susceptible to believing misinformation. When institutions are not transparent, people may find it difficult to know whom to trust, making them more likely to believe misinformation that aligns with their beliefs or prejudices.

Therefore, as is the case with the European approach, transparency should play a key role in the Macedonian approach to tackling disinformation and be considered a key tool for addressing the problem of disinformation, as it allows users to identify sources of information and make informed decisions about the reliability of the information they encounter online.

Overall, transparency should be considered a tool for dealing with disinformation, as it helps create a more open, accountable and trustworthy information environment and supports the efforts of policymakers, companies and civil society organizations to address the challenges posed by disinformation.

The fight against disinformation is a complex process that neither the media, institutions, civil society organizations, and, least of all, citizens themselves can cope with alone. More importantly, it is a long-term process in which one of the key factors is general and media literacy.

That is why we need a strategic plan with good measures that will be consistently implemented. Of course, with a clear definition of disinformation, we can avoid the "trap" of its free, voluntaristic interpretation and call into question the creation of efficient and coordinated policies and measures to prevent the spread of disinformation.

In order to regulate disinformation, it is necessary to be aware of the risks, the greatest of which are censorship and the restriction of freedom of speech. Given the potential risks, the best approach to dealing with disinformation should aim to reduce the conditions for creating and spreading disinformation rather than censoring it.

The best way to achieve this is to be proactive rather than reactive, which includes some of the following approaches:

1. Increasing media literacy and institutional transparency,
2. Open cooperation between different stakeholders, including governments, technology companies, media and civil society organizations,
3. Locating and monitoring the problem,
4. Encouraging self-regulation, especially among the media and online media,
5. Investing in research and reducing the structural economic benefits of the spread of disinformation.

State of Media and Democracy: Case of North Macedonia

The survey of trust in the media was conducted within the project "Resistance to disinformation and hate speech: Civil society action to reaffirm media freedom and prevent disinformation and hate propaganda in the Western Balkans and Turkey".

The data is from 2020, and the situation in seven countries was analyzed - Albania, Bosnia and Herzegovina, Kosovo, N. Macedonia, Serbia, Turkey and Montenegro (Macedonian Institute of Media, 2022).

The survey results in the mentioned countries show a pronounced division of the public in terms of the sources of information they use and the trust in the information they present.

In North Macedonia, television is considered the main source of information, represented by 52%. Social media (Twitter, Facebook, Instagram, YouTube, etc.) are followed by about 25% of citizens, followed by online media (blogs, online magazines, information portals) with 12%, and print media and radio as a source of information is represented by 1% and 2%, respectively.

Trust in television is ambivalent, with only 50% of those who watch television believing or mostly trusting the information they receive on this medium. That is not surprising, given the existing financial and political influence, which reduces trust and the quality of media reporting.

Trust in public service in our country is 51%, and media outlets engaged in investigative journalism have lower trust at 36%.

In terms of social networks and trust in them, this research showed that social networks are not trustworthy and that most citizens believe that political propaganda, misinformation and hatred are spread through them. Social networks are most often used for entertainment, socializing and the need to belong to a certain group.

In terms of the research methodology, I would like to note that the public opinion poll was conducted in six countries: Albania, Bosnia and Herzegovina, Kosovo, Montenegro, North Macedonia and Serbia.

The sample size in North Macedonia was 1,002 respondents, while the data were collected using a mixed method (telephone and online) from 1-15 March 2021.

The questionnaire consists of three groups of questions, which relate to:

1. Media use of news;
2. Trust in the media and
3. Citizens' attitudes and experiences with the media.

The first group of questions explores the frequency of citizens' use of information, news sources for political and social events, and their main sources of information.

The second topic examines trust and distrust in different media types regarding full, accurate and fair reporting and the reasons for trust and distrust in the media, including the public broadcasting service.

The third group of questions concerns citizens' opinions about the media serving the public interest, media freedom and independence, as well as the role of the media in spreading hatred, propaganda and disinformation.

According to the Reporters Without Borders report, N.Macedonia ranks 36th in the annual Media Freedom Index out of 180 countries covered in the survey (Radio Free Europe, 2024). The country has jumped two places compared to last year, but deep political polarization is also noted.

The problem is that Reporters Without Borders notes the high distrust in the media: "Although journalists do not work in a hostile environment, widespread disinformation and the lack of professionalism contribute to the decline in society's trust in the media, which exposes independent media to threats and attacks".

Regarding the political climate, it is noted that the overall environment is favorable for media freedom, but on the other hand, critical journalism is increasingly susceptible to attacks.

Reporters Without Borders warns that the media may be under pressure from the authorities, politicians and business people due to the strong political polarization.

"The two largest parties (in power and opposition) are creating parallel media systems that exercise their political and economic influence. The public broadcasting service lacks editorial and financial independence".

The report also expresses concern that the law has once again allowed national and local authorities to advertise in private media, which could lead to influence in the media.

In assessing the media landscape in North Macedonia, Reporters Without Borders also notes that although television is the dominant choice of information, online media also plays an important role.

When it comes to the economic situation in the media, it is noted that the editorial offices of some of the main television stations are exposed to economic pressure from their owners.

State funding, as indicated, is limited and non-transparent, and "independent media rely heavily on donors." The report emphasizes that foreign grants for projects received by the media contribute only to survival, not to further development.

The basic principles and conditions for performing media activities are defined in the Law on Media of the Republic of North Macedonia adopted in 2013 (Law on Media 2013). The law is not extensive; it has 35 articles, but they are sufficient to regulate the behavior and work of all parties involved in this important profession.

Ethics in Reporting by Journalists and Media Workers

The freedom of journalists to report in media outlets is an inviolable right. Journalists have a role in conveying information, ideas, opinions, and the right to comment. All of their activities must be carried out with respect to ethical values and professional standards in conveying information, whereby journalists must be honest, objective and accurate. These standards are part of the codes of ethics of professional organizations of journalists but also of Article 16 of the Constitution of the RSM.

The right and duty of journalists is to strive to prevent censorship and distortion of the news. Their role in building democracy and civil society is to defend human rights, dignity and freedom, respect the pluralism of ideas and opinions, and contribute to strengthening the rule of law and controlling government and other subjects of public life.

A journalist has the right to free access to all sources of information that are of public interest. This opportunity gives him great privileges and the responsibility to publish accurate, verified information without concealing essential data and falsifying documents. This should be said and published if the information cannot be confirmed or is an assumption or speculation. The accuracy of the information should be checked as much as possible.

Journalists, even if they are prevented from obtaining certain information, have the opportunity and right to inform the public about it. The obligation to indicate the source of the information is valid only if it follows the source. Otherwise, if the source requests to remain anonymous, the journalist is obliged to protect it.

There is another side to the ethical behavior of journalists. Namely, they, like other citizens, must respect positive legal regulations. The public interest is primary, and a journalist will not publish or conceal anything contrary to the public interest.

The media should generally be in the interest of the social community, and journalists must not use the medium to publish or conceal information for personal gain. Bribery, corruption and extortion are incompatible with the journalistic profession. Advertising and other commercial motives must not be allowed to influence the freedom of information. The manner of informing in accidents, natural disasters, wars, family tragedies, illnesses, and court proceedings must be free from sensationalism. In court proceedings, the principle of presumption of innocence should be respected, all parties involved in the dispute should be informed, and a verdict should not be suggested.

Adherence to generally accepted social standards of decency and respect for ethnic, cultural and religious diversity in North Macedonia is an obligation in the behavior of every journalist. Also, the culture of speech, ethics, and appropriate communication with the public are of essential importance and significance in the everyday life of a journalist, regardless of what media he is employed in (electronic, print or online).

Freedom of the media requires responsibility. A journalist is, at the same time, a citizen and, even when performing his profession, can play a role in resolving political crises and conflicts. A journalist should always know his work's possible positive and negative impacts. This means his words and tone must be as neutral and sober as possible, regardless of the topic. This also implies reasonableness when reporting topics that can incite incidents or conflicts, such as stigmatization or labeling of individuals or groups.

European Regulation on Disinformation and Transparency

The European Union's approach to disinformation is particularly relevant for the Republic of S. Macedonia as a candidate country for EU membership. Disinformation is a global challenge, and the EU faces similar issues but has far more advanced institutional mechanisms for dealing with these processes.

A comprehensive strategy to tackle disinformation is important, including adopting and implementing new regulations primarily aimed at greater transparency of major platforms and content moderation and algorithms, investment in fact-checking, media literacy and support for independent media. Access to these resources, as well as the expertise of EU institutions and member states in the fight against disinformation, can offer solutions that are also relevant to the Macedonian context, especially since the EU's approach to tackling disinformation is based on shared democratic values, such as freedom of expression, media pluralism and the protection of fundamental rights.

Respect for these values is important for EU candidate countries, as they are part of the democratic membership criteria that must be met. In EU documents and policies, disinformation is disseminating false or inaccurate content for economic or political gain. At the same time, it can cause harm to public life and pose a threat to democracy, security, and the health of citizens. Disinformation is a major challenge, requiring a coordinated response from institutions, online platforms, media and citizens.

As key acts in the EU for preventing disinformation, it can be stressed:

1. Communiqué of the European Commission on tackling disinformation from 2018. It is a document that represents a collection of tools for effectively preventing the spread of disinformation and protecting the values of the EU (European Commission, 2018),
2. Action Plan against disinformation from 2018 as a comprehensive set of measures adopted by the European Commission to strengthen the EU's ability to prevent, detect and respond to disinformation (Action Plan Against Disinformation, 2018).
3. The European Democracy Action Plan for 2020 focuses on protecting free and fair elections, strengthening media freedom and pluralism, and preventing disinformation (European Commission, 2020).
4. The Enhanced Code of Practice against Disinformation of 2018 and 2022. These are voluntary self-regulatory measures agreed by the European Commission and major online platforms to combat disinformation. (The Strengthened Code of Practice on Disinformation, 2022).
5. The Digital Services Act of 2020 aims to protect internet users by establishing a new standard for the transparent operation of online platforms (European Commission, 2020).
6. The European Media Freedom Act of 2022. The European Media Freedom Act (EMFA) is a set of EU rules to protect media pluralism and independence. It focuses on ensuring that media can operate effectively within the EU single market without undue pressure and taking into account the digital transformation of the media landscape
7. The European Media and Audiovisual Action Plan of 2021. This is a package of measures adopted by the European Commission to support the recovery and transformation of the European media and audiovisual sector, including measures to combat disinformation. The European Commission aims to support projects that promote a free, diverse and pluralistic media environment and/or address structural challenges of media sectors.
8. European Digital Media Observatory from 2021 as a platform established by the European Commission to monitor and analyze the online environment and identify trends, risks and opportunities related to digital services.

The EU approach to preventing the spread of disinformation makes a clear distinction between the media, especially public service, and social media as a potential source or transmitter of disinformation. One of the most important specifics of EU policies is that the media are treated as partners in preventing the spread of disinformation. For these reasons, the European approach to preventing disinformation is accompanied by measures and policies to strengthen democracy, including protecting the journalistic profession. These measures are particularly important and guide national strategies and policies to prevent disinformation in the Republic of North Macedonia.

It must be noted that attention should be paid to European measures to protect journalists from online threats. It is necessary to harmonize national media-related legislation with European regulations (the Audiovisual Media Services Directive, the Digital Services Act, the draft Act on Freedom of the Media in Europe, etc.) and with other European standards, self-regulatory and co-regulatory acts, as well as with the recommendations of the Council of Europe. Also, the EU Directive on preventing the possibility of initiating and abusing legal proceedings against journalists should be fully integrated into national strategies and policies. This abuse is called Strategic Lawsuits against Public Participation. The Directive treats strategic lawsuits as a special form of harassment, which relies on unfounded or excessive legal proceedings, which state authorities, powerful companies or individuals most often initiate (EU Directive 2024/1069).

The issue of transparency of the EU institutions gains constitutional weight with the Lisbon Treaty, the principles of which are specified in the Rules of Procedure of the Council and the European Council.

The Directive on Open Data and Reuse of Public Sector Information, which aims to reusable public sector and publicly funded data, is also relevant in this context. The Directive is based on two key principles of the European market: transparency and fair competition. The Directive also provides for strengthening the transparency of public-private partnership agreements involving public sector information and the avoidance of exclusive arrangements.

Transparency plays a key role in the European approach to tackling disinformation. It is considered a key tool for addressing the problem of disinformation, as it allows users to identify the sources of information and make informed decisions about the reliability of the information they encounter online.

In this context, transparency is considered a key element of the European approach to tackling disinformation, as it helps to create a more open, accountable and trustworthy information environment and supports the efforts of policymakers, companies and civil society organizations to address the challenges posed by disinformation.

In EU documents and policies, disinformation is defined as the dissemination of false or inaccurate content to obtain economic or political gain while simultaneously causing harm to public life, posing a threat to democracy, security and the health of citizens.

It is treated as a major challenge, requiring a coordinated response from institutions, online platforms, media and citizens.

The main objectives of the so-called European approach to tackling disinformation are:

1. To strengthen the resilience of democratic societies against disinformation.
2. To support free and independent media and quality journalism.
3. To promote transparency and accountability in online platforms and advertising.
4. To strengthen cooperation and coordination between EU Member States and international partners.
5. To empower citizens by improving media literacy and critical thinking skills.

Overall, the current approach can be seen as primarily designed to prevent illegal micro-targeting of voters by protecting personal data and combating disinformation by increasing the transparency of online platforms.[1]

Another important aspect of the European approach is the emphasis on cooperation between different stakeholders, including governments, technology companies, media and civil society organizations.

CONCLUSION

In conclusion, combating disinformation is a complex and ongoing challenge that no single actor—media, institutions, or civil society—can tackle alone. It requires a comprehensive, long-term strategy grounded in a clear definition of disinformation and a commitment to protecting media freedom while ensuring the public can access accurate and verified information. Central to this effort is transparency, which must go beyond merely publishing information to include open, accountable decision-making processes with mechanisms for correction and responsibility.

Only through such genuine transparency can citizens feel included rather than excluded from governance, reducing their vulnerability to manipulation and falsehoods. Furthermore, effective countermeasures should emphasize prevention by fostering media literacy, promoting institutional accountability, encouraging cooperation among all stakeholders, and supporting responsible media self-regulation.

The European approach, which treats media as partners in preventing disinformation rather than as part of the problem, offers a valuable model—one that contrasts with less coordinated efforts seen elsewhere, such as in North Macedonia, where ambiguities and controversial measures risk undermining media freedom.

Ultimately, addressing disinformation demands inclusive, participatory solutions that engage institutions and citizens alike. Only by building such an environment can societies become resilient against misinformation and uphold the values of truth, responsibility, and democratic integrity in all facets of life.

REFERENCES

Abramowicz, M., & Ho, D. (2020). Transparency and trust in the digital age. *Harvard Journal of Law & Technology.*

Ali, M. (2015). Governance and good governance: A conceptual perspective. *The Dialogue, 10*(1), 65–77. https://www.qurtuba.edu.pk/thedialogue/The%20Dialogue/10_1/Dialogue_January_March2015_65-77.pdf

Arendt, H. (1994). *Truth and lies in politics*. Filip Višnjić.

Badiou, A. (2020). *A brief overview of metapolitics*. FPZ, Political Thought Library.

Bayet, N.. (2019). *Disinformation in the Western Balkans*. EU Institute for Security Studies.

Birkinshaw, P. (2006). *Freedom of information: The law, the practice and the ideal*. Cambridge University Press.

Borr, D. (1998). Transparency in government. *Public Administration Review, 58*(4), 347–356.

Bradshaw, S., & Howard, P. N. (2019). *The global disinformation disorder: 2019 global inventory of organized social media manipulation* (Working Paper 2019.2). Oxford: Project on Computational Propaganda.

Chayko, M. (2019). *Superconnected: Internet, digital media and techno-social life*. White City: Clio.

Commission of the European Union. (2021). *Commission recommendation of 16.9.2021 on ensuring the protection, safety and empowerment of journalists and other media professionals in the European Union* (C(2021) 6650). https://digital-strategy.ec.europa.eu/en/library/recommendationprotection-safety-and-empowerment-journalists

Commission of the European Union. (2022a). *Proposal for a directive of the European Parliament and of the Council on protecting persons who engage in public participation from manifestly unfounded or abusive court proceedings ("Strategic lawsuits against public participation")* (COM(2022) 177 final). https://eur-lex.europa.eu/legal-content/EN/TXT/?uri=CELEX:52022PC0177&from=EN

Commission of the European Union. (2022b). *2022 strengthened code of practice on disinformation*. https://digital-strategy.ec.europa.eu/en/library/2022-strengthened-code-practice-disinformation

Commission of the European Union. (2022c). *Proposal for a regulation of the European Parliament and of the Council on a single market for digital services (Digital Services Act) and amending Directive 2000/31/EC* (COM/2020/825 final). https://eur-lex.europa.eu/legal-content/EN/TXT/PDF/?uri=CELEX:52020PC0825&from=en

Commission of the European Union. (2022d). *European Media Freedom Act (draft presentation).* https://ec.europa.eu/commission/presscorner/detail/en/ip_22_5504

Cooper, T., & Yodder, S. (2012). *Transparency in the EU: A critical analysis.* Oxford Policy Papers.

Edson, R., et al. (2017). The new age of disinformation. *Journal of Information Warfare.*

Etzioni, A. (2016). The limits of transparency. *Public Administration Review, 66*(6), 1–11.

Fishkin, J. S. (2008). Realizing deliberative democracy: Virtual and face-to-face possibilities. *Political Thought, 45*(3–4), 7–26.

Grbeša Zenzerović, M., & Nenadić, I. (2022). *Strengthening society's resistance to disinformation: Analysis of the situation and guidelines for action.* https://www.aem.hr/wp-content/uploads/2022/09/Studija_dezinformacije_2-izdanje.pdf

Hillebrandt, M. Z., Curtin, D., & Meijer, A. (2014). *Transparency in the EU Council of Ministers: An institutional analysis.* University of Amsterdam. https://pure.uva.nl/ws/files/1541494/135720Transparency_in_the_EU_Council_of_Ministers_manuscript.pdf

Hoboken, J., & Fathaigh, R. (2021). Regulating disinformation in Europe: Implications for speech and privacy. *UC Irvine Journal of International, Transnational, and Comparative Law, 6*(1), 9. https://scholarship.law.uci.edu/ucijil/vol6/iss1/3

Law on Media. (2013). *Official Gazette of the Republic of Macedonia,* No. 184/2013.

Lowe, E. (2013). *Media and the political process.* Faculty of Political Sciences, University of Belgrade.

Lux, S. (2006). Power: A radical understanding. *New Serbian Political Thought, 13*(1–4), 69–119.

Martens, B.. (2018). *The digital transformation and disinformation.* European Commission.

Moskovisi, S. (1997). *Age of the crowd, I.* Belgrade: Biblioteka XX vek.

Orlović, S. (2013). Critical thinking and public action of a political scientist (intellectual): Ten theses about a holy calling in difficult times. In Podunavac, M., & Paunović, Ž. (Eds.), *Politics: Science and profession* (pp. xx–xx). University of Belgrade, Faculty of Political Sciences.

Orlović, S. (2020). The decline of democracies and the reduction of human rights: The case of Serbia. *Political Life*, July 18.

Pankovski, M., & Recica, V. (2022). *Suppression of disinformation in North Macedonia: How can Sobranie respond to the challenge?* Institute for Democracy, CEBS Public Policy Brief. https://idscs.org.mk/wp-content/uploads/2022/02/CESSPolicy-Brief_6-2022_MAC.pdf

Pinter, H. (2005). *Art, truth & politics: Nobel lecture.* NobelPrize.org.

Rosenfeld, S. (2018). *Democracy and truth: A short history.* University of Pennsylvania Press.

Sartori, G. (2003). *Comparative constitutional engineering: Citizens in the age of misinformation.* Filip Višnjić.

Shapiro, I., & Macedo, S. (Eds.). (2000). *Designing democratic institutions.* New York University Press.

Stanovčić, V. (2006). *Political theory.* Official Gazette.

Transparency Index. (2022). Center for Civic Communication, Skopje. https://www.ccc.org.mk/images/stories/akt22.pdf

Vaidyanathan, S. (2018). *Anti-social networks: How Facebook divides us and undermines democracy.* Clio.

KEY TERMS AND DEFINITIONS

Accountability: Denotes the obligation of institutions to explain and justify their decisions and actions to the public. Accountability is a practical component of transparency, enabling citizens to scrutinize authorities and demand responsibility. It reinforces democratic legitimacy and encourages ethical governance.

Corruption and Clientelism: These phenomena thrive in environments lacking transparency. When institutional processes are hidden from public view, the risk of abuse of power for private or political gain increases significantly.

Democratic Governance: A system based on transparency, accountability, and citizen participation. In democratic contexts, institutional legitimacy relies on openness and responsiveness to public needs. Without transparency, democracy loses its foundational capacity to reflect the people's will.

Digital Technologies and Social Networks: While offering significant benefits for information access, these technologies also facilitate the rapid spread of disinformation. Their global reach and algorithmic nature amplify false narratives and complicate the public's ability to distinguish facts from manipulations.

Disinformation: Defined as the intentional dissemination of false or manipulative content aimed at deceiving the public, undermining institutional trust, or securing political and economic gain. Disinformation directly threatens democracy and impedes citizens' ability to make informed decisions.

Fake News: Forms of disinformation that create an alternative, distorted reality, which often appears more credible than truth. These forms of manipulation generate fear, confusion, and mistrust and seriously affect public discourse and democratic stability.

Information: In the contemporary world, information is no longer merely a communication or data exchange tool. It has become a fundamental prerequisite for accumulating and exercising political and economic power. Institutions cannot make legitimate decisions or formulate public policies without access to accurate, timely, and verified information. Information underpins informed decision-making processes and serves as the foundation for governance in the public interest.

Informed Citizenship: Refers to citizens who possess access to relevant and credible information and can participate consciously and critically in societal processes. Informed citizenship is a cornerstone of democratic societies, as only informed citizens can monitor institutions, engage in political decision-making, and exercise responsibility in democratic processes.

Institutional Trust and Stability: These phenomena thrive in environments lacking transparency. When institutional processes are hidden from public view: the risk of abuse of power for private or political gain increases significantly.

Law on Free Access to Public Information: A legal framework that guarantees citizens the right to receive information from public institutions. It is a concrete instrument for achieving transparency.

Public Participation: Refers to the active involvement of citizens in decision-making processes, particularly in areas affecting public interest. Transparency creates space for participation and empowers citizens to influence public policy and institutional behavior.

Public Records and Digital Accessibility: Examples of practical tools for transparency – publishing documents, databases, and information available online.

Transparency: Represents openness and the availability of institutional information to the public. It is not merely an administrative obligation but a fundamental democratic value that fosters trust between institutions and citizens. Transparency involves access to public records, explanation of procedures, and proactive institutional communication. It allows for public oversight and compels institutions to act with integrity.

ENDNOTES

1 Measures for transparency in the European approach include requirements for an online platform to disclose information on the sources of political advertising and news content, as well as measures to improve the transparency of algorithms and data collection practices.

Chapter 11

The Role of Education in Combating Cybercrime in the Asia-Pacific: Tackling Misinformation and Disinformation in Australia

Leo S. F. Lin
https://orcid.org/0000-0003-3684-5403
Charles Sturt University, Australia

Geberew Tulu Mekonnen
https://orcid.org/0000-0001-7672-3609
Charles Sturt University, Australia

Mladen Zecevic
https://orcid.org/0009-0002-1455-2992
Charles Sturt University, Australia

Duane Aslett
0000-0003-1540-7180
Charles Sturt University, Australia

Douglas M. C. Allan
https://orcid.org/0000-0003-0616-5546
Charles Sturt University, Australia

ABSTRACT

This chapter examines how education serves as a key strategy to combat cybercrime by specifically analysing misinformation and disinformation issues in Australia. The

DOI: 10.4018/979-8-3693-9601-8.ch011

chapter analyses complex elements of the subject area to provide valuable insights which can shape upcoming educational approaches and inform policymaking decisions. Through education priority, the chapter supports an adaptive and practical cybercrime approach that respects ethical standards to protect individual rights. This research aims to build an essential basis for enhancing educational methods and policy systems across the Asia-Pacific region. This chapter points out that digital literacy and critical thinking skills must be developed in individuals because these abilities are essential for navigating and fighting against misinformation and disinformation in the digital environment. These educational programs prove essential because they teach citizens to identify trustworthy information, which helps build societal defences against cybercrime in the region.

INTRODUCTION

The current digital era witnesses a rapid spread of misinformation and disinformation, which creates complicated global challenges for societies (Bennett & Livingston, 2020; Petratos, 2021). This circumstance distorts public perception and damages the reputation of institutions and systems. The United Nations has drafted a Cybercrime Convention that offers a framework for international cooperation to combat cybercrime threats (Lin et al., 2024b). Emerging technologies offer opportunities and challenges, particularly in mitigating the spread of false information.

Misinformation and disinformation have had profound consequences on public trust, decision-making, and societal stability, making individuals more susceptible to manipulation, fraud, and other cyber-related threats (Ma & McKinnon, 2021; Wilson et al., 2024). Equipping individuals with fact-checking technologies and critical thinking skills enables them to identify credible information, thereby reducing the impact of misinformation and disinformation. Educational initiatives play a pivotal role in fostering these competencies, ensuring individuals can navigate the digital information landscape effectively.

In Australia, misinformation and disinformation have become pressing concerns, affecting democracy, public health, education, and social cohesion. In response to this threat, the Australian government is developing a multifaceted approach aimed at enhancing public trust and the individual capacity to critically assess online information. This approach has been shaped by policy development, legislative reforms, curriculum integration, and community engagement programs.

This chapter examines the Australian government's strategic response to misinformation and disinformation through a two-pronged approach: (1) the development and implementation of policy and legislative measures, and (2) the integration of digital literacy and critical thinking education into school curricula and public awareness campaigns. By exploring these efforts, this research highlights the essential role of education in combating cybercrime, providing valuable insights for future policy development and educational strategies in the Asia-Pacific region.

The arrangement of this chapter is as follows: After the Introduction, this chapter provides a literature review that analyses current studies on misinformation and disinformation together with their societal impacts and connections to cybercrime during the digital era. In this section, we explore essential theories and research results that clarify how misinformation operates and demonstrate how cybercriminals take advantage of these weaknesses. The chapter presents its research methodological framework, followed by a description of data collection and analysis methods for evaluating educational strategies that enhance digital literacy. The following section examines Australia's cybercrime legal environment while outlining major national policies and international agreements, including the UN Cybercrime Convention. This section examines how educational programs can be incorporated into legislation to create curricula promoting students' critical thinking and media literacy skills. The final section of this chapter evaluates challenges, pressing issues,and the impact of these findings on educational leaders and policymakers and proposes new research paths that could enhance efforts to counter misinformation and disinformation throughout the Asia-Pacific.

LITERATURE REVIEW

Cybercrime and Risks of Emerging Technologies

Cybercriminals are increasingly leveraging a variety of emerging technologies to spread misinformation and disinformation to deceive the public (Oancea, 2024; Tamilselvan & Biswal, 2024). These technologies include advanced artificial intelligence (AI) tools to create deepfake videos and voice clones, making it highly realistic fake content (Lin et al., 2024a; Tamilselvan & Biswal, 2024). Social media bots are also employed to amplify false narratives, creating the illusion of widespread support or belief in misleading information. As Lai et al. (2023) stated, sophisticated phishing and spoofing techniques are being used to trick individuals into revealing personal information. In addition, Figueira and Oliveira (2017) noted that news websites and manipulated images or videos are designed to mislead viewers and create confusion. By exploiting these technologies, cybercriminals can effectively manipulate public opinion, discredit individuals, and perpetrate various forms of fraud. In the era of digitalisation, emerging technologies have been pervading many aspects of civil society (Vecchio, 2020).

However, to this day, many companies are making efforts to enhance technologies for automatic fact-checking. For example, Ünver (2023) noted that Artificial Intelligence (AI) and Natural Language Processing (NLP) have revolutionised fact-checking processes, enabling the analysis of vast amounts of textual data in real time. Levy et al. (2017) also mentioned that automatic claim detection is used to mine claims regarding a topic of consideration automatically. This trend indicates that the demand for these technologies is increasing due to the rapid spread of fake news.(Vecchio, 2020). Public awareness about the presence and use of emerging technologies for fact-checking misinformation and disinformation is crucial (Zeiger & Gyte, 2020). The public needs awareness-raising and training to tackle fake news and false information that individuals disseminate for personal motives.

Concept of Misinformation and Disinformation

The concepts of misinformation and disinformation are very complex today, especially in this digital age. To understand how misconceptions towards knowledge are developed, it is essential to analyse the source of disinformation, misinformation, and fake news (Lecheler & Egelhofer, 2022). Lecheler and Egelhofer (2022) state that misinformation and disinformation are key concepts that explain the processes of false information in the current media environment. Misinformation is defined by Rubin (2022) as the unintentional dissemination of wrong information, while disinformation is the intentional generation and propagation of false information. The current study is based on Lecheler and Egelhofer (2022) shows how different actors, such as political leaders, the media, and public participants, become involved in the production of these falsehoods. Thus, the interaction between the real and the perceived misinformation and disinformation is challenging for researchers and therefore calls for more research in this field (Aïmeur et al., 2023; Tudjman & Mikelic, 2003).

Misinformation has become more prevalent in society, especially during the COVID-19 pandemic. Ceylan et al. (2023) highlighted that "the online sharing of misinformation has become a worldwide concern with serious economic, political, and social consequences. Most recently, misinformation has hindered acceptance of COVID-19 vaccines and mitigation measures" (p. 1). As pointed out by Tandoc et al. (2018), misinformation can be defined in various ways, and it can be of two types:one is false news, which refers to the lack of factual accuracy and a biased perspective (i.e., partisan-biased news). According to the American Psychological Association (2024), misinformation consists of false or inaccurate information, whereas disinformation is intentional and includes harmful content like fraud, spear phishing, and propaganda. This type of information presents panic and distrust among the public.

Lecheler and Egelhofer (2022) explained how the fake news genre intersects with various related concepts as indicated in Figure 1 below:

Figure 1. Misinformation and disinformation trends (Egelhofer & Lecheler, 2019)

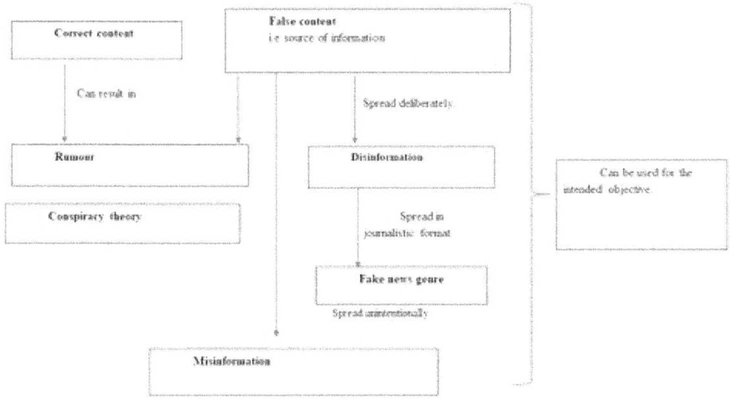

As shown in Figure 1, misinformation and disinformation emerge from false content. The figure differentiates between accurate and false information, highlighting that false content comes from unreliable sources (Egelhofer & Lecheler, 2019; Lecheler & Egelhofer, 2022). Within the category of fake news, it identifies conspiracy theories, which are intentionally spread to deceive, and rumours, which often circulate unintentionally and without verification. As Egelhofer and Lecheler (2019) noted, disinformation refers to false information presented in a journalistic format with the intent to mislead, while misinformation pertains to incorrect information shared unintentionally. Furthermore, in relation to the mechanisms of information spread, information can be shared deliberately for specific purposes or unintentionally due to a lack of verification. This classification clarifies the different types of false information and their methods of dissemination.

The World Economic Forum (2024) reports that the rise of false content is eroding global trust in institutions, with only 40% of people consistently trusting the news. The Global Risks Report of 2024 indicated that disinformation is viewed as the world's top risk over the next two years and the fifth global risk over the next decade. Combating disinformation requires a collaborative effort from various stakeholders, including governments, media outlets, tech firms, and civil society (Koulolias et al., 2018). Each stakeholder needs to take a collective approach to build a strong defence against the spread of false information. The key strategies include educating internet users on media literacy, ensuring the independence and sustainability of news organisations, and utilising technology to differentiate between credible journalism and disinformation (UNESCO, 2018).

In response to the significant threats posed by cybercrime, Australia passed the 2013 National Plan to Combat Cybercrime (Australian Government Department of Home Affairs, 2022). Reports from the Australian Cyber Security Centre (ACSC) indicated that Australia lost AU$33 billion during the 2020–21 financial year, underscoring the urgent need to combat criminal activities and support the community. Since the release of the 2013 National Plan, the Australian government has implemented various measures to address the evolving cybercrime threats. For instance, the government has fostered strong collaboration with industry to protect the community from malicious SMS messages, established the ReportCyber online reporting system, and established the Office of the eSafetyCommissioner, among other initiatives (Australian Government Department of Home Affairs, 2022).

Based on the existing literature, the following differences between misinformation and disinformation have been identified.

Table 1. Differences between misinformation and disinformation

Aspect	Misinformation	Disinformation
Definition	False or inaccurate information spreads without harmful intent.	Deliberately created false information and spread to deceive or mislead.
Intent	Unintentional	Intentional
Dissemination	spreads due to misunderstanding or lack of knowledge.	spread with the purpose of manipulating public opinion or causing harm
Source	Often from individuals who believe the information to be true.	Often originates from organised groups or individuals with specific agendas.
Impact	Cause confusion and spread false beliefs unintentionally.	Cause significant harm, including undermining trust in institutions and inciting conflict.
Examples	Sharing a false news story without realising it's fake.	An example includes creating and distributing fake news stories to influence an election/cause crime.
Detection	It can be corrected through education and fact-checking	Detect through more sophisticated methods, such as tracking the origin and intent of the content.

(Caled & Silva, 2022; Princeton Public Library, 2024)

RESEARCH METHOD

This chapter uses a qualitative case study method that examines existing literature, policy documents, and legal frameworks to analyse how education, legislation, and technology work together to fight misinformation and disinformation. The research depends on secondary data compiled through thoroughly examining academic literature, government documents, global guidelines, and crucial legal documentation. A qualitative method enables researchers to examine the wide-reaching socio-political, legal, and technological environment within which countermeasures against misinformation and disinformation operate.

The research team conducted an extensive literature review that examined multiple aspects of cybercrime and misinformation and their connection to new technological developments. The review examined important policy documents like the UN Cybercrime Convention together with various national laws and regulations related to online safety standards and digital literacy education. Reports from government agencies and international organisations, along with scholarly expert opinions in cybersecurity law education and media studies, served as key sources.

The manuscript investigates different case studies together with current educational programs that work toward tackling misinformation and disinformation. Both government-established programs include media literacy campaigns and instructional resources for teachers and students, combined with industry-created solutions such as the Digital Industry Group Inc. (DIGI) Code. The case studies provide real-world examples of stakeholders' actions toward tackling the issue and their implementation challenges.

The study uses thematic analysis for data examination using qualitative software MAXQDA, which enables the identification of main themes, trends, and gaps within existing methods to fight misinformation and disinformation from secondary collected data. Through thematic analysis, researchers could identify recurring concepts in legal frameworks, educational policies, and technological interventions, which helped to evaluate how these initiatives tackle digital misinformation challenges.

The research evaluates existing legislative efforts through a comparative analysis of the UN Cybercrime Convention and national laws to determine their potential to strengthen global collaboration against cyber threats. The comparative analysis demonstrates both positive aspects and weaknesses in existing legal structures and emphasises the necessity for increased international coordination efforts.

The research combines its analytical results to create practical policy recommendations. The identified recommendations target key improvement areas, such as better media literacy education methods, stronger legal structures, and new technology integration to reduce disinformation spread.

The UN Cybercrime Convention and the Role of Education in Tackling Misinformation and Disinformation

The UN Cybercrime Convention: Recent Development

Information and communications technologies (ICT) have become integral to everyday life, as evidenced by the rapid growth of the internet and social networks (Broadhurst & Chang, 2013). While technological advancements have brought numerous benefits, they have also created opportunities for criminal exploitation (Chang & Coppel, 2020). Consequently, cyberspace is increasingly viewed as a battleground against cybercrime, which involves criminal activities where computers or networks serve as tools, targets, or venues for illegal actions (Chang & Coppel, 2020).

The scale of cybercrime has expanded significantly, leading to the misuse of information and technology for various malicious activities, including stealing, identity theft, fraud, and, in some cases, corporate surveillance. (Chang & Coppel, 2020; Oreku & Mtenzi, 2017). In the digital age, cybercrime poses a growing threat to individuals, businesses, and governments (AllahRakha, 2024). For this reason, strong cybercrime legislation is essential (AllahRakha, 2024). On May 26, 2021, the United Nations adopted a resolution ona new convention on cybercrime (United Nations, 2021). This proposed global convention aims to combat the rising threat of cybercrime by fostering international collaboration (Lin et al., 2024c; United Nations, 2021). It stands out as the first legally binding agreement on cybercrime, developed through extensive negotiations among UN member countries, with input from civil society, academia, and the private sector. The convention seeks to establish a coordinated global response to the criminal misuse of information and communication technologies (Lin et al., 2024c).

In December 2024, the United Nations General Assembly adopted the United Nations Convention against Cybercrime, marking a significant step forward in global efforts to combat cyber threats. This landmark treaty is designed to enhance international cooperation, facilitate the exchange of electronic evidence, and provide technical assistance, particularly to developing nations, to strengthen their capacity to prevent and address cybercrime. The United Nations Office on Drugs and Crime (UNODC), the secretariat during negotiations, has positioned the treaty as the first international crime-focused agreement in over two decades. This is a crucial step in tackling crimes such as online child exploitation, sophisticated financial fraud, and money laundering.

Philémon Yang, President of the General Assembly, highlighted the importance of the new convention. He states:

"We live in a digital world, one where information and communications technologies have enormous potential for the development of societies, but also increase the potential threat of cybercrime... With the adoption of this Convention, Member States have at hand the tools and means to strengthen international cooperation in preventing and combating cybercrime, protecting people and their rights online" (United Nations, 2024).

The convention will be open for signature in 2025 at a formal signing ceremony hosted by Vietnam, followed by additional signing opportunities at UN Headquarters in New York until December 31, 2026. For the treaty to take effect, at least 40 States must ratify, accept, approve, or accede to it. Once this threshold is met, a Conference of the States Parties will be convened to oversee implementation, facilitate cooperation, and enhance global capacity to combat cybercrime effectively.

However, the convention has raised significant concerns about its broad scope, potential impacts on privacy and human rights, and the risk of compromising state sovereignty. Despite various treaties and conventions related to cybercrime, there is currently no specific UN legal instrument dedicated to this issue (United Nations, 2021). As cybercriminals increasingly use technology for scams (Allah Rakha, 2024), it is essential to educate the public and implement measures to protect individuals and institutions against such fraud (Chang et al., 2021; Chang & Coppel, 2020).

Considering these challenges, international collaboration stands as an essential strategy to achieve equilibrium between security measures and fundamental human rights. The success of the UN Cybercrime Convention in addressing cyber threats relies on whether states choose to synchronise their legal systems and maintain human rights protections. An ongoing research process and stakeholder dialogues involving governments, academic institutions, civil society groups, and private sector entities must continue to develop cybersecurity policies that function well and maintain ethical standards. Educational curricula that integrate cybercrime awareness programs will provide individuals with essential knowledge and skills to navigate risks in today's digital society.

The Role of Education in Tackling Misinformation and Disinformation

The UN Cybercrime Convention marks a major international initiative to address cybercrime activities like fraud, online exploitation, and identity theft. In the digital environment, the propagation of false information stands as one of the most widespread complex problems thatdamage institutional trust and enable cyber offences like scams and political meddling. The convention creates a legal framework for dealing with cyber threats, but legal responses fail to address the societal damage caused by false information. Education, digital literacy, and public awareness must be strengthened to combat the negative consequences of misinformation and disinformation. Australia and other global entities like New Zealand, the UK, and the European Union have acknowledged the need for dual strategies. They are developing policies that combine legislative and educational solutions. Educational reinforcement of public resilience allows individuals to evaluate information critically, which helps protect them from manipulation and cyber threats.

Various initiatives have gained momentum over the years in response to the urgent need to tackle the growing challenges of disinformation and misinformation. One notable example is the Australian Code of Practice on Disinformation and Misinformation (the Code), which was released by Digital Industry Group Inc. (DIGI) in February 2021 (Commonwealth of Australia, 2024). This Code requires a diverse array of technology companies to reduce the risks associated with online misinformation and disinformation that could harm Australians. These efforts involve legislative actions from different national governments and initiatives by tech companies such as Facebook, X (formerly Twitter), and YouTube to identify and remove fake news from circulation. The New Zealand Ministry of Justice (2015) introduced legislation to tackle harmful digital communications. The Harmful Digital Communications Act 2015 (NZ) section explicitly outlines its purpose as to "... (a) deter, prevent, and mitigate harm caused to individuals by digital communications; and (b) provide victims of harmful digital communications with a quick and efficient means of redress"(New Zealand Ministry of Justice, 2015, p. Article 3). In the context of New Zealand, certain forms of misinformation may be deemed illegal. Similarly, in 2019, the UK introduced the Online Harm Reduction Bill to establish statutory duties of care for social media platforms, aiming to mitigate the harms associated with internet use (UK Parliament, 2020, p. Article 1). In addition, the European Union (2022) passed a regulatory framework that require the member countries to tackle disinformation. The framework stipulates that "Member States are increasingly introducing, or are considering introducing, national laws on the matters covered by this Regulation, imposing, in particular, diligence requirements for providers of intermediary services as regards the way they should tackle illegal content, online disinformation or other societal risks" (European Union, 2022, p. Article 2)

In an effort to introduce legislation addressing misinformation and disinformation, it has been identified that providing essential support to enhance the credibility and reliability of sources is crucial. (Kyza et al., 2020). Despite the introduction of legislation aimed at tackling misinformation and disinformation, several studies have highlighted a persistent lack of public awareness regarding these issues (Dame Adjin-Tettey, 2022; Egelhofer & Lecheler, 2019; Kyza et al., 2020; Shu et al., 2020; Vintilă, 2024). This lack of awareness leads many people to struggle to distinguish between accurate information and falsehoods. This means legislative measures alone are insufficient to address the problem. Effective solutions require a combination of legal frameworks, public education, and media literacy initiatives to help individuals critically evaluate the information they encounter. Studies by researchers such as Dame Adjin-Tettey (2022) and Egelhofer and Lecheler (2019) stressed the need for comprehensive strategies that include educational programs to enhance public understanding of misinformation. Similarly, Kyza et al. (2020) and Shu et al. (2020) argued for the development of tools and resources that empower individuals to verify the credibility of information sources. Vintilă (2024) further stated the importance of ongoing public engagement and awareness campaigns to mitigate the evolving tactics used in spreading disinformation.

Australian Government's Approach to Combat Online Misinformation and Disinformation

The continuous growth of the digital realm makes the swift dissemination of misinformation and disinformation a significant challenge for Australia's government and its population. The emergence of social media platforms, the spread of false news, and online manipulation tactics have produced extensive negative impacts on Australia's democratic processes, public health systems, educational institutions, and social unity. The Australian government understands the significant dangers these phenomena present and has implemented active measures to lessen the damaging effects of online misinformation and disinformation.

Australia has designed an extensive and multi-layered strategy to build public resilience while rebuilding trust within the information ecosystem and responding to current challenges. The strategy includes policy frameworks, legislative reforms, curriculum adjustments, and community outreach programs. The government suppresses misinformation while teaching citizens how to evaluate the information they find online critically.

The following section examines how Australia implements a dual approach to solve this issue. The investigation begins by reviewing how policy development and legislative reforms provide the foundation for the government's response to misinformation and disinformation. This segment will analyse the incorporation of these initiatives into school programs and public domains to build a society that is better informed and more capable of critical thinking and resilience.

Inquiries, Policy Frameworks and Legislation

The Australian government has emphasised a response to online disinformation and misinformation that embeds principles of transparency, accountability,and collaboration. Recognising that effective solutions must balance freedom of expression with harm mitigation, Australia has focused on fostering resilience to mis and disinformation rather than direct censorship. Key inquiries, policies, and legislation include the *Digital Platforms Inquiry,* the *Disinformation Code of Practice, the 2023-2030 Australian Cyber Security Strategy,* the *Online Safety Act 2021* and the *Communications Legislation Amendment (Combatting Misinformation and Disinformation) Bill 2024.*

Digital Platforms Inquiry

The Digital Platforms Inquiry served as a decisive shift point for Australian strategies to combat misinformation and disinformation. The investigation demonstrated that digital platforms influence public discussions and therefore called for active and organised methods to tackle misinformation and deceptive information. In 2017, the Australian government directed the Australian Competition and Consumer Commission (ACCC) to conduct a Digital Platforms Inquiry. The scope of the inquiry was to examine the impact of online platforms on media, competition, and the supply of news. The final report, delivered in 2019, revealed that digital platforms such as Meta (formerly Facebook), Twitter, and Google had become primary sources of information for most Australians, creating pathways for spreading false and misleading content due to algorithm-driven prioritisation of engagement over accuracy.

The relevant recommendation of this report included increased transparency and oversight through a regulatory framework Government support for media literacy initiatives. Consideration of the approach to digital media literacies in the Australian curriculum, and the creation of a digital platform code of conduct to counter disinformation.

Government funding and partnerships with civil society organisations enabled this inquiry to expand community-based interventions. The programs provided people with essential understanding and resources to handle the challenges of the digital world better. Government-backed educational campaigns seek to educate citizens about false information while building their ability to resist deceptive online materials.

The Digital Platforms Inquiry established a regulatory framework combining governmental oversight with industry self-governance and public educational efforts. The Australian government understands that fighting misinformation demands legal measures and community-based initiatives to boost digital literacy and public understanding.

The Disinformation Code of Practice

One of the significant outcomes of the Digital Platforms Inquiry was the adoption of the *Australian Code of Practice on Disinformation and Misinformation* (the Code). Launched in 2021, this Code was developed by the Digital Industry Group Inc. (DIGI), a non-profit industry association, in response to the Australian Government's support of a voluntary digital platform code of conduct to hold digital platforms accountable for the spread of disinformation and misinformation. The Code is voluntary and platforms such as Adobe, Apple, Facebook, Google, Legitimate, Microsoft, Redbubble, TikTok and Twitch have committed to implementing measures to:

- Provide transparency about actions taken to reduce misinformation,
- Collaborate with fact-checkingorganisations,
- Prioritise credible and trusted information sources, and
- Offer tools for users to report and identify harmful content.

Although the focus of the Code is platform-level accountability, increased transparency aligns with the government's broader efforts to educate the public. This approach encourages a shared responsibility between the platforms that provide information and the public, thus maintaining freedom of speech while allowing Australians to evaluate online information critically. Collaborative efforts to create transparency reports, label false content, and promote credible sources are all positive steps towards risk mitigation. However, one significant limitation of the Code is its voluntary nature, meaning that principles may not be applied, prioritised, or applied inconsistently. For example, while transparency reports may be encouraged, they may lack standardised metrics, making it difficult to measure impact.

The Australian government understands the inadequacies of voluntary frameworks and seeks fortified regulatory approaches to ensure platform accountability. The Australian Communications and Media Authority (ACMA) received broader authority in 2023 to supervise digital platforms' work against misinformation and disinformation and determine its effectiveness. The expanded powers granted to ACMA enabled them to request data from platforms and monitor their compliance while offering legislative recommendations to the government when needed. The government prefers industry-led solutions but indicates it will consider mandatory codes of practice should voluntary efforts prove insufficient. The changing regulatory framework demonstrates a continuous movement towards stricter measures to fight misinformation online while preserving freedom of expression and digital rights.

The Code, DIGI and ACMA (Australian Communication and Media Authority)

As a result of its general role in regulating communications and media industries in Australia, ACMA was tasked with monitoring the Code's implementation and evaluating its effectiveness. In June 2021, ACMA submitted its first report to the government on the effectiveness of the platform's measures to address mis and disinformation based on implementing the DIGI code. ACMA proposed several measures to enhance the effectiveness of the Code:

- Encouraging DIGI to consider ACMA's findings in the following review of the Code.
- Granting ACMA information-obtaining powers to oversee digital platforms more effectively.
- Granting the ACMA thepowers to enforce code compliance.
- Establishment of formal standards for digital platforms, and
- Establishment of an action group to support collaboration between platforms, government agencies, researchers, and NGOs.

In December 2022, DIGI finalised a review of the Code, implementing changes to address feedback and international standards. The changes included:

- Encouraging greater code adoption by smaller digital platforms
- Updating the definition of 'harm' about mis and disinformation to address concerns regarding requisite thresholds
- Further commitments related to recommender systems
- Reaffirm that professional news content does not fall under the umbrella of misinformation under the Code.
- Greater transparency of products and services that are within the scope of the Code

DIGI also expressed in-principlesupport for expanding ACMA's oversight powers. Although enhancements have been made, the Code's effectiveness continues to face scrutiny due to enforcement issues and sustainability concerns. The lack of mandatory compliance mechanisms makes critics doubt digital platforms' ability to consistently honour their commitments while addressing harmful content that falls outside policy violations. The DIGI revisions adhere to international best practices, but since the framework is voluntary, enforcement depends on industry goodwill instead of regulatory obligations. The evolution of misinformation through AI-generated content and deepfakes leads to increasing demands for enforceable legal standards to improve accountability. The Australian government should contemplate a hybrid strategy to enhance ACMA's regulatory authority and sustain industry-driven adaptability to confront new digital challenges.

2023-2030 Australian Cyber Security Strategy

Although the Australian government's cybersecurity strategy details the response to the growing cybercrime threat, it briefly notes that the government will empower vulnerable communities to improve their cyberliteracy. This goal will be achieved through funded grant programs that deliver cyber awareness campaigns tailored to different cohorts; achieved through collaboration with community leaders to effectively develop strategies to engage the varied community cohorts.

This approach to cyber literacy and community engagement becomes indispensable for building public defences against deceptive online content while addressing misinformation and disinformation. Digital literacy deficiencies allow misinformation initiatives to target vulnerable populations, necessitating precise awareness programs to combat online harms. The Australian government collaborates with educators, civil society organisations, and community leaders to train people to evaluate digital content critically while identifying manipulation techniques for better online decision-making processes. The government's digital resilience agenda supports this approach because cybersecurity now protects more than infrastructure and includes information integrity management in a complex digital environment.

The Online Safety Act 2021

Enacted in 2021, the *Online Safety Act 2021* (the Act) was the Australian Government's response to harmful online content. The Act provides for the eSafety Commissioner to collaborate with industry, online platforms, educational institutions, and the community to reduce the risk of online harms, including misinformation and disinformation. Overall, the legislation primarily addresses online bullying, image-based abuse, violent content, etc. However, it also provides for the eSafety Commissioner to support, encourage, conduct, and evaluate initiatives to educate and empower individuals about online harm minimisation. The Act complements existing policies by promoting digital resilience and safety education through the Safety Commissioner. This includes programs such as online safety courses for parents, teachers, and students, emphasising safe online practices and identifying misinformation.

In November 2024, the Australian Government also proposed a 'Digital Duty of Care' regulatory model, which was to include:

- An age restriction (16 years of age minimum) to access social media.
- Fast tracking of the Communications Legislation Amendment (Combatting Misinformation and Disinformation) Bill 2024, and
- Commencement of 'deepfake' legislation to introduce 'criminal offences to ban the sharing of non-consensual deepfake sexually explicit material.'

The Minister for Communication, Ms Rowland MP, explained during a speech at the Sydney Institute regarding the governance of digital platforms: He states, "the Online Safety Act has been a crucial tool for incentivising digital platforms to remove illegal content, usually applied remedially and case by case. However, it does not, in a fundamental sense, incentivise the design of a safer, healthier, digital platforms ecosystem. What's required is a shift away from reacting to harms by relying on content regulation alone and moving towards systems-based prevention, accompanied by a broadening of our perspective of what children experience online harms."

The Digital Duty of Care framework introduces a new preventative systems-based approach to managing online safety and misinformation governance. The Australian government has launched age restrictions for social media platforms to protect young users from psychological damage and societal issues caused by misinformation, cyberbullying, and harmful online behaviour.In the 2021 High Court decision in Fairfax Media Publications Ltd v Dylan Voller, media outlets were responsible for defamatory third-party comments on their social media pages. This judicial case has established a crucial precedent on media publisher liability in online misinformation contexts.The accelerated passage of the Combatting Misinformation and Disinformation Bill 2024 demonstrates the urgent need to strengthen oversight of digital platforms so they actively work to stop harmful content from spreading. The government acknowledges new digital threats by introducing deepfake legislation addressing how AI-generated content can deceive and damage individuals. The government now adopts a more interventionist position through these measures, transitioning from self-regulation towards a mixed regulatory framework that combines platform responsibility with law enforcement and educational programs.Notably, the Office of the Australian Information Commissioner (OAIC) supports the legal action against Facebook over privacy breaches linked to misinformation and data misuse, making social media platforms accountable for breaches of Australian privacy law (OAIC 2023). However, legal experts and civil societies have raised some concerns about this legislative endeavour, highlighting potential risks to freedom and challenging effective enforcement. The concerns show the importance of striking a balance between combating misinformation and safeguarding fundamental rights.

Communications Legislation Amendment (Combatting Misinformation and Disinformation) Bill 2024

As a direct result of ACMA reports to develop formal standards for digital platforms and enforcement powers, as well as the 'Digital Duty of Care Commitment', in September 2024 the Australian government commenced the 'fast-tracking' of the Communications Legislation Amendment (Combatting Misinformation and Disinformation) Bill 2024 (the Bill) to the House of representatives. The Australian government's intent through this Bill was to increase transparency and accountability of digital platforms, ACMA information gathering and record keeping powers, code and standard-making powers, enforcement and review of legislation, and impact on freedom of expression.

Referred to Senate Environment and Communications Committee 19/9/24; report presented 25/11/24.

The explanatory memorandum of the Bill suggested that the Bill is compatible with human rights and freedoms under the Human Rights (Parliamentary Scrutiny Act) 2011 and that the imposed burdens onrights to privacy and freedoms of expression are only to the extent that it imposes:

"...obligations on digital communications platform providers (and provides the ACMA with regulatory powers) that pertain to information disseminated on digital communication platforms. The Explanatory Memorandum outlined that the Bill's limitations on the right to privacy have been imposed in pursuit of a legitimate objective, are necessary and proportionate to the achievement of that objective, and have appropriate protections in place for individuals."

The Bill was subsequently referred to the Senate Environment and Communications Committee, which recommended that the Bill be withdrawn.

Ultimately, the attempt to reach support for the passage of the Bill failed largely due to political, media, expert and public concerns over freedom of expression; the possibility of suppression of online content, suppression of legitimate discourse and the vagueness and broadness of terms defined in the Bill (definition of terms such as 'false', 'misleading', 'harmful').

The failure of the Combatting Misinformation and Disinformation Bill 2024 demonstrates the intricate challenge of balancing governmental regulation with freedom of speech in the modern digital environment. The legislative proposal sought to improve digital platform transparency and accountability, yet faced criticism because its wide-ranging definitions and enforcement strategies might unintentionally suppress valid public discussions. Media organisations and civil rights advocates expressed fears that the Bill may enable government or platform regulators to suppress content arbitrarily judged as "false" or "harmful" without using consistent standards. Detractors highlighted the absence of independent supervision and the risk of content regulation becoming politically biased, which could damage democratic debate instead of safeguarding it. The Bill's withdrawal shows how challenging it is to fight misinformation while safeguarding fundamental freedoms. It indicates that future laws will require refined consultation and rights-based methods to protect online information integrity.

The Australian School Curriculum

The Curriculum

The Australian Curriculum (v9) provides, at face value, a robust framework for embedding digital literacy and critical thinking across subject areas. The curriculum is currently separated into three dimensions: learning areas, general capabilities, and cross-curriculum priorities. Throughout the different dimensions, students are taught to analyse the credibility of information sources (literacy and science), discuss the potential spread of misinformation (whether automatically generated or intentionally posted (digital technologies), apply digital information security practices and identify the impacts of information and communication technology in society (general capability ICT), how to identify, process and evaluate information (general capability, critical and creative thinking) etc.

Media Literacy in Australian Schools Programs

Various programs have been implemented to provide Australian students with media literacy skills that enable them to critically analyse digital content because of the vital role media literacy plays in fighting misinformation. These programs extend past standard educational content by offering specific resources to tackle misinformation challenges. The eSmart Media Literacy Lab represents one such initiative created by the Alannah & Madeline Foundation. This platform stands as the initial e-learning system developed to assist students in understanding online media intricacies. The interactive modules assist students in recognising trustworthy sources while teaching them how algorithms influence online content and how to evaluate the reliability of digital information. Through this program, students learn to participate in digital spaces as responsible citizens while developing their ability to analyse online information with increased awareness and discernment.

Teacher Training and Professional Development

To effectively deliver education pertaining to digital and media literacy, teachers require access to professional development opportunities, knowledge of current trends, and time to deliver activities. Initiatives such as the eSafety Commissioner training for educators provide education professionals at all levels with webinars, lectures, toolkits, and online learning modules, alongside classroom activities and assessment tools focused on media literacy. Unfortunately, despite the fact that the availability of resources and the willingness to teach media literacy skills amongst Australian teachers is high, the ability to do so faces significant barriers as 'teachers lack direction about how news should be taught to young people, the curriculum is already crowded, limiting opportunities to address news, and teachers lack access to relevant professional development.'

The swift advancement of digital misinformation strategies presents educators with substantial challenges in tracking new threats. The increasing use of artificial intelligence (AI) technologies and advanced content manipulation methods requires teachers to receive continual support and access to updated instructional resources. Media literacy education becomes obsolete without consistent curriculum upgrades and financial support, preventing students from critically analysing modern digital deception. The solution to these educational deficiencies demands a united commitment from governments, schools, and tech firms to deliver ongoing teacher training programs that build a robust and responsive education system.

Digital Platform Third-Party Fact-Checking

The DIGI Code prompts digital platforms to develop strategies that diminish the presence and distribution of false information. Digital platforms should partner with independent fact-checking organisations to improve content verification. Meta has established partnerships for fact-checking purposes in Australia with the following organisations:

- AFP – Hub
- The Australian Associated Press (AAP)
- RMIT FactLab (formerly, now replaced by the RMIT Lookout project)

The Code underlines the importance of creating long-lasting connections with fact-checking entities to enable users to make decisions based on verified information. The sustainability of Meta's fact-checking partnerships encountered problems when allegations of political bias led to Meta suspending RMIT FactLab. Meta's suspension of RMIT FactLab demonstrates how fact-checking initiatives face contentious challenges regarding impartiality and credibility that can undermine digital platform interventions. Following its suspension, RMIT FactLab gave way to the new RMIT Lookout project, demonstrating continued efforts to enhance fact-checking systems throughout Australia.

Community Campaigns and Digital Literacy Initiatives

The Australian government, in accordance with the 2023-2030 Australian Cyber Security Strategy, has funded outreach programs that reach seniors, culturally diverse populations, Indigenous communities, and regional Australians because these groups face higher risks from online scams and incorrect information. These programs work to close the digital gap by providing essential digital literacy training to every Australian regardless of their background or where they live.

The Be Connected program, alongside the Good Things Foundation, offers digital literacy workshops together with interactive learning modules and practical resources that enable individuals to use the internet safely. The programs provide foundational digital skills training which covers identifying reliable sources and verifying online material and scam recognition alongside critical thinking skill enhancement. The Be Connected project from the Australian government alongside the eSafety Commissioner, delivers complimentary online lessons and on-the-ground guidance to enable seniors to become confident digital device users while ensuring safe online interactions.

Access to digital literacy education has increased through partnerships between communities and institutions such as local libraries, multicultural organisations, and Indigenous advocacy groups. First Nations Media Australia offers programs that match cultural needs to improve media and information literacy for Indigenous communities. This enables people to thoroughly analyse digital materials while keeping community wisdom and viewpoints intact.

The Australian government collaborated with services for migrants and refugees to create multilingual tools thathelp new Australians from different cultures recognise and fight against misinformation. Multiple language workshops and outreach programs overcome language barriers that block access to accurate news and digital safety education.

Private-sector partnerships have become more prominent than ever in their financial support for grassroots initiatives and government actions. Major technology corporations and telecommunications companies have joined forces with NGOs and advocacy organisations to provide no-cost or discounted internet services, educational workshops, and verification tools. These initiatives build community defences against digital dangers while promoting good digital behaviour among users.

Challenges and Pressing Issues

The Australian government has taken active measures against online misinformation yet faces numerous substantial challenges which hinder effective problem resolution. The difficulties presented by online misinformation and disinformation span across legal, technological, social, and political areas. The solution calls for an integrated collaborative framework involving government policies, industry regulations, public education efforts, and international partnerships.

Freedom of Expression vs. Regulation

Combating misinformation presents a major challenge when reconciling free speech protection with regulatory requirements. The introduction of the Communications Legislation Amendment (Combatting Misinformation and Disinformation) Bill 2024 has led to widespread discussions about its potential to restrict genuine communication. Critics warn that these wide-ranging misinformation definitions, including "false," "misleading," and "harmful", may serve as tools to suppress political dissent alongside marginalised voices and independent journalism. Enforcing misinformation standards becomes difficult because the current definitions lack clarity and consistency, which could unintentionally lead to civil rights violations and reduced expression diversity.

The Rapid Evolution of Digital Threats

Digital misinformation and disinformation tactics are advancing quickly because technological innovations like artificial intelligence (AI), deepfakes, and automated bots are driving this evolution. The development of new technologies enables the production and spread of advanced fake content, which is challenging to identify and fight. Deepfake technology enables the production ofgenuine-looking fake videos that harm public confidence, interfere with political activities, and harm reputations. The increasing accessibility of deceptive technologies, alongside their growing difficulty in detecting, demands that government initiatives to monitor and prevent disinformation must continually evolve to confront new challenges. The government's current comprehensive strategy faces problems in matching the fast-changing landscape of digital manipulation.

Platform Accountability and Self-Regulation

The voluntary self-regulation system used by digital platforms under Australia's Code of Practice on Disinformation and Misinformation presents a significant ongoing challenge. Meta, Google, and TikTok have promised to combat misinformation, yet their initiatives have shown inconsistent results and lack strong oversight. The Code's voluntary status prevents legal enforcement for full implementation by platforms, which results in possible uneven approaches to misinformation control across different platforms. The lack of standardised measurement methods for disinformation mitigation strategies makes it challenging for regulators to monitor progress and evaluate the effectiveness of current measures.

Misinformation and Disinformation Targeting Vulnerable Populations

Seniors and culturally diverse communities and populations from rural or remote areas face special risks from online misinformation and disinformation. Specific groups lacking essential skills for evaluating online information have limited access to digital literacy resources. Misinformation campaigns that target vulnerable groups play upon their weaknesses to drive social division, institutional distrust, and dangerous behaviours, including vaccine reluctance and online fraud. Government investment in programs like Be Connected and digital literacy initiatives falls short of providing adequate coverage to tackle this issue, which persists, especially in remote regions.

International Cooperation and Regulation

Misinformation online exists beyond national boundaries because the content is transmitted internationally in seconds, complicating the efforts of individual countries to handle the challenge alone. Due to their global operations, digital platforms need internationally harmonised regulatory frameworks to function effectively. Challenges to coordinated global action emerge from the disparities in national laws, political objectives, and regulatory frameworks. Australia's misinformation fight sits within global conversations, yet requires international governments and tech firms to work together on common digital content standards and transparent accountability measures for successful enforcement.

Resource Constraints and Funding Limitations

Despite the Australian government's substantial investments in digital literacy programs and policy frameworks, the resources available to tackle online misinformation remain minimal. Significant funding is necessary for community outreach programs, educator training, and platform regulation, but these areas face resource competition from other public policy priorities. The fast-evolving technological landscape and increasingly complex disinformation tactics necessitate continuous investment to create cutting-edge solutions while building public awareness and establishing effective regulations. Without consistent financial support and strategic planning, the government's initiatives will fail to progress substantially.

Public Trust and Media Literacy

A crucial current challenge involves regaining public confidence in digital media while ensuring its trustworthiness. Educational efforts must address the erosion of trust in traditional media outlets and scientific expertise by political institutions alongside misinformation and disinformation to rebuild public confidence. School curricula and community outreach media literacy programs equip individuals to assess online content critically. The general public's distrust of mainstream information providers and fact-checking entities continues to hinder the broad implementation of media literacy programs. Addressing misinformation demands improved public recognition skills and a stronger emphasis on the importance of credible information sources.

Policy Implications for the Asia-Pacific Region

The evolution of digital technologies demands that educational leaders and policymakers take vital steps to combat the increasing problems of misinformation and disinformation. School curricula must prioritize digital literacy integration to effectively address these contemporary challenges. Educational programs that integrate critical thinking and media literacy skills will enable students to evaluate the trustworthiness of online content. Educational systems must advance beyond source evaluation to teach students skills for analysing the purpose behind the information they come across. Professional development for educators remains crucial because it prepares teachers to understand emerging misinformation trends and develop their media literacy teaching abilities. Establishing an inquiry-based environment in educational institutions enables students to interact with digital content actively and critically instead of being passive recipients.

Educational strategies to combat misinformation receive crucial support and reinforcement from policymakers. A national strengthening of digital literacy efforts can result from developing thorough frameworks integrating digital literacy across all educational levels as a fundamental skill. Through legislation, policymakers can secure financial support for teacher training programs alongside educational resources and community outreach efforts that reach beyond regular classrooms. Partnering with technology firms and non-profit groups strengthens educational efforts through customized workshops and materials that reach varied groups such as parents and local communities. National initiatives that teach media literacy and digital citizenship responsibilities will create a public that is better informed and more resistant to misinformation. Regional cooperation through network building among Asia-Pacific educational institutions enables effective counter-misinformation strategy development and best practices sharing.

The fast-paced changes in the digital world require educational leaders and policymakers to adapt their strategies accordingly. Ongoing assessments and evaluations of digital literacy initiatives will maintain their relevance and effectiveness over time. Education systems must integrate discussions about emerging technologies that contribute to thespread because this will equip students with the necessary skills to handle complex information environments. Policymakers and educators who engage in proactive and coordinated actions can build stronger societal defences against misinformation and disinformation, which will lead to cultivating a more knowledgeable and participatory citizen population throughout the Asia-Pacific region.

CONCLUSION

The chapter highlights that education serves as a vital tool to combat misinformation and disinformation challenges associated with cybercrime throughout Australia and the Asia-Pacific region. The widespread spread of misleading information harms public trust and societal stability while impairing decision-making processes. The UN Cybercrime Convention helps establish international strategies against cyber threats, but it fails to handle the wider societal effects of misinformation. Legal actions must work alongside strong educational programs to fight false information successfully.

Education is a fundamental tool in tackling these challenges because it helps individuals traverse the intricate digital environment with better proficiency. Educational programs that teach digital literacy and critical thinking skills help citizens distinguish between trustworthy and deceptive information while diminishing their vulnerability to manipulation and fraud. These programs help individuals by teaching them essential assessment skills and creating a citizenry that is both more knowledgeable and active in civic life.

The chapter argues thatgovernments should produce a comprehensive strategy against misinformation that merges policy creation with educational curriculum and community involvement. This approach seeks to raise public awareness while equipping people with essential tools to engage with information critically. Effective cybercrime legislation and improved educational practices lead to stronger individual skills and collective resilience to misinformation. Educational initiatives and legal frameworks are essential for protecting democratic operations and maintaining institutional trust within a well-informed community.

This chapter identifies multiple significant domains that require future research exploration. One important avenue is evaluating policy implementation. A study reviewing the execution of national and international misinformation policies in educational contexts would reveal effective strategies and obstacles faced during implementation. Research in this field stands to provide essential data that will shape future policy development and enhance anti-misinformation efforts.

It remains crucial to investigate the effects of technological progress in artificial intelligence and machine learning technologies on misinformation distribution. Understanding the role of evolving technologies in producing and spreading misleading content remains essential. Research must investigate how educational systems can adjust to current changes to enable students and the public to develop abilities that help them identify and tackle new disinformation techniques.

Cross-national comparative studies represent a significant research direction with valuable potential. By analysing misinformation education strategies from different countries and regions, researchers can determine effective educational models for global adoption. Examining various legal, cultural, and technological contexts reveals important lessons for global policymakers and educators about integrating misinformation education.

Research into how media literacy education affects public trust over time represents a vital field of study. Research that examines the effects of improved digital literacy on public views regarding media trustworthiness and institutional credibility, together with society's ability to counter misinformation, will reveal how education helps to form social attitudes. Extended research over time in media literacy education will yield important findings about its sustained impact and offer strategic guidance for future misinformation countermeasures.

REFERENCES

Aïmeur, E., Amri, S., & Brassard, G. (2023). Fake news, disinformation and misinformation in social media: A review. *Social Network Analysis and Mining*, *13*(1), 30. DOI: 10.1007/s13278-023-01028-5 PMID: 36789378

AllahRakha, N. (2024). Global perspectives on cybercrime legislation. *Journal of Infrastructure. Policy and Development*, *8*(10), 6007.

American Psychological Association. (2024). *Misinformation and disinformation.* Retrieved 16 from https://www.apa.org/topics/journalism-facts/misinformation-disinformation

Australian Government Department of Home Affairs. (2022). *National Plan to Combat Cybercrime 2022.* https://www.homeaffairs.gov.au/criminal-justice/files/national-plan-combat-cybercrime-2022.pdf

Bennett, W., & Livingston, S. (2020). *The disinformation age.* Cambridge University Press.

Broadhurst, R., & Chang, L. Y. C. (2013). Cybercrime in Asia: Trends and Challenges. In Liu, J., Hebenton, B., & Jou, S. (Eds.), *Handbook of Asian Criminology* (pp. 49–63). Springer New York., DOI: 10.1007/978-1-4614-5218-8_4

Caled, D., & Silva, M. J. (2022). Digital media and misinformation: An outlook on multidisciplinary strategies against manipulation. *Journal of Computational Social Science*, *5*(1), 123–159. DOI: 10.1007/s42001-021-00118-8 PMID: 34075349

Ceylan, G., Anderson, I. A., & Wood, W. (2023). Sharing of misinformation is habitual, not just lazy or biased. *Proceedings of the National Academy of Sciences of the United States of America*, *120*(4), e2216614120. DOI: 10.1073/pnas.2216614120 PMID: 36649414

Chang, L. Y., Mukherjee, S., & Coppel, N. (2021). We are all victims: Questionable content and collective victimisation in the digital age. *Asian Journal of Criminology*, *16*(1), 37–50. https://doi.org/https://doi.org/10.1007/s11417-020-09331-2. DOI: 10.1007/s11417-020-09331-2 PMID: 33042290

Chang, L. Y. C., & Coppel, N. (2020). Building cyber security awareness in a developing country: Lessons from Myanmar. *Computers & Security*, *97*, 101959. https://doi.org/https://doi.org/10.1016/j.cose.2020.101959. DOI: 10.1016/j.cose.2020.101959

Commonwealth of Australia. (2024). *Online misinformation and disinformation reform: Impact analysis* Retrieved from https://shorturl.at/DFaT9

Dame Adjin-Tettey, T. (2022). Combating fake news, disinformation, and misinformation: Experimental evidence for media literacy education. *Cogent Arts & Humanities*, *9*(1), 2037229. DOI: 10.1080/23311983.2022.2037229

Egelhofer, J. L., & Lecheler, S. (2019). Fake news as a two-dimensional phenomenon: A framework and research agenda. *Annals of the International Communication Association*, *43*(2), 97–116. DOI: 10.1080/23808985.2019.1602782

European Union. (2022). *Legal documents on The Digital Services Act.* Retrieved from https://commission.europa.eu/publications/legal-documents-digital-services-act_en

Figueira, Á., & Oliveira, L. (2017). The current state of fake news: Challenges and opportunities. *Procedia Computer Science*, *121*, 817–825. DOI: 10.1016/j.procs.2017.11.106

Harmful Digital Communications Act. 2015, (2015). https://www.legislation.govt.nz/act/public/2015/0063/latest/whole.html

Koulolias, V., Jonathan, G. M., Fernandez, M., & Sotirchos, D. (2018). *Combating Misinformation: An ecosystem in co-creation.* OECD Publishing.

Kyza, E. A., Varda, C., Panos, D., Karageorgiou, M., Komendantova-Amann, N., Coppolino Perfumi, S., Shah, S. I. H., & Hosseini, A. S. (2020). Combating misinformation online: Re-imagining social media for policy-making. *Internet Policy Review*, *9*(4), 1–24. DOI: 10.14763/2020.4.1514

Lai, W. L., Goh, V. T., Yap, T. T. V., & Ng, H. (2023). Phishing and Spoofing Websites: Detection and Countermeasures. *International Journal on Advanced Science, Engineering and Information Technology*, *13*(5), 1672–1678. DOI: 10.18517/ijaseit.13.5.19037

Lecheler, S., & Egelhofer, J. L. (2022). Disinformation, misinformation, and fake news: Understanding the supply side. *Knowledge resistance in high-choice information environments*, 69-87.

Levy, R., Gretz, S., Sznajder, B., Hummel, S., Aharonov, R., & Slonim, N. (2017). Unsupervised corpus–wide claim detection. *Proceedings of the 4th Workshop on Argument Mining*, Copenhagen, Denmark. DOI: 10.18653/v1/W17-5110

Lin, L. S., Aslett, D., Mekonnen, G., & Zecevic, M. (2024a). The dangers of voice cloning and how to combat it. *The Conversation.* https://theconversation.com/the-dangers-of-voice-cloning-and-how-to-combat-it-239926

Lin, L. S., Aslett, D., Mekonnen, G., & Zecevic, M. (2024b). The UN Cybercrime Convention: What it Means for Policing and Community Safety in Australia. *Australian Outlook*. https://www.internationalaffairs.org.au/australianoutlook/the-un-cybercrime-convention-what-it-means-for-policing-and-community-safety-in-australia/

Ma, K. W. F., & McKinnon, T. (2021). COVID-19 and cyber fraud: Emerging threats during the pandemic. *Journal of Financial Crime*, *29*(2), 433–446. DOI: 10.1108/JFC-01-2021-0016

Oancea, M. (2024). AI and Deep Fake-Video and Audio Manipulation Techniques Capable of Altering the Political Process. *Revista de Stiinte Politice*, (81), 70–82.

Office of the Australian Information Commissioner. (2023, March 7). *High Court clears way for OAIC case against Facebook to proceed.* https://www.oaic.gov.au/news/media-centre/high-court-clears-way-for-oaic-case-against-facebook-to-proceed

Oreku, G. S., & Mtenzi, F. J. (2017). Cybercrime: Concerns, Challenges and Opportunities. In Alsmadi, I. M., Karabatis, G., & Aleroud, A. (Eds.), *Information Fusion for Cyber-Security Analytics* (pp. 129–153). Springer International Publishing., DOI: 10.1007/978-3-319-44257-0_6

Parliament, U. K. (2020). *Online Harms Reduction Regulator (Report) Bill [HL].* Retrieved from https://bills.parliament.uk/bills/2546

Petratos, P. N. (2021). Misinformation, disinformation, and fake news: Cyber risks to business. *Business Horizons*, *64*(6), 763–774. https://doi.org/https://doi.org/10.1016/j.bushor.2021.07.012. DOI: 10.1016/j.bushor.2021.07.012

Princeton Public Library. (2024). *Misinformation, disinformation & malinformation: A guide*. Retrieved 16/12/2024 from https://princetonlibrary.org/guides/misinformation-disinformation-malinformation-a-guide/

Rubin, V. L. (2022). *Misinformation and disinformation*. Springer. DOI: 10.1007/978-3-030-95656-1

Shu, K., Bhattacharjee, A., Alatawi, F., Nazer, T. H., Ding, K., Karami, M., & Liu, H. (2020). Combating disinformation in a social media age. *Wiley Interdisciplinary Reviews. Data Mining and Knowledge Discovery*, *10*(6), e1385. DOI: 10.1002/widm.1385

Tamilselvan, G., & Biswal, M. (2024). Voice Cloning & Deep Fake Audio Detection Using Deep Learning. *International Journal of Advanced Research and Interdisciplinary Scientific Endeavours*, *1*(2), 22–26. https://doi.org/doi.org/10.61359/IJARISE2408

Tandoc, E.Jr, Lim, Z. W., & Ling, R. (2018). Defining "Fake News". *Digital Journalism (Abingdon, England)*, *6*(2), 137–153. DOI: 10.1080/21670811.2017.1360143

Tudjman, M., & Mikelic, N. (2003). Information science: Science about information, misinformation and disinformation. *Proceedings of Informing Science+ Information Technology Education, 3*, 1513-1527.

UNESCO. (2018). *Journalism, fake news & disinformation: handbook for journalism education and training*. UNESCO.

United Nations. (2021). *Resolution adopted by the General Assembly on May 26 2021*https://documents.un.org/doc/undoc/gen/n21/133/51/pdf/n2113351.pdf

United Nations. (2024). UN General Assembly adopts milestone cybercrime treaty. https://news.un.org/en/story/2024/12/1158521

Ünver, A. (2023). Emerging technologies and automated fact-checking: Tools, techniques and algorithms. *Techniques and Algorithms (August 29, 2023)*. https://edam.org.tr/Uploads/Yukleme_Resim/pdf-28-08-2023-23-40-14.pdf

Vecchio, L. (2020). *Misinformation: A Threat to Digital Governance*. Invictus Corporation Ltd.

Vintilă, D. (2024). Public Libraries–Key Actors in Fighting Misinformation in the Future Digital Society. *Culture. Society. Economy. Politics (Culture-SEP), 4*(1), 24-31. https://doi.org/https://doi.org/10.2478/csep-2024-0003

Wilson, S., Hassan, N. A., Khor, K. K., Sinnappan, S., Abu Bakar, A. R., & Tan, S. A. (2024). A holistic qualitative exploration on the perception of scams, scam techniques and effectiveness of anti-scam campaigns in Malaysia. *Journal of Financial Crime*, *31*(5), 1140–1155. DOI: 10.1108/JFC-06-2023-0151

World Economic Forum. (2024). *Disinformation is a threat to our trust ecosystem. Experts explain how to curb it.* https://www.weforum.org/stories/2024/03/disinformation-trust-ecosystem-experts-curb-it/

Zeiger, S., & Gyte, J. (2020). *Prevention of radicalization on social media and the internet*. International Centre for Counter-Terrorism (ICCT).

KEY TERMS AND DEFINITIONS

Crime Prevention in Cyberspace: This term refers to strategies and measures aimed at reducing the risk and impact of cybercrime. This includes public education, law enforcement, policy development, and technological solutions to protect individuals and communities from online threats.

Cybercrime: This term refers to criminal activities carried out using computers or the internet, including online harms such as scams, cyberbullying, data interference, computer-related fraud, and the spread of malicious or false information.

Digital Literacy: This term refers to the ability to effectively and critically navigate, evaluate, and create information using digital technologies. Digital literacy includes recognizing trustworthy sources, understanding online risks, and practicing safe behaviors in the digital environment.

Disinformation: This term refers to the deliberate and coordinated dissemination of false or misleading information with the intent to deceive, manipulate, or cause harm to individuals, groups, organisations, or countries.

Education in Cybercrime Prevention: This term refers to the process of developing knowledge, skills, and critical thinking abilities in individuals to help them recognise, resist, and respond to cyber threats, such as misinformation, disinformation, and online scams.

Misinformation: This terms refers to the spread of inaccurate, misleading, or false information without the intention to cause harm.

Policing in Cyberspace: This term refers to the activities of law enforcement agencies in monitoring, investigating, and responding to cybercrimes. Policing includes collaboration with other sectors, adopting new technologies, and implementing legal frameworks to address evolving cyber threats.

Chapter 12
Evaluating the Impact of Education on Misinformation Suppression: A Stock-and-Flow Simulation Approach

Ilija S. Hristoski
https://orcid.org/0000-0002-9291-7873
University "St. Kliment Ohridski", Bitola, North Macedonia

ABSTRACT

In the digital age, the rapid spread of misinformation via online platforms poses significant challenges because the rising interconnectivity allows false information to circulate quickly and widely. This study proposes a Stock-and-Flow simulation model to evaluate the educational interventions' impact on misinformation, featuring three stocks: Misinformed Individuals, Well-Informed Individuals, and Educational Resources, with various flows governed by rates including the Misinformation Spread, Education Effectiveness, Resource Utilization, Resource Growth, and Decay Rates of both Misinformed and Well-Informed Individuals. The simulation explores how education reduces misinformation and how resource availability affects outcomes. While education can significantly lower misinformation, success depends on resource replenishment and Education Effectiveness Rate. Well-Informed Individuals can help counteract misinformation, underlining the importance of sustained educational efforts. The model provides insights for policymakers to design effective strategies for combating misinformation.

DOI: 10.4018/979-8-3693-9601-8.ch012

INTRODUCTION

The fabrication of information, including misinformation, disinformation, false narratives, and propaganda, has been a part of human previous eras since at least the time of ancient Rome. The documented history of fake news and disinformation dates back to 44 BC, when Emperor Octavian launched a propaganda campaign against Mark Antony using brief, defamatory slogans inscribed on coins to damage his rival's reputation (Fisher, 2023). It continued with the Great Moon Hoax of 1835, when the *New York Sun* published six fabricated articles about life on the Moon, falsely attributed to astronomer Sir John Herschel (Young, 2017). Another iconic example is the 1938 U.S. radio broadcast of *The War of the Worlds*, which convinced many listeners that Earth was under Martian attack (Schwartz, 2016). Throughout the 20th century, including World Wars I and II, regional conflicts, and the Cold War, fabricated information remained a powerful strategic weapon, with propaganda and manipulation used by governments and military leaders to influence both domestic audiences and enemy forces.

The advent of the Web 2.0 paradigm in the early 2000s marked a transformative shift toward a more interconnected, collaborative, and interactive Web, characterized by vast volumes of user-generated content via blogs, social media, and online news platforms. This accelerated the global spread of fake news, making false information widespread across Web 2.0 platforms (Gohil & Nightingale, 2023). In this environment, falsehoods often circulate rapidly through digital channels, outpacing the truth and deceiving even the most vigilant readers due to the difficulty of detecting and preventing misinformation (Juul & Ugander, 2021).

During the COVID-19 pandemic, disinformation and conspiracy theories regarding the virus scope, origin, prevention, and treatment, spread widely across social media, messaging platforms, and mass media. Alarmingly, not only celebrities, politicians, and influencers, but also governments contributed to their dissemination (Kassam, 2020). Today, large-scale information fabrication continues around major geopolitical events.

The timeline of modern-day *information disorder*, a term coined to describe 21st-century global *information pollution*, has become increasingly crowded with events. This concept encompasses all the challenges posed by misinformation, disinformation, and malinformation, especially given the unprecedented scale and complexity of information flows in a hyperconnected yet polarized world. *Misinformation* refers to false information shared without intent to harm or deceive, typically resulting from unintentional errors; *Disinformation* is false information, a deliberately fabricated or manipulated content, spread with the intent to deceive or cause harm for political, financial, or social gain; *Malinformation* involves genuine content shared to inflict harm to a person's reputation, a deliberately exposed private information for personal or corporate interest, based on altering its context, timing or meaning (Wardle, 2018). *Propaganda*, distinct yet related, includes true or false information spread to influence audiences, often politically and state-driven. The famous Russian chess grandmaster Garry Kasparov once said, "*The point of modern propaganda isn't only to misinform or push an agenda. It is to exhaust your critical thinking, to annihilate truth.*" Society's priority should not be to avoid offense when truth is spoken, but to protect individuals from harm when truth is silenced.

The extensive spread of all kinds of false information can have severe and far-reaching consequences: eroding social intelligence, skepticism, and trust in public institutions; influencing elections; and endangering public health (Ecker et al., 2024). Such information poses a major obstacle to building trust and credibility, as it can irreparably damage the reputations of individuals and communities (Olan et al., 2024). Harmful content undermines democratic processes by polarizing societies, fueling extremism and hate speech, and diminishing public trust (CoE, 2024). It also impairs individuals' ability to understand the world accurately, make informed decisions, and engage effectively in civic life.

The advent of generative AI in the Web 3.0 era has significantly amplified disinformation spread (Goldstein et al., 2024). Large Language Models offer powerful tools to combat misinformation, yet they also pose a paradox: can they effectively counter falsehoods without becoming sources of misinformation themselves? (Chen & Shu, 2024). This technology not only accelerates and lowers the cost of producing disinformation but also undermines public trust in authentic media and information sources (Elliott, 2023).

The ever-evolving and resilient nature of false information highlights its ability to persist and spread, despite its detrimental societal impact and the continuous advancements in fact-checking and verification technologies; its adaptive characteristics enable it to evolve in response to countermeasures, ensuring its ongoing influence (Bragazzi & Garbarino, 2024). In today's hyper-digitalized world, where information floods in freely and rapidly from countless sources and where having no information is a better choice than having false information, the pressing challenge is distinguishing truth from deception, and more urgently, combating misinformation, disinformation, and related false narratives (Radu & Petcu, 2024a).

Education, in its many forms, plays a vital role in empowering individuals to discern truth from falsehood. It is increasingly viewed as a cornerstone for developing knowledge, media and information literacy, critical thinking, evidence-based evaluation, source verification, awareness of cognitive biases, analytical reasoning, and responsible mindsets, essential for resisting all forms of false information (EC, 2022a; EC, 2022b).By fostering curiosity and independent thought, education equips individuals to navigate complex information landscapes and make informed decisions in all areas of life (Nygren & Ecker, 2024).As false information spread has become a top political concern globally, it has prompted governments and institutions, from primary schools to universities, to develop and implement strategies to combat misinformation, disinformation and all other kinds of false narratives through education (Radu & Petcu, 2024b).

In this context, British philosopher Anthony C. Grayling aptly stated: "*True education is the process of learning to think for oneself, to draw one's own conclusions, and not be swayed by the opinions of others*", a principle vital for discerning truth from false information. Similarly, psychology professor Gregory Feist emphasized, "*The more I've been teaching, I realize it's really about teaching how to think rather than what to think*" (Pappas, 2022). Imeri (2024) stresses the vital role of education and effective teaching methods in building digital skills, media and information literacy, and critical thinking among children and young adults. These competencies empower them to become active, engaged, informed, and responsible citizens capable of resisting the harmful effects of false information on democracy, public health, and society (Shyh et al., 2023; Radu & Petcu, 2024b). Gross & Balaban (2025) found that educational interventions significantly increase perceived media literacy and reduce belief in conspiracy theories. Blanc (2023) identifies education and access to knowledge as essential tools against disinformation, which are simple in theory but quite challenging to put into practice. As technologies like the Internet and AI evolve, investing in critical thinking is more urgent than ever. According to the Council of Europe, analytical and critical thinking, and understanding the role of language and communication are central to citizenship education and media literacy, while educational institutions are key to fostering these abilities, laying the foundation for digital citizenship and ongoing critical engagement in society (CoE, 2024).

The interplay between educational efforts and false information is complex, due to their multifaceted nature. While misinformation spreads rapidly via social networks, education requires time, sustained engagement, and gradual cognitive development (Bateman & Jackson, 2024).Furthermore, educational efforts are not uniform in their reach or effectiveness; they vary in reach and effectiveness, influenced by educational resources' availability, content quality, and individuals' capacity to apply critical thinking (Javornik & Klemenčič Mirazchiyski, 2023). While education can strengthen information assessment skills, its impact depends on how well initiatives are designed and tailored to their audience (Ali & Qazi, 2023).

Considering the previous discussion, and acknowledging that education is widely recognized as a key instrument for countering the generation and spread of false information, this research is motivated by the need to better understand how education can mitigate misinformation.

This paper aims to propose a streamlined simulation model as a theoretical framework to quantify and assess the impact of education in combating misinformation. By analyzing how variations in educational resources and their effectiveness influence transitions between misinformed and well-informed populations, the model offers valuable insights for policymakers and educators. To the author's knowledge, this is the first model to explicitly incorporate educational parameters (resources, growth rate, utilization rate, and effectiveness) into the dynamics between misinformed and well-informed individuals.

The paper is organized as follows: Section 2 reviews recent research on misinformation, disinformation, and false narratives, with a focus on System Dynamics and Stock-and-Flow simulation models. Section 3 outlines the research problem, questions, objectives, hypotheses, and methodology. Section 4 details the proposed Stock-and-Flow model and the Causal Loop Diagram. Section 5 presents simulation results across two scenarios and four cases, including sensitivity analysis, and a results summary. Section 6 discusses the model's limitations, benefits, verification and validation, and provides recommendations. The final section concludes with suggestions for future research.

RELATED RESEARCH

As proliferation of false information emerges as a major societal challenge in the digital age, modeling and simulation have become vital tools for predicting and mitigating its effects. Strategies in those models typically include blocking harmful rumors, promoting counter-rumors, and disseminating verified facts, as noted by Ojha et al. (2023). Comprehensive systematic reviews by Valverde-Berrocoso et al. (2022) and López et al. (2024) offer detailed insights into existing models and simulations addressing misinformation. Broadly, these models fall into six categories: Epidemiological models; Agent-based models; Game-theoretical models; Bayesian inference models; Machine Learning models; and System Dynamics models.

System Dynamics (SD) modeling, including Stock-and-Flow (S&F) simulations and Causal Loop Diagrams (CLDs), is a powerful approach for analyzing complex systems characterized by feedback loops, nonlinearity, and dynamic interdependencies, rooted in the Systems Thinking theory. As other research approaches lie beyond this study's scope, this section concentrates solely on studies employing SD approach to address misinformation. It reviews key recent efforts applying this methodology to similar challenges and underscores its value in modeling misinformation dynamics.

Using SD, Zhu & Liu (2017) developed a rumor makers' behavior evolution model, starting with a CLD based on key behavioral drivers. S&F simulations in Vensim PLE software showed that negative attitudes are central to disinformation behavior, with personal factors having greater impact than societal or governmental influences.

Ammara et al. (2020) proposed the Systems Thinking approach, using tools like CLDs and S&F models in Stella software, as a comprehensive method to simulate misinformation dynamics. They showed the value of simplified simulations in understanding the misinformation ecosystem and testing interventions, highlighting the risk of naïve interventions in complex systems causing unintended consequences.

In their study, Zawadzki et al. (2020) simulated a model of information war, based on the SD approach, using Lanchester equations and the SIR epidemic spread model, to predict causes and effects of disinformation campaigns.

Gao et al. (2021) applied the SIR model within a SD framework to analyze interactions between vaccine-related tweets and user exposure to misinformation during late 2020. Findings showed that more frequent messaging and higher retweet activity by agencies significantly reduced anti-vaccine misinformation exposure. Huang et al. (2021) used Python to build a SD model analyzing how individual actions and governmental policies shaped online public sentiment in China during COVID-19. Results showed that government responsiveness boosts both positive and negative sentiment, while positive individual actions reduce negativity and promote positivity.

Mumtaz et al. (2022) explored the effect of misinformation spread on infectious disease transmission by combining into a single model the spread of misinformation and the disease, using SD. Besides proposing a combined misinformation/disease SIR model, their work also provided a CLD, along with the results of several scenarios and sensitivity analyses.

Using SD, the study of Guzmán Rincón et al. (2022)modeled and simulated disinformation scenarios driven by disinformation agents' activity. Their mathematical framework illustrated disinformation dynamics and simulated the effects of varying bot activation and deactivation rates, underscoring the pivotal role of social networks in regulating bot-driven disinformation spread.

Concepcion & Sy (2022) used SD to model false news victims' behavior and platforms facilitating their spread. By evaluating existing and proposed solutions, they recommended strategies like combating confirmation bias, revising social media recommendation algorithms, and fostering public trust in news organizations. Later on, they introduced a SD-based rumor propagation model utilizing the SDILR epidemiological framework to analyze false news spread on social media using the Stella software. S&F simulations identified user biases, post sharing, and algorithmic ranking as factors influencing rumor spread (Concepcion & Sy, 2023).

Guzmán Rincón et al. (2023) used a SD model to simulate the spread of disinformation in social networks as a diplomacy strategy. By examining misinformation spread techniques, echo chambers, and bot outreach, their results revealed that disinformation spreads efficiently via bots, while significant changes occurred in the absence of paid outreach, bots, and trolls.

Table 1 compares this study with previous research, highlighting similarities and differences.

Table 1. Comparison between previously published related studies and this study (Source: The Author)

Study	Methodology	Stock & Flow model	Causal Loop Diagram	Software / Method
Zhu & Liu (2017)	SD	YES	YES	Vensim PLE® simulations
	Other models/ methods used:	NO		
	Key concepts:	Rumors; Rumor makers' behavior; Disinformation driving factors		
	Education included:	YES / Education level		
Ammara et al. (2020)	SD	YES	YES	Stella® simulations
	Other models/ methods used:	NO		
	Key concepts:	False information archetypes; Resource allocation; Effects of innovations in technology; Future levels of misinformation		
	Education included:	NO		
Zawadzki et al. (2020)	SD	YES	YES	4th-order Runge-Kutta method
	Other models/ methods used:	Lanchester equations; SIR epidemic spread model		
	Key concepts:	Information war; Causes and effects of disinformation campaigns; Counter-measures; General society wealth; Anti-propaganda campaigns		
	Education included:	NO		
Gao et al. (2021)	SD	YES	YES	Vensim PLE® simulations
	Other models/ methods used:	SIR epidemic spread model; Support Vector Machine (SVM) classifier		
	Key concepts:	Online health misinformation; COVID-19 vaccine; Twitter message dissemination; Misinformation types; Credible information types		
	Education included:	NO		
Huang et al. (2021)	SD	NO	YES	Python programming
	Other models/ methods used:	NO		
	Key concepts:	Online public sentiment; Individual behavior; Cross-validation		
	Education included:	NO		

continued on following page

Table 1. Continued

Study	Methodology	Stock & Flow model	Causal Loop Diagram	Software / Method
Mumtaz et al. (2022)	SD	YES	YES	Unspecified
	Other models/ methods used:	SIR epidemic spread model; Loops That Matter (LTM) method		
	Key concepts:	Misinformation effects; Infectious disease transmission		
	Education included:	NO		
GuzmánRincón et al. (2022)	SD	YES	YES	Stella Architect® simulations; SPSS®
	Other models/ methods used:	SIR epidemic spread model; Kolmogorov-Smirnov statistics; Wilcoxon signed rank test; Euler integration method		
	Key concepts:	Disinformation propagation; Social networks; Activation and deactivation rates of bots		
	Education included:	NO		
Concepcion &Sy (2022)	SD	N/A	N/A	N/A
	Other models/ methods used:	N/A		
	Key concepts:	False news; Social networks; False news' victim behavior		
	Education included:	NO		
GuzmánRincón et al. (2023)	SD	YES	NO	Stella® Architect simulations; SPSS®
	Other models/ methods used:	Ordinary differential equations (ODEs); Kolmogorov-Smirnov statistics; Wilcoxon signed rank test		
	Key concepts:	Disinformation propagation; Social networks; Diplomacy strategy; Susceptible population; Uninformed population; Misinformation techniques; Echo chamber		
	Education included:	NO		
Concepcion &Sy (2023)	SD	YES	YES	Stella® simulations
	Other models/ methods used:	SDILR (modified SIR) epidemic spread model;		
	Key concepts:	False news propagation; Social networking sites; Online users' behavior; Echo chambers		
	Education included:	NO		

continued on following page

Table 1. Continued

Study	Methodology	Stock & Flow model	Causal Loop Diagram	Software / Method
This study	SD	YES	YES	InsightMaker® simulations
	Other models/ methods used:	NO		
	Key concepts:	Misinformed individuals; Well-informed individuals; Education resources; Education resource growth rate; Education resource utilization rate; Education effectiveness rate; Decay rate of Misinformed individuals; Decay rate of Well-informed individuals; Misinformation spread rate		
	Education included:	YES / Education resources; Education resources growth rate; Education resources utilization rate; Education effectiveness rate		

Table 1 confirms that:

- all studies are based on the SD methodology;
- all studies, except one, leverage S&F simulation models;
- all studies, except one, include CLDs;
- all studies utilize different simulation software or evaluation approach;
- two studies, including this one, are not based on any additional models or methods;
- all studies, except this one, are focused on some aspect of false information propagation via social networking sites;
- only one study mentions 'education level' as a parameter in their S&F model;
- only this study takes into account and focuses explicitly on education and its associated aspects (education resources, education resource growth rate, education resource utilization rate, education effectiveness rate) as a highly important countermeasure against the spread of all kinds of false information.

Research Problem, Questions, Objectives, Hypotheses, and Methodology

Research Problem

This study presents a relatively simple yet expressive Stock-and-Flow simulation model, offering a novel conceptual framework specifically designed to capture the dynamics of misinformation spread and its mitigation through education. Its uniqueness lies in addressing a critical empirical gap in the literature, the lack of evidence explaining how the effectiveness of educational systems, with their dynamic and renewable resources, can influence the suppression of misinformation. By focusing on the role of education, an aspect overlooked and underexplored in prior models, this work highlights its potential as a central mechanism in combating misinformation.

Research Questions

Based on the defined research problem, while seeking to address the identified gap, this research aims to answer the following research questions:

- *RQ1*: How does a lack of educational resources, combined with low educational effectiveness rate, influence the spread of misinformation and the dynamics of well-informed and misinformed populations?
- *RQ2*: Can a high educational effectiveness rate partially mitigate the negative impact of scarce educational resources on combating misinformation and increasing the well-informed population?
- *RQ3*: How does a low educational effectiveness rate affect the ability of an educational system with abundant educational resources to combat misinformation and enlarge the well-informed population?
- *RQ4*: To what extent can a high educational effectiveness rate, combined with abundant educational resources, maximize the suppression of misinformation and enhance the growth of well-informed population?

Research Objectives

To address these research questions, the objectives of the research are:

- *RO1*: To develop a Stock-and-Flow simulation model that captures the dynamic relationships between misinformed population, well-informed population, and availability of educational resources;
- *RO2*: To simulate different scenarios reflecting varying levels of educational effectiveness and availability of educational resources;
- *RO3*: To analyze the model's behavior and identify conditions under which educational interventions are most successful;
- *RO4*: To support policy formulation by providing insights into which factors most significantly influence misinformation reduction;
- *RO5*: To conduct sensitivity analysis to evaluate the robustness of the simulation outcomes.

Research Hypotheses

Based on the structure and logic of the simulation model and the previously stated research questions, the following hypotheses are proposed:

- *RH1*: A combination of scarce educational resources and low educational effectiveness rate leads to a sustained increase in the misinformed population and a corresponding decline in the well-informed population over time;
- *RH2*: Even under conditions of scarce educational resources, a high educational effectiveness rate can partially mitigate the spread of misinformation and result in moderate growth of the well-informed population;
- *RH3*: The availability of abundant educational resources alone, regardless of the effectiveness of their use, is sufficient to significantly reduce the spread of misinformation and increase the well-informed population;
- *RH4*: When educational resources are abundant and the educational effectiveness rate is high, the spread of misinformation is significantly suppressed, and the well-informed population grows at a markedly faster rate.

Methodology

The scientific methodology employed in this research is based on System Dynamics (SD) modeling, specifically utilizing a Stock-and-Flow (S&F) simulation approach. The methodology follows a structured process consisting of the following stages:

- *Problem identification*: The study identifies the problem of misinformation and its connection to education. For clarity and ease of presentation, all forms of false information are collectively referred to as misinformation, irrespective of intent;
- *Model formalization*: A quantitative Stock-and-Flow model is proposed, comprised of three stocks and six parameters. The dynamics of the system is governed by five flows, all defined by mathematical expressions;
- *Model conceptualization*: A conceptual, qualitative model is developed using a CLD to map relationships among S&F model's key components;
- *Simulation implementation*: The formalized model is implemented using InsightMaker®, a cloud-based platform for SD simulations;
- *Scenario analysis*: Two simulation scenarios are designed by varying combinations (low vs. high) of *Education Resource* availability and *Education Effectiveness Rate* to understand how different conditions affect the misinformation spread/suppression;

- *Sensitivity analysis*: An univariate sensitivity analysis is performed to examine how changes in one key parameter affect the model's outputs;
- *Interpretation of results*: Simulation outputs are analyzed to identify conditions that foster the transition from a misinformed to a well-informed society. The insights are used to derive implications for educational policy and strategic planning.

The model-based, simulation-driven approach is both exploratory and explanatory, enabling hypothesis testing, behavioral analysis, and intervention evaluation in a risk-free virtual setting. By integrating qualitative Systems Thinking (CLDs) with quantitative Stock-and-Flow modeling, it effectively captures complex socio-cognitive dynamics of misinformation spread and education's impact.

The Proposed Model

The S&F model is based on three key assumptions:

- Misinformation spreads through networks of people, i.e., through society as people share incorrect information, often influenced by false narratives;
- Education can neutralize or decrease susceptibility to misinformation, as well as the belief in, or sharing of, misinformation;
- The effectiveness of education in combating misinformation depends not only on the quality of education but also on the availability, growth, and sustainable utilization of educational resources.

The Stock-and-Flow Simulation Model

Emerging in the late 1950s, System Dynamics (SD) has become a powerful methodology for modeling and understanding the behavior of complex systems, making it valuable for decision-making, policy analysis, and strategic planning across varied domains.

Stocks and flows form the core of SD modeling, providing a visual and quantitative way to analyze how different elements of a system interact. Stocks represent accumulations within a system, its current state, and act as reservoirs that store the net difference between inflows and outflows over time. Flows represent the rates at which stocks change, functioning as either inflows or outflows. They drive system's dynamics by transferring quantities between stocks, determining the pace of change (Bala et al., 2017). Additionally, SD models incorporate variables, either constants or dynamically computed values, and links, which connect model primitives, enabling equations to reference and influence one another.

The proposed Stock-and-Flow model was developed using InsightMaker®, a Web-based, general-purpose tool for building and simulating SD models in a SaaS environment (IMOW, n.d.; IMM, n.d.; Gonczi, 2022; Wijnhoven, 2023). InsightMaker® provides a streamlined, accessible platform suitable for broad modeling needs, enabling users to explore dynamic behaviors of modeled systems over time.

The basic building blocks of the proposed S&F model include:

- Stocks:
  - *Misinformed Individuals*; Population segment currently holding and potentially spreading false narratives;
  - *Well-Informed Individuals*; Individuals educated to critically assess and reject misinformation, no longer contributing to its spread;
  - *Education resources*; Pool of assets (personnel, materials, programs, funding…), allocated to initiatives aimed at enhancing public resilience to misinformation.
- Variables:
  - *Resource Growth Rate* (α); Governs the rate at which educational resources increase in response to the gap between *Misinformed* and *Well-Informed Individuals*;
  - *Misinformation Spread Rate* (β); Determines the speed at which misinformation propagates among susceptible individuals;
  - *Education Effectiveness Rate* (γ); Captures how successfully educational efforts convert *Misinformed Individuals* into *Well-Informed* ones;
  - *Decay Rate of Misinformed Individuals* (δ); Reflects how quickly misinformation is corrected or abandoned due to peer influence or fact-checking;
  - *Decay Rate of Well-Informed Individuals* (θ); Represents the rate at which *Well-Informed Individuals* lose awareness or vigilance, potentially reverting to *Misinformed Individuals*;
  - *Resource Utilization Rate* (κ); Indicates how quickly *Education Resources* are used to counter misinformation.
- Flows:
  - *Increase in Educational Resources* (inflow into the stock of *Education Resources*);
  - *Resource Utilization* (outflow from the stock of *Education Resources*);
  - *Spread of Misinformation* (inflow into the stock of *Misinformed Individuals*);
  - *Reversion to Well-Informed Individuals* (inflow into the stock of *Well-Informed Individuals*; outflow from the stock of *Misinformed Individuals*);

- o *Reversion to Misinformed Individuals* (outflow from the stock of *Well-Informed Individuals*; inflow into the stock of *Misinformed Individuals*).

The five flows and their governing algebraic expressions, detailed per stock below, form the core of the simulation model's dynamics. These expressions are derived through the process of *empirical modeling*, i.e., *functional relationship derivation*, which defines functional relationships using domain expertise, observed patterns, and logical reasoning rather than explicit time-dependent formulations. This method emphasizes steady-state or generalized system behavior, prioritizing clarity and computational efficiency by including only the most impactful variables and parameters. Well-suited for systems with hard-to-measure or less critical time-based dynamics, it enables rapid model prototyping and intuitive analysis.

- **The Education Resources Stock**

The 'Increase in Educational Resources' inflow into the stock of *Education Resources* is represented by Eq. 1:

$$\begin{aligned}&\text{Increase in Educational Resources} =\\&= \alpha \cdot (1-\kappa) \cdot \gamma \cdot \left(1 - \frac{\text{Misinformed Individuals}}{\text{Well-Informed Individuals} + \text{Misinformed Individuals} + 1}\right)\end{aligned} \tag{1}$$

The 'Resource Utilization' outflow from the stock of *Education Resources* is expressed by Eq. 2:

$$\begin{aligned}&\text{Resource Utilization} =\\&= \kappa \cdot \text{Education Resources} \cdot (1+\gamma) \cdot\\&\cdot \left(\frac{\text{Misinformed Individuals}}{\text{Well-Informed Individuals} + \text{Misinformed Individuals} + 1}\right)\end{aligned} \tag{2}$$

- **The Misinformed Individuals Stock**

The 'Spread of Misinformation' inflow into the stock of *Misinformed Individuals* is defined by Eq. 3:

$$\begin{aligned}&\text{Spread of Misinformation} =\\&= \beta \cdot \text{Misinformed Individuals} \cdot (1-\gamma) \cdot\\&\cdot \left(1 - \frac{\text{Well-Informed Individuals}}{\text{Well-Informed Individuals} + \text{Misinformed Individuals} + 1}\right)\end{aligned} \tag{3}$$

- **The Well-Informed Individuals Stock**

The 'Reversion to Well-Informed Individuals' inflow to the stock of *Well-Informed Individuals*, originating from the stock of *Misinformed Individuals*, is calculated using Eq. 4:

$$\text{Reversion to Well-Informed Individuals} = \\ = \delta \cdot \text{Misinformed Individuals} \cdot (1+\gamma) \cdot \\ \cdot \left(\frac{\text{Well-Informed Individuals}}{\text{Well-Informed Individuals} + \text{Misinformed Individuals} + 1}\right) \tag{4}$$

Eq. 5 provides the expression for calculating the 'Reversion to Misinformed Individuals 'inflow to the stock of *Misinformed Individuals*, originating from the stock of *Well-Informed Individuals*:

$$\text{Reversion to Misinformed Individuals} = \\ = \theta \cdot \text{Well-Informed Individuals} \cdot (1-\kappa) \cdot \\ \cdot \left(\frac{\text{Misinformed Individuals}}{\text{Well-Informed Individuals} + \text{Misinformed Individuals} + 1}\right) \tag{5}$$

Implementation

The InsightMaker® model, portrayed in Figure 1, integrates all identified stocks, variables, and flows. The Web-based software tool provides an interactive interface enabling users to adjust initial stock and variable values via sliders within their predefined ranges.

The three stocks can be set interactively within the 0–1,000 range (step of 50), allowing for flexible exploration of model dynamics. The six variables are interactively adjustable within the 0.05–0.95 range (step of 0.01), rather than the full 0.00–1.00 range, to avoid extremes that may: represent unrealistic boundary conditions; cause numerical instability or unrealistic transitions; obscure the interplay among variables; and exaggerate certain processes. The 0.05–0.95 interval ensures a stable, realistic framework, with edge cases (0.00–0.05 or 0.95–1.00) that can be explored independently and systematically if needed.

Figure 1. The proposed stock-and-flow simulation model (Source: The Author, using InsightMaker®)

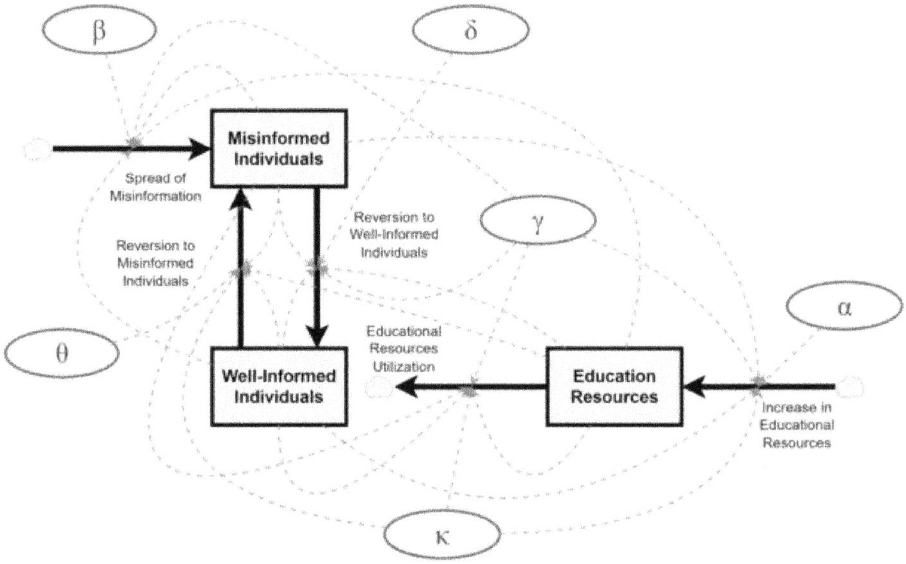

In Figure 1, stocks are represented by rectangles, variables by colorless ovals, information flows (links) by gray dashed arrows, and inflows/outflows by thick solid black arrows pointing to/from stocks.

Causal Loop Diagram

Widely used in SD, Causal Loop Diagrams (CLDs) visually represent complex systems' structure, emphasizing feedback loops and their impact on system behavior. The aim of creating a CLD for this model is to visually illustrate key relationships and feedback loops between stocks and variables in misinformation spread/suppression due to education (Figure 2).

Figure 2. Causal loop diagram of the proposed model, illustrating the impact of education on misinformation spread (Source: The Author)

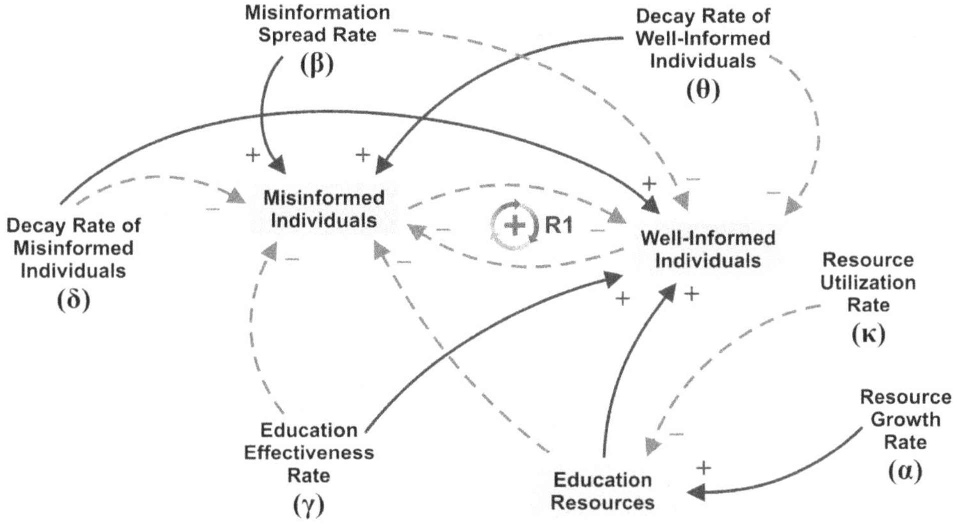

Arrows in Figure 2 represent causal links between variables/stocks, with solid lines for positive and dashed lines for negative influences. The CLD shows both stock relationships and all relevant variable-driven influences.

The CLD portrayed in Figure 2hasone positive (reinforcing) loop and zero negative (balancing) loops:

- *Reinforcing loop R1 (Misinformed Individuals → Well-Informed Individuals → Misinformed Individuals)*: Increased *Misinformed Individuals* reduce *Well-Informed Individuals*, further increasing *Misinformed Individuals*; conversely, fewer *Misinformed Individuals* raise *Well-Informed Individuals*, decreasing *Misinformed Individuals*.

Reinforcing loop R1 highlights the system's dual behavior:

- Positive feedback: Unchecked misinformation amplifies its spread, leading to an exponential rise in *Misinformed Individuals*.
- Negative feedback: Effective educational interventions stabilize the system, increasing *Well-Informed Individuals* and reducing misinformation.

Simulation Results

This section presents the results from running the Stock-and-Flow simulation model. Two scenarios are analyzed: Scenario #1 with limited educational resources and Scenario #2 with abundant resources. Each scenario is further examined under low and high *Education Effectiveness Rates* (γ). The findings are expected to highlight how varying *Education Resources* availability and *Educational Effectiveness Rate* can influence the balance between *Misinformed* and *Well-Informed Individuals* over time, offering insights for effective strategies to combat misinformation.

Table 2 presents the initial parameter values used for the two scenarios.

Table 2. Specification of the initial working parameters (Source: The Author)

			Scenario #1		Scenario #2	
Type	**Name**	**Notation**	**Case 1.1**	**Case 1.2**	**Case 2.1**	**Case 2.2**
Stock	Education Resources		50	50	500	500
Stock	Misinformed Individuals		500	500	500	500
Stock	Well-Informed Individuals		100	200	100	300
Variable	Education Effectiveness Rate	γ	0.20	0.80	0.20	0.80
Variable	Resource Growth Rate	α	0.05	0.05	0.10	0.10
Variable	Resource Utilization Rate	κ	0.10	0.10	0.05	0.05
Variable	Decay Rate of Misinformed Individuals	δ	0.05	0.30	0.10	0.40
Variable	Misinformation Spread Rate	β	0.40	0.20	0.30	0.10
Variable	Decay Rate of Well-Informed Individuals	θ	0.10	0.05	0.05	0.05

Scenario #1: Lack of Education Resources

This scenario models a limited initial stock of *Education Resources*, mirroring real-world challenges where efforts to counter misinformation face severe constraints. Two cases are examined: (1) Case 1.1 assumes a *low Education Effectiveness Rate* (γ), capturing poorly designed or ineffective education; (2) Case 1.2 assumes a *high Education Effectiveness Rate* (γ), reflecting well-executed strategies that suppress misinformation effectively. These two cases allow for assessing the relative importance of educational resource scarcity versus educational effectiveness and how their interplay shapes the evolution of *Misinformed* and *Well-Informed Individuals* over time.

Case 1.1: Low Education Effectiveness Rate (γ). The first case of Scenario #1 assumes a relatively low *Education Effectiveness Rate* ($\gamma = 0.20$) and scarce *Education Resources* (50), a combination representing the most unfavorable conditions in a society: a severe lack of educational resources, which are also used in a highly ineffective way to combat the misinformation spread. Simulation results for Case 1.1 are portrayed in Figure 3.

Figure 3. Simulation results for Scenario #1, Case 1.1 (Source: The Author, InsightMaker® Output)

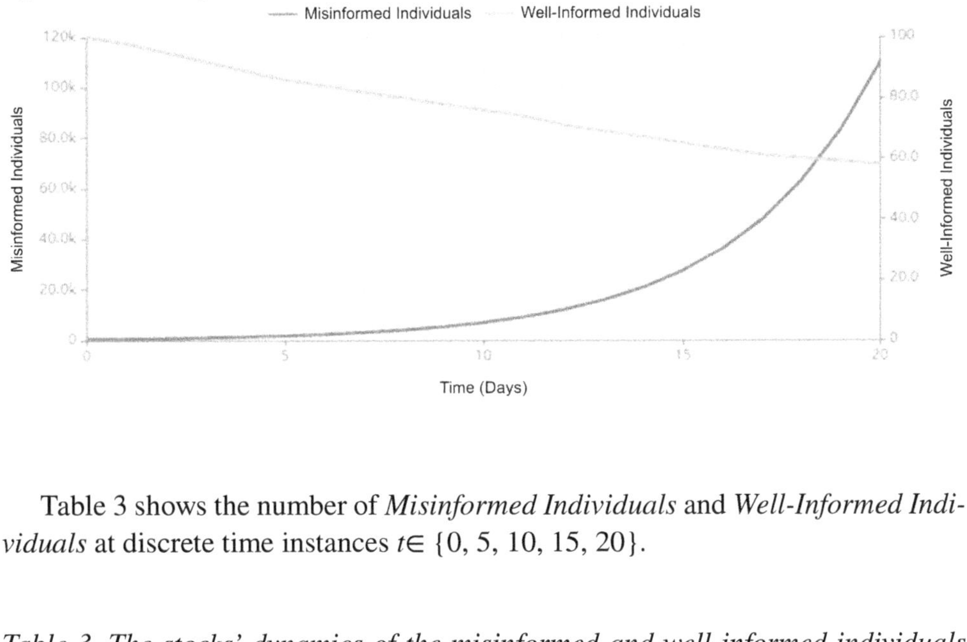

Table 3 shows the number of *Misinformed Individuals* and *Well-Informed Individuals* at discrete time instances $t \in \{0, 5, 10, 15, 20\}$.

Table 3. The stocks' dynamics of the misinformed and well-informed individuals (Scenario #1, Case 1.1) at discrete time instances (Source: The Author)

Time instance (t)	0	5	10	15	20
Misinformed	500	1,774	6,886	27,398	109,625
Well-Informed	100	86	76	65	58

Figure 3 and Table 3 show that under severe constraints, low *Education Resources* and low *Education Effectiveness Rate* (γ), society fails to suppress the spread of misinformation. The number of *Well-Informed Individuals* declines nonlinearly from 100 ($t = 0$) to 76 ($t = 10$), and 58 ($t = 20$), eventually stabilizing at just 27 by $t = 45$ (not shown).In contrast, the number of *Misinformed Individuals* surges exponentially, from 500 (t = 0), to 6,886 (t = 10), 109,625 (t = 20), and an overwhelming 113,257,822 by t = 45 (not shown). This explosive growth highlights the system's inability to counter misinformation, further aggravated by the reversion of *Well-Informed Individuals* back to *Misinformed Individuals*.

Case 1.2: High Education Effectiveness Rate (γ). The second case of Scenario #1 assumes high *Education Effectiveness Rate* (γ = 0.80), whilst initial *Education Resources* are still highly limited (50).

Figure 4 presents the simulation output for Case 1.2, with specific values at selected time points $t \in \{0, 5, 10, 15, 20\}$ detailed in Table 4.

Figure 4 and Table 4 indicate that despite *Education Resources* scarcity, high *Education Effectiveness Rate* moderately, still successfully, enables society to effectively counter misinformation. The number of *Misinformed Individuals* drops sharply from 500 (t = 0) to 7 (t = 10), reaching zero by t = 13 time units. Conversely, *Well-Informed Individuals* rise nonlinearly from 200 (t = 0) to 734 (t = 10), stabilizing at 741 (from t = 13 onwards). A well-functioning educational system can offset limited resources, improving reversion to *Well-Informed Individuals*, though still constrained by *Education Resource* availability.

Figure 4. Simulation results for Scenario #1, Case 1.2 (Source: The Author, InsightMaker® Output)

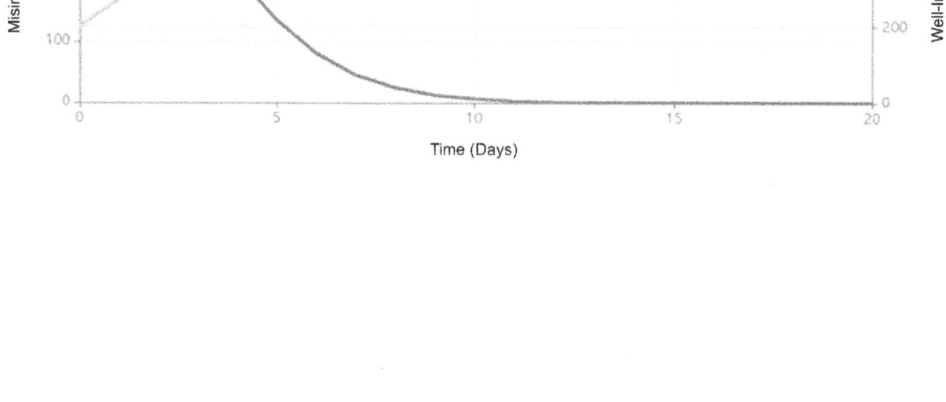

Table 4. The stocks' dynamics of the misinformed and well-informed individuals (Scenario #1, Case 1.2) at discrete time instances (Source: The Author)

Time instance (t)	0	5	10	15	20
Misinformed	500	136	7	0	0
Well-Informed	200	604	734	741	741

Scenario #2: Abundance of Education Resources

Scenario #2 contrasts Scenario #1 by assuming a high initial stock of *Education Resources*, reflecting ample capacity to counter misinformation. As in Scenario #1, two cases are examined: (1) Low *Education Effectiveness Rate* (γ), representing underutilized or ineffective education; (2) High *Education Effectiveness Rate* (γ), reflecting strategic and impactful educational efforts. This scenario underscores that educational effectiveness is key to leveraging resource abundance, revealing whether high educational resource levels alone suffice or whether the success hinges on their strategic and effective deployment.

Case 2.1: Low Education Effectiveness Rate (γ). The first case of Scenario #2 assumes relatively low Education Effectiveness Rate ($\gamma = 0.20$) and plenty of *Education Resources* (500).

Figure 5 displays the simulation output for Case 2.1, while Table 5 shows the number of *Misinformed* and *Well-Informed Individuals* at discrete time points $t \in \{0, 5, 10, 15, 20\}$.

Figure 5. Simulation results for Scenario #2, Case 2.1 (Source: The Author, InsightMaker® Output)

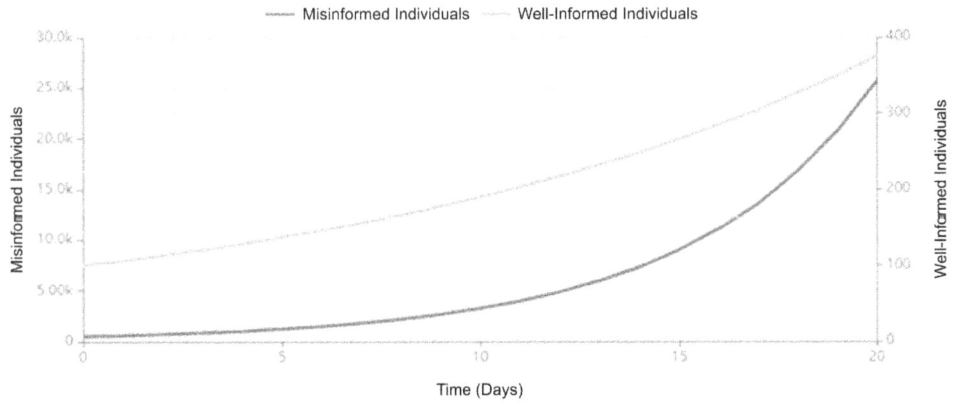

Table 5. The stocks' dynamics of the misinformed and well-informed individuals (Scenario #2, Case 2.1) at discrete time instances (Source: The Author)

Time instance (t)	0	5	10	15	20
Misinformed	500	1,226	3,244	9,001	25,656
Well-Informed	100	137	190	266	375

Figure 5 and Table 5 indicate that abundant *Education Resources* alone cannot effectively combat misinformation. Despite a steady increase in *Well-Informed Individuals*, from 100 ($t = 0$) to 375 ($t = 20$), the stock of *Misinformed Individuals* grows sharply due to the low *Education Effectiveness Rate* (γ), from 500 ($t = 0$) to 25,656 ($t = 20$). The low *Education Effectiveness Rate* significantly hinders the system's ability to mitigate misinformation, limiting the growth of *Well-Informed Individuals* and leading to underutilized *Education Resources*.

Case 2.2: High Education Effectiveness Rate (γ). The second case of Scenario #2 assumes high *Education Effectiveness Rate* ($\gamma = 0.80$), whilst initial *Education Resources* are still abundant (500). This combination of values resembles the most favorable conditions in a society: there are plenty of educational resources and they are spent in a highly effective way in combating misinformation spread.

The simulation output for Case 2.2 is shown in Figure 6, with specific values at discrete time instances $t \in \{0, 5, 10, 15, 20\}$ listed in Table 6.

Figure 6. Simulation results for Scenario #2, Case 2.2 (Source: The Author, InsightMaker® Output)

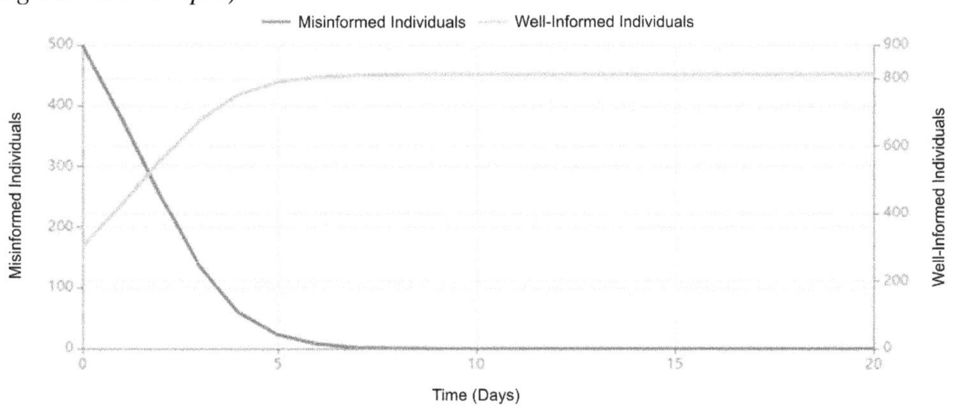

Table 6. The stocks' dynamics of the misinformed and well-informed individuals (Scenario #2, Case 2.2) at discrete time instances (Source: The Author)

Time instance (t)	**0**	**5**	**10**	**15**	**20**
Misinformed	500	23	0	0	0
Well-Informed	300	789	812	812	812

Figure 6 and Table 6 show that the ideal societal conditions rapidly suppress misinformation.

The stock of *Well-Informed Individuals* grows nonlinearly from 300 ($t = 0$) to a maximum of 812 (from $t = 9$ onwards), while *Misinformed Individuals* drop from 500 ($t = 0$) to 0 (from $t = 9$ onwards). This case highlights the effectiveness of the combination of abundant educational resources and high education quality in driving substantial growth in *Well-Informed Individuals*, while effectively restricting misinformation spread.

Sensitivity Analysis

Given the importance of the *Education Effectiveness Rate* (γ) in scenario analyses, it was selected for univariate sensitivity analysis to assess how changes in this parameter affect the number of *Misinformed Individuals* and *Well-Informed Individuals*.

The analysis, conducted for Scenario #2, Case 2.2, tests the model's reliability by varying the *Education Effectiveness Rate* (γ) within the plausible range [0.05, 0.95] in steps of 0.05, while holding other parameters constant.

The results are shown in Figure 7 and Figure 8.

Figure 7. Sensitivity analysis examining the impact of education effectiveness rate on the stock of misinformed individuals (Source: The Author)

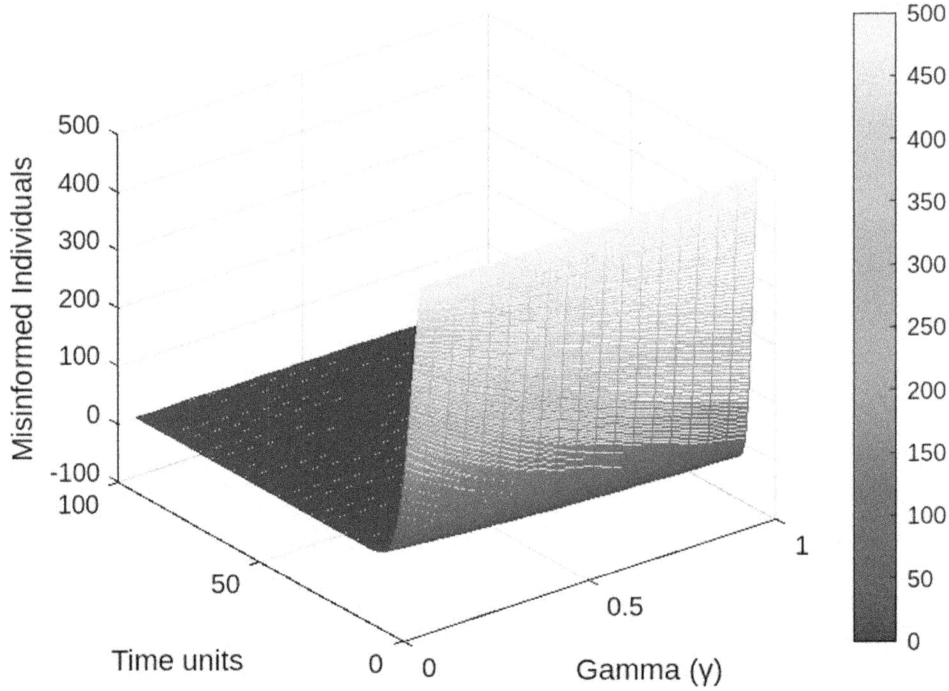

Figure 8. Sensitivity analysis examining the impact of education effectiveness rate on the stock of well-informed individuals (Source: The Author)

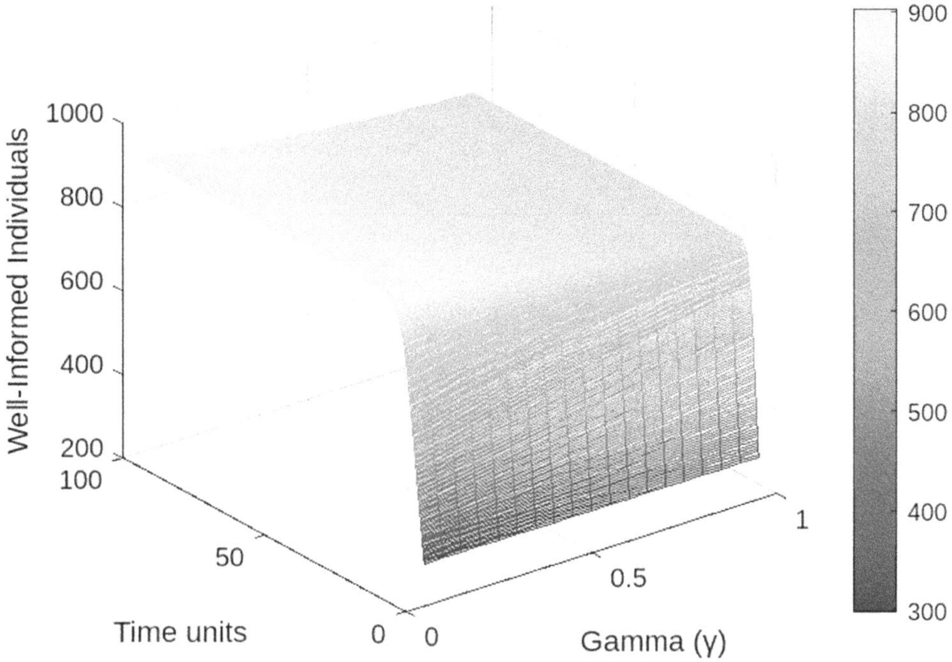

The smooth surfaces portrayed in Figure 7 and Figure 8, with no threshold effects or anomalies, indicate that the model's results for the analyzed scenario are realistic, reliable, and robust.

Results Summary

Given the previously formulated research hypotheses, this subsection provides a concise summary of the key findings from the simulation runs, as presented by Table 7.

Table 7. Research Hypotheses vs. Simulation Results (Source: The Author)

Research hypothesis	Definition	Status	Explanation
RH1	A combination of scarce educational resources and low educational effectiveness rate leads to a sustained increase in the misinformed population and a corresponding decline in the well-informed population over time.	Confirmed	The most unfavorable combination, assuming relatively low Education Effectiveness Rate ($\gamma = 0.20$) and scarce Education Resources (50 out of 1,000), leads to a nonlinear decline of Well-Informed Individuals to only 27 in 45 time units. At the same time, the number of Misinformed Individuals grows in a non-linear manner exponentially reaching 113,257,822. The system is unable to counter misinformation spread.
RH2	Even under conditions of scarce educational resources, a high educational effectiveness rate can partially mitigate the spread of misinformation and result in moderate growth of the well-informed population.	Confirmed	A more favorable combination, assuming relatively high Education Effectiveness Rate ($\gamma = 0.80$), but still scarce Education Resources (50 out of 1,000), leads to a positive outcome, since the number of Misinformed Individuals drops to 0 in 13 time units, while the number of Well-Informed Individuals rise nonlinearly to 741.Despite Education Resources scarcity, high Educational Effectiveness Rate moderately, yet successfully, limits the misinformation spread.
RH3	The availability of abundant educational resources alone, regardless of the effectiveness of their use, is sufficient to significantly reduce the spread of misinformation and increase the well-informed population.	Not confirmed	Also a favorable combination, assuming plenty of Education Resources (500 out of 1,000), but relatively low Education Effectiveness Rate ($\gamma = 0.20$), leads toa situation when both stocks of Well-Informed and Misinformed Individuals rise, however, with different dynamics. While the number of Well-Informed Individuals rises nonlinearly to 375 in 20 time units, the number of Misinformed Individuals rises, in a nonlinear fashion, even faster, to 25,656. So, the availability of abundant Education Resources alone is not sufficient to hinder system's ability to suppress the misinformation spread entirely due to the low Education Effectiveness Rate.
RH4	When educational resources are abundant and the educational effectiveness rate is high, the spread of misinformation is significantly suppressed, and the well-informed population grows at a markedly faster rate.	Confirmed	The most favorable combination, assuming relatively high Education Effectiveness Rate ($\gamma = 0.80$) and abundant Education Resources (500 out of 1,000), leads to rapid suppression of misinformation spread, since the stock of Misinformed Individuals drops sharply and nonlinearly to 0 in just 9 time units, while the number of Well-Informed Individuals grows quickly in a nonlinear fashion to 812. This outcome means an effective restriction and a complete annihilation of misinformation spread.

DISCUSSION

This section delves into the key issues that have shaped the development of the proposed model, positioning it within broader academic, theoretical, and practical contexts.

General Considerations

The proposed S&F model is designed to reveal systemic patterns and strategic insights into the interplay between education, misinformation, and individual reversion, focusing on understanding dynamics rather than predicting precise outcomes.

All model variables are deliberately bounded within the interval [0.05, 0.95] to ensure interpretability, clarity, and consistency. The rationale for this constraint is detailed as follows:

- Scaling all variables to a [0.05, 0.95] range normalizes values, enabling consistency, comparability across different units, and easier interpretation of interactions. This supports flexible scenario analysis and credible sensitivity testing by ensuring practical, stable, and interpretable simulations;
- The theoretical range [0.00, 1.00] represents natural bounds for model variables, which are *de facto* rates or probabilities and thus inherently confined to this interval;
- Normalized variables simplify the construction and implementation of equations, especially those involving fractions, ratios, or nonlinear terms, by ensuring consistent, meaningful inputs for modeling stock inflows and outflows. They ensure adaptability and generalizability across diverse scenarios, contexts and scales.

A key consideration is the trade-off between simplicity and accuracy. The five stock equations are limited to include a maximum of three rates to maintain clarity. While more variables could enhance realism, they would also increase complexity.

The ratios $W / (W + M + 1)$ and $M / (W + M + 1)$, where $W$and M denote *Well-Informed Individuals* and *Misinformed Individuals*, respectively, capture their relative proportions within the population. The stabilizing constant (+1) prevents division by zero and ensures both ratios remain bounded between 0 and 1.These expressions normalize the system dynamics and model the dynamic tension between misinformation and education.

Limitations

The presented Stock-and-Flow model has several notable limitations, necessitating cautious interpretation and application of its results:

- A major limitation of the model is the oversimplification of inherently complex real-world misinformation dynamics, potentially overlooking nuances like cultural differences, psychological factors, digital literacy, public policies, and the role of media;
- A significant limitation of the model lies in the assumptions that may not universally apply: all its predefined parameters (i.e., rates) remain fixed and do not update during simulations, which disregards the reality that these values fluctuate over time;
- Another key limitation is the lack of feedback loops beyond the reinforcing one between the stocks of *Misinformed Individuals* and *Well-Informed Individuals*, which restricts the model's ability to capture more complex effects, such as misinformation's impact on the availability or effectiveness of educational resources;
- Moreover, the model omits external factors, such as economic conditions, policy changes, digital literacy levels, and technological advancements, that could significantly influence system behavior and outcomes;
- Additionally, reducing the *Reversion to Well-Informed Individuals* flow to the sole countermeasure fostering the misinformation decay may oversimplify the variety of mechanisms that mitigate misinformation spread in practice;
- Relying on linear relationships for flows between stocks may oversimplify complex real-world interactions by assuming constant proportionality. Introducing nonlinear equations could better reflect dynamic behaviors and uncover critical policy thresholds, such as points at which increased education resources significantly curb misinformation;
- The model lacks a mechanism to translate real-world conditions into specific rate values within the [0.05, 0.95] range, limiting its applicability for empirical calibration;
- Time-lagged effects of both long-term education and immediate educational interventions are overlooked; temporal nuances (delays, oscillations) are omitted;
- Ultimately, the reliability of simulation outcomes hinges on initial assumptions and parameter choices; unrealistic inputs can produce misleading results;

Benefits

The model offers several notable strengths, including:

- The use of linear and simple nonlinear terms in the mathematical equations enhances clarity, streamlines simulations, and ensures interpretability. Such quasi-linear structure promotes computational efficiency and model stability, making it particularly suitable for educational use and early-stage exploration;
- The visual clarity of the Stock-and-Flow model facilitates intuitive understanding of system dynamics by clearly representing the interactions among stocks, flows, and variables;
- The model abstracts individual-level behavior to focus on aggregate dynamics of misinformation spread and suppression, emphasizing the systemic impact of education over time;
- The model supports flexible scenario analyses, enabling the exploration of policy strategies to combat misinformation and providing actionable insights for decision-makers;
- The mathematical framework enables quantitative simulation, allowing researchers to predict system behavior and assess the effectiveness of different educational approaches in reducing misinformation.

Verification and Validation

The verification process addressed the question, '*Is the model built right?*' by confirming its mathematical accuracy and internal consistency. Structural verification showed that the S&F architecture accurately reflects the intended conceptual framework. The model was verified as structurally sound, logically consistent, and well-aligned with its theoretical and conceptual design.

The validation process, addressing the question '*Is the right model built?*' assesses how accurately the model reflects real-world dynamics. Practical validation of the proposed model, however, was not feasible due to several justifiable constraints: the absence of reliable, high-quality data capturing the interaction between misinformation and education systems; the model provides a theoretical framework, validated conceptually rather than empirically; the inherently fluid nature of misinformation and the delayed impact of countermeasures limit the availability of stable historical benchmarks; ethical and logistical barriers to real-world experimentation make large-scale data collection impractical; simulation testing across four cases validated the model's robustness and computational performance, yielding consistent, yet predictable results in line with expectations.

Recommendations

Drawing on simulation outcomes and system behavior across varied scenarios, several actionable recommendations, summarized in Table 8, emerge to strengthen strategies for combating misinformation and fostering a well-informed society through education. Recommendations are paired with practical implementation mechanisms, ensuring relevance and applicability within real-world educational and policy contexts.

Table 8. Key recommendations and practical mechanisms for their implementation (Source: The Author)

	Recommendation	Rationale	Practical implementation mechanisms
1.	Prioritize sustained investments in educational resources	Simulation results showed that even with high educational effectiveness, combating misinformation is significantly hindered when educational resources are scarce.	• *Public funding*: Governments should allocate a consistent portion of national or local budgets to education, media literacy, and information campaigns; • *Public-private partnerships*: Collaboration with tech companies and NGOs to co-develop educational materials and digital learning platforms; • *Infrastructure development*: Investments in schools, libraries, digital access points, and training for educators in underserved communities.
2.	Increase the effectiveness of education	The model clearly showed that *Education Effectiveness Rate* plays a critical role in determining how well the system can transition individuals from *Misinformed* to *Well-Informed* ones.	• *Curriculum reforms*: Integration of critical thinking, media and information literacy, and fact-checking skills into primary, secondary, and tertiary education; • *Interactive learning tools*: Individuals should use gamified applications, multimedia, and other types of interactive learning tools to increase engagement and retention of knowledge; • *Training programs*: Governments and universities should offer professional development for educators to adopt effective teaching methods that combat misinformation.
3.	Reinforce the role of *Well-Informed Individuals* as social correctives	The reinforcing loop R1 in the CLD shows that *Well-Informed Individuals* reduce the spread of misinformation and increase reversion to informed states.	• *Ambassador programs*: Community leaders, influencers, and educators should be trained as ambassadors for factual information; • *Social media campaigns*: *Well-Informed Individuals* should be mobilized through coordinated digital campaigns to counteract viral misinformation in real time; • *Peer learning*: Community workshops and peer-led initiatives should be established to encourage knowledge-sharing in informal settings.

continued on following page

Table 8. Continued

	Recommendation	Rationale	Practical implementation mechanisms
4.	Monitor and mitigate the spread of misinformation dynamically	Since the *Spread of Misinformation* flow is influenced by the *Misinformation Spread Rate* and the stock of *Misinformed Individuals*, dynamic monitoring is needed.	• *Early warning systems*: Development and deployment of AI-driven systems that track and flag misinformation trends online; • *Regulatory frameworks*: Implementation of policies that require online social media platforms to label or remove false content while preserving freedom of speech; • *Fact-checking networks*: Independent fact-checking organizations should be fully supported and integrated into all kinds of digital platforms for faster responses.
5.	Employ sensitivity analysis for policy design	The sensitivity analysis helps in identifying which model parameters most affect the outcome, thus helping to prioritize policy measures.	• *Scenario planning*: Simulation tools should be used to test various policy scenariosunder different parameter settings before real-world deployment; • *Parameter tuning*: Policy interventions should be focused on the most sensitive variables (γ, α, κ) to maximize impact; • *Iterative feedback*: Real-world data should be consistently collected in a systematic way to refine simulation assumptions and continuously adjust policies to combat false information effectively across platforms.

CONCLUSION

In today's information-saturated environment, flooded with content from both reliable and unreliable sources, there is an urgent need for coordinated, pragmatic strategies to confront the escalating threat of information disorder. Misinformation, disinformation, and false narratives erode political stability, undermine public trust, weaken economic resilience, disrupt social cohesion, and impair informed decision-making. Addressing these challenges requires inclusive collaboration among researchers, policymakers, and technology developers to design adaptable, evidence-based frameworks that match the scale and complexity of the problem. While fully eliminating false information may be unrealistic, its spread can be significantly reduced by empowering individuals through education and critical thinking. As people develop the ability to assess information critically, they become more adept at identifying misleading content, evaluating source credibility, and making informed choices. Education thus plays a pivotal role in advancing digital literacy and cultivating a vigilant public capable of detecting and limiting the spread of falsehoods. A proactive educational approach, integrating media literacy, practical tools, and ongoing learning, enables individuals to navigate digital environments more effectively. Beyond limiting misinformation, such strategies also combat news fatigue by equipping users to manage information overload and engage more deeply with credible sources.

The proposed Stock-and-Flow simulation model provides a robust framework for analyzing dynamics of misinformation, focusing on education's role in both its spread and suppression. It introduces a novel conceptual structure centered on the stock of *Education Resources* and three key parameters: *Resource Growth Rate* (α), *Resource Utilization Rate* (κ), and *Education Effectiveness Rate* (γ). These variables underscore education as a critical force in combating misinformation, enabling evidence-based strategy development. The model captures interactions among *Education Resources*, *Misinformed Individuals*, and *Well-Informed Individuals* through five flows and six dynamic rates, ensuring theoretical coherence and interpretability. Simulations across two scenarios, with varying levels of resources and education effectiveness, yield outcomes consistent with real-world expectations. Designed for extensibility, the model can accommodate additional components or refined relationships, while further feedback loops could enhance realism and predictive power. It also offers a foundation for future comparison with existing models, highlighting its novelty and potential to address current research gaps.

Future research may explore more complex nonlinear modeling, empirical validation and calibration, or application to specific misinformation events to test robustness. Policy-focused simulations could assess interventions like education campaigns, fact-checking, or misinformation source regulation. Resource optimization under budget constraints could enhance impact, while sensitivity analyses may reveal key parameters and long-term intervention effects. Integrating complementary approaches and leveraging machine learning for parameter estimation, calibration, and strategy optimization would further strengthen the model. Together, these directions advance societal resilience, with education as a central pillar in combating misinformation.

REFERENCES

Ali, A., & Qazi, I. A. (2023). Countering misinformation on social media through educational interventions: Evidence from a randomized experiment in Pakistan. *Journal of Development Economics, 163*, 103108. DOI: 10.1016/j.jdeveco.2023.103108

Ammara, U., Bukhari, H., & Qadir, J. (2020).Analyzing Misinformation through the Lens of Systems Thinking.*Proceedings of the 2nd Conference on Truth and Trust Online* (TTO 2020), Boston, MA, USA, 55–63.

Bala, B. K., Arshad, F. M., & Noh, K. M. (2017).*System Dynamics: Modelling and Simulation*. Springer Texts in Business and Economics. Springer, Singapore. DOI: 10.1007/978-981-10-2045-2

Bateman, J., & Jackson, D. (2024).Countering Disinformation Effectively: An Evidence-Based Policy Guide.https://carnegieendowment.org/research/2024/01/countering-disinformation-effectively-an-evidence-based-policy-guide?lang=en

Blanc, Y. (2023, August 11). Education and critical thinking as tools in the battle against fake news.https://world-education-blog.org/2023/08/11/education-and-critical-thinking-as-tools-in-the-battle-against-fake-news/

Bragazzi, N. L., & Garbarino, S. (2024). Understanding and Combating Misinformation: An Evolutionary Perspective. *JMIR Infodemiology, 2024*(4), e65521. DOI: 10.2196/65521 PMID: 39466077

Chen, C., & Shu, K. (2024). Combatting misinformation in the age of LLMs: Opportunities and challenges. *AI Magazine, 45*(3), 354–368. DOI: 10.1002/aaai.12188

CoE. (2024). Dealing with propaganda, misinformation and fake news – intro. Council of Europe.https://www.coe.int/en/web/campaign-free-to-speak-safe-to-learn/compendium/-/asset_publisher/V117nfhFNH6d/content/dealing-with-propaganda-misinformation-and-fake-news-intro

Concepcion, A., & Sy, C. (2023). Modeling the Spread of Fake News on Social Networking Sites Using the System Dynamics Approach. *ASEAN Engineering Journal, 13*(4), 69–78. DOI: 10.11113/aej.v13.19251

Concepcion, A. R., & Sy, C. L. (2022).A System Dynamics Model of False News on Social Networking Sites.*Proceedings of the 2022 IEEE International Conference on Industrial Engineering and Engineering Management* (IEEM 2022), Kuala Lumpur, Malaysia, 786–790. DOI: 10.1109/IEEM55944.2022.9989859

EC. (2022a). *Final report of the Commission expert group on tackling disinformation and promoting digital literacy through education and training: Final report*. European Commission.Publications Office of the European Union.DOI: 10.2766/283100

EC (2022b).*Guidelines for teachers and educators on tackling disinformation and promoting digital literacy through education and training*.European Commission. Publications Office of the European Union.DOI: 10.2766/28248

Ecker, U. K. H., Lewandowsky, S., Cook, J., Schmid, P., Fazio, L. K., Brashier, N., Kendeou, P., Vraga, E. K., & Amazeen, M. A. (2022). The psychological drivers of misinformation belief and its resistance to correction. *Nature Reviews Psychology*, *1*(1), 13–29. DOI: 10.1038/s44159-021-00006-y

Elliott, V. (2023, December 28). Generative AI Learned Nothing From Web 2.0. https://www.wired.com/story/generative-ai-web-2-mistakes/

Fisher, M. (2023, March 15). Octavian, Mark Antony and the Ancient Battle of "Fake News".https://martinifisher.com/2023/03/15/octavian-mark-antony-and-the-ancient-battle-of-fake-news/

Gao, S., Wang, Y., & Platt, L. S. (2021). Modeling U.S. Health Agencies' Message Dissemination on Twitter and Users' Exposure to Vaccine-related Misinformation Using System Dynamics. In A. Adrot, R. Grace, K. Moore, &C. Zobel (Eds.),*Proceedings of the 18th International Conference on Information Systems for Crisis Response and Management* (ISCRAM 2021), Blacksburg, VA, USA, 333−344.

Gohil, K., & Nightingale, P. (2023, July 7). Demystifying Web 2.0 and Web 3.0: Understanding the Evolution of the World Wide Web. https://www.shoosmiths.com/insights/articles/demystifying-web-2-and-web-3-understanding-the-evolution-of-the-world-wide-web

Goldstein, J. A., Chao, J., Grossman, S., Stamos, A., & Tomz, M. (2024). How persuasive is AI-generated propaganda? *PNAS Nexus*, *3*(2), pgae034. Advance online publication. DOI: 10.1093/pnasnexus/pgae034 PMID: 38380055

Gonczi, A., Palosaari, C., Mayer, A., & Urban, N. (2022). From User to Creator: Helping Students See Inside the "Black Box" with Insight Maker. *Science Teacher (Normal, Ill.)*, *89*(3), 32–37. https://www.nsta.org/science-teacher/science-teacher-januaryfebruary-2022/user-creator. DOI: 10.1080/00368555.2022.12293666

Gross, E.-C., & Balaban, D. C. (2025). The Effectiveness of an Educational Intervention on Countering Disinformation Moderated by Intellectual Humility. *Media and Communication*, *13*, 9109. Advance online publication. DOI: 10.17645/mac.9109

Guzmán Rincón, A., Barragán Moreno, S., Rodríguez-Canovas, B., Carrillo Barbosa, R. L., & Africano Franco, D. R.GuzmánRincón. (2023). Social Networks, Disinformation and Diplomacy: A Dynamic Model for a Current Problem. *Humanities & Social Sciences Communications, 10*(1), 505. DOI: 10.1057/s41599-023-01998-z

Guzmán Rincón, A., Carrillo Barbosa, R. L., Segovia-García, N., & Africano Franco, D. R.GuzmánRincón. (2022). Disinformation in Social Networks and Bots: Simulated Scenarios of Its Spread from System Dynamics. *Systems, 10*(2), 34. DOI: 10.3390/systems10020034

Huang, H., Chen, W., Xie, T., Wei, Y., Feng, Z., & Wu, W. (2021). The Impact of Individual Behaviors and Governmental Guidance Measures on Pandemic-Triggered Public Sentiment Based on System Dynamics and Cross-Validation. *International Journal of Environmental Research and Public Health, 18*(8), 4245. DOI: 10.3390/ijerph18084245 PMID: 33923746

Imeri, L. (2024). The Role of Education in the Fight against Fake News.https://f2n2.mk/en/the-role-of-education-in-the-fight-against-fake-news

IMM. (n.d.). InsightMaker Manual. https://insightmaker.com/help

IMOW. (n.d.).InsightMaker Official Website.https://insightmaker.com/

Javornik, Š., & Klemenčič Mirazchiyski, E. (2023). Factors Contributing to School Effectiveness: A Systematic Literature Review. *European Journal of Investigation in Health, Psychology and Education, 13*(10), 2095–2111. DOI: 10.3390/ejihpe13100148 PMID: 37887149

Juul, J. L., & Ugander, J. (2021). Comparing information diffusion mechanisms by matching on cascade size. *Proceedings of the National Academy of Sciences of the United States of America, 118*(46), e2100786118. DOI: 10.1073/pnas.2100786118 PMID: 34750252

Kassam, N. (2020, March 25). Disinformation and coronavirus.*The Interpreter*.Lowy Institute.https://www.lowyinstitute.org/the-interpreter/disinformation-coronavirus

López, A. B., Pastor-Galindo, J., & Ruipérez-Valiente, J. A. (2024). Frameworks, Modeling and Simulations of Misinformation and Disinformation: A Systematic Literature Review. arXiv:2406.09343. /arXiv.2406.09343DOI: 10.48550

Mumtaz, N., Green, C., & Duggan, J. (2022). Exploring the Effect of Misinformation on Infectious Disease Transmission. *Systems, 10*(2), 50. DOI: 10.3390/systems10020050

Nygren, T., & Ecker, U. K. H. (2024).*Education as a countermeasure against disinformation*.Working Paper 2024:3.Lund University Psychological Defense Research Institute, Lund University, Lund, Sweden.https://uu.diva-portal.org/smash/get/diva2:1915602/FULLTEXT01.pdf

Ojha, R. P., Srivastava, P. K., Awasthi, S., Srivastava, V., Pandey, P. S., Dwivedi, R. S., Singh, R., & Galletta, A. (2023). Controlling of Fake Information Dissemination in Online Social Networks: An Epidemiological Approach. *IEEE Access : Practical Innovations, Open Solutions, 11*, 32229–32240. DOI: 10.1109/ACCESS.2023.3262737

Olan, F., Jayawickrama, U., Arakpogun, E. O., Suklan, J., & Liu, S. (2024). Fake News on Social Media: The Impact on Society. *Information Systems Frontiers, 26*(2), 443–458. DOI: 10.1007/s10796-022-10242-z PMID: 35068999

Pappas, S. (2022, January 1). Fighting fake news in the classroom. *Monitor on Psychology, 53*(1). https://www.apa.org/monitor/2022/01/career-fake-news

Radu, A. F., & Petcu, I. (2024a). Digital Technologies Used to Combat Disinformation and FakeNews. *Romanian Cyber Security Journal, 6*(1), 15–28. DOI: 10.54851/v6i1y202402

Radu, A. F., & Petcu, I. (2024b). *The Education System, The Way to Fight Fake News. Proceedings of the 5th International Conference on Machine Intelligence & Security for Smart Cities "Securing Smart Cities International Conference (SSCIC)* (Vol. 1). Security Above All., https://scrd.eu/index.php/trust/article/download/545/510/1085

Schwartz, A. B. (2016). *Broadcast Hysteria: Orson Welles's War of the Worlds and the Art of Fake News* (reprint ed.). Hill and Wang, New York, NY, USA.

Shyh, T. H., Hin, H. S., & Ju, H. T. Y. (2023). Combat Fake News: An Overview of Youth's Media and Information Literacy Education. In F. Mustaffa (ed.), *Proceedings of the 3rd International Conference on Creative Multimedia 2023* (ICCM 2023), *Advances in Social Science, Education and Humanities Research 786*, 47–61. DOI: 10.2991/978-2-38476-138-8_6

Valverde-Berrocoso, J., González-Fernández, A., & Acevedo-Borrega, J. (2022). Disinformation and multiliteracy: A systematic review of the literature. *RevistaComunicar, 70*(XXX), 93–105. DOI: 10.3916/C70-2022-08

Wardle, C. (2018, July 9). Information Disorder, Part 1: The Essential Glossary. https://medium.com/1st-draft/information-disorder-part-1-the-essential-glossary-19953c544fe3

Wijnhoven, F. (2023).*InsightMaker Introduction Course: Manual.* https://insightmaker.com/sites/ Introduction_Manual.pdf

Young, K. (2017, October 21). Moon Shot: Race, a Hoax, and the Birth of Fake News. *The New Yorker*.https://www.newyorker.com/books/page-turner/moon-shot-race-a-hoax-and-the-birth-of-fake-news

Zawadzki, T., Wałęcki, T., Świeboda, H., Szpyra, R., Kuczabski, M., & Stobiecki, P. (2020). Introduction to Methods of Modelling Information Warsas a 21st Century Threat. *European Research Studies Journal, 23*(2), 1011–1026. DOI: 10.35808/ersj/1922

Zhu, X., & Liu, F. (2017).Research on Behavior Model of Rumor Maker Based on System Dynamics.*Complexity, 2017*(1), 5094218, 9 pages.DOI: 10.1155/2017/5094218

ADDITIONAL READING

Abrams, Z. (2024, September 1). How to teach students critical thinking skills to combat misinformation online.https://www.apa.org/monitor/2024/09/media-literacy-misinformation

Akademie, D. W. (2024, March 17). How media and information literacy can fight disinformation. https://akademie.dw.com/en/how-media-and-information-literacy-can-fight-disinformation/a-67980301

Brown, C., & Holloman, S. (n.d.). Information Overload: Combating Misinformation with Critical Thinking. https://cpet.tc.columbia.edu/news-press/information-overload-combating-misinformation-with-critical-thinking

Charlton, E. (2019, May 21). How Finland is fighting fake news - in the classroom. https://www.weforum.org/stories/2019/05/how-finland-is-fighting-fake-news-in-the-classroom/

Fraser, N. (2023, October 30). Media literacy and misinformation.https://www.aph.gov.au/About_Parliament/Parliamentary_departments/Parliamentary_Library/Research/FlagPost/2023/October/media-literacy

Leedom, M. (2024, February 29). Building media literacy into school curriculums worldwide.https://news-decoder.com/building-media-literacy-into-school-curriculums-worldwide/

Oxland, E. (2018). Fighting 'Fake News' in the Classroom.https://etfovoice.ca/feature/fighting-fake-news-classroom

Salzburg Global. (n.d.). When the Truth Is Attacked, Education Fights Back. https://www.salzburgglobal.org/news/regions/article/when-the-truth-is-attacked-education-fights-back

Terada, Y. (2022, May 26). What Fact-Checkers Know About Media Literacy—and Students Should, Too. https://www.edutopia.org/article/what-fact-checkers-know-about-media-literacy-and-students-should-too

KEY TERMS AND DEFINITIONS

Causal Loop Diagrams: Causal Loop Diagrams (CLDs) are visual tools in System Dynamics that illustrate relationships, feedback loops, and causal interactions within a system, offering a qualitative framework to understand how components influence each other and drive dynamic behavior over time. Core elements include:*variables*, representing system elements or factors; *causal links*(*arrows*), showing the direction and polarity (positive or negative) of influence between variables;*feedback loops*, representing closed chains of variables and causal links, categorized as reinforcing (amplifying changes and promoting growth) or balancing (resisting change and maintaining equilibrium); and *delays*, representing time lags between a cause and its effect.

Education Resources: Education resources encompass the tools, materials, infrastructure, and support systems that enable effective teaching and learning. These include: *tangible assets*(textbooks, digital content, instructional materials, physical infrastructure such as schools, libraries, laboratories, ICT components including computerhardware, computer networks, Internet access, and educational software; *intangible assets*(educators' expertise, training, pedagogical strategies, curricula, policies, funding, and administrative support); and *targeted interventions* (media literacy programs, fact-checking tools, and awareness campaigns) to foster critical evaluation skills and resistance to false content.

Education: Education is the complex and long-lasting process of learning, acquiring knowledge, skills, values, and habits through methods such as teaching, training, and research.It serves as a foundation for personal development/growth, critical thinking, and informed decision-making.Education occurs both*formally* (in schools and universities)and*informally* (through self-study and societal interactions).

Information Pollution: Information pollution refers to the spread of misinformation, disinformation, and malinformation, along with the proliferation of hate speech and propaganda, particularly in online environments.It undermines citizens' ability to make informed decisions, fosters social divisions, erodes trust in public institutions, and complicates efforts to promote civic engagement, informed discourse, and collective problem-solving.

Misinformed Individuals: Misinformed individuals hold beliefs misaligned with verified facts due to exposure to inaccurate or misleading information. Unlike deliberate spreaders of falsehoods, they typically act without realizing their information is incorrect. Key traits include: belief in falseinformation; unintentional spread of falsehoods; high susceptibility to misinformation; and reversibility to well-informed individuals.

Stock-and-Flow Simulations: A core part of System Dynamics, Stock-and-Flow (S&F) simulations are used to quantify and model how resources, information, or entities accumulate (stocks) and move (flows) within a system over time. Key elements include: *stocks*, representing quantities accumulated at a given moment; *flows*, representing rates of change (inflows increase and outflows decrease stocks); *auxiliary variables*, representing factors influencing flows or connecting stocks indirectly, such as rates or proportions; and *feedback loops*, representing sequential connections of stocks and flows.S&F models enable visualization of system behavior over time and support scenario testing by adjusting parameters and observing outcomes.

System Dynamics (SD): A modeling methodology for analyzing and simulating complex, non-linear, and interdependent systems over time. It focuses on feedback loops, time delays, and structural drivers of dynamic behavior, helping researchers and policymakers explore scenarios. SD is now widely applied in economics, ecology, social sciences, and policy analysis.

Well-Informed Individuals: Well-informed individuals base their beliefs, decisions, and actions on accurate, evidence-based information. They verify sources, resist misinformation, and embody the following traits: access to accurate information; critical thinking; digital literacy; resilience tomisinformation; positive social impact; and engagement in lifelong learning.

Chapter 13
Exploring the Legal Framework and Education for Protection and Promotion of Truthful Information

Pranjal Khare
https://orcid.org/0000-0002-9937-9588
O.P. Jindal Global University, India

Vishambhar Raghuwanshi
https://orcid.org/0009-0009-1365-1850
Manipal University Jaipur, India

Paridhi Sharma
https://orcid.org/0009-0005-3373-0557
O.P. Jindal Global University, India

ABSTRACT

The widespread dissemination of misinformation, amplified by social media, presents a significant threat to democracies and societies globally. False narratives distort reality, manipulate public opinion, and undermine trust in institutions. Addressing this challenge requires a dual approach that combines legal regulation and educational empowerment. This chapter examines existing and emerging legal frameworks aimed at curbing the spread of harmful misinformation, alongside educational strategies designed to enhance individuals' critical thinking skills and their ability to discern fake news. It also reviews the roles of international organizations and

DOI: 10.4018/979-8-3693-9601-8.ch013

governments in implementing solutions such as stricter regulations on social media platforms, accountability measures for content, public awareness campaigns, media literacy programs, and fact-checking initiatives. By integrating legal and educational efforts, societies can become better equipped to navigate the complex information environment of the digital age and foster a more informed and resilient citizenry.

INTRODUCTION

Misinformation in the new age of the internet is one of the major antagonists the world faces today having gained momentum and coverage. Such complete misinformation distorts almost every aspect of human endeavor, politics, health, financial markets and the international system. The how and when of fake news tells even more: in the context of the extremely fast sharing of information that does not undergo any verification, coupled with the multiple embedding of the misinformation in cultural, political, and economic realities, it has become clear that there is a desperate need for scientific and efficient protection of truths. Social media has rapidly turned into a source of institutionalized misinformation and its costs are not marginal; they are becoming existential, which means that they are undermining the basis of informed societies.

The problem is all the more daunting, especially given its dimensions. In a world where billions of people have one form of interaction with the other through electronic media then it becomes very easy to spread a wrong narrative, which is a kryptonite to the traditional structures of information control. While miscreances have always been part of societies around the globe, such deceptive information disseminates rapidly and without any sort of control due to internet and social media. Thus, popular algorithms that aim at enhancing people's interest unintentionally amplify sensational or emotion-provoking material, which is often blatant misinformation. Such has been this digital architecture that there is an architecture that fosters misinformation, subtly negotiating public perception of realities. Misinformation has shown the ability to distort lives, intensify division, and erode sound deliberation, the very decisions necessary for democratic governance, right from the possibly manipulated portrayal of electoral results to the false health information (Eyal, 2024).

It means much, especially in democratic nations where good, credible information is the foundation of good citizenship and leadership. The Democratic system requires citizens to make rational choices in exercising their accountability on leaders and in developing policies which meet public desires. If false information misleads the public, then there is danger of diluting democracies. For instance, amorphous information on candidates standing for election or on electoral process disorients eligible voters or paints a picture, which, if misleading may influence the voters' decision and thereby compromise election results. Moreover, fake news leads tomore hatred, increases sectionalism and political polarization, and instills suspicion of institutions, all of which undermine democracy.

Another clear area where undue reliance on unreliable sources can lead to severe penalties is public health. The COVID-19 crisis proved that, in the field of public health, it is crucial to use data as the primary source of information. False news regarding vaccines, treatments and preventive measures are produced and disseminated in social media which negatively influences the efforts of the authorities and the population in receiving vaccines. This caution, or lack of confidence arising mainly from fake news, was bringing about real life, quantifiable consequences on the uptake of vaccines, thereby elongating the pandemic and claiming more lives. The current social problems threaten public health and call for collective actions and confidence in scientific expertise, while disinformation has revealed itself as capable of rupturing trust, hindering response efforts, and undermining the safety of the populaces (Fernandez & Alani, 2018).

Social relations are not immune to the negative impact of misinformation either, let alone international relations. Lies and propaganda, consciously or unconsciously used, can provoke hostile attitudes between countries, dictate peoples' opinions in hostile manner, and also incite conflicts. Over the political landscapes, misinformation is employed to shift the perception of individuals in the international systems, rupture partnerships and launch hostile actions. This explains why misinformation and the forces related to it within conflicts, especially when states or non-state actors leverage them for political advantage have led to appreciating the idea of it as a weapon of psychological and cultural warfare. Foreign policy decision-makers and global institutions and actors have begun to realize that misinformation is not only a problem for a particular state but also for the stability of the international system (Broda & Stromback, 2024).

To this multifaceted challenge, the next sections zoom in legal and educational approaches as means for encouraging the use of adequate and reliable information to counteract fake news. National and international laws also have crucial assignments to define the measures of accuracy in disseminating information and penalizing the individuals who post misinformation knowingly. Over the past few years, some countries have passed legislation targeting information that is considered fake, but such laws differ in the approach they take: some address content moderation, while others address the platform's liability. Nonetheless legislative measures raise some issues which induce problems regarding freedom of speech and jurisdiction of enforcement. The fact that contemporary misinformation is published in the digital space and affects countries and states worldwide increases the difficulties in enforcing national legislation and promotes the need for the development of interstate cooperation and gradual alignment of legislation in this area.

Legal measures, although required, cannot address this problem on their own as the problem of mis/disinformation is very widespread at the present. Education is found to be no less important, if not more so as a method of building human capacity in defense against such false narratives. Media literacy, for instance, prepares people to discern articles, evaluate them, look at the sources of information, and determine where to get accurate information other than from the article. In portraying education as a means of critical and skeptical belief structure nurturing, common people can effectively defend themselves from manipulation by scandals or sensationalism (Torkington, 2024). Further, through the inclusion of information literacy of learners at the different levels of education, primary, secondary and tertiary level, future generations to embrace complex information environments.

Finally, there is no one single method by which the modern man can seek information that is entirely truthful. Legal measures have to be targeted so as not to restrict some liberty might still be a beneficial one, in the process of suppressing mis-/disinformation. At the same social time Education is to be valued as a tool of nurturing a society that can distinguish between truth and falsity. Altogether, these may go some ways toward assisting the formation of an enlightened public, toward making the democratic process less volatile, toward making the world itself safer. The recipes for circulating misconceptions have not stopped changing and hence the postures of defense cannot lack reminiscence of law, education, and technology. This chapter attempts to make a modest contribution towards that discourse by examining the practical measures which center on the use of legal and educational instruments in the fight against dissemination of incorrect information.

UNDERSTANDING MISINFORMATION AND FALSE NARRATIVES

Fake news, misinformation, and disinformation are widely seen as values antithetical to democratic pluralism and destabilizing agents accountable for sowing social discord, economic disruption, and personal misery. Even though commonly these two terms are considered to be synonyms, in fact, they denote two different subtypes of fake or misleading information, which, of course, has different impacts on society. Fake information is a lie or a story that is not a true one, and it is launched with no malicious intention in mind. While information and misinformation are the spreading of honest information, disinformation is the spreading of information that is clearly fake with malicious purpose. While malinformation is the act of sharing actual information in a misleading or harmful way with intent to cause harm to an individual, group or even a nation. These distinctions are important also in comprehending the system of fake stories and their effects on different spheres of the population's life (Green et al., 2023).

Misinformation has been realized to manifest in different domains with political, social, and economic misinformation being common. Political misinformation for instance consists of lies that change people's perception of political leadership, elections and policy making. The example of the Donald Trump campaign and Brexit mentions a great many instances where planned misinformation was used and backed by external parties with the full objective of manipulating opinions and thereby sparking even higher levels of polarization. In these cases, false information circulation via social networks and internet influencing exacerbation of social splits made the questions of process' democratic nature acceleration.

Social misinformation, in the same way, is a distortion of common knowledge about any given society, this constitutes what that particular society believes in, their norms and their ways of conducting themselves. For example, rumors about vaccine efficiency or side effects during the COVID-19 pandemic brought numerous problems to public health, as people's logs about the vaccine made the COVID-19 pandemic longer and more people got sick or died from diseases that could be prevented. In some countries, such mistrust led to attacks on Health Care Workers and other staff that worsened the health predicament in affected areas. Given that social media moves in cultural and religious context, it is common for misinformation to tap into culturally or religiously sensitive issues making it even harder to deal with because it plays on the thematic tuning of the population (Krasadakis, 2024).

Economic misconceptions are related to falsehoods about financial security, employment opportunities and personal spending. For instance, fake news concerning stock market or even concern trades from cryptocurrency sites or groups instituted online have provoked great losses among people. The events at the beginning of 2021, the GameStop case, revealed that retail investors easily become locked into a stratagem since partial or misleading information can cause chain behavior with significant outcomes. Thus, misconceptions in economics lead to fluctuation in the market, social discredit of financial companies, and personal consequences.

These different types of fake news create deep social, economic and psychological impact in the society. Socially, misinformation erodes society's trust in received information from the media, governmental agencies, and scientific organizations. This deterioration of trust can trigger mistrust and in fact hostility towards the original authoritative sources and their messages preparing the ground for conspiracy theories, other explanations and views. For instance, climate change denial has, over years propagated fake news that has created an anti-science belief system that has slowed down policy measures for realizing environmental goals. As the knowledge learnt from such experts is ignored or not sought, then societies break apart revealing different groups with different beliefs as the bond holding them together disappears (Ecker et al., 2022).

In terms of the economy, misinformation can have awful outcomes. Several kinds of false information that deceive customers or investors have skewed markets, influenced improper economic decisions, and sometimes led to economic losses at the national level. For example, fake news, particularly on social media about the dangers of certain foods have been seen to greatly reduce people's consumption, to the detriment of producers in the agriculture value chain. Likewise, if perceptions are formed about the financial solidity using incorrect information like a bank being insolvent; people are likely to engage in panicky-like behavior like a run on the bank, which only worsens the problem. In an increasingly integrated global economy, distortions are created by misinformation that can propagate through different markets, manipulating supply chain and trading relationships across nations.

The classification of fake news into political, social, and economical contexts as well as the differences between misinformation, disinformation, and malinformation give a structure on how fake news exists in many aspects of life. As it has earlier been discussed, fake news distribution now transcends geographical boundaries; distorting political systems, the credibility of the democratic process, and even diplomacy. Propaganda strategies are common especially on sensational objectives like immigration or national identity in order to create confusion on the societal structures and manipulate the ledge. For instance, in Europe the far-right groups have continued to exploited disinformation that gives immigration a negative connotation as a death knell to cultural set-up. Such campaigns do affect voting, albeit in a manner that leaves societies polarized and this renders popular consensus decision making unsustainable (Ochoa et al., 2024)

Technologically driven social misinformation is the spread of erroneous information within social networks, with the simultaneous potential of endangering the lives of individuals within a given society at any given time when such posts are crafted to address topics associated with health or safety concerns. Sometimes the ignorance associated with the subject provokes public panic in connection with the identification of the virus and circulation of myths regarding its transmission and treatment during the Ebola virus epidemic in West Africa, leading to the abandonment of treatment, quarantine measures and isolation (Wardle, 2023). Similar patterns were seen during the COVD-19 pandemic when quack remedies such as ingesting hydroxychloroquine or bleach also emerged as potential treatments and resulted in hospitalizations and deaths. Misinformation of social issues also tends to take advantage of societal susceptibility including prejudice or fear, to influence people's perception and behavior. Indeed, bearing on these vulnerabilities, when false information is nursed the impact is exponential: the community is split on all fronts and may lead to violence (Beauvais, 2022).

Misinformation about economies can have the capacity to destabilize an economy together with bringing about change in the economic activities that go round all through the financial market procedures which is facilitated through the digitized platforms. Frauds that boast of high rates of return appear on the social networks, which lots of people contribute serious money and lose their money. This kind of economic interference is most lethal to the new or ignorant persons in the market since they lack adequate appreciation regarding tendentious securities. Misinformation is therefore used to manipulate economic information hence taking advantage of information asymmetry whereby particular individuals have superior knowledge to other people hence taking advantage of the later through unscrupulous means that could potentially harm society.

Analyzing the social, economic, and psychological impact of misinformation, one understands that misinformation is a multi-dimensional problem. In its long-term constellation, misinformation becomes capable of eroding key societal values embedded in commonly shared constructs of social norms, institutional trust and collective problem-solving capacity. According to the information, the perception of such a generation might be distorted as long as rather popular with youth channels are being used to spread unreliable information. As a result, there are potential ramifications for the overall process of democratic participation and governance, as the audience continuously obtains distorted narratives, either in regard to an individual politician or political parties and candidates in general, to be disillusioned with formal democratically established processes, not to solely distance themselves from voting, but to potentially subscribe to the use of extralegal force (Anderson & Rainie, 2017).

Thus, misinformation, disinformation, and malinformation do not represent a single united phenomenon but a cascade of threats with numerous negative implications for people and society in general. Studying the peculiarities of these information types, as well as the range of domains they influence, provides the opportunity for elaborating a more complex strategy for combating misinformation. Reducing the spread of misinformation requires a multimodal approach that is enforceable through law, taught in school and augmented through technology with special techniques for addressing each type of misinformation. It is only when these impacts are seen as interconnected that societies can muster sufficient action against the dangers from fake and deceptive information.

Legal Framework for Combating Misinformation

This influence of fake news has elicited a wide range of actions at the international and national levels, nuclear and acting, given that the policy makers, legal scholars and human rights activist aim at advocating and balancing between right to freedom of expression and right to truthful information. Several codes and standards, based on the recommendations of the United Nations, UNESCO activities, and certain conventions, relate misinformation to human rights. National responses differ a lot and are influenced by differences in legal frameworks, cultural prejudices, and democratic ideals. This paper investigates the international standards and conventions on misinformation and how the five major jurisdictions of the world, the United States, the European Union, Australia, India, and Brazil are seeking to ban this problem while upholding freedom of rights.

The United Nations has come out strongly as an active organization that has responded proactively to ensure it halts any actions that promote threats possible by misinformation especially to human rights and democracy. Resultantly, the UN Human Rights Council's advancement for Promoting and Protecting the Right to Freedom of Opinion and Expression (year 2021) enunciates the stance of the organization for the misconception regularization at equilibrate level and ensuring the right to freedom of expression. The UN guidelines which prescribe ways of addressing fake news are clear that curbing such information cannot encroach upon democratic liberties or let governments escalate unjust restrictions on opposition (Zimdars & Mcleod, 2020). The report also insists that any limitation of misinformation should fulfil the principles of lawfulness, immediacy, and dips offence, this to ensure that counteractions to misinformation do not occasion inhibition.

Expanding on the above, the UN Secretary-General's Digital Cooperation Roadmap offers a blueprint to address the vice in question with a special note that platforms must be held to account within the space. Noting that the spread of correct and false information is carried out largely through social networks, the existence of a detailed plan for the further actions of states, companies, and public organizations for raising digital literacy and popularizing truthful data is produced. This set of guidelines also includes counter-speech as an efficient non- interfering measure against misinformation and emphasizes that nations should work to ensure that the latter's anti-fake news policies promote accurate rather than suppress false narratives.

UNESCO has been one of the pioneers in advocacy towards Media and Information Literacy as a proactive process against fake news. In its Global Media and Information Literacy Week and in associated activities such as the MIL CLICKS social media project, UNESCO has underlined the importance of information literacy. UNESCO Internet Universality ROAM-X indicators based on Rights Openness Access for All and Multi-stakeholder participation gives frames the Internet environment should support an informed active citizenship. These efforts are made in accordance with UNESCO's work on Article 19 of the Universal Declaration of Human Rights entitling every individual the right "to seek, receive and impart information and ideas through any media (Ordway, 2017).

Another program under UNESCO is media literacy because UNESCO believes that informed citizens cannot easily be misled. At the same time, UNESCO takes necessary steps by helping people get prepared to analyze information and consequently the idea of emerging as a protective shield will be less required and people will be able to act more freely. UNESCO has also partnered with social media companies to convene social media that supports posting of education-related content and engaging social media platforms to support fact-checking work. Nevertheless, UNESCO does not rush to support too severe limitations as long as the regulation of misinformation violates the rights of individuals and has significant negative effects on freedom of speech (Singh & Sunil, 2020).

Besides UN and UNESCO activities, more and more treaties and agreements discuss misinformation from the human rights perspective. The International Covenant on Civil and Political Rights (ICCPR) is basic in this regard because Article 19 of ICCPR guarantees the right to freedom of expression, whilst setting out the circumstances under which freedoms can be restricted for the purpose of respecting the principles of national security, public order, health or morals. Paragraph 34 of the ICCPR provided an elaboration on aforesaid observation that any restriction hence to speech /information including misinformation, should be so designed as to prevent the freedom of ideas (Galligher & Tanner, 2024).

Regional treaties also follow this approach too. In accordance with the ECHR under Article 10 freedom of expression can be restrained if this measure is legal, proportional and serves a legitimate interest. Over the years, the Council of Europe has issued some guidelines for combating the flow of fake news on the Internet with the governments being urged not to interfere too much with online communication. They do so to reaffirm the principle in international law whereby freedom of expression is protected, but concurrently, measures should be taken to prevent different forms of hostile false information by adopting policies which are proportional and necessary.

As to legal regulation of misinformation, such measures adopted in countries have been varied, which can be explained by the differences in the legal systems of countries: their philosophical orientations that are the basis of legal systems of various countries, one is free speech or freedom of information, while the other is the principle of the truth.

The constitution of liberal democracy in the United States of America presents essential protective rights of speech to free speech, and thus it becomes difficult for the government to regulate misinformation. As in the New York Times Co. v. Sullivan (1964) case, the US Supreme Court set up high barriers to control speech, especially on public matters. However, with the advent of fake news, there has been discussions on The Section 230 of The Communications Decency Act through which online services do not take legal responsibility for the content created by its users.

New misinformation threats drive some members of the United States Congress to push for changes in Section 230 which protects the companies from legal responsibility when their platform hosts dangerous content (Banchio, 2024). However, any legislative actions must tread carefully on constitutional First Amendment protections, due to the United States' policy of freedom of speech.

The most active regulatory approach has been developed by the European Union represented by the Digital Services Act (DSA) and the Code of Practice on Disinformation. The DSA imposes clear obligations for platforms to reveal recommendation or demotion systems that either favor or disadvantage certain content. Moreover, underneath the EU Code of Practice, that is merely guidelines, recommends social media companies to work with fact-checkers and give a label to misinformation. This is contrary to the US reporting of laws on free speech where the EU's regulatory perspective takes an overarching approach to freedom of speech (Gaur, 2021). It is equally worth pointing out that the EU's GDPR also combats misinformation by obligating platforms to safeguard consumers' information from being exploited or inappropriately used, thus making cyberspace safer overall.

An example of a correct approach is how Australia has adopted legislation against misinformation through the News Media Bargaining Code that compelled the major technology companies to pay for news content, with the latter indirectly supporting trusted information outlets. The Australian Communications and Media Authority (ACMA) has also come up with what it terms misinformation code to assist the digital platforms to detect and prevent fake content. Furthermore, Australia has Section 79 of the Criminal Code Act that establishes as a criminal offence to make a communication falsehood knowing it is communicated in relation to a scheme of operations and the circumstances include a health risk scheme of operations or a natural disaster scheme of operations. This legal framework shows that the country supports media accountability and at the same time protects its citizens from wrong sources of information as well as protect journalism (Funke & Flamini, 2024).

The issues of misinformation to some extent are unique to Indian context because of the huge population, the heterogeneity in terms of languages spoken, and a very active presence on social media. The Information Technology (Intermediary Guidelines and Digital Media Ethics Code) Rules, 2021 now force the social media platforms to take down competitive content that the government considers fake or potentially damaging. However, these regulations have raised the questions of over-regulation because the rules provide the government with great power over the meant digital contents. Even the Indian Supreme Court has realized that right to information is inherent in Article 19 regarding freedom of speech and expression but there remains question on how much regulation is acceptable (Jens, 2024). India has adopted similarly lion something which tries to reel in misinformation while not encroaching on the rights of the populace.

The Fake News Bill that was proposed in Brazil also known as the Brazilian Law on Freedom, Responsibility and Transparency, requires social media providers to remove and inform users of false information concerning the elections and the public health crises. This legislation also makes demands for the platforms' presentations where sponsored content comes from. The bill has not been spared criticism among civil rights activists who claim that the bill threatens to curtail freedom of digital expression through over regulation. However, by now, Brazil presents a very engaged position when it comes to misinformation, especially when there are threats to the lives of its people or the country's democracy.

The regulation of misinformation at the international and national levels shows how free speech interferes with the suppression of the exchanges of truthful information and vice versa. The legal frameworks include ICCPR and ECHR to determine legal limits to free speech restrictions. At the national level, the approaches differ greatly, the U.S has high levels of free speech protection, EU enacted legislation that encompasses all the internet elements, the countries like Australia, India and Brazil have rules that can be adapted to the political, social and legal situation in these states. Because misinformation will persist to change, these frameworks shall have to change with it in order to address the risks of misinformation whilst not infringing on rights. Collectively, as a rights-based society, we can fight hard for the legal and regulatory reform that will uphold the principles of truthful information in a people's polity.

Role of Technology and Digital Tools

New media technologies have accelerated the flow of information through social media to incredible levels. While social media has made it easier for people to access information it has also made it easier to disseminate fake news due to extensive impacts on society. At the heart of this process are the algorithms that drive engagement and which in essence, promote provocative or outright fake news. It is for this complex interaction between social media, interaction between algorithmic and the spread of fake news that the legal and ethical questions of responsibility and disclosure of the platforms have been raised. As for these challenges, artificial intelligence has appeared as a measure to fight false information using NLP, along with image checking. This discussion, therefore, focuses on the effects of social networking in the dissemination of information, additional concerns of social media platform responsibility, ethic and legal, and challenges that artificial intelligence can solve in internetworked information systems.

Information dissemination through social media platforms has enhanced the creation of information platforms that are easy to access, interactive and real time. Social sites such as Facebook, Twitter, Instagram and YouTube have provided people an opportunity to disseminate /receive information in the blink of an eye to audiences all around the globe. That said, this connectivity opens great opportunities for information sharing while making misinformation particularly pathological. Due to the fact that social media is much more engaging to users than traditional media by the very process of interaction it engages emotions, and people share posts without confirming whether the information provided is true or not. Therefore, lies spread more easily and widely on social networks than on mass media and present several difficulties for regulators and society.

The wall also presents the decisions made by algorithm in terms of which posts go viral from likes, shares, and comments from users on the social media platforms. The algorithms developed to engage the users of such platforms put into consideration the content that causes extreme effects such as extreme polarization; and thus sensationalism, is boosted. This is well observed in conditions like the elections, where fake political information goes viral, or in the case of the current pandemic, where fake treatment or vaccine information spreads. Studies have shown that entertaining algorithms are more likely to foment polarization or offend someone, as such posts will gain more attention. In this sense, users' desire to spend more time on these sites and the need of social media companies to satisfy this desire, may override the societal need for accurate information (Radu & Petcu, 2024).

In addition, algorithms, which generate filter bubbles and echo chambers, maintain users' own opinions and do not allow exposure to other views. Filter bubbles are generated by recommending content based on the user's previous activity that effectively promotes some ideas. While embedding content which has the higher likelihood of engagement and which is preferred due to the user's past actions, algorithms reinforce the misinformation to a wide audience.

This is why social media platforms have shifted more to be legally and ethically questionable for the spread of misinformation. Chief of these is the question of whether social media firms bear responsibility for the content they transmit or if they are mere carriers. In countries like the United States, for example, they are protected by Section 230 of the Communications Decency Act that say that the platform is not liable for the content provided by users of the site. Thus, while such provision helped foster the emergence of online platforms, critics suggest it allows big corporations to avoid accountability for the social value that fake news erode. Democrats have recently urged the Congress to change Section 230 to make platforms accountable for the distribution of fake or damaging information relate to the presidential elections, shows increasing concern toward the influence these sites have on societies (Kreps, 2020).

In the European Union, the Digital Services Act (DSA) appears as an attempt to improve transparency and accountability. The DSA also ensures that the social media companies reveal some information concerning the contents placed on the channels which the companies own and manage, especially on the algorithms which they employ in the ranking of certain contents for presentation or entirely banning from the Chanel. It also makes them estimate and address risks from misinformation, putting pressure on massive platforms to address measures for the public interest. Similarly, the EU's Code of Practice on Disinformation include recommendations requiring platforms to engage with verified fact-checkers and to prevent the distribution of misinformation and the promotion of reliable sources as a non-binding code of conduct. These regulations are heads towards a more civil and responsible process which intended to decrease the ill consequences of fake news but does not limit the people's rights to express their opinion (Li & Callegari, 2024).

Ethical questions add to the interaction of responsibility allegiances even more. Social media applications introduce trends to the public, but the decision-making process in this case is not transparent. Ethical issues are observed as to how much such private firms should regulate the information dissemination that does not always meet the common good. For instance, the algorithms that aim at increasing engagement may suggest articles that erode trust or articles that encourage violence. This tension becomes the ethical conflict of interest at play; between the industry profit and informing the citizens responsibly. Demands for Algorithmic audits, insisting that firms open the way algorithms work, characterizes the emerging acknowledgment that companies require the public to be accountable to fight against misinformation (Unver, 2023).

Although social networking sites are among the primary purveyors of fake news, and algorithms linked to it, Artificial Intelligence shows the potential of becoming effective solutions. Other technologies like NLPs and image verification also present various capabilities to detect and prevent fake information and bring solutions generally manageable and versatile in many situations. To this end, AI may enable the filtering of a large volume of content in real time and therefore prevent possible tendencies to misinformation hence minimizing the effect of such influences on the overall population (Khare, 2025).

Textual misinformation detection finds significant use of natural language processing. The main methods of NLP include determining the presence of false information by analyzing the language patterns and mathematical calculation of such parameters as morphological and syntactical complexity, and semantic density. For example, existing NLP algorithms can consider marking posts that contain conspiracy theories, abusive language, or misinformation that defies approved sources. Currently, Facebook and Twitter use NLP-based tools to flag and categorize fake news, although the effectiveness is targeting language dependent as well as the context. NLP algorithms can also detect patterns of these misinformative posts so platforms can more effectively detect new narratives as well. Still, there are context and subtlety issues, inability to interpret satire, opinion, or sarcasm as misinformation rather than a signal of opinion divergent from information (Singh, 2023).

As deepfakes and manipulated media spread, image verification has become critical to fighting misinformation and AI-powered tools have emerged as a first line of defense. Such tools work by checking on metadata related to the image together with pixel coherence and numerous visual characteristics in order to flag those images that have been digitally manipulated or misrepresented. For instance, it has been established that platforms employ reverse image searching algorithms to ascertain whether images that have gone viral are used in a different context and, thereby, to detect instances of manipulations. Image verification throughout the COVID-19 situation showed that AI does have the potential to fight false visual information by suppressing several fake images regarding the virus and its treatments. However, as deepfake technology becomes more sophisticated, it is still difficult to create methods by which they can be effectively verified. Due to the arms race between the sides creating and fighting misinformation and the constant invention of new means of manipulation, AI has to be developed constantly (Kanozia, 2019).

However, there are certain drawbacks of AI in their attempt to combat fake news as we shall discover below. One of the biggest issues that must be overcome is the ability to reduce the likelihood of blocking legitimate material while still claiming high degrees of accuracy. AI systems might fail at understanding subtle cases or such cases as satire and can be blamed for overacting and frequently potentially censoring necessary and important information. In addition, there is a concern that those algorithms are themselves trained on media content that tends to reflect a particular point of view, and therefore when the system turns to searching for fake news, it fails to recognize the content from the side that shares its own bias. Making AI-driven misinformation control fair and transparent needs to be thoroughly tested and improved for a long time due to such a high probability of ethical violation.

In addition to detection, AI is also used in response and awareness campaigns too. AI can be employed in platforms to provide media literacy in terms of resources, to put an issue into context or to give the right information when a hoax one was provided. For instance, recommendation-based mechanisms can work to subsequently recommend learning material from reliable sources to alter and destabilize filter bubbles and echo chambers.

These aspects of society such as social media presence, algorithm and AI in the distribution and regulation of fake news present an advance view of the information generation and distribution system in the age of information (Khare & Raghuwanshi, 2025). So called engagement-based social media platforms have enabled the spread of false information by design: legal and ethical implications. Honest speech initiatives like the EU's Digital Services Act are indicative of a new zeitgeist which has begun to explicitly consider the value of free speech against the need for truthful speech.

At the same time, AI has been providing useful technologies for misinformation, ranging from NLP to image, with the advanced technology that should be applied prudently for mis-categorization or deploying bias. Finally, since the problem of combating fake news is still very relevant to present-day society, the further progress of modern society in this issue will require integrated work, the results of which will have to include transparent legislation, ethical standards, and the development of artificial intelligence. We have seen that through combined efforts one can design the digital environment in a way that the freedom of expression is supported though the information integrity is protected.

Case Studies of Legal and Educational Misinformation

Sometime, but not always, misinformation or misinformation has been a massive problem in crises, particularly in the context of health and elections, threatening governance, public confidence, and social cohesion. In the past few years especially the storyline of the COVID 19 pandemic, false news that circulate in the social networks poses a potentially deleterious threat to public health intervention as well as vaccination campaigns. Just like disinformation in elections have had similar impacts towards destabilizing democratic systems in other countries by eroding public trust in electoral systems and fueling political polarization. In response, the societies of the countries worldwide have introduced a variety of legal and educational measures with the focus on the fight against fake news, wanting to maintain the rights of citizens and the democracies' health while paying regard to people's freedom. These are discussed in this section along with global measures to combat health and electoral misinformation and misinformation that fueled conflicts as case studies are the follow up legal and educational measures taken (Samdani & Dimri, 2024).

Because the problem of health misinformation during COVID-19 was global, the legal actions to counter it were taken with different levels of strictness across countries. Governments of the countries such as Germany and France passed bills that allowed repression of fake news that posed an immediate threat to human life. Such measures are in Germany where the Netz DG Act was further upgraded to force the social media platforms to remove the violate contents including the unhealthy health news within a realization period of 24 hours. France also acted to make new laws for governing bodies to penalize social media which do not limit fake news and disinformation on COVID-19. These laws are intended to ensure that platforms take measures against the lies that fueled their sites and react more nimbly to toxic speech. The same was done in Singapore where the Protection from Online Falsehoods and Manipulation Act (POFMA) enabled the government to direct individuals and social media providers stating health misinformation to issue correction orders. This legal structure allowed Singaporean authorities to give source information together with or instead for such posts, which was going to prevent public confusion as the law intended without completely censoring speech.

However, educational approaches were incorporated as a part of health mis/disinformation intervention since governments, and global institutions embarked on massive awareness creation. Many such campaigns were aimed at disseminating scientifically sound factual data over the commonly accessible channels as often the users found themselves under the information overload stream. So, WHO started its activity with the MythBusters campaign through social media platforms to combat the myths surrounding the Coronavirus pandemic and encourage people to stick strictly to real and accurate health information. Governments all across the globe collaborated with the tech giants to boost such authentic content. For instance, both Twitter and Facebook have set up COVID-19 information hubs which allowed users to receive trusted data from the WHO and other national health organizations (Pappas, 2022). These information centers not only provided users with fact-based data but also provided them with information about how to avoid fake news, and how readers should live without blindly spreading information acquired on the web.

Another clear example of disinformation during the pandemic is the flood of anti-vaccine posts which rose to popularity through social media and some news channels. The process of vaccine reluctance, particularly in the United States, was fueled by various myths regarding COVID-19 vaccines, which contributed to the long lasting of pandemic, additionally to reach herd immunity. Consequently, the U.S government launched an elaborate campaign intended to popularize the COVID19 vaccine asserting that it was safe and effective, it employed the help of local leaders and other influential figures to persuade those who were hesitant about getting vaccinated. As part of educational measures, data practices were combined with the identification of mis- and disinformation trends by health authorities as well as the targeting of addressing specific issues arising among certain demographics. This is why it was the case where misinformation compounded a health crisis, which can only be addressed through legal, social and educational solutions (Nealon, 2024).

Aside from health field, misinformation has greatly affected electoral process resulting in political instability and aforementioned democratic institutions. Sowing of wrong information during votes mainly refers to the provision of wrong information to do with how to vote, background information about candidates as well as wrong information concerning the results of votes. Legal and educational responses to electoral misinformation have therefore become crucial for the defense of democracies and for an enlightened citizenship.

To diminish the level of misinformation in the EU, the mentioned Code of Practice on Disinformation has been the key policy focused on the regulation of electoral interference. While it is still voluntary, the Code calls for social medial firms to be forthcoming about political ads purchasing on their platforms, work with third-party verification services and shut down accounts that traffic in fake news. The Code has performed well especially in cases of electoral misinformation during the European Parliament elections, Facebook Twitter took pro-active measures to make sure and verify political content and reduce visibility of false information. EU's obsession with free and open information system has extended such debates on how other related electoral laws should guard against fake news without infringing on freedom of speech (Tan, 2022).

In the case of the United States, mis/disinformation regarding the 2020 presidential election led to ones of the biggest tests for the country's democratic institutions. Lies about election fraud swirled through social media discrediting the election to a high extent with voters and leading to violent consequences such as the attack on the Capitol on January 6th, 2021. As a result, the US government launched probes of the sources and boosters of disinformation, and most of the largest social networks put brakes on non-linked profiles related to the matter of the election fraud. Legal initiatives were also pursued at the state level: several states passed laws that require the political ads to be 'Made in Washington' to be more transparent in social media.

Brazil also represents another valuable case because false information has become an incredibly significant factor that determines the perception of the population during the elections. Given the rising threat of fake news, the Brazilian Superior Electoral Court (TSE) developed collaborations with social media platforms to counteract the problem during the 2018 and 2022 electoral campaigns. The TSE had put in place measures of fact-checking and brought out information crusade for efficient flow of right information with a lot of emphasis on the electronic media users/voters. The latter shows that the work of the TSE illustrates the need for cooperation between legal establishments and new technologies in the countries where misinformation has deepened the political polarization. This example goes to show that fighting electoral misinformation in law and education needs dynamism because the approaches employed must deal with different sociopolitical conditions of the countries in question (Sharevski & Loop, 2024).

Apart from distorting health and electoral matters, falsehood has deepened hostility in conflicts and crises and at some point, catalyzes violence. Sometimes, fake news has helped fan ethnic, religious, or political tensions in some places, requiring immediate legal and educational actions. For instance, false news on the social media in, led to increased escalation of violence against the Rohingya minority in Myanmar. Rumors and fake news spread rapidly, and hatred grew, and as a result people supported prejudice measures. In turn Facebook responded and began to address the issue of being responsible for the moderation of content in the country. Internal cases remain relatively small due to Myanmar's political condition but there has been a push from the international human rights organizations demanding better regulation of hate speech for conflict regions.

It is like what has been happening in India where fake news regarding the religious groups has been at large especially on the WhatsApp. These narratives have sometimes resulted in mob action which poses danger to life and exacerbates conflict along social lines. In response, the Indian government has passed legal approaches that compelled the platforms to trace the sources of the viral messages despite sparking privacy and free speech issue. In addition to practicing legal measures, changes in people's awareness and more disciplined approach to interacting in cyber-space through educational campaigns with the goal to teach people to distinguish the difference between fake and genuinely factual news has been initiated in order to prevent the consequences of misinformation when it comes to relations in the communities.

Besides, conflicts have also occasionally been accompanied by misrepresentation, which has attracted the international systems' attention. To counteract misinformation, the UN has already started using such projects as the Verified campaign aimed at combating COVID-19 misinformation and later broadened to other focal areas. Identifying misinformation, the campaign offers credible information on certain topics that prevents tensions resulting from false information. A number of global organizations including UNESCO have ramped up such campaigns through promotion of media and information literacy especially among such nations at the risk of being fed with hybrid warfare propaganda. All these efforts are aimed at pointing out the place of the international society in combating the vice especially in situations that endanger human security (Jiang & Wang, 2024).

This means that the fight against misinformation in health, electoral, and conflict contexts needs to be legal actioned with education. As shown in the COVID-19 pandemic, when fake news arises and spreads in the context of health issues, efforts to protect the population's health suffer, so it takes quick action from lawyers and huge public awareness campaigns with factual data. Therefore, with support from legal frameworks in Education, Media literacy programs can be enhanced to grow the societies of each country when interconnecting the world by helping them to overcome the difficulties of misinformation. When the peoples of the world continue to do as they have done here today and work together, the common good will be to have a more truthful presentation of the world which minimizes the effects associated with it.

CONCLUSION AND THE WAY FORWARD

Misinformation is not set in stone; on the contrary, misinformation is malleable and changes with alacrity as new technologies and media come on stream to spread falsehoods at a higher octane. This plasticity can only mean that such work has to go on and laws and educational endeavors have to be anticipatory and assertively responsive to filter out misconceptions. Dispelling misinformation is not an end-point or linear process of policy formulation or even international collaboration but requires a society of media and policy majors, political leaders, and citizens.

An enlightened citizenry continues to be the foundation of democracy, societal recovery, and world peace. Misinformation is a problem to these foundations by providing wrong and skewed knowledge in the populace and organization decision-making procedures and undermining their trust. A society that is informed and critical in its reception of media and with an understanding of the dangers of misinformation is better placed to be an active participant in the democratic project, protect the health of the society, and to support social cohesion. Here, then, one can see the roles that the legal systems and educational facilities perform, on the one hand, countering fake news, and, on the other hand, cultivating the reader and the consumer of the information. However, as misinformation forms continue to change, it does imply that the same must apply to the tools that we use in containing it.

If the legal measures against misinformation are to be effective in the first place, then they should be sufficiently adaptive to respond to the developing nature of popular technologies and the increasing complexity and malice of misinformation strategies. It is becoming rather difficult for current laws to crumble to contain misinformation since most of them lag far behind updated technology. For example, the use of deep fakes, synthetic media, in which a person's image is cloned onto another person's body has only recently been banned in many countries. However, as the regulating agencies try to design regulations concerning synthetic media, the technology expands, developing new problems of identification and legal responsibility. To address such challenges, countries should adopt a process that can be referred to as a cycle, where problems arising in the technological field can be reflected in the legislation and corrected at a certain stage, after they have accumulated sufficient experience in this field.

States like the US and EU have already set laws regulating how social media should handle false information that endangers the populace. Although the emphasis should shift from penalties as the sole strategy, extensible to encompass a variety of preventive legal measures that promote responsibility for content distribution. One of them could be the channelization to require 'openness' from those that serve to filter and popularize content on the site so as not to contribute to spreading false information. One could involve the enhancement of labeling or flagging policies in order to enhance user understanding of information credibility.

Furthermore, it means that any legal solution should preserve the right to Freedom of speech that is regarded as one of the primary human rights, as well as restrain cyber manipulation. Over these two objectives, there is always some tension, and these two objectives must be balanced in a way that upholds public confidence in the legal systems. Governments should investigate regulating some misinformation as less severe or harmless (for instance non-partisan satire) and others as being highly dangerous; for instance, an unverified health or an unverified message before an election. This stratified model would enable fine grades of distinction with aims to honor the liberty of speech when policing harmful misinformation. Additionally, independent regulatory authorities can also equally review other legal measures as to their compliance with free speech principles and engage in checks and balances systems over regulatory authorities.

Although legal activities are helpful, informative activities are also demanding for forming a lasting solution to the problem of false information. It is therefore important through education a person is armed with means, criterion, and practices that enable him or her to scrutinize information, recognize or possible fakes, and where to find authentic information. To accomplish this means, curricula must include media literacy and critical thinking from an early stage and allow students to comprehend the difficulties of the present information environment. For example, any set of lessons on media literacy could contain lessons on identifying formal fallacies, sources' reliability, and the reasons behind creating different kinds of content. This education must be cyclical, in responding to the fresh forms of media and strategies of misinforming launched on the public by various stakeholders.

In particular, the focus should shift toward the role of universities and tertiary learning institutions within society. Education for primary and secondary level is clear cut and straightforward in its purpose. It could also be useful to introduce into university curricula, general themes of digital literacy and such a theme as misinformation, within particular strings of learning. For example, political science students may analyze the consequences of false information in electoral campaigns, students of healthcare may, the consequences of health misinformation.

The use of public education is also a part of the educational intervention in cases of misrepresentation. For details, governments together with NGOs and tech platforms can run campaigns, targeting people with the purpose of raising awareness of the dangerous outcomes of fake news and teaching people how to act properly online. For instance, the campaigns that encourage people to verify the information they received before sharing it or the campaigns that demonstrate how deepfakes and other examples of synthetic media work can help to increase user's awareness. These campaigns should be as naturalistic as possible – with super simple text, and straightforward graphics – to attract everybody from uneducated individuals with low-tech literacy.

Misinformation is a global problem that requires collective actions by governments, technology organizations, schools, and NGOs. As a human, it disappointingly reduces my expectations for human civilization where people are no longer bound by national borders and national boundaries hence it spreads through networks and online platforms. Therefore, there is a need for unity, cooperation and cooperation of all countries to work towards the formulation of standard and standard procedure to use while disseminating information while respecting cultural and political diversities. For such cooperation, inter alia, international organizations like the UN and UNESCO are in a good starting position in order to define common frameworks and requirements, provide advisory services and work as a discussion platform for the member states.

A potential policy suggestion implies the creation of a legal definition for misinformation on the international level comparable to the GDPR across the European Union. A common framework for how platforms should regulate content could establish a base line standard Content Regulation Policy addressing the conceptual issues of Content Moderation, Transparency, and Responsibility that would be acceptable to all countries and technology companies around the world. This global framework can be underpinned by regional treaties which address the regional specificities but at the same time provide for necessary adaptability when addressing fake news problem as the worldwide commitment.

To reiterate, given that tech companies serve as central informational platforms, they also must doubly shoulder the blame for misinformation. This is an area that needs to be transparent; the platforms should be forced to explain how they handle the contents especially fake news. This could include mundane reports on the kind of content that has been banned or deleted, the reason for doing so and the procedure for appealing the content ban. Third, the level of platform accountability could be increased via third party audits of algorithms for harm-causing misinforming reinforcement. A coordinated push for algorithmic transparency would enable academic and policymakers to determine whether information firm practices are consistent with the public's best interest and enhance the veracity of information.

Education centers and NGOs can extend the effect of combating misinformation on the global level by exchanging experience, carrying out investigations, and developing interdisciplinary and international cooperation. For instance, it is possible to imagine universities and research institutes specifically dealing with the effects of misinformation to create international consortia aimed at analyzing how misinformation works in different cultures and to better understand the distinctions that might help to create countermeasures for a specific region. The logical progression of NGO involvement with educational institutions could be for these NGOs help in creating localized programs which would then go into providing media literacy training to communities which often has had inadequate access to education.

That is when nations, technology platforms, educational institutions, and NGOs come together so that truth can triumph over falsehood and help develop better democracies, healthier societies, and a more stable world. This way, the global community establishes the framework for the socially proactive, evidence-based policy, as well as encouraging critical thinking and inquiry – this society will better face the challenges of contemporary info-sphere. By continued hard work and collaboration with counterparts from around the world we can look forward to an informational sphere that can foster the citizen's informed decision making and thus democratic and civil society.

REFERENCES

Anderson, J., & Rainie, L. (2017). The Future of Truth and Misinformation Online. *Pew Research Center*. https://www.pewresearch.org/internet/2017/10/19/the-future-of-truth-and-misinformation-online/

Banchio, P. R. (2024). Legal Framework to Combat Disinformation and Hate Speech on Digital Platforms. *SSRN*. https://papers.ssrn.com/sol3/papers.cfm?abstract_id=4879162

Beauvais, C. (2022). Fake news: Why do we believe it? *Joint, Bone, Spine*, *89*(4), 105371. DOI: 10.1016/j.jbspin.2022.105371 PMID: 35257865

Broda, E., & Stromback, J. (2024). Misinformation, disinformation, and fake news: Lessons from an interdisciplinary, systematic literature review. *Annals of the International Communication Association*, *48*(2), 139–166. DOI: 10.1080/23808985.2024.2323736

Ecker, U. K. H., Lewandowsky, S., Cook, J., Schmid, P., Fazio, L. K., Brashier, N., Kendeou, P., Vraga, E. K., & Amazeen, M. A. (2022). The psychological drivers of misinformation belief and its resistance to correction. *Nature Reviews Psychology*, *1*(1), 13–29. DOI: 10.1038/s44159-021-00006-y

Eyal, J. (2024). The Global Challenge of Fake News. *Carter Ruck*. https://www.carter-ruck.com/insight/fakes-news-authentic-views/the-global-challenge-of-fake-news/

Fernandez, M., & Alani, H. (2018). *Online Misinformation: Challenges and Future Directions*. ACM Digital Library., DOI: 10.1145/3184558.3188730

Funke, D., & Flamini, D. (2024). A guide to anti-misinformation actions around the world. *Poynter*. https://www.poynter.org/ifcn/anti-misinformation-actions/

Galligher, R., & Tanner, S. (2024). A Guided Tour of Disinformation Policy: Framework and Legal Action. *GDIL*. https://gdil.org/a-guided-tour-of-disinformation-policy-framework-and-legal-action/

Gaur, A. (2021). Towards policy and regulatory approaches for combating misinformation in India. *Yale Law School*. https://law.yale.edu/isp/initiatives/wikimedia-initiative-intermediaries-and-information/wiii-blog/towards-policy-and-regulatory-approaches-combating-misinformation-india

Green, Y., Gully, A., Roth, Y., Roy, A., Tucker, J. A., & Wanless, A. (2023). Evidence-Based Misinformation Interventions: Challenges and Opportunities for Measurement and Collaboration. *Carnegie Endowment for International Peace*. https://carnegieendowment.org/research/2023/01/evidence-based-misinformation-interventions-challenges-and-opportunities-for-measurement-and-collaboration?lang=en

Jens, S. (2024). Why laws to combat misinformation can do more harm than good. *Scroll.in*. https://scroll.in/article/1066180/why-laws-to-combat-misinformation-can-do-more-harm-than-good

Jiang, B., & Wang, D. (2024). Perception of misinformation on social media among Chinese college students. *Frontiers in Psychology*, *15*, 1416792. Advance online publication. DOI: 10.3389/fpsyg.2024.1416792 PMID: 39027055

Kanozia, R. (2019). Analysis of Digital Tools and Technologies for Debunking Fake News. *Journal of Content, Community & Communication, 9*(5), 114-122. https://www.amity.edu/gwalior/jccc/pdf/jccc%20june%202019%20final-114-122.pdf

Khare, P. (2025). Investigating the Influence of AI in Social Media Governance. *IGI Global Scientific Publishing*, 365-388. https://doi.org/DOI: 10.4018/979-8-3693-9904-0.ch015

Khare, P. & Raghuwanshi, V. (2025). Legal Frameworks Surrounding the Use of AI in Online Content Moderation. *IGI Global Scientific Publishing*, 235-260. https://doi.org/DOI: 10.4018/979-8-3693-9904-0.ch011

Krasadakis, G. (2024). Fake News and Misinformation: How digital tech can help. *Innovation Mode*. https://www.theinnovationmode.com/the-innovation-blog/misinformation-online-a-solution-powered-by-state-of-the-art-tech

Kreps, S. (2020). The Role of Technology in Online Misinformation. *Brookings*. https://www.brookings.edu/wp-content/uploads/2020/06/The-role-of-technology-in-online-misinformation.pdf

Li, C., & Callegari, A. (2024). Stopping AI disinformation: Protecting truth in the digital world. *World Economic Forum*. https://www.weforum.org/stories/2024/06/ai-combat-online-misinformation-disinformation/

Nealon, D. (2024). What's at Stake with the U.S. Supreme Court Case on Misinformation? *Harvard Medical School*. https://hms.harvard.edu/news/whats-stake-us-supreme-court-case-misinformation

Ochoa, A. G., Khare, P., & Setia, S. (2024). Expanding Environmental Education in Honduras: A Holistic Approach for Sustainable Development. *IGI Global Scientific Publishing,* 153-170. https://doi.org/DOI: 10.4018/979-8-3693-2577-3.ch010

Pappas, S. (2022). Fighting fake news in the classroom. *American Psychological Association.* https://www.apa.org/monitor/2022/01/career-fake-news

Radu, A., & Petcu, I. (2024). Digital Technologies Used to Combat Disinformation and Fake News. *ResearchGate.* https://www.researchgate.net/publication/380987988_Digital_Technologies_Used_to_Combat_Disinformation_and_Fake_News

Samdani, A., & Dimri, S. (2024). Syrian Refugees and the Digital Misinformation Crisis: Legal Challenges and Policy Solutions. *Journal of Informatics Education and Research*, *4*(2). Advance online publication. DOI: 10.52783/jier.v4i2.1231

Sharevski, F., & Loop, J. V. (2024). Children, Parents, and Misinformation on Social Media. *ResearchGate.* https://www.researchgate.net/publication/381002519_Children_Parents_and_Misinformation_on_Social_Media

Singh, M. (2023). Combating Fake News And Misinformation On Social Media With Tech. *RipenApps.* https://ripenapps.com/blog/combating-fake-news-misinformation-on-social-media-with-tech/

Singh, P., & Sunil, S. (2020). Towards A Legal Framework To Tackle Fake News. *Live Law.* https://www.livelaw.in/lawschool/articles/towards-a-legal-framework-to-tackle-fake-news-155556

Tan, C. (2022). The curious case of regulating false news on Google. *Computer Law & Security Review*, *46*, 105738. Advance online publication. DOI: 10.1016/j.clsr.2022.105738

Torkington, S. (2024). These are the 3 biggest emerging risks the world is facing. *World Economic Forum.* https://www.weforum.org/stories/2024/01/ai-disinformation-global-risks/

Unver, A. (2023). The Role of Technology: New Methods of Information, Manipulation and Disinformation. *EDAM.* https://edam.org.tr/en/cyber-governance-digital-democracy/the-role-of-technology-new-methods-of-information-manipulation-and-disinformation

Wardle, C. (2023). Misunderstanding Misinformation. *Issues.*https://issues.org/misunderstanding-misinformation-wardle/

Zimdars, M., & Mcleod, K. (2020). Fake News: Understanding Media and Misinformation in the Digital Age. *MIT Press Direct*. https://direct.mit.edu/books/edited-volume/4625/Fake-NewsUnderstanding-Media-and-Misinformation-in

KEY TERMS AND DEFINITIONS

Digital Services Act (DSA): A legislative framework developed by the European Union aimed at increasing transparency and accountability of digital platforms, especially concerning misinformation and content moderation.

Disinformation: Deliberately fabricated or manipulated information intended to deceive or cause harm. It is a more malicious form of misinformation, often used for political or ideological agendas.

Echo Chamber: A digital or social environment where individuals are only exposed to information or opinions that reflect and reinforce their own. This limits exposure to diverse perspectives and amplifies biases.

Fake News: Completely or partially fabricated news stories spread with or without intent. It includes misinformation, disinformation, and malinformation and is a threat to democratic and social structures.

Filter Bubble: A state of intellectual isolation resulting from personalized search algorithms, which selectively guess what information users want to see, often based on past behavior.

Malinformation: Genuine information used out of context or with intent to cause harm. Unlike misinformation or disinformation, the content is true but used manipulatively.

Media Literacy: The ability to access, evaluate, and create media in a variety of forms. It empowers individuals to critically assess sources and recognize misinformation.

Misinformation: False or misleading information shared without intent to deceive. It can distort facts unintentionally and has wide-reaching consequences in politics, health, economy, and society.

Chapter 14
Influenced by the Group:
AI Misinformation Detection by Prospective Teachers

Gamze Türkmen
https://orcid.org/0000-0002-4695-9159
Manisa Celal Bayar University, Turkey

ABSTRACT

This study examined how group discussions affected prospective teachers' metacognitive confidence and decision accuracy when classifying AI-based educational technology news as real or fake. A quasi-experimental design was used with 20 prospective teachers. Before evaluating the news, participants completed measures of news media and AI literacy. They then classified eight news articles individually, in groups, and again individually. Findings showed that group discussions significantly affected confidence and accuracy, with group confidence exceeding individual confidence after discussion. However, accuracy was more consistent for real news than fake news. News media and AI literacy had a small effect on initial judgments and a limited effect after discussion. The results highlight the need to integrate media and AI literacy into teacher education to improve decision making in collaborative learning, while highlighting the complexity of group dynamics in addressing misinformation about AI.

INTRODUCTION

News has the potential to influence people's perceptions and decisions. This potential can have positive or negative consequences. Negative consequences may include the spread of fake news and the content of the news being considered real because it cannot be understood by people. In recent times, with the increase in

DOI: 10.4018/979-8-3693-9601-8.ch014

the frequency of news about artificial intelligence (AI) and the widespread use of this concept in society, it may become difficult for people to distinguish between what is real and what is fake in news related to this concept. It has been said that overcoming this difficulty in distinguishing may be directly related to literacy skills. With the spread of AI-based educational technologies used in the field of education, fake news spreading may cause ethical concerns and a negative attitude towards AI technologies among people (Wilner, 2018; Al-Asadi & Tasdemir, 2021; Monteith et al., 2023; Williamson & Prybutok, 2024). Such negative attitudes may be one of the obstacles to parents not allowing the use of these technologies in classroom environments and benefiting from their potential benefits. Similarly, teachers' negative attitudes and lack of use of technologies may hinder their professional development. Therefore, it is argued that media and AI literacy can play an important role in dealing with such fake news (Adjin-Tettey, 2022; Jang & Kim, 2017; Jones-Jang et al., 2019; Washington, 2023).

Based on this information, it is said that individual information literacy can help in identifying fake news, but there is no support for finding media and AI literacy (De Paor & Heravi, 2020; Williamson & Prybutok, 2024). In addition, there is no evidence on how a person's ability to distinguish fake and false news in group dynamics is observed at individual levels belonging to these literacy types. While people have the potential to make more consistent decision evaluations when alone, they can change their initial decisions by adapting to other opinions in a group. It is important to understand how decision changes regarding the detection of fake news affect individuals' metacognitive confidence decisions and decision accuracy in a group decision-making process. Abels et al. (2024) emphasizes in a study that cognitive biases are effective in group decisions and can affect the decision made by the group. It has been found that by using adaptive machine learning models (such as MetaCMAB and ExpertiseTree), there are ways to enhance the decision-making process by preventing biases, thus improving group decision accuracy (Abels et al., 2024).

News about AI-based educational technology is important for the people of the country to learn about the developments. However, the fact that the news is fabricated or does not reflect the truth may cause people to worry about the applicability of these developments in daily life. For prospective teachers, it is important to examine such news critically in the long term so that it does not create different biases and prevent them from developing professional development. For them who have not received any literacy training from any official institution, it is important to evaluate whether such news is real so that it does not become an obstacle to their professional development in the long term. However, although the decisions that individuals make alone when evaluating the reality of the news are correct, these decisions can be turned wrong with group discussions. It is important to be able to look at the relationships between the literacy levels declared individually by prospective teachers who have not received any literacy training and the accuracy of the decisions they make in individual and group discussions. Because it is known that individual biases can affect group decisions and have the potential to change personal decisions (Hart et al., 2009). In Hart et al. (2009)'s studies based on selective exposure theory, it was found that individuals tend to prefer information that supports their beliefs. However, this tendency was found to decrease with defensiveness when commitment to beliefs is weak, information quality is low, or the individual is more open-minded. On the other hand, it was stated that individuals can also turn to information that is contrary to their beliefs with the motive of truth when it is necessary to achieve a certain goal. In long-term analyses, it is of research value to look at the decision changes before and after the group in order to understand such biases for fake news detection (Ostillio, 2019; French et al., 2023). However, not only decision accuracy but also the change in the level of confidence that individuals and groups have in their decisions is very important in order to understand this process more comprehensively.

Therefore, understanding how individual biases are shaped by group interaction and its impact on decision accuracy and confidence levels becomes a critical area of research for distinguishing accurate information in news about AI-based educational technologies. This study aims to identify the factors that affect the final decisions of prospective teachers in the process of distinguishing fake and real news in AI-based educational technologies news. And it tries to understand how news media or AI literacy shapes this process by giving importance to it. It plans to provide insights into the effect of individual literacy on decision making by examining factors such as individual and group confidence levels, perceived difficulty and decision accuracy before and after the group discussion.

BACKGROUND

The Role of News Media Literacy in Education

In this information age, where news spreads rapidly and misinformation can easily circulate on digital platforms, media literacy has become a cornerstone of educational practices. While Potter (2004) presented a basic cognitive model that includes seven skills: analysis, evaluation, classification, inference, induction, synthesis, and abstraction; Potter and Thai (2016) later emphasized the practical difficulties in distinguishing and assessing these skills. These difficulties pose obstacles to designing valid and reliable measurement tools for media literacy, especially in educational contexts. However, existing studies show that media literacy not only helps students interact meaningfully with information but also provides them with the skills to identify reliable sources and reduce the potential impact of misinformation (Ulu-Aslan & Baş, 2022). In addition, there are findings in the literature that it improves students' critical thinking and decision-making skills, especially their ability to detect false or misleading news (Hobbs, 2004; Ulu-Aslan & Baş, 2022).

In this context, potential teachers play an important role. The ability to critically engage with media content is seen as important not only for their own professional development, but also for developing similar competencies in their future students. As Cherner and Curry (2019) argue, developing media literacy among future educators can contribute to the prevention of misinformation and prepare them to act responsibly in a technology-driven society. Furthermore, the rapid advancement of AI technologies and their integration into educational systems make it even more imperative that teachers are equipped with the skills to accurately assess and interpret AI-related content.

In addition, the rise of algorithm-driven news delivery systems, such as social media feeds and personalized recommendations, can reinforce existing biases by increasing the risk of selective exposure and filter bubbles (Hart et al., 2009). This highlights the importance of not only having general media literacy but also developing a critical media literacy perspective that includes awareness of structural power dynamics, commercial agendas, and the role of algorithms in shaping news access. Therefore, it is considered important to develop thoughtful and reflective media engagement habits among potential teachers. This can help them not only understand how media functions to shape public discourse but also design learning experiences that prepare students for informed citizen participation in a digital society. This study hypothesizes that the media literacy levels that potential teachers self-report when evaluating AI-based e-tech news, especially when influenced by group dynamics, may be related not only to the accuracy of their judgments but also to their confidence in those judgments.

AI Literacy and Decision-Making

With its increasing presence in educational technologies, AI literacy has emerged as a critical 21st-century skill that complements media literacy to help individuals navigate a complex digital environment. AI literacy is often defined as understanding what AI is, how it works, what it can and cannot do, and how it is applied in various fields (Long and Magerko, 2020). In educational contexts, it also includes the capacity to critically evaluate AI tools, reflect on their pedagogical implications, and use them responsibly and effectively in teaching and learning. However, as AI becomes more integrated into both daily life and education, the abundance of news and content surrounding these technologies, often infused with misinformation, makes it increasingly difficult for individuals to distinguish reliable information from false or misleading claims. This challenge is compounded when individuals rely not only on their own understanding but are also influenced by group dynamics, peer input, and social norms.

While previous research has shown that AI literacy enhances individuals' ability to make informed decisions about AI-related technologies (Ng et al., 2021), most of these studies focus on individual cognition and behavior. There is a significant gap in understanding how AI literacy interacts with social and collaborative decision-making processes, particularly in educational settings where group discussions and consensus play a central role. Therefore, this study aims to investigate the impact of AI literacy on decision-making at both individual and group levels. By examining how preservice teachers evaluate the credibility of AI-based educational technology news in independent and group discussions, it aims to reveal whether AI literacy contributes not only to decision accuracy but also to individuals' confidence in their decisions before and after group interaction. In doing so, AI literacy addresses a critical gap in the literature at the intersection of misinformation detection and collaborative reasoning.

Metacognitive Confidence Judgement and Perceived Difficulty in Decision-Making

Metacognitive confidence judgments encompass an individual's self-assessment of their knowledge and cognitive processes and often guide both individual behavior and social influence in group settings. In educational contexts, especially for preservice teachers, such judgments are critical not only for personal reflection but also for effective pedagogical decision-making. Research suggests that individuals with higher confidence are more likely to influence group decisions, even if their actual expertise is limited (Koriat, 2012; Zarnoth & Sniezek, 1997). This can lead to disproportionate weight being given to individuals with higher confidence in collaborative settings, sometimes resulting in overconfidence and reduced group accuracy (Heidhues et al., 2019; Bahrami et al., 2010). In this direction, Kolić-Vehovec et al. (2021) show that metacognitive awareness and how well individuals align their confidence with actual performance (calibration accuracy) play an important role in students' learning and reasoning processes. When confidence is not well calibrated, individuals may either overestimate their understanding or fail to make accurate judgments. Both situations can impair the overall quality of group decision-making. These findings are of particular importance for preservice teachers who are expected to make sound judgments in uncertain information contexts and guide others accordingly.

In addition, the perceived difficulty of a task interacts significantly with metacognitive monitoring. When individuals evaluate a task as complex, they tend to report lower confidence and, in many cases, exhibit lower performance accuracy (Ackerman and Thompson, 2017). These dynamics may be particularly evident in evaluating AI-based edtech news, as they may be associated with the perceived difficulty of the novelty and technicality of the content.

Furthermore, in group discussions, confidence can be socially transmitted or reinforced; this phenomenon is called "confidence contagion" (Peker and Tezcan, 2009). Such effects can disrupt group consensus, especially when individuals defer to seemingly confident peers without critically evaluating the basis of their confidence. Therefore, examining both individual and group-level confidence judgments and the perceived difficulty of evaluating news is seen as important for understanding how preservice teachers form their judgments under uncertainty.

Therefore, the other purpose of this study is to examine how preservice teachers perceived difficulty and trust judgments interact in individual and group contexts when evaluating the credibility of AI-based educational technology news, thereby contributing to a better understanding of how metacognitive factors affect decision making in educationally important but cognitively challenging situations.

Technology-Enhanced Literacy Education

As misinformation in the context of AI-generated content becomes increasingly sophisticated, educational interventions that leverage technology have come to the fore. Technology-enhanced literacy education refers to the use of digital tools, including AI-enabled platforms, to teach media, digital, and AI literacy in ways that actively engage students and support critical evaluation skills. Recent studies suggest that integrating AI-enabled tools, such as fact-checking aids or adaptive learning systems, into curricula can enhance individuals' ability to recognize false content and enhance their epistemic alertness (Ng et al., 2021; Williamson and Prybutok, 2024). These tools not only provide immediate feedback but can also adapt to the user's existing knowledge and cognitive patterns, enabling a more personalized learning experience.

Furthermore, research in democratic and civic education emphasizes the need to prepare individuals (especially future educators) to become resilient to misinformation and manipulation (Kahne and Bowyer, 2017). Such approaches aim to move beyond technical literacy by developing reflective and participatory practices that help students become active agents in digital environments. Technology-enhanced literacy education for pre-service teachers holds promise not only for developing their own media and AI literacy, but also for designing classroom practices that develop these skills in students. Educators are seen as having the potential to facilitate deeper engagement with the complexities of information reliability and credibility in digital spaces by exposing them to real and AI-driven news scenarios supported by interactive tools.

In this context, the development of targeted literacy programs using AI-based teaching tools is thought to serve as a meaningful intervention to reduce the impact of conformity bias and overconfidence in group decision-making. Future research is seen as having the potential to further investigate how such interventions affect both individual and collaborative decision-making processes.

Research Questions

In line with the literature mentioned above, it is thought that media and AI literacy in educational settings are related to metacognitive confidence judgments and decision accuracy. However, there is not enough evidence on how these factors interact in group contexts, especially when pre-service teachers evaluate the accuracy of news about AI-based educational technology. This study aims to fill this gap by investigating how individual literacy levels affect decision accuracy and confidence in decisions before and after group discussions. In order to make a comprehensive evaluation, individual and group evaluations of this news are also important. Thus, it is thought that the results of this study can contribute to the design of educational programs that develop critical thinking and decision-making skills in collaborative learning environments.

In this study, one of the key objectives is to understand how the individual decisions of prospective teachers regarding the detection of fake news related to AI-based educational technologies are shaped by group decisions. The research questions are listed below:

1. How do confidence judgment levels and decision accuracy evolve before and after group discussions, and to what extent do media and AI literacy predict individual and group decision-making accuracy in the context of real and fake news?
2. How does group confidence judgement influence the accuracy of individuals' decision-making in the context of identifying the correctness of AI-based educational technology news, and to what extent do media literacy, AI literacy, perceived difficulty of the news and individual confidence judgement contribute to this process?

3. How do decisions change and the type of news (real vs. fake) affect students' confidence levels and decision accuracy, and why do these effects differ across initial, group, and final confidence judgements?
4. How do students' levels of news media and AI literacy influence their ability to evaluate the accuracy of news, both before and after group discussions? To what extent do these literacy levels determine the impact of students on decision changes within the group, and how do social interactions within the group contribute to decision changes?

METHODS

In this research, a quasi-experimental design was employed. Approval of the research was obtained from the Human Ethics Committee, and the students participating in the course took part in the study on a voluntary basis as part of the course. A total of 20 students (16 female, 4 male) were initially asked to complete the News Media Literacy Scale (Güdekli et al., 2022) and the AI Literacy Scale (Polatgil & Güler, 2023). The News Media Literacy Scale consists of 9 items and includes two sub-dimensions: self-efficacy and critical performance. All items load onto the sub-dimensions with factor loadings above 0.5, and the fit indices from the confirmatory factor analysis are within acceptable limits. The AI Literacy Scale consists of 12 items and is divided into four sub-dimensions: awareness, usage, evaluation, and ethics. Cronbach's alpha values for all sub-dimensions were found to be greater than 0.85.

For the news items, the headlines and content were generated using ChatGPT 4.0. During the generation process, the model was expected to produce both real and potentially fake news related to AI-based educational technologies. Out of the 20 generated news articles, 4 real and 4 fake articles were selected, and the authenticity of these articles was verified by two experts in the field of educational technology.

Due to the random assignment of student groups and the evaluation of the group discussion intervention, this study can be classified as a quasi-experimental design. The quasi-experimental procedure was implemented in three stages. In the first stage, each student individually assessed eight news items, determining whether they believed the news was real or fake. They also rated their confidence in their judgments on a scale of 1 to 5 and assessed the perceived difficulty of determining the news' authenticity using the same scale. In the second stage, students were randomly assigned to groups of 3-4 members. Within these groups, they re-evaluated the same news items, again indicating whether they thought the news was real or fake, and rated their confidence and the difficulty of verifying the news on a 1 to 5 scale. In the third and final stage, students returned to individual assessments, re-evaluating the news items and rating their confidence levels as they did in the first stage (see Figure 1).

Figure 1. Three-Stage quasi-experimental design for evaluating the impact of group discussions on confidence and accuracy in classifying AI-based educational news

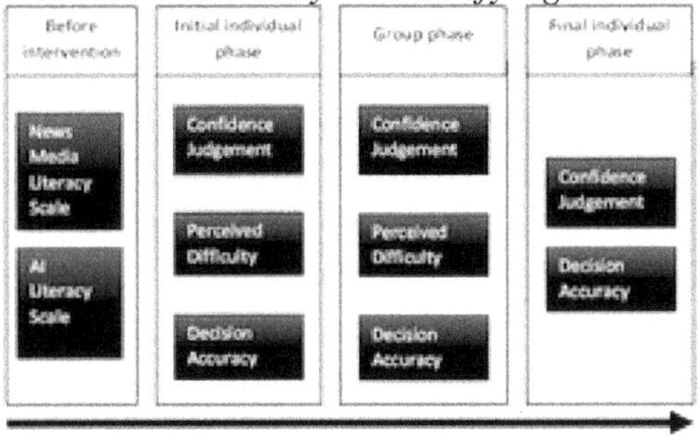

Data Analysis

The data collected from the students were coded into an Excel file as student number, group number, order of news items, news type categorized as fake or real, initial individual decision accuracy, final individual decision accuracy, group decision accuracy, initial perceived difficulty level, final confidence level, perceived difficulty level within the group and group confidence level. The responses of the students to the media literacy and AI literacy scales were stored in separate sheets and the average scores of these responses per student were included in the analysis. Data analysis was performed using the Python programming language via Google Colab.

Data analysis for RQ1 aimed to explore participants' confidence judgment levels, decision accuracy, and their relationship with media and AI literacy in three main stages. These stages were named as pre-group discussion, during group discussion, and post-group discussion, respectively. Various statistical methods were used to gain a deeper understanding of how group interactions and literacy levels affect decision-making processes. Descriptive statistics were first calculated to summarize the mean confidence levels and standard deviations in the real and fake news categories for each stage. Then, a Friedman test suitable for repeated measures design was applied to assess differences in confidence levels across the three stages. Cochran's Q test was then used to assess differences in decision accuracy across stages. Finally, accuracy rates for real and fake news were compared at each stage to track participants' ability to correctly identify the news type over time, and to provide insights into the role of group discussions in increasing decision accuracy.

In the data analysis phase for RQ2, it was attempted to understand the effect of the confidence judgments of the groups determining the accuracy of the AI-based educational technology news on the individual decision accuracy. In addition, it was attempted to understand to what extent variables such as media literacy, AI literacy, perceived difficulty of the news and individual confidence levels contribute to this process. Therefore, forward stepwise logistic regression was used to determine the significant predictors of the final individual decision accuracy from a set of candidate variables including media literacy, AI literacy, individual confidence level before the group discussions, perceived difficulty and group confidence level.

Data analysis for RQ3 aimed to understand the impact of decision change and news type on participants' confidence levels and decision accuracy. This analysis prioritized three stages based on confidence level before group discussion, group confidence, and individual confidence level after group discussion. Thus, it was thought that it would be possible to examine how decision change and exposure to real or fake news affected participants' confidence levels and their ability to correctly identify the news type. Descriptive statistics were calculated to summarize the mean confidence levels and standard deviations for real and fake news types based on decision changers and non-changers in all three stages. Thus, a clear overview of participants' confidence levels at different stages was provided. The Mann-Whitney U test was used to assess the statistical significance of the differences between decision changers and non-changers and between real and fake news types. The reason for using this non-parametric test is that the confidence level data is not normally distributed.

The analysis of RQ4 allows to understand how people evaluate the accuracy of news before and after the group discussions where they will see the news media and AI literacy. It continues to extract the social influence network to expand and investigate how this literacy levels affect decision making and social influence in group settings. Finally, descriptive statistics were used to find out how confidence is affected by decision changes, especially in the changes in the level of confidence for the distribution of decisions after the group discussions.

RESULTS

Preliminary Analysis Results

The preliminary analysis of the study aims to understand how confidence levels change before and after group discussions and to explore the relationships between confidence levels and news media and AI literacy. Additionally, it examines the extent to which AI and news media literacy levels predict the accuracy of the initial individual, group, and final individual choices. In doing so, it allows for the observation of changes in these literacy levels across different sessions for the first time.

A Friedman test was conducted to assess the differences in confidence levels across three phases: before group discussion, during group discussion, and after group discussion. The test indicated a statistically significant difference in confidence levels among the phases, χ^2 (2, N = 160) = 12.1, p = 0.0024. The mean ranks for the phases were as follows: initial individual confidence level before group discussion had a mean rank of 1.83, group confidence level had a mean rank of 2.13, and final individual confidence after group discussion, the mean rank was 2.04. The corresponding rank sums were 293.5, 340.5, and 326.0, respectively. In terms of descriptive statistics, the mean confidence levels were 3.89 (SD = 0.97) for the pre-discussion phase, 4.18 (SD = 0.88) for the group discussion phase, and 4.10 (SD = 0.93) for the post-discussion phase. These findings suggest that the confidence levels changed significantly across the phases, with the highest confidence being observed during the group discussion phase (see Table 1).

Table 1. Mean confidence judgement levels and Friedman test results across phases

Phase	Mean Rank	Rank Sums	Mean	Std	χ^2 ANOVA	*p*-value
Individual confidence level before group discussion	1.83	293.5	3.89	0.97	12.1	0.00**
Group confidence level	2.13	340.5	4.18	0.88		
Individual confidence level after group discussion	2.04	326.0	4.10	0.93		

Note. ***p* < .01.

Since it was important to understand the relationships between the news media and AI literacy levels, as self-reported by the students prior to the intervention, and their individual and group confidence levels, a Spearman correlation analysis was conducted (see Table 2). The analysis examined the relationship between confidence levels and both news media literacy and AI literacy. The results revealed a significant positive correlation between media literacy and the initial individual confidence level, with a correlation coefficient of 0.21 ($p = 0.01$). However, no significant correlations were found between news media literacy and group confidence level ($r = -0.00$, $p = 0.96$) or final individual confidence level ($r = 0.01$, $p = 0.89$). Similarly, AI literacy was significantly positively correlated with initial individual confidence level ($r = 0.17$, $p = 0.03$), but no significant correlations were observed between AI literacy and group confidence level ($r = 0.02$, $p = 0.82$) or final individual confidence level ($r = -0.99$, $p = 0.96$). These findings suggest that media and AI literacy are more strongly associated with initial individual confidence levels, while they have little to no impact on confidence levels in group settings or after group discussions.

In conclusion, the results of the Spearman correlation analysis indicate that AI literacy is significantly correlated with initial individual confidence levels but not with final individual or group confidence levels. News media literacy similarly shows a significant correlation with initial individual confidence, but no significant correlation with final or group confidence levels. Additionally, comparing confidence levels based on the type of news is also crucial for understanding the distinction between real and fake news, as well as the opinions formed about these types of news.

Table 2. Spearman correlation coefficients between media and ai literacy with initial, group, and final individual confidence levels

Type of literacy	Phase	Correlation coefficient	p-value
News Media	Individual confidence level before group discussion	0.21	0.01*
	Group confidence level	-0.00	0.96
	Individual confidence level after group discussion	0.01	0.89
Artificial Intelligence	Individual confidence level before group discussion	0.17	0.03*
	Group confidence level	0.02	0.82
	Individual confidence level after group discussion	-0.00	0.96

Note. $*p < .05$.

Table 3 shows a comparison of confidence levels across phases for fake and real news types. Before the group discussion, the mean confidence level for participants exposed to fake news was 3.76 ($SD = 0.91$), whereas those exposed to real news had a higher mean confidence level of 4.06 ($SD = 1.02$). This suggests that participants were slightly more confident in their initial judgments when dealing with real news compared to fake news. For the group discussion phase, the mean confidence level for the fake news group increased to 4.01 ($SD = 0.91$), while the real news group showed a more substantial increase to 4.38 ($SD = 0.82$). This indicates that group discussions significantly boosted confidence, particularly in the real news condition. After the group discussion, the mean confidence levels remained relatively stable, with participants exposed to fake news reporting a mean of 4.06 ($SD = 0.96$), and those exposed to real news reporting a mean of 4.13 ($SD = 0.92$). The slight change in confidence levels after the discussion suggests that group discussions helped maintain high confidence levels across both news types, though the difference between real and fake news persisted.

Table 3. Comparison of mean and standard deviation for confidence levels across fake and real news types

		Fake	Real
Individual confidence level before group discussion	Mean	3.76	4.06
	Std	0.91	1.02
Group confidence level	Mean	4.01	4.38
	Std	0.91	0.82
Individual confidence level after group discussion	Mean	4.06	4.13
	Std	0.96	0.92

In addition to confidence levels, it is also important to understand the accuracy rates in these phases and the differences between them. The Cochran's Q test was employed to evaluate the consistency of decision accuracy across three phases: before group discussion, during group discussion, and after the group discussion. The analysis revealed a significant difference in accuracy rates across these phases, with Cochran's Q (2) = 9.48, $p = 0.0087$. The findings suggest that the accuracy of participants' decisions varied significantly, particularly during and after group discussions, indicating that the group setting had a notable influence on individual decision-making. Specifically, the proportion of correct responses was higher during and after the group discussion compared to the individual decisions made before the discussion. This demonstrates the importance of collaborative group discussions in enhancing decision accuracy and suggests that group dynamics can positively impact participants' ability to arrive at correct conclusions. In conclusion, the results emphasize the role of group interactions in improving decision-making processes (see Table 4).

Table 4. Cochran's Q test results: Comparison of decision accuracy across phases before, during, and after group discussion

Phase	Incorrect	Correct	Cochran's Q Test Statistic	*p*-value
Individual decision accuracy before group discussion	32	128	9.48	0.00**
Group decision accuracy (Group_Choice)	19	141		
Individual decision accuracy after group discussion	21	139		

Note. $^{**}p < .01$.

Impact of Group Confidence on Final Answer Correctness (Results for RQ2)

A forward stepwise logistic regression was conducted to identify potential predictors of the second answer correctness from a set of candidate variables: news media literacy, AI literacy, initial individual confidence level, perceived news difficulty, group confidence level, and perceived news difficulty among group. At each step, variables were added based on statistical significance, and the Akaike Information Criterion (AIC) was used to evaluate model improvement and determine the final inclusion of variables (see Table 5).

In Step 1, news media literacy and AI literacy were included in the model. The resulting pseudo-R-squared was 0.007, indicating that these variables explained less than 1% of the variance in the second answer correctness. Neither news media literacy ($p = 0.512$) nor AI literacy ($p = 0.97$) was statistically significant, and the overall model was not significant ($p = 0.65$), suggesting that these variables alone did not meaningfully predict the outcome.

In Step 2, initial individual confidence level and perceived difficulty were added to the model. The pseudo-R-squared increased slightly to 0.036, explaining about 3.6% of the variance. Although the model improved slightly, none of the predictors were statistically significant, with first news difficulty ($p = 0.087$) approaching significance. The overall model remained statistically insignificant ($p = 0.345$), indicating that these additional variables provided limited predictive value.

Table 5. Stepwise logistic regression results predicting second answer correctness based on news media literacy, ai literacy, confidence judgement, and perceived difficulty

Variables	Category	Coefficient	Change in -2 Log Likelihood	*p*-value	Significance
News Media literacy	Literacy	-0.449	0.65	0.51	
AI literacy	Literacy	-0.021		0.97	
Confidence level before group discussion	Individual	0.086	0.34	0.73	
Perceived news difficulty before group discussion	Individual	-0.330		0.09	
Group confidence level	Group	1.519	0.00	0.00	***
Perceived news difficulty during group discussion	Group	-0.261		0.40	
Confidence level after group discussion	Individual	0.134	0.00	0.65	
Constant		-1.480			

Note. ***$p < .001$.

In Step 3, group confidence level, and perceived news difficulty were introduced. This step resulted in a significant improvement, with the pseudo-R-squared rising to 0.32, explaining approximately 32% of the variance. Group confidence level was a highly significant predictor ($p = 0.00$), with a positive coefficient of 1.519, suggesting that higher group confidence strongly increased the likelihood of a correct second answer. In addition, the group perceived news difficulty was not significant ($p = 0.40$). The overall model was significant ($p < 0.00$), indicating that group-related variables, particularly group confidence level, played a critical role in predicting the second answer correctness.

In Step 4, individual confidence level for second run was added. The pseudo-R-squared remained nearly the same at 0.32, and individual confidence level was not a significant predictor ($p = 0.65$). Group confidence level remained significant ($p = 0.00$). The addition of second individual confidence level did not significantly improve the model, which remained significant overall ($p < 0.00$).

To sum up, the most important predictor in this stepwise regression was group confidence level, which consistently showed a strong and significant influence on second answer correctness. Neither news media literacy, AI literacy, nor individual confidence variables had a significant impact on the outcome. These findings suggest that group dynamics, particularly group confidence judgement, play a critical role in determining the correctness of individual decisions, while individual-level factors like confidence and literacy were not influential in this context.

Influence of Group Discussion and News Type on Confidence and Decision Accuracy (Results for RQ3)

The Mann-Whitney U-test revealed several significant differences between students who changed their decision after group discussion and those who did not, as well as differences based on the type of news (real vs. fake) (see Table 6). Regarding the decision change, no significant difference was found in the first individual confidence level between students who changed their decision and those who did not ($U = 1511.0, p = 0.5457$). This indicates that initial confidence before the group discussion was not influenced by whether students later decided to change their decision. However, a significant difference was observed in the group confidence level between these two groups ($U = 892.5, p < 0.00$), with students who changed their decision exhibiting different confidence levels during the group discussion compared to those who maintained their original stance. Additionally, a significant difference was also found in the final individual confidence level ($U = 994.0, p = 0.00$), suggesting that decision changers had different confidence levels in their final decision compared to non-changers. In addition, in terms of answer correctness, there was a significant difference between the two groups ($U = 1324.0, p = 0.01$), implying that decision change might have affected whether students provided a correct response after the group discussion.

Table 6. Mann-Whitney U test results comparing decision change and news type effects on confidence levels and answer correctness

Category	U-statistics	*p*-value
Decision changer vs non-changer		
Initial individual confidence level before group discussion	1511.0	0.55
Group confidence level	892.5	0.00***
Final individual confidence level after group discussion	994.0	0.00***
Final individual decision accuracy	1324.0	0.01*
Real vs. Fake		
Initial individual confidence level before group discussion	3818.0	0.03*
Group confidence level	3960.5	0.01*
Final individual confidence level after group discussion	3300.5	0.71
Final individual decision accuracy	3640.0	0.01

Note. *$p<.05$, ***$p < .001$.

When examining differences based on news type, a significant difference was found in the initial individual confidence level between students exposed to real and fake news ($U = 3818.0, p = 0.03$), suggesting that students approached real and fake news with different initial confidence levels. Similarly, a significant difference in group confidence was observed between the two groups ($U = 3960.5, p = 0.01$), indicating that group discussions led to varying confidence levels depending on whether the news was real or fake. However, no significant difference was found in the final individual confidence level between students exposed to real and fake news ($U = 3300.5, p = 0.71$), implying that the final decision confidence judgement was not influenced by the type of news encountered. In contrast, a significant difference was found in answer correctness between students exposed to real and fake news ($U = 3640.0$, $p = 0.01$), indicating that the ability to correctly classify news was affected by whether the news was real or fake.

To sum up, the analysis shows that decision change significantly impacted group confidence level, final individual confidence level, and answer correctness, while the type of news significantly influenced initial individual confidence level, group confidence level, and decision accuracy. However, the final initial confidence level was not affected by news type, suggesting that while students may approach real and fake news differently initially, their final confidence judgement in their decision remains similar regardless of the news type after the group discussion.

Observational Findings for the Role of News Media and AI Literacy in Group Decision-Making (Results for RQ4)

This research question investigates whether students with higher levels of news media and AI literacy are more influential in group settings, and how these levels affect the likelihood of decision changes (such as correcting wrong answers or changing correct answers to incorrect ones after group discussions) and social influence (i.e., who influences whom in the decision-making process). The group-wise graphs provided below offer a detailed explanation of the students within each group who are influencers and those who are influenced.

Figure 2. Group-wise social influence network for Group 1

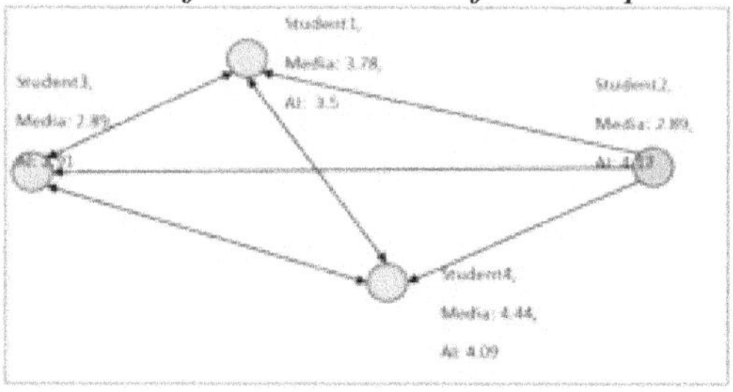

When examining the network diagram of the first group, it is observed that Student2 has a significant influence on other students in changing their responses. However, there is no clear distinction in this student's reported levels of news media and AI literacy compared to the other students (see Figure 2). Student2 appears to have a positive impact on correcting the wrong answers provided by other students during their initial individual evaluations. Nonetheless, the reported confidence level and the media and AI literacy levels of this student do not seem to be higher than those of the other students.

Figure 3. Group-wise social influence network for Group 2

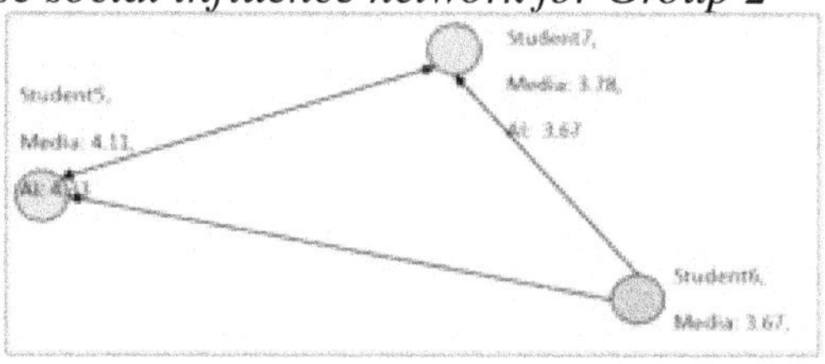

When examining the network diagram of the second group, it is observed that Student6 influences the responses of two other students. However, similar to the first group, Student6's reported levels do not appear to be higher than those of the other students (see Figure 3). It is noted that this student positively influences the other students in one of the fake news responses. However, within the same group, Student5, who had correctly answered one of the fake news items, changed their answer to incorrect after the group decision, influenced by both Student7 and Student6. This could be connected to following the majority's decision, which might be linked to the consensus bias. Additionally, it is observed that after changing their answer, Student5's confidence level decreased.

Figure 4. Group-wise social influence network for Group 3

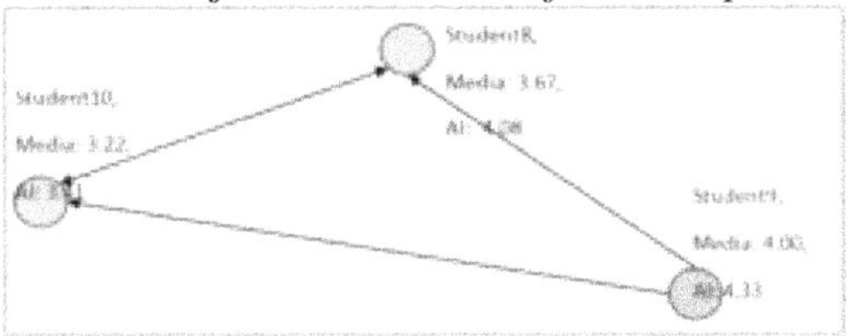

In the third group, it is observed a different profile compared to the first two groups. Student9's reported levels of news media and AI literacy appear to be higher than those of the other students (see Figure 4). However, when examining the level of influence, it can be seen that Student9's incorrect assessment of two fake news items led to the group also incorrectly assessing them. For instance, Student8 changed her correct answer to incorrect in the second round based on the group decision, whereas Student10, contrary to the group decision, did not change her correct answer. However, similar to the second group, Student10's confidence in their second response decreased compared to her first response.

Figure 5. Group-wise social influence network for Group 4

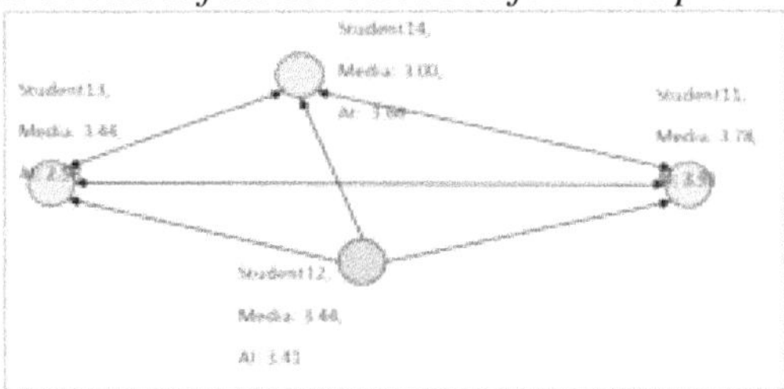

When examining Group 5, it is once again an observational evident that news media and AI literacy levels do not play a significant role in influencing the decision-making process (see Figure 5). Here, it is observed that Student12 negatively influenced the group's decision. Student12 misclassified a real news item as fake and similarly convinced other students that the news was fake. Additionally, as seen in the other two groups, students who changed their answers experienced a decrease in their confidence levels for the second response. This indicates that, even though they followed the group decision, there was a noticeable decline in the confidence students had in their answers after changing them.

Figure 6. Group-wise social influence network for Group 5

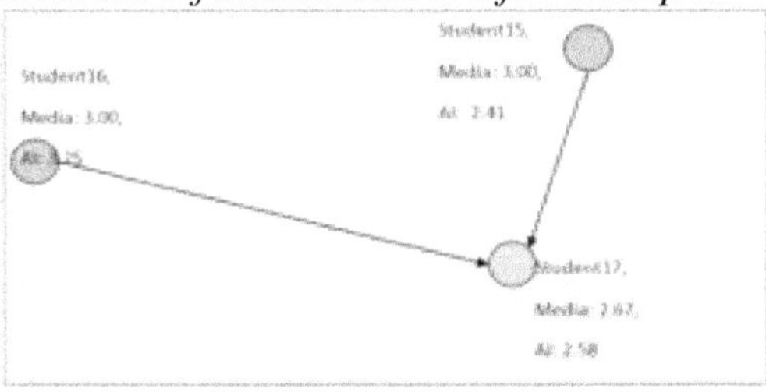

When examining the influence dynamics of Group 5, it is observed that Student15 and Student16 influenced Student17 (see Figure 6). However, similar to the other groups, Student15 and Student16 made an incorrect individual assessment of a fake news item, negatively impacting Student17, who had initially made the correct judgment. Here, only the student who changed their answer experienced a decrease in confidence in their response.

Figure 7. Group-wise social influence network for Group 6

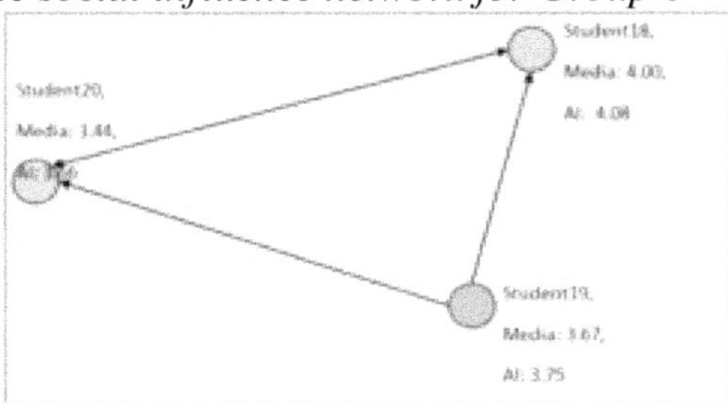

When examining Group 6, it is observed that Student19 positively influenced Student18 and Student20, leading them to change their answers correctly (see Figure 7). Although all students made correct group decisions and second responses, there was still a decrease in confidence levels among those who changed their answers. This suggests that, regardless of whether the answer was correct or incorrect, students tend to experience a decline in confidence when they change their decisions. Additionally, it can be noted that news media and AI literacy levels did not have a significant impact on students' influence within the group.

To further detail these graphics, it is important to explore the impact of news media and AI literacy on the accuracy of initial responses. Examining the correlations, the findings reveal a modest but notable relationship between news media literacy and the accuracy of students' initial decision accuracy. A positive correlation ($r = 0.17$) suggests that students with higher news media literacy are somewhat better at distinguishing between fake and real news. Although the effect size is small, this relationship underscores the role of news media literacy in fostering critical evaluation skills in news classification. In contrast, AI literacy shows a weaker correlation with accuracy (r = 0.12), reflecting a lesser influence on students' ability to correctly identify fake or real news. This disparity suggests that while AI literacy contributes to decision-making, news media literacy has a stronger impact on students' evaluative abilities in this domain. However, this conclusion applies specifically to the accuracy of the initial individual responses. When examining the effect on the accuracy of second individual responses after group discussions, a different result emerges.

Following group discussions, the influence of news media and AI literacy on the accuracy of students' second choices diminishes compared to their initial decisions. The correlation between news media literacy and second-choice accuracy (r = 0.08) weakens, indicating a reduced role in guiding post-discussion decisions. Conversely, AI literacy maintains a slightly stronger but still modest correlation (r = 0.10), suggesting a continued, though less pronounced, positive effect on decision accuracy after group discussions. These findings imply that while both news media and AI literacy play a role in individual decision-making, their effects are more pronounced in solo judgments and tend to be diluted in collaborative settings.

In summary, news media literacy has a greater influence on the correctness of students' first choices, but this influence diminishes after group discussions. AI literacy, while less impactful, shows a stable influence on correctness across both individual and group settings. Similar to observational findings stated in above graphics, group discussions seem to dilute the impact of both literacies, reducing their role in determining accuracy in collaborative decision-making contexts.

CONCLUSION AND SUGGESTIONS

This study examined the effects of group discussions among prospective teachers on individuals' decision accuracy and metacognitive confidence judgments while classifying AI-based educational technology news as true or false. The findings reveal that group discussions can have a significant impact on individuals' decisions. However, when looking at the findings, while a general increase in confidence levels was observed during group discussions, this increase did not always translate into decision accuracy. In particular, despite the increase in group confidence, the probability of making wrong decisions when faced with fake news also increased. This observation suggests that individuals may develop overconfidence when working in groups, and this may negatively affect the accuracy of their decisions. Similarly, in their study by Blanchard et al. (2020), dyadic groups exhibited more confidence, lower control thresholds, and more inconsistent decisions compared to individuals, and as a result, a higher rate of decision errors was observed. In another study, Kolić-Vehovec et al. (2021) found that although collaborative learning improved students' conceptual understanding and comparison ability; It has been found that it can also lead to bias, especially during explanation tasks. This may be due to the risks of students' overconfidence. Kolić-Vehovec et al. (2021) mention that warning students about the risks of overconfidence has no positive effect on their performance.

The results of this study show that while initial decisions are shaped by individuals' levels of news media and AI literacy, this effect diminishes after group discussions. While students who reported higher levels of literacy reached more accurate conclusions during their initial decisions, this advantage was observed to disappear in group settings. This suggests that group dynamics can override individual literacy and potentially lead to the spread of incorrect decisions. Although group discussions give individuals the chance to reconsider their choices, dominant voices or majority opinions can distract individuals from their correct decisions. However, another issue to be noted here is that while conforming to majority opinions seems to negatively affect individual decision accuracy in the short term, the accuracy of declared literacy levels may also be due to discussion. On the other hand, similar findings can be observed for other factors affecting decision-making rather than literacy levels. For example, Chen et al. (2024) found that digital literacy improved older users' risk perception, self-efficacy, and subjective norms, which are key to recognizing misinformation on social media. However, although digital literacy has been found to improve critical thinking, perceived behavioral control is said to not strongly affect intentions to identify false content. Another possible reason may be that the lack of technical knowledge about AI technologies in education hinders students' ability to critically analyze news, leading them to evaluate based on perception rather than comprehensive assessment. Similar findings can be observed in studies focusing on political contexts. For example, Pennycook and Rand (2021) suggest that the difficulty in distinguishing between true and false news is largely due to poor judgment and lack of knowledge in the relevant field rather than political bias. Instead, they mention that individuals tend to rely on mental shortcuts such as familiarity, which can lead to errors when evaluating news content. However, Sniezek and Henry (1989) found that group judgments are generally more accurate than individual judgments, and that there is a significant reduction in bias. In one-third of the cases they examined, group decisions can overshadow the best individual judgment within the group. But from a different perspective, relying on group judgment during challenging times may be more effective for long-term problem solving. Similarly, Hastie and Kameda (2005) found that purely irrational majority rules can be quite effective in group decision making during times of uncertainty.

In the last research question of the study, although it was observed that majority answers within the group influenced the answers of other students and this sometimes led to negative results, thinking about majority decisions itself can serve the learning process. For example, Michinov et al. (2020) found that providing guidance on interpreting collective feedback during peer tutoring reduced group conformity and improved learning outcomes. In addition, students who were encouraged to critically evaluate feedback were found to be less likely to follow incorrect majority answers and more likely to engage in meaningful peer discussions, resulting in greater consensus on correct answers and better learning. Therefore, it is thought that interventions aimed at reducing conformity bias can improve group decision-making processes, even if individuals deviate from the correctness of their decisions due to being influenced by the group.

This study also revealed that students who changed their decisions after group discussions experienced a significant decrease in their confidence levels. This finding suggests that individuals were not completely confident in their choices, despite being in line with group decisions. The decrease in confidence among students who changed their decisions highlights the impact of incorrect group decisions on individuals. It was found that although both individuals and groups had high confidence levels, this did not guarantee decision accuracy, especially when dealing with fake news. In addition, it was found that in the AI-based educational technology news presented to students, confidence levels and accuracy rates in detecting real news were higher compared to fake news. Considering the nature of these news items and the fact that the students did not receive any literacy training, it can be argued that the tasks were perceptual in nature. Lundie (2022) emphasized that the relationship between decision accuracy and confidence levels varied according to the task type. In perceptual tasks, participants were more sensitive to disconfirming evidence by adjusting their confidence after incorrect decisions, while in analytical tasks, confidence levels were observed to be more resistant to change even when faced with contradictory information. In line with this finding, preparing news sets that students can evaluate analytically in future studies may help establish this relationship more easily.

Another important finding from this study is that the difficulty of news affects how decisions are made in groups. When news is complex or ambiguous, both individuals and groups have difficulty making correct decisions. This may indicate that complex information can disrupt the decision-making process and lead to the spread of false ideas in group discussions. Due to the need to process more information, people in groups may become more open to the opinions of others. Schwarz and Jalbert (2021) state that when information is difficult to process, people tend to examine it more closely, while simpler information is more easily accepted without further scrutiny. This "processing fluency" suggests that difficult information leads to more careful group analysis, while groups may be more likely to reach incorrect conclusions when misleading information is presented.

In conclusion, this study highlights the complex dynamics of group discussions when distinguishing between real and fake AI-based edtech news. While group discussions may have an impact on increasing confidence, they may not always lead to more accurate decisions, especially when dealing with fake news. The findings suggest that group environments can foster overconfidence and make individuals more susceptible to incorrect decisions driven by group conformity. Additionally, the perceived difficulty of news can add another layer of complexity that leads to more collective processing without necessarily increasing decision accuracy. Implementing strategies to reduce conformity bias and promote critical thinking through AI and news media literacy programs may help mitigate these issues and improve decision making in educational contexts.

LIMITATIONS

The limitations of this study can be summarized under six issues. First, the small sample size of the study, consisting of 20 prospective teachers, is limited in its generalizability as it cannot be extrapolated to a larger population. Second, since it was conducted in a specific educational setting where prospective teachers did not have formal news media and AI literacy training, the findings may not be applicable to other contexts with different curriculum structures. Third, a quasi-experimental setting may not fully capture the complexities of real-world group decision-making processes when prospective teachers evaluate AI-based educational technology news. Fourth, self-reported measures of news media and AI literacy may not accurately represent the participants' actual competencies as the scales used may not capture the full complexity of literacy in rapidly evolving digital environments. Fifth, since the study focused on short-term outcomes, it is not possible to understand the long-term effects on confidence and decision accuracy. Finally, the study did not investigate the reasons behind why groups classified the news as real or fake, nor was any discourse collected for analysis to understand the arguments or rationales underlying their decisions.

FUTURE RESEARCH DIRECTIONS

Future research focusing on the long-term effects of group discussions on individual decision-making processes regarding AI-based educational technology news may encourage suggestions that could improve the field. While the current study provides insights into short-term decision changes, it does not provide any evidence on how these changes evolve over time. Longitudinal studies could examine how potential teachers' media and AI literacy skills develop and whether these developments lead to more accurate decision making in group settings. In addition, investigating the role of group dynamics in affecting decision accuracy (especially the influence of dominant individuals within a group) could provide a deeper understanding of how social interactions shape collective judgments. Methods such as social network analysis are among the methods suggested for examining the extent to which specific individuals disproportionately influence group decisions and whether this influence leads to more accurate or biased conclusions.

Another promising avenue for future research is the idea that AI-supported interventions could be integrated into media literacy education. It is thought that investigating whether AI-powered fact-checking tools enhance individuals' ability to critically evaluate news and how such tools interact with group decision-making dynamics could provide valuable insights into the effectiveness of technology-based interventions. Furthermore, examining how different media formats (e.g., text-based, visual, or video news) affect individuals' perceptions of credibility and susceptibility to misinformation in group discussions could further advance our understanding of media literacy education. By addressing such research gaps, future studies could contribute to the development of evidence-based educational programs aimed at strengthening critical thinking and decision-making skills in collaborative learning environments.

ADDITIONAL READINGS

Jang, S. M., & Kim, J. K. (2017). Third person effects of fake news: Fake news regulation and media literacy interventions. *Computers in Human Behavior, 80*, 295–302. DOI: 10.1016/j.chb.2017.11.034

Jones-Jang, S. M., Mortensen, T., & Liu, J. (2019). Does media literacy help identification of fake news? Information literacy helps, but other literacies don't. *The American Behavioral Scientist, 65*(2), 371–388. DOI: 10.1177/0002764219869406

Pennycook, G., & Rand, D. G. (2019). Fighting misinformation on social media using crowdsourced judgments of news source quality. *Proceedings of the National Academy of Sciences of the United States of America, 116*(7), 2521–2526. DOI: 10.1073/pnas.1806781116 PMID: 30692252

Pennycook, G., & Rand, D. G. (2021). The psychology of fake news. *Trends in Cognitive Sciences, 25*(5), 388–402. DOI: 10.1016/j.tics.2021.02.007 PMID: 33736957

Williamson, S. M., & Prybutok, V. (2024). The era of artificial intelligence deception: Unraveling the complexities of false realities and emerging threats of misinformation. *Information (Basel), 15*(6), 299. DOI: 10.3390/info15060299

REFERENCES

Abels, A., Domingos, E. F., Nowé, A., & Lenaerts, T. (2024). Mitigating biases in collective decision-making: Enhancing performance in the face of fake news. *arXiv (Cornell University)*. https://doi.org//arxiv.2403.08829DOI: 10.48550

Ackerman, R., & Thompson, V. A. (2017). Meta-Reasoning: Monitoring and control of thinking and reasoning. *Trends in Cognitive Sciences, 21*(8), 607–617. DOI: 10.1016/j.tics.2017.05.004 PMID: 28625355

Adjin-Tettey, T. D. (2022). Combating fake news, disinformation, and misinformation: Experimental evidence for media literacy education. *Cogent Arts & Humanities, 9*(1), 2037229. Advance online publication. DOI: 10.1080/23311983.2022.2037229

Al-Asadi, M. A., & Tasdemir, S. (2021). Using AI against the phenomenon of fake news: A systematic literature review. In *Studies in computational intelligence* (pp. 39–54). https://doi.org/DOI: 10.1007/978-3-030-90087-8_2

Bahrami, B., Olsen, K., Latham, P. E., Roepstorff, A., Rees, G., & Frith, C. D. (2010). Optimally interacting minds. *Science*, *329*(5995), 1081–1085. DOI: 10.1126/science.1185718 PMID: 20798320

Blanchard, M. D., Jackson, S. A., & Kleitman, S. (2020). Collective decision making reduces metacognitive control and increases error rates, particularly for overconfident individuals. *Journal of Behavioral Decision Making*, *33*(3), 348–375. DOI: 10.1002/bdm.2156

Chen, L., Jia, J., Xiao, M., Wu, C., & Zhang, L. (2024). A study on the influence of digital literacy on elderly user's intention to identify social media false information. *The Electronic Library*, *42*(5), 701–721. Advance online publication. DOI: 10.1108/EL-10-2023-0257

Cherner, T. S., & Curry, K. (2019). Preparing pre-service teachers to teach media literacy: A response to "fake news". *The Journal of Media Literacy Education*, *11*(1), 1–31. DOI: 10.23860/JMLE-2019-11-1-1

De Paor, S., & Heravi, B. (2020). Information literacy and fake news: How the field of librarianship can help combat the epidemic of fake news. *Journal of Academic Librarianship*, *46*(5), 102218. DOI: 10.1016/j.acalib.2020.102218

French, A. M., Storey, V. C., & Wallace, L. (2023). The impact of cognitive biases on the believability of fake news. *European Journal of Information Systems*, •••, 1–22. DOI: 10.1080/0960085X.2023.2272608

Güdekli, A., Van Het Hof, S. D., Eser, M., & Oruç, M. S. (2022). News media literacy scale: Validity and reliability. *Journal of Economy Culture and Society*, *66*(1), 61–80. DOI: 10.26650/JECS2021-837512

Hart, W., Albarracín, D., Eagly, A. H., Brechan, I., Lindberg, M. J., & Merrill, L. (2009). Feeling validated versus being correct: A meta-analysis of selective exposure to information. *Psychological Bulletin*, *135*(4), 555–588. DOI: 10.1037/a0015701 PMID: 19586162

Hastie, R., & Kameda, T. (2005). The robust beauty of majority rules in group decisions. *Psychological Review*, *112*(2), 494–508. DOI: 10.1037/0033-295X.112.2.494 PMID: 15783295

Heidhues, P., Kőszegi, B., & Strack, P. (2019). Overconfidence and prejudice. *arXiv (Cornell University)*. https://doi.org//arxiv.1909.08497DOI: 10.48550

Hobbs, R. (2004). A Review of school-based initiatives in media literacy education. *The American Behavioral Scientist*, *48*(1), 42–59. DOI: 10.1177/0002764204267250

Jang, S. M., & Kim, J. K. (2017). Third person effects of fake news: Fake news regulation and media literacy interventions. *Computers in Human Behavior, 80*, 295–302. DOI: 10.1016/j.chb.2017.11.034

Jones-Jang, S. M., Mortensen, T., & Liu, J. (2019). Does media literacy help identification of fake news? Information literacy helps, but other literacies don't. *The American Behavioral Scientist, 65*(2), 371–388. DOI: 10.1177/0002764219869406

Kahne, J., & Bowyer, B. (2017). Educating for Democracy in a Partisan Age: Confronting the Challenges of Motivated Reasoning and Misinformation. *American Educational Research Journal, 54*(1), 3–34. DOI: 10.3102/0002831216679817

Kolić-Vehovec, S., Pahljina-Reinić, R., & Zubković, B. R. (2021). Effects of collaboration and informing students about overconfidence on metacognitive judgment in conceptual learning. *Metacognition and Learning, 17*(1), 87–116. DOI: 10.1007/s11409-021-09275-7

Koriat, A. (2012). When are two heads better than one and why? *Science, 336*(6079), 360–362. DOI: 10.1126/science.1216549 PMID: 22517862

Long, D., & Magerko, B. (2020). What is AI Literacy? Competencies and Design Considerations. In *CHI '20: Proceedings of the 2020 CHI Conference on Human Factors in Computing Systems*. https://doi.org/DOI: 10.1145/3313831.3376727

Lundie, M. J. (2022). *The metacognitive underpinnings of confirmation bias and its political consequences.*https://hdl.handle.net/10735.1/9662

Michinov, N., Anquetil, É., & Michinov, E. (2020). Guiding the use of collective feedback displayed on heatmaps to reduce group conformity and improve learning in Peer Instruction. *Journal of Computer Assisted Learning, 36*(6), 1026–1037. DOI: 10.1111/jcal.12457

Monteith, S., Glenn, T., Geddes, J. R., Whybrow, P. C., Achtyes, E., & Bauer, M. (2023). Artificial intelligence and increasing misinformation. *The British Journal of Psychiatry, 224*(2), 33–35. DOI: 10.1192/bjp.2023.136 PMID: 37881016

Ng, D. T. K., Leung, J. K. L., Chu, S. K. W., & Qiao, M. S. (2021). Conceptualizing AI literacy: An exploratory review. *Computers and Education Artificial Intelligence, 2*, 100041. DOI: 10.1016/j.caeai.2021.100041

Ostillio, T. (2019). The trigger effect: Cognitive biases and fake news. *Hybris, 44*(1), 86–104. DOI: 10.18778/1689-4286.44.06

Peker, M., & Tekcan, A. İ. (2009). The role of familiarity among group members in collaborative inhibition and social contagion. *Social Psychology (Göttingen)*, *40*(3), 111–118. DOI: 10.1027/1864-9335.40.3.111

Pennycook, G., & Rand, D. G. (2021). The psychology of fake news. *Trends in Cognitive Sciences*, *25*(5), 388–402. DOI: 10.1016/j.tics.2021.02.007 PMID: 33736957

Polatgil, M., & Güler, A. (2023). Adaptation of artificial intelligence literacy scale into Turkish. *Journal of Quantitative Research in Social Sciences*, *3*(2), 99–114.

Potter, W. (2004). *Theory of Media Literacy: A Cognitive Approach*. https://doi.org/ DOI: 10.4135/9781483328881

Schwarz, N., & Jalbert, M. (2021). When (fake) news feels true: Intuitions of truth and the acceptance and correction of misinformation. In C. Mc Mahon (Ed.), *Psychological insights for understanding COVID-19 and media and technology* (pp. 9–25). Routledge/Taylor & Francis Group. https://doi.org/DOI: 10.4324/9781003121756-2

Sniezek, J. A., & Henry, R. A. (1989). Accuracy and confidence in group judgment. *Organizational Behavior and Human Decision Processes*, *43*(1), 1–28. DOI: 10.1016/0749-5978(89)90055-1

Ulu-Aslan, E., & Baş, B. (2022). Popular culture texts in education: The effect of tales transformed into children's media on critical thinking and media literacy skills. *Thinking Skills and Creativity*, *47*, 101202. DOI: 10.1016/j.tsc.2022.101202

Washington, J. (2023). Combating misinformation and fake news: the potential of AI and media literacy education. SSRN *Electronic Journal*. https://doi.org/DOI: 10.2139/ssrn.4580385

Williamson, S. M., & Prybutok, V. (2024). The era of artificial intelligence deception: Unraveling the complexities of false realities and emerging threats of misinformation. *Information (Basel)*, *15*(6), 299. DOI: 10.3390/info15060299

Wilner, A. S. (2018). Cybersecurity and its discontents: Artificial intelligence, the Internet of Things, and digital misinformation. *International Journal (Toronto, Ont.)*, *73*(2), 308–316. DOI: 10.1177/0020702018782496

Zarnoth, P., & Sniezek, J. A. (1997). The social influence of confidence in group decision making. *Journal of Experimental Social Psychology*, *33*(4), 345–366. DOI: 10.1006/jesp.1997.1326 PMID: 9247369

KEY TERMS AND DEFINITIONS

Artificial Intelligence Literacy: The understanding of AI concepts, capabilities, limitations, and ethical considerations.

Cognitive Biases: Systematic patterns of deviation from rationality in judgment and decision making.

Fact-Checking Tools: AI-powered or human-driven systems designed to verify the truthfulness of news and information.

Group Decision Making: A process in which multiple individuals collaborate to reach a decision, typically involving discussion, information sharing, and consensus building.

Media Literacy: The ability to access, analyze, evaluate, and create media in a variety of formats.

Metacognitive Confidence Judgment: A self-assessment of one's own knowledge, understanding, and decision accuracy.

Misinformation: False or misleading information that is disseminated regardless of intent.

Perceived Difficulty: Involves a subjective assessment of how difficult a task or decision is perceived to be.

Social Influence in Group Discussions: The process by which individuals' opinions and decisions are shaped by the presence and actions of others in a group.

Compilation of References

Abramowicz, M., & Ho, D. (2020). Transparency and trust in the digital age. *Harvard Journal of Law & Technology.*

Agarwal, S., Farid, H., & Guo, H. (2019). Protecting world leaders against deep fakes. *Proceedings of the IEEE Conference on Computer Vision and Pattern Recognition Workshops,* 38-45.

Aïmeur, E., Amri, S., & Brassard, G. (2023). Fake news, disinformation and misinformation in social media: A review. *Social Network Analysis and Mining, 13*(1), 30. DOI: 10.1007/s13278-023-01028-5 PMID: 36789378

Ajder, H. (2020, July 9). Tracer newsletter #58 (09/07/20)-deepfake threat intelligence: A statistics snapshot from June 2020. *Sensity.* https://medium.com/sensity/tracer-newsletter-58-09-07-20-deepfake-threat-intelligence-a-statistics-snapshot-from-june-2020-1af7052e724a

Ajder, H., Patrini, G., Cavalli, F., & Cullen, L. (2019). The State of Deepfakes: Landscape, Threats, and Impact. Available: https://regmedia.co.uk/2019/10/08/deepfake_report.pdf

Alarcón, B., & Hidalgo, M. (2024). Venezuela: La lógica de la supervivenciaautocrática. *Revista de Ciencia Política, 44*(2), 463–489. DOI: 10.4067/s0718-090x2024005000121

Algorithm watch (2023). Generative AI and elections: Are chatbots a reliable source of information for voters? Available from: https://algorithmwatch.org/en/wp-content/uploads/2023/12/AlgorithmWatch_AIForensics_Bing_Chat_Report.pdf

Ali, A., & Qazi, I. A. (2023). Countering misinformation on social media through educational interventions: Evidence from a randomized experiment in Pakistan. *Journal of Development Economics, 163*, 103108. DOI: 10.1016/j.jdeveco.2023.103108

Ali, M. (2015). Governance and good governance: A conceptual perspective. *The Dialogue*, *10*(1), 65–77. https://www.qurtuba.edu.pk/thedialogue/The%20Dialogue/10_1/Dialogue_January_March2015_65-77.pdf

AllahRakha, N. (2024). Global perspectives on cybercrime legislation. *Journal of Infrastructure. Policy and Development*, *8*(10), 6007.

Allcott, H., & Gentzkow, M. (2017). Social media and fake news in the 2016 election. *The Journal of Economic Perspectives*, *31*(2), 211–236. https://www.jstor.org/stable/44235006. DOI: 10.1257/jep.31.2.211

Al-Nimr, A. M. I. (2024). The relationship between college students' personal anxiety resulting from deepfake threats and the privacy of social media data management. *The Egyptian Journal of Media Research*, *2024*(88), 127–189.

Alsat.mk. (2024, December 30). *Balanserotzaminuvavoistorijata [The balancer goes into history]*. Retrieved from https://alsat.mk/mk/balanserot-zaminuva-vo-istorijata/

Alt News. (n.d.). *Methodology for fact checking*. https://www.altnews.in/methodology-for-fact-checking/

Altuncu, E., Franqueira, V., & Li, S. (2022). Deepfake: Definitions, performance metrics and standards, datasets and benchmarks, and a meta-review. arXiv. org.

Al-Zaman, M. S. (2021). Social media fake news in India. *Asian Journal for Public Opinion Research*, *9*(1), 25–47. DOI: 10.15206/ajpor.2021.9.1.25

American Library Association. (2020). Media literacy for adults. Architecture of the internet: Programming guide. https://www.ala.org/sites/default/files/tools/content/!%20Media-Lit_Prac-Guide_FINALWEB_112020_0.pdf

American Library Association. (2021). Promising practices: Educational research applied to the shared foundations. https://www.ala.org/sites/default/files/2024-04/AASL_ClassIIResearch_Book_0.pdf

American Psychological Association. (2024). *Misinformation and disinformation*. Retrieved 16 from https://www.apa.org/topics/journalism-facts/misinformation-disinformation

Ammara, U., Bukhari, H., & Qadir, J. (2020).Analyzing Misinformation through the Lens of Systems Thinking.*Proceedings of the 2nd Conference on Truth and Trust Online* (TTO 2020), Boston, MA, USA, 55–63.

Amorín, S. (2022). Uruguay y la "cuestióncubana":Diplomacia, movilizaciónpolítica y radicalizaciónanticastrista en los sesenta. *EncuentrosUruguayos*, *15*(1), 90–124. DOI: 10.55509/ayer/896

Anders, B. (2023). *ChatGPT AI in Education: What it is and How to Use it in the Classroom*. Sovorel Publishing.

Anderson, J., & Rainie, L. (2017). The Future of Truth and Misinformation Online. *Pew Research Center*. https://www.pewresearch.org/internet/2017/10/19/the-future-of-truth-and-misinformation-online/

Anderson, J., Rainie, L., & Vogels, E. A. (2021). *Experts say the'new normal'in 2025 will be far more tech-driven, presenting more big challenges* (Vol. 18). Pew Research Center.

Annotation to thedraftlaw "Amendments to thePre-electionCampaignLaw". Available: https://titania.saeima.lv/LIVS14/saeimalivs14.nsf/webSasaiste?OpenView&restricttocategory=523/Lp14

Apostolov, G., & Jankulovski, M. (2018). Media literacy and fake News in North Macedonia. *The Journal of Medical Research*, *11*(3), 56–72.

Arendt, H. (1994). *Truth and lies in politics*. Filip Višnjić.

Arksey, H., & O'Malley, L. (2005). Scoping studies: Towards a methodological framework. *International Journal of Social Research Methodology*, *8*(1), 19–31. DOI: 10.1080/1364557032000119616

Article 19 (2011) General Comment No.34: Article 19: Freedoms of opinion and expression, available at https://www.refworld.org/docid/4e38efb52.html

Article 19 (2012) International standards: Regulation of media workers, available at https://www.article19.org/resources/international-standards-regulation-media-workers/

Ashley, S., Maksl, A., & Craft, S. (2017). News media literacy and political engagement: What's the connection? *The Journal of Media Literacy Education*, *9*(1), 79–98. DOI: 10.23860/JMLE-2017-9-1-6

Aspen Institute. (2022). Medienkompetenz meistern: Tipps von Schüler*innen für Schüler*innen. https://www.aspeninstitute.de/wp-content/uploads/Aspen-Institute-Germany-Handbuch-Medienkompetenz-meistern-Tipps-von-SchuelerInnen-fuer-SchuelerInnen.pdf

Aufderheide, P., & Firestone, C. (1993). Media literacy: A report of the national leadership conference on media literacy. The Aspen Institute. https://www.medialit.org/reading_room/pdf/358_AspenFrwd_Firestone.pdf

Australian Government Department of Home Affairs. (2022). *National Plan to Combat Cybercrime 2022*. https://www.homeaffairs.gov.au/criminal-justice/files/national-plan-combat-cybercrime-2022.pdf

Babulík, M. (2024). China's influence in the Western Balkans. *Strategic Analysis*. Retrieved May 24, 2025, from https://www.strategicanalysis.sk/chinas-influence-in-the-western-balkans/

Badiou, A. (2020). *A brief overview of metapolitics*. FPZ, Political Thought Library.

Baines, P., & O'Shaughnessy, N. (2020). Towards the measurement of Islamist propaganda effectiveness: A marketing perspective. In Baines, P., O'Shaughnessy, N., & Snow, N. (Eds.), *The SAGE handbook of propaganda* (pp. 223–242). SAGE Publications. DOI: 10.4135/9781526477170.n15

Bala, B. K., Arshad, F. M., & Noh, K. M. (2017).*System Dynamics: Modelling and Simulation*. Springer Texts in Business and Economics. Springer, Singapore. DOI: 10.1007/978-981-10-2045-2

Bali, A., & Desai, P. (2019). Fake news and social media: Indian perspective. *Media Watch, 10*(3). Advance online publication. DOI: 10.15655/mw/2019/v10i3/49687

Balkan Investigative Reporting Lab. (2021). BIRN presents online platform on China's activities in Western Balkans. https://balkaninsight.com/2021/12/15/birn-presents-online-platform-on-chinas-activities-in-western-balkans/

Balkans, We. (2023). Serbia's leap into the Erasmus Plus programme: Fostering mutual understanding and opportunities. https://webalkans.eu/en/stories/serbias-leap-into-the-erasmus-plus-programme-fostering-mutual-understanding-and-opportunities/

Balkans, We. (2024). Discover the YEA Network. https://webalkans.eu/en/yea/

Balkin, J. (2018). Free speech is a triangle. *Columbia Law Review, 118*(7), 2032–2033.

Banchio, P. R. (2024). Legal Framework to Combat Disinformation and Hate Speech on Digital Platforms. *SSRN*. https://papers.ssrn.com/sol3/papers.cfm?abstract_id=4879162

Bateman, J., & Jackson, D. (2024).Countering Disinformation Effectively: An Evidence-Based Policy Guide.https://carnegieendowment.org/research/2024/01/countering-disinformation-effectively-an-evidence-based-policy-guide?lang=en

Battista, D. (2024). Political communication in the age of artificial Intelligence: an overview of deepfakes and their Implications. *Society Register*, Vol. 8 No. 2 (2024). Available: https://www.ceeol.com/search/article-detail?id=1251211

Bayet, N.. (2019). *Disinformation in the Western Balkans*. EU Institute for Security Studies.

Beauvais, C. (2022). Fake news: Why do we believe it? *Joint, Bone, Spine*, *89*(4), 105371. DOI: 10.1016/j.jbspin.2022.105371 PMID: 35257865

Beck, J., Stern, M., & Haugsjaa, E. (1996). Applications of AI in Education. *XRDS: Crossroads. The ACM Magazine for Students*, *3*(1), 11–15.

Bedi, S. (2021). The myth of the chilling effect. *Harvard Journal of Law & Technology*, *35*(1). https://jolt.law.harvard.edu/assets/articlePDFs/v35/Bedi-The-Myth-of-the-Chilling-Effect.pdf

Benkler, Y., Faris, R., & Roberts, H. (2018). *Network propaganda: Manipulation, disinformation, and radicalization in American politics*. Oxford University Press. DOI: 10.1093/oso/9780190923624.001.0001

Bennett, W., & Livingston, S. (2020). *The disinformation age*. Cambridge University Press.

Bhadoria, S. (2024, February 25). *How AI will be a double edged sword in the upcoming Lok Sabha polls*. Mint. https://www.livemint.com/news/india/lok-sabha-elections-2024-how-ai-will-be-a-double-edged-sword-to-boost-fake-news-curb-voting-manipulations-11708705430974.html

Bhalli, N. N., Naqvi, N., Evered, C., Mallinson, C., & Janeja, V. P. (2024). Listening for Expert Identified Linguistic Features: Assessment of Audio Deepfake Discernment among Undergraduate Students. arXiv preprint arXiv:2411.14586.

Birkinshaw, P. (2006). *Freedom of information: The law, the practice and the ideal*. Cambridge University Press.

Blanc, Y. (2023, August 11). Education and critical thinking as tools in the battle against fake news.https://world-education-blog.org/2023/08/11/education-and-critical-thinking-as-tools-in-the-battle-against-fake-news/

Blazhevski, T., & Rizankoska, J. (2020). Social media disinformation during COVID-19: A case study of North Macedonia. *Southeast European and Black Sea Studies*, *20*(4), 595–617.

Bond, S. (2020, December 10). ‘The perfect storm’: How vaccine misinformation spread to the mainstream. *NPR*. https://www.npr.org/2020/12/10/944408988/the-perfect-storm-how-coronavirus-spread-vaccine-misinformation-to-the-mainstrea

Borr, D. (1998). Transparency in government. *Public Administration Review*, *58*(4), 347–356.

Borz, G., & De Francesco, F. (2024). Digital political campaigning: Contemporary challenges and regulation. *Policy Studies, 45*(5), 677–691. DOI: 10.1080/01442872.2024.2384145

Bradshaw, S., & Howard, P. N. (2019). *The global disinformation disorder: 2019 global inventory of organized social media manipulation* (Working Paper 2019.2). Oxford: Project on Computational Propaganda.

Bradshaw, S., & Howard, P. N. (2019). *The global disinformation order: 2019 global inventory of organised social media manipulation*. Project on Computational Propaganda.

Brady, A. M. (2008). *Marketing dictatorship: Propaganda and thought work in contemporary China*. Rowman&Littlefield.

Bragazzi, N. L., & Garbarino, S. (2024). Understanding and Combating Misinformation: An Evolutionary Perspective. *JMIR Infodemiology, 2024*(4), e65521. DOI: 10.2196/65521 PMID: 39466077

Broadhurst, R., & Chang, L. Y. C. (2013). Cybercrime in Asia: Trends and Challenges. In Liu, J., Hebenton, B., & Jou, S. (Eds.), *Handbook of Asian Criminology* (pp. 49–63). Springer New York., DOI: 10.1007/978-1-4614-5218-8_4

Broda, E., & Stromback, J. (2024). Misinformation, disinformation, and fake news: Lessons from an interdisciplinary, systematic literature review. *Annals of the International Communication Association, 48*(2), 139–166. DOI: 10.1080/23808985.2024.2323736

Brodsky, J. E., Brooks, P. J., Scimeca, D., & Galati, P. (2021). Improving college students' fact-checking strategies through lateral reading instruction in a general education civics course. *Cognitive Research: Principles and Implications, 6*(1), 1–18. DOI: 10.1186/s41235-021-00291-4 PMID: 33788064

Brown, T. B.. (2020). Language models are few-shot learners. *Advances in Neural Information Processing Systems, 33*, 1877–1901.

Brumfiel, G. (2021, June 14). Anti-vaccine activists use a federal database to spread fear about covid vaccines. *NPR*. https://www.npr.org/sections/health-shots/2021/06/14/1004757554/anti-vaccine-activists-use-a-federal-database-to-spread-fear-about-covid-vaccine

Buckingham, D. (2019). Teaching media in a 'post-truth' age: Fake news, media bias and the challenge for media literacy education. Cultura y Educación, 31(2), 1–19. https://davidbuckingham.net/wp-content/uploads/2019/10/post-truth-buckingham.pdf

Buckingham, D., Banaji, S., Carr, D., Cranmer, S., & Willett, R. (2005). *The media literacy of children and young people: A review of the research literature*. Ofcom.

Buka, A., Schewe, C., & Strazdiņš, Ģ. (2020). European Union law. Section I. Institutional Law. Second revised edition. In scientific editorial of K. Gailitis, A. Buka, C. Schewe. *Riga: Publishing house "Tiesunamuagentura"*.

Burkhardt, J. M. (2017). Chapter 1. History of fake news. *Library Technology Reports*, *53*(8), 5–9. https://journals.ala.org/index.php/ltr/article/view/6497

BuzzFeedVideo. (2018, April 17). You Won't Believe What Obama Says In This Video! YouTube. https://www.youtube.com/watch?v=cQ54GDm1eL0

Caled, D., & Silva, M. J. (2022). Digital media and misinformation: An outlook on multidisciplinary strategies against manipulation. *Journal of Computational Social Science*, *5*(1), 123–159. DOI: 10.1007/s42001-021-00118-8 PMID: 34075349

Camero Guevara, Y., Chaguaceda Noriega, A., Diaz Torres, I., González Arenas, B., González Marrero, C., Hernández, H. E., Puerta Riera, M. I., & Thiemann, L. (2023). *Sharp power y redes intelectuales: La presencia de Cuba en América Latina* [Sharp power and intellectual networks: Cuba's presence in Latin America]. Editorial Dunken.

Carter Center. (2024, July 30). Statement on Venezuela's 2024 presidential election [Press release]. *The Carter Center.* https://www.cartercenter.org/news/pr/2024/venezuela-073024.html

Centenera, M., Mella, C., & Gómez Vega, R. (2024, July 28). Sólo el 1% de los venezolanos en el exterior puede votar en las elecciones presidenciales. *El País.* https://elpais.com/america/2024-07-27/solo-el-1-de-los-venezolanos-en-el-exterior-puede-votar-en-las-elecciones-presidenciales.html

Ceylan, G., Anderson, I. A., & Wood, W. (2023). Sharing of misinformation is habitual, not just lazy or biased. *Proceedings of the National Academy of Sciences of the United States of America*, *120*(4), e2216614120. DOI: 10.1073/pnas.2216614120 PMID: 36649414

Chaguaceda, A., & Rouvinski, V. (2024, September 10). Russia's capture of intellectual elites in Latin America. *Wilson Center.* https://www.wilsoncenter.org/blog-post/russias-capture-intellectual-elites-latin-america

Chang, L. Y. C., & Coppel, N. (2020). Building cyber security awareness in a developing country: Lessons from Myanmar. *Computers & Security*, *97*, 101959. https://doi.org/https://doi.org/10.1016/j.cose.2020.101959. DOI: 10.1016/j.cose.2020.101959

Chang, L. Y. C., Mukherjee, S., & Coppel, N. (2021). We are all victims: Questionable content and collective victimisation in the digital age. *Asian Journal of Criminology*, *16*(1), 37–50. DOI: 10.1007/s11417-020-09331-2 PMID: 33042290

Chayko, M. (2019). *Superconnected: Internet, digital media and techno-social life*. White City: Clio.

Chen, C., & Shu, K. (2024). Combatting misinformation in the age of LLMs: Opportunities and challenges. *AI Magazine*, *45*(3), 354–368. DOI: 10.1002/aaai.12188

Chesney, R., & Citron, D. (2019). Deepfakes and the new disinformation war: The coming age of post-truth geopolitics. *Foreign Affairs*, *98*(1), 147–155.

China Daily. (2015). Chinese art troupe presents gala performance in Albania. https://www.chinadaily.com.cn/culture/2015-10/26/content_22287211.htm

Cho, H., Cannon, J., Lopez, R., & Li, W. (2024). Social media literacy: A conceptual framework. *New Media & Society*, *26*(2), 941–960. DOI: 10.1177/14614448211068530 PMID: 38328341

Chu-Ke, M.F, C. & Dong, Y.. (2024). Misinformation and Literacies in the Era of Generative Artificial Intelligence: A Brief Overview and a Call for Future Research. *Emerging Media* 2(1).

CilanoPeláez. J., Chaguaceda, A., Puerta, M., VieraCañive, E., & González, C. (2021). *Cuba en Latinoamérica: Presencia e influencia cubanas en espacios académicos y plataformas generadoras de pensamiento*. Gobierno y AnálisisPolítico AC.

Cipers, S., Meyer, T., & Lefevere, J. (2023). Government responses to online disinformation unpacked. *Internet Policy Review*, *12*(4). Advance online publication. DOI: 10.14763/2023.4.1736

CISA. (n.d.). *Election security rumor vs. Reality*. https://www.cisa.gov/topics/election-security/rumor-vs-reality

Clarín. (2024, April 25). Encuentro para una Alternativa Social Mundial del ALBA CTP reunió en Caracas a los pueblos del sur global. *Clarín*.https://www.elclarin.cl/2024/04/25/encuentro-para-una-alternativa-social-mundial-del-alba-ctp-reunio-en-caracas-a-los-pueblos-del-sur-global/

Clarke, L. (2025). Nobody was tricked into voting for Trump: Why the disinformation panic is over. https://www.politico.eu/article/nobody-tricked-vote-donald-trump-disinformation-panic-over/

Clegg, N. (2024). Labeling AI-GeneratedImagesonFacebook, InstagramandThreads. Meta. Available: https://about.fb.com/news/2024/02/labeling-ai-generated-images-on-facebook-instagram-and-threads/

Clemente, D. (2017). El regionalismo post-hegemónico en perspectiva crítica: Una mirada neogramsciana. Brasil, Venezuela y la opción contra-hegemónica. *Observatorio Latinoamericano y Caribeño*, *1*(1), 110–130.

CNTI – Center for News. Technology and Innovation. (2025). *Artificial Intelligence in Journalism.* Retrieved from: https://innovating.news/article/ai-in-journalism/ on 19.3.25.

Cochran, J. D., & Napshin, S. A. (2021). Deepfakes: Awareness, concerns, and platform accountability. *Cyberpsychology, Behavior, and Social Networking*, *24*(3), 164–172. DOI: 10.1089/cyber.2020.0100 PMID: 33760667

CoE. (2024). Dealing with propaganda, misinformation and fake news – intro. Council of Europe.https://www.coe.int/en/web/campaign-free-to-speak-safe-to-learn/compendium/-/asset_publisher/V1l7nfhFNH6d/content/dealing-with-propaganda-misinformation-and-fake-news-intro

Cohen-Almagor, R. (2014). After Leveson: Recommendations for Instituting the Public and Press Council' 19. *The International Journal of Press/Politics*, *202*(2), 207. DOI: 10.1177/1940161213516680

Coie, P. (2022). *The EU's Digital Services Act: A Paradigm Shift for Online Intermediaries.* Retrieved from: https://perkinscoie.com/insights/update/eus-digital-services-act-paradigm-shift-online-intermediaries

COM (2023) 637: Proposal for a DIRECTIVE OF THE EUROPEAN PARLIAMENT AND OF THE COUNCIL establishing harmonised requirements in the internal market on transparency of interest representation carried out on behalf of third countries and amending Directive (EU) 2019/1937/ (2023/0463(COD)).

Commission of the European Union. (2021). *Commission recommendation of 16.9.2021 on ensuring the protection, safety and empowerment of journalists and other media professionals in the European Union* (C(2021) 6650). https://digital-strategy.ec.europa.eu/en/library/recommendationprotection-safety-and-empowerment-journalists

Commission of the European Union. (2022a). *Proposal for a directive of the European Parliament and of the Council on protecting persons who engage in public participation from manifestly unfounded or abusive court proceedings ("Strategic lawsuits against public participation")* (COM(2022) 177 final). https://eur-lex.europa.eu/legal-content/EN/TXT/?uri=CELEX:52022PC0177&from=EN

Commission of the European Union. (2022b). *2022 strengthened code of practice on disinformation.* https://digital-strategy.ec.europa.eu/en/library/2022-strengthened-code-practice-disinformation

Commission of the European Union. (2022c). *Proposal for a regulation of the European Parliament and of the Council on a single market for digital services (Digital Services Act) and amending Directive 2000/31/EC* (COM/2020/825 final). https://eur-lex.europa.eu/legal-content/EN/TXT/PDF/?uri=CELEX:52020PC0825&from=en

Commission of the European Union. (2022d). *European Media Freedom Act (draft presentation).* https://ec.europa.eu/commission/presscorner/detail/en/ip_22_5504

Commonwealth of Australia. (2024). *Online misinformation and disinformation reform: Impact analysis* Retrieved from https://shorturl.at/DFaT9

Concepcion, A. R., & Sy, C. L. (2022).A System Dynamics Model of False News on Social Networking Sites.*Proceedings of the 2022 IEEE International Conference on Industrial Engineering and Engineering Management* (IEEM 2022), Kuala Lumpur, Malaysia, 786–790. DOI: 10.1109/IEEM55944.2022.9989859

Concepcion, A., & Sy, C. (2023). Modeling the Spread of Fake News on Social Networking Sites Using the System Dynamics Approach. *ASEAN Engineering Journal, 13*(4), 69–78. DOI: 10.11113/aej.v13.19251

Cooper, T., & Yodder, S. (2012). *Transparency in the EU: A critical analysis.* Oxford Policy Papers.

Cope, B., & Kalantzis, M. (2009). Multiliteracies: New literacies, new learning. *Pedagogies, 4*(3), 164–195. DOI: 10.1080/15544800903076044

Coper, E. (2022). *Facts and other lies. Welcome to the disinformation age.* Allen & Unwin Book Publishers.

Cornelisse, D. (2018) An intuitive guide to Convolutional Neural Networks, Available: https://www.freecodecamp.org/news/an-intuitive-guide-to-convolutional-neural-networks-260c2de0a050/

Correspondent, H. T. (2024, March 17). 'Myth vs Reality': EC lays down steps to curb fake news. *Hindustan Times*. https://www.hindustantimes.com/india-news/myth-vs-reality-ec-lays-down-steps-to-curb-fake-news-101710615785656.html

Council of Europe (CoE). (2017) Dominika Bychawska-Siniarska, Protecting the right to freedom of expression under the European convention on human rights: A handbook for legal practitioners, available at https://rm.coe.int/handbook-freedom-of-expression-eng/1680732814

Council of Europe (CoE). (2017) Dominika Bychawska-Siniarska, Protecting the right to freedom of expression under the European convention on human rights: A handbook for legal practitioners, https://rm.coe.int/handbook-freedom-of-expression-eng/1680732814

Council of Europe (CoE). (2018) Factsheet on memory laws available at https://rm.coe.int/factsheet-on-memory-laws-july2018-docx/16808c1690

Council of Europe (CoE). (2019) Focus on defamation: a new Council of Europe study draws attention to dangers of 'forum shopping' in defamation cases, https://www.coe.int/en/web/freedom-expression/-/focus-on-defamation-a-new-council-of-europe-study-draws-attention-to-dangers-of-forum-shopping-in-defamation-cases

Council of Europe. (2017). Study on the use of internet in electoral campaigns, DGI(2017)11. Available: https://rm.coe.int/study-on-the-use-of-internet/1680796298

Council of Europe. (2023) Council of Europe report on the freedom of artistic expression- Free to create: Artistic freedom in Europe, https://rm.coe.int/free-to-create-council-of-europe-report-on-the-freedom-of-artistic-exp/1680aa2dc0#:~:text=Protection%20of%20freedom%20of%20artistic,rights%20as%20provided%20under%20human

Council of Europe. (CoE. Int) (2023) Margin of appreciation, available at https://www.coe.int/t/dghl/cooperation/lisbonnetwork/themis/echr/paper2_en.asp

Cull, N. J. (2008). *The Cold War and the United States Information Agency: American propaganda and public diplomacy, 1945–1989*. Cambridge University Press. DOI: 10.1017/CBO9780511817151

Cunliffe-Jones, P., Diagne, A., Finlay, A., Gaye, S., Gichunge, W., Onumah, C., Pretorius, C., & Schiffrin, A. (2018). Misinformation: One part of a wider information disorder. In *Misinformation policy in Sub-Saharan Africa: From laws and regulations to media literacy* (pp. 114–117). University of Westminster Press. https://www.jstor.org/stable/j.ctv1v3gqw5.20

Cvetkovska, S., Belford, A., Silverman, C., & Methodieva, A. (2021). *Russian disinformation networks in the Balkans: A study of media manipulation in North Macedonia, Serbia, and Kosovo*. Digital Forensic Research Lab.

Dame Adjin-Tettey, T. (2022). Combating fake news, disinformation, and misinformation: Experimental evidence for media literacy education. *Cogent Arts & Humanities, 9*(1), 2037229. DOI: 10.1080/23311983.2022.2037229

deeptomcruise. (2021, February 25). I love magic! Video]. TikTok. https://www.tiktok.com/@deeptomcruise/video/6933305746130046214

Delchev, K., Safieddine, F., & Hammad, R. (2024). Identification of AI generated deep fake video by Higher Education Students. Lecture Notes in Networks and Systems, 473–489. https://doi.org/DOI: 10.1007/978-3-031-62281-6_33

Digital News Report (2023). Available: https://reutersinstitute.politics.ox.ac.uk/digital-news-report/2023

Dobber, T., Metoui, N., Trilling, D., Helberger, N., & de Vreese, C. (2021). Do (Microtargeted) Deepfakes Have Real Effects on Political Attitudes? *The International Journal of Press/Politics, 26*(1), 69–91. DOI: 10.1177/1940161220944364

Doss, C., Mondschein, J., Shu, D., Wolfson, T., Kopecky, D., Fitton-Kane, V. A., Bush, L., & Tucker, C. (2023). Deepfakes and scientific knowledge dissemination. *Scientific Reports, 13*(1), 13429. Advance online publication. DOI: 10.1038/s41598-023-39944-3 PMID: 37596384

Downs, A. (1957). *An economic theory of democracy*. Harper &Row.

Dukalskis, A. (2021). *Making the world safe for dictatorship*. Oxford University-Press. DOI: 10.1093/oso/9780197520130.001.0001

Đurić, L. (2023) Do Companies Have Human Rights? https://geciclaw.com/companies-human-rights/

Eberl, A., Kühn, J., & Wolbring, T. (2022). Using deepfakes for experiments in the Social Sciences - a pilot study. *Frontiers in Sociology, 7*, 907199. Advance online publication. DOI: 10.3389/fsoc.2022.907199 PMID: 36524213

EC (2022b).*Guidelines for teachers and educators on tackling disinformation and promoting digital literacy through education and training*.European Commission. Publications Office of the European Union.DOI: 10.2766/28248

EC. (2022a). *Final report of the Commission expert group on tackling disinformation and promoting digital literacy through education and training: Final report*. European Commission.Publications Office of the European Union.DOI: 10.2766/283100

ECHR. (1979) case of Sunday Times v. The United Kingdom, 6538/74, Council of Europe: European Court of Human Rights, 29 March 1979, https://www.refworld.org/jurisprudence/caselaw/echr/1979/en/14995

ECHR. (1991) The Observer and Guardian v. The United Kingdom, 51/1990/242/313, Council of Europe: European Court of Human Rights, 24 October 1991, https://www.refworld.org/jurisprudence/caselaw/echr/1991/en/18238

Ecker, U. K. H., Lewandowsky, S., Cook, J., Schmid, P., Fazio, L. K., Brashier, N., Kendeou, P., Vraga, E. K., & Amazeen, M. A. (2022). The psychological drivers of misinformation belief and its resistance to correction. *Nature Reviews Psychology*, *1*(1), 13–29. DOI: 10.1038/s44159-021-00006-y

Edison Research. (2024). *Edison Researchconductsexitpoll in Venezuela* [Report]. Edison Research.https://www.edisonresearch.com/edison-research-conducts-exit-poll-in-venezuela/

Edith Cowan University. (2024). *Hidden Biases: Midjourney's Portrayal of Olympic Athletes by Country.* ECU Online. Retrieved from: https://studyonline.ecu.edu.au/blog/hidden-biases-ai-portrayal-olympic-athletes on 4.1.25.

Editorial. (2019, February 15). Can social media be democratised? *Economic and Political Weekly*. https://www.epw.in/journal/2019/7/editorials/can-social-media-be-democratised.html

Edson, R., et al. (2017). The new age of disinformation. *Journal of Information Warfare*.

Education Department of the Embassy of the People's Republic of China in the Republic of Serbia. (2015). Introduction to Chinese Government Scholarships. https://serbia.lxgz.org.cn/serbia/lxzg/2021090910330183206/index.html

Egelhofer, J. L., & Lecheler, S. (2019). Fake news as a two-dimensional phenomenon: A framework and research agenda. *Annals of the International Communication Association*, *43*(2), 97–116. DOI: 10.1080/23808985.2019.1602782

El País. (2024a, July 30). La OEA denuncia la aberrante manipulación de las elecciones de Venezuela en un proceso sin garantías. *El País*.https://elpais.com/america/2024-07-30/la-oea-denuncia-la-aberrante-manipulacion-de-las-elecciones-de-venezuela-en-un-proceso-sin-garantias.html

El País. (2024b, October 15). La ONU acusa al gobierno de Maduro de cometer crímenes de lesa humanidad en las elecciones. *El País*.https://elpais.com/america/2024-10-15/la-onu-acusa-al-gobierno-de-maduro-de-cometer-crimenes-de-lesa-humanidad-en-las-elecciones.html

Elliott, V. (2023, December 28). Generative AI Learned Nothing From Web 2.0. https://www.wired.com/story/generative-ai-web-2-mistakes/

Ellner, S. (2014). *LatinAmerica's radical left: Challenges and complexitiesofpolit-icalpower in thetwenty-firstcentury.* Rowman&Littlefield.

Erickson, K. (2016) Defining the public domain in economic terms: Approaches and consequences for policy, available at https://papers.ssrn.com/sol3/papers.cfm?abstract_id=2777407

Etzioni, A. (2016). The limits of transparency. *Public Administration Review, 66*(6), 1–11.

Europarl (2025). *EU AI Act: first regulation on artificial intelligence.* Retrieved from: EU AI Act: first regulation on artificial intelligence | Topics | European Parliament on 20.3.25.

European Association for Viewers Interests (EAVI). (2017). Media literacy network in the Republic of Macedonia. https://eavi.eu/media-literacy-network-in-the-republic-of-macedonia/

European Commision. (2019). Joint communication to the European Parliament, the European Council, the Council, the European Economic and Social Committee and the Committee of the Regions. Report on the implementation of the Action Plan Against Disinformation, JOIN/2019/12 final. Available: https://eur-lex.europa.eu/legal-content/EN/ALL/?uri=comnat:JOIN_2019_0012_FIN

European Commision. (2020). Joint communication to the European Parliament, the European Council, the Council, the European Economic and Social Committee and the Committee of the Regions, Tackling COVID-19 disinformation - Getting the facts right. Join(2020) 8 final. Available: https://eur-lex.europa.eu/legal-content/LV/TXT/?uri=CELEX:52020JC0008

European Commission (2018). Communication from the Commission to the European Parliament, the Council, the European Economic and Social Committee and the Committee of the Regions.

European Commission, Directorate-General for Education, Youth, Sport and Culture, & PPMI. (2025). Report on the outcomes and transformational potential of the European Universities initiative (Authors: Manja Klemencic, Sabine Hoidn, Hanne Shapiro, Dragana Avramov, Hans de Wit, Simone Ravaioli NC-02-24-860-EN-N). Publications Office of the European Union. https://doi.org/DOI: 10.2766/32313

European Commission, Directorate-General for Education, Youth, Sport and Culture. (2024). *European universities: A key pillar of the European education area*. Publications Office of the European Union. https://data.europa.eu/doi/10.2766/521265

European Commission. (2018). Code of practice on disinformation. https://digital-strategy.ec.europa.eu/en/library/2018-code-practice-disinformation

European Commission. (2020). *EU–Western Balkan cooperation through Erasmus+*. https://ec.europa.eu/assets/eac/erasmus-plus/factsheets/regional/westernbalkans-regional-erasmusplus-2020.pdf

European Commission. (2021). Erasmus+ program impact report: Western Balkans. https://ec.europa.eu/assets/eac/erasmus-plus/factsheets/regional/westernbalkans-regional-erasmusplus-2020.pdf

European Commission. (2021). *North Macedonia 2021 Report: Progress on media freedom and pluralism* (SWD(2021) 294 final). Brussels: European Commission.

European Commission. (2022). Strengthened code of practice on disinformation. https://digital-strategy.ec.europa.eu/en/library/2022-strengthened-code-practice-disinformation

European Commission. (2023). Annual progress reports on countering hybrid threats. Retrieved from https://defence-industry-space.ec.europa.eu/eu-defence-industry/hybrid-threats_en

European Commission. (2024a). Erasmus + programme guide, Version 1 (2024): 28-11-2023 (p. 326). https://erasmus-plus.ec.europa.eu/sites/default/files/2023-11/2024-Erasmus%2BProgramme-Guide_EN.pdf

European Commission. (2024b). The European Universities alliances in action. https://education.ec.europa.eu/education-levels/higher-education/european-universities-initiative/about

European Court of Human Rights (ECHR). (1976) Handyside v. the United Kingdom, 5493/72, Council of Europe: European Court of Human Rights, 4 November 1976, available at https://www.refworld.org/jurisprudence/caselaw/echr/1976/en/40705

European Court of Human Rights (ECHR). (1995) Vogt v. Germany Application no. 17851/91, https://globalfreedomofexpression.columbia.edu/wp-content/uploads/2021/09/CASE-OF-VOGT-v.-GERMANY.pdf

European Court of Human Rights (ECHR). (2022) Factsheet – Derogation in time of emergency https://www.echr.coe.int/documents/d/echr/FS_Derogation_ENG

European Court of Human Rights (ECHR). (2022) Guide on Article 10 of the European Convention on Human Rights - Freedom of expression https://www.echr.coe.int/documents/d/echr/guide_art_10_eng

European External Action Service (EEAS). (2023). *1st EEAS report on foreign information manipulation and interference threats: Towards a frameworkfornetworkdefence.*EEAS. https://www.eeas.europa.eu/sites/default/files/documents/2023/EEAS-DataTeam-ThreatReport-2023.pdf

European Parliament. (2022). China's strategic interests in the Western Balkans – Briefing (p. 6). https://www.europarl.europa.eu/RegData/etudes/BRIE/2022/733558/EPRS_BRI%282022%29733558_EN.pdf

European Parliament. Directorate-General for Internal Policies of the Union, Wieworra, L., & Godlovitch, I. (2021). The Digital Services Act and the Digital Markets Act: a forward-looking and consumer-centred perspective, European Parliament. https://data.europa.eu/doi/10.2861/447141

European Training Foundation. (2024). Taking forward Youth Guarantee schemes in the Western Balkans. https://www.etf.europa.eu/en/news-and-events/news/taking-forward-youth-guarantee-schemes-western-balkans

European Union. (2022). *Legal documents on The Digital Services Act.* Retrieved from https://commission.europa.eu/publications/legal-documents-digital-services-act_en

European Union. (2023). EU annual report on human rights and democracy in the world 2022 country updates (pp. 12-13). https://www.eeas.europa.eu/sites/default/files/documents/2023/2022%20EU%20Annual%20Human%20Rights%20and%20Democracy%20Country%20Reports_0.pdf

EuropeanParliament. (2024). Jointmotionfor a resolutiononRussiagate: possibleRussian interference inthedemocraticprocessesoftheEuropeanUnion. (2024/2548(RSP)) Available: https://www.europarl.europa.eu/doceo/document/RC-9-2024-0124_LV.html

Eyal, J. (2024). The Global Challenge of Fake News. *Carter Ruck.* https://www.carter-ruck.com/insight/fakes-news-authentic-views/the-global-challenge-of-fake-news/

Faizan, N., & Hussain, E. (2022). Fake news in India during COVID-19: Legal study on the spread of fake news via social media. *Jus Corpus*, *3*(1), 254–273.

Federal Register. (2025). 2025 Donald J. Trump executive orders. https://www.federalregister.gov/presidential-documents/executive-orders/donald-trump/2025

Federal Trade Commission (FTD). (2015) Native Advertising: A Guide for Businesses https://www.ftc.gov/business-guidance/resources/native-advertising-guide-businesses

Fernandez, M., & Alani, H. (2018). *Online Misinformation: Challenges and Future Directions*. ACM Digital Library., DOI: 10.1145/3184558.3188730

Figueira, Á., & Oliveira, L. (2017). The current state of fake news: Challenges and opportunities. *Procedia Computer Science, 121*, 817–825. DOI: 10.1016/j.procs.2017.11.106

Finchelstein, F. (2024). *The wannabe fascists: A guide to understanding the greatest threat to democracy*. University of California Press.

Finkelstein, R., & Tiffen, R. (2015). When does press self-regulation work? *Melbourne University Law Review, 38*, 944–967.

Fisher, M. (2023, March 15). Octavian, Mark Antony and the Ancient Battle of "Fake News".https://martinifisher.com/2023/03/15/octavian-mark-antony-and-the-ancient-battle-of-fake-news/

Fishkin, J. S. (2008). Realizing deliberative democracy: Virtual and face-to-face possibilities. *Political Thought, 45*(3–4), 7–26.

Flick, D. (2017). Combatting fake news: Alternatives to limiting social media misinformation and rehabilitating quality journalism. *SMU Science and Technology Law Review, 20*(2), 375. https://scholar.smu.edu/scitech/vol20/iss2/17

Fokus.mk. (2024, December 30). *(ИНТЕРВЈУ) Мицкоски: ДУИ јазагрозуваинтеретничкатаслика и претставуваzаканапомирот и стабилноста! [Interview - Mitskoski: DUI endangers the interethnic image and poses a threat to peace and stability].* Retrieved from https://fokus.mk/intervju-mitskoski-dui-ja-zagrozuva-interetnichkata-slika-i-pretstavuva-zakana-po-mirot-i-stabilnosta/

Freedom House. (2020). Freedom in the World reports – China, 2020. https://freedomhouse.org/country/china/freedom-world/2020

Freedom House. (2024). *Venezuela: Freedom in theWorld 2024* [Report]. Freedom House.https://freedomhouse.org/country/venezuela/freedom-world/2024

Freelon, D., & Wells, C. (2020). Disinformation as political communication. *Political Communication, 37*(2), 145–156. DOI: 10.1080/10584609.2020.1723755

Fudan University. (2025). International students office – Scholarships. https://iso.fudan.edu.cn/isoenglish/16210/list.htm

Funk, A., Vesteinsson, K., & Baker, G. (2024). T*he Struggle for Trust Online*. Retrieved from: https://freedomhouse.org/report/freedom-net/2024/struggle-trust-online on 28.1.25.

Funke, D., & Flamini, D. (2024). A guide to anti-misinformation actions around the world. *Poynter*. https://www.poynter.org/ifcn/anti-misinformation-actions/

Galligher, R., & Tanner, S. (2024). A Guided Tour of Disinformation Policy: Framework and Legal Action. *GDIL*. https://gdil.org/a-guided-tour-of-disinformation-policy-framework-and-legal-action/

Gao, S., Wang, Y., & Platt, L. S. (2021). Modeling U.S. Health Agencies' Message Dissemination on Twitter and Users' Exposure to Vaccine-related Misinformation Using System Dynamics. In A. Adrot, R. Grace, K. Moore, &C. Zobel (Eds.),*Proceedings of the 18th International Conference on Information Systems for Crisis Response and Management* (ISCRAM 2021), Blacksburg, VA, USA, 333–344.

Gaur, A. (2021). Towards policy and regulatory approaches for combating misinformation in India. *Yale Law School*. https://law.yale.edu/isp/initiatives/wikimedia-initiative-intermediaries-and-information/wiii-blog/towards-policy-and-regulatory-approaches-combating-misinformation-india

Georgiadou, E. (1995). Marshall McLuhan's 'global village' and the Internet [Unpublished manuscript]. https://www.researchgate.net/publication/274383916_Marshall_McLuhan's_'global_village'_and_the_Internet

Gilboa, E. (2008). Searchingfor a theoryofpublicdiplomacy. *The ANNALS ofthe American AcademyofPolitical and Social Science, 616*(1), 55–77. https://doi.org/ DOI: 10.1177/0002716207312142

Gillespie, T. (2022). Donotrecommend? Reduction as a formofcontent moderation. *SocialMedia + Society*, *8*(3), 20563051221117552. DOI: 10.1177/20563051221117552

Gohil, K., & Nightingale, P. (2023, July 7). Demystifying Web 2.0 and Web 3.0: Understanding the Evolution of the World Wide Web. https://www.shoosmiths.com/insights/articles/demystifying-web-2-and-web-3-understanding-the-evolution-of-the-world-wide-web

Goldstein, J. A., Chao, J., Grossman, S., Stamos, A., & Tomz, M. (2024). How persuasive is AI-generated propaganda? *PNAS Nexus*, *3*(2), pgae034. Advance online publication. DOI: 10.1093/pnasnexus/pgae034 PMID: 38380055

Gonczi, A., Palosaari, C., Mayer, A., & Urban, N. (2022). From User to Creator: Helping Students See Inside the "Black Box" with Insight Maker. *Science Teacher (Normal, Ill.)*, *89*(3), 32–37. https://www.nsta.org/science-teacher/science-teacher-januaryfebruary-2022/user-creator. DOI: 10.1080/00368555.2022.12293666

Gonzalez, A. (2025, January 9).¿Cómo llegó Nicolás Maduro al poder en Venezuela y cuánto tiempo lleva?*CNN*.https://cnnespanol.cnn.com/2025/01/09/venezuela/como-llego-maduro-poder-venezuela-orix

Goodfellow, I., Pouget-Abadie, J., Mirza, M., Xu, B., Warde-Farley, D., Ozair, S., & Bengio, Y. (2014). Advances in Neural Information Processing Systems: Vol. 27. *Generative adversarial nets.*, Available https://arxiv.org/abs/1406.2661

Goodman, E. (2021). Media literacy in Europe and the role of EDMO. *European Digital Media Observatory*. https://edmo.eu/wp-content/uploads/2022/02/Media-literacy-in-Europe-and-the-role-of-EDMO-Report-2021.pdf

Gov. UK. (n.d.). *Fact sheet on the CDU and RRU*. https://www.gov.uk/government/news/fact-sheet-on-the-cdu-and-rru

Granderath, J. S., Sondermann, C., Martin, A., & Merkt, M. (2021). Actual and perceived knowledge about COVID-19: The role of information behaviour in media. *Frontiers in Psychology*, *12*, 778886. Advance online publication. DOI: 10.3389/fpsyg.2021.778886 PMID: 34975667

Grandjean, M. (2016). A social networkanalysisof Twitter: Mappingthe digital humanitiescommunity. *Cogent Arts & Humanities*, *3*(1), 1171458. DOI: 10.1080/23311983.2016.1171458

Grant, M. J., & Booth, A. (2009). A typology of reviews: An analysis of 14 review types and associated methodologies. *Health Information and Libraries Journal*, *26*(2), 91–108. DOI: 10.1111/j.1471-1842.2009.00848.x PMID: 19490148

Grbeša Zenzerović, M., & Nenadić, I. (2022). *Strengthening society's resistance to disinformation: Analysis of the situation and guidelines for action*. https://www.aem.hr/wp-content/uploads/2022/09/Studija_dezinformacije_2-izdanje.pdf

Green, Y., Gully, A., Roth, Y., Roy, A., Tucker, J. A., & Wanless, A. (2023). Evidence-Based Misinformation Interventions: Challenges and Opportunities for Measurement and Collaboration. *Carnegie Endowment for International Peace*. https://carnegieendowment.org/research/2023/01/evidence-based-misinformation-interventions-challenges-and-opportunities-for-measurement-and-collaboration?lang=en

Green, B. N., Johnson, C. D., & Adams, A. (2006). Writing narrative literature reviews for peer-reviewed journals: Secrets of the trade. *Journal of Chiropractic Medicine*, *5*(3), 101–117. DOI: 10.1016/S0899-3467(07)60142-6 PMID: 19674681

Gross, E.-C., & Balaban, D. C. (2025). The Effectiveness of an Educational Intervention on Countering Disinformation Moderated by Intellectual Humility. *Media and Communication*, *13*, 9109. Advance online publication. DOI: 10.17645/mac.9109

Gubbala, R. W. Laura Silver, Janell Fetterolf, Christine Huang, Sarah Austin, Laura Clancy and Sneha. (2022, December 6). Social media seen as mostly good for democracy across many nations, but u. S. Is a major outlier. *Pew Research Center*. https://www.pewresearch.org/global/2022/12/06/social-media-seen-as-mostly-good-for-democracy-across-many-nations-but-u-s-is-a-major-outlier/

Guess, A. M., Nagler, M. H., Tucker, J., Reifler, J., & Sircar, N. (2020). A digital media literacy intervention increases discernment between mainstream and false news in the United States and India. *Proceedings of the National Academy of Sciences of the United States of America*, *117*(27), 15536–15545. DOI: 10.1073/pnas.1920498117 PMID: 32571950

Gürkan, H. (2017) The Portrayal of Journalists in Turkish Cinema: A Study about Journalism Ethics through Cinema, available at https://hrcak.srce.hr/file/284649

Guzmán Rincón, A., Barragán Moreno, S., Rodríguez-Canovas, B., Carrillo Barbosa, R. L., & Africano Franco, D. R.GuzmánRincón. (2023). Social Networks, Disinformation and Diplomacy: A Dynamic Model for a Current Problem. *Humanities & Social Sciences Communications*, *10*(1), 505. DOI: 10.1057/s41599-023-01998-z

Guzmán Rincón, A., Carrillo Barbosa, R. L., Segovia-García, N., & Africano Franco, D. R.GuzmánRincón. (2022). Disinformation in Social Networks and Bots: Simulated Scenarios of Its Spread from System Dynamics. *Systems*, *10*(2), 34. DOI: 10.3390/systems10020034

Halili, A., Palloshi-Disha, E., Bajrami, D., & Ibrahimi, Sh. (2023). Media and information literacy education in the age of disinformation: SEEU professor and student perceptions. *Media and Communication Review*, *2*, 56–65.

Harmful Digital Communications Act. 2015, (2015). https://www.legislation.govt.nz/act/public/2015/0063/latest/whole.html

Harnecker, M. (2004). *Venezuela: Una revolución sui géneris*. El Viejo Topo.

Harper, T., Aboulafia, A., & Linzer, I. (2024). GeneratingConfusion, Stress-testing AI ChatbotResponsesonVotingwith a Disability, CenterforDemocracy&Technology. Available: https://cdt.org/wp-content/uploads/2024/09/updated-508-Prep-CDT-Issue-Brief-Chatbot-Responses-on-Disability-Rights-and-Voting-FINAL.pdf

Heiss, R., Nanz, A., & Matthes, J. (2023). Social media information literacy: Conceptualization and associations with information overload, news avoidance and conspiracy mentality. *Computers in Human Behavior*, *148*, 107908. Advance online publication. DOI: 10.1016/j.chb.2023.107908

Helmus, C. T. (2022). Artificial intelligence, deepfakes, and disinformation: A primer. *RAND Corporation.* Retrieved from: https://www.rand.org/content/dam/rand/pubs/perspectives/PEA1000/PEA1043-1/RAND_PEA1043-1.pdf on 15.1.25.

Heyneman, S. P. (2021). Fake news, fake truth: A new purpose for public schooling. *International Journal of Educational Development*, *87*, 102496. Advance online publication. DOI: 10.1016/j.ijedudev.2021.102496

Hillebrandt, M. Z., Curtin, D., & Meijer, A. (2014). *Transparency in the EU Council of Ministers: An institutional analysis*. University of Amsterdam. https://pure.uva.nl/ws/files/1541494/135720Transparency_in_the_EU_Council_of_Ministers_manuscript.pdf

Hilmansyah, I., Wiryawan, D., & Hartono, H. (2024). Analysis of student trust in the credibility of Deepfake video information on Social Media. 2024 9th International Conference on Information Technology and Digital Applications (ICITDA), 1–6. https://doi.org/DOI: 10.1109/ICITDA64560.2024.10810015

Hoboken, J., & Fathaigh, R. (2021). Regulating disinformation in Europe: Implications for speech and privacy. *UC Irvine Journal of International, Transnational, and Comparative Law, 6*(1), 9. https://scholarship.law.uci.edu/ucijil/vol6/iss1/3

Hoferer, M., Böttcher, L., & Hans, J. (2020). The impact of technologies in political campaigns. *Physica A*, *538*, 122795. Advance online publication. DOI: 10.1016/j.physa.2019.122795

Huang, H., Chen, W., Xie, T., Wei, Y., Feng, Z., & Wu, W. (2021). The Impact of Individual Behaviors and Governmental Guidance Measures on Pandemic-Triggered Public Sentiment Based on System Dynamics and Cross-Validation. *International Journal of Environmental Research and Public Health*, *18*(8), 4245. DOI: 10.3390/ijerph18084245 PMID: 33923746

Huguet, A., Kavanagh, P. B., Sultana, A., Leung, T., Tran, L. M., Rosen, M. L., & Downey, G. (2022). Evaluating the effectiveness of digital media literacy programs: A systematic review and meta-analysis. *Psychological Bulletin*, *148*(3), 193–226.

Human Rights Watch. (2019a). China: Government threats to academic freedom abroad. https://www.hrw.org/news/2019/03/21/china-government-threats-academic-freedom-abroad

Human Rights Watch. (2019b). The Chinese government cannot be allowed to undermine academic freedom. https://www.hrw.org/news/2019/11/08/chinese-government-cannot-be-allowed-undermine-academic-freedom

Ilik, G., & Shapkoski, V. (2022). The EU's response vs. Chinese vaccine diplomacy in Central and Eastern Europe. *Eastern Journal of European Studies*, 13(2), 99–115. https://doi.org/https://ejes.uaic.ro/articles/EJES2022_1302_ILI.pdfDOI: 10.47743/ejes-2022-0205

Ilik, G., & Adamczyk, A. (2017). Finalité politique or just a step forward: The Lisbon Treaty and the identity of the European Union as a global actor. *Journal of Liberty and International Affairs*, *3*(Supp. 1), 9–25. https://e-jlia.com/index.php/jlia/article/view/89

IMA.mk. (2024, August 21). *(ANALIZË) Media njësojsipolitika: Përplasjeetnikem-biçështjetëndjeshme [(ANALYSIS) Media as politics: Ethnic clashes over sensitive issues].* Retrieved from https://ima.mk/sq/2024/08/21/analize-media-njesoj-si-politika-perplasje-etnike-mbi-ceshtje-te-ndjeshme/

IMA.mk. (2024, August 31). *ПремиеротМицкоскикакоизворнанепотврдениинформацииздржавендолг, инфлација, дестабилизација [Prime Minister Mickoski as a source of unconfirmed information about state debt, inflation, destabilization].* Retrieved from https://ima.mk/2024/08/31/premierot-miczkoski-kako-izvor-na-nepotvrdeni-informaczii-za-drzhaven-dolg-inflaczija-destabilizaczija/

Imeri, L. (2024). The Role of Education in the Fight against Fake News.https://f2n2.mk/en/the-role-of-education-in-the-fight-against-fake-news

IMM. (n.d.). InsightMaker Manual. https://insightmaker.com/help

IMOW. (n.d.).InsightMaker Official Website.https://insightmaker.com/

Infobae. (2024a, September 11). El derroche de Maduro en la campaña electoral ahora es la nueva amenaza para su régimen. *Infobae*.https://www.infobae.com/venezuela/2024/09/11/el-derroche-de-maduro-en-la-campana-electoral-ahora-es-la-nueva-amenaza-para-su-regimen/

Infobae. (2024b, May 16). El régimen de Maduro clausuró un hotel para evitar que Edmundo González y María Corina Machado se hospeden en su visita al estado Aragua. *Infobae*.https://www.infobae.com/venezuela/2024/05/16/el-regimen-de-maduro-clausuro-un-hotel-para-evitar-que-edmundo-gonzalez-y-maria-corina-machado-se-hospeden-en-su-visita-al-estado-aragua/

Infobae. (2024c, July 28).El chavismo difundió en las redes sociales resultados de falsos boca de urna de una encuestadora que no existe. *Infobae*.https://www.infobae.com/venezuela/2024/07/28/el-chavismo-difundio-en-las-redes-resultados-falsos-de-boca-de-urna-de-una-encuestadora-que-no-existe/

Institute for Strategic Dialogue (ISD). (2020, June 25). *Anatomy of a disinformation empire: Investigating NaturalNews*. https://www.isdglobal.org/wp-content/uploads/2021/10/20211013-ISDG-NaturalNews-Briefing.pdf

Inter-American Court of Human Rights (IACHR). (1985) Compulsory Membership in an Association Prescribed by Law for the Practice of Journalism, Advisory Opinion OC-5/85 of 13 November 1985, Series A. No. 5, available at https://www.corteidh.or.cr/docs/opiniones/seriea_05_ing.pdf

Intersoft Consulting. (2013) General Data Protection Regulation (GDPR). Available at: https://gdpr-info.eu (Access 9.01.2025).

IREX. (2020). *Media Sustainability Index 2020: North Macedonia*. IREX.

Isaac, M., & Schleifer, T. (2025). Meta says it will end its fact-checking program on social media posts. New York Times. https://www.nytimes.com/live/2025/01/07/business/meta-fact-checking

Iskandarov, K., & Gawliczek, P. (2022). Economic coercion as a means of hybrid warfare: The South Caucasus as a focal point. Security and Defence Quarterly. Retrieved from https://securityanddefence.pl/Economic-coercion-as-a-means-of-hybrid-warfare-The-South-Caucasus-as-a-focal-point,151038,0,2.html

Islam, M. S., Sarkar, T., Khan, S. H., Mostofa Kamal, A.-H., Hasan, S. M. M., Kabir, A., Yeasmin, D., Islam, M. A., Amin Chowdhury, K. I., Anwar, K. S., Chughtai, A. A., & Seale, H. (2020). COVID-19-related infodemic and its impact on public health: A global social media analysis. *The American Journal of Tropical Medicine and Hygiene*, *103*(4), 1621–1629. DOI: 10.4269/ajtmh.20-0812 PMID: 32783794

Jade Gilbourne PhD Candidate in Sociology. (2025, January 29). *Taylor Swift Deepfakes: A legal case from the singer could help other victims of AI pornography*. The Conversation. https://theconversation.com/taylor-swift-deepfakes-a-legal-case-from-the-singer-could-help-other-victims-of-ai-pornography-222113

Jain, D. (2024, March 22). Supreme Court transfers petitions pending before various HCs against its rules 2021 to Delhi High Court. *Livelaw*. https://www.livelaw.in/top-stories/supreme-court-petitions-against-it-rules-2021-transferred-delhi-hc-253147

Jain, S. (2023, November 30). The rise of deepfakes: 25 percent of videos that people watch are later found to be fake. *Forbes India*. https://www.forbesindia.com/article/news/the-rise-of-deepfakes-25-percent-of-videos-that-people-watch-are-later-found-to-be-fake/90077/1

Jang, S. M., & Kim, J. K. (2017). Third person effects of fake news: Fake news regulation and media literacy interventions. *Computers in Human Behavior, 80*, 295–302. DOI: 10.1016/j.chb.2017.11.034

Javornik, Š., & Klemenčič Mirazchiyski, E. (2023). Factors Contributing to School Effectiveness: A Systematic Literature Review. *European Journal of Investigation in Health, Psychology and Education, 13*(10), 2095–2111. DOI: 10.3390/ejihpe13100148 PMID: 37887149

Jazeera, A. (2023) Denmark proposes bill that could see ban on Quran burnings, available at https://www.aljazeera.com/news/2023/8/25/danish-government-proposes-bill-that-would-ban-

Jens, S. (2024). Why laws to combat misinformation can do more harm than good. *Scroll.in*. https://scroll.in/article/1066180/why-laws-to-combat-misinformation-can-do-more-harm-than-good

Jiang, B., & Wang, D. (2024). Perception of misinformation on social media among Chinese college students. *Frontiers in Psychology, 15*, 1416792. Advance online publication. DOI: 10.3389/fpsyg.2024.1416792 PMID: 39027055

JOE.ie. (2025, January 24). Video]. Facebook. https://www.facebook.com/reel/28397734073174759

Jones-Jang, S. M., Mortensen, T., & Liu, J. (2019). Does media literacy help identification of fake news? Information literacy helps, but other literacies don't. *The American Behavioral Scientist, 65*(2), 371–388. DOI: 10.1177/0002764219869406

Jonins E. (2021). Cīņa Ar Dezinformāciju Latvijā (I). Journal JuristaVārds, 03.08.2021., No 31 (1193), pp. 11.-18.

Jonins E., Dvorovijs M. (2024). Dezinformācija Latvijā un Ukrainā. Journal JuristaVārds, No 13/14 (1331/1332), pp.11.-16.

Judgment of the Senate of the Republic of Latvia of 6 March 2017 in Case No SKC-98/2017 (C17150712).

Juul, J. L., & Ugander, J. (2021). Comparing information diffusion mechanisms by matching on cascade size. *Proceedings of the National Academy of Sciences of the United States of America, 118*(46), e2100786118. DOI: 10.1073/pnas.2100786118 PMID: 34750252

Kajosevic, S. (2020). Montenegro forced to extend deadline for Chinese to finish highway. *BIRN*. https://balkaninsight.com/2020/09/30/montenegro-forced-to-extend-deadline-for-chinese-to-finish-highway/

Kalathil, S., & Boas, T. C. (2003). *Open networks, closed regimes: The impact of the internet on authoritarian rule*. Carnegie Endowment for International Peace.

Kanozia, R. (2019). Analysis of Digital Tools and Technologies for Debunking Fake News. *Journal of Content, Community & Communication, 9*(5), 114-122. https://www.amity.edu/gwalior/jccc/pdf/jccc%20june%202019%20final-114-122.pdf

Kaplan, A. M., & Haenlein, M. (2010). Users of the world, unite! The challenges and opportunities of Social Media. *Business Horizons, 53*(1), 59–68. DOI: 10.1016/j.bushor.2009.09.003

Kaplan, J. (2024). *Generative Artificial Intelligence: What Everyone Needs to Know*. Oxford University Press.

Kassam, N. (2020, March 25). Disinformation and coronavirus. *The Interpreter*. Lowy Institute. https://www.lowyinstitute.org/the-interpreter/disinformation-coronavirus

Katkovska M. (2024). Kā Atpazīt Dezinformāciju. Journal JuristaVārds No 13/14 (1331/1332), pp. 35.-38.

Kertysova, K. (2018). Artificial Intelligence and Disinformation: How AI Changes-theWay Disinformationis Produced, Disseminated, and Can Be Countered. *Security and HumanRights, 29*(1-4), 55–81. DOI: 10.1163/18750230-02901005

Keyes, R. (2004). *The post-truth era: Dishonesty and deception in contemporary life*. St. Martin's Press.

Khan, M. L., & Idris, I. K. (2019). Recognise misinformation and verify before sharing: A reasoned action and information literacy perspective. *Behaviour & Information Technology, 38*(12), 1194–1212. DOI: 10.1080/0144929X.2019.1578828

Khare, P. & Raghuwanshi, V. (2025). Legal Frameworks Surrounding the Use of AI in Online Content Moderation. *IGI Global Scientific Publishing*, 235-260. https://doi.org/DOI: 10.4018/979-8-3693-9904-0.ch011

Khare, P. (2025). Investigating the Influence of AI in Social Media Governance. *IGI Global Scientific Publishing*, 365-388. https://doi.org/DOI: 10.4018/979-8-3693-9904-0.ch015

Killion, V. (2019) Cong. Research Serv., The First Amendment: Categories of Speech, available at https://crsreports.congress.gov/product/pdf/IF/IF11072

Kingsbury, D. V. (2016). Frompopulismtoprotagonism (and back?) in Bolivarian Venezuela: Rethinking Ernesto Laclau'sOnPopulist Reason. *Journal of Latin American Cultural Studies, 25*(4), 495–514. DOI: 10.1080/13569325.2016.1230939

Klan Macedonia, T. V. (2024, December 30). *Minçevndryshoillogaritjetpërbalancuesin, uletpërqindja e shqiptarëve, rritet e maqedonasve [Mincev changed the calculations for the balancer, Albanian percentage decreases, Macedonian increases].* Retrieved from https://tvklan.mk/mincev-ndryshoi-llogaritjet-per-balancuesin-ulet-perqindja-e-shqiptareve-rritet-e-maqedonasve/

Knight, W. (2018, May 23). The US military is funding an effort to catch deepfakes and other AI trickery. *MIT Technology Review*. https://www.technologyreview.com/2018/05/23/142770/the-us-military-is-funding-an-effort-to-catch-deepfakes-and-other-ai-trickery/

Koperniak, S. (2022). *Fostering media literacy in the age of deepfakes*. MIT Open Learning.

Koulolias, V., Jonathan, G. M., Fernandez, M., & Sotirchos, D. (2018). *Combating Misinformation: An ecosystem in co-creation*. OECD Publishing.

Krasadakis, G. (2024). Fake News and Misinformation: How digital tech can help. *Innovation Mode*. https://www.theinnovationmode.com/the-innovation-blog/misinformation-online-a-solution-powered-by-state-of-the-art-tech

Kreps, S. (2020). The Role of Technology in Online Misinformation. *Brookings*. https://www.brookings.edu/wp-content/uploads/2020/06/The-role-of-technology-in-online-misinformation.pdf

Krippendorff, K. (2013). *Content Analysis: An Introduction to Its Methodology* (3rd ed.). SAGE Publications.

Krstinovska, A. (2022a). Chinese influence in North Macedonia. *Center for European Policy Analysis (CEPA)*. https://cepa.org/comprehensive-reports/chinese-influence-in-north-macedonia/

Krstinovska, A. (2022b). China's development assistance to the Western Balkans and its impact on democratic governance and decision-making. *Journal of Liberty and International Affairs*, *8*(1), 229–242. DOI: 10.47305/JLIA2281229k

Krutka, D. G., Manca, S., Galvin, S. M., Greenhow, C., Koehler, M. J., & Askari, E. (2019). Teaching "against" social media: Confronting problems of profit in the curriculum. *Teachers College Record*, *121*(14), 1–42. DOI: 10.1177/016146811912101410

Kurtzleben, D. (2017, February 17). With 'fake news,' Trump moves from alternative facts to alternative language. *NPR*. https://www.npr.org/2017/02/17/515630467/with-fake-news-trump-moves-from-alternative-facts-to-alternative-language

Kyza, E. A., Varda, C., Panos, D., Karageorgiou, M., Komendantova-Amann, N., Coppolino Perfumi, S., Shah, S. I. H., & Hosseini, A. S. (2020). Combating misinformation online: Re-imagining social media for policy-making. *Internet Policy Review*, *9*(4), 1–24. DOI: 10.14763/2020.4.1514

Lai, K., Queiroz, L., Shmerko, V., Sundberg, K., & Yanushkevich, S. (2023) Post-Pandemic Follow-Up Audit of Security Checkpoints.

Lai, W. L., Goh, V. T., Yap, T. T. V., & Ng, H. (2023). Phishing and Spoofing Websites: Detection and Countermeasures. *International Journal on Advanced Science, Engineering and Information Technology*, *13*(5), 1672–1678. DOI: 10.18517/ijaseit.13.5.19037

Law on Media. (2013). *Official Gazette of the Republic of Macedonia*, No. 184/2013.

Law, D. "Amendments to the Criminal Law" (No: 535/Lp14). Available: https://titania.saeima.lv/LIVS14/SaeimaLIVS14.nsf/0/F49CCF01C82F5C2AC2258AD20025B611?OpenDocument

Law, D. "Amendments to the Pre-election Campaign Law". Available: https://titania.saeima.lv/LIVS14/saeimalivs14.nsf/webSasaiste?OpenView&restricttocategory=523/Lp14

Leary, T. (1994). *Chaos and cyberculture*. Ronin Publishing.

Lecheler, S., & Egelhofer, J. L. (2022). Disinformation, misinformation, and fake news: Understanding the supply side. *Knowledge resistance in high-choice information environments*, 69-87.

Lee, J., Kalny, C., Demetriades, S., & Walter, N. (2024). Angry content for angry people: How anger appeals facilitate health misinformation recall on social media. *Media Psychology*, *27*(4), 639–665. DOI: 10.1080/15213269.2023.2269084

Lee, N. M., & Xenos, M. (2023). Toward a global understanding of media literacy education: Insights from cross-cultural research. *Communication Education*, *72*(1), 1–21.

Letter from the Latvian Advertising Association. "Proposals to the Draft Law "Amendments to the Pre-election Campaign Law" (No 523/Lp14)". (2024). Available: https://titania.saeima.lv/LIVS14/saeimalivs14.nsf/0/A67A48F4C9B7DDE4C2258B230029D3BD?OpenDocument

Letter from the Public Policy Centre Providus. "On the Need to Clarify the Legal Framework on the Use of Artificial Intelligence and Deep Learning Technologies in Election Campaigning", (2024). Available: https://titania.saeima.lv/LIVS14/saeimalivs14.nsf/0/41EF917932E7BBBDC2258B0100451C4D?OpenDocument

Letter from the State Chancellery. "On the Draft Law "Amendments to the Pre-election Campaign Law" (No 523/Lp14)". (2024). Available: https://titania.saeima.lv/LIVS14/saeimalivs14.nsf/0/EE83C25EC0BE43D5C2258B1F004792D0?OpenDocument

Levits, E. (2024). The European Union, democracy and the risks of populism. *Journal. JuristaVards*, *18/19*(1336/1337), 13–18.

Levy, R., Gretz, S., Sznajder, B., Hummel, S., Aharonov, R., & Slonim, N. (2017). Unsupervised corpus–wide claim detection. *Proceedings of the 4th Workshop on Argument Mining*, Copenhagen, Denmark. DOI: 10.18653/v1/W17-5110

Lewandowsky, S., Ecker, U. K. H., & Cook, J. (2017). Beyond misinformation: Understanding and coping with the "post-truth" era. *Journal of Applied Research in Memory and Cognition*, *6*(4), 353–369. DOI: 10.1016/j.jarmac.2017.07.008

Li, C., & Callegari, A. (2024). Stopping AI disinformation: Protecting truth in the digital world. *World Economic Forum*. https://www.weforum.org/stories/2024/06/ai-combat-online-misinformation-disinformation/

Lin, L. S., Aslett, D., Mekonnen, G., & Zecevic, M. (2024a). The dangers of voice cloning and how to combat it. *The Conversation*. https://theconversation.com/the-dangers-of-voice-cloning-and-how-to-combat-it-239926

Lin, L. S., Aslett, D., Mekonnen, G., & Zecevic, M. (2024b). The UN Cybercrime Convention: What it Means for Policing and Community Safety in Australia. *Australian Outlook*. https://www.internationalaffairs.org.au/australianoutlook/the-un-cybercrime-convention-what-it-means-for-policing-and-community-safety-in-australia/

Liuliu, X., Wenwen, W., & Wei, F. (2023). Falling in love with Chinese language. *Global Times*. https://www.globaltimes.cn/page/202309/1298681.shtml

Liu, M. Y., & Tuzel, O. (2016). Coupled generative adversarial networks. *Advances in Neural Information Processing Systems*, ●●●, 29.

Livelaw News Network. (2023, August 14). *Supreme court issues alerts about fake news falsely quoting CJI; it says legal action is being taken.* https://www.livelaw.in/top-stories/supreme-court-issues-alert-about-fake-news-being-spread-falsely-quoting-cji-says-legal-action-being-taken-235161

Livelaw News Network. (2023, December 2). *'There's no market place of facts': CJI DY Chandrachud expresses concerns about online disinformation & hate speech.* https://www.livelaw.in/top-stories/cji-dy-chandrachud-expresses-concerns-about-online-disinformation-hate-speech-243497

Livingstone, S. (2004). Media literacy and the challenge of new information and communication technologies. *Communication Review*, *7*(1), 3–14. DOI: 10.1080/10714420490280152

Loomba, S., de Figueiredo, A., Piatek, S. J., de Graaf, K., & Larson, H. J. (2021). Measuring the impact of COVID-19 vaccine misinformation on vaccination intent in the UK and USA. *Nature Human Behaviour*, *5*(3), 337–348. DOI: 10.1038/s41562-021-01056-1 PMID: 33547453

Lopatovska, I., Fenton, M. R., & Campot, S. (2012). Examining preferences for search engines and their effects on information behavior. *Proceedings of the American Society for Information Science and Technology*, *49*(1), 1–11. DOI: 10.1002/meet.14504901110

López, A. B., Pastor-Galindo, J., & Ruipérez-Valiente, J. A. (2024). Frameworks, Modeling and Simulations of Misinformation and Disinformation: A Systematic Literature Review. arXiv:2406.09343. /arXiv.2406.09343DOI: 10.48550

Lowe, E. (2013). *Media and the political process.* Faculty of Political Sciences, University of Belgrade.

Lux, S. (2006). Power: A radical understanding. *New Serbian Political Thought*, *13*(1–4), 69–119.

Mahitha, D. S. (2021). Social media and its regulations in India. *International Journal of Law Management & Humanities*, *4*(6), 1560–1572. https://doij.org/10.10000/IJLMH.112426

Majhosev, A., & Bakev, M. (2019). Media freedom and disinformation in North Macedonia: Challenges and perspectives. *Balkan Social Science Review*, *13*(1), 63–80.

Ma, K. W. F., & McKinnon, T. (2021). COVID-19 and cyber fraud: Emerging threats during the pandemic. *Journal of Financial Crime*, *29*(2), 433–446. DOI: 10.1108/JFC-01-2021-0016

Malhotra, P., Zhong, R., Kuan, V., Panatula, G., Weng, M., Bras, A., Sehat, C. M., Roesner, F., & Zhang, A. (2023). User experiences and needs when responding to misinformation on social media. *Harvard Kennedy School Misinformation Review*. Advance online publication. DOI: 10.37016/mr-2020-129

Manca, S., Bocconi, S., & Gleason, B. (2021). "Think globally, act locally": A glocal approach to the development of social media literacy. *Computers & Education*, *160*, 104025. https://www.researchgate.net/publication/344340527_Think_globally_act_locally_A_glocal_approach_to_the_development_of_social_media_literacy. DOI: 10.1016/j.compedu.2020.104025

Margolin, J., & Bruggeman, L. (2020, June 11). Intel bulletin warns of 'malign actors' targeting US over George Floyd fallout. *ABC News*. https://abcnews.go.com/US/intel-bulletin-warns-malign-actors-targeting-us-george/story?id=71184163

Marin, V. V., & Koivula, A. (2022). Media literacy education in Finland: Integrating critical thinking and digital skills. *The Journal of Media Literacy Education*, *14*(1), 1–15.

Martens, B.. (2018). *The digital transformation and disinformation*. European Commission.

Martinez-Costa, C., & Rodriguez, R. (2021). Media literacy in formal education: Challenges and opportunities. *Comunicar*, *29*(66), 9–19.

Marton, P., & Navarro, M. (2024). At thecrossroads: The Cuban American NationalFoundation and theendoftheColdWar. In Thomasen, G., Békés, C., & Rácz, A. (Eds.), *ThePalgravehandbookofnon-stateactors in East-West relations* (pp. 277–292). Palgrave Macmillan., DOI: 10.1007/978-3-031-40546-4_14

Mawad, T. F. (2024). Maduro, las elites y la «perestroika» venezolana. *Nueva Sociedad*.https://nuso.org/articulo/venezuela-elites-Maduro-fedecamaras/

Mayring, P. (2014). *Qualitative Content Analysis: Theoretical Foundation, Basic Procedures and Software Solution*. Beltz.

McBride, J. (2021) The doctrines and methodology on the interpretation of European Convention on Human Rights by the European Court of Human Rights, Council of Europe, https://rm.coe.int/echr-eng-the-doctrines-and-methodology-of-interpretation-of-the-europe/1680a20aee

McBride, J., Berman, N., & Chatzky, A. (2023). China's massive Belt and Road Initiative. *Council of Foreign Relations*. https://www.cfr.org/backgrounder/chinas-massive-belt-and-road-initiative

McGrew, S., Breakstone, J., Ortega, T., Smith, M., & Wineburg, S. (2018). Can students evaluate online sources? Learning from assessments of civic online reasoning. *Theory and Research in Social Education*, *46*(2), 165–193. DOI: 10.1080/00933104.2017.1416320

McGrew, S., & Wineburg, S. (2023). Improving students' ability to identify misinformation online: Lessons from the COR curriculum. *The Journal of Media Literacy Education*, *15*(1), 1–15.

McKew, M. (2017) "The Gerasimov Doctrine" https://www.politico.eu/article/new-battles-cyberwarfare-russia/

McLuhan, M. (1964). *Understanding media: The extensions of man*. McGraw-Hill.

McLuhan, M. (1967). *The medium is the massage: An inventory of effects*. Penguin Press.

Medianálisis. (2023, December 13).#CiberAlianzaAlDescubierto: Desinformación y ataques en línea con tinte de género.*Medianálisis*.https://www.medianalisis.org/ciberalianzaaldescubierto-desinformacion-y-ataques-en-linea-con-tinte-de-genero/

Meinrath, S. D., Losey, J., & Pickard, V. (2024). Digital feudalism. *Advances in Computers*, *81*, 237–287. DOI: 10.1016/B978-0-12-385514-5.00005-7

Mejías, U., & Vokuev, N. E. (2017). Disinformation and the media: The case ofRussia and Ukraine. *Media Culture & Society*, *39*(7), 1027–1042. DOI: 10.1177/0163443716686672

Melikyan, G. (2023) Commentary: Navigating Hybrid Threats in the South Caucasus,available at https://www.commonspace.eu/commentary/commentary-navigating-hybrid-threats-south-caucasus

META. mk Network. (2023). *Fact-checking initiatives in North Macedonia: Annual report 2023*. Skopje: META.

Miklaucic, M. (2011) NATO countering the hybrid threat https://www.act.nato.int/nato-countering-the-hybrid-threat

Mishra, N. K. (2008). Governmental Threats for Media Freedom : Comparative Study of Asian Countries. *Indian Journal of Poultry Science*, *69*(1), 149–156. http://www.jstor.org/stable/41856399

Misinformation - Research and data from pew research center. (2024, October 10). *Pew Research Center*. https://www.pewresearch.org/topic/news-habits-media/media-society/misinformation/

Mitchell, D.-G. (2014). Here Today, Gone Tomorrow? Assessing How Timing and Repetition of Scandal Information Affects Candidate Evaluations. *Political Psychology, 35*(5), 679–701. http://www.jstor.org/stable/43783812. DOI: 10.1111/pops.12095

Mitra, A., Mohanty, S. P., & Kougianos, E. (2024). The world of generative ai: Deepfakes and large language models. *arXiv preprint arXiv:2402.04373*.

Mitra, H. (2024, February 24). Fact Check: Video claiming farmers joining protest in exchange for money turns out to be fake | Know truth. India Today. https://www.indiatvnews.com/fact-check/fact-check-video-claiming-farmers-joining-protest-in-exchange-for-money-turns-out-to-be-fake-know-truth-2024-02-24-918426

Mondal, A. (2024, March 19). India: Deciphering Deepfakes: Navigating The Legal Implications Of Digital Deception. *Mondaq*. https://www.mondaq.com/india/new-technology/1441788/deciphering-deepfakes-navigating-the-legal-implications-of-digital-deception

Monde, L. (2005) L'enfer des bonnes intentions, par Françoise Chandernagor https://www.lemonde.fr/idees/article/2005/12/16/l-enfer-des-bonnes-intentions-par-francoise-chandernagor_722124_3232.html

Moskovisi, S. (1997). *Age of the crowd, I.* Belgrade: Biblioteka XX vek.

Mukaddam, F. (2017). *UK Government seeks to tackle the "fake news" problem.* Global law firm. https://www.nortonrosefulbright.com/en/knowledge/publications/4a0c020f/uk-government-seeks-to-tackle-the-fake-news-problem

Mumtaz, N., Green, C., & Duggan, J. (2022). Exploring the Effect of Misinformation on Infectious Disease Transmission. *Systems, 10*(2), 50. DOI: 10.3390/systems10020050

Mundo, B. B. C. (2020, December 7). Venezuela:Laoposiciónlograuna victoria histórica al ganar las eleccionesparlamentarias.*BBC Mundo*.https://www.bbc.com/mundo/noticias-america-latina-55212032

Munn, L. (2020). Angry by design: Toxic communication and technical architectures. *Humanities & Social Sciences Communications, 7*(1), 53. Advance online publication. DOI: 10.1057/s41599-020-00550-7

Murillo-Ligorred, V., Ramos-Vallecillo, N., Covaleda, I., & Fayos, L. (2023). Knowledge, Integration and Scope of Deepfakes in Arts Education: The Development of Critical Thinking in Postgraduate Students in Primary Education and Master's Degree in Secondary Education. *Education Sciences*, *13*(11), 1073. DOI: 10.3390/educsci13111073

Musiol, M. (2024). *Generative AI - Navigating the Course to the Artificial General.* New Jersey.

Nagy, S. G. (2020). Maduro Venezulája [Maduro's Venezuela]. In Zs. Csikós& E. Horváth (Eds.), *Diktátorokésdiktatúrák a Karibtérségben* [Dictators and dictatorships in theCaribbeanregion] (pp.131-145). L'HarmattanKiadó.

Nan-Run, Z., Tian-Feng, Z., Xin-Wen, X., & Jun-Yun, W. (2023). Hybrid quantum-classical generative adversarial networks for image generation via learning discrete distribution. *Signal Processing: Image Communication,* Volume 110, 2023, 116891, ISSN 0923-5965. Available: https://doi.org/DOI: 10.1016/j.image.2022.116891

NATO. (2010) NATO's Bi-Strategic Command Capstone Concept of 2010 https://www.act.nato.int/images/stories/events/2010/20100826_bi-sc_cht.pdf

Nealon, D. (2024). What's at Stake with the U.S. Supreme Court Case on Misinformation? *Harvard Medical School.* https://hms.harvard.edu/news/whats-stake-us-supreme-court-case-misinformation

Nenovski, B., Ilijevski, I., & Stanojoska, A. (2023). *Strengthening Resilience Against Deepfakes as Disinformation Threats.* Poland's Experience in Combating Disinformation.

Nickerson, R. S. (1998). Confirmation bias: A ubiquitous phenomenon in many guises. *Review of General Psychology*, *2*(2), 175–220. DOI: 10.1037/1089-2680.2.2.175

Nistori. (2024, December 30). *Opozitë e pozitë, partitëshqiptareireagojnë Maksim Dimitrievskitpërflamurinshqiptar [Opposition and position, Albanian parties react to Maksim Dimitrievski about the Albanian flag].* Retrieved from https://nistori.com/opozite-e-pozite-partite-shqiptare-i-reagojne-maksim-dimitrievskit-per-flamurin-shqiptar/

Noble, S. U. (2018). *Algorithms of Oppression: How Search Engines Reinforce Racism.* NYU Press. DOI: 10.18574/nyu/9781479833641.001.0001

NPR. (2022). *Deepfake video of Zelensky could be 'tip of the iceberg' in info war, experts warn.* Retrieved from: https://www.npr.org/2022/03/16/1087062648/deepfake-video-zelenskyy-experts-war-manipulation-ukraine-russia on 17.12.24.

Nye, J. S. (2012). China and soft power. *The South African Journal of International Affairs, 19*(2), 151–155. DOI: 10.1080/10220461.2012.706889

Nygren, T., & Ecker, U. K. H. (2024).*Education as a countermeasure against disinformation.*Working Paper 2024:3.Lund University Psychological Defense Research Institute, Lund University, Lund, Sweden.https://uu.diva-portal.org/smash/get/diva2:1915602/FULLTEXT01.pdf

Oancea, M. (2024). AI and Deep Fake-Video and Audio Manipulation Techniques Capable of Altering the Political Process. *Revista de Stiinte Politice*, (81), 70–82.

Ochoa, A. G., Khare, P., & Setia, S. (2024). Expanding Environmental Education in Honduras: A Holistic Approach for Sustainable Development. *IGI Global Scientific Publishing,* 153-170. https://doi.org/DOI: 10.4018/979-8-3693-2577-3.ch010

OECD. (2021). *Lobbyinginthe 21st century: Transparency, Integrityand Access.* OECD Publishing., DOI: 10.1787/c6d8eff8-

OECD. (2024). *Facts not Fakes: Tackling Disinformation, Strengthening Information Integrity.* OECD Publishing., DOI: 10.1787/d909ff7a-

OECD. (2024). Recommendation of the Council on Information Integrity, OECD/LEGAL/0505, Adopted on: 17/12/2024. Available: https://legalinstruments.oecd.org/en/instruments/OECD-LEGAL-0505

Ofcom. (2021, January 27). *Understanding online false information in the UK.* Economist discussion paper series, Issue number 2. Ofcom UK. https://www.ofcom.org.uk/siteassets/resources/documents/research-and-data/economic-discussion-papers-/understanding-online-false-information-uk.pdf?v=325850

Office of the Australian Information Commissioner. (2023, March 7). *High Court clears wayfor OAIC case against Facebook to proceed.* https://www.oaic.gov.au/news/media-centre/high-court-clears-way-for-oaic-case-against-facebook-to-proceed

Ojha, R. P., Srivastava, P. K., Awasthi, S., Srivastava, V., Pandey, P. S., Dwivedi, R. S., Singh, R., & Galletta, A. (2023). Controlling of Fake Information Dissemination in Online Social Networks: An Epidemiological Approach. *IEEE Access : Practical Innovations, Open Solutions, 11*, 32229–32240. DOI: 10.1109/ACCESS.2023.3262737

Olan, F., Jayawickrama, U., Arakpogun, E. O., Suklan, J., & Liu, S. (2024). Fake News on Social Media: The Impact on Society. *Information Systems Frontiers, 26*(2), 443–458. DOI: 10.1007/s10796-022-10242-z PMID: 35068999

Olaniran, B., & Williams, I. (2020). Social media effects: Hijacking democracy and civility in civic engagement. In Jones, J., & Trice, M. (Eds.), *Platforms, Protests, and the Challenge of Networked Democracy* (pp. 77–94). Springer International Publishing., DOI: 10.1007/978-3-030-36525-7_5

Online, E. T. (2024, February 24). Fake Lok Sabha Election schedule alert! ECI warns against misinformation. *The Economic Times*. https://economictimes.indiatimes.com/news/elections/lok-sabha/india/fake-lok-sabha-election-schedule-alert-eci-warns-against-misinformation/articleshow/107965334.cms?from=mdr

Oreku, G. S., & Mtenzi, F. J. (2017). Cybercrime: Concerns, Challenges and Opportunities. In Alsmadi, I. M., Karabatis, G., & Aleroud, A. (Eds.), *Information Fusion for Cyber-Security Analytics* (pp. 129–153). Springer International Publishing., DOI: 10.1007/978-3-319-44257-0_6

Organization of American States (OAS). (1969) "American Convention on Human Rights." Treaty Series, No. 36

Orlović, S. (2020). The decline of democracies and the reduction of human rights: The case of Serbia. *Political Life*, July 18.

Orlović, S. (2013). Critical thinking and public action of a political scientist (intellectual): Ten theses about a holy calling in difficult times. In Podunavac, M., & Paunović, Ž. (Eds.), *Politics: Science and profession* (pp. xx–xx). University of Belgrade, Faculty of Political Sciences.

Orosz, G., Faragó, L., Paskuj, B., & Krekó, P. (2024). Strategies to combat misinformation: Enduring effects of a 15-minute online intervention on critical-thinking adolescents. *Computers in Human Behavior, 159*, 108338. Advance online publication. DOI: 10.1016/j.chb.2024.108338

OSCE. (2008) The Media Self-Regulation Guidebook, available at https://www.osce.org/files/f/documents/1/d/31497.pdf

Oxford English Dictionary. (2016). Post-truth. https://www.oxfordlearnersdictionaries.com/us/definition/english/post-truth

Oxford English Dictionary. (2016). Word of the year. https://languages.oup.com/word-of-the-year/2016/

Pankovski, M., & Recica, V. (2022). *Suppression of disinformation in North Macedonia: How can Sobranie respond to the challenge?* Institute for Democracy, CEBS Public Policy Brief. https://idscs.org.mk/wp-content/uploads/2022/02/CESSPolicy-Brief_6-2022_MAC.pdf

Pappas, S. (2022). Fighting fake news in the classroom. *American Psychological Association*. https://www.apa.org/monitor/2022/01/career-fake-news

Pappas, S. (2022, January 1). Fighting fake news in the classroom. *Monitor on Psychology, 53*(1). https://www.apa.org/monitor/2022/01/career-fake-news

Pariser, E. (2011). *The filter bubble: What the Internet is hiding from you*. Penguin Press.

Parliament, U. K. (2020). *Online Harms Reduction Regulator (Report) Bill [HL]*. Retrieved from https://bills.parliament.uk/bills/2546

Paul, R., & Elder, L. (2014). *Critical Thinking: Tools for Taking Charge of Your Professional and Personal Life*. Pearson.

Pennycook, G., & Rand, D. G. (2019). Fighting misinformation on social media using crowdsourced judgments of news source quality. *Proceedings of the National Academy of Sciences of the United States of America, 116*(7), 2521–2526. DOI: 10.1073/pnas.1806781116 PMID: 30692252

Pennycook, G., & Rand, D. G. (2021). The psychology of fake news. *Trends in Cognitive Sciences, 25*(5), 388–402. DOI: 10.1016/j.tics.2021.02.007 PMID: 33736957

Petkova, M. (2021). The environmental impact of Chinese projects in the Western Balkans. *Association for International Affairs (AMO)*. https://chinaobservers.eu/wp-content/uploads/2021/11/CHOICE_policy-paper_Environmental-Impact_A4_07_web.pdf

Petratos, P. N. (2021). Misinformation, disinformation, and fake news: Cyber risks to business. *Business Horizons, 64*(6), 763–774. https://doi.org/https://doi.org/10.1016/j.bushor.2021.07.012. DOI: 10.1016/j.bushor.2021.07.012

PEW Research Centre. (2020) Concerns about democracy in the digital age, available at https://www.pewresearch.org/internet/2020/02/21/concerns-about-democracy-in-the-digital-age/

Pinter, H. (2005). *Art, truth & politics: Nobel lecture*. NobelPrize.org.

Pleps, J., Engīzers, K., & Soņeca, V. (2024). *Latvija. The 2023 Global Review of Constitutional Law*. Published by the Constitutional Studies Program at the University of Texas at Austin. U of Texas Law, Legal Studies Research Paper., Available https://papers.ssrn.com/sol3/papers.cfm?abstract_id=5046787

Polegkyi, O. (2023). Russiandisinformation and propaganda before and after theinvasionofUkraine. *RocznikInstytutuEuropyŚrodkowo-Wschodniej, 21*(1), 91–107. DOI: 10.36874/RIESW.2023.1.6

Ponniah, T., & Eastwood, J. (2011). *Therevolution in Venezuela: Social and politicalchangeunder Chávez*. Harvard UniversityPress.

Poposka, V. (2024) A Primer on Hybrid Threats to Critical Infrastructurepublished by PRESPA Institute, available at http://www.prespa-institute.mk/wp-content/uploads/2024/02/EN_Informirana-odbrana_01.pdf

Poposka, V. (2021). *Меѓународно-правни аспекти за заштита на критичната инфраструктура од современи безбедносни закани, " International Legal Aspects of the Critical Infrastructure Protection Against Contemporary Security Threats"- published by International Vision University*. North Macedonia.

Potter, W. J. (2016). *Media Literacy*. SAGE Publications.

Preu, E., Jackson, M., & Choudhury, N. (2022, October). Perception vs. Reality: understanding and evaluating the impact of synthetic image deepfakes over college students. In 2022 IEEE 13th Annual Ubiquitous Computing, Electronics & Mobile Communication Conference (UEMCON) (pp. 0547-0553). IEEE.

Princeton Public Library. (2024). *Misinformation, disinformation & malinformation: A guide*. Retrieved 16/12/2024 from https://princetonlibrary.org/guides/misinformation-disinformation-malinformation-a-guide/

Pupillo, L., Fantin, S., Ferreira, A., & Polito, C. (2021). *Artificial Intelligence and Cybersecurity. Technology, Governance and Policy Challenges*. Centre for European Policy Studies., Available https://www.ceps.eu/ceps-publications/artificial-intelligence-and-cybersecurity-2/

Puyosa, I. (2023, September 6). Pro-Russian BRICS narratives in LatinAmerica-prosperedduringsummit lead-up. *DFRLab*.https://dfrlab.org/2023/09/06/pro-russian-brics-narratives-in-latin-america-prospered-during-summit-lead-up/

Puyosa, I., Marín Vázquez, M., & Fivenson, A. (2023), *Contrarrestar las operaciones de información de actoresautoritarios en Latinoamérica*(pp. 18–30). NationalEndowmentforDemocracy (NED Studies). https://www.ned.org/wp-content/uploads/2023/12/NED_FORO-Countrarestar-Operaciones-AMLAT.pdf

Puyosa, I. (2017). Political bots on Twitter in #Ecuador2017 presidential campaigns. *Contratexto*, *27*(027), 39–60. DOI: 10.26439/contratexto.2017.027.002

Radford, A., Narasimhan, K., Salimans, T., & Sutskever, I. (2018). Improving Language Understanding by Generative Pre-Training. *Technical Report, OpenAI*. Available: https://cdn.openai.com/research-covers/language-unsupervised/language_understanding_paper.pdf

Radford, A., Metz, L., & Chintala, S. (2015). Unsupervised representation learning with deep convolutional generative adversarial networks. Available: https://arxiv.org/abs/1511.06434

Radu, A., & Petcu, I. (2024). Digital Technologies Used to Combat Disinformation and Fake News. *ResearchGate*. https://www.researchgate.net/publication/380987988_Digital_Technologies_Used_to_Combat_Disinformation_and_Fake_News

Radu, A. F., & Petcu, I. (2024a). Digital Technologies Used to Combat Disinformation and FakeNews. *Romanian Cyber Security Journal*, *6*(1), 15–28. DOI: 10.54851/v6i1y202402

Radu, A. F., & Petcu, I. (2024b). *The Education System, The Way to Fight Fake News. Proceedings of the 5th International Conference on Machine Intelligence & Security for Smart Cities "Securing Smart Cities International Conference (SSCIC)* (Vol. 1). Security Above All., https://scrd.eu/index.php/trust/article/download/545/510/1085

Ramachandran, V., Hardebolle, C., Kotluk, N., Ebrahimi, T., Riedl, R., Jermann, P., & Tormey, R. (2023). A multimodal measurement of the impact of deepfakes on the ethical reasoning and affective reactions of students

Rāviņa, K., Šantare, G. (2024) Sabiedrības tiesības saņemt patiesu informāciju demokrātiskā, tiesiskā valstī. Journal JuristaVārds, No13/14 (1331/1332), pp. 31.-34.

Ray, P. P. (2023). ChatGPT: A comprehensivereviewonbackground, applications, keychallenges, bias, ethics, limitationsandfuturescope. *Internet of Things and Cyber-Physical Systems*, *3*, 121–154. https://www.sciencedirect.com/science/article/pii/S266734522300024X. DOI: 10.1016/j.iotcps.2023.04.003

REDH. (2023, August 9). A 20 años de la fundación de la Red de Intelectuales y Artistas en Defensa de la Humanidad y a 40 años de la democracia en Argentina. *Humanidad en Red*.https://humanidadenred.org/a-20-anos-de-la-fundacion-de-la-red-de-intelectuales-y-artistas-en-defensa-de-la-humanidad-y-a-40-anos-de-la-democracia-en-argentina/

Report "On the role of extra-institutional actors in the democratic system (lobbying)", adopted by the Venice Commission at its 94th Plenary Session (Venice, 8-9 March 2013). CDL-AD(2013)011.

Report on the Public Consultation for the European Democracy Action Plan (EDAP), (2020). Available: https://commission.europa.eu/document/fe30817d-9ea1-4ec7-ae2b-f80b301df8f7_en

Reuters (2021, August 18). *Facebook removes dozens of vaccine misinformation 'superspreaders'*. https://www.reuters.com/technology/facebook-removes-dozens-vaccine-misinformation-superspreaders-2021-08-18/

Reuters. (2024, July 26). Venezuelans abroad say they are struggling to register to vote. *Reuters*.https://www.reuters.com/world/americas/venezuelans-abroad-say-they-are-struggling-register-vote-2024-07-26/

Riedel, A., Whittaker, L., Barnes, R., & Mulcahy, R. (2024, November 20). *Disinformation and deepfakes played a part in the US election. Australia should expect the same*. The Conversation. http://theconversation.com/disinformation-and-deepfakes-played-a-part-in-the-us-election-australia-should-expect-the-same-243373

Rini, R. (2020). Deepfakes and the Epistemic Backstop. *Philosophers' Imprint, 20*(24), 1–16.

Robin, M. (2024). Are propagandistscombatants?Analysingtheethical status of propagandists in warfare. *Reviewof International Studies,* 1–20. https://doi.org/DOI: 10.1017/S0260210524000044

Rochlin, N. (2017). Fake news: Belief in post-truth. *Library Hi Tech, 35*(3), 386–392. https://www.researchgate.net/publication/318709609_Fake_News_Belief_in_Post-Truth. DOI: 10.1108/LHT-03-2017-0062

Roese, V. (2018). You won't believe how co-dependent they are: Or: Media hype and the interaction of news media, social media, and the user. In Vasterman, P. (Ed.), *From Media Hype to Twitter Storm* (pp. 313–332). Amsterdam University Press., DOI: 10.2307/j.ctt21215m0.19

Rojas, N., & Ángel, S. (2017). "Estancamiento paradójico": La ciencia política en los tiempos de la Revolución Bolivariana. *Anuario Latinoamericano: Ciencias Políticas y Relaciones Internacionales, 5*, 157–172. DOI: 10.17951/al.2017.5.157

Rosenfeld, S. (2018). *Democracy and truth: A short history*. University of Pennsylvania Press.

Roth, Y., & Pickels, N. (2020, May 11). *Updating our approach to misleading information*. X Blog. https://blog.twitter.com/en_us/topics/product/2020/updating-our-approach-to-misleading-information

Rouvinski, V. (2022). Russia in LatinAmerica: A frameworkofanalysis. In *Rethinking post-ColdWarRussian–Latin American relations* (1.ª ed., p. 17). Routledge. https://doi.org/DOI: 10.4324/9781003183372

Rubin, V. L. (2022). *Misinformation and disinformation*. Springer. DOI: 10.1007/978-3-030-95656-1

Russell, S. J., & Norvig, P. (2020). *Artificial Intelligence: A Modern Approach* (4th ed.). Pearson.

Ryan, T. J. (2012). What makes us click? Demonstrating incentives for angry discourse with digital-age field experiments. *The Journal of Politics*, *74*(4), 1138–1152. DOI: 10.1017/S0022381612000540

Sakya, S. M., Scoy, L. J. V., Garman, J. C., Miller, E. L., Snyder, B., Wasserman, E., Chinchilli, V. M., & Lennon, R. P. (2021). The impact of COVID-19-related changes in media consumption on public knowledge: Results of a cross-sectional survey of Pennsylvania adults. *Current Medical Research and Opinion*, *37*(6), 911–915. DOI: 10.1080/03007995.2021.1901679 PMID: 33840315

Samdani, A., & Dimri, S. (2024). Syrian Refugees and the Digital Misinformation Crisis: Legal Challenges and Policy Solutions. *Journal of Informatics Education and Research*, *4*(2). Advance online publication. DOI: 10.52783/jier.v4i2.1231

Sanchez, G. R., & Middlemass, K. (2022, July 26). *Misinformation is eroding the public's confidence in democracy*. Brookings. https://www.brookings.edu/articles/misinformation-is-eroding-the-publics-confidence-in-democracy/ (Sanchez & Middlemass, 2022)

Sartori, G. (2003). *Comparative constitutional engineering: Citizens in the age of misinformation*. Filip Višnjić.

Schreier, M. (2012). *Qualitative Content Analysis in Practice*. SAGE Publications. DOI: 10.4135/9781529682571

Schwartz, A. B. (2016). *Broadcast Hysteria: Orson Welles's War of the Worlds and the Art of Fake News* (reprint ed.). Hill and Wang, New York, NY, USA.

Scott, M. (2020, January 1). *Russia and China target U.S. protests on social media*. Politico. https://www.politico.com/news/2020/06/01/russia-and-china-target-us-protests-on-social-media-294315

Semana. (2015, December 6). Elecciones en Venezuela: Oposición gana Asamblea Nacional 17 años después. *Semana*. https://www.semana.com/mundo/articulo/elecciones-en-venezuela-oposicion-gana-asamblea-nacional-17-anos-despues/452639-3/

Serafimovska, E., & Cherepnalkova-Trajkoska, J. (2023). (2023). Vulnerability to Disinformation of Diverse Groups of Citizens in North Macedonia. *Institute of Communication Studies*https://cdn.iks.edu.mk/wp-content/uploads/2023/04/ranlivost-na-dezinformacii-en.pdf?_gl=1*b38uyy*_ga*MTU1NTQ0O TU4MC4xNzE2NjMzMzI2*_ga_0E19CX2514*MTczNTI0MDMwMi 4xMC4xLjE3MzUyNDA0NDIuNTguMC4w

Shalevska, E. (2024). The Future of Political Discourse: AI and Media Literacy Education. *Journal of Legal and Political Education*, *1*(1), 50–61. Advance online publication. DOI: 10.47305/JLPE2411050sh

Shapiro, I., & Macedo, S. (Eds.). (2000). *Designing democratic institutions*. New York University Press.

Sharevski, F., & Loop, J. V. (2024). Children, Parents, and Misinformation on Social Media. *ResearchGate*. https://www.researchgate.net/publication/381002519_Children_Parents_and_Misinformation_on_Social_Media

Sharf, Z. (2019). Deepfake Porn Videos Are Using Scarlett Johansson's Face, but She Says It's Useless to Fight Back. IndieWire. Available: https://www.indiewire.com/features/general/scarlett-johansson-deepfakes-face-porn-videos-1202031678/

Shu, K., Bhattacharjee, A., Alatawi, F., Nazer, T. H., Ding, K., Karami, M., & Liu, H. (2020). Combating disinformation in a social media age. *Wiley Interdisciplinary Reviews. Data Mining and Knowledge Discovery*, *10*(6), e1385. DOI: 10.1002/widm.1385

Shumei, L., & Yuwei, H. (2021). Chinese COVID-19 vaccines gain more international recognition. https://www.globaltimes.cn/page/202101/1213083.shtml

Shyh, T. H., Hin, H. S., & Ju, H. T. Y. (2023). Combat Fake News: An Overview of Youth's Media and Information Literacy Education. In F. Mustaffa (ed.), *Proceedings of the 3rd International Conference on Creative Multimedia 2023* (ICCM 2023), *Advances in Social Science, Education and Humanities Research 786*, 47–61. DOI: 10.2991/978-2-38476-138-8_6

Sidharth, A. (2019, November 21). How misinformation is being used to undermine JNU students' protest: Alt News compilation, *Alt News*. https://www.altnews.in/how-misinformation-is-being-used-to-undermine-jnu-students-protest-alt-news-compilation/

Silverman, H. (2019). *Helping fact-checkers identify false claims faster*. Meta. https://about.fb.com/news/2019/12/helping-fact-checkers/

Singh, M. (2023). Combating Fake News And Misinformation On Social Media With Tech. *RipenApps*. https://ripenapps.com/blog/combating-fake-news-misinformation-on-social-media-with-tech/

Singh, P., & Sunil, S. (2020). Towards A Legal Framework To Tackle Fake News. *Live Law*. https://www.livelaw.in/lawschool/articles/towards-a-legal-framework-to-tackle-fake-news-155556

Sitel.mk. (2024, December 30). *Мицкоски: Запрена е инфлацијата, серабoти настабилизацијанаинституциите [Mickoski: Inflation has been stopped, work is being done on stabilization of institutions].* Retrieved from https://sitel.com.mk/mickoski-zaprena-e-inflacijata-se-raboti-na-stabilizacija-na-instituciite

Skrabut, S. (2023). *80 Ways to Use ChatGPT in the Classroom: Using AI to Enhance Teaching and Learning*. Stan Skrabut: Self Published.

SlobodenPečat. (2024, December 30). *РаздорвоВладатапоради ЗНАМ(е) посамо 8 дена [Discord in the Government over the flag after only 8 days].* Retrieved from https://www.slobodenpecat.mk/razdor-vo-vladata-poradi-zname-po-samo-8-dena/

Small, T. A. (2011). What the hashtag? *Information Communication and Society*, *14*(6), 872–895. DOI: 10.1080/1369118X.2011.554572

Snyder, T. (2017). *On tyranny: Twenty lessons from the twentieth century*. Crown.

Snyder, T. (2018). *The road to unfreedom*. Europe, America. Tim Duggan Books.

Song, Y., & Tian, X. (2020). Managerial Responses and Customer Engagement in Crowdfunding. *Sustainability (Basel)*, *12*(8), 3389. DOI: 10.3390/su12083389

Spencer, J. (2016). Fake news is a real problem. Here's how students can solve it. https://spencerauthor.com/fake-news-is-a-real-problem-heres-how-students-can-solve-it/

Ss. Cyril and Methodius University Skopje, Institute of Economics. (2017). International cooperation. https://www.ek-inst.ukim.edu.mk/en/international-collaboration

Stanovčić, V. (2006). *Political theory*. Official Gazette.

Steffen, S. (2024, July 11). *Fact check: Disinformation's impact on the US election*. Dw.Com. https://www.dw.com/en/fact-check-what-role-did-disinformation-play-in-the-us-election/a-70729575

Stępińska, A. (2021). Factors Affecting Self-Censorship Among Polish Journalists. *Zeszyty Prasoznawcze*, *64*(2 (246)), 49–63. DOI: 10.4467/22996362PZ.21.010.13475

Suárez Pérez, D., & Ponce de León Rosas, E. (2021, March). *Digital autocracy: Maduro's control of the Venezuelan information environment*. Atlantic Council, DFRLab. https://dfrlab.org/wp-content/uploads/2021/04/DigitalAutocracyVEN-FINAL.pdf

Sudarsanan, T., & Yamuna, S. (2020). 'Fake news' in India – a legal approach. *International Journal of Law Management & Humanities*, *3*(3), 86–94.

Sukumaran, A. (2023. December 07). Deepfakes: Clear and present danger. *India Today*. https://www.indiatoday.in/india-today-insight/story/deepfakes-clear-and-present-danger-2473187-2023-12-07

Sule, A. (2020). COVID-19 and Infectious Misinformation. *Economic and Political Weekly*, *24*(13), 54.

Sun, Y., & Xie, J. (2024). Who shares misinformation on social media? A meta-analysis of individual traits related to misinformation sharing. *Computers in Human Behavior*, *158*, 108271. https://www.researchgate.net/publication/380409062_Who_Shares_Misinformation_on_Social_Media_A_Meta-analysis_of_Individual_Traits_Related_to_Misinformation_Sharing. DOI: 10.1016/j.chb.2024.108271

Tackling online disinformation: a European Approach, COM(2018)236. Available: https://eur-lex.europa.eu/legal-content/EN/TXT/?uri=celex:52018DC0236

Tagg, C., & Seargeant, P. (2021). Context design and critical language/media awareness: Implications for a social digital literacies education. *Linguistics and Education*, *62*, 100776. Advance online publication. DOI: 10.1016/j.linged.2019.100776

Tahiru, F. (2021). AI in Education: A Systematic Literature Review. *Journal of Cases on Information Technology*, *23*(1), 1–20. DOI: 10.4018/JCIT.2021010101

Tambini, D. (2017). *The attention economy and the law*. Media Policy Brief 22. London School of Economics and Political Science.

Tamilselvan, G., & Biswal, M. (2024). Voice Cloning & Deep Fake Audio Detection Using Deep Learning. *International Journal of Advanced Research and Interdisciplinary Scientific Endeavours*, *1*(2), 22–26. https://doi.org/doi.org/10.61359/IJARISE2408

Tan, C. (2022). The curious case of regulating false news on Google. *Computer Law & Security Review*, *46*, 105738. Advance online publication. DOI: 10.1016/j.clsr.2022.105738

Tandoc, E. C., Jr., Yee, A., Ong, J., Lee, J., Duan, X., Zheng, H., Matthew, C., Ng, J., Lim, C., Cheng, L., & Cayabyab, M. (2021). Developing a perceived social media literacy scale: Evidence from Singapore. International Journal of Communication, 15, 2484–2505. https://www.researchgate.net/publication/352118340_Developing_a_Perceived_Social_Media_Literacy_Scale_Evidence_from_Singapore United Nations Educational, Scientific and Cultural Organization. (2012). Media and information literacy: Curriculum for teachers. https://iite.unesco.org/publications/3214706/

Tandoc, E. C.Jr, Goh, Z. H., Wong, D. K. J., & Zhang, L. (2023). The good, the bad, and the Internet: Investigating the impact of online prosocial and anti-social behaviours on well-being. *Cogent Social Sciences*, *9*(1), 2225834. Advance online publication. DOI: 10.1080/23311886.2023.2225834

Tandoc, E. C.Jr, Lim, Z. W., & Ling, R. (2017). Defining "fake news": A typology of scholarly definitions. *Digital Journalism (Abingdon, England)*, *6*(2), 137–153. DOI: 10.1080/21670811.2017.1360143

Taylor, P. M. (2011). Ethics and international propaganda. In Fortner, R. S., & Fackler, P. M. (Eds.), *The handbook of global communication and media ethics* (Vol. II, pp. 912–932). Wiley-Blackwell. DOI: 10.1002/9781444390629.ch46

teknoius. (2023, July 23). *This is not Morgan Freeman - A Deepfake Singularity* [Video]. YouTube. https://www.youtube.com/watch?v=cJ80z_CzFRA

The CommLaw Group. (2025). *U.S. Copyright Office Releases Reports Addressing Digital Replicas and Copyrightability of AI-Generated Content.* Retrieved from: U.S. Copyright Office Releases Reports Addressing Digital Replicas and Copyrightability of AI-Generated Content—Part 3 Covering AI Model Training Remains to Be Published | The CommLaw Group on 20.3.25.

The Geopost. (2024). Expansion of the Confucius Institute in Serbia despite controversies in Europe and the USA. https://thegeopost.com/en/news/expansion-of-the-confucius-institute-in-serbia-despite-controversies-in-europe-and-the-usa/

The Guardian. (2016) How Facebook powers money machines for obscure political 'news' sites, available at https://www.theguardian.com/technology/2016/aug/24/facebook-clickbait-political-news-sites-us-election-trump

The Guardian. (2021) Sugar-coated propaganda? Middle East taps into power of influencers, https://www.theguardian.com/world/2021/jan/29/sugar-coated-propaganda-egypt-taps-into-power-instagram-influencers

The New York Times. (2023) Denmark Moves to ban Quran Burning after Muslim Outrage, available at https://www.nytimes.com/2023/08/25/world/europe/denmark-quran-burning.html

The Sun. (2019, September 25). *Boris Johnson's speech on Brexit, AI robots and chicken at the UN* [Video]. YouTube. https://www.youtube.com/watch?v=XaN-MbGV4dY

The Telegraph. (2020, April 5). *"We will succeed": Watch the Queen's speech on coronavirus in full* video]. YouTube. https://www.youtube.com/watch?v=_d1YEkcbFwk

The Wired. (2019) The WIRED Guide to Influencers - Everything you need to know about engagement, power likes, sponcon, and trust available at https://www.wired.com/story/what-is-an-influencer/

Theobalt, C. (2018). Lip-syncingthanks to artificial intelligence. Max - Planck - Gesellschaft. Available: https://www.mpg.de/12226519/synchronisation-facial-expressions-video

Thies, J., Zollhöfer, M., Stamminger, M., Theobalt, Ch., & Nießner, M. (2016). *"Face2Face: Real-Time Face Capture and Reenactment of RGB Videos". 2016 IEEE Conferenceon Computer Vision and Pattern Recognition (CVPR)*. IEEE.

Time.mk. (2024, December 30). *Димитриевски: ЗНАМ ќеизлезеодВладатаако повторноминистритеодВредиистакнаталбанскозname [Dimitrievski: ZNAM will leave the government if VREDI ministers display the Albanian flag again]*. Retrieved from https://time.mk/c/e7085289af/dimitrievski-znam-ke-izleze-od-vladata-ako-povtorno-ministrite-od-vredi-istaknat-albansko-zname.html

Tiwari, S. (2024, March 20) Fact Check: Did CJI walk away while Tushar Mehta was speaking? NO, viral claim is false. *India Today*. https://www.indiatoday.in/fact-check/story/fact-check-did-cji-walk-away-while-tushar-mehta-was-speaking-no-viral-claim-is-false-2516874-2024-03-19

Todd, J. T., & Woodhouse, J. (2024, January 15). *Preventing misinformation and disinformation in online filter bubbles*. UK Parliament House of Commons Library. https://commonslibrary.parliament.uk/research-briefings/cdp-2024-0003/

Topsümer, F., Durmuş, Y., & Yılmaz, B. A. (Eds.). (2023). *Media and Communication in the Digital Age: Changes and Dynamics*. Özgür Publications., DOI: 10.58830/ozgur.pub234

Torkington, S. (2024). These are the 3 biggest emerging risks the world is facing. *World Economic Forum*. https://www.weforum.org/stories/2024/01/ai-disinformation-global-risks/

Transparency Index. (2022). Center for Civic Communication, Skopje. https://www.ccc.org.mk/images/stories/akt22.pdf

Transparency International Macedonia. (2024). *(Dis)information spread online in the pre-election period.* https://transparency.mk/wp-content/uploads/2024/05/disinformation-spread-online-in-the-pre-election-period.pdf

Trimble, L., & Sampert, S. (2010). *Mediating Canadian politics.* Pearson Prentice Hall.

Trpevska, S., & Micevski, I. (2022). *Digital media manipulation in the Balkans: Mapping disinformation ecosystems in North Macedonia.* Southeast European Media Observatory.

Tudjman, M., & Mikelic, N. (2003). Information science: Science about information, misinformation and disinformation. *Proceedings of Informing Science+ Information Technology Education, 3*, 1513-1527.

Tully, S. (2014). People you might know: Social media in the conflict between law and democracy. In Patmore, G., & Rubenstein, K. (Eds.), *Law and Democracy: Contemporary Questions.* ANU Press., DOI: 10.22459/LD.12.2014.09

TV21. (2024, December 30). *Përplasjemes VLEN dhe ZNAM: Ulja e përfaqësimit-tëshqiptarëvenëadministratëshkaktonrevoltëtepartnerët e koalicionitqeverisës [Clash between VLEN and ZNAM: Reduction of Albanian representation in administration causes revolt among government coalition partners].* Retrieved from https://tv21.tv/perplasje-mes-vlen-dhe-znam-ulja-e-perfaqesimit-te-shqiptareve-ne-administrate-shkakton-revolte-te-partneret-e-koalicionit-qeverises/

Ubertalli, O. (2025, January 17). Quand le dictateur Maduro fait la « leçon » au « Point ».*Le Point.* https://www.lepoint.fr/monde/quand-le-dictateur-maduro-fait-la-lecon-au-point-17-01-2025-2580184_24.php

UN GeneralAssemblyResolutionof 09.04.2015 on "HumanRights, Democracy-andtheRuleofLaw", A/HRC/RES/28/14.

Unesco, (2023). SSurvey on the impact of online disinformation and hate speech. Available at: https://www.unesco.org/sites/default/files/medias/fichiers/2023/11/unesco_ipsos_survey.pdf

UNESCO. (2018). *Journalism, fake news & disinformation: handbook for journalism education and training.* UNESCO.

UNESCO. (2025). *UNESCO-MICA hold summit on media and information literacy in AI age.* Retrieved from: https://www.unesco.org/en/articles/unesco-mica-hold-summit-media-and-information-literacy-ai-age on 20.3.25.

UNESCO. (n.d.) *Media and Information Literacy.* Retrieved from: https://www.unesco.org/en/media-information-literacy on 5.1.25.

United Nations Human Rights Committee. General Comment No. 34: Article 19: Freedoms of opinion and expression, (CCPR/C/GC/34). Available: https://www2.ohchr.org/english/bodies/hrc/docs/gc34.pdf

United Nations. (2021). *Resolution adopted by the General Assembly on May 26 2021*https://documents.un.org/doc/undoc/gen/n21/133/51/pdf/n2113351.pdf

United Nations. (2024). UN General Assembly adopts milestone cybercrime treaty. https://news.un.org/en/story/2024/12/1158521

United Nations. (General Assembly) (1966) "International Covenant on Civil and Political Rights." https://www.equalityhumanrights.com/en/our-human-rights-work/monitoring-and-promoting-un-treaties/international-covenant-civil-and#:~:text=ICCPR%20is%20an%20international%20human,fair%20trial%20rights

United States China Economic and Security Review Commission. (2023). Section 2: Battling for overseas hearts and minds: China's united front and propaganda work (p. 37). https://www.uscc.gov/sites/default/files/2023-11/Chapter_2_Section_2--Chinas_United_Front_and_Propaganda_Work.pdf

United States Department of State. (2024, February 8). Disarming Disinformation: Our Shared Responsibility. *Global Engagement Center.*https://www.state.gov/disarming-disinformation/

United States Department of State. (2024, June 7). Russia spreads disinformation to cover up its use of chemical weapons in Ukraine. *Global Engagement Center.*https://www.state.gov/russia-spreads-disinformation-to-cover-up-its-use-of-chemical-weapons-in-ukraine/

University "Ss. Cyril and Methodius" in Skopje. (2025). Confucius Institute. https://ukim.edu.mk/en/sostav/nauchni-instituti/institut-konfucij/

University of Sarajevo. (2025). The Confucius Institute of the Sarajevo University successfully held the 2025 Spring Festival Gala event. https://www.unsa.ba/en/novosti/confucius-institute-sarajevo-university-successfully-held-2025-spring-festival-gala-event

Ünver, A. (2023). Emerging technologies and automated fact-checking: Tools, techniques and algorithms. *Techniques and Algorithms (August 29, 2023)*. https://edam.org.tr/Uploads/Yukleme_Resim/pdf-28-08-2023-23-40-14.pdf

Unver, A. (2023). The Role of Technology: New Methods of Information, Manipulation and Disinformation. *EDAM*. https://edam.org.tr/en/cyber-governance-digital-democracy/the-role-of-technology-new-methods-of-information-manipulation-and-disinformation

USG (United States Government Office) Russian intervention in European elections hearing before the select committee on intelligence of the United States Senat, one hundred fifteenth congress, first session Wednesday, june 28, 2017 available at https://www.intelligence.senate.gov/wp-content/uploads/2024/08/sites-default-files-hearings-s-hrg-115-105.pdf

Vaccari, C., Chadwick, A. (2020). Deepfakes and Disinformation: Exploring the Impact of Synthetic Political Video on Deception, Uncertainty, and Trust in News. *Social Media + Society, 6*(1). https://doi.org/ (Original work published 2020)DOI: 10.1177/2056305120903408

Vaidyanathan, S. (2018). *Anti-social networks: How Facebook divides us and undermines democracy*. Clio.

Valverde-Berrocoso, J., González-Fernández, A., & Acevedo-Borrega, J. (2022). Disinformation and multiliteracy: A systematic review of the literature. *RevistaComunicar, 70*(XXX), 93–105. DOI: 10.3916/C70-2022-08

Van Huijstee, M., Van Boheemen, P., & Das, D. (2021). *Tackling deepfakes in European policy*. European Parliament.

Vanderhoven, E., Raes, A., Montrieux, H., Rotsaert, T., & Schellens, T. (2021). Developing a media literacy program for secondary education: Challenges and opportunities. *The Journal of Media Literacy Education, 13*(1), 1–13.

Vecchio, L. (2020). *Misinformation: A Threat to Digital Governance*. Invictus Corporation Ltd.

Vecer.mk. (2024, December 30). *Димитриевски: Акоповторносеистакнеалба нскотозname, ЗНАМ ќејанапуштиВладата [Dimitrievski: If the Albanian flag is displayed again, ZNAM will leave the Government]*. Retrieved from https://www.vecer.mk/makedonija/dimitrievski-ako-povtorno-se-istakne-albanskoto-zname-znam-kje-ja-napushti-vladata/

Vest.mk. (2024, December 30). *Димитриевски: Акоповторносеистакнеалбан скотозname, ЗНАМ ќејанапуштиВладата [Dimitrievski: If the Albanian flag is displayed again, ZNAM will leave the Government].* Retrieved from https://vest.mk/dimitrievski-ako-povtorno-se-istakne-albanskoto-zname-znam-kje-ja-napushti-vladata/

Vicent, M. (2006, August 7). Chávezcalifica a Fidel Castro de "Papa de los revolucionarios": Cuba se mantieneatenta a los mensajes sobre la saluddelcomandante.*El País*.https://elpais.com/diario/2006/08/07/internacional/1154901612_850215.html

Vintilă, D. (2024). Public Libraries–Key Actors in Fighting Misinformation in the Future Digital Society. *Culture. Society. Economy. Politics (Culture-SEP), 4*(1), 24-31. https://doi.org/https://doi.org/10.2478/csep-2024-0003

Vishwanath, A., Neo, L. S., Lee, J., Goh, P., & Khader, M. (2020). Cyber hygiene: The concept, its measure, and its initial tests. *Decision Support Systems*, *128*, 113160. Advance online publication. DOI: 10.1016/j.dss.2019.113160

Vlada na Republika Severna Makedonija [Government of the Republic of North Macedonia]. (2024, December 30). *ВладанаРепубликаСевернаМакедонија: Балансеротзаминувавоисторијата [Government of the Republic of North Macedonia: The balancer goes into history].* Video]. YouTube. https://www.youtube.com/watch?v=P5Pq739NbSA

Vosoughi, S., Roy, D., & Aral, S. (2018). The spread of true and false news online. *Science*, *359*(6380), 1146–1151. DOI: 10.1126/science.aap9559 PMID: 29590045

Vuorikari, R., Kluzer, S., & Punie, Y. (2022). *DigComp 2.2: The digital competence framework for citizens—With new examples of knowledge, skills and attitudes (EUR 31006 EN)*. Publications Office of the European Union., DOI: 10.2760/115376

Walker, C., & Ludwig, J. (2017). *Sharp power: Rising authoritarian influence.* National Endowment for Democracy. https://www.ned.org/wp-content/uploads/2017/12/Sharp-Power-Rising-Authoritarian-Influence-Full-Report.pdf

Walker, M., & Mitchell, A. (2021, August 18). More Americans now say government should take steps to restrict false information online than in 2018. *Pew Research Center*. https://www.pewresearch.org/short-reads/2021/08/18/more-americans-now-say-government-should-take-steps-to-restrict-false-information-online-than-in-2018/

Wang, S., Wang, O., Zhang, R., & Tao, X. (2020). CNN-generated images are surprisingly easy to spot... for now. *Proceedings of the IEEE/CVF Conference on Computer Vision and Pattern Recognition*, 8692-8701. DOI: 10.1109/CVPR42600.2020.00872

Wardle, C. (2018, July 9). Information Disorder, Part 1: The Essential Glossary. https://medium.com/1st-draft/information-disorder-part-1-the-essential-glossary-19953c544fe3

Wardle, C. (2020, February 23). Essential guide to understanding information disorder. First Draft News. https://firstdraftnews.org/wp-content/uploads/2019/10/Information_Disorder_Digital_AW.pdf:contentReference[oaicite:2]{index=2}

Wardle, C. (2023). Misunderstanding Misinformation. *Issues.*https://issues.org/misunderstanding-misinformation-wardle/

Wardle, C., & Derakhshan, H. (2017). *Information disorder: Toward an interdisciplinary framework for research and policy making*. Council of Europe Report DGI(2017)09.

Wardle, C., & Derakhshan, H. (2017). *Information Disorder: Toward an Interdisciplinary Framework for Research and Policy Making*. Council of Europe.

Wei, L., Gong, J., Xu, J., Abidin, N. H., & Apuke, O. D. (2022). Do social media literacy skills help in combating fake news spread? Modelling the moderating role of social media literacy skills in the relationship between rational choice factors and fake news sharing behaviour. *Telematics and Informatics*, *76*, comprobating101910. https://www.researchgate.net/publication/365290679_Do_social_media_literacy_skills_help_in_combating_fake_news_spread_Modelling_the_moderating_role_of_social_media_literacy_skills_in_the_relationship_between_rational_choice_factors_and_fake_news_shari. DOI: 10.1016/j.tele.2022.101910

Wendling, M. (2024, November 3). Whirlwind of misinformation sows distrust ahead of US election day. *BBC*. https://www.bbc.com/news/articles/czj7eex29r3o

West, D. M. (2024, November 7). *How disinformation defined the 2024 election narrative*. Brookings. https://www.brookings.edu/articles/how-disinformation-defined-the-2024-election-narrative/

Westerlund, M. (2019). The Emergence of Deepfake Technology: A Review. Technology Innovation Management Review. Available: https://timreview.ca/article/1282

Westerlund, M. (2019). The emergence of deepfake technology: A review. *Technology Innovation Management Review*, *9*(11), 39–52. DOI: 10.22215/timreview/1282

Western Balkans University. (2024). WBU has signed a cooperation agreement with Zhejiang Normal University in China. https://wbu.edu.al/en/news/wbu-has-signed-a-cooperation-agreement-with-zhejiang-normal-university-in-china

Whittaker, L., Mulcahy, R., Letheren, K., Kietzmann, J., & Russell-Bennett, R. (2023). Mapping the deepfake landscape for innovation: A multidisciplinary systematic review and future research agenda. *Technovation*, *125*, 102784. DOI: 10.1016/j.technovation.2023.102784

Wijnhoven, F. (2023).*InsightMaker Introduction Course: Manual.* https://insightmaker.com/sites/ Introduction_Manual.pdf

Williamson, S. M., & Prybutok, V. (2024). The era of artificial intelligence deception: Unraveling the complexities of false realities and emerging threats of misinformation. *Information (Basel)*, *15*(6), 299. DOI: 10.3390/info15060299

Wilson, S., Hassan, N. A., Khor, K. K., Sinnappan, S., Abu Bakar, A. R., & Tan, S. A. (2024). A holistic qualitative exploration on the perception of scams, scam techniques and effectiveness of anti-scam campaigns in Malaysia. *Journal of Financial Crime*, *31*(5), 1140–1155. DOI: 10.1108/JFC-06-2023-0151

Wingström, R., Hautala, J., & Lundman, R. (2023). Redefining Creativity in the Era of AI? Perspectives of Computer Scientists and New Media Artists. *Creativity Research Journal*. Advance online publication. DOI: 10.1080/10400419.2022.2107850

Wordorigins.org. (n.d.). Truthiness. https://www.wordorigins.org/big-list-entries/truthiness

WordPress. 2U. (2020, May 28). The evolution of social media: How did it begin, and where could it go next? *Maryville University Online*. https://online.maryville.edu/blog/evolution-social-media/

World Economic Forum. (2024). *Disinformation is a threat to our trust ecosystem. Experts explain how to curb it.* https://www.weforum.org/stories/2024/03/disinformation-trust-ecosystem-experts-curb-it/

www.europarl.europa.eu. (n.d.) Texts adopted – Artificial intelligence in education, culture and the audio-visual sector. 19.05.2021. Available at: https://www.europarl.europa.eu/doceo/document/TA-9-2021-0238_EN.html (Access 9.01.2025).

Yenduri, G., Srivastava, G., Maddikunta, P. K. R., Jhaveri, R. H., Wang, W., Vasilakos, A. V., & Gadekallu, T. R. (2023). Generative pre-trained transformer: A comprehensive review on enabling technologies, potential applications, emerging challenges, and future directions. *arXiv preprint arXiv:2305.10435.*

Young, K. (2017, October 21). Moon Shot: Race, a Hoax, and the Birth of Fake News. *The New Yorker*.https://www.newyorker.com/books/page-turner/moon-shot-race-a-hoax-and-the-birth-of-fake-news

Yousman, B. (2008). Media literacy: Creating better citizens or better consumers? In Andersen, R., & Gray, J. (Eds.), *Battleground: The media* (pp. 238–247). Greenwood Press., https://newmediagr.wordpress.com/wp-content/uploads/2009/10/17171370-battleground-themedia.pdf

Yuwei, H. (2023). China-Serbia ironclad friendship sets a model of shared fulfillment: Serbian deputy PM. *Global Times*. https://www.globaltimes.cn/page/202305/1291032.shtml

Zawadzki, T., Wałęcki, T., Świeboda, H., Szpyra, R., Kuczabski, M., & Stobiecki, P. (2020). Introduction to Methods of Modelling Information Warsas a 21st Century Threat. *European Research Studies Journal, 23*(2), 1011–1026. DOI: 10.35808/ersj/1922

Zeiger, S., & Gyte, J. (2020). *Prevention of radicalization on social media and the internet*. International Centre for Counter-Terrorism (ICCT).

Zeneli, V. (2023, June 23). Chinese influence in the Western Balkans and its impact on the region's European Union integration process. *Europe's Futures*. https://www.iwm.at/blog/chinese-influence-in-the-western-balkans-and-its-impact-on-the-regions-european-union

Zeneli, V., & Mejdini, F. (n.d.). Countering Beijing's regional influence. *Per Concordiam*. Retrieved May 24, 2025, from https://perconcordiam.com/china-in-the-balkans/

Zhang, B., & Thompson, A. (2022). Deepfakes and media literacy: Toward a framework for navigating synthetic media. *New Media & Society, 24*(5), 1165–1182.

Zhu, X., & Liu, F. (2017).Research on Behavior Model of Rumor Maker Based on System Dynamics.*Complexity, 2017*(1), 5094218, 9 pages.DOI: 10.1155/2017/5094218

Zimdars, M., & Mcleod, K. (2020). Fake News: Understanding Media and Misinformation in the Digital Age. *MIT Press Direct*. https://direct.mit.edu/books/edited-volume/4625/Fake-NewsUnderstanding-Media-and-Misinformation-in

ZNM. (2017) Freedom of expression through the practice of the European Court of Human Rights https://znm.org.mk/wp-content/uploads/2020/04/Freedom-of-expression-through-the-practice-of-the-European-Court-for-Human-Rights-December-2017.pdf

Zuboff, S. (2019). *The age of surveillance capitalism: The fight for a human future at the new frontier of power*. Profile Books.

About the Contributors

Goran Ilik is a full professor and Vice-Rector for Science at the University St. Kliment Ohridski in Bitola (North Macedonia). From 2012 to 2016, he served as a Senator in the Senate of the University St. Kliment Ohridski in Bitola, and from 2013 to 2017, he held the position of Vice-Dean for Science and International Cooperation at the Faculty of Law - Kicevo. In 2017, Prof. Dr. sc Goran Ilik was elected Dean of the Faculty of Law - Kicevo for the first time, while on January 15, 2021, he was re-elected as Dean of the Faculty of Law - Kicevo for the second time. The academic background includes BA in Law, MA in Political Science, and PhD in Political Science. The publication list contains papers, chapters, and monographs emphasizing the role of the European Union in international relations, the institutional architecture of its foreign policy, the EU's constitutional law and constitutionalism, the EU's axiological performances, and its political power. Also, many papers treat the EU's role in the new international context concerning the contemporary challenges of the liberal world order and the EU's role and place in it. He is the author of the books: "Europe at the Crossroads: The Treaty of Lisbon as a Basis of European Union International Identity", "EUtopia: The International Political Power of the EU in the Process of Ideeologization of the Post-American World", and "International Relations and the European Union: Values before Power". Prof. Dr. sc. Goran Ilik is a lecturer/trainer at the State Academy of Judges and Public Prosecutors "Pavel Shatev" – Skopje (North Macedonia). Also, Prof. Dr. sc. Goran Ilik is co-founder of the Institute for Research and European Studies – Bitola and Editor-in-Chief of the international academic journals "Journal of Liberty and International Affairs" and "Journal of Legal and Political Education". Since October 2019, Prof. Dr. sc. Goran Ilik has been engaged as an expert in the project ANETREC, which is focused on academic cooperation and post-conflict reconciliation in the Western Balkans region. He is a member of ISCOMET – Institute for Ethnic and Regional Studies (Maribor, Slovenia). He also completed a post-doctoral fellowship at the "Mediterranea" International Centre for Human

Rights Research in Italy (2020-2021). In August 2021, Prof. Dr. sc. Ilik became a coordinator of the sub-thematic area "International Public Law" at the post-doctoral program in "New Technologies and Law", organized by the "Mediterranea" International Centre for Human Rights Research at the University Mediterranea of Reggio Calabria (Italy). Prof. Dr. sc. Goran Ilik has been engaged as an expert by the Institute for Global Analytics in Sofia (Bulgaria), which is an independent, nonpartisan, and nonprofit organization. Furthermore, Prof. Dr. sc. Goran Ilik has been appointed as an expert for the "Cross-Border Complex Floods and Forest Fires: Prevention and Management - SOLVE" project within the framework of the Interreg IPA CBC "Greece and North Macedonia" program 2014-2023. Additionally, he brings extensive experience from his involvement in international projects and those supported by the European Union.

Mladen Karadjoski graduated at the Interdisciplinary studies for Public administration in the University of "St. Kliment Ohridski"- Bitola as the best student of the first generation. Became MA in public administration at the Faculty of administration and MIS. Acquired PhD degree in 2011 in the area of public administration. Dr. Mladen Karadjoski is an Associate Professor at the University of "St.Kliment Ohridski" – Bitola. In his academic career he participated at a numerous scientific conferences, seminars, forums, workshops, etc. He is an author and co-author of many published articles. Some of them are: "Dicrepancies between anti-corruption legislation and practice in Macedonia", 10th Cross-border Crime Colloquium, 10th edition, Crime, money and criminal mobility in Europe, Wolf legal publishers, Nijmegen, Netherlands, 2009;"Public administration in the Republic of Macedonia – legal aspects, reforms, management processes", Scientific Journal, Warsaw, Poland, 2010;"Functional characteristics of the informational system of finance in transition countries", Book of papers from the 5th International Science Conference of ASECU, Tirana, Albania, 2010;"Eurocentrism and the obstacles for entrance of Western Balkans and Turkey in the European Union", Scientific Journal - European Perspectives, Ljubljana, Slovenia, 2011;"Fulfillment of the Madrid criteria through the reforms of the public administrations of the countries from the Western Balkans" NISPA Journal, 2011;"Democracy in the countries of the Western Balkans: nominal or crucial transformation of the political systems after the end of communism", Scientific journal – Revista de stiinte politice, University of Craiova, No.33-34, 2012.

Ice Ilijevski is born on 29.06.1986 in Bitola. He has finished security studies, has defended his Master thesis titled „Sources of financing terrorism - criminalistics, criminological and criminal-legal characteristics" and has defended his doctoral thesis titled „Control and oversight of the security system in the Republic of

Macedonia - with particular reference to Ministry of Interior“ at the Faculty of security - Skopje, University “St. Kliment Ohridski” in Bitola and gain the scientific title doctor of sciences in the field of security. Ice Ilijevski has worked at the Faculty of security – Skopje for 10 years. Now he is associate professor at the Faculty of Law, University “St. Kliment Ohridski” in Bitola. Ice Ilijevski has written several books, handbooks, papers and articles in the field of security as author and co-author and has been participant at many national and international scientific conferences, seminars, symposiums etc. Also, he was member of several teams for conducting surveys and researches for citizens' perceptions about security, safety and rule of law in the country. He is an expert witness and a former member of the Council for Civil Supervision established by the Assembly of the Republic of North Macedonia. His field of interest is control and oversight of the security sector and the fight against different types of illegal trafficking, terrorism, corruption, and organized crime.

Blagoj Nenovski is Assistant Professor at the Faculty of Law, “St. Kliment Ohridski” University – Bitola, Republic of North Macedonia. He graduated from the Technical faculty with a degree in IT (2009) and obtained his Msc in IT from the same faculty (2012). In 2020 he received his PhD in Information and Computer Technologies from the Faculty of Information and Communication Technologies. He teaches Informatics 1 and Informatics 2 at the Faculty of Law on the first cycle of studies, Computer security at the second cycle and Application of ICT in scientific research work at the third cycle of studies. His research interests are in ICT, ICT in education, augmented reality and computer and network security, areas on which he has published multiple papers. He is a coordinator for the department of ICT preparation of lawyers at the Faculty of Law.

***

S. M. Aamir Ali is presently an Assistant Professor at Symbiosis Law School Pune, Symbiosis International (Deemed University), Pune. He is currently pursuing his PhD at the West Bengal National University of Juridical Sciences (WBNUJS), Kolkata. He has completed his LL.M. at the National Law School of India University (NLSIU), Bengaluru, with a specialization in Human Rights Law. Mr. Ali has been teaching across specializations in Constitutional Law, Human Rights, and Criminal Law at the undergraduate and postgraduate levels since 2019.

Douglas M.C. Allan earned his PhD in Criminology from the Regulatory Institutions Network at the Australian National University. He is currently the Acting Head of the Australian Graduate School of Policing and Security at Charles Sturt University, managing a portfolio of undergraduate and postgraduate programs in law enforcement, national security, emergency management, law and financial crime. He has published in multiple areas, including education, financial crime, criminology and cybercrime.

Duane Aslett earned his doctoral degree in Law from North-West University (NWU), South Africa, with a thesis on combating organized crime, and now serves as Associate Professor and Director of the Centre for Law and Justice at Charles Sturt University, Australia, where he teaches Policing Studies and coordinates the program with a focus on integrating practical and academic approaches to law enforcement. His research interests include financial crime, corruption, money laundering, and organized crime, with notable contributions, including presentations before the Financial Action Task Force in 2019 and publications in these fields. Dr Aslett's extensive career includes roles as an Inspector in the South African Police Service, Senior Public Prosecutor in the National Prosecuting Authority, forensic investigator at PricewaterhouseCoopers, and leadership positions at NWU, including Programme Leader of Forensic Accountancy and Director of Strategy. In his spare time, he writes crime fiction, publishing novels and short stories in Afrikaans.

Avni Avdiu was born on January 10, 1973, in Kumanovo, North Macedonia. He completed his primary education in his hometown and his secondary education in Gjilan, Republic of Kosovo, graduating with exemplary success. He earned his degree in philosophy, journalism, and sociology from the University of Pristina. He completed his Master's studies in media sociology in Tirana, Albania, and holds two doctoral degrees: one in political philosophy from Skopje and another in media sociology from Tirana. He has lectured at the University of Pristina and several private colleges in Kosovo. He is currently a professor at the Department of Media and Intercultural Communication at Mother Teresa University in Skopje, Republic of North Macedonia. With over 30 years of experience in journalism, he has worked as an announcer, journalist, reporter, and translator across various media platforms, including radio, television, newspapers, and magazines, in both Kosovo and North Macedonia. He is the author of five books, three of which focus on media-related topics.

Goran Bandov, PhD, Lawyer and Political Scientist, World Academy of Art and Science Fellow, Global Young Academy Alumni Plus Fellow, Inter-Academy Partnership's Development and Program Committee on Policy Advice, Croatian Club of Rome President, Rotary Peace Fellow and Rotary Peace Activator, International Relations and Sustainable Development University Department Head at the University of Zagreb, former Vice Dean at Dag Hammarskjöld University College of International Relations and Diplomacy in Zagreb (2009-2019) and former

Research Fellow at the Institute for Peace and Security Studies of the University of Hamburg (2009-2014) is a European expert in Diplomacy, International Relations and International Law, Peace and Conflict Studies, Migration and Sustainable Development. Bandov is a member of the Foreign Affairs Committee of the Croatian Parliament from the academic community in the third mandate. In this role, he serves as an active adviser to the Croatian Parliament in the fields of foreign and security policy. Previously, he served as a member of the Committee for European Policies in the Croatian Parliament, where he advised on positions related to EU policies. He is deeply committed to public science communication in his fields of expertise, with over a thousand media appearances and public speeches in the last couple of years. In that area, he hosts a weekly radio show on Croatian Radio, where he promotes science, peace, and diplomacy.

Juan Cristóbal Demian holds a degree in Political Science from the Pontificia Universidad Católica de Chile and a Master's degree in Security, Defense, and International Relations from the National Academy of Political and Strategic Studies (ANEPE), Chile. He is currently pursuing a PhD in World Economics at Corvinus University of Budapest.

Anuttama Ghose is an Assistant Professor of Law and Program Coordinator of BA LLB (Hons.) Program at the School of Law, Dr. Vishwanath Karad MIT World Peace University, Pune, India. She is also currently heading the Centre for Innovation, Incubation, and Intellectual Property Laws (CIIIPL) at the MIT WPU School of Law. She has completed her BA LLB (IPR Hons.) from the School of Law, KIIT University, Bhubaneshwar and an LL.M with specialization in the field of Intellectual Property Laws from Symbiosis Law School, Pune, India. She has completed her PhD in the field of Protection of Non-Conventional Trademarks from the School of Law and Justice at Adamas University, Kolkata. She has previously worked as Vice-Principal and Assistant Professor of Law at the Indian Institute of Legal Studies, Darjeeling, West Bengal. Apart from being an IPR enthusiast, she is a keen researcher with over 25 academic publications in National and International Journals to her credit.

Nikolina Herceg Kolman is a doctoral candidate at the Faculty of Political Science, University of Zagreb, and is currently in the final stage of her studies, preparing her doctoral dissertation on the Europeanization of human rights. She has extensive experience in European and foreign affairs, human rights, and sustainability, as well as policy planning, having worked as a policy advisor to the Minister of Foreign and European Affairs, a policy advisor in the Croatian Parliament, Office of MEP, and policy consultant to international foundations (NDI,

Friedrich Naumann Stiftung). Herceg Kolman is the author, co-author, and co-editor of several scientific articles and books in the fields of foreign and European policy, UN policy, sustainable development, and theory of democracy. She has also served as a lecturer for the "UN 2030 Program" course at the Dag Hammarskjöld College of International Relations and Diplomacy in Zagreb, as well as a guest lecturer at the Faculty of Political Science and Libertas University in Zagreb.

Ilija Sotir Hristoski earned his Ph.D. in Technical Sciences from "St. Kliment Ohridski" University in Bitola, North Macedonia, in 2013. He currently serves as a full-time Professor at the Faculty of Economics in Prilep, within the same University. Dr. Hristoski teaches a variety of ICT-focused courses across all three ECTS cycles, including "Database Systems" and "Internet Technologies" at the undergraduate level, "Advanced Internet Technologies" at the Master's level, as well as "Information Management" and "Big Data Technologies" at the doctoral level. He has authored over 90 peer-reviewed scientific papers published in international journals and conference proceedings. Additionally, he has written two textbooks in Macedonian: Business Informatics (2010, Faculty of Economics, Prilep) and the two-volume series Relational Databases Design, Volume 1: Conceptual and Logical Design and Volume 2: Physical Design and Implementation (2022, Faculty of Economics, Prilep). His research primarily focuses on the application of Petri Nets, Relational and NoSQL Graph-based databases, Discrete-event simulations, System Dynamics, and Systems Thinking.

Pranjal Khare is a distinguished corporate lawyer and currently works as a law faculty member at O.P. Jindal Global University, India. He specializes in Property Law, Corporate laws, Intellectual Property Rights, and International Law. Mr. Pranjal is a highly regarded scholar who has published extensively on various issues related to international affairs, economics, politics, data and privacy, artificial intelligence, and intellectual property disputes. He is also a frequent speaker at legal conferences and has served as a consultant to numerous law firms and corporations.

Agron Kurtishi is a Lecturer and Head of the Department of Media and Intercultural Communication at the Faculty of Social Sciences, University "Mother Teresa" in Skopje. He holds a PhD in Media, Journalism and Mass Communication from the University "St. Kliment Ohridski" in Sofia. He earned two Master's degrees in Media and Intercultural Communication—one from Europa-Universität Viadrina in Germany and another from the University "St. Kliment Ohridski" in Sofia. Additionally, he completed an Integrated Master's program in Media Planning, Development, and Advising at the University of Siegen in Germany.

Leo S.F. Lin holds a PhD in International Development and Security Studies from the University of Southern Mississippi. He is a Senior Lecturer at Charles Sturt University's School of Policing Studies. With over 20 years of experience in policing and security, he has taught undergraduate and postgraduate courses in criminal justice, security studies, and emergency management across various institutions. His research focuses on transnational security, cybercrime, AI-enabled offenses, and emergency management in the Indo-Pacific. Dr. Lin has published numerous journal articles, book chapters, and four books, including an edited volume on Asia-Pacific security, and is currently authoring and editing two books on crime and security. He leads innovative research on cybercrime and risk policy, contributing to advancements in criminology and emergency management policy and practice.

Geberew Tulu Mekonnen is a Lecturer at the School of Policing Studies at Charles Sturt University. He holds a PhD in Education from the University of Tasmania (UTAS), with a focus on the impact of the Bologna Process on Ethiopian higher education. Dr Mekonnen is engaged in criminology research, collaborating with colleagues on topics such as youth crime and education, cybercrime, cryptocurrencies, combating misinformation and disinformation, and deepfake technology. His broader academic contributions include publications on student learning and assessment, higher education governance, pedagogy, and leadership, reflecting his significant impact in these fields. Before joining Charles Sturt University, Dr Mekonnen held various roles at the University of Tasmania, including Sessional Academic Staff, Research Assistant, Research Outputs Officer, and Research Funding Officer. He also taught and conducted research at Addis Ababa University (AAU), Ethiopia. During his time at AAU, he served in administrative leadership positions, including Associate Dean for Undergraduate Programs, College Managing Director, and Program Coordinator.

Michel Navarro is a doctoral candidate in International Relations and Securitization at Corvinus University of Budapest. He previously lectured in Latin American Studies and Geopolitics at Budapest Metropolitan University and his alma mater. His research focuses on the foreign policy strategies of authoritarian regimes, with particular emphasis on disinformation, lobbying, and influence operations. He has published extensively on these subjects in peer-reviewed outlets and is actively engaged in several departmental research initiatives at his University.

Pallav Pallav is a Junior Research Fellow (UGC) and PhD Scholar at The West Bengal National University of Judicial Sciences (NUJS), Kolkata. He has completed a PG Diploma in Media Laws From NALSAR, Hyderabad. He has qualified for the Prestigious UGC NET with JRF. He has practicing experience as an Advocate at

Patna High Court. He has also completed an LLM with a specialization in Human Rights. He has completed a BBA and LL.B. (Constitutional Law Honors) from the School of Law, KIIT University, Bhubaneswar.

Vesna Poposka completed her formal education in the field of law at the "Iustinianus Primus" Faculty of Law in Skopje, where she later obtained a Master's degree at the Department of International Law and International Relations. She completed her Doctoral Studies at the "General Mihailo Apostolski" Military Academy in Skopje, where she defended her Thesis titled "International Legal Aspects for the Protection of Critical Infrastructure from modern security threats". To date, she is the only woman to have earned a PhD at the Academy, where she serves as associate professor of international law and international relations. Her research interests include international law, hybrid threats, disinformation, and foreign and security policy. She was actively involved in civil society in various areas, including democracy, human rights, the rule of law, and gender equality. She served as a consultant, trainer, facilitator, and researcher for various project activities, including those funded by the NATO Science for Peace and Security Program and Public Diplomacy.

Vishambhar Raghuwanshi has been pursuing his doctoral degree in Criminal Law from the Faculty of Law, part of the Manipal University, since January 2025. He is currently an Assistant Professor at the Faculty of Law at the same University. He teaches Banking Law and Environmental Law to law students and Business Law to MBA students. His research interests include geopolitics, International Relations, and International Politics, areas on which he has published multiple papers. He is a coordinator for the Centre for Alternate Dispute Resolution at the Faculty of Law with a special focus on the intersection of Arbitration and Law.

Elena Shalevska, born on August 17, 1995, is a researcher and a lecturer at the University "St. Kliment Ohridski" - Bitola. She holds an MA in English Language and is currently a PhD candidate conducting research in AI, Linguistics, Literature, and TESOL. She works as a lecturer in the English Language and Literature Department at the Faculty of Education, and her research interests encompass English Linguistics, Artificial Intelligence, Literature, Language Teaching, as well as Media and Communications.

Vesna Shapkoski is a PhD student at the Faculty of Law, "St. Kliment Ohridski" University in Bitola (North Macedonia), enrolled in the International Law and International Politics study program. She holds a BA in Law and an MA in Business Law. Her primary research interests include the European Union, foreign and security policy, the protection of fundamental rights, and access to justice. She is also an experienced NGO activist, particularly in the field of legal empowerment and access to justice for citizens from marginalized communities. In this capacity, she has participated in numerous trainings, workshops, and courses related to human rights, legal empowerment, advocacy, and European policies.

Paridhi Sharma is a dedicated legal scholar and educator at OP Jindal Global University, where she imparts her expertise in law to aspiring students. Her commitment to the field is further evidenced by her numerous publications in reputed academic journals, reflecting her insightful contributions to legal discourse.

Viktorija Soņeca is a PhD candidate in Legal Sciences at the University of Latvia, with her defense scheduled for November 5, 2025. She currently serves as an advisor to the Supreme Court of Latvia on matters concerning European Union law. Previously, she led the European Court of Justice Department at the Ministry of Justice of the Republic of Latvia, where she represented the country before the Court of Justice of the European Union. Additionally, she worked as the legal editor for the national journal Jurista Vārds and served as a national expert on digital issues for the OECD. Currently, she serves as a guest lecturer at the Riga Graduate School of Law and is a researcher specializing in European Union law, civil law, lobbying, and artificial intelligence.

Angelina Stanojoska, Ph.D., is a Full Professor of Criminology and Basic Criminalistics Theory and the acting Vice-Dean for Science and International Cooperation at the Faculty of Law, University "St. Kliment Ohridski" – Bitola, North Macedonia. She graduated from the Police Academy in Skopje, earned her MSc and PhD in Security Sciences at the Faculty of Security in Skopje, and is a Fulbright Visiting Scholar Alumnus, having researched GST and substance abuse at UMSL, USA. In 2023, she received the Chevening Western Balkans Cybersecurity Fellowship. Dr. Stanojoska has authored several criminology textbooks, a monograph on criminological theories, two works on criminal sanctions in North Macedonia, and numerous scientific articles. Her expertise includes female criminality, violent crimes, treatment of incarcerated women, and online gender-based violence. She has also coordinated projects funded by the US and British Embassies in Skopje, focusing on strengthening the digital skills of incarcerated women and empowering students to combat gender-based violence.

Gamze Türkmen has been working as a researcher at Manisa Celal Bayar University. She completed her PhD in 2020 in the Department of Computer Education and Instructional Technology at Middle East Technical University. She also holds an MSc from the Cognitive Science department, earned in 2013. Her research focuses primarily on metacognition-centered instructional design in science centers, teacher trust in artificial intelligence, and debugging processes in programming education.

Svetlana Veljanovska, PhD, is a Full Professor of Law at the Faculty of Law in Kicevo. She was born in Kicevo, Republic of Macedonia. Since 2009, as a member of the academic community at the University "St. Kliment Ohridski" in Bitola, she has served as both President and member of the University Senate. At the Faculty of Law, she has held various leadership roles, including Head of the Second Cycle of Studies, and currently serves as the Dean of the Faculty, now in her second term. Professor Veljanovska actively participates in numerous conferences, symposiums, and other scholarly gatherings. She is the author and co-author of a substantial number of scientific papers and has published seven peer-reviewed books and textbooks designed for law students. She plays an integral role in developing curricula for the first, second, and third cycles of legal education at the Faculty of Law in Kicevo. Prof. Veljanovska is also a member of the Joakim Krčoski Scientific Society in Kicevo. Among her most meaningful recognitions are those awarded by her students, who named her "Favorite Professor" in 2020 and honored her as the "Most Inspiring and Motivating Professor" in 2022. She is fluent in English, French, and all South Slavic languages.

Agron Vrangalla, born on July 3, 1989, in Kicevo, North Macedonia, is a PhD candidate at South East European University, pursuing doctoral studies in the Faculty of Languages, Cultures, and Communication, with a focus on Media and Communication. He previously served as an Assistant Professor at the State University of Tetovo, Faculty of Law, in the Journalism Department. Currently, he holds the position of Assistant Professor at the University "Mother Teresa" in Skopje, Faculty of Social Sciences, Department of Media and Intercultural Communication.

Arta Xhelili is a lecturer at Mother Teresa University, Faculty of Social Sciences, in the Media and Intercultural Communication study program. She received her Ph.D. in Social Sciences, with an emphasis in Communication, from Ss. Cyril and Methodius University in Skopje, and her MA in Organizational and Professional Communication and Training Development from Ball State University, Indiana. Her research interests include Communication, gender studies, and media.

Mladen Zecevic is a Lecturer at the School of Policing Studies, Charles Sturt University. He holds a Master of Education from Charles Sturt University. His work focuses on cybercrime and education.

Index

H

I

K

L

M

N

P

R

S

T

W

www.ingramcontent.com/pod-product-compliance
Ingram Content Group UK Ltd.
Pitfield, Milton Keynes, MK11 3LW, UK
UKHW050949290926
15470UKWH00005B/1720